Saul Alinsky and the Dilemmas of Race

Saul Alinsky and the Dilemmas of Race

Community Organizing in the Postwar City

MARK SANTOW

The University of Chicago Press
Chicago and London

The University of Chicago Press, Chicago 60637
The University of Chicago Press, Ltd., London
© 2023 by The University of Chicago
All rights reserved. No part of this book may be used or reproduced in any manner whatsoever without written permission, except in the case of brief quotations in critical articles and reviews. For more information, contact the University of Chicago Press, 1427 E. 60th St., Chicago, IL 60637.
Published 2023
Printed in the United States of America

32 31 30 29 28 27 26 25 24 23   1 2 3 4 5

ISBN-13: 978-0-226-82627-1 (cloth)
ISBN-13: 978-0-226-82628-8 (e-book)
DOI: https://doi.org/10.7208/chicago/9780226826288.001.0001

Library of Congress Cataloging-in-Publication Data

Names: Santow, Mark E., 1967– author.
Title: Saul Alinsky and the dilemmas of race : community organizing in the postwar city / Mark Santow.
Description: Chicago : The University of Chicago Press, 2023. | Includes bibliographical references and index.
Identifiers: LCCN 2022043291 | ISBN 9780226826271 (cloth) | ISBN 9780226826288 (ebook)
Subjects: LCSH: Alinsky, Saul D., 1909–1972. | Back of the Yards Neighborhood Council (Chicago, Ill.) | Organization for the Southwest Community (Chicago, Ill.) | Woodlawn Organization. | Community organization—Illinois—Chicago—History—20th century. | Segregation—Illinois—Chicago. | Black people—Segregation—Illinois—Chicago. | Chicago (Ill.)—Race relations. | Chicago (Ill.)—History—20th century.
Classification: LCC HM766 .S36 2023 | DDC 361.809773/11—dc23/eng/20221018
LC record available at https://lccn.loc.gov/2022043291

♾ This paper meets the requirements of ANSI/NISO Z39.48-1992 (Permanence of Paper).

Contents

Introduction 1

1. "Americanism in the Truest Sense?"
   Alinsky and Race in Packingtown   17

2. "Dissolving the Walls of Racial Partition"
   The 1957 General Report   51

3. Chicago's "Great Question"
   Racial Geography and the Creation of the Organization for the
   Southwest Community, 1958–1959   79

4. The "Benign Quota," Racial Liberalism, and the OSC   109

5. "And Just All of a Sudden, They Left"
   The OSC and the Challenges of Neighborhood Integration, 1961–1969   146

6. "We Will Not Be Planned For"
   The Creation of the Woodlawn Organization   184

7. Truth Squads and Death Watches
   TWO, Schooling, and Spatial Strategy   206

8. Maximum Feasible Alinsky
   TWO and the War on Poverty   229

9. Model Cities, TWO, and the Spatial Dilemmas of Metropolitan
   Segregation   262

Conclusion: Mending Walls and Building Bridges 295

Acknowledgments 319
Notes 323
Index 397

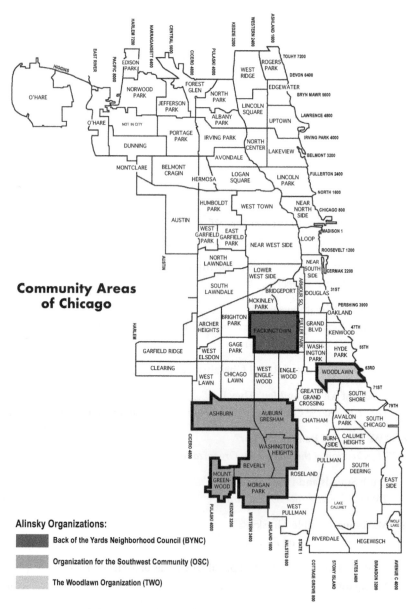

FIGURE 0.1. Map of Chicago community areas, highlighting areas covered by Saul Alinsky's three neighborhood organizations. Map created by Shana Santow.

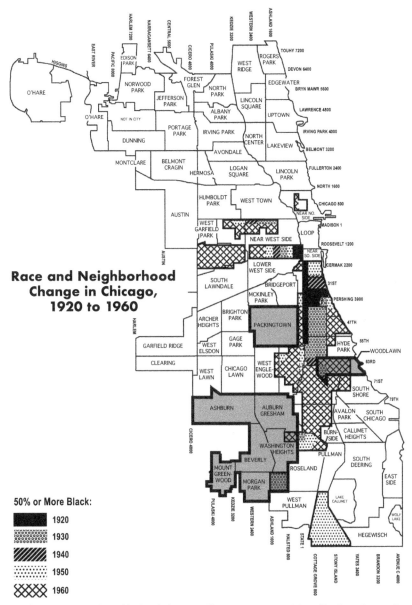

FIGURE 0.2. Race and Neighborhood Change in Chicago, 1920 to 1960. Adapted by Shana Santow, from Brian J. L. Berry, *The Open Housing Question: Race and Housing in Chicago 1966–1976*, Ballinger Publishing, Cambridge, MA (1979), fig. 1-1, p. 6.

Introduction

> The really big problem is that the deprived have no power over their lives, and they know it. . . . Show them how to get what they need and want, not what someone else thinks is enough for them, and they will uplift their communities themselves.
> SAUL ALINSKY, March 1966

President Lyndon Johnson formed the National Advisory Commission on Civil Disorders in late July 1967 to investigate the causes of the riots that had engulfed black neighborhoods in more than one hundred cities that summer, and in the three preceding years. It held closed hearings from August to December, with over 130 witnesses, including Martin Luther King, Robert F. Kennedy, Stokely Carmichael, and Chicago-based community organizer Saul Alinsky. Members visited eight cities and did field surveys in twenty-three others. In its March 1968 report, the Kerner Commission, as it was informally called, famously warned that if conditions were not changed, the nation would be "moving toward two societies, one black, one white—separate and unequal."

It was clear that the nation could no longer hold the "wolf by the ear," as in Thomas Jefferson's evocative description of the American dilemma. A critical point had been reached. Despite legislative and judicial victories over Jim Crow in the South, the reduction of open racial discrimination in the North, the softening of white racial attitudes, and years of economic growth, the black urban condition appeared to be deteriorating. Racial segregation was expanding, whites continued to resist the passage of even the most minimal fair housing laws, and the War on Poverty seemed unable to arrest rising levels of unemployment and concentrated poverty in black neighborhoods. As jobs left the city, young blacks in particular were trapped in overcrowded and inadequate schools, with rapidly diminishing hope of stable employment and upward mobility.

The Kerner Report responded with appropriate urgency. One suggested alternative to the status quo, the authors noted, was to concentrate massive public and private resources on inner-city communities, and to abandon metropolitan desegregation as an unobtainable goal. This "enrichment" approach—often referred to at the time as "gilding the ghetto"—had support from across the political spectrum (and across racial lines), but the commission nonetheless opposed it. If implemented alone, commission members warned, the policy would have "ominous consequences for our society," because "equality cannot be achieved under conditions of nearly complete separation." It involved "choosing a permanently divided country" while doing little to "arrest the deterioration of life in central city ghettos." While "large-scale improvement in the quality of ghetto life" was essential, this could be only an "interim strategy." Metropolitan segregation threatened to further isolate black ghetto residents politically and economically, continually undermining any progress that massive investments in their neighborhoods might create.

If the primary goal was to create a "single society, in which every citizen will be free to live and work according to his capabilities and desires, not his color," the Kerner Report concluded, metropolitan desegregation and ghetto enrichment had to be undertaken together and with equal vigor. Neither could succeed without the other. Enrichment had to be paired with "substantial Negro movement out of the ghettos" and the elimination of all barriers to free choice in employment, education, and housing. Federal housing programs needed to encourage or directly construct millions of low- and moderate-income units in the suburbs, and Congress needed to pass a strong fair housing law that included single-family housing. America had to affirmatively open up the suburbs. "Integration," the Kerner Commission concluded, "is the only course which explicitly seeks to achieve a single nation." The nation could no longer maintain the illusion that economic growth, nondiscrimination laws, and goodwill would unwind the racial status quo.

President Johnson made his choice when he refused to even acknowledge the report. After a brief flurry of hopeful judicial, administrative, and legislative action between 1968 and 1975, the nation largely rejected it as well. The issue of metropolitan segregation disappeared from national politics, along with the idea that there might be something fundamentally wrong with existing conditions, something that required strong governmental action. The issue was replaced by a belief that everything reasonable had been done, and that civil rights policies might have gone so far as to be unfair to whites.

Segregation by class as well as race remains a fundamental fact of life in the nation's cities and suburbs in the twenty-first century, and thus in its public schools as well, concentrating people of color in low-opportunity urban and increasingly suburban communities, across multiple generations. Black political action has once again reminded the nation of this fact, and its corrosive consequences, in the wake of police violence against young black men in Ferguson, Baltimore, Minneapolis, and elsewhere.

Even a brief journey through America's largest metropolitan areas reveals an unmistakable connection between where (and how) people live and who they are. I have taught American urban history in universities across the country. My students can quickly identify which groups of people live where in their city. How they map the surrounding geography—how they see it, understand it, and place themselves within it—is profoundly shaped by race as well as class. The *other side of the tracks*, the *inner city*, *white flight*, the *Black Belt*, the *lily-white suburbs*—all these terms are geographic, at once describing places, people, social processes, and history. Urban scholars generally refer to this relationship between place, identity, and social structure as social geography. It has been said that one of the best ways to understand a society is to look at what it takes for granted. Social geography is taken for granted. It is like air—natural, immutable—or so it seems.

In reality, of course, land-use patterns are not the result of unencumbered individual choices, random selection, or free markets. They are shaped by laws, political choices, social processes, and power relations, just as workplaces and families are. How people understand and react to these arrangements can both reproduce and challenge social processes and power relations. To put it somewhat differently, social structures and hierarchies shape people's lives, possibilities, and worldviews through *space*. Space is a critical part of the concrete lived world, and of how people behave as social and political actors. It frames social life—even though the constraints of that frame often pass unnoticed.[1]

This insight is particularly vital for making sense of American race relations. People don't experience racial hierarchy in general; they experience it in particular places, at particular times. What power is, and how it is experienced and cognitively understood, is tied to how it finds its way into the built environment, where people live, and how they think of property, community, and social belonging. Race has helped to shape metropolitan space, and the spatial development of cities and suburbs along racial (and class) lines has deeply affected what opportunities are available for different groups, as well as how they define themselves. Whiteness, for example, has been defined and defended through its spatial expressions, often with support from the law and the state. It is evident in more local and individual actions, too, from the residential and educational choices of white families, to the legal and extralegal ways in which groups and communities of whites have sought to exclude others. As Patrick Sharkey, Sean Reardon, Robert Sampson, and other scholars have argued, the overall level of economic advancement of African

Americans since the civil rights era has been remarkably limited because of how racial inequality is tied to—and reproduced by—racial spatialization.[2]

Accordingly, black political thought and action has long grappled with what the legal scholar David Delaney has called the "spatial conditions of liberation." By the mid-1960s, portions of the Black Freedom Movement and the broader left had developed a sophisticated and historically informed understanding of how racial and class privilege shaped—and was shaped by—metropolitan space. For a brief time, as the Kerner Report demonstrates, this insight appeared ready to erupt into the national policy discourse. But just as quickly, the moment passed. It took a long time and much effort to create the patterns of segregation by class and race that we see around us today. It will take a long time and much effort to unravel these patterns, if we wish to do so. But first we must see them for what they are: a tightly wound human construct, creating and amplifying—but also obfuscating—inequality for generations of Americans. For this, the study of history is indispensable.[3]

More than almost any other American public figure of the past century, the community organizer Saul Alinsky was keenly aware of and grappled with the relationship between social geography, activism, and the pursuit of racial justice. Most accounts of his activism and ideas focus on tactics and the practicalities of community organizing, not on race. Rarely is Alinsky taken seriously as a thinker and man of thoughtful action. This is unfortunate, because his insights and his activism, as well as his oversights and failures, have much to teach us. Alinsky possessed a keen sociological imagination, honed by the white-hot heat of Chicago's inflamed racial politics. This book is an attempt to explain and explore that imagination, the actions it inspired, and the lessons it may have to teach us about the struggle for social justice.

Most of Alinsky's adult life was caught up in an effort to understand racial segregation and inequality in his native Chicago and to find a way for grassroots activism to challenge that inequality, rather than reinforce it. He was hardly alone in this effort; many of his peers also contemplated the causes and consequences of racial segregation, white flight, and the poverty and powerlessness that seemed to concentrate in black ghetto areas. However, because Alinsky confronted these issues on paper and in the streets, on both sides of the color line, in the halls of power and at the grass roots, in Chicago and in Washington, and over a thirty-year period, his story gives us unique access to the racial politics of the era. Alinsky's ideas, actions, and organizations provide us with a comprehensive understanding of the politics of race, poverty, and social geography in the United States in the three decades after World War II. Through Alinsky, and his organizations in Chicago's Back of the Yards, Southwest Side, and Woodlawn, we can see how the metropolitan color line was constructed, contested, and maintained—on the streets, nationwide, and among white and black alike. We can perhaps also discern the hazy contours of paths that were not taken but perhaps should have been—and still could be.

While we are supposedly now living in a post–civil rights era, much of what Alinsky struggled against—and for—remains painfully relevant in the early twenty-first century. Metropolitan racial segregation is still a powerful generator of inequality in American life, too often distracting us from the atrophy of the nation's opportunity structure in the previous four decades. As of this writing, however, events have provided some hope for meaningful change, and for the first time in almost five decades. Black activism in the wake of police brutality and unrest in Baltimore in 2015 prompted some sectors of the American media to begin to investigate the connections between racial inequality and housing segregation for the first time in more than a generation. Many of these journalists sought to understand how places like Ferguson and West Baltimore came to be by exploring some of the historical writing on race and place of the previous two decades—work that had transformed scholarly understandings of racial inequality but had otherwise failed to penetrate the national conversation. Newspapers, magazines, online publications, and even television news stations were suddenly filled with people talking about redlining, the Fair Housing Act, and the intersection of racial segregation and the criminal justice system.[4] Then came the massive outpouring of protest in the wake of George Floyd's murder by a Minneapolis police officer in 2020. Citizen activism, scholarship, and state action all seem to have converged to give the American people yet another chance to address the issues that Alinsky and his colleagues grappled with decades ago. As the poet Claudia Rankine put it, "History's authority over us is not broken by maintaining a silence about its continued effects." Recent events have breached that silence. This book was written in the spirit of widening that breach.[5]

Who Was Saul Alinsky?

During his life Saul Alinsky was the most famous—and notorious—community organizer in America, a man who almost single-handedly invented a new political form: the community federation, a kind of neighborhood trade union. In a controversial career spanning more than three decades, Alinsky and his Industrial Areas Foundation (IAF) organized Eastern European meatpackers in Chicago, Kansas City, Buffalo, and St. Paul; Mexican Americans in California and Arizona; white middle-class homeowners on the edge of Chicago's

South Side black ghetto; and African Americans in Rochester, Buffalo, Chicago, and other cities. Alinsky groups also took on environmental pollution, redlining and urban disinvestment, and corporate hiring practices.

In the 1940s and again during the 1960s, he achieved national celebrity with his controversial writings, attention-grabbing tactics, abrasive rhetoric, and political effectiveness. In the New Deal era, he tried to build a racially progressive and integrated community organization in the shadow of Chicago's packinghouses, which had exploded in a brutal racial pogrom just a few decades earlier. As American race relations reached a flashpoint in the mid-1960s, Alinsky simultaneously spoke out for black militants and "backlash" whites—and sought to bring them together, in common cause against the haves, and in defense of livable and integrated urban neighborhoods.

Alinsky was friend, student, and biographer of the union leader John L. Lewis and a mentor to several generations of organizers. Directly and indirectly, he influenced the activism of Cesar Chavez, Gail Cincotta, Paul Wellstone, Heather Booth, Hillary Clinton—and Barack Obama. His ideas and organizations shaped the civil rights movement, the federal War on Poverty, environmental organizations, community development corporations, social ministry, and countless activists in communities around the country.

Inspired by a basic belief in the critical importance of citizens acting collectively through voluntary associations, Alinsky helped to build large and influential neighborhood groups, with indigenous leaders and organizations fighting for local needs. While the IAF's approach to organizing has changed substantially since his death, it has helped to create dozens of effective community organizations around the country, improving the lives of hundreds of thousands of Americans. IAF affiliates helped to give birth to the living-wage movement, to build thousands of units of inner-city affordable housing through the Nehemiah Housing projects, and to give Mexican Americans a seat at the table in Texas politics. The IAF has also trained thousands of ordinary citizens in organizing, coalition building, and social analysis.

In recent decades, most Americans who encountered Alinsky did so through his two insightful and provocative books. In *Reveille for Radicals* (1946) and *Rules for Radicals* (1971), Alinsky reveled in the messy, conflicted, and never-ending process of democratic politics, insisting that if citizens didn't collectively tinker with the machinery of power, the promise of American life would wither and die. In *Reveille*, his praise for town-meeting-style deliberation and his ability to see beauty in the local, as well as his lament about the growing power of big institutions, anticipated the Port Huron Statement of the early 1960s. He also took to task many of his allies on the left who idealized the virtues of downtrodden people.

Rules, most famously, recounted a series of hilarious direct-action tactics that his organizations had used or contemplated, many of them scatological. I first encountered Alinsky in the summer after my senior year in high school, in 1985, when I took a job canvassing for a Connecticut organization working on consumer and environmental issues. My nineteen-year-old "trainer" tossed a dog-eared copy of *Rules* in my lap and told me not to return until I had read it. Alinsky convinced this young activist that fighting for social justice was not only eminently possible—it was quintessentially American.

Even better, it was a blast. You could tell fart jokes and still fight the power. As *Playboy* put it in 1972, Alinsky "looks like an accountant and talks like a stevedore." Alinsky looked and sounded like my Chicago-born father and his brothers, who also came from the Jewish West Side. Same nasal Midwestern twang, same wicked sense of humor, same love for the city's steak and rib houses (and the White Sox). When young New Leftists encountered him, *Rolling Stone* quipped, "they asked, who is that masked Jewish uncle? He's a revolutionary?" When his organizing protégé Nicholas Von Hoffman first met him in 1953, Alinsky "wore glasses that shielded exophthalmic eyes and his every grey hair was smoothed into place. I had been promised a firecracker, but what I was getting was a middle-aged businessman."[6]

Alinsky certainly had his vices; he enjoyed scotch and a steak at the Palmer House Grill, a popular Mafia hangout. He was easily bored, which made him a lousy administrator and fundraiser. He was frequently profane, a bit of a misogynist, and was always ready with a cutting quip for friends and foes alike. "Saul had a bit of the boy prankster in him," Von Hoffman recalls. "We got a kick out of watching prissy-pants people go flying off in hysteria." Despite his scholarly demeanor, his personal charisma was apparently undeniable, particularly as he aged. "There is a tremendous vitality about Alinsky, a raw, combative ebullience, and a consuming curiosity about everything and everyone around him," Rabbi William Berkowitz wrote in 1972. "Add to this a mordant wit, a monumental ego coupled with an ability to laugh at himself and the world in general, and you begin to get the measure of the man."[7]

Early in his organizing career Alinsky was apparently a bit of a "hothead," telling Von Hoffman that he once had "an innermost core made liquid by the heart of anger." "I hate people who act unjustly and cause many to suffer," he confessed to the Catholic theologian Jacques Maritain. "I become violently angry when I see misery and am filled with a bitter vindictiveness toward those responsible." But by the mid-1950s, Alinsky had become a master at "goading the other side to lose its cool" while keeping his own. Often, he said incendiary things just for the fun of it. He meant everything he said—he once told a reporter "every fucking word I say is for the record"—although he didn't always

FIGURE 0.3. Saul Alinsky's playful irreverence. Box 169, folder 1727, Saul Alinsky Papers, Special Collections, University of Illinois Chicago.

say everything he meant. In the end, Von Hoffman concluded that "he was a conventional middle-class man, a non-bohemian like the non-bohemian masses whom he strove to organize . . . he did not come to destroy the social order, but to perfect it." Whatever his shortcomings (and they were several), he was an engaged intellectual, a patriot, and a serious moral being.[8]

Contrary to popular belief, Alinsky was no nihilist. He came of age during a time when ideology and moral certainty had led to the deaths of tens of millions of people. As a result, he became a lifelong skeptic of the singular power of ideas and moral passion to remake societies. "Dogma," he wrote in *Rules*, "is the enemy of human freedom . . . the human spirit glows from that small inner doubt of whether we are right, while those who believe with complete certainty that they possess the right are dark inside and darken the world with cruelty, pain and injustice." The organizers' first responsibility was to the people he recruited, he instructed Von Hoffman; they didn't sign up "to be used in behalf of a grander cause."[9]

Alinsky went out of his way rhetorically, at least in public, to disassociate himself from any ideology or worldview. He was, Von Hoffman observed, "the least doctrinaire of men." He had "no truck with . . . the kamikaze idealism of projects that he knew would fail." This tendency was reinforced by his encounters with the New Left of the 1960s, which he found too dogmatic and too willing to idealize the have-nots. As a result, Alinsky tended to downplay moral purpose and to fetishize tactics. But organizing was never an end in itself for him and the groups he helped to create. It was technique, not telos. Alinsky had witnessed the transformation of his first organizing project, the Back of the Yards Neighborhood Council, into a segregationist group in the 1950s—and an effective one, at that. He knew full well that effective organizing had to be rooted in humane values for democracy to flourish. "If a state voted for school segregation or a community organization voted to keep blacks out, and claimed justification by virtue of the 'democratic process,'" he argued, "then this violation of the value of equality would have converted democracy into a prostitute."[10]

So who was Saul Alinsky? What did he stand for? Traditional political labels tend to shed a great deal of heat without providing much illumination. He was deliberately imprecise, even obtuse, when asked to describe his politics. Sometimes he grabbed on to a political model or label for aesthetic reasons—to gauge their effect on the listener—as much as for moral reasons. Early in his career, very much an intellectual and political child of the Popular Front–era labor movement, Alinsky described himself as a "professional anti-fascist." As a Jew in polyglot Chicago and an activist in union organizing campaigns, he was intimately familiar with how prejudice and intolerance blinded people. He also worried that individuals and their communities—particularly the have-nots—would be lost in an America increasingly defined by large institutions. As the resonance of the term *anti-fascist* faded, he took to calling himself an "urban populist . . . rooted in an American radical tradition, not in a Marxist tradition." Alinsky was particularly fond of the word *radical*, largely because of his preferred Latinate definition: someone who gets to the "root of things."[11]

In his writings, he evoked Thomas Paine, St. Paul—and Satan. Because of his Orthodox Jewish upbringing, and his close relationships with Catholic clergy and theologians, he was far more conversant with biblical figures and parables than he was with Marxist texts. Indeed, his private correspondence and public utterances reveal no familiarity with the latter at all, much to the chagrin of some of his leftist critics.

He fired many verbal barbs at his presumptive allies, liberals and the New Left. The farther American liberalism drifted from the New Deal–era labor movement, Alinsky believed, the more unwilling it had become to afflict the comfortable, and to see conflict as the inevitable source of democratic energy and social justice. Liberals had become too enamored of big government, legal action, and the ideas of experts, and too fearful of the popular use of power. They lacked moral courage and conviction, and had a "tender-minded, overly romantic image of the poor" that too often led them to dismiss their ideas, institutions, and actions. Liberals "are a strange breed of hybrids," he wrote in 1946, "with radical minds and conservative hearts."

In contrast, he found the New Left to be overly ideological and too impatient with the inconclusive messiness of the democratic process and institution building. "Their problem is that they always want the third act—the resolution, the big drama," he said in 1965. "They want to skip the first act, the second act, the tediousness, the listening . . . you do more organizing with your ears than with your tongue." "It would be great if the whole system would just disappear overnight," he said in 1972, "but it won't, and the kids on the New Left sure as hell aren't going to overthrow it. Shit, Abbie Hoffman and Jerry Rubin couldn't organize a successful luncheon, much less a revolution."[12]

Ultimately, Alinsky is fascinating because he doesn't fit the standard liberal-conservative-radical typology. One need look only at the criticisms he received from all three groups. Conservatives tended to see him as a communist agitator during the Cold War—many still do. The New Left saw him as an ideologically naïve supporter of the status quo, who simply organized the have-nots to get more scraps from the American table rather than kicking it over. Liberals were uncomfortable with his advocacy of conflict and power, the incivility of his rhetoric, his open skepticism of government, and—in a few cases—his close relationship with the Archdiocese of Chicago. By the early 1960s, his understanding of race, power, and privilege also tended to clash with liberal views, which attributed racial inequality primarily to individual white prejudice and black pathology. In his writings and especially his public statements he was blunt and often crude, convinced that the more threatening and egotistical he sounded, the more powerful his community organizations would seem. He was personally indifferent to criticism and brilliant at using the media to shape his public reputation in ways he thought useful.

Perhaps the best way of approaching Alinsky's politics is instead to consider how he believed the world worked (his sociological imagination) and how he believed it should work (his moral imagination). To that end, he is best understood as a left communitarian and a moral pragmatist. As World War II ended, Alinsky saw a crisis in American civic life approaching, and he dedicated himself to overcoming it—by experimenting with new ways of creating, sustaining, and empowering communities and citizens in urban neighborhoods, through the creation of what he called People's Organizations.

"Democracy as a way of life has been intellectually accepted, but emotionally rejected" by most Americans, Alinsky argued. "Multitudes of our people have been condemned to urban anonymity—to living the kind of life where many of them neither know nor care about their own neighbors." Isolated from the life of their community and their nation, they "find themselves driven by social forces beyond their control into little individual worlds in which their own individual objectives have become paramount to the collective good. Social objectives, social welfare, the good of the nation, the democratic way of life—all these have become nebulous, meaningless, sterile phrases," he concluded.

In contrast to many postwar political theorists, who viewed democracy as simply a mechanism through which political consumers could register their desires and interests by choosing and authorizing governments run by elites, Alinsky argued for a democracy that placed heavy emphasis on local civil society, democratic talk, and the experience of community participation and empowerment.[13] Alinsky worried especially about what he saw as the increasing atrophy of civil associations. Echoing Alexis de Tocqueville, one of his favorite writers, he saw such organizations as crucial parts of a modern, urbanized democracy. His People's Organizations were intended to be "the extension of the principles and practices of organized collective bargaining beyond their present confines of the factory gate" and to serve as schools of public life for the poor and working classes by providing participatory local forums through which they could learn how to practice democracy.[14]

The French theologian Jacques Maritain—who knew the organizer well—believed that Alinsky's organizations and ideas embodied the Catholic idea of subsidiarity. According to Robert Vischer, subsidiarity "is a principled tendency toward solving problems at the local level and empowering individuals, families and voluntary associations to act more efficaciously in their own lives." A just and democratic society requires a thriving civil sector of mediating institutions, to foster self-empowerment, belonging and civic purpose, and a sense of responsibility for oneself and the common good. It also required what Maritain referred to as a "dynamic leaven or energy . . . a prophetic factor" that inspired people to pursue justice. It had to be "rooted in free initiative" and thus couldn't be imposed from above. Maritain believed that Alinsky's organizations embodied this energy.[15]

While in recent decades American conservatives have used the principle of subsidiarity to defend the free market and to advocate the devolution and privatization of state functions—to drown the government in the bathtub, as Grover Norquist so sourly put it—Catholic Church teaching on subsidiarity fully recognizes the necessity of robust government action in pursuit of individual empowerment, the strengthening of mediating institutions, and the common good. Its demand that people have access to everything they need to lead a humane existence—even if this requires curtailing the operation of the "free" market—provided a moral foundation for the New Deal–era Popular Front intellectual and political milieu out of which Alinsky emerged.

The emphasis of subsidiarity on the importance of civic associations and the habits of self-government and social cooperation sustained by participation in them mirrors Tocqueville's analysis of antebellum American democracy, which heavily influenced Alinsky. "The more government takes the place of associations," the Frenchman warned, "the more will individuals lose the idea of forming associations and need the government to come to their help."[16] Humans are by nature social beings, Alinsky argued, but they require mediating structures—families, neighborhoods, churches—to empower individual action and link them to society as a whole. Where such structures can effectively address a problem, they should. Where they cannot, city, state, and finally national governments should intervene. The state should do whatever most justly and effectively supported human dignity and self-government, not ideology.[17]

Alinsky's moral imagination was informed by religion, reading, close observation of human behavior, and personal tragedy. His relationship to his own religion was not atypical of Jewish intellectuals of his generation. He was raised in a strictly Orthodox Jewish household in Lawndale, on Chicago's West Side. As an adult Alinsky clung tightly to a skeptical (and private)

Judaism, and he openly expressed distrust of religious talk, as well as moral and spiritual motives. He tended to find self-proclaimed religious people, clergy and laity alike, to be morally hypocritical; as he once put it in a letter to Maritain, "Christianity is certainly an unpopular subject in many parts of the Church."[18]

Alinsky was no philosopher, but his ethical yardstick generally measured people by their congruence in words and action, a pragmatic passion for social justice, and a moral humility fueled by doubt. Dismissive of those Panglossian optimists who held that God would provide, Alinsky measured moral authenticity in terms of action: "You've got to be a part of the world," he once told a group of seminary students. That meant having the moral courage to pursue justice under imperfect conditions, and to accept that a "free and open society is an on-going conflict."

Democratic politics, for Alinsky, was not about perfectionism. It was about process. "You never have the best course of action. You always have to pick the least bad," he cautioned. "Do you know any permanent solutions? We'll always have problems! We always will." When pushed he would acknowledge that his approach to organizing implied some basic moral commitments about human interactions and institutions, but he otherwise insisted that "you've got to start with the world as it is." All life is a "series of revolutions," Alinsky argued, "each bringing society a little bit closer to the ultimate goal of *real* personal and social freedom." Along the way "the values of humanism and social justice . . . take shape and change and are slowly implanted in the minds of all men, even as their advocates falter and succumb." "Can you imagine," he asked *Rolling Stone*, "anything that's more of a drag than a so-called perfect world? What the fuck are you going to do in it?"[19]

Alinsky was entirely comfortable with conflict and the language of power politics, believing that both were vital to democracy and human creativity. "If one were to project the democratic way of life in the form of a musical score," he wrote in 1969, "its major theme would be the harmony of dissonance." Because he was fond of provocative pronouncements about the role of self-interest in human motivation, it is not surprising that many of his readers have thought of him as a pure materialist—or, less charitably, a nihilist. We live in "a world not of angels, but of angles," he wrote in *Rules*. Morality is merely a "rhetorical rationale for expedient action and self-interest."

At the same time—and in the same section of the book—Alinsky could elegantly expound upon the ethical sensibility at the core of community organizing. His work was "anchored in optimism" and premised on the "belief that if people have the power to act, in the long run they will, most of the time, reach the right decisions." Because of this belief, he had the responsibility to organize them "so that they will have the power and opportunity to best meet each unforeseeable future crisis as they move ahead, in their eternal search for those values of equality, justice, freedom, peace, a deep concern for the preciousness of human life." Democracy, he argued, "is the best means toward achieving these values."

At first blush these appear to be contradictory positions—both angles and angels. But Alinsky's approach to organizing was essentially pedagogical: he wanted to help people to understand the institutions that governed them. "Real education," he wrote, is the means by which people "begin to make sense out of their relationship as individuals . . . to the world they live in, so that they can make informed and intelligent judgments." If you want people to do social analysis, they have to be able to discern the role of self-interest and power in institutional arrangements. Perhaps it is obvious that people in power often use moral pronouncements to justify their elevated status, and that in so doing, they often deceive others (and themselves). But that level of social analysis isn't always easy to achieve when it is aimed at powerful institutions and ideas, by people with lives defined by impoverishment and disempowerment.[20]

Throughout his life, Alinsky lamented that the "vast mass" of Americans did not participate in the "endless responsibilities of citizenship." Whether they were thwarted by lack of interest or opportunity, the majority seemed "resigned to lives determined by others," he wrote. Alinsky believed that all people had to be given the power and responsibility to act politically—to be citizens, in other words—if we wanted to live in a society in which human goodness flourished. "There can be no darker or more devastating tragedy than the death of man's faith in himself and in his power to direct his future," he argued. "To lose your identity as a citizen of democracy is but a step from losing your identity as a person."

To Alinsky the great virtue of democracy (and community organizing) was that because it served as a constant reminder of human interdependence, it pushed citizens toward a more enlightened form of self-interest. "A major revolution to be won in the immediate future," Alinsky argued, "is the dissipation of man's illusion that his own welfare can be separate from that of all others." Man will become "his brother's keeper" when he sees that he must. "People cannot be free unless they are willing to sacrifice some of their interests to guarantee the freedom of others," he insisted. "The most practical life is the moral life, and the moral life is the only road to survival." "Man . . . is beginning to learn that he will either share part of his material wealth, or lose all of it," he said. Alinsky acknowledged that this was a "low road to morality," but he didn't see another path.[21]

Publicly, Alinsky was disdainful of idealism and approaches to social change that seemingly depended upon faith in the essential goodness of human beings. In his writings, speeches, and organizational work, his emphasis was on individual and institutional self-interest as the prime motivator of action. He was often criticized (and still is) for having an amoral, materialistic approach that justified virtually any means as long as it was in service to a desired end. Privately, however, Alinsky acknowledged the necessary role that emotion (anger, but also love) and a vision of human goodness played in driving his work.

Those who knew him best had little difficulty seeing Alinsky's moral core. Most attributed to him a spirituality that he would almost certainly have denied. Maritain in particular believed that Alinsky's democratic faith was unavoidably rooted in a deeper faith in human goodness, calling him a "practical Thomist." In a letter to the University of Chicago president Robert Hutchins, Maritain described Alinsky as "a great soul, a man of profound moral purity ... whose natural generosity is quickened, though he would not admit it, by genuine evangelical brotherly love." "You act and fight ... for the recovery by man of his inner, moral dignity," Maritain wrote to Alinsky. "That is to say, finally, even if you do not have such a purpose in your mind, for his spiritual redemption." He continued, "All your fighting effort as an organizer is quickened *in reality by love for the human being, and for God,* though you refuse to admit it." Fr. John Egan, who worked with Alinsky on a daily basis, which Maritain did not, claimed to have "never seen him violate the moral law or advocate the violation of it." In 1969, a coalition of Catholic groups in Iowa gave Alinsky its Pacem in Terris Peace and Freedom Award, named after Pope John XXIII's encyclical on war, peace, and social justice.

Alinsky's faith, ultimately, was in democracy, not in dogmas or deities. Tom Gaudette, who worked with Alinsky in the 1960s, recalled his mentor tearing up at annual conventions of his organizations. "Look at that," Alinsky shouted excitedly. "It works! Isn't it great? Democracy works. That's the fight. That's democracy at work." Late in his life, Alinsky described having developed an empathetic imagination, in large part because of tragedies in his personal life. "When you are cursed with that kind of imagination, you see people suffering, you identify," Alinsky told Rabbi William Berkowitz. "This makes you very angry, and you want to do something about it to relieve your own self-pain, because their pain becomes part of you." The key to being an effective organizer, Alinsky believed, was to demonstrate "respect for the dignity of the individual you're dealing with."[22] While he was a man of considerable ego, his work was nonetheless informed by a deeply held moral humility and a skepticism that indicated not amorality or cynicism but rather an amalgam of existential self-doubt and an unshakable respect for individual human dignity. According to Fr. John Egan, Alinsky defined the true radical as "that person for whom the common good is the greatest personal good."[23]

Despite his demanding moral skepticism—or perhaps because of it—"religiously motivated people buzzed around Saul as though he were loaded with pollen," as Von Hoffman put it. Many of them were struck by the man's spiritual depth, hard-won through a series of awful tragedies that struck almost every woman he loved. "I had nuns tell me that he was a saint and ministers explain that he was a 'true' Christian," Von Hoffman wrote. Since I began working on this project in the mid-1990s, I have rarely met a Jesuit or priest over the age of seventy who doesn't have an "Alinsky story" to tell. Somewhat puckishly, Alinsky took to calling himself the "Kosher Cardinal."

He was, of course, neither. He was a citizen.[24]

1

"Americanism in the Truest Sense?"

Alinsky and Race in Packingtown

> The achievements of the Back of the Yards Movement open a new road to real democracy, and show us the only way in which that deep need for communion ... can be satisfied in freedom and through freedom, in and through genuine respect for the human person, in and through actual and living trust in the people.
> CATHOLIC THEOLOGIAN JACQUES MARITAIN, 1946

> The negro citizen in search of a decent home in Chicago and in the many other big cities soon discovers that ... [e]very alternative is fraught with troubles which spring directly from the inability of many whites to concede that a Negro should have the right to live where he chooses, granting his ability to pay the freight.
> "OUR OPINIONS: ANY WAY YOU TURN YOU'RE WRONG,"
> *Chicago Defender*, December 9, 1950

In the first two decades after World War II, population movements and federal policies profoundly racialized Chicago's social geography. The Second Great Migration of Southern blacks to Northern cities was overlapped by a kind of "third" Great Migration, one of jobs and white Americans to the urban fringe and the suburbs. Chicago changed from 8 percent black in 1940 to 23 percent in 1960; more than a quarter million whites left the city from 1950 to 1956 alone.[1]

While the aggregate numbers reveal a profound change, they tell us little about how these transformations were experienced in Chicago's neighborhoods. Like other Northern cities, Chicago had a dual housing market: one for blacks and one for whites. By the late 1940s, aided by federal housing, banking, and transportation policies, aspiring white homeowners had begun to move to the suburbs, which were largely closed to black families regardless of income or assets. While discrimination continued to limit where black families could affordably live, white flight opened up Chicago's housing market for the first time in a generation. Overcrowding, opportunity, and social mobility pushed many black families to seek housing beyond the boundaries of the traditional Black Belt, in previously all-white neighborhoods.[2]

In Alinsky's time, Back of the Yards (also known then as "Packingtown") was an overwhelmingly Catholic working-class neighborhood on the South Side. Saul Alinsky began his career as a community organizer there in the

Back of the Yards Neighborhood Council (BYNC)

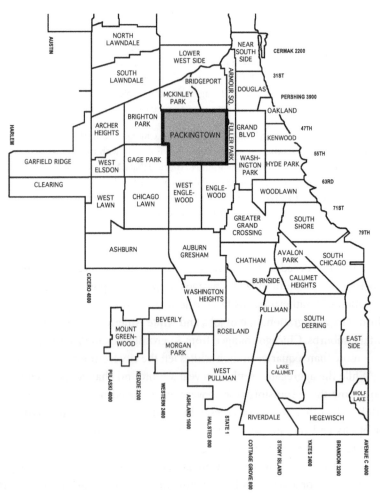

FIGURE 1.1. The territory of the Back of the Yards Neighborhood Council.

late 1930s, helping to create the Back of the Yards Neighborhood Council (BYNC), a coalition of Catholic priests, union leaders, small businessmen, and residents dedicated to bridging ethnic differences, improving social conditions, and unionizing the meatpacking workforce. Both the union (the Packinghouse Workers Organizing Committee, or PWOC) and the BYNC took progressive stances on racial issues in the 1940s in an effort to build solidarity within the increasingly interracial packinghouse workforce. Yet by the late 1950s, the BYNC had become powerfully (and effectively) opposed to neighborhood integration, and also dedicated to keeping Packingtown white. The BYNC's "conservation" program generated national attention in the 1950s and 1960s because the issues that gave rise to it emerged in virtually every city with a growing black population. When Alinsky started his work in the late 1930s, he had little sense of how much race had come to define the social geography of his city. By the mid-1950s, convinced that a just and democratic Chicago could never be created without confronting the city's combustible color line, Alinsky had launched himself into a lifelong effort to enable that confrontation with grassroots organizing on both sides of that line—and across it.

Why did Packingtown and other South Side white communities react so negatively to the possibility of black neighbors in the first two decades after World War II? The broad contours are clear: the conditions that tended to encourage BYNC member organizations to see common interests across racial lines weakened or disappeared altogether, and those that gave rise to racialized ways of seeing and thinking moved to the foreground. The ecology of racial politics, in short, had changed.

Back of the Yards

Immortalized in Upton Sinclair's muckraking novel *The Jungle*, Back of the Yards was one of Chicago's most infamous neighborhoods. It was also one of the poorest, a status greatly exaggerated by the unemployment of the Depression decade. When Alinsky came on the scene in 1938, the Yards was a neighborhood of ethnic division, economic privation, decrepit housing, and political powerlessness.

Long a point of entry for immigrants, the area was divided culturally, institutionally, and geographically by ethnicity, and it lacked any kind of community-wide infrastructure or identity, save perhaps that created by common misery. Packingtown grew up around the Union Stockyards, which opened in 1865 and at one point employed nearly seventy-five thousand workers. By the time of Alinsky's arrival, it was an area of nearly four square miles, familiar to the senses of Chicagoans for the domes and spires of its impressive churches and the fetid odors emanating from the Yards—including Bubbly Creek, a tributary of the South Branch of the Chicago River into which packers dumped waste.[3]

Work and religion, the two central institutions of daily life regardless of ethnic background, did not serve to unite residents; indeed, they further divided them. The packing companies dominated local life and continuously sought both to encourage ethnic, racial, and occupational divisions among their employees and to undermine occasional attempts to organize unions. Every decade or so, workers in the Yards would succeed in building a union movement to bring the various groups together, only to have it splinter and collapse.

Even in good times, work in the stockyards was generally temporary, low paying, and dangerous. Most packinghouse workers were common laborers, subject to the low wages of an overcrowded labor market and without job security. Unable to fully mechanize production, the packers tried to make profits by keeping wages low and the shop floor under management control. As a result, workers experienced stagnant wages, casual labor, the arbitrary rule of foremen, and the frequent speeding up of the assembly line.[4]

Although more than 90 percent of local residents were Catholic, religious identity did little to bridge ethnic differences. They worshipped in eleven different ethnically segregated parishes run by priests who rarely communicated with one another. In John McGreevy's wonderfully visual words, each parish was "a small planet whirling through its orbit, oblivious to the rest of the ecclesiastical solar system." The PWOC organizer Herbert March described the parishes as "little autonomous empires." Parishes were intensely focused not only on spirituality but also on maintaining and transmitting ethnic language, culture, and tradition. As scholars have shown, ethnic nationalism in Chicago seemed to intensify over time, particularly after World War I. This is evident in the low percentage of residents who participated in English and naturalization classes. An abundance of foreign-language newspapers complemented the other ethnically separate social institutions, including taverns. The overwhelming majority of children attended parish schools, and few adults married outside their own ethnic group. Everything in Back of the Yards continuously reinforced ethnic divisions and a strong sense of territorial identity.[5] Shortly before Alinsky's arrival in 1938, according to historian Robert Slayton, "it looked as though no power, no institution, could unite the neighborhood."[6]

High rates of home ownership, strongly encouraged by parish priests, reinforced this strong identification with place; the ownership of a home in

Catholic Chicago, according to Thomas Dyja, was "less the American Dream than the Vatican's." A remarkable 57 percent of homes in Back of the Yards were owned by residents in 1919; 90 percent of owners were foreign born. "The ambition of the immigrant to own property in America is one of his most striking characteristics," Louise Montgomery noted in her 1913 study of Packingtown. "He will make almost unbelievable sacrifices both of his own comfort, and that of his wife and children" to purchase a home. Home ownership generally reinforced ethnic segmentation, rather than undermining it, by tightly binding residents to their parishes.[7]

Back of the Yards also had a long-standing and well-deserved reputation as a hotbed of racism and violent hostility to blacks. It was common knowledge on the South Side that any black person caught in the neighborhoods surrounding the Union Stockyards after dark risked physical attack. As the black population in the neighborhoods surrounding Packingtown began to increase, James Grossman argues, "whites became still less likely to tolerate a black neighbor and more actively began to resist black settlement in their neighborhoods."[8]

Much of the hostility to blacks stemmed from confrontations between white packinghouse workers and black scabs during a series of unsuccessful strikes earlier in the century. According to the historian William Tuttle, as early as 1904 the words *negro* and *scab* had become synonymous to white workers in the area.[9] The period during and immediately after World War I was especially critical in the formation of racial identities and perceptions in the area. With immigration from Europe closed off, the packers turned to Southern blacks as a source of labor. In a remarkably short span, the packinghouse workforce changed from 3 percent to 25 percent black. Packing company manipulation of racial and ethnic differences, most famously, had contributed to the bloody race riot of 1919, much of which took place on Packingtown's fringes. The riot brought an organizing drive of the Stockyards Labor Council to an end and exacerbated racial tensions that persisted into the 1930s and beyond. For many black packinghouse workers, therefore, race seemed to be a more salient identity than class in determining their interests and loyalties. Unionism, according to Grossman, "had yet to prove its efficacy as a solution to a racial problem."[10]

In the wake of the first Great Migration of African Americans to the urban North, and particularly the Midwest, Chicago's social geography became increasingly racialized. Racial segregation in Chicago and elsewhere in the early twentieth century was largely maintained through a combination of local violence, the policing of racial boundaries by neighborhood associations, the assumptions and practices of real estate institutions and banks, and the court system. As early as 1910, according to Margaret Garb, Chicago's neighborhoods "came to be associated with the racial identity of their residents," as homeowners and real estate salesman linked property values to race. Even before the mass migration from the South, blacks in Chicago "faced organized campaigns to define and enforce racial boundaries of neighborhoods." By the end of World War I, Chicago had a racially divided housing market with an increasingly overcrowded black ghetto on the South Side.[11]

By the 1920s most professional real estate practitioners had come to believe that racial homogeneity was critical to the viability of urban neighborhoods and that property values were determined as much by who lived in the community as by the quality of the dwelling itself. The closer white communities were to a concentrated black settlement, the less stable property values were believed to be. The presence of black families in a white neighborhood was seen as a sign of instability and decline. This "racial theory of value" led real estate agents to see the protection of all-white communities and their property values as obligatory and in the public interest. In daily practice this meant refusing to show or sell properties to blacks in white or mixed areas. It also led real estate agents to encourage neighborhood groups to insert racially restrictive covenants into property deeds that prohibited property owners from selling or renting to blacks. By the late 1920s, according to the *Hyde Park Herald*, racially restrictive covenants were draped "like a marvelous delicately woven chain of armor" over much of the South Side. By 1930, two-thirds of all Chicago blacks lived in neighborhoods that were at least 90 percent black.[12]

Property was about more than just shelter: it generated social relationships and marked one's place in the moral economy. Encouraged by real estate agents, white neighborhood associations asserted a property right in the stability and value of the community as a whole. Racial segregation was considered common sense, as property was the "material foundation for creating and maintaining the proper social order." The market interventions necessary to maintain that racialized social order were justified because they were presumed to foster security and predictable risk. For real estate agents, segregation was profitable, and it would remain so for decades to come. For white homeowners, segregation became an expectation—even an entitlement—that was hard to separate from property rights themselves and was generally honored and enforced by the state. The housing market itself became a "race-making situation," creating racial identities and interests through its day-to-day operations.[13]

Racial segregation reinforced ethnic and racial ways of constructing identities, articulating interests, and mapping the city more generally. For European immigrants (and their children), striving to define and defend their identity as Americans, whiteness was an asset. It purchased market privileges in housing and labor that generated wealth and opportunity across generations. It offered the possibility of economic security. It also symbolized citizenship and a stable and legitimate place in the nation's moral economy. It was a marker of "worthiness." The whiteness of the "new" immigrants and their children was both contested and emergent in the decades before World War II. As Arnold Hirsch argues, it was used "as both a shield and a club, fending off challenges from above, and lashing out at those below."[14]

Organizing in Packingtown: The Creation of the BYNC

Alinsky went to Back of the Yards in the fall of 1938 to do fieldwork on juvenile delinquency, under the direction of Clifford Shaw's Chicago Area Project.[15] The Packinghouse Workers Organizing Committee was in the midst of a difficult unionizing campaign in the stockyards. Alinsky met a number of union organizers and began to attend mass meetings and take a more active role in the campaign. Convinced that problems with crime and juvenile delinquency were directly tied to the economic and political weakness of Packingtown's residents, Alinsky began to advocate the creation of a kind of "community union" to parallel the one being created in the meatpacking plants.

Alinsky met Joseph Meegan, the son of an Irish packinghouse worker, who introduced him to a group of young, America-born priests who were interested in bringing the ethnic enclaves together to support the PWOC. Packingtown's older priests were red-baiting the union from the pulpit, which was hurting the organizing campaign. Alinsky saw Meegan as a crucial community contact. Meegan also had connections in the Catholic hierarchy. His brother was the secretary for Bishop Bernard Sheil, the founder of the Catholic Youth Organization, who was an outspoken advocate for workers' rights and the hero of socially active priests throughout the city.[16]

With Sheil's help, in the spring and summer of 1939, Alinsky and Meegan began to talk to local priests and parishes, as well as social clubs, women's groups, youth organizations, and businesspeople about their common interest in the economic security and community power that an alliance between the PWOC and a multiethnic neighborhood group could create. Alinsky strongly believed in the value of conflict and confrontational tactics for building neighborhood unity, community organization, and collective power. Organization and conflict would lead a community group to ever-broader issues and identities as participants became aware of the relationships between local and larger units of the social structure—in this case, between neighborhood problems and economic powerlessness. Nearly four out of every five local

FIGURE 1.2. Saul Alinsky and Joseph Meegan. Box 171, folder 1737, Saul Alinsky Papers, Special Collections, University of Illinois Chicago.

families depended on packinghouse jobs in 1939, creating a strong economic interest in the union drive, which Alinsky hoped to mobilize. In that same year, a group of young women in the local Communist Party convinced the PWOC to sponsor a youth committee with representatives from community institutions to deal with juvenile delinquency and teenage unemployment—an issue that crossed ethnic lines. This youth committee became the organizational core of Alinsky's efforts.[17]

Alinsky viewed organizing as similar to social-science field research, in that listening, observing, and learning—rather than rabble-rousing—were essential to learning the lay of the land. He then used this knowledge to try to overcome fragmented loyalties and mobilize community-wide sentiments and interests. It was only by investigating a neighborhood's social structure—its traditions, viewpoints, and leadership (both formal and informal)—that an organizer could determine which forces pushed toward constructive democratic action and which ones promised to obstruct it. As Alinsky put it, "Those who build People's Organizations begin realistically with what they have. It does not matter whether they approve or disapprove of local circumstances, traditions, and agencies; the fact remains that this is the material that must be worked with. Builders of People's Organizations cannot indulge in the sterile, wishful thinking of liberals who prefer to start where they would like to begin rather than with actual conditions as they exist."[18]

Alinsky and Meegan sought to bring churches, unions, athletic clubs, cultural associations, block clubs, and business groups together into an "organization of organizations" for a common dialogue about shared problems. Such associations, Alinsky later argued, were "the very skeleton of democracy" and thus had to be used in the construction of a neighborhood organization, which could then quickly tap into and mobilize local resources. However poor and divided Packingtown was, it had a rich network of voluntary associations, which knit residents together in relationships of trust, dependency, and reciprocity. When the people of Packingtown eventually participated in the organization Alinsky and Meegan were building, they would bring with them what they had learned in their lodges, athletic clubs, and church societies. A community-wide group would be able to move these experiences onto a broader stage and take aim at more powerful targets.[19]

On July 14, 1939, over three hundred delegates representing seventy-six local groups assembled to create the BYNC, founded "for the purpose of uniting all of the organizations within that community known as the Back of the Yards, in order to promote the welfare of all residents of that community regardless of their race, color, or creed, so that they may all have the opportunity to find health, happiness and security through the democratic way of life." Local churches were prominently represented at the Community Congress, as was the PWOC, ending decades of clerical hostility to union efforts at the stockyards.[20] The alliance of churches, community groups, and the PWOC resulted in a rapid organizing victory for the union within days of the council's first Community Congress, as well as immediate economic benefits for residents.

Alinsky and Meegan had tried to organize residents through these civic associations rather than as members of ethnic blocs. This proved a wise choice, because it enabled the council (and the PWOC) to draw upon the rooted power of local civil society, creating a community-wide public while also broadening social identities and interests.[21] The BYNC was aided in this effort by a number of emerging changes in the nature of local ethnic and class identities. The new mass culture of the 1920s, employer efforts to stave off unionization, and the daily routine of work in gigantic mass-production factories spawned a new workplace culture and collective identity, particularly among younger workers. At the same time, the Great Depression undermined traditional sources of support and authority in ethnic communities.

The PWOC (and the Congress of Industrial Organizations—or CIO—with which it was affiliated) offered a new language for younger workers, a new way of envisioning themselves as Americans. Most of Packingtown's immigrants were introduced to the American political and economic system—and the meaning and significance of race—at union meetings. Immigration from Eastern Europe was largely cut off after 1924, so the white packinghouse workforce was increasingly made up of the native born. While this second generation of white workers remained closely tied to their parish-centered ethnic and spiritual lives, they also very much chafed at being seen as hyphenated Americans. The Great Depression, the labor movement, and the New Deal all helped to make their self-images as ethnic and working class more compatible with one another and with increasingly assertive forms of collective action. Particularly within the milieu of CIO-affiliated unions, they made use of the political discourse of what James Barrett calls "working-class Americanism," which strongly emphasized free speech, an "American standard of living," and cultural pluralism. The BYNC was the beneficiary of these shifts, in large part because Alinsky's organizing strategy was compatible with them. The process of "Americanization from the bottom up" took place within the PWOC and the BYNC simultaneously.[22]

As a result of the BYNC's success, Alinsky became a strong believer in the value of territorial identities and the power of local civic groups. In the future, he would always try to layer his People's Organizations on top of a neighborhood's civic groups rather than supplant them. This approach had the virtue of embedding his organizations deeply into local life, thus providing them with resources and legitimacy. For him the greatest obstacles to the empowerment of the urban poor were ethnic division and apathy. The remedy was to organize people locally, to politicize problems that had previously been seen as private, and to foster a sense of territorial unity and interest that would allow Chicago's ethnic working class to get its share of public and private resources. Unfortunately, as Alinsky would soon discover, racial identities and interests were very difficult to separate from how and where people lived, how they thought of one another, and how they thought of themselves. By using geographic identities and interests as an organizational template, Alinsky's method could easily reinforce the parochialism and territorial defensiveness that he most desired to overcome. This was especially true—and dangerous—with regard to race.

"Planting The Seed of Unity": The BYNC and Race in the 1940s

As the percentage of black packinghouse workers increased in the early 1940s, Alinsky and the PWOC worked hard to keep the BYNC progressive on racial issues. The early success of the PWOC was heavily dependent on the ability of the BYNC to pacify or redirect the racial identities and animosities of white workers and residents. Communists within the PWOC in particular had strongly emphasized interracial cooperation since the early 1930s. Using both the union hall and the University of Chicago Settlement House, black workers and their families were brought into the Back of the Yards as visitors for the first time. The PWOC carefully constructed a "culture of unity," integrating social activities and desegregating many of the bars near the stockyards, while blacks held leadership positions in the union in virtually every plant.

By the start of the Great Depression, black packinghouse workers had become seasoned, veteran workers with many of the same work-related grievances as their white counterparts. The cause of the black slaughterhouse worker was slowly becoming aligned with the overall interests of their neighborhoods, much as it had always been for white workers. The form that the rebirth of worker organization in the stockyards took in the 1930s—with a strong emphasis on direct action and control of the production process—also helped to build ethnic and racial cooperation, by allowing workers to voice and immediately act on shared grievances. Within the PWOC, shop-floor committees and executive boards were frequently racially integrated.[23]

The growing perception among both whites and blacks that the protection of their communities and their economic security required interracial cooperation was aided by the temporary calcifying of racial boundaries on the South Side during the Depression. As both black migration and the housing market ground to a halt, few blacks moved into white neighborhoods. The lessening of this threat made it possible for white packinghouse workers to see blacks as akin to another ethnic enclave, one that just happened to be located on the other side of Wentworth Avenue. It may also have tempered or delayed the widespread adoption of a white racial consciousness by Packingtown residents. As Arnold Hirsch and others have pointed out, Southern and Eastern Europeans appeared to stand outside of the "color-based, two-tiered social hierarchy" of racial identity. Nativists assigned them to "the peculiar racial purgatory of the middle tier," not black but not fully white either. And many of the immigrants themselves resisted the "reflexive assumption of a racist posture" that so powerfully shaped Chicago after World War I. Poles and other new immigrants witnessed the 1919 racial pogroms in their midst with a mixture of "empathy, minority identification and resistance to an all-embracing 'whiteness.'" This liminal period of racial formation allowed for the possibility of common interest across the color line, at least for a time.[24]

According to Rick Halpern, PWOC organizers eventually succeeded in building a coalition across ethnicity and race within the plants "not by supplanting bonds of ethnicity or dissolving ties to specific community institutions, but by forging a 'culture of unity' that linked material well-being with solidarity and empowerment at the workplace." Alinsky pushed the same message in the BYNC.[25]

This culture of unity was reinforced by political developments. By the end of World War II, racial liberalism had emerged as an important and increasingly influential political force in the urban North. It was premised on the belief that racism was a problem of white attitudes, not black capacities, and that only education, interracial contact, and state protection of individual rights and opportunities could end it. Sparked by black political mobilization and informed by a decided optimism about the use of state power to protect individual rights, broadly distribute opportunity, and encourage upward social mobility, a coalition of liberal and leftist activists sought to use the labor movement and the New Deal state to achieve racial justice.

While postwar racial liberalism was stronger, broader, and longer lasting in cities like New York and Philadelphia, Chicago emerged from the war with its own influential interracial coalition during the administration of Mayor Edward Kelly (1933–1946). Much like the BYNC itself, Kelly took strong positions in favor of civil rights during World War II. He was reportedly inspired by the struggle against fascism; no doubt the possibility of capturing Chicago's expanding black vote lifted his spirits as well. Kelly backed up his belief in open housing with action, ordering city police to protect blacks when they moved into previously all-white neighborhoods. He created the Mayor's Committee on Race Relations in 1943, with Alinsky as an early member. As the war came to an end, Kelly sought to address the critical issues of employment discrimination, housing, and education. He steered a local fair employment practices law through City Council in 1945 and appointed liberal whites and blacks to lead both the Chicago Housing Authority (CHA) and the public schools.[26]

Even though integrated teams of door-to-door union organizers sometimes had to dodge bricks and stones, and white workers had to escort blacks through some parts of Packingtown, significant progress was made. The *Chicago Defender*, a black newspaper, noted in 1939 that before the PWOC, the folk wisdom was that "no Negro had better show his face west of Ashland Avenue after dark." But conditions had changed: "Today because the PWOC planted the seed of unity in the stony soil of Packingtown, Negroes walk freely and safely . . . on the very streets where danger once lurked at every corner for Negroes, colored men stop for long chats about baseball with Polish or Irish workers." The story of the union was also "the story of the successful fight waged by its Negro and white members to abolish discrimination and racial terror in Packingtown." "Isn't this Americanism in the truest sense?" asked Oscar Wilson, a black union officer.[27]

The BYNC aided in sowing that seed of unity. The council joined the union in fighting for racial equality, using protests to open local retail businesses, restaurants, and theaters to blacks and playing a leading role in the fight for state laws against employment discrimination. It created its Race Relations Committee, charged with bringing white and black packinghouse workers together to discuss union and workplace issues, and also dealing with rumors in the community. Through the committee, the council worked closely with union representatives to "counteract the racial and national antipathies" by showing movies, offering lectures, and distributing pamphlets.[28] Individuals found "guilty of spreading rumors that foment hatred" were reprimanded publicly and threatened with social ostracism and the cancellation of union membership. When a story began to circulate in Packingtown that blacks were "pushing white people around" on buses, six priests in civilian clothes rode the buses and trolleys for a week and reported from the pulpit that they had seen no such offenses take place. Meegan and the council discredited rumors that black families were moving into the neighborhood in the local paper. The BYNC also organized trips through the Black Belt for clergy and local leaders to expose them to black living conditions. Priests active in the group frequently spoke out from the pulpit against racial prejudice as unchristian. "I witnessed racial integration to a degree which I have never seen before or since," Alinsky later wrote.[29]

Gary Gerstle describes an ongoing tension in the past century between "racial nationalism" and "civic nationalism." In the New Deal and especially during World War II, American identity was redefined, often from the bottom up, as racially and ethnically pluralistic and inclusive. The BYNC typified this 1940s-era civic nationalism, inviting Packingtown's immigrants and their children to see tolerance and interracial cooperation as a significant step toward adopting and defining an American identity that would include them as equals. A flyer inviting residents to the BYNC's 1943 Community Congress asked, "Do you believe that religious and racial prejudices are wholly foreign and repulsive to the very spirit of America? If so, your place is in the BYNC, which has unswervingly carried on the fight against those purveyors of the Hitlerite poison." In his invocation address, Bishop Bernard Sheil echoed this sentiment, declaring, "We know now, as never before, that this world cannot be half free and half slave." He praised the council for standing "squarely on these democratic principles of truth, and it is for that reason that prejudice, either based on religion or color, has not and never can have any place in your hearts or minds. You appreciate what it is to be part of a minority."[30]

Importantly, however, the BYNC's interest in the welfare of black citizens did not include welcoming them to live in Packingtown. Its racial liberalism depended largely upon the leadership of Alinsky and PWOC organizers, the need for unity at the workplace, the wartime housing shortage, and the council's studied silence on the question of blacks as neighbors. When the war ended and the South Side's racial boundaries began to rapidly change, the council quickly abandoned its interest in interracialism, as Packingtown residents began to see the expanding ghetto as a threat. The volatility of the South Side's racial boundaries threatened the homogeneity and cultural security of the area; blacks and Mexicans (many of them packinghouse workers) were moving into nearby Englewood and Kenwood in increasing numbers. The surrounding areas had begun to change from white to black largely because white housing demand had evaporated with the first rumors of a black influx. Meegan feared the same outcome in Packingtown. Other white communities (such as Hyde Park) were in the process of putting together conservation and rehabilitation programs to try to forestall racial change. The BYNC followed suit.

Why did the BYNC become a force for racial segregation in the early 1950s? At the macro level, the Chicago area's racial geography was transforming rapidly and violently, with the state playing a greatly expanded role in legitimizing and exacerbating racial segregation. More locally, the conditions that had led to some degree of interracial solidarity in Packingtown began to disappear. The packinghouse workforce became increasingly black, as did the union. At the same time, the broader political milieu of racial liberalism had begun to atrophy, overpowered by red-baiting and racialized struggles. This altered racial ecology, when combined with the precarious status of Packingtown's overwhelmingly Catholic and immigrant population, led the BYNC to see keeping blacks out of the neighborhood as a legitimate and necessary undertaking. Much to his chagrin, Alinsky's hard work helped them succeed.

The Changing Politics of Race and Place in Chicago

The Great Migration of African Americans from the South to the urban Northeast and Midwest began during World War I, lapsed during the Depression decade, and then began again in the 1940s and continued until the end of the 1960s, changing forever both the nature and the spatial expression of

American race relations. In the 1930s and early 1940s, Chicago's racial boundaries were mostly frozen in place. This provided part of the context for interracial union organizing in meatpacking and other industries, as well as for the BYNC's liberal positions on race. The end of the war, however, set Chicago's racial boundaries moving once again. Aided by the lifting of wartime rent controls, the resumption of housing construction in outlying city areas and in the suburbs in the late 1940s, long bottled up during the Depression and the war, opened up Chicago's housing market for white home buyers for the first time in a generation. The population of Chicago's suburbs grew by a remarkable 72 percent during the 1950s, while the population of the city fell slightly. Just over three hundred thousand new housing units were constructed in the suburbs during the 1950s, more than twice as many as were built in the city. Between 1945 and 1959 more than 77 percent of the new units built in the Chicago area were located in the suburbs. These units were almost entirely closed to black families through the next decade. Those whites who could move to the urban fringe or leave the city altogether did so at an extraordinary rate: more than 270,000 whites left Chicago from 1950 to 1956 alone. The pace continued in the 1960s, when the white population of the city fell by nearly five hundred thousand. The city's share of the metropolitan area population decreased from 74 percent in 1940 to 57 percent in 1960. By the early 1960s, the housing shortage for whites had ended.[31]

The rapid expansion of the white housing market initiated a filtering process through which upwardly mobile blacks began to move into the older and formerly white neighborhoods surrounding the traditional Black Belt. The result was a wave of contested and often violent racial change in Chicago's neighborhoods in the first two postwar decades. Nearly fifteen thousand black families purchased or occupied dwellings beyond previously established black areas during the 1940s, resulting in a rash of violent confrontations between blacks and whites. In the late 1940s, 485 racial incidents were reported to the Chicago Commission on Human Relations (CCHR), most of them directly related to housing or residential property—and located on the fringes of black concentrations.[32] As Charles Abrams later described it, the monthly reports of the CCHR "read like field bulletins in a war." Blacks walking through white South Side neighborhoods faced real physical danger, even during daylight. The process only accelerated in the 1950s and 1960s, with the expansion of the racially exclusive suburbs. The number of black homeowners in the city grew fivefold from 1950 to 1970, with the huge majority of the new purchases in neighborhoods that were previously all white. In the 1960s alone, 128,829 units were transferred from white to black occupancy in Chicago.[33]

The area of black settlement expanded for three reasons. First, the Second Great Migration was causing black housing demand to grow rapidly, while supply within the boundaries of the traditional Black Belt was substandard and overcrowded. At the same time, supply *beyond* the ghetto was restricted—in part by Chicago's overall housing shortage, but mainly by decades of racial discrimination in the city and its suburbs. The result of increasing demand and stagnant supply, not surprisingly, was tremendous overcrowding and exploitative rents in black areas. When the war ended, three hundred thousand blacks were packed into an area seven miles long and a mile and a half wide; population density on the black South Side was ninety thousand people per square mile versus twenty thousand for adjacent white areas.

As late as 1950 there were only 114,000 housing units available for the half a million blacks living in Chicago's Black Belt, with over half of these in poor physical condition. Just thirteen thousand units were owner-occupied. The vacancy rate was only 1 percent, and these were largely substandard units. Neither private nor federal lending agencies would finance the construction or rehabilitation of homes in the ghetto, other than public housing. If black families aspired to decent housing in Chicago, let alone homeownership, there was nowhere to go but out of the traditional Black Belt.[34]

Second, by the early 1950s there was actually somewhere for the South Side's aspiring black middle class to go. The enormous growth in the white suburban housing market—as well as the *Shelley v. Kraemer* (1948) Supreme Court decision invalidating court enforcement of racially restrictive covenants—greatly expanded the available housing supply for Chicago blacks. The flight of whites to the suburbs and the urban fringe loosened the housing market for the first time in decades, providing black families with access to a large number of good-quality units in previously white areas. Despite persistent discrimination in the realty and credit markets, Chicago's black middle class increasingly took the financial and physical risks necessary for homeownership beyond the boundaries of the traditional Black Belt. For example, middle-class black families began to move west and south out of the Grand Boulevard neighborhood, on Packingtown's eastern border, starting in the early 1950s. It quickly depopulated, as slum clearance programs reduced the number of housing units, while white flight and economic mobility provided tens of thousands of black families with an opportunity to improve their surroundings. By 1970, the population within the boundaries of the 1960 Black Belt had fallen by 19 percent, as an ever-larger proportion of Chicago's black families improved their housing standards by fleeing the traditional South Side ghetto.[35]

West Englewood, just south of Packingtown, is a useful example. Racial conflict and rapid population change there would help to frame BYNC's approach to the issue in the early 1950s. Englewood and other Southwest Side neighborhoods originally emerged as suburbs of the stockyard district in the early twentieth century. Generations of skilled workers in the packinghouses tended to follow one another to Englewood and other areas to the west. By 1920 it had become a neighborhood of Catholic homeowners. The Depression hit Englewood hard, leading to a collapse of the business district, and the deterioration of the housing stock. As in so many other older white neighborhoods, this deterioration began *before* black families began to arrive, although blacks were generally blamed after the fact.[36]

Black stockyard workers began to move into Englewood from Grand Boulevard during the war, and their numbers increased in peacetime. This was matched by a rapid and virtually complete out-migration of whites from the area. On a November night in 1949, a crowd of violent whites surrounded Aaron Bindman's home at Fifty-sixth and Peoria. Bindman, a union activist, had invited eight black shop stewards and ten whites to his home, sparking rumors that he had sold his house to a black family. The mob was at least ten thousand strong at its peak.[37]

The BYNC had good reason to believe that what was happening in Englewood would soon happen in Packingtown. In the 1950s alone, fourteen thousand whites left western Englewood. Many of them moved to the newer sections of the Southwest Side, where they would encounter Saul Alinsky and his Organization for the Southwest Community in the early 1960s. Neighborhoods to the west of Western Avenue (like Marquette Park and Gage Park, where Martin Luther King Jr. would later lead open housing marches in 1966) reacted defensively to West Englewood's growing black population, as did Packingtown. Blacks had been just over 2 percent of Englewood's population in 1940; by 1960, the community was nearly 70 percent black. The possibility of a black influx into Packingtown provided an important context for the BYNC's conservation program.[38]

Third, the housing market in the suburbs and the urban fringe were almost entirely closed to black families, forcing those seeking to improve their housing situation into previously white neighborhoods in such large numbers that black demand swamped both white demand and the housing supply. It was in older communities adjacent to the ghetto where housing was generally available for black pioneers, often either on installment or at very high rents. Neighborhoods that bordered on predominantly black areas found it difficult to keep or attract white residents, as mortgages and loans for home improvements dried up in anticipation of transition. Long-term investment would be postponed, and many supporting services and institutions would depart. Young white families with school-age children were often the first to leave. Others, stirred by rumors of increasing crime and decreasing property values, would contemplate both resistance and flight. Once a block in a white neighborhood had been "busted," real estate agents and speculators had a strong financial interest in catering to potential black buyers and tenants, since the dual housing market allowed them to profit. Local neighborhood-improvement associations, frequently encouraged by parish priests, furiously embarked upon conservation campaigns to avoid redlining and the transition and flight that was presumed to (and often did) follow from it.

Racial segregation was imprinted on the urban and suburban landscape, while neighborhood after neighborhood rapidly (and often violently) turned over from white to black. The segregated housing market created a demand differential: the supply available to blacks was concentrated in limited parts of the city only, whereas whites (particularly wealthier ones) could purchase homes virtually anywhere in the metropolitan area. Racial discrimination thus created financial incentives for the rapid transition of white neighborhoods—popularly referred to as blockbusting—since sellers could get more money from black buyers than from white. It served as a kind of racial centrifuge, heightening awareness among whites (and blacks) of their racial identities and interests while making interracial organizing extremely difficult. It also naturalized racial segregation and made the notion of a stable, integrated neighborhood seem impossible.

Segregation also contributed to a context of economic and social precariousness, particularly in white neighborhoods on the edge of the ghetto. For white working-class homeowners in these areas, issues of race quickly became enmeshed in larger questions of property, community, social acceptance, moral desert, the state, and the divide between public and private. Whites and blacks thus encountered one another—and shaped their perceptions of one another and themselves—in a race-making context that whites in particular perceived as a kind of zero-sum game. According to Arnold Hirsch, the white racial consciousness that emerged was "both an act of self-defense and a conscious grasping for the advantage that came with entry into the 'white' clubroom." This was particularly true for "ethnic" Catholics, like those who populated Packingtown.[39]

The role of the state at all levels was critical. Housing markets, like all markets, are social creations governed by politically and legally determined rules, by market institutions and actors, and by the assumptions, interests, and identities that shape them. They constitute, reflect, and reinforce power relations. Similarly, in creating and defending property rights the law draws boundaries and enforces or reorders existing regimes of power. Throughout Chicago's South Side, white homeowners defended the racial homogeneity of their neighborhoods and community institutions because they believed that something valuable was at stake and that their defense of it was sanctioned by public opinion, economic common sense, and the law. For Catholics, these beliefs were strengthened by the intense territoriality of their faith and its surrounding social and institutional practices.

Federal policies, court rulings, and political action have all shaped the racial geography of American metropolitan areas in the twentieth century, especially since World War II. Racially restrictive covenants were legally enforceable and widespread in Chicago, particularly on the South Side, until 1948, when the US Supreme Court in *Shelley v. Kraemer* ruled them unconstitutional. This gave the close identification of race with place, and of racial homogeneity with economic and social security, a significant degree of legitimacy. In particular, it naturalized residential segregation and encouraged the creation of identities and interests bound up in its preservation. It also tacitly condoned and encouraged white violence.[40]

In the 1930s and 1940s, federal housing policy greatly amplified the connections between race, place and security in Chicago and other cities, embedding race ever deeper into urban geography and the social identities and perceptions surrounding it. The loan and mortgage insurance guidelines of the Federal Housing Administration, the Home Owners' Loan Corporation, the Veterans Administration, and other government agencies followed the racial theory of value assumed by most housing market actors and stressed the importance of racial homogeneity for neighborhood stability in urban areas. Because private assessors and government agencies did not believe that neighborhoods inhabited by or adjacent to black settlements were stable or creditworthy, federally insured mortgages after the war were overwhelmingly located in the suburbs, from which black families were generally excluded. In effect, government housing programs joined locally organized efforts to resist integration to both the law and the national purpose with regard to housing. These policies punished whites that lived in racially diverse neighborhoods by devaluing their homes and by raising the opportunity costs of denying the racial privileges upheld by segregation.[41]

By the late 1950s the federal government had created a two-tiered housing policy that subsidized suburban homeownership for whites while consigning blacks to segregated urban neighborhoods. It was reinforced by action in other realms, from taxation to transportation to the welfare state, racializing perceptions of the moral economy, liberalism, and government.

White homeowners perceived their houses and communities as a private, market-based reflection of their own virtues (hard work, lawfulness, patriotism, faith) and blacks as demanding (and receiving) things that they hadn't earned, which to them simultaneously threatened the security of those who had "played by the rules."[42]

The rules and assumptions embedded in government policies and the practices of housing market actors, when combined with the impressions presented to many white urbanites by the concentrated poverty of nearby black settlements, and the racist images that permeated politics and the culture generally, were clear: blacks moving in to white neighborhoods were a financial and social threat. The state-structured housing market established clear and unmistakable incentives for white homeowners to resist integrated living. And they did so, in Packingtown and countless other white neighborhoods in Chicago and elsewhere. Not surprisingly, white resistance to black proximity in the late 1940s and early 1950s altered Chicago politics, which in turn changed the relationship of city government to issues of race and geography. The BYNC's interracial unity, always weak, was fatally undermined—threatening not only Alinsky's reputation but also his faith in the possibility of grassroots solutions to Chicago's injustices and inequalities.

Packingtown's Shifting Ground

The state, the labor market, and the politics of Chicago's postwar racial geography powerfully shaped the context in which the BYNC devised its conservation program. Neighborhood racial homogeneity was framed as a valuable and politically legitimate entitlement worth fighting for. At the same, the political ecology shifted at the local level in the first decade after the war, foregrounding racial identities and weakening the conditions that had earlier made interracial coalition building possible.

Mayor Kelly's public stances on race contributed to two important developments in Chicago politics: the shift of black voters into the local Democratic Party and the emergence of race and housing as a pivotal political issue. As Arnold Hirsch describes it, "Fatefully, at the precise moment South Side ethnics were demonstrating their mortal fear of an expanding Black Belt, Kelly issued a public statement guaranteeing blacks 'their right to live peaceably anywhere in Chicago.'" Ward politicians encouraged white resistance, hoping to break Kelly's patronage stranglehold. When the increasingly unpopular (and corrupt) Kelly was forced out in 1946, the space for racial liberalism he had created in government and politics rapidly diminished. Kelly shouldn't be idealized, of course; his corruption weakened the alliance between civil rights advocates and white anti-machine elements. The city's changing social geography increasingly racialized Chicago politics, and red-baiting crippled the more assertive wing of the civil rights coalition. The most prominent black political figure in the city, Congressman William Dawson, chose to avoid racial issues in favor of increasing his power within the Democratic Party's machine. An incipient interracial coalition for civil rights, which had been nurtured by the wartime politics of "civic nationalism," vanished from Chicago politics—with dire consequences in the decades to follow. The period that Chicago writer Nelson Algren referred to as a "fresh time" had come to an end.[43]

The BYNC had reason to believe that Chicago's political elite saw racial containment as a legitimate undertaking. In the wake of the *Shelley* ruling in 1948 and violent resistance by white homeowners to residential integration in South Deering, Englewood, and Chicago Lawn in the early 1950s, state and city politicians responded to popular pressures by utilizing the CHA to shore up segregation and by creating an institutional and financial infrastructure to support conservation and slum clearance efforts aimed at containing the Black Belt. In 1948 the state took the power to choose public housing sites away from the CHA and gave it to City Council. Encouraged by Kelly's successor, Martin Kennelly, the City Council overwhelmingly rejected a 1949 ordinance proposed by black alderman Archibald Carey that would have required nondiscrimination in all housing built with municipal funding, or on land acquired through the city's power of eminent domain. The City Council also rejected efforts by CHA executive director Elizabeth Wood to build public housing on vacant sites in outlying (and white) areas, forcing future construction back into the expanding ghetto.[44]

Left without political cover, the CHA's independence on racial issues came under heavy attack in the early 1950s. Alinsky, as president of the Public Housing Association (PHA)—a federation of Chicago's racially liberal groups—led a valiant campaign in support of the Carey Ordinance and the CHA's efforts to scatter project sites around the city, but to no avail. School superintendent Harold Hunt's story closely mirrored that of Wood. When he sought to implement a redistricting plan in 1950—which was aimed primarily at overcrowding in black schools, not racial dispersion—Hunt faced powerful and effective opposition. Teachers and school administrators hesitated to implement the changes, and white parents long accustomed to having their racial preferences informally accommodated reacted angrily. A frustrated Hunt resigned in 1953. Benjamin Willis succeeded him. Much to the delight of the machine and white neighborhood activists, Willis openly championed the neighborhood school and denied the existence of racial segregation, describing it as "a circumstantial thing."[45]

Aided by federal housing laws passed in 1949 and 1954, Chicago and other cities utilized urban renewal, public housing, and conservation to maintain the walls of racial segregation. Frank Horne, of the US Housing Authority, worried that cities would try to use federal money to clear black neighborhoods and "crystallize patterns of racial or nationalistic separation by allowing private developers . . . to prohibit occupancy in new developments merely on the basis of race." Federal funds and powers might be used to "harden into brick and mortar the racially restrictive practices of private real estate and lending operations." Horne's fears proved prophetic. Chicago city officials used slum clearance and public housing (both enabled by the 1949 housing law) to protect downtown interests, displace black families, and reinforce racial segregation. The 1954 Federal Housing Act, which funneled money into nonresidential development and nonslum areas, marked a policy shift from urban redevelopment to urban renewal and conservation. Its stated purpose was to rehabilitate downtown business districts and "save" threatened neighborhoods. In reality it provided cities with tools to contain and displace areas of concentrated black residence.[46]

In Chicago, the 1955 mayoral election was an important watershed. Stung by the race-baiting rhetoric of Kennelly's campaign, black voters swung their electoral support to the Democratic machine (and Richard Daley) in large numbers for the first time. While black voters were never as loyal to the machine as is commonly believed—they consistently gave national Democratic candidates more support, and wards with a strong middle-class presence were often in play—they were critical to Daley's first three elections.

Their trust was not rewarded. Under Daley, the CHA quickly became a bulwark of segregation in the city, while conservation and urban renewal projects were increasingly directed toward protecting downtown business interests and pacifying white homeowners. Racial containment united both constituencies, although the former was much better served by the Daley regime than the latter, in the end. All these measures served to reinforce Chicago's racialized housing market and white expectations of racial homogeneity. High schools in the city rapidly segregated and inequality increased, while Willis and the Chicago Board of Education stonewalled.[47]

By the early 1950s, there was little space in Chicago politics for interracial advocacy of racial liberalism and civil rights. The combination of white resistance, black political powerlessness, and Cold War red-baiting had essentially sidelined it. Chicago's best-known white novelist at the time, Nelson Algren, lamented the deterioration of race relations in the city: "The Christianity of the white American middle class had lost its nerve; now we saw it to be a coast-to-coast fraud. And the fraud lay in this: that property was more valuable than people." There was little impetus from outside Packingtown to keep the BYNC tied to its wartime racial liberalism. There was even less impetus from the inside.[48]

Changes in the meatpacking workforce also undermined the racial openness of the BYNC. Jobs in the industry were increasingly filled by blacks. By the end of World War II, half of the union's members were black, and this percentage increased in the postwar decade. By the time the plants began to close in the late 1950s and early 1960s, almost all the workers were black. Few whites in Packingtown worked in the stockyards anymore; very few young whites did so. With the closing of the plants, according to the union activist Herbert March, "the social basis for positive relations between black and white workers simply disappeared." Fred Hoehler, a union activist observing the area in 1947, noted that while "ethnics are in a closer working relationship than ever before," all whites still had "great antipathies toward the Negro population living directly to the east." Even in the late 1940s, when the BYNC still made public stands for racial equality, most of those who attended local union meetings in Packingtown were black, and they faced growing hostility during their several-block walk into and out of the area—a fact that eventually led to the removal of union headquarters to a black neighborhood. According to March, even during the height of local work on racial cooperation, "people didn't go to each other's homes or churches or social clubs. It just wasn't done." Black workers heading to union affairs in the Back of the Yards could do so, but "had their destination been anything but the Union's headquarters there would have been an immediate, and negative reaction in the community."[49]

Union activists had always dominated the BYNC's Race Relations Committee, and it began to lose local support as early as 1946. In the wake of white violence against a black family trying to move into the Airport Homes apartments on the Far South Side in 1946, Alinsky told the National Conference of Christians and Jews that the Back of the Yards had become a racial "powder keg" that could explode at any moment. The council was "taking extraordinary measures to nip any outbreak in the bud," he told the gathering. This took the form of "anti-bigotry sermons preached from local pulpits and fair play discussion groups and anti-rumor activities have been initiated among adults and children." In 1948, when Chicago hosted the CIO's national convention, violence erupted in nearby Bridgeport when a white delegate invited a black worker to spend the night at his home.[50]

Without the common bond of the killing floor and the union hall, whites in Packingtown increasingly identified the stability, viability, and desirability of their parishes and neighborhoods with racial homogeneity, much as whites did elsewhere on the South Side. In the 1940s the United Packinghouse Workers Association (UPWA, successor to the PWOC) was part of a CIO-led Popular Front coalition dedicated to eradicating racial discrimination as an act of class solidarity and democratic progress. It found a relatively friendly climate within Chicago politics, as well. The BYNC plugged into this coalition, interacting extensively with its interracial leadership and tentatively expanding the wartime civic nationalism that had brought its own ethnic enclaves together to include blacks as fellow workers in search of a full American life. While the BYNC was a place-based organization from its inception, deriving its identity and interests from the commonality of geography first and foremost, its connection to an ideologically and institutionally broader social movement that was not geographically defined enabled it to be substantively progressive on racial issues. In the early 1950s changes at the workplace and the politics of racial geography began to separate the BYNC from this coalition; simultaneously, the coalition itself began to weaken.

For black workers, the union continued to be a vehicle to pursue a wider agenda that touched on both race and class, including housing discrimination in the neighborhoods around the stockyards. The UPWA was at the forefront of Chicago's Black Freedom Movement in the late 1940s and early 1950s, fighting for laws against employment and housing discrimination. Black union activists like Charles Hayes, who had worked with Alinsky in the early 1940s, took leadership positions in the National Association for the Advancement of Colored People (NAACP) and other civil rights groups.

The BYNC, however, was no longer an ally. By the early 1950s the BYNC had changed its official symbol from a priest surrounded by a black worker and a white worker to one that portrayed the priest between a white worker and a white businessman.[51] The official symbol is of some consequence. In 1940, the notion of a boss and a worker making common cause would have seemed alien to BYNC members, their shared skin color notwithstanding. A decade later, a kind of inward-looking whiteness and Catholicism had literally become the face of the organization. Packingtown was certainly not unique in this respect.

For Catholics, who not only predominated in Packingtown but also throughout the white South Side well into the postwar era, racial formation was intertwined with a religiously sanctioned territorial sensibility centered on the parish. Alinsky understood the spiritual and institutional commitments of the urban church well. When queried about his explanation of the council's segregationism by Gurney Breckenfeld in 1960, Alinsky explained that racial transition threatened the very existence of Catholic parishes: "When a community changes from white to Negro, the Catholic church is in a different position from the Protestant and Jewish churches. It has a bigger real estate investment. Thus it is in double jeopardy." Black "invasion" of neighborhoods like Packingtown seemed to threaten more than just property values, in the conventional sense; it jeopardized the Catholic civil society that had taken decades of sacrifice to construct.

Pastors often commanded their parishioners to buy homes in the parish and emphasized the religious meanings of territorial identity. Catholics in Chicago and other Northern cities tended to stay longer in their neighborhoods, had more friends within walking distance, attended church more frequently, and were more likely to own their own homes and to be involved in local institutions than non-Catholics. Alinsky had built the BYNC largely on the returns to this parish-centered investment. The New Deal state offered home ownership as a crucial component of American social citizenship, and unions advocated it as the material precondition of an "American standard of living." These two related notions of property generally found willing listeners in Packingtown. Long accustomed to seeing the ownership of property as a critical component of their religious expression, in the postwar context the available resource of whiteness invited them to see it as a way to claim American identity.[52]

The PWOC brought packinghouse workers of different races and European ethnicities together as Americans striving for the rights and security promised by the New Deal and necessary for full membership and acceptance in American society. For a time, the BYNC fought the same battle, with the same language of "working-class Americanism." By the late 1940s, a union contract, a home in a stable neighborhood, and the right to choose one's associates all seemed to be a part of full membership in American society to which all—including Catholics—were entitled. Home ownership, in particular, gave Packingtown residents a place in the moral economy decidedly more stable and secure than had existed before the war. It was a marker of their acceptance as Americans and a symbol of their hard work; at the same time, the precariousness of their new status was strongly related to their proximity to the ghetto.[53]

When the boundaries of Chicago's Black Belt were shattered in the late 1940s, the value of whiteness in that moral economy became readily apparent. For the residents of Packingtown, who had spent the better part of the previous decade (with Alinsky's help) believing that territorial unity, unionization, and community improvement would cement their full membership in the American polity, while still ensuring the viability of their religious practices, black proximity was seen as a profound threat. The BYNC's conservation program was intended to meet this threat; Alinsky's prowess in helping to develop a multiethnic sense of territorial identity in Packingtown unwittingly made this effort an effective one.

"An Island of Comfort and Contentment": The Segregationist Turn

The Back of the Yards Neighborhood Council never publicly declared itself opposed to residential integration, and it never took or endorsed specific steps to prevent black families from moving into Packingtown and its adjacent neighborhoods. Its efforts to keep the area white instead took the form of a campaign to improve and upgrade the infrastructure and housing stock of the neighborhood. Rather than preventing black families from moving in—which steering by real estate agents and the threat (and occasional reality) of violence against black "pioneers" largely took care of—the council concentrated on keeping and attracting white families.

But much of the housing stock was run down, young families were moving to the suburbs, and illegal conversions were creating congested and inferior housing. Packingtown had a long and well-deserved reputation for decrepit housing; in 1918, a lawyer for the packers said that the only solution to it was "absolute destruction of the district." Private builders shunned the area after World War II, in part because banks and federal housing agencies had, too. Fewer than a dozen new homes had been built in the area since before the Great Depression; as a result, much of the housing was old and substandard.[54]

Packingtown residents were not alone in their fears of "blight." Housing stock and infrastructure in Chicago's older South Side neighborhoods had become run down, and courts and building inspectors rarely enforced relevant laws. Yet while blight was certainly real, it was more often than not falsely conflated with black occupancy (or proximity). The entrance of black families into formerly all-white communities tended to follow physical deterioration rather than cause it. But discussions of blight and decay were thoroughly infused with racist assumptions. Neighborhood decline was seen as a function of age, as proximity to black communities, or as a condition of black life per se, not as a symptom of social inequality originating in the segregation of housing and labor markets, and of the unequal distribution of political and economic power. As a metaphor, according to Thomas Dyja, blight "allowed politicians, journalists, and civic do-gooders to rail against the visible effects of poverty without having to address its uncomfortable causes."[55]

The use of organic language like *blight* and *decay* was itself indicative of the perception that processes beyond the control of white communities were undermining their surroundings. Run-down buildings, parks, streets, and schools threatened a "contagion" that could leave the community vulnerable to the "infection" of black proximity. Homeowners, downtown real estate interests, and public officials offered a variety of different programs to preserve and renew Chicago after World War II. Virtually all of them involved containing the growing black population in some fashion. The Federal Housing Act of 1949 provided funding for slum clearance and public housing construction, and the 1954 Housing Act shifted federal and local resources into urban renewal and conservation. In city after city, including Chicago, public officials and housing market institutions used federal resources to reinforce racial segregation.

Like dozens of other neighborhoods, the BYNC launched a conservation program in 1953 to upgrade the physical infrastructure of the neighborhood, to keep white families in place, to reinforce private investments in the area, and to head off deterioration of housing. "We are trying to keep people in the neighborhood, not keep them out," Meegan told the *Chicago Daily News* in the late 1950s. "Negroes don't have anything in common with the people who live here."[56]

Two sets of institutions in particular were financially dependent on the stability of Packingtown: Catholic churches and banks. Meegan decided to take advantage of the large number of financial institutions in the Back of the Yards—by one estimate the neighborhood contained 10 percent of all the banks and savings and loans in Cook County—and lobby for them to stop financing flight. He called a meeting at the Stockyards Inn in July 1953 to persuade residents to stay and remodel their properties, and to push bankers to reinvest in the community. With seventy-one representatives from labor, business, banks, churches, and the Federal Housing Administration in the audience, Meegan made his pitch. According to one banker, Meegan "told us that we would either lend money for remodeling and new home construction right here in the yards, or we'd see all our depositors disappear to the suburbs. And he was right. We'd been taking deposits from these people for years and we were making all our mortgage loans in the suburbs."[57]

The council's conservation program had four components: first, the group used its political pull to get housing and zoning codes enforced, especially on absentee owners, to prevent an increase in housing conversions and rooming houses. Second, the council pushed City Hall to make long overdue capital improvements, such as street widening, new lights, and park construction. Third, Meegan convinced churches, businesses, and banks that the future of Packingtown would be a stable one, if they improved their properties and financed homeowner efforts to rehabilitate older housing. Finally, to keep young families in the area, the council purchased vacant lots and arranged for new reasonably priced and financed homes to be constructed.

At the same time, however, the packing industry was beginning to disappear. By all accounts the neighborhood should have declined. Nonetheless, the BYNC succeeded spectacularly. The Back of the Yards became widely known as a "model urban working-class community." When houses went on sale, parish churches worked to find local whites to buy them. The council stopped real estate agents who tried to panic property owners into selling their homes. In the first year, local banks made 560 home improvement loans, many at rates below standard. Real estate values jumped 30 percent in two years; by 1963, more than ten thousand homes (90 percent of the entire housing stock) had been upgraded. Over four hundred storefronts were converted to apartments, and over eight hundred homes were constructed from 1953 to 1972. The council also sponsored a housing development, Destiny Manor, whose buildings tripled in value in ten years. By the mid-1950s, the BYNC had attracted nationwide attention as a model of local democracy. As Slayton puts it, the council had "met and overcome all other bases of power in the community, and had become a recognized force in Chicago." Upton Sinclair's "jungle" had become, in the words of one observer, "an island of comfort and contentment" for nearly one hundred thousand residents.[58]

But it was an island in another sense as well: the Back of the Yards remained almost entirely white. Hal Barron of the Chicago Urban League described the neighborhood as a "hotbed of segregationist feeling." Joseph Meegan denied that the BYNC was racist, claiming, "We are trying to keep people in the neighborhood, not keep them out," and that blacks had chosen not to live there and their absence was "just happenstance," a dubious claim at best. Gurney Breckenfeld was certainly skeptical, observing in 1960 that "race tensions are still little mentioned in the millions of words now being spoken and written on rehabilitation and urban renewal . . . yet the racial situation has a great deal to do with the outcome of a rehabilitation program."[59]

By the early 1960s, a South Side real estate speculator observed that the Back of the Yards Neighborhood Council had managed to keep Packingtown "all white" through a system of "unique authoritarian control extending through stores, banks, churches, and industry." Breckenfeld found few residents who would speak on the issue publicly—but quite a few did so anonymously. Bank officials, businessmen, and homeowners told him that they were "determined to keep Negroes out." The vice president of a lending institution hoped some other neighborhood would absorb the growing black population, and thus relieve the pressure on Packingtown. A highly placed city official told Breckenfeld that in Back of the Yards a "covenant of violence" had replaced the racially restrictive covenants outlawed by the US Supreme Court in 1948. The Chicago Commission on Human Relations, charged with investigating racial conflict and discrimination, described the area as a "white enclave surrounded by straining-at-the-bit Negroes . . . where anti-Negro feeling is strong and where racial incidents occur regularly." The CCHR was "watching closely."[60]

The lack of black residents was not simply the random result of the housing market and consumer choice, as Meegan insisted. The neighborhood was directly in the line of Black Belt expansion west and south, while the packinghouse workforce by the end of the 1950s was nearly all black, making Packingtown—at least in theory—an attractive neighborhood for black families. Indeed, given the restricted housing market for Chicago blacks, a rehabilitated neighborhood was more likely to attract blacks, not less. The fact that the BYNC program did not coincide with (or contribute to) an increase in the black population indicates that nonmarket forces were at work.

While there is no evidence that the council participated in, sponsored, or condoned violence and physical threats, it was undoubtedly at the center of all other local efforts at racial containment—and its seemingly race-neutral programs rested heavily on both implicit violence and a belief in the desirability of racial homogeneity. Meegan's claim that the council's conservation program was merely intended to make life better for residents, and thus had no discriminatory intent, rang hollow to knowledgeable observers—and it still does. While Packingtown's housing stock was indeed in need of rehabilitation, the timing of the council's program made its intent unmistakable. The *Chicago Daily News* reported in 1963 that observers "are not certain which way the Council will go if a Negro does move in." The fact that no black family had even attempted to do so is itself evidence of the effectiveness of the BYNC's program. Breckenfeld, seemingly without irony, referred to the council as "a kind of interdenominational Great White Father to its people."[61]

By the late 1950s Chicago was home to two nationally prominent neighborhood conservation efforts: the BYNC's and the University of Chicago's attempts to shape the Hyde Park neighborhood that surrounded it. The exclusionary intent of the BYNC's efforts was abundantly clear, and Alinsky had no desire to be associated with it. Unlike the BYNC, however, the university's work in Hyde Park (where Alinsky and his family lived) was widely praised for its racial openness. It was touted not only as a model but also as a virtuous contrast to the kind of "keep 'em out" motives that informed the BYNC's conservation program. As Alinsky dug further into how racial segregation worked, however, he became a fierce critic of the Hyde Park project, too.

The Hyde Park "Model" and the Limits of Conservation

As the boundaries of the Black Belt moved closer to Hyde Park and its surrounding neighborhoods in the 1930s and 1940s, the University of Chicago organized and subsidized local groups to devise and maintain restrictive covenants in its surrounding neighborhoods. Nonetheless, black families began to move across the traditional racial boundary of Cottage Grove Avenue into the Washington Park neighborhood during the Depression decade, and into western Hyde Park after the war. Despite their continued participation in the preservation of local segregation, by the late 1940s university administrators knew that their policies were failing.[62]

The university's chancellor Robert Hutchins initiated a program of real estate accumulation and began to utilize the school's power over the local housing market to demolish run-down buildings and control the composition of the local population through manipulation of rent levels. Just as important, university officials and local alderman Robert Merriam began to lobby at all levels of government for new urban redevelopment laws focused on conservation and slum prevention, rather than just clearance. A crime scare in early 1952 sparked demands for a university response from faculty, students, local churches, and the Hyde Park–Kenwood Community Conference (HP-KCC). As a result, the university created the South East Chicago Commission (SECC) to serve as its community arm.[63]

The HP-KCC was a racially liberal group formed in 1949. Unlike the SECC and the university, it called for an "interracial community of high standards," and set out to welcome incoming blacks, keep whites, and preserve Hyde Park as a stable and integrated middle-class neighborhood. It took a liberal stance in the wake of the *Shelley* decision and was one of the first white community groups in the city to advocate an open occupancy law. Arguing that "interracialism" was inevitable, and that the community needed to mobilize its better instincts in response, the HP-KCC reflected the general sense among Hyde Park's racial liberals that the law, the public mood, and demographic change would create the foundations for interracial living.[64]

However, as black families moved into the neighborhoods surrounding Hyde Park in ever-greater numbers, the conference was faced with a dilemma. Its executive director Julia Abrahamson realized that if the HP-KCC made no effort to control the local housing market, keep whites in the area, and attract new white residents, the chances of creating an interracial community would be undermined. Because of metropolitan housing segregation and discrimination, many of Hyde Park's whites would take advantage of their ability to buy or rent housing elsewhere while black families desperate for housing would move in. The inevitable result would be racial transition and segregation. But she also worried that deliberate efforts to "secure a balanced turnover in tenancy would appear to be abandoning the open occupancy ideal for Hyde Park–Kenwood while advocating it for other communities"—a frequent criticism of the conference, by Alinsky and others.[65] By the mid-1950s, in the absence of any changes to the broader patterns of racial segregation and discrimination in the city and in the metropolitan area as a whole, the HP-KCC ultimately acquiesced to the university's more aggressive efforts at keeping poor blacks out of Hyde Park. Forced to choose between ideological consistency and their continued residence in the area, the members of the conference chose the latter.[66]

Using the SECC, in the mid-1950s the university "sunk hundreds of thousands of dollars in order to hire lawyers, real estate men, building inspectors, policemen, public relations men and many other kindred functionaries." It enlisted the help of Chicago's newspapers, sent lobbyists to Springfield to enact new legislation, and lobbied in Washington. According to Alinsky, the university put "crushing political pressure" on the city to enforce building codes and punish offenders, all while using its economic power to control the local housing market. School administrators discussed the seemingly race-neutral tool of conservation publicly—but privately, Chancellor Kimpton hoped to upgrade Hyde Park's housing stock as "an effective screening tool" and a way of "cutting down [the] number of Negroes" living in the area.[67] The SECC's urban renewal plan, revealed in 1958, called for demolishing about twenty thousand homes in western Hyde Park, about one-fifth of the neighborhood's buildings. Mayor Richard Daley helped to shepherd the plan through the City Council and secured the federal and local funds needed to implement it. Most of the twenty thousand citizens evicted were poor and black. The Urban League criticized the program for "chasing slums around" by pushing the dislocated into already-overcrowded black neighborhoods and pricing black residents out of the area. Very little effort was made to find them adequate housing, public or private, elsewhere in the neighborhood.[68]

University officials wanted an economic upgrade of the area first and foremost. If improving the neighborhood meant accepting the inevitability of some black middle-class residents, and thus helped to inspire community support, so much the better. By avoiding the appearance of racism, the university was able to mobilize public officials, government money, and racial liberals in support of its efforts, in the process elevating an "unwanted fait accompli into a daring achievement." In part because of the visibility of the liberal HP-KCC, as well as the national reputation of University of Chicago, this effort avoided many of the public criticisms that similarly situated (but less wealthy and powerful) working-class neighborhoods elsewhere on the South Side—like Back of the Yards—faced.[69]

Initially, Alinsky himself—who lived in Hyde Park—was caught up in the purported idealism of the project. He had played a critical role in inspiring and designing conservation programs for Catholic parishes throughout the South Side in the early 1950s. And of course, his most famous organizing project had received national attention for its conservation efforts. But by the end of the 1950s, Alinsky had become a sharp public critic of conservation in general and of the Hyde Park "experiment" in particular. The Packingtown experience had taught him that such efforts were both segregationist and doomed.[70] The problem with conservation, ultimately, was that it did nothing to address the structural racism of metropolitan Chicago's dual housing and credit markets. This was as true for the much-praised Hyde Park experiment as for BYNC's cruder efforts. While communities that utilized conservation might succeed in stabilizing their populations and housing markets, such local efforts only made things worse for other neighborhoods, in the absence of the construction of more low-income public and private housing and a more open metropolitan housing market.

Alinsky's intellectual engagement with both Packingtown and Hyde Park led him to the conclusion that conservation at the local level was not a generalizable strategy as long as black housing supply was limited and discrimination rendered both fair rents and mortgages and large swaths of the Chicago metropolitan area off-limits to economically capable black families. The integrationist or segregationist intent of local efforts, in a sense, was beside the point. Conservation in white neighborhoods would restrict the supply of housing available to Chicago's poor blacks while shifting pressures for racial transition to those areas without the power or resources to successfully stop or manage it. It would accelerate racial turnover and reinforce segregation.

The BYNC had "retreated into the classic posture of the Three Monkeys, 'See No Negroes, Hear No Negroes, and Speak No Negroes,'" Alinsky observed. "A lot of Back of the Yards people think conservation will keep Negroes out. It won't."[71] To overcome this dilemma and succeed in the long term, conservation would have to be part of a larger program, both in ambition and in geographic focus, designed to open up the suburbs along lines of race and class, increase supply at the lower end of the housing market, and transform the rules of access to that market.

Conclusion

While the Hyde Park "experiment" was bound to provoke Alinsky's legendary intolerance for moral self-righteousness, the BYNC's racial exclusion pained him personally. His name was attached to it, after all. However, out of loyalty to Meegan and other friends, through the early 1960s he refused to publicly disassociate himself from the group or declare it a failure, although behind the scenes he did try to push the BYNC away from segregation.[72] For years, when publicly questioned about the council's segregationist activities, he would somewhat defensively refer back to its earlier racial liberalism. Alinsky told the IAF's board in 1961 that the accusations of segregation, while accurate, did not "take into consideration the fact that the Back of the Yards areas' race relations record in all areas of discrimination, with the exception of residential restriction, is a very good one." The neighborhood wasn't any more segregated than any other white area in the city, Alinsky insisted. What made it "conspicuous in not having made any adjustments in the field of racial integration" was its success. This was of course a somewhat disingenuous statement, given that the council's liberalism with regard to race was at the time more than a decade in the past, and that housing segregation was the paramount racial issue on the South Side. To praise the council for "allowing" black packinghouse workers from nearby Englewood to walk to work unmolested through the neighborhood—a notable accomplishment a decade or two earlier, to be sure—was to damn with faint praise, indeed.[73]

Late in his life, Alinsky became more reflective—and self-critical. "Last time I was in Back of the Yards," he told an interviewer from *Playboy* magazine, "a good number of the cars were plastered with Wallace stickers. I could have puked." He and Von Hoffman fantasized for years about trying to challenge or reform the BYNC in some way. "I could have gone back in and reorganized it," he later confessed, after a half decade of organizing in black neighborhoods, "but my ego was tied up in it, so I didn't." It is also very doubtful that he had the power to reshape the BYNC in a meaningful way. "We would brainstorm about some other way to insert the knife to shuck that oyster," Von Hoffman later recalled, "but we could not come up with a feasible way to open up the area. With the BYNC we failed." Alinsky, for his part, never saw it as a failure, "only a challenge." Democracy didn't make angels out of people, he pointed out, and the expansion of "humanism and social justice" was a slow and never-ending process.[74]

Alinsky also slowly recognized the extent to which his organizing approach itself contributed to both the ability and willingness of the council to engage in racial containment. Set up to enhance and draw upon territorial identity in a deeply and increasingly segregated city, the council did little to resist the growing association of race, property, religion, and citizenship. Indeed, it strengthened it. The BYNC had used the democratic power of Alinsky's organizing work to protect and preserve an island of segregation. What had made it successful in conserving the neighborhood and retaining its middle class was precisely the community identity and parochialism that Alinsky had done so much to foster.

Alinsky was relentlessly and purposefully nonideological. His organizing methods focused on the process of building communities of citizens, and he strongly believed that it was not his role to prejudge or determine their values and interests. Alinsky's religion, to the extent that he had one, was the democratic faith. But what if the people democratically choose to pursue goals that are hostile to freedom, and even democracy itself? The BYNC experience didn't cause Alinsky a loss of faith, but it did raise some doubts. "There are values that cannot be compromised," he concluded. "You cannot justify a democratic process, just process, over the goals. You cannot, for example, have a people in any place in the country meeting democratically, and by democratic vote, deciding to segregate another people—because this is the end of the whole democratic idea . . . you don't have a free society anymore." Alinsky would spend the next two decades trying to work out the challenge that race (and racism) seemed to present to his democratic faith and the role that community organizing might play in meeting that challenge.[75]

2

"Dissolving the Walls of Racial Partition"

The 1957 General Report

> Our task is to change the prevailing social patterns so that Negroes and whites come into contact with one another on a new basis . . . in which both sides need each other and must, for their respective self-interests, treat each other with equality.
> SAUL ALINSKY, *The General Report*, 1957

> Chicago must integrate its neighborhoods or it will become as racially schizophrenic as any city of the old South.
> EDWIN BERRY, Chicago Urban League, 1963

Alinsky's success in Packingtown stemmed from his ability to use familiar institutions and social networks to create new forms of territorial identity that crossed class and ethnic lines. By the end of the war, however, in the Back of the Yards and elsewhere, territorial identity was becoming increasingly intertwined with race. For Alinsky, the emergence of community-wide leadership, the development of social capital, and the broadening of identities and interests had all enabled the BYNC to succeed in its early years. Unfortunately, these things had also enabled the organization to become fiercely and successfully segregationist by the 1950s.

Alinsky became increasingly skeptical of the utility and morality of local conservation efforts and worried about the "community chauvinism" that neighborhood conservation groups might embrace to "save" their neighborhoods. By ignoring what goes on outside the neighborhood, Alinsky argued, even a powerful organization "will eventually find itself caught in the vortex of swirling forces about which it has no understanding and no control, with the final end of catastrophe." While he was confident that "the night of segregation is gone and the day is here in which our people must learn to live together in racially integrated communities," a parochial conservation program would delay progress, and with dangerous consequences.[1]

As the BYNC came under increasing public scrutiny, Alinsky desperately sought a way for "People's Organizations" to become racially progressive. The massive *General Report of the Industrial Areas Foundation for the Archdiocese* (1957) was the culmination of a fifteen-year intellectual journey for Alinsky to determine the relevance and role of community organizing for race relations in the postwar city. It is also provides a unique analytical window on an important transitional period in Chicago's history. Alinsky and his staff used a keen sociological and political eye to describe the effects of migration, racial transition, and the dual housing market on local politics and institutions, and also on the archdiocese and its interests. In the process, Alinsky acquainted himself with the particular problems and possibilities of black Chicago and the dilemmas that segregation posed for justice.

Racial issues, of course, had been a constant source of tactical and intellectual concern for Alinsky for some time. Asked by Ben Burns, the editor of *Negro Digest*, to write an entry for the publication's 1946 "If I Were a Negro" series, Alinsky readily agreed. "We know you to be a friend of the darker brother," Burns wrote. Alinsky's essay reflected his belief at the time that a Popular Front–style interracial alliance would eliminate prejudice and segregation. He disdained the idea of a separate black community organization and declared black machine politicians and "the tolerant middle-of-the-roader who boasts of his liberal attitudes" to be the true enemies of black progress. Black Chicagoans should "repudiate the immoral and cowardly 'peace in our time' way," Alinsky concluded. "It is far better to have war in our time and peace for our children." Although his radicalism would never abate, his views on race and organizing would change.[2]

Through his participation in the Public Housing Association and the Committee to End Mob Violence, he had a front-row seat for the bloody neighborhood racial conflicts of the late 1940s and early 1950s. He also worked closely with Catholic parishes on approaches to racial transition and white flight. More personally, the BYNC began to come under heavy criticism for its racism, and his own neighborhood of Hyde Park was in the midst of a heavily contested integration experiment. So Alinsky was understandably anxious to engage the issue of race more deeply. But it was only with the *General Report* that Alinsky began to see the "Negro problem" as something other than one of just trying to manage white prejudice. Ultimately the information and analysis in the report became the intellectual basis for the Organization for the Southwest Community (OSC) and the Woodlawn Organization (TWO), two of Alinsky's most successful ventures.

The Origins of the General Report

Each spring in the 1940s and early 1950s, the rector of Chicago's Catholic seminar sent a small group of promising graduates to spend a few hours with Alinsky. Fr. John Egan attended the 1943 session. "On the day that you're ordained," Alinsky told him, "make up your mind whether you want to be a priest or a bishop. Everything else will follow." Egan made up his mind and committed his life to the pursuit of social justice. At the suggestion of a mutual friend, philosopher Jacques Maritain, Egan invited Alinsky to lunch in 1954. The meal launched a lifelong friendship. "Saul just loved Egan, loved him as a priest," Alinsky's protégé Tom Gaudette recalled. "Saul knew what a priest was . . . 'But there's so few of them around,' he'd say."[3]

Alinsky was struggling to find a post-BYNC project, and Egan opened some doors in the archdiocese's Chancery office. As Egan put it, "Maybe the one great contribution I made . . . was to help Saul . . . begin another career."[4] Egan introduced Alinsky to Cardinal Stritch, and to two young organizers, Nicholas Von Hoffman and Lester Hunt. Von Hoffman and Hunt enrolled in what passed for Alinsky's organizer training course, consisting mostly of late-night bull sessions several times a week at his home.

Egan and Alinsky began to meet regularly with Msgr. Edward Burke, chancellor of the archdiocese, and Msgr. Vincent Cooke, the head of Chicago Catholic Charities, to create a proposal that Stritch would be willing to fund. The biggest issue for the archdiocese, they concluded, was black migration and its related issues—the spread of the ghetto, white racial violence, and the depopulation of established parishes. A citywide study of the impact of black migration on the church and the city was needed, so the archdiocese and the Industrial Areas Foundation (IAF) could take appropriate action.

In the spring of 1957, they proposed a three-year study to Stritch, which would conclude with recommendations for action. The cardinal gave Alinsky $118,800 to study changing areas and the impact of population movements on local institutions, power arrangements, and social programs. Stritch also requested that Fr. Egan spend a year with the IAF as a "priest-intern," which would allow him to train other priests as organizers and report back on the state of the parishes. The end goal, according to Alinsky, was to develop "the most feasible plans for community organizing under these circumstances."[5]

This was far and away the IAF's largest undertaking yet. It offered secure funding and institutional support for Alinsky's work, providing him with staff and resources. As Alinsky informed the IAF board in late 1957, "A major experimental approach in community organizing in the area of race relations . . . has a high place on the agenda for the coming year." The ideas that emerged from the survey would define Alinsky's work for the next decade.[6]

The *General Report*: An Overview

The purpose of the IAF report, Alinsky wrote, would be to determine "why Chicago is more segregated than ever before, why it is as violent as ever before, and why so much money spent on education campaigns and other devices for so many years has failed to yield results." He would propose a pioneering "program of action," including the creation of a black community organization in Grand Boulevard on the South Side and an effort to create and sustain integrated neighborhoods on the edge of the ghetto through grassroots interracial alliances.[7]

He also recommended that the archdiocese commit itself fully to fighting racial segregation, since conservation had been a failure. The only way for the archdiocese to ensure the long-term viability of its parish infrastructure was to take an active role in breaking down segregated housing markets. It was in the institutional interests of the Church to take a stand for integration.

Racial segregation caused the overcrowding of ghettos, with all the suffering, social costs, and truncated opportunities that entailed. It put enormous pressure on white neighborhoods adjacent to the expanding ghetto, leading to deterioration, violence, and flight. And it made integration "immeasurably more difficult," by encouraging the belief "on the part of most white Chicagoans that moving a single Negro into their neighborhood heralds the immediate transition of the community from a white to a black one." This self-fulfilling prophecy brought with it "the consequent loss of their homes, investments, small businesses," leaving the "fabric of communities, something particularly dear to a city of homey neighborhoods . . . rent and torn to pieces." Last, segregation was underwriting Chicago's political system, which systematically excluded and underserved the growing black population. The housing crisis, Alinsky insisted, could not be solved until "the walls of racial partition have been at least partly dissolved."[8]

The archdiocese's emphasis at the time on conservation was not only bound to fail; it would also, like the BYNC's campaign, reinforce racial segregation. Indeed, by adopting a fundamentally defensive approach, the archdiocese was both fanning the flames of white resistance and accelerating the speed of turnover. Black Chicagoans were ill housed, overcrowded, and segregated, and they welcomed any and all opportunities to obtain quality housing. A legal and nonviolent method had to be found that would allow housing markets to find an interracial equilibrium; for Alinsky, the preferred solution was a democratic, locally organized one.[9]

Alinsky's Critique of Liberal Racial Orthodoxy

To Alinsky, the ongoing moral and political dilemma of racial segregation in Chicago was rooted in two problems: the lack of a grassroots black community organization and a flawed analysis of the political ecology of race by even the most well-intentioned observers and activists. Alinsky had been critical of mainstream social analysis for decades, both as a criminologist and as an activist. He deplored the professional stance of objectivity and noninvolvement, arguing that it blinded social analysts to the workings of power by favoring a more psychological approach that tended to reinforce the status quo. In the *General Report* he extended these criticisms to the field of race relations. Programs and groups organized by outside professionals, Alinsky argued, offer little more than therapy. *Democracy* is a "political term meant to describe the use and distribution of power," not the existence of group opportunities for conversation and "self-expression." Their professional training, he continued, prevents them from seeing that it is not the individuals who are sick, but "the world they live in . . . the whole analogy between health and sickness is misapplied when speaking of the slum." Ghetto residents needed to be made "powerful, not 'well.'"[10]

As he had in Packingtown, Alinsky drew a direct line between apathy and the lack of opportunities for the exercise of real power. Apathy, he surmised, was a reasonable response to an immovable status quo. Given a lever for change (as the emerging civil rights movement in the South made clear), local residents would—with prodding from professional organizers—put their shoulders to the wheel. Conversely, Alinsky argued, if people believe that things were hopeless, why exercise responsibility? A locally controlled mass community organization would create an effective political technology for getting things done, thus "redeeming individual responsibility by allowing a person to exercise it in fact as well as in name." Involvement would teach locals how to exercise responsibility and citizenship, and help them to understand their problems as essentially political and thus amenable to change.[11]

Liberal thinking about race relations had undergone subtle but important shifts in the decades following World War II. Many cities, including Chicago, had responded to race riots in Detroit and elsewhere during the war by creating municipal interracial commissions. During the war Alinsky himself served as a consultant to the Mayor's Committee for Home Front Unity in Los Angeles. Chicago's wartime group, the Mayor's Committee on Race Relations, was renamed the Chicago Commission on Human Relations (CCHR) in 1947 and made an official city department. Alinsky served on the commission briefly after the war. Its primary purpose was to prevent racial violence; in the late 1940s it also fought discrimination in conjunction with Chicago's broader civil rights coalition. In addition to the NAACP and the Chicago Urban League (CUL), other groups concerned with racial issues were organized, including the Committee to End Mob Violence and a Chicago branch of the Catholic Interracial Council (CIC). All these groups concentrated heavily on racially restrictive covenants and the administration of public housing.[12]

In the late 1940s, however, groups began to shift from fighting discrimination to managing white prejudice, and from political action to education. Increasingly, the CCHR viewed "the Negro problem" as a result of irrational white fears, which might be changed through education and interracial contact. According to Arnold Hirsch, postwar white violence left racially liberal groups defensive and in a "desiccated state" by the mid-1950s. Like the Chicago Housing Authority (CHA), the CCHR "was first subdued and then enlisted in the struggle to maintain the racial status quo." Its primary purpose had always been the preservation of racial peace, not the struggle for racial justice. The commission's annual reports in the late 1940s are striking for their lack of detailed analysis of the housing market, its long history of racial discrimination and violence, and the extent to which the problems of race and housing were systemic, not simply temporary and exceptional deviations from an otherwise just status quo. By the mid-1950s, the CCHR was increasingly criticized for its "do nothing" stance; its tentative advocacy of "race mixing" had all but disappeared. By the end of the decade, it actively defended the city against charges of segregation.[13]

Liberal efforts to fight racism in the Chicago public schools after World War II were in many ways typical of the analytically simplistic ideas of race that dominated the era. Race-relations experts tended to explain white resistance and violence in psychological terms, characterizing participants in racial turf battles as irrational, hysterical, and bigoted—but aberrational, and open to persuasion and change, through proper instruction.[14] Prejudice was thought to result from ignorance and a lack of intergroup contact. The solution was the creation of educational programs, and "intercultural" and "brotherhood" groups designed to bring willing whites and blacks together. School superintendent Harold Hunt thus implemented a program of intercultural education to promote tolerance among teachers and students. Although it did tame some of the sharper edges of public speech and expression in the schools, it was grounded in the psychological theories of race relations. Hunt's efforts highlighted great achievements by blacks and encouraged teachers to talk about racial differences as shallow or illusory. There was little effort to grapple with the lived experience of race that surrounded students and teachers; housing segregation, racial transition and violence, and labor market discrimination were not discussed.[15]

Alinsky found these therapeutic and educational approaches infuriating, later referring to organizations like the CCHR and the CIC as "highly paid professional propagandists for the status quo" and little more than "zookeepers . . . trying to keep the animals quiet." "The frank truth," he reported, "is that most of Chicago's interracial organizations are futile, tiresome, ineffectual, meddlesome, presumptuous and will shortly reach the dangerous point of being just plain boring. They boast of a long history of getting nothing done quickly."[16]

Financial support from government and the private sector had encouraged the institutionalization and professionalization of the "science" of race relations, pushing it away from political confrontation. Alinsky criticized the CIC, for example, for choosing to ally itself with "inter-group experts" rather than using "the ancient art of statesmanship, which includes familiarity and understanding of the prevailing power pattern."[17] Violent white resistance to neighborhood change had also become more virulent and visible, making white racism—not discrimination and structural inequality—seem to be the main problem. Moreover, red-baiting and factionalism had substantially weakened the ability of civil rights groups to keep issues of discrimination and inequality on the table.[18]

The shift in focus of the CCHR and the CIC echoed larger trends in both social science and racial liberalism. When scholars did focus on blacks, it was usually to point out the harms inflicted upon them by white prejudice. The idea that segregation and discrimination imposed psychological "damage" on black Americans—which only integration and uplift could alleviate—was the dominant conceptual framework shaping liberal racial thought by the mid-1950s. It powerfully influenced the 1954 Brown decision, in particular. This framing easily lent itself to blaming the victim; the CCHR, for example, partly attributed racial divisions to "antisocial" behaviors by Chicago blacks. Some of this was motivated by the desire to shock whites into remedial action, but it was also based on the assumption that political reform was a project for experts, not mass action.[19]

Alinsky viciously criticized the political and social shallowness of this approach in the *General Report*, describing efforts of "group workers" and "inter-relations experts" to "eradicate prejudice from the human soul" as "benignly futile." They provide an "escape hatch for its members guilt which might otherwise have expressed itself constructively." All the "ululations from all the anguished pulpits in America" had accomplished little more. Alinsky believed this approach to be naïve and ineffective.[20]

The *General Report* provided a detailed mix of data and analysis on black Chicago generally, and on the Grand Boulevard neighborhood more specifically. Fr. Egan and Lester Hunt had visited almost every home, store, church, and business in the area, talking to State Street ministers, real estate agents, and barbershop clients and owners about the housing situation. They then compiled nightly reports for Alinsky. At the end of each week Alinsky would read them and check whether they had followed up on various meetings or had double-checked their facts.[21]

Doing a survey was the first step in organizing, Alinsky argued, because it allowed the IAF staff to plot the local power structure, analyze its leadership, and determine whether existing organizations can adequately and democratically represent the people of Grand Boulevard. Black institutions were deeply rooted, of great importance to Grand Boulevard residents, and the only locally legitimate vehicles for empowering them, Alinsky insisted. In this sense Chicago's black communities were no different from white ones like Packingtown. An IAF-sponsored community organization would not try to "build up an exclusive allegiance between the individual and itself which shortcuts vital local institutions." Rather, it would try to work through the "social fabric of a neighborhood," such as churches, clubs, and associations, to reinvigorate it—not replace it.

While many social scientists and liberal whites saw the cultural and social institutions that maintained local patterns of social trust, reciprocity, and daily survival as the greatest impediment to black advancement, Alinsky argued that the final success of any organizing project in black Chicago rested upon "the health and strength of a community's constituent parts."[22] Chicago had been plagued by almost constant violence over racial matters "in spite of the fact that never before has so much money, government and private, been spent on dissuading people from the ways they have." Less costly and more useful methods needed to be found, Alinsky argued, and "no other is known aside from having people look after themselves." Blacks in Chicago were denied dignity "as a man alike by those who hate him and those who would help him ... it is they who have given him what he might have earned for himself; they who often render him a permanent hat-in-hand client in the vestibules of the social agencies; they who have come in the guise of 'human relations experts,' as 'inter-group or interracial relations experts' ... to tell him what to do, how to think, how to arrange his affairs, and who in a word would manage everything for the Negro people."[23]

"'Interracial' or 'integrated' communities do not exist in Chicago," Alinsky wrote. "Once a corner of the city has a Negro population in excess of fifteen or twenty per cent, the whites decamp." But if a balance between housing supply and demand could be created, "then it might be possible to conceive of a neighborhood in which only a restricted number of Negroes might move in and live," he argued. However, segregation "brought with it huge profits for certain people and groups." As a result, "immediate residential integration is not possible ... unless certain prior steps are taken and certain conditions exist."

The most important step was the creation of a powerful black community organization. Given the persistence of segregation, "a pressing necessity for integration must exist if there is to be any," Alinsky reported. Only the self-interest of whites, under pressure from a powerful black organization, could produce this necessity. The desire of blacks for equal treatment would not be sufficient, he argued, because they were too weak and disorganized to satisfy or threaten white self-interest.[24]

A large, independent black mass organization would have the power to force larger changes. It "will not be a step towards bolstering segregation, no matter what it may look like," Alinsky argued. Rather, it is "the weapon that Negroes and whites need to break up the racial island."[25] A powerful, representative, and responsive organization "is the only means we can envisage of coming to grips with the great pressures and problems bearing on Negro communities, which in turn react with such disastrous effect upon the white neighboring areas."[26] Alinsky proposed such a group for Grand Boulevard.

Organizing in Bronzeville

Located just east of Packingtown, Grand Boulevard had undergone rapid racial change after World War I. By the beginning of the Great Depression, 60 percent of Chicago's blacks lived there and in an adjoining neighborhood, Washington Park. "City-wide housing segregation . . . has kept families in the area which would otherwise have moved out as the neighborhood buildings have deteriorated," Alinsky wrote.[27] The violent containment of the "Black Belt" had one virtue: it allowed for the development of a mixed-income neighborhood in Grand Boulevard, with a vibrant associational life and an entertainment and retail district that drew black migrants from around the country.

Much of the residential housing in Grand Boulevard had been constructed before the turn of the century, and little had been built since. Segregation and continued in-migration led to overcrowding, driving up rents and encouraging property owners to subdivide their buildings. In 1930, Grand Boulevard had 87,000 residents. By 1950, the population was 114,557—an extraordinary density given the complete lack of high-rises in the area. What had once been an area of one-, two-, and three-story brick units, many originally built as single-family homes, had by 1950 becoming a rooming-house district.[28] The eastern section of Grand Boulevard (adjacent to Hyde Park and Kenwood) largely retained its status as the black Gold Coast while the western edge (along Federal Street) became increasingly poor.

After the US Supreme Court declared state enforcement of racially restrictive covenants unconstitutional in 1948, many middle-class and wealthier blacks started to move to formerly white communities below Sixty-Third Street, like Englewood and Chatham. During the 1950s the population of

Grand Boulevard fell by nearly one-third. Yet at the same time, racial and class segregation increased. The number of blacks and the black poor more than doubled in the city as a whole from 1950 to 1966, while the geographic size of the ghetto more than tripled—leading to greater economic differentiation within black communities, as well as an increasing concentration of poverty in older areas. Grand Boulevard became the fifth-poorest community in the entire Chicago metropolitan area.[29]

Alinsky was aware of the neighborhood's increasing poverty and the flight of its middle class. Nonetheless, he concluded, Grand Boulevard was "still predominantly a neighborhood where you move when you have made some money and have gotten established in the city." Relative to other black neighborhoods, Grand Boulevard had a stable population.[30] The clock, however, was clearly ticking. Plans were underway to clear the Federal Street district and build the largest public housing project in the world—the Robert Taylor Homes, on a site a quarter mile wide and two miles long. The sheer size of the proposed project (it would eventually house close to forty thousand people in twenty-eight high-rises) both sped up the flight of middle-class blacks and greatly escalated the fears of neighboring white areas. In the 1960s and 1970s, Grand Boulevard and Washington Park together would lose almost forty thousand residents, along with much of their institutional and commercial infrastructure. The geographically concentrated poverty of Grand Boulevard in general, and the Taylor Homes in particular, would come to symbolize the risks of residential integration for white Chicagoans.[31]

Grand Boulevard and Black Politics

The gradual impoverishment of Grand Boulevard was only barely visible to Alinsky and his staff in the summer of 1957. John Egan and Lester Hunt began their survey with a visit to Chicago's black political kingpin, Congressman William Dawson, at his Forty-seventh Street office. Born in Georgia, Dawson was a decorated veteran of World War I and a graduate of Fisk University and Northwestern University Law School. Elected to City Council as a Republican in 1933, Dawson switched parties in 1939. He was elected to Congress in 1942 and gradually attained a position of considerable power in the Cook County Democratic Party, as well as the Democratic National Committee. Power in Grand Boulevard, Alinsky believed, resided in the "Dawson Empire... when there is something which he does not want done, it does not happen." The congressman was bound to be "the strong enemy of any community organization which should develop," Alinsky warned, because it would be "a real threat to his power."[32]

At the height of Dawson's power in the mid-1950s, with six wards under his control, the IAF had little chance of putting together a powerful and representative community group if Dawson chose to obstruct the effort.[33] Dawson had first gained congressional office by defeating Earl Dickerson. One of Dawson's lieutenants ousted Dickerson from City Council the next year. Dickerson, the first black graduate of the University of Chicago Law School, was a progressive attorney who strongly believed in the importance of black political independence. He had helped to organize the NAACP's Legal Defense and Educational Fund in 1939, and he served on the organization's national board. As alderman, he had frequently spoken out on civil rights issues. In 1940, after successfully arguing the *Hansberry v. Lee* restrictive covenant case before the US Supreme Court, he called a City Council hearing to investigate the widespread use of covenants in Chicago, which covered almost half the homes on the white South Side. Angry white aldermen maneuvered to replace him with Dawson in 1942. "I recognize what is happening here," Dickerson scolded Dawson. "I have been trying to make the Negro people independent and self-movers, not slaves to the political system that dominates this city . . . I did that. You don't want that."[34]

In many ways the transition from Dickerson to Dawson symbolized the limited black politics created by racial segregation, which Alinsky was seeking to undo.[35] The prescience of Dickerson's 1942 warning became abundantly clear in 1946, as white ward politicians successfully pushed a retreat on racial issues under Mayor Martin Kennelly, symbolized by the reining in of Elizabeth Wood and the CHA in 1954. Richard Daley would further limit black political power in the late 1950s. Within a month of taking office, Daley gave each alderman the power to veto any project in his ward, effectively restricting all public housing occupied by blacks to the ghetto. In the 1950s and 1960s, Arnold Hirsch argues, Daley "ruthlessly subordinated blacks, and raised the Democratic edifice on a barely concealed social fault line. It was a settlement that left black leadership fragmented, the masses apathetic, and black concerns unaddressed." Although the machine would most definitely pursue black votes, it would never again pursue black interests.[36]

For all of his power, Dawson did not marshal greater resources or opportunity for black Chicagoans. For Alinsky, this was one of the most pernicious consequences of segregation: it had helped to prolong the life of Chicago's racialized political system. "With hundreds of thousands of Negroes walled into their ghetto, cut off from others, and thrust back on themselves without resources or power," Alinsky argued, "it cannot be surprising to learn of the existence of political empires which are nurtured by their constituents impotence." Dawson's ability to turn out the black vote garnered him patronage to distribute, but it came with rather taut strings: his position was solid as long as he didn't push too hard on racial issues that might alienate the machine's white working-class base. Dawson obliged, in virtually every case. "His entire history," Alinsky wrote, "is one long acquiescence to the party line."[37] As a result, policy issues of concern to the growing black community were ignored. In the sharp words of Milton Rakove, Dawson and other black machine politicians would "rather gild the ghetto than break it up," because it would "insure their tenures of office, indebt their constituencies to them, and enable them to advance themselves within the Democratic machine."[38]

The machine abetted racial discrimination in housing, schools, and the labor market, with no opposition from Dawson or his underlings. In 1949 civil rights activists proposed requiring that "all housing conveyed to private interests by the city's power of eminent domain be made available for ownership, use, or occupancy without discrimination or segregation on the basis of race, creed, color, or national origin or ancestry." Offered at the very beginning of large-scale federally supported urban redevelopment, such an ordinance might have altered the course of black life and politics in Chicago in the coming decades. Dawson, following Mayor Kennelly, refused to support it. He spoke out against the CHA's efforts to integrate public housing, arguing that it "forces people on other people"—precisely the "forced housing" language used by white neighborhood groups to oppose open housing over the following two decades. This particularly angered Alinsky, who was president of the Public Housing Association at the time. The CHA rapidly became one of the largest bricks in the wall of racial segregation.[39]

And that segregation simply served to extend Dawson's power, Alinsky argued, by creating more black wards. "Vertical ghettoes" like the Taylor Homes became made for easy vote canvassing. As the black population expanded and wards were depopulated of whites in the 1950s, they became for Dawson "like so many conquered provinces." The Fifth Ward alderman Leon Despres, the City Council's lone racial liberal in the late 1950s and early 1960s, concurred with Alinsky's assessment: Dawson "simply awaited the steadily expanding ghetto, which slowly gave him more wards he expected to control." Dawson of course didn't create racial segregation in Chicago, and he almost certainly didn't have the power to halt it or roll it back. Nonetheless, he had little incentive to expend his political capital trying to break the dual housing market.[40]

Dawson's "submachine" was one of the key reasons Chicago blacks remained politically disorganized, Alinsky asserted. It had become increasingly clear by the late 1950s that Dawson's role in the machine was to contain black political power. Dawson didn't just use his leverage to keep policy issues off the table; he also sought to undermine any potential competitors.

Both the Urban League and the NAACP were disciplined by Chicago's political machine in the 1950s. When racial violence over housing reached epidemic proportions in 1947, Sidney Williams of the Chicago Urban League led a coalition of black and white civil rights activists that demanded that Mayor Kennelly reaffirm his predecessor's stance against racial discrimination. He refused.[41] In response, Williams organized an interracial coalition of 125 organizations to pressure the city, the Committee to End Mob Violence (CEMV). In December 1949, the CEMV called for Kennelly's impeachment because of his "failure to halt increasing mob violence against Negroes and Jews." It also strongly criticized the unwillingness of Chicago newspapers to cover housing violence, and the complacency of the CCHR. "For too many years we Negro citizens have been plagued by the 'hush-hush' policy of our daily newspapers," Williams argued. Alinsky worked with the CEMV to put together its Statement of Principles, which strongly criticized riot coverage.[42]

A combination of mayoral hostility, red-baiting, and factionalism doomed the CEMV and Williams's leadership of the CUL. The presence of leftists in the CEMV left it vulnerable to attack, as a number of Chicago's white-dominated racially liberal groups backed away from the group. It created divisions within the CUL, as moderate blacks, conservative labor leaders, and white Catholics left the board. The Community Fund, which provided the CUL with more than half of its funding, lost $300,000 a year in contributions. The fund asked the national office of the Urban League to investigate the Chicago branch. The CUL was temporarily shut down, and Williams was fired. Dawson was silent.[43]

Similarly, as neighborhood racial conflict heated up in the summer of 1957, Mayor Daley's response was to clamp down on civil rights activism within the Chicago branch of the NAACP, which had become increasingly assertive under the leadership of labor activist Willoughby Abner. The chapter's focus on segregation and inequality in public schools in particular was attracting strong support in the black community.[44] Following the 1957 release of a scathing NAACP report, Dawson took out memberships for hundreds of his precinct captains just before the branch held elections. Their candidate, loyal and moderate Theodore Jones, defeated Abner for the presidency. Most of Abner's union allies were ousted as well.[45]

Most of Chicago's interracial organizations, Alinsky reported, were ineffective. Dawson sought to weaken potentially countervailing sources of power in the black community, and too many organizations that aspired to represent black Chicago—including the NAACP and the CUL—were dependent upon the largesse of wealthy whites. An effective black community organization would have to be black controlled and hostile to Dawson, Alinsky argued.

The Dawson machine was a part of the problem. Beyond poverty and white racism, Alinsky insisted that the "abominably inferior public school system, the inadequate police, the absence of adequate recreational facilities, and the lack of a dozen and one other municipal services that are considered essential in white communities can be laid at the door of the Negro politicians who have failed and have, indeed, frequently not even tried to procure them." While the point was a bit overstated, Alinsky's argument that political powerlessness was at the root of black economic powerlessness was a useful one. It would be echoed repeatedly in the coming decades—by Alinsky's Woodlawn Organization, by the Black Panther Party, and by Harold Washington, among others.[46]

Grand Boulevard, Alinsky reasoned, was an ideal place for the IAF to organize a mass-based black community group. It was peppered with locally controlled churches, union activists, and middle-class social institutions that had already begun to resist the Dawson submachine. The residents of Grand Boulevard, Alinsky concluded, were "looking for a fiery leadership that will command by charting a course that flows from the aspirations of a people who refuse to be denied much longer." The residents were both middle and working class, and there were fewer recent Southern migrants than in other Black Belt neighborhoods.[47] The majority of the population was made up of "toiling, unskilled manual laborers," but Alinsky expected leadership to come from the middle class, which has "an intrepid perseverance, a moral tenacity and a kind of collective consciousness of purpose which seem to explain the growing numbers of exceptional persons in all walks of life issuing from it." The working and middle classes are "joiners par excellence." To belong to an organization of some kind "is a very important thing to most Grand Boulevard people, and a great deal of their social life takes place in their organizations," Alinsky found. But their groups and associations "are so many islets in the broad ocean. They are not joined and connected . . . their members may harbor the same sentiments on important issues but no way exists that allows them to unite in common action." The "new generation of Negro leaders" will come from this group, Alinsky insisted, but only with a mass organization "that can act as a vehicle" for them.[48]

While Grand Boulevard and Packingtown could not have been more different, the solution for Alinsky was similar. Any successful black community group, he concluded, would have to be "tightly bound" to black churches and unions. Churches, Alinsky argued, "represent the basis for whatever social cohesion there is, and organized labor is the principal hope for raising the standard of living to a degree that the other major problems, born of poverty, can be attacked practically." These two institutions were key for an independent, cross-class alliance capable of defeating the machine and cracking Chicago's system of residential apartheid.[49]

Grand Boulevard's 204 Protestant churches were the "best organized, the most numerous and the potentially most powerful forces in the community," Alinsky wrote. In addition to having a "splendid tradition of leadership" and a dense network of social organizations similar to many Catholic parishes, they were also the only institutions in Grand Boulevard that were "solely and purely Negro," a quality that Alinsky found to be very powerful for many Grand Boulevard residents. The ministers of the larger Baptist churches were among the best-known, vocal, and popular leaders in the community. Most of them were "perpetually concerned about the problems of discrimination and the advancement of the race," the IAF found. Poverty had enticed many ministers to participate in the Dawson machine in the past, but the growing black middle class was increasingly enabling churches to stand on their own financially. Given someplace other than Dawson to turn, "their independence from political domination would increase."[50]

There were some caution flags, however, as revealed by the survey. Many of the larger and more economically stable churches were losing parishioners. Grand Boulevard was rapidly becoming a "slum" area in the eyes of many of its residents, particularly the section closest to the Dan Ryan Expressway. Many Grand Boulevard residents saw themselves as temporary members of the community, hoping to accumulate enough capital to purchase a home farther south or even outside the city limits. Grand Boulevard was well on its way to becoming the prototypical government-sponsored "second ghetto": public money and power used to facilitate private development, with older low-income housing replaced by public housing high-rises, packed together a significant distance from predominantly white neighborhoods. But this also created an opportunity for an IAF-derived organization. Many ministers were angry with Dawson for doing nothing to stop this process, and a new organization might serve as the base for a community rebellion for political independence. As for the middle class, enough of it remained, Alinsky believed, to serve as the organizational base for a new group.[51]

Unions could serve as the other critical component of such an organization, Alinsky felt, even though local meetings were poorly attended, and leaders rarely lived in Grand Boulevard—they had joined the middle-class exodus southward. Worse, most union leaders seemed to be under "the illusion that the 'political realm' is capable of solving all their problems," despite the "terrific beating" Dawson and Daley had inflicted on Abner in the recent NAACP election. Alinsky could see that the unions were inept at "mobilizing their memberships for anything other than purely union activities," but he also held out hope for them "creating, principally by means of alliances with the churches, a politically independent force" which might "force Dawson to come to terms or to defeat him." The declining power of the United Packinghouse Workers Association (UPWA), tied to the decline of the Chicago meatpacking industry generally, probably should have given Alinsky pause.[52] Nonetheless, his optimism was based on some preliminary organizing work in the neighborhood that Lester Hunt had undertaken in late 1957. With help from the Emil Schwarzhaupt Foundation, Alinsky and Hunt put together an adult education program in Grand Boulevard to lay the groundwork for a future community organization. Hunt worked with the four largest UPWA locals for three months to create a course designed to get members talking about community problems.[53]

Hunt found that participants initially believed that their unions were suited only to "bargain for contracts and handle grievances." They could see that union-sponsored voting drives weren't appreciably changing neighborhood conditions, and as a result, most of them focused their community energies on other institutions—like churches. After a few weeks of the course, however, they began to discuss pushing community issues in their locals and agitating within their other membership organizations as well. All the ministers and union people could see the advantage of a church-labor alliance, Alinsky argued, "but it was quite obvious also that unless someone such as ourselves were to come in and do the leg work and the organizing of these alliances that not much was going to get done." Much like the churches, Grand Boulevard union locals would move only if given a powerful alternative.[54]

The creation of an effective mass-based black community organization, the organizer insisted, "will depend in large measure on our handling of bread and butter issues." More pointedly, each of the issues enumerated by residents to Egan and Hunt revolved around a "sizeable surge in the standard of living . . . housing, health, not to say the intellect's and soul's refinement eventually repose on a base of wealth." This was one of the critical reasons for including union locals. A black community organization would have to attack all these issues at once, while inventing ways of "getting immediate, real things done quickly."[55]

What issues would work to create a sense of territorial identity and mutual interest in Grand Boulevard? In theory, Alinsky's approach called for community groups to generate their own issues through organizing and institution building. In practice, however, he delineated a list of critical issues as he saw them. First and foremost, a new community group would have to quickly deal with housing. It would have to clean up the worst slums, keep other areas from getting worse, reduce overcrowding, and "rectify a very disadvantageous and illegitimate rent structure." If this weren't addressed immediately, Alinsky argued, the institutional core of Grand Boulevard—and any potential organization—would dissipate. Churches would lose their more economically stable congregants and unions would see their members scattering outward, making them harder to organize.

Politics was clearly another issue of importance, Alinsky found. A new community organization would have to obtain improved city services, respect the need for black control of community institutions and representatives, and attack segregation and housing discrimination throughout the city. According to Alinsky, ministers of some of the larger and more independent Baptist churches were already focusing on the poor quality of city services, leading to a growing spirit of political insurgency among Grand Boulevard's middle class.

IAF researchers found that the most stinging criticism leveled at Dawson, local businesses, unions, and even the Urban League and the NAACP was that they were not sufficiently independent of white political and economic elites. As Alinsky put it, "It is difficult to overemphasize how important this issue is in the Negro community." Any community organization that expected to have mass support "must be a Negro organization, controlled and responsible to the Negro community . . . there can be no substitute for this." Furthermore, the group would have to "take a strong position on this issue elsewhere, and see that those who represent the Negro community outside of it are chosen and responsible to it."[56] The IAF staff, of course, was all white (and male), but Alinsky didn't see this as a long-term problem. It would quickly move toward an all-black staff in Grand Boulevard. "With a crack Negro staff that is not above saying it is planning on using the white man's money to get the operation going and then dumping the parent outfit," he wryly predicted, "the chances of success are promising."[57]

Finally, this black-controlled community organization had to take a "strong and uncompromising position" on segregation and discrimination throughout the region, particularly in housing. Alinsky was reluctant to admit this as an immediate goal because he strongly believed that community organizations were best assembled around local issues. They would attack broader ones when they had the power to do so and a more precise sense of which institutions and individuals to attack. Few residents of Chicago's Black Belt, Alinsky argued, were interested in housing in general—"only a house."[58] But he also understood the extent to which the restricted opportunities in Grand Boulevard were maintained by larger structures of housing, politics, and employment. And his conversations with middle-class residents convinced him that the experience of being black in Chicago was shaped far more by race than by the specifics of place. This was particularly true for the middle class, Alinsky believed, because "being on the borderline," they perhaps "feel discrimination . . . a good deal more than other groups, and it is very much in their minds." To many of them, Grand Boulevard symbolized their plight as black Chicagoans as much as it did their resiliency and resourcefulness in the face of discrimination.[59]

Alinsky's solution was patience. "Setting out to organize with the intention of pulling down the ghetto's walls now is succumbing to the lure of fool's gold," he argued. "Only the slowest changes" would be possible in the next decade or so, and "there will be very little anyone can do about it." Without attacking both the black housing shortage and segregation throughout the metropolitan area, Alinsky warned, little progress in housing was likely to occur in Grand Boulevard in the near future. "There is not now nor is there any prospect of there being any sufficiently strong organized power in the area which could even begin to do something about it," he continued, without challenging the structural forces that "have created this abysmal housing situation." Only a strong, mass-based organization would be able to "enforce the building of additional housing in Chicago. This, coupled with a vigorous attack on the segregated housing situation[,] would relieve a good deal of the pressures which prohibit anything being done in Grand Boulevard."[60]

The final piece of the puzzle for Alinsky involved an alliance between a Grand Boulevard organization and a comparably powerful white one elsewhere on the South Side: the BYNC. In a sense this was his last effort to try to redeem the fruit of his early career. It was terribly unrealistic. But he saw it as the primary way for his community organizations to address broader structural issues. Alinsky envisioned a corporatist arrangement of organized racial groups negotiating with one another to their mutual benefit while simultaneously redeeming the increasingly negative image of the BYNC. Allied, he insisted, the two groups "would constitute . . . the first real force working for some forms of integration" in Chicago.[61] Only this coalition would be enough to break down the dual housing market, stop the speculation and flight that was destroying neighborhoods, and open the door for racial integration. It would bring the races together in mutual self-interest and for the purpose of reforming the housing market.

After all the academic research into race relations, Alinsky argued: "We know what we did when we started out twenty years ago: people like and respect the people they know. They hate, fear, despise and disdain the people they do not know." Segregation was so pernicious because it "has so constructed things that Negroes and whites have almost no opportunity to become friends." When they did meet, "it is in postures of subordinate and superordinate." Race-relations professionals had assumed that simply putting blacks and whites together in the same room would break down racism, but "conditions must be such that the normal ambit of life brings individuals together." "Our task," Alinsky offered, "is to change the prevailing social patterns so that Negroes and whites come into contact with one another on a new basis . . . in which both sides need each other and must, for their respective self-interests, treat each other with equality."[62]

Bringing Grand Boulevard and the Back of the Yards together, in particular, would go a long way toward "breaking the log-jam" in Chicago race relations. Each in its own way, Alinsky pointed out, represented the "difficult extremes." Packingtown had been the "seed-bed and major trouble spot in the 1919 race riots and . . . has always been considered one of the city's most violently anti-Negro sections." However, he continued, "in the minds of many [white] Chicagoans it is precisely the sort of persons who populate the Grand Boulevard section that make desegregation a practical impossibility." Organized, mass-based cooperation between the two neighborhoods would change whites' perceptions of blacks while also providing a real opportunity to bring about residential integration.[63]

The arrangement could begin with racially mixed committees in both communities and lead to more and different kinds of "elbow rubbing." While the participants would experience a limited sort of social integration, meetings wouldn't deal directly with the topic of residential integration. Rather than dealing with such a "distant abstraction," Alinsky argued, the groups would meet to work out "more immediate and important (for them) problems." In particular, Alinsky believed, both organizations would find mutual interest in an expanded housing supply available to blacks in Grand Boulevard, which would relieve the pressure on (and lessen the speculative opportunities in) Packingtown.[64]

By its very nature a community organization "touches upon the many facets of social life, not simply the situation on the job." As a result, the two groups would quickly find themselves "working together on such a variety of programs and projects that it would be almost impossible to unscramble each race and separate it from the other." Over time, they would move from "partial cooperation to a sort of fusion in which the classic categories of extremes, black and white, melt into a gray."[65]

Under his proposed arrangement, the two organizations could take an "enormous step in favor of eventual residential integration" by avoiding the "cloying artificiality of forcing people together for no better reason than that they have different skin pigmentations," as the so-called brotherhood groups tried to do. Posing the question of race relations as a moral problem "would be replaced by the more effective and sure propulsive power of self-interest." Two organized communities, one white and one black, could find "areas of agreement and mutual interest" and "discover [that] their combined power would win for each other more than their separate power could."[66]

Learning, he argued, "takes place through a natural experience." You could not convert a white person to "pro-black" simply by pointing out the error of their ways. The people of the Back of the Yards and Grand Boulevard "can never be expected to learn to know and respect each other because they are of different races. They must have more compelling reasons to meet." However, Alinsky believed, once they had met, worked, and associated with one another, "they will no longer be able to look upon each other as white and black." Cooperation under these conditions would give these leaders a chance to work "in areas of interest where the traditional antipathies, prejudices and revulsions are absent," thus allowing them to "shake off the trammels of their present positions and to accomplish many things that the fear and hate in these communities currently makes impossible."[67]

Only a "pressing necessity" for integration would bring it about, Alinsky insisted. "The problem of white hatred for Negroes is insoluable by any other means than members of both races meeting one another" under circumstances that would allow "getting acquainted and knowing each other as individuals." Such an encounter cannot be arranged through the programs of "good will groups," because only the "tiny, unprejudiced minority of whites attend such affairs."[68]

Clearly Alinsky was drawing on the experience of ethnic coalition in the formation of the BYNC, when he, union organizers, and Packingtown's parish priests brought ethnic groups together to pursue common interests. They focused on specific issues of concern, like juvenile delinquency, housing, and union campaigns, which allowed them to break down prejudices and cultural misunderstandings that had previously divided neighborhood residents. Alinsky saw no reason blacks in Grand Boulevard and whites in Packingtown couldn't also build institutional relationships through the pursuit of shared interests while also respecting differences.

Was this a valid analogy? While one could easily find common interests among Grand Boulevard blacks and Packingtown whites in the late 1950s, their positions in the city and the housing market were fundamentally different. They also lacked the context of a larger social movement or a hospitable political situation. The experience of the UPWA in Packingtown may be a more useful example, as white and black workers had joined together to further their interests as workers. Particularly as blacks became more numerous on the killing floor and in union offices, the UPWA became one of Chicago's most assertive civil rights organizations. However, there were clear limits to interracial cooperation, and these quickly came into focus in the late 1940s and early 1950s. As whites were leaving the slaughterhouses and the union, their perceptions of a common class interest with black workers atrophied. At the same time, the union movement stepped back from its pursuit of social transformation and community activism. The BYNC rapidly abandoned its alliance of necessity with black workers in favor of defending a white Packingtown. The likely future of a Grand Boulevard–BYNC alliance (assuming one could be assembled) was similar, without a broader diminution of racial segregation across the metropolitan area. Alinsky's idea was premised on the notion that residents of both neighborhoods could keep race and segregation off the table long enough to build common institutions and interests. On the South Side in the late 1950s, that was a fantastically tall prospect.

Open Occupancy or Gilding the Ghetto?

Could a powerful community organization in Grand Boulevard simultaneously break down the walls of segregation in Chicago and improve daily life for all classes of local residents? The focus of many of the more middle-class organizations, especially those that had attained some measure of independence, was on structural and citywide racial issues. Upwardly mobile families didn't want to "gild the ghetto"; they wanted an opportunity for a better life, regardless of the neighborhood. The bulk of Grand Boulevard residents, however, were desperately poor, suffered from high unemployment, and lived in conditions that were bad and getting worse. Creating interracial alliances would be tremendously challenging, but trying to hold together a coalition across class lines within Grand Boulevard promised to be difficult as well, particularly without a broader social movement to provide some kind of cultural and moral coherence.

Should a black community organization seeking racial justice try to improve conditions in the ghetto in the here and now, or should it strive to open up opportunities on a nonracial basis throughout the city? On the one hand, organizing to improve Grand Boulevard for those who lived there might relieve pressure on nearby white neighborhoods and incrementally make it a better place to live, but it might also be seen as implicitly maintaining segregation. It would leave the dual housing market in place and the economic difficulties and disinvestments that in part derived from it.

On the other hand, breaking down racial barriers regionwide might provide the black middle class with an opportunity to flee the ghetto, thus weakening the neighborhoods and institutions left behind without addressing the desperate material conditions of most residents. This was not an either-or issue, of course. Alinsky saw no way to break down segregation in Chicago without the creation of a powerful black community organization. But this strategic dilemma clearly indicated that that organization would face limits to its power, no matter how well organized, without alliances across neighborhood boundaries and racial lines.

Black leadership in Chicago was itself divided over this question, in terms of both class and ideology. A good portion of the South Side's black middle class had an inherent interest in stabilizing and improving Grand Boulevard: aldermen were elected by all-black districts, black businesspeople depended on a geographically concentrated market, and clergy relied upon a steady pool of nearby congregants. In contrast, as upwardly mobile beneficiaries of the postwar economic boom and the opening of the housing market, many middle-class families aspired to a future outside the traditional Black Belt and favored whatever measures promised to make those opportunities manifest. Regardless of how they felt about living in the Black Belt, virtually all could agree with John St. Clair Drake that they "resent being *forced* to live there."

This dilemma was perhaps most clearly posed by the work of the University of Chicago and the Hyde Park–Kenwood Community Conference (HP-KCC) in the 1950s. In that case, the question was whether controlled integration was a valid goal if discrimination against low-income black households was the only way to bring it about. The dilemma in Hyde Park was especially acute for the area's middle-class blacks because it thrust their racial and class interests into sharp contrast. As it became increasingly clear that the Hyde Park–Kenwood urban renewal plan was specifically designed to exclude poor blacks and to accept middle-class blacks as a necessary evil, blacks both in Hyde Park and in the city as a whole divided over the contradictions between race and class.[69] The comedian Mike Nichols described the essence of the Hyde Park experiment: "Whites and Blacks, shoulder to shoulder against the lower classes."[70]

The sociologist James Wilson, drawing upon interviews with dozens of black South Side political, civic, and religious leaders in the late 1950s, interpreted this dilemma as a choice between welfare goals and status goals. Those who stressed the former sought to tangibly improve the daily life of the community and its individuals through better services, enhanced living conditions, and increased political representation. Black elected officials certainly fell into this category; by seeking to build a community group through success in dealing with such issues, Alinsky inevitably did as well, even if his long-term goal was broader. The bulk of the black community was in desperate need of more schools, regardless of where they were located; of more public housing, even if it were built in the ghetto; and of an increased supply of private housing, even if white flight and ghetto expansion were the direct result. Ending barriers to black home ownership in white areas tended to benefit a small and relatively privileged group, at least in the near term. "The most important thing," one black activist informed Wilson, "is to give people a roof over their heads, *not* integration . . . if in the process of putting roofs over their heads, you see that the houses are all going to one race, then you just have to live with it."

Another told Wilson that "there is no organized, expressed demand for integration" on the black South Side. "They want *things*, and integration comes second." For most residents of Grand Boulevard the "housing problem" was limited to the obstacles to ghetto expansion and "only theoretically a free real estate market with Negroes moving unhampered throughout the city in search of homes." Immediate material needs, it was argued, should not be put off for remote ends that tended to benefit only a small and relatively privileged part of the community.

Status ends, however, were at the core of postwar racial liberalism and the "black civic ideology" dominant among Chicago's black intellectuals and social reformers, if not its politicians. It involved the integration of blacks into "all phases of community life" in accordance with their proportion of the general population, on the principle of equality and color-blind opportunity. Segregation entailed subordination, and any spatial strategy that tried to turn separation to its advantage was bound to lead to deterioration, not improvement. To some extent, this was the basis of black middle-class criticism of Dawson; to an even greater extent, it informed liberal white criticism of Alinsky's proposals for a black community organization. Successful instances of residential integration, even if accomplished only through economic rather than racial discrimination, were thus valued as important precedents that taught white homeowners that racial propinquity was not inherently threatening. Arguing that black progress could come only through unwavering support for legally defined civil rights and the establishment of social equality and equal access to opportunity, liberal black leaders (such as Archibald Carey, Robert Weaver, and the local NAACP) strongly advocated the scattering of racially mixed public housing projects, the integration of public schools, and the establishment of the principle of open occupancy in the private real estate market. Welfare ends, from this perspective, could only institutionalize and perpetuate racial segregation.[71]

Alinsky sought, in his Grand Boulevard project, to use welfare means toward status ends. Or rather, he viewed welfare goals as having tactical value in the pursuit of a broader strategy. While the creation of a black community group had intrinsic worth, it was intended to serve as the first stage in the long march toward the creation and maintenance of interracial neighborhoods. He didn't want his organization to simply be a more effective Dawson machine. And he worried—justifiably—that Chicago's white liberals would see a mass-based black community organization as a force for preserving the ghetto, not destroying it. Where they saw Grand Boulevard as a disorganized, often pathological way station to eventual assimilation, Alinsky saw it as an institutionally rich community deprived of opportunity, material resources, and political power. He saw segregation as the ultimate cause of this condition but despaired of the range of solutions thus far attempted. None of them seemed to recognize the investment so many whites had in segregation, which education and the law couldn't touch. Nor did they understand the need for black autonomy and empowerment—valuable intrinsically and as a means to achieving an integrated Chicago. The same debates would be replayed in the next decade by white liberals and advocates of "black power." Critics might accuse Alinsky of "gilding the ghetto," but he at least was attempting to come up with a political technology to address the dilemmas that legalism and moral suasion had failed to resolve. A community organization in Grand Boulevard—or any other black area—would inevitably run into this dilemma because it was an unavoidable part of Chicago's racial geopolitics.

Organizing on the Edge of the Ghetto

Alinsky's second idea for furthering residential integration was to organize blacks and whites together in an area of racial transition, such as the Auburn-Gresham section of the Southwest Side. This was probably the more realistic proposal. Black families leaving Grand Boulevard were more likely to head for Woodlawn, Hyde Park, Chatham, Auburn-Gresham, or Englewood than they were to move into the older and more physically dangerous Back of the Yards. Meegan and the BYNC had successfully excluded blacks altogether and had little incentive to work with a black community group. Organizing in a transition area was both more feasible and replicable. Every few months the racial geography of some South Side neighborhood was thrown into flux, with little reaction from whites other than "fight or flight." Black newcomers were even less organized, and few instruments existed for bringing the races together to mutually redefine their geography.

The success of this second proposal, Alinsky argued, would ironically lie in capitalizing on the fears of both sides: blacks who had just moved and were afraid the slum would follow them, and whites worried that blacks would bring the ghetto with them. Unlike in the Grand Boulevard–Packingtown proposal, the races in a transitional area could not be organized separately. Any white organization built under such conditions would become "virulently anti-Negro." Complete racial transition would surely follow, because "sooner or later . . . doom comes" to such white groups. However, organizing an area that had recently "turned" black would be extremely difficult, because most residents would have arrived too recently to have established a "community life," or a territorial identity or allegiance.

The inducement for whites was the creation of what Alinsky called a "buffer state." In return for negotiating with blacks and "associating with them organizationally," whites would achieve a buffer area "between them and the ghetto's heaviest push outward." The new black community alone would not have the power to prevent the expansion of the ghetto, but "in conjunction with a more easily organized and more powerful neighbor," the necessary force could be exercised "to keep the slums out of the buffer section."

The problem with Alinsky's Auburn-Gresham proposal, of course, is that it was unclear what blacks would gain from the arrangement. Alinsky anticipated that by seeking to limit the extent and speed of ghetto expansion, such a project would be criticized as a way of maintaining segregation, but he argued that the choice was not between integration and this proposal; it was between segregation and the creation of a mass-based force for racial balance. Racial boundaries, Alinsky continued, always move. The only chance an area like Auburn-Highland had for permanent racial stability was if the housing shortage and segregation elsewhere eased. In the meantime, partial solutions had to be found. The creation of several such border organizations, he argued, would help to bring two "warring populations into partial and harmonious relations" and present the possibility of the "pacification of the white working-class elements in the city." Working-class whites are "the heart and soul of racial warfare in Chicago." If the goal was to reach them, Alinsky concluded, this would seem to offer them a compromise they could accept.[72]

It remained to be seen, however, whether this strategy could resolve the contradictions of Chicago's racial geography. For blacks those contradictions were connected to questions of spatial strategy—the geographic conditions of liberation and racial progress. While most of Chicago's black leaders agreed with the general principle of open occupancy, they were deeply divided over the definition of integration and its utility in the near term. Did integration mean actual mixing and dispersion, or just the opportunity for blacks to buy or rent anywhere in a color-blind private market? There was also little agreement on just what alleviation of the housing problem required. Was it enough to eliminate the violence and organized resistance that impeded the expansion of the ghetto? Should the priority be the elimination of obstacles to blacks in all-white neighborhoods, not just those adjacent to the ghetto? Did it matter where new public and private housing was constructed? Should a black neighborhood organization concentrate on local institution building and community improvement, or should it seek to hammer down the walls of racial separation regionwide? Was the creation of an integrated neighborhood important enough to accept restrictions on the expansion of the ghetto? Should blacks moving into previously all-white neighborhoods concern themselves with white flight and integration, even if doing so meant excluding economically capable and needy black families?[73]

White neighborhoods on the edge of the ghetto could have controlled integration or nondiscrimination, but not both. A policy of racial openness made rapid racial transition a certainty. Wealthier communities could use class as a proxy for race and claim a "victory" for integration. For most of Chicago's neighborhoods, this wasn't an option. For them, absent dramatic changes in the housing market across the region, negotiated residential integration would require some kind of racial containment and exclusion, thus making the creation and protection of an island of racial balance a higher priority than the immediate housing needs of black families. Regardless of which project Alinsky undertook next, these dilemmas would be unavoidable. Because his approach revolved around the construction of territorial identities, and his funding and reputation were heavily dependent upon evidence of tangible benefits to particular neighborhoods and their institutions, whatever group Alinsky launched was bound to emphasize welfare goals first and foremost. Yet pursuing these goals in racialized Chicago threatened to perpetuate, not end, racial segregation, unless the organization remained strategically consistent. Alinsky understood the dilemmas but had no means for resolving them other than his basic faith in the outcome of organized democratic deliberations.

Conclusion

Late in 1958, Alinsky invited himself and Fr. Egan to dinner with Joseph Meegan, the director of the BYNC and a close friend, at Meegan's house on Garfield Boulevard, one of Chicago's racial boundaries. After the meal, Alinsky proposed that Meegan arrange to have some houses that the Council was developing sold to blacks. The neighborhood would not panic, Alinsky said, because Meegan could convince them that the black families would be at the same economic level and that he and the council could control the number of black newcomers. He had his Grand Boulevard project clearly in mind, of course. But Meegan brought the difficulty of the plan immediately into focus.

The meeting ended in shouting and yelling; Egan concluded that they had asked for the impossible, the unrealistic.[74]

Researching the *General Report* had taught Alinsky that his traditional organizing methods were not enough. Racial conflict and the decline of neighborhoods and parishes could not be overcome by constructing parochial, intensely local organizations intent on creating islands of safety. Conservation, which had guided the city, the archdiocese, and BYNC through the thicket of race and space during the first postwar decade, had not been the answer. Indeed, Alinsky had learned, it threatened to make the situation worse. A democratic approach to housing and race relations required two parties, organized for power, and prepared to negotiate a solution. But the BYNC would not be one of them.

Meegan's reaction was emblematic of the larger problems facing Alinsky's vision of democratically controlled residential integration. White homeowners asserted a right to choose their neighbors, preserve the social and cultural capital of their communities, and uphold the value of their homes, a value that was perceived to be heavily dependent upon the discrimination and segregation that ensured racial homogeneity. These rights, long recognized and guaranteed by real estate agents, local banks, neighborhood associations, courts, and politicians, were considered critical pillars of social and economic security. In conjunction with racially inflected federal programs like the GI Bill, these perceived rights gave millions of white Americans access to the middle class.

While many white Chicagoans were willing to concede the principle of nondiscrimination in public life, homes and neighborhoods were seen as a private sphere earned and protected by meritorious hard work and beyond the jurisdiction of governments and "social engineers." Organized efforts on behalf of integration or open occupancy were thus not only inherently political; they were also perceived as an illegitimate interference with private property and the bundle of rights and protected privileges stemming from it. These perceptions were reinforced by the territorial sensibilities of urban Catholicism. This racial geopolitics was a formidable barrier for any community organization Alinsky hoped to create.

Alinsky was anxious to get a project up and running, but Cardinal Stritch balked at funding either of his projects—and then he died, in the fall of 1958. Alinsky's friend Msgr. John O'Grady immediately wrote to the new archbishop, Albert Meyer. One of the "most significant features of Cardinal Stritch's work," the priest insisted, "has been his very great appreciation of the contribution of the Industrial Areas Foundation," which has had a "rather far-reaching influence on local self-help organizations in Chicago." Its principles, he concluded, "are in line with many statements in regard to neighborhood self-help made by our Most Holy Father during the past ten years."[75] Fr. Egan, in the meantime, gave Meyer a guided tour of Chicago's poorer neighborhoods and encouraged him to follow Alinsky's advice and come out strongly against racial segregation.[76]

Meyer agreed, appointing Egan to lead the new Office of Urban Affairs (OUA) for the archdiocese. Joining him in the OUA would be Fr. Martin Farrell of Woodlawn (an increasingly black neighborhood adjacent to Hyde Park) and Msgr. John McMahon of St. Sabina's, an Auburn-Gresham parish facing racial transition. Like Egan, both men were interested in building bridges—between Catholics and Protestants, and whites and blacks. McMahon and Farrell had another thing in common: by 1959, both were trying to get Alinsky to organize in their neighborhoods. Both would succeed.[77]

3

Chicago's "Great Question"

Racial Geography and the Creation of the Organization for the Southwest Community, 1958–1959

> The place names change, but for 40 years the cry has been the same. "They'll never pass 35th street." "They'll never pass 47th street." "You'll never see 'em east of South Park... of Cottage Grove... of Woodlawn... of Stony Island... You'll never see one west of Halsted... of Ashland... of Damen, of Western, of California, Kedzie... of Pulaski... Every Chicagoan knows who "They" and "Us" are.
> NICHOLAS VON HOFFMAN, 1963

The process of racial containment, white flight, and resegregation—what *Chicago Daily News* reporter M. W. Newman referred to in 1960 as "Chicago's 'Great Question'"—is of vital importance for understanding the racial and political dynamics of metropolitan areas in postwar America.[1] Even a brief perusal of city newspapers from the late 1950s and early 1960s reveals that the Great Question was hardly specific to Chicago. Mobility, racial containment, transition, and flight—experienced by millions of Americans, white and black—and their related structural inequalities serve as both the foundation of modern American urban and suburban politics and the prism through which many whites and blacks map metropolitan space, creating racial and territorial identities.[2]

More than almost any other urbanist of his day, Saul Alinsky was keenly aware of the intersection of race, place, and social belonging. His vision of the democratic city and his methods for sustaining and advancing it relied heavily upon the creation and nurturing of territorial identities. As Alinsky began to learn more about the causes and consequences of racial segregation during the 1950s, however, he became increasingly worried that community organizations in Chicago's white neighborhoods would inevitably become white first and foremost. Following the lead of the housing market, the New Deal state, and the political culture more generally, many of Chicago's white homeowners in the postwar decades had come to believe that owning a house in a neighborhood of their choice was the mortar that held American citizenship and security together, and that interracial living was a profound threat to that mortar; this became a self-fulfilling prophecy. Armed with a variety of

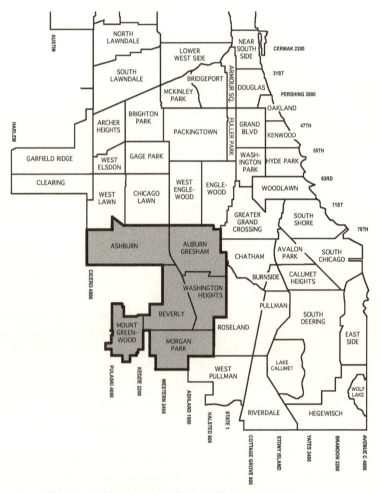

FIGURE 3.1. The territory of the Organization for the Southwest Community.

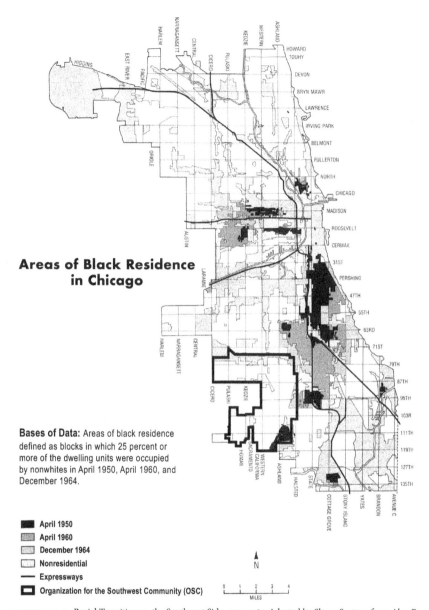

FIGURE 3.2. Racial Transition on the Southwest Side, 1950–1964. Adapted by Shana Santow, from Alan B. Anderson and George W. Pickering, *Confronting the Color Line: The Broken Promise of the Civil Rights Movement in Chicago*, University of Georgia Press, Athens (1986), 74–75.

legally and politically sanctioned and economically viable ways of fighting or avoiding integration, countless white homeowners concluded that the racial politics of housing was a zero-sum game.

Any community organization that sought to further housing integration had to deal with this. In this and the following two chapters, we explore the possibilities and limits of locally initiated residential integration in the 1950s and 1960s, and Saul Alinsky's bold attempt to use his place-based organizing methods to foster interracial living, through the creation of the Organization for the Southwest Community (OSC), on Chicago's South Side. By knitting together whites and blacks through local churches, homeowner associations, businesses, and social groups into a representative community organization on the predominantly middle-class and Catholic Southwest Side, Alinsky hoped to attain democratic control over the local housing market and use some form of housing quotas to foster racial balance.

Such experiments have much to teach us about the ways that markets are politically and socially constructed, and about the politics of racial geography in postwar America. The history of the OSC also demonstrates, tragically, the extent to which metropolitan residential segregation limited the efficacy of local efforts to foster interracial living. Alinsky and the OSC tried to emphasize territorial identities in a metropolitan context that seemed to racialize those identities faster than he could change them.

"Like a Thief in the Night": Transition and White Flight on the Southwest Side

An overwhelmingly white, mostly Catholic, and predominantly middle-class area of the city, the Southwest Side was made up of close-knit parish-centered neighborhoods settled in the 1920s. The population had tripled during the decade before the Great Depression, as Irish, Germans, and Swedes moved south from the stockyards area—in part to capture a piece of the American Dream but also to flee the growth of the Black Belt. The Southwest Side was economically—if not racially—diverse, ranging from the simple bungalows and twenty-five-foot lots in Englewood to the north, to the mansions of Beverly Hills near the city limits. The majority of the area's two hundred thousand residents, scattered over fifteen square miles, owned their own homes and attended some of the largest and wealthiest parishes in the city.[3]

A twenty-year hiatus in housing construction, caused by the Great Depression and World War II, contributed to the flowering of a deep-rooted and intricate local Catholic life, centered on the parish and its institutions. White homeowners—accustomed to racially homogeneous neighborhoods, the social and equity capital presumed to stem from them, and the protection of that capital by real estate agents, bankers, courts, and politicians—looked upon the expansion of the ghetto as a threat to their hard-won security. In the late 1940s, the border communities of Auburn Park, South Englewood, East Gresham, West Chatham, and Washington Heights increasingly found themselves being "redlined" by banks and lending agencies that were anticipating an influx of black residents. Young upwardly mobile white families began to leave for Beverly, Mount Greenwood, and the suburbs beyond.[4]

By the late 1950s nearby Chatham and Grand Crossing were in the midst of an extraordinarily rapid turnover of their populations from white to black, while a small number of blacks had begun to move into Englewood and Auburn-Gresham. Blockbusters—real estate speculators—were spreading fear, and banks were refusing to lend money for home improvements. While blacks were still only 9 percent of the area population, approximately forty black families were moving into the Southwest Side each month.[5] The result was a growing sense of panic among white homeowners as the Black Belt approached, block by block.

In areas with a high percentage of rental housing, the transition from white to black happened fairly quickly. In his fascinating memoir *Revolution in the City* (1961), the Catholic youth worker Vincent Giese recounts how the western section of Chatham, a mostly middle-class apartment community, was transformed almost overnight in the late 1950s from an overwhelmingly white neighborhood to a predominantly black and middle-class one. While residents were aware of rapid changes in Englewood to the west and Grand Crossing to the north, when blacks started moving in to Chatham in 1956 there was little organized resistance. According to Giese, the change was first seen in the commercial district along Cottage Grove Avenue. Black faces were more evident at busy intersections, and white merchants, fearing a change of clientele, began to move, rendering the district a kind of "ghost town." Not enough blacks had moved to the area to justify black merchants coming in, but not enough whites remained to sustain white-owned stores. The transformation of the Cottage Grove strip—and the replacement of many shops with taverns and storefront "fly-by-night" realty offices "prepared for the big financial kill opening up to them"—was the first step in getting people to think about leaving.[6]

While West Chatham's white and predominantly middle-class residents had established some degree of community identity through shared use of churches, schools, parks, and stores, few owned homes. Apartment buildings, which varied from two-flats to hundred-unit complexes, were generally owned by outsiders through anonymous trusts and operated by real estate management firms. As a result, once whites began to "press the panic button," there was little to hold them in Chatham. Most could afford to leave, and they did so. Managers of Chatham's large buildings held vacancies for a few months, hoping for white renters; but then they rented to blacks (or sold the buildings to them), often at increased rents—which pushed the remaining white residents out.[7]

Giese believed that youth, sexuality, and violence were especially important in the rapid population turnover. As in most of Chicago's transitional areas, racial change took place in the public schools first. A large number of white children attended Catholic schools, whereas black families moving into previously all-white communities tended to be younger than their new white neighbors, so had more children of school age. White parents who believed that an increased black presence in schools would lead to lower standards and pose a danger to white female teenagers were often the first to flee. Such families associated blacks with crime, and in particular with sexual predators, and they feared that both large apartment complexes and high schools would pose a threat to wives and daughters. Opinion polls in the 1950s indicated an almost universal dislike of interracial marriage among whites nationally; racial fears and fears of sexual intimacy were hopelessly intertwined for whites in transition areas.

Crime rates increased in Chicago beginning in the late 1950s and greatly accelerated throughout the following decade. Indeed, many blacks tried to move out of the South Side ghetto for precisely that reason. Media coverage of racial transition tended to associate racial integration with crime and violence, however, which fed (and confirmed) white fears. With the white suburbs beckoning, many whites perceived themselves as "victims." According to Richard Taub, "once individuals decided that their neighborhood has begun to decline, they became more generally helpless and more generally fearful, and they selected evidence around them that reinforced this view." Racial turnover in Chatham came "like a thief in the night," Giese remembered, with such "fantastic" speed that interracial living was never given a chance to "set in." A community that had been over 99 percent white in 1950 was two-thirds black ten years later—with much of the change taking place in just the last few years of the decade.[8]

In neighborhoods of homeowners, the process had a different and much slower course. Real estate speculators would encourage whites to sell their property to them rather than to blacks—thus avoiding the social approbation of 'busting' their block. Often egged on by speculators' attempts to induce a panicked sell-off, whites would unload their homes for less than they were worth; they would then be sold to blacks at higher prices. In 1959, the *Chicago*

Daily News described residents of the predominantly single-family-home section of East Chatham as "jittery, confused, and generally unwilling to accept Negroes." Blacks had crossed Cottage Grove and Seventy-ninth—a long-maintained racial barrier—in 1959, and whites were scared: as one elderly white housewife put it, "We can't afford to move again. We've been driven out twice before. The Negroes are coming. They'll run us off the streets. What are we to do?" Even those sympathetic to the black need for housing feared being "flooded." All that was needed to "set up" the community, according to the *Daily News*, was for "a few buildings to go. They went—and organized scare salesmen moved in, as if on signal, to do the rest."[9]

White homeowners were being "hounded day and night to sell" by real estate firms trying to create a "fear market," lamented George Murphy, the president of the all-white Chatham Improvement Association.[10] Unnerved by the rapid increase in vacancies and For Sale signs well before blacks began to move in, by the fall of 1959 whites were abandoning the area. Homeowners often received dozens of calls a night informing them that nearby houses had already been sold to blacks and encouraging them to sell now and "get their price." Residents believed the calls were coming from real estate offices, because "mop-up salesmen" often came around the next day, asking them to list their property. One owner, on the 8000 block of Drexel, showed reporters ninety-three calling cards left by salesmen in the previous three months. Some real estate agents placed conspicuous Sold signs on buildings—a violation of zoning laws, which the City Building Department did not enforce. Others went to greater lengths to foment panic, hiring blacks to walk all-white blocks or to stage loud fights in alleys, "complete with cries of 'don't shoot!'"[11]

The biggest local speculator was Benjamin "Benny the Broker" Klein, who turned $10,000 down into $114,000 in sales in one block alone. Chatham was already besieged by rumors in the spring of 1958 when Klein went to work on the first block in the area to have a black resident, offering homeowners "quick deals for hard cash." He snapped up three three-flats and covered up the ownership in secret land trusts through the Cosmopolitan National Bank. Within a year, the buildings had been sold to blacks, at a total markup of $32,000; one of the units had been marked up from $26,500 to $37,500. Klein claimed to have "nothing to be ashamed of."[12]

According to future Alinsky organizer Thomas Gaudette, the president of the interracialist Chatham–Avalon Park Community Council, the pattern of phone calls indicated which blocks "panic peddlers" intended to hit next. Even blacks who had recently settled just west of Cottage Grove were receiving calls, attempting to drive them into all-white areas and accelerate the pace of property turnover.[13] Gaudette's organization, a small group of white activists, attempted to attract black middle-class newcomers through block clubs, as a forum through which old and new residents could get acquainted and find common interests.[14] Giese was a member of a similar, albeit short-lived group, the West Avalon Community Association, which declared that "the Negroes are here and we want them to work with us to maintain this fine neighborhood."[15]

The West Avalon Community Association and the Chatham–Avalon Park Community Council organized block clubs to monitor code violations, serve as conduits for complaints about city services, and uphold housing standards. The hope was that the similar class backgrounds of white residents and black newcomers would reveal common ground regarding schools, prohibition of taverns, and zoning enforcement. More bluntly, neither group wished to live in or near the ghetto; as one black newcomer put it, "I'd rather have a decent white family next to me than some Negro family fresh from the slums." Chicago's black middle class had always struggled to maintain exclusive and stable class space. Wherever the black middle class moved, the black poor tended to follow. So it is hardly surprising that black pioneers tended to value efforts at neighborhood stabilization, especially given the lack of a suburban alternative. The stakes were higher for them than for their new white neighbors. Even liberal whites always had the option of exit. Neither group succeeded in maintaining an interracial neighborhood, although both did slow the transition enough to uphold the economic stability of the neighborhood.[16]

Blacks, for their part, found the flight of white owners, often at a financial loss, a mystery. Generally, black "pioneers" in previously all-white communities had higher incomes and more education than their new white neighbors. This was particularly the case on the Southwest Side, but frightened whites seemed to be unaware of it. As Louis Rosen recalled, in predominantly Jewish Calumet Heights, just east of Chatham, many black pioneers found the departure of their white neighbors an inexplicable and personal affront. A black teacher there told Rosen: "It was like having a tooth pulled for no reason . . . I couldn't understand why people kept leaving, why the individuals who didn't leave right away couldn't see that those of us moving in were at the same economic level—that we had similar values." A young male high school student agreed: "I couldn't understand it. If you have a home, and you have a community, and you have businesses there, where you goin'? . . . I'm not gonna break into your garage and steal your lawnmower. We got two lawnmowers, okay?"[17]

Chatham's most famous new black resident was the world-renowned gospel singer Mahalia Jackson. In the spring of 1956, Jackson took $40,000 in cash out of her bra and handed it to the white owner of a red brick ranch house at 8353 S. Indiana, then moved in. Neighbors shot out her windows, broke into the house, and attempted to drive her out. "I hadn't intended to start a one-man crusade," she said in 1963. "All I wanted was a quiet, pretty home to live in." Shortly after she moved to Chatham, the actor Sidney Poitier tried to convince her to play the role of Walter Younger's mother in a new play, *A Raisin in the Sun*, which depicted the struggles of a black South Side family that was contemplating a move to a white neighborhood much like Jackson's. Despite—or possibly because of—her experiences, she declined. It premiered on Broadway in the spring of 1959, shortly after the few remaining white families on Jackson's block had moved out. "The same birds are in the trees," she later reflected. "I guess it didn't occur to them to leave just because we moved in."[18]

While many black pioneers weren't necessarily motivated by the desire to live in a racially integrated community, most were well aware of what tended to follow racial turnover. Once an area had been written off as a "Negro district," the police would appear more rarely, broken streetlamps would go unrepaired, trash service became less reliable, and the most experienced teachers often transferred out. Taverns filled newly empty storefronts. As Carl Rowan put it in August 1958, black pioneers "have concluded that it is not a coincidence that the schools are more rundown, more crowded, the teaching inferior, in predominantly Negro areas. They see it as a standard pattern for the snowplow, the street repair crew, the garbage collector, to get to the 'colored section' last if at all."[19]

Giese found that while black newcomers tended to be younger, have larger families, and have less job security than their new white neighbors, they were more highly educated, and generally "fit into the neighborhood pattern." Despite high payments, Giese found that Chatham's black families often took advantage of their first opportunity to own a home, "taking to the new experience in urban living with zest and pride." Chatham resident Nellie Dora agreed, telling the Chicago Commission on Human Relations that her new black neighbors had greatly improved their homes, by hanging awnings, enclosing open porches, and landscaping their yards.[20] Newman and Swegle, who found the black area to the west of Cottage Grove to be "as respectable and law-abiding as most white sections, if not more so," were baffled. Apparently, they concluded, this was "not the yardstick by which the average white person judges Negroes."[21]

Most whites in Chatham did not want to leave, Newman and Swegle argued, but they seemed to fear that even middle-class blacks would "bring with them problems often associated with the Negro 'ghetto': slums, overcrowding, skidding property values, unemployment, crime, dope." The tragedy for black pioneers, of course, was that they moved precisely to escape these things themselves. They generally found themselves squeezed between an expanding ghetto and unresponsive white neighbors, elites, and institutions. Despite the unfair payment burdens thrust upon them by credit discrimination and the dual housing market, many black newcomers joined block clubs and worked to improve their properties. As one black resident of the 8200 block of Maryland put it: "Negroes are getting better buildings and are keeping them better. It makes you think different if you can get out of the jam [of the Black Belt]."[22]

The perception among whites that black neighbors threatened property values, neighborhood stability, and community safety stemmed in large part from the way the dual housing market operated: because of racial discrimination, the "jam" tended to follow blacks out of the ghetto. With banks unwilling to loan them money outside of black or transition areas, and facing a restricted housing market, many blacks were forced to buy or rent from speculators at exorbitant prices. As effective as covenants occasionally had been, informal collusion among real estate agents, bankers, builders, and individual property owners not to sell or make loans to blacks was especially successful in maintaining segregation. It was exceedingly difficult for even middle-class black families to keep up payments and maintenance.

The installment contract was a common means for black families shut out of the traditional credit market to purchase homes. They would purchase a home for a low down payment but at a very high rate of interest—with the speculator keeping title to the property. A study during the 1950s by the Chicago Commission on Human Relations revealed the frequent use of this financing method in South Englewood, as well as the extraordinary rapidity of speculator-aided racial turnover. The CCHR discovered that while mortgage loans were readily available to speculators seeking to buy properties from white owners, twenty-four of the twenty-nine blacks who tried to buy homes in the area from 1953 to 1961 were forced to do so on installment. Speculators were ubiquitous, secret, and remarkably successful: of the twenty-three mortgage and trust deeds taken out on the twenty-nine homes sold in the area, only seven were made to owner-occupants. The rest were granted to nonresident buyers, who quickly resold the properties on installment, at an average profit of 73 percent. Trust agreements, in which banks act as trustees for a purchaser, tended to conceal the identity of speculators, and they were entirely legal—as were installment contracts. The unwillingness of local lending agencies to extend mortgages to black buyers made such contracts common, and the high payments—with no equity—tended to accelerate the deterioration of areas with new black residents. Eighty-five percent of the buildings acquired by black Chicagoans outside the Black Belt in late 1950s were bought on installment.

Blacks could not build equity in homes bought this way, and the high interest payments made it difficult to maintain the property—leading to illegal conversions, overcrowding, resales, and what white homeowners generally perceived as the expansion of the ghetto. While speculators were easily vilified, the burden of responsibility for their practices was widely shared, if rarely acknowledged. The Federal Housing Administration, redlining banks, real estate agents, exclusive suburbs, and white homeowners all shaped the racial geopolitics which led to the fleecing of countless black families. Thousands of Chicago's white professionals were also implicated in this exploitation through their purchase of contract paper in the secondary market. In many cases that secondary market provided the capital for further speculation.[23]

Unable to see the structural limits imposed by the dual housing market, many whites associated the physical deterioration of their neighborhoods with the social and moral dispositions of blacks. The conditions produced by speculation and discrimination gave visible "proof" to the common belief that black "invasion" meant the creation of new slums and the destruction of beloved communities. They saw in the crime, overcrowding, poverty, and disorder of black areas to the north and east of them both the antithesis of their own neighborhoods and a grim prophecy. Rather than blaming landlords, city officials, increasing black joblessness, or racial discrimination, most whites interpreted poor housing conditions as a sign of black personal failure and "family breakdown." Because home ownership was, in Tom Sugrue's words, a "powerful symbol of 'making it' for immigrant and working-class families," Southwest Side whites tended to see poor blacks in particular as a direct threat to their own hard-won and precarious place in society. When the black pioneer J. Saunders Redding moved into a white neighborhood, he later recalled, it felt "almost like stealing." Given the value of whiteness as the coin of the American realm, his temporary white neighbors probably agreed. The pace of racial transition in Chicago accelerated throughout the postwar decades. The "fight or flight" mentality took stronger hold on the Southwest Side.[24]

"Choose Your Neighbor": Racial Containment before the OSC

The Southwest Side had long been a haven for organized and sometimes violent resistance to black newcomers. These efforts were generally initiated by property owners' associations of various kinds, which began to emerge in the

1920s and 1930s with the encouragement of the Chicago Real Estate Board. The area was among the most closely organized in the city, with twelve such groups in Washington Heights–Morgan Park alone as early as 1927. Initiated by organizations such as the Englewood Civic Association, the Morgan Park Improvement Association, the South Town Planning Association, and the Beverly Area Planning Association, racial restrictive covenants had blanketed the area into the 1950s, and the northern and eastern borders were frequent sites of violence against black homeowners and their property.

Racial boundaries (in terms of both identity and territory) were most fiercely policed by young white working-class men, who embodied broader racial anxieties. For many this task enacted masculine honor and perhaps alleviated some of the powerlessness they experienced in the wake of Chicago's industrial deconcentration. Worried about personal downward mobility and community decline, they focused their anger and blame on black newcomers. According to Andrew Diamond, white working-class youth subcultures were fundamental to racial violence on the Southwest Side, as well as the "overall atmosphere of white hostility that African Americans encountered in neighborhoods outside the Black Belt." The Southwest Side was "honeycombed with a dozen varieties of segregation conspiracies, some brutal and stupidly ineffectual, some intelligent and quite effective in their own way," Saul Alinsky wrote to the IAF Board in 1960. "The situation was, if a black family moved in . . . and their house were to catch fire, the fire engines would not come," Nicholas Von Hoffman recalled.[25]

Methods of racial containment tended to vary by neighborhood and by class. In the wealthier—and less threatened—southern end of the Southwest Side, Morgan Park and Beverly Hills, many local property associations belonged to the Beverly Area Planning Association (BAPA).[26] BAPA, led by the real estate agent William Groebe, assisted associations in opposing black occupancy and had played a key role in defeating alderman Archibald Carey's proposed 1949 ordinance that would have prohibited racial discrimination in all housing constructed on land conveyed to private interests by the Chicago Housing Authority and the Land Clearance Commission. Mayor Kelly had famously rebuked white Morgan Park parents during the war for pulling their children out of the public schools when a small number of black students enrolled. Morgan Park and Beverly Hills had similar economic and topographical qualities. Morgan Park, affectionately referred to as the "Suburb in the City," was made up of elegant homes on a forty-foot ridge and a valley to the east that had housed a sizable and growing homeowning enclave of black house servants and railroad workers since the 1920s. More than four out of every five housing units in Beverly were owner-occupied in 1960, and in 1970 the community had the second-highest median income and percentage of professional workers in the city. Both neighborhoods were heavily Catholic, with a high degree of homeownership, low residential mobility, and conservative political leanings but also strong allegiance to the local Democratic Party, many of whose leaders lived in the area.[27]

Neighborhood groups in Englewood, Auburn-Gresham, Highland, and other communities in the upper reaches of the Southwest Side tended to affiliate with either the Southwest Neighborhood Council—a federation of twenty property owners' groups formed in 1949 largely to fight public housing—or the older and larger South Town Planning Association (SPA). BAPA and the SPA aided local groups in creating and enforcing restrictive covenants, and in crafting political, social, and economic responses to the *Shelley* ruling. The Brainerd Civic Association, one of the larger groups in the area—and a center of resistance to Alinsky's organizing—belonged to BAPA, as did the Morgan Park Improvement Association, while the Englewood Civic Association, among others, was affiliated with SPA.[28]

While most local groups focused on the basics of community maintenance, such as street repair, snow removal, recreational improvements, social activities, and the enforcement of zoning laws and building codes, keeping blacks out was of primary importance. Racial exclusion tended to be the most reliable way to get broad-based support for and participation in neighborhood groups; the only block captain in the Morgan Park Improvement Association to get 100 percent membership in 1950 was a man who focused his recruiting pitch on the danger of blacks moving in. Most homeowner groups on the Southwest Side were at some point involved in adopting and maintaining restrictive covenants, usually drawn up by a local real estate agent, in cooperation with the Chicago Real Estate Board (CREB) and Chicago Title and Trust. For the less "threatened" areas, covenants often served as a rallying point for community unity and the development of sentiment for segregation, rather than as a legal device with real teeth. South Side groups closer to the edges of the Black Belt spent more of their time raising funds to pay the legal costs of covenant enforcement.[29]

The SPA was incorporated in 1939 in Englewood. Founded and run predominantly by real estate agents, bankers, and the local chambers of commerce, the SPA devoted most of its time and resources to the creation and maintenance of restrictive covenants, as a buffer between black settlements and the white Southwest Side. Frank Rathje, president of two community banks, past president of the American Bankers Association, and onetime vice president of the Chicago Planning Commission, was the leading spirit of the SPA, alongside William McDonnell, editor of the *Southtown Economist*.[30]

Population growth in Englewood and West Englewood during the 1930s had led to an increase in housing conversions and a decline in the quality of housing stock. White middle-class families began to move south, to Morgan Park and Beverly Hills or beyond, while blacks spread west, as far as Ashland Avenue, and south to Sixty-Seventh Street. The black population of Englewood, many of them packinghouse workers who could not find homes in the Back of the Yards, increased fivefold in the 1940s, to slightly less than 10 percent of the population.[31]

The SPA played a key role in the passage of the Illinois Redevelopment Act of 1941, which allowed the group to create the Southtown Realty and Development Corporation, empowered to eliminate "blight" in its neighborhoods. In 1946 the SPA launched a "build the Negroes out of Englewood campaign" and used the development corporation to demolish the increasingly black northeastern corner of Englewood (Ogden Park) in favor of a large middle-income (and all-white) apartment building. The SPA even formulated a bizarre colonization scheme that would relocate the displaced black residents to the suburb of Robbins. While neither the development nor the relocation took place, the SPA continued to extol the virtues of covenants to its member clubs, as part of its 1947 "Choose Your Neighbor" campaign.[32] That year the association allotted half of its budget—$30,000—for contracting and enforcing its covenants, which covered roughly 60 percent of the area.[33]

The SPA began to expand its activities in the wake of *Shelley* and the resumption of housing construction regionally. Englewood's businesspeople and property owners saw their community as the gatekeeper for the Southwest Side; as one SPA activist put it in June 1950, "if Englewood's residential areas remain healthy and stable, all areas of the south and west will also maintain their integrity." Financial contributions from Sears, Chicago City Bank and Trust, Wieboldt's department stores, and the *Southtown Economist* helped to make the SPA one of the wealthiest federations in the city—albeit one increasingly dominated by the area's larger economic and land interests.[34]

After the 1948 *Shelley* decision, associations and homeowner groups began to wage an "economic cold war" against blacks, gradually replacing covenants with organized efforts to buy up available property to prevent its sale to blacks seeking to "leapfrog" into the community.[35] The Southtown Land and Building Corporation continued to buy houses and apartment buildings and hold them for demolition or rehabilitation, and also purchased property from blacks who had bought into the area. BAPA also attempted for a time to buy property from blacks or those who planned to sell to them. The East Gresham Community Association, led by James Norris, worked with neighborhood banks to buy homes and keep them off the market until white buyers could be found. This method was expensive, however, and few associations had the resources or power base to sustain it.³⁶

Violence and intimidation also remained primary weapons, especially near the advancing Black Belt. A 1957 Chicago Urban League study found racial violence increasing along the periphery of the black ghetto, especially in Chatham and Grand Crossing.³⁷ Alinsky described the Southwest Side as "impervious to the promotion of actual racial equality . . . the community's fears of Negroes coming in [have] resulted in innumerable bombings, arsons, and other attacks against persons and property."³⁸ Englewood in particular was a site of racial violence: as many as ten thousand rioters, spurred on by rumors of the sale of a house to a black family, and organized by priests, block clubs, and the SPA, attacked property and individuals in November 1949. Aside from Wentworth Avenue along the boundary of the old Black Belt, no Chicago neighborhood suffered as many racial incidents in the late 1940s.³⁹

Violence, inflicted mostly by white youth, had reached worrisome levels in Auburn-Gresham by 1959, leading to lurid press reports of a crime wave that accelerated the flight of whites from the area. Talk of flight among white residents was ubiquitous. In 1960 Nicholas Von Hoffman found vacancy rates as high as 30 percent in some blocks, as real estate agents, blockbusters, and lenders conspired to price young white homebuyers out of the area while simultaneously gouging black families desperate for quality housing in a restricted market. As of 1960 there were no integrated blocks in the area, other than those in some kind of temporary balance before total transition.⁴⁰

Racial transition wasn't only causing flight. It was also causing a breakdown in the communication and trust that had formerly sustained many Southwest Side neighborhoods, as suspicion and distrust set neighbor against neighbor. Since no one wanted to be the first to move out, and no one wanted to be the last, families gradually and silently slipped away, one by one. The apparent lack of options led to helplessness and a sense of impending, unavoidable doom. By the late 1950s few methods appeared to be working, and most local institutions lacked either the power or the interest to move in a new direction.

The "Analogy of Vaccination": Religion, Race, and the Origins of the OSC

Neighborhoods on the Southwest Side had few institutions that could stabilize the local housing market. Political representatives were unlikely to take the necessary risks to stop the transformation of the community, and many real estate agents and bankers had a material interest in selling and reselling white homes in transitional areas. The methods of neighborhood associations had proved illegal, expensive, ineffective, or (to some) morally abhorrent. Large corporations with plants in the area took little interest in local affairs, and merchants struggling to make a profit often lacked the time and resources for meaningful political action.[41]

Churches, however, had money, members, and recognized and respected leaders with connections outside the community. Msgr. John McMahon, pastor of St. Sabina's in Auburn-Gresham, took a particularly prominent leadership role on the question of containment and transition. St. Sabina, which later became the organizational heart of the community group, had around 3,500 mostly middle-class families in the 1950s. The church was at the center of a vibrant and predominantly Irish Catholic social and cultural life, which cradled residents from childhood to marriage and beyond; in the decades after the war, as priest Tom McMahon put it, "everything was centered around the parish." In 1960, slightly more than one thousand children attended St. Sabina's parish school, while only forty-six went to the local public school. Most went on to Catholic high schools, reinforcing parish values, identity, and experience. While Protestants were a significant percentage of the local population, intermarriage was rare, and social and institutional life was segregated. The parish community center and parochial school together created an insulated set of social activities. The result, as historian Eileen McMahon concluded, was a "protected and defensive" Catholic world that was "defined by locality and mutual devotions, values and sentiments."[42] As an increasing number of non–Irish Catholics moved into the parish in the late 1940s and early 1950s, that world became less specifically Irish and more generally Catholic and white, even as the expanding Black Belt moved closer.[43]

McMahon was appointed to St. Sabina in 1952 and had an immediate impact. Conservation and stabilization of Auburn-Gresham became McMahon's primary social concern. While the area was mostly middle class, both its population and its housing stock were aging, and violent racial skirmishes to the north and east—and McMahon's previous experience with a racially changing parish on the West Side—pushed the integrationist priest to prepare his parishioners for interracial living.[44] McMahon faced an uphill battle: many upwardly mobile locals had previously fled transitioning parishes near the stockyards and did not look forward to doing so again. Many were on fixed incomes—the most frequently cited occupation was "retiree"—and thus could not move again, even if they wanted to. Most had assumed that blacks would never come that far south and west; as one parishioner told Eileen McMahon, "we thought we were safe."

By the late 1950s, however, as blacks started to move into the area, violence, deterioration, and flight—especially near the parish itself—were creating heightened tensions. As one Catholic put it, parishioners had serious doubts about blacks as neighbors: "These stories about the blacks don't keep up their property and all that. We'd see that going down on the 'el' . . . when whites were there, it was an old neighborhood, but a good neighborhood. And then [blacks] took it over and it was burned out . . . they were ghettoes right away." McMahon interpreted growing "pockets of blight" around the church as a danger sign.[45]

With advice from Msgr. John O'Grady, Fr. John Egan, and Alinsky, McMahon began a parish conservation program as soon as he arrived. Because banks were increasingly reluctant to provide mortgages and improvement loans in the area, McMahon encouraged the Holy Name Society to organize a credit union in 1953.[46] McMahon used his considerable clerical authority to fight housing deterioration, often walking his dog through the neighborhood to check for signs of neglect and deterioration. He met with small groups and encouraged members of devotional societies to get involved in block clubs, in order to watch for illegal home conversions.[47] In the parish newsletter, *Seraph*, McMahon also warned against the rumors and gossip that tended to accelerate deterioration and flight: "Neighborhoods have been wrecked because of idle conversations in supermarkets, beauty parlors, taverns or street corners . . . to start a rumor is criminal, to pass it on is no less so."[48] He also spoke out against racist white neighborhood groups, although he was careful to avoid racial issues in his sermons, choosing instead to remind parishioners of the good reasons for staying.

By the late 1950s, however, McMahon was convinced that he would need greater organizational power to stop speculators and blockbusters. Conservation would not be enough. In the fall of 1958, he approached John Egan and began to press Msgr. Vincent Cooke of Chicago Catholic Charities for money to fund an Alinsky project.[49] When Cooke promised McMahon that money would be forthcoming, Egan arranged a dinner with McMahon, local banker Donald O'Toole, and Alinsky.[50]

But Alinsky didn't like the idea at all; as Egan described it, he "fought McMahon's proposal every step of the way."[51] The Southwest Side was outside of the IAF's Grand Boulevard survey, and he felt that organizing a white middle-class area would be a step backward in his integration plans. He believed he was on the verge of getting church funding for Grand Boulevard, which was on the border of an already-organized white community—Back of the Yards. But McMahon gradually persuaded Egan to make the case to Alinsky, in particular by emphasizing the growing violence and terrorism against blacks in his neighborhood. Cardinal Meyer instructed McMahon to call a summit meeting of Southwest Side pastors at Christ the King's rectory in Beverly for early 1959. Egan convinced Alinsky to attend, and to present a plan for a possible organizing project. The gathering took place that January 6.[52]

Egan and Alinsky explained to the ten priests in attendance that an overall, interdenominational community organization could stabilize the area, preserve Catholic parishes, and prevent racial violence. As he had done in the Back of the Yards, Alinsky decided to approach the pastors with a pragmatic, institutional argument for limited integration and interreligious cooperation, rather than a moral one. The community organization would approach racial integration in a strictly utilitarian manner, emphasizing the "analogy of vaccination," or "the idea of being inoculated with a certain quota of Negroes for white immunity." Alinsky hoped to sell the new organization as a force for stabilization, not integration. Even while Alinsky, Von Hoffman, McMahon, and Egan privately all hoped that the new community group would be integrationist, they also knew that before it could even attempt to control the local housing market, it would have to accumulate broad-based local power and support. As in Back of the Yards, Alinsky believed this could be done only by focusing on a variety of relatively noncontroversial issues that directly addressed the interests of local institutions. Encouraged (and funded) by Cardinal Meyer, the IAF accepted the project.[53]

Alinsky sent Von Hoffman to survey the area, along with two new twenty-nine-year-old organizers: ex-seminarian Edward Chambers and Joe Villemas, whom Alinsky had hired away from the Welfare Council of Chicago. Egan, who had served at the Southwest Side's St. Justin Martyr, took an active role as "advisor, consultant, catalyst, and interpreter" for the trio—in particular by using his local connections to bring Protestant and Catholic clergy (and their money) together.[54] Chambers focused on the Protestant churches, and Villemas and Von Hoffman on the Catholic ones, with Egan shuttling between them. The three organizers worked an area fifty blocks long by thirty blocks wide, bounded by Sixty-Seventh Street on the north, State Street to the east, Western Avenue to the west, and the city limits at the south. They spoke to more than one thousand people in just three months, and they found small groups of liberal interracialists and a larger number of racial conservatives amid a vast majority that was content with their community and generally moderate on race. Throughout the spring of 1959, the organizers built up personal relationships with both Protestant and Catholic clergy.[55]

As anticipated, the issue of integration was at the center of virtually every discussion, although IAF staffers tried to avoid it. While Alinsky's traditional organizing method called for a "survey" of local issues, on the Southwest Side this canvass served largely to legitimize the IAF's presence. The true goal, never openly acknowledged, was to create a community organization powerful enough to deal with racial conflict, white flight, and neighborhood stability. A traditional Alinsky survey might reveal other issues to address, but Von Hoffman and the others recognized that such things were useful only insofar as they might build the new group.

As a result, the organizing strategy blended a large dose of pragmatism with a slightly smaller amount of subterfuge. Von Hoffman later described it as "organizing by bamboozle." "Viewed from the twenty-first century, what we did . . . may seem indefensible," he admitted in 2010. "But you had to have been there. . . . Saul's belief that in the long run people allowed to make their own decisions will make the right choice did nothing for the short run, which was a problem." As the future staff organizer Peter Martinez recalled, the idea was to "get everybody involved and to pull known racists into the organization . . . you had to keep all these people in the same arena . . . that way you'd get a very realistic perspective . . . [otherwise] the solutions that would come out of this would have a narrow basis of support. They would lose their credibility."[56] Although race inevitably came up as an issue, Alinsky's organizers promised neither integration nor segregation. As one organizer recounted to clergyman and activist John Fish, they would talk to potential recruits about the problems of the expanding ghetto and ask for suggestions; the general sentiment was "to keep the community white, but they would accept half a loaf. We would say, 'there is no way to keep it white but maybe we can keep it stable and healthy.'"[57]

As Alinsky often stressed, demonstrating an ability to solve local problems quickly was also crucial if a new organization were to take root. Bringing panic peddling and blockbusting to a halt became a useful issue for the organizers: as Alinsky preferred, it was dramatic, it was a part of many residents' immediate experience, and it focused on easily identified villains. For Chambers, addressing the question of violence was first and foremost. As he told Fr. David Finks, "All we tried to do during the first year was to put together an organization of moderate residents and church groups to get control over this racial transition and stop the violence." He and the organizers worked to prevent black visitors from being harassed and their new homes from being vandalized. Within three or four months, according to Chambers, "we knew who the bombers were, in whose kitchens the tactics were planned—it was like the White Citizens Council in the South."[58]

The problem with such an approach, however, was that neither insiders nor outsiders had any sense of the organization's true purpose. Chicago's

Great Question was the central issue, yet the new group refused to take a public position on it. This opened it up to criticisms from all sides. While Alinsky believed that a broad base was essential for the formation of an effective collective bargaining agent for the community, some who might otherwise have been sympathetic were put off by it—including the editors of the liberal *Christian Century* and Christ the King's assistant pastor Andrew Greeley. Conservatives active in local block clubs and improvement associations were also skeptical, though for different reasons.

To get local conservatives on board and to forestall red-baiting, Alinsky's organizers needed to court the more skeptical clergy. McMahon gave Von Hoffman and Villemas ready access to lay club leaders, each of whom provided lists of others to talk to. Things were more difficult, however, at other parishes: St. Barnabas and Christ the King in upper-middle-class Beverly were run by conservative pastors and attended by many bigwigs in the Democratic Party, while St. Brendan's in South Englewood and Little Flower in Highland were more directly and immediately threatened by racial transition and feared the new community organization. Von Hoffman quickly discovered that any attempt to circumvent the more skeptical priests by appealing directly to their parishioners was "pipe-dreaming," because "in nine cases out of ten" the people were "staunchly behind their anti-Negro pastors with all their anti-Negro selves."[59]

With a few notable exceptions, most of the local homeowners' groups were also dedicated to keeping blacks out; thus, if the IAF organizers were going to tap into a significant organizational base, it would have to be through the parishes' significant network of lay clubs that had membership lists, resources, meeting places, and the social capital necessary for risky collective action. But leaders of many parish clubs were also important players in the homeowner groups, putting the IAF organizers in the uncomfortable position of having to consider circumventing them as well and trying to put together their own neighborhood entities—a daunting task.

Alinsky's preferred method would not work here. As long as a number of pastors held out, local associations would continue to feel threatened by the presence of a new supergroup and seek to undermine it.[60] Chambers and Von Hoffman were certain that James Norris, an ironworker and president of the powerful and all-white East Gresham Community Association, was working behind the scenes with local lending institutions and the police and fire departments to keep blacks out of the area, in addition to red-baiting the IAF organizers. As Chambers told Alinsky biographer Sanford Horwitt, Norris "was raising havoc with us . . . every place we'd go, he would come behind or he'd been there before, saying 'Watch out for these Alinsky communist organizers.'" Chambers made the recruitment of Norris his personal mission, but the association president avoided him throughout the spring of 1959.[61]

Von Hoffman was not optimistic about his progress with the Catholic priests either. As he told Alinsky, "With certain notable exceptions, the pastors out on the Southwest side are practically a caricature, a cartoon, of the sins of omission and commission of the Irish Roman Catholic clergy." He found two of them to be "out and out lushes," and another to be a "psychopath." The pastor at St. Kilian's reportedly spent six months of every year away from his parish working on his golf game. All in all, Von Hoffman found few "cooperative, far-seeing, dependable pastors." Fr. Egan reluctantly agreed, finding that despite Meyer's endorsement, many clergy and laypeople were infected with what he called the "virus of anti-Communism" and equated integration with "fellow traveling."[62]

The most powerful of the more conservative parish priests was Msgr. Patrick Molloy of St. Leo's, a quintessentially Irish character who in many ways (and much to the chagrin of the IAF organizers) became the pivotal figure in the early years of the OSC. St. Leo's, at Seventy-eighth and Emerald in the southeastern corner of Auburn Park—directly in the path of the advancing ghetto—was reputed to be the largest, richest, and greatest parish in the world, with more than five thousand families, a grammar school, a high school, a hospital, and a football field. Graced with a booming voice, an overbearing manner, a taste for liquor, and a wavering commitment to his vow of celibacy, Molloy ruled his parish like his close friend Richard Daley ruled the city—with huge building programs and brooking no compromises. "We had to have him," Von Hoffman recalled. "He was a major power ... with the cops, with the fire department, with organized crime and with financial institutions in some of which he had very large deposits."[63]

Molloy was by all accounts a racist; he generally responded to an influx of blacks into his parish by arranging to have their blocks transferred to the parish to the north, St. Brendan's, in increasingly black Englewood. When a black woman came to register her child at St. Leo's school in 1960, he informed her that no room existed for "you people," despite the recent order to integrate the parish schools. He occasionally ordered "burrheads" out of his church, and his parish bulletins reflected a deep sense of fear and panic about racial transition, warning his parishioners not to "sell your birthright to some real estate man and then lament your loss throughout your lives!" A black family moving into his parish "would be like the barbarian Mongols breaching the Great Wall of China," Von Hoffman remembered.[64]

Like McMahon, Molloy took an active interest in conservation, though for different reasons. Through the *St. Leo Weekly*, Molloy encouraged his readers to "clean up, paint up and brush up and keep your property as models of our Chicagoland." Parishioners who would not toe the line would quickly find their pastor "going to court in order to have these houses eliminated."[65] He helped to organize the Auburn-Highland Improvement Association, and advised his flock "if you don't move out, they can't get in."[66] Von Hoffman successfully used Molloy's fear of racial transition and violence to convince him that only through a broad community group could he hope to maintain a stable parish.

Throughout the spring and summer of 1959, Von Hoffman built up a productive relationship with the priest. He asked Alinsky to come to Molloy's lavish rectory for a chat, in order to seal the relationship. Over a bottle of bourbon, the organizer and the priest broke bread while discussing the White Sox and their mutual friends in the Mob. Alinsky then "turned the conversation," Von Hoffman recalled. A black family would inevitably move in to Molloy's parish, Alinsky pointed out. If someone set fire to the house, white families would immediately flee, destroying the parish—and the value of its real estate. Molloy would then be in trouble; his influence over area police and firefighters ensured that he would be held responsible by the press, the mayor, and the cardinal. By August, Molloy had personally given $5,000 to the new group and played a crucial role in deflecting anticommunist criticisms.[67]

As Fr. Egan recounted, a number of other reluctant pastors followed suit.[68] Once Von Hoffman and Chambers could tell area ultraconservatives that they were working with Molloy to "stabilize the neighborhood," they could develop relationships.[69] Molloy's participation was especially important for getting Norris's attention; the local leader became increasingly involved in the organizing effort as the summer progressed.

There were some early successes. The IAF organizers went to work on the local Protestant clergy, most of whom also looked on in dread as blacks moved closer their neighborhoods: unlike the Catholic pastors, Protestant ministers held their posts at the discretion of their congregations, making it very difficult for them to forcefully step forward on racial issues. Alinsky tried to use this as a selling point: group action would give them safety in numbers, in addition to stabilizing the area. IAF organizers also played on interdenominational fears, warning ministers that in their absence, Catholics would dominate the group.[70]

In February 1959, Chambers, Von Hoffman, and Alinsky called on Rev. Robert Christ of the mostly lower-middle-class Seventh Presbyterian Church in Gresham. Christ immediately hit it off with them and quickly became the key Protestant figure in the project. While his congregation differed little from Catholics in their "apprehensive and head-in-the-sand" approach to racial transition, the Seventh Presbyterian Church did have a particularly territorial identity and focus. This allowed Christ to convince many of his parishioners that the church "has a mission to its immediate community," and thus involve them in the creation of a new community organization. Christ offered what the IAF most needed: resources and organized activists with a moral and material stake in the community. He brought the project to the local ministerial association and to the Chicago Presbytery, which gave him $1,000 to donate to the project.[71]

The IAF organizers also succeeded in gaining the support of banker Donald O'Toole. President of the local Standard State Bank and a native of Woodlawn, which experienced almost complete racial turnover during the 1950s, O'Toole was a former real estate agent who was deeply concerned about the role of panic peddlers in scaring whites out of the community. In the late 1940s, O'Toole had financed and constructed a private housing development for blacks outside the boundaries of the South Side ghetto, and the experience had taught him about the ways the dual housing market restricted both races and threatened the maintenance of stable interracial communities.[72] O'Toole became a conduit between IAF organizers and local businessmen and merchants, and he quickly became the most prominent lay leader in the new community group.

McMahon, O'Toole, and other local leaders decided in April 1959 to move ahead with plans to create the Provisional Organization for the Southwest Community (POSC). The organization was formally established on May 25, with more than three hundred leaders representing eighty local groups (all of them white) in attendance. Like Alinsky's other projects, the POSC was going to be an "organization of organizations," in which member groups sent delegates to an annual congress that would decide policy, authorize programs, and elect officers. An executive committee of fifteen individuals, working closely with IAF staffers, would oversee the project. A monthly council of elected officers and a carefully balanced delegation of Protestants and Catholics would do the day-to-day work. Each congregation was given one vote at the council meetings (giving the smaller but more numerous Protestant churches an edge), and delegations to the annual congress were to be allotted by the size of each congregation (giving Catholics the advantage). The Executive Committee would have a balanced ticket, with two priests and two ministers.[73] Half of those at the meeting signed on to work with a variety of committees empowered to lay the groundwork for a Community Congress in October.[74]

O'Toole was elected to head the POSC, and he informed the *Chicago Daily News* that the new group would maintain standards, not "try to stop the unstoppable."[75] While much of the meeting centered on the excitement of interreligious cooperation, those present knew that a summer of controversy and conflict awaited them.

The Hyde Park Model?

Chicago had only one other community on the edge of the ghetto that had attempted, with some success, to foster residential integration: Hyde Park, where Alinsky and his family lived. For many racial liberals in Chicago and elsewhere, efforts by the University of Chicago and the Hyde Park–Kenwood Community Conference (HP-KCC) to sustain white housing demand and foster interracial living were instructive. Was Hyde Park a useful model for Alinsky and the POSC?

There were some similar circumstances. Hyde Park and the upper reaches of the Southwest Side were situated on the edge of the expanding black ghetto and were experiencing rapid white flight. Racial turnover in nearby neighborhoods during the 1950s had been extraordinarily rapid: near Hyde Park, Woodlawn and North Kenwood witnessed an almost complete transformation of their populations; East Washington Heights, Chatham, North Englewood, and Grand Crossing experienced similar changes on the Southwest Side. Both communities had been using a variety of racial containment methods (such as restrictive covenants and the organization of property associations) for decades—Hyde Park since World War I, and the Southwest Side since the 1930s. (Violence, however, was not generally used to keep blacks out of Hyde Park and its surrounding neighborhoods.) With the *Shelley* decision of 1948, however, black in-migration accelerated, and leaders and institutions scrambled to respond.

The perceived nature of the "threat" to each community was also similar. Since the housing stock in both communities had aged considerably in the previous three decades, property owners feared that the more blighted areas of their neighborhoods were a profound threat to racial homogeneity because they tended to be the first blocks vacated by white families. Institutions that were deeply and immovably invested in Hyde Park and the Southwest Side (the University of Chicago and parish churches, respectively) worried about the effects of blight, flight, and turnover on the value of their real estate holdings, their attractiveness to clients, and their ability to carry out their respective missions. Priests and school officials were concerned that economic and racial instability would pose a profound threat to the social and cultural atmosphere essential to the effective operation of their respective institutions: for the university, a predominantly white community of open-minded cosmopolitanism, and for the parish, a territorially centered Catholic identity and cultural life.

In other respects, however, Hyde Park and the Southwest Side were faced with very different dilemmas, stemming largely from their economic and cultural differences. While Hyde Park had both homeowners and Catholics, it had far fewer of each than did most of the Southwest Side. This had a profound effect on the way residents viewed the "threat" of interracial living, and on the approaches of community organizations to racial containment. The HP-KCC was led mainly by Jews and Quakers who lived in apartment districts surrounding the campus. They valued the intellectual liberalism of the neighborhood and saw no reason an expansion of Hyde Park's black middle-class should pose a threat to their identities and interests. Indeed, given the emerging intellectual orthodoxy of racial liberalism, a hard-and-fast opposition to black families would have been a difficult position for the leaders of the conference to maintain—although university administrators did not find it quite as troubling. Some degree of tolerance and openness was an important part of the social and self-identities of most of the conference's leaders.

In contrast, while Alinsky's organizers found most of the residents of the Southwest Side to be moderate on racial issues and interested in stability above all else, their cultural, economic, and institutional attachments differed in important ways from those of the residents of Hyde Park. Auburn-Gresham and other Southwest Side neighborhoods were populated largely by Catholic homeowners. Most had moved to the area as a first step on the ladder of social mobility; many had also done so in part because of perceived racial threats to their old communities and parishes. Their neighborhoods were valued because homeownership in a parish-centered community grounded their cultural identities and life courses. While property owners in both places feared the effect that black neighbors would have on their investments, Southwest Side Catholics also perceived a threat to their cultural and institutional life.

Economic security was also an important difference between the two communities. While residents of the Southwest Side were not poor, much of their wealth and sense of economic stability was tied up in home ownership. Auburn-Gresham—where the POSC's support was the deepest—consisted mostly of small, older homes of average value. The population tended to be older as well, with many residents on a fixed income. Whether they found integration desirable or not, many Southwest Side home owners did not feel comfortable enough economically to ignore the "common wisdom" about race and property values. While most Hyde Park residents were not wealthy, they tended to be younger renters with higher incomes who did not feel as keen a sense of economic threat from interracial living. The University of Chicago may have felt such a threat, but its predatory actions to uphold property values in the area allowed many members of the conference to keep the relationship between their economic well-being and the presence of black neighbors in the background of their thinking.[76]

For this reason, openness to interracial living appeared to come at a higher cost on the Southwest Side than in Hyde Park. It wasn't until the founding of the POSC that white community leaders on the Southwest Side began to publicly argue that a policy of total containment threatened to impose even higher costs than one of interest-based flexibility. Hyde Park liberals could afford to be more open to residential integration because poor blacks didn't have the financial resources to move there, and because liberals who compared the responses of whites in both communities to racial issues mistook the motives of each: they saw Catholic homeowners (and the archdiocese) as self-interested and ignorant, the university and the conference as altruistic and open-minded.[77] Editorials in *Christian Century* in 1959, for example, described the University of Chicago as advocates of the "open city." Alinsky, the POSC, and the archdiocese, in contrast, were accused of trying to build an "iron community curtain" to keep blacks out.

Stability and racial containment were the goals for both communities, but there were important differences in the resources available to each. While the larger apartment population of Hyde Park made it easier for its white residents to flee, it also provided the university and the conference with greater opportunities to control local occupancy. Apartment rentals could be manipulated through monopoly control over property ownership or management. The only reason whites had remained in Hyde Park was the University of Chicago's economic and political power, which enabled it to remove and exclude poor black families, Alinsky argued. "There is only one University of Chicago, willing and able to spend money as though they printed it on the premises," Alinsky wrote. The integrationist dreams of the HP-KCC had nothing to do with it.[78]

The decisions of individual homeowner families to stay or sell, while made within a social context that defined price and the market, were much harder for a community group or institution like the POSC to regulate or control. However, the large percentage of homeowners on the Southwest Side presented the POSC with a population that desperately wanted to avoid abandoning their homes, churches, and neighbors. Black newcomers, in turn, generally sought that kind of stability. While the POSC could not monopolize the local housing market, most of the people it was trying to organize had deep economic, emotional, and spiritual ties to the community. Chicago neighborhoods that had tried to maintain some kind of economic (and racial) stability in the past had frequently run aground when confronted with properties owned by absentee landlords. The Southwest Side had few of these.

Clearly, the primary difference between Hyde Park and the Southwest Side was the University of Chicago itself. As Alinsky acknowledged, his alma mater was "unrivaled in its power and influence" in the community. "When it acts," Alinsky told the Chicago chapter of the National Association of Housing and Redevelopment Officials, "the local banks, the real estate agencies, the insurance companies, a significant part of its population which is on its payroll, and a more substantial part of the population to whom status in the University society is of major concern, moves with it as its shadow." In Hyde Park, he concluded, "the University of Chicago is omnipotent."[79] While Alinsky may have exaggerated somewhat, there can be no question that the political and economic resources possessed by school administrators, trustees, and alumni both locally and citywide were hugely important to the ability of the university and the conference to sustain an interracial middle-class community.

Alinsky intended for the Catholic Church and the POSC to play a role on the Southwest Side similar to that of the University of Chicago and the conference in Hyde Park. Like the university, parishes had planted deep economic and cultural roots in the community that could not be abandoned. Parish priests and institutions potentially had the economic and leadership resources—and respect—to anchor their neighborhoods, inspire committed action by their parishioners, and provide the social security and spiritual sanction needed for them to welcome black neighbors. They offered the possibility of asserting conscious social control over the local housing market. Parishes would allow a community of homeowners to see the value of their property, their block, and their neighbors in a social and moral context. Thus, local churches would hopefully provide the POSC a crucial resource: motivated and organized citizens with an attachment to territorial identity. The parishes would provide the POSC with money and foot soldiers while providing a spiritual sanction for organizational activities without resting them solely on the thin ice of racial tolerance and understanding. That could come later.

While individual parishes may not have had the money or the power to launch a coordinated program, the archdiocese did. When the POSC got up and running, its close alliance with parishes (and thus the archdiocese) would keep it connected to the larger political and structural issues affecting the potential for a stable, integrated community. His commission for the *General Report*, as well as Cardinal Meyer's interest in race relations, encouraged

Alinsky to believe that the POSC could leverage the resources and power necessary for controlled integration.

Yet the archdiocese was not the University of Chicago. While the university was a large and powerful local institution with citywide (indeed, nationwide) influence, the archdiocese was a citywide institution with local outposts. School officials could use their power to leverage resources and legislation for the benefit of Hyde Park, and without any obligation to justify its use to others, but the archdiocese constantly had to balance the interests and viewpoints of Catholics throughout the city—as well as the prejudices of non-Catholics. Complicating matters, many Catholics (both clergy and laity) were ambivalent at best about the virtues of open occupancy and residential integration. Taking an aggressive stance on the issue threatened to undermine the authority of the archdiocese among its parishioners.

Alinsky was highly skeptical of the organizational methods of the HP-KCC. Poor blacks were almost completely excluded from it.[80] Little effort was made to include some of Hyde Park's more powerful and racially conservative elements, such as businesspeople, large property owners, and even the university. Alinsky believed that no individual membership community organization could effectively represent local residents, because its self-selecting structure would lead it to take hard-and-fast ideological positions born of individual moral commitments rather than engage in a democratic process of debate, interest aggregation, and compromise. Such groups would inevitably advocate strong moral positions that might be admirable, but they were also often politically naïve or beyond its power to implement.[81] When the group found that its combination of citywide lobbying, local organizing, and moral education was not working in the late 1950s, it readily abandoned its democratic goals in favor of an alliance with university officials to "save" the neighborhood—even if a few thousand black families were displaced in the process. Egan and Von Hoffman convinced Alinsky that a more desirable approach would create a mass-based neighborhood group and include local blacks of all classes in it from the beginning.

Alinsky believed it to be critically important for a fledgling community organization dealing with sensitive racial issues to be broadly representative. This was especially crucial on the Southwest Side, where the POSC did not have a large, well-organized, and politically self-aware constituency already committed to interracialism. While the inclusion of more conservative elements might have a dampening effect on the pace of change and the moral consistency of a community group's pronouncements and positions, the changes that were implemented promised to have broader and longer-lasting support. For Alinsky, Hyde Park was a cautionary lesson in the limits of racial liberalism. He believed that in the long run his organizing methods would advance residential integration in a way that was more democratic, replicable, and effective than one that married good intentions to a fundamental lack of local power.[82]

Conclusion

In April 1959, the Chicago Commission on Human Relations convened a workshop, "Management of Neighborhood Change," in Lake Geneva, Wisconsin, a few hours north of the city. The 123 delegates, representing thirty-five Chicago neighborhoods and ten suburbs, listened while experts, public officials, and local activists discussed race relations and neighborhood stabilization in four Chicago communities: Lawndale, on the West Side; Lincoln Park, on the North Side; and Chatham and Winneconna Lakes, both within the boundaries of the POSC.[83]

John Lee, an Irish Catholic homeowner in Winneconna Lakes and a past president of the Auburn-Highland Community Council as well as the Winneconna Lakes Area Improvement Association (WLAIA), told the assembly that most white residents were convinced that the neighborhood would become all black in the near future. His neighbors had little knowledge of or experience with blacks, aside from the "sensational news stories" that informed them of "the number of Negroes on relief, the number of illegitimate Negro children receiving ADC [Aid to Dependent Children]," and of the high crime rate in the Black Belt. Because of these stereotypes, Lee observed, his neighbors "do not believe that there is any workable plan to keep the neighborhood in a condition that would be livable for them." In the previous year and a half, Winneconna Lakes had been "swarming with real estate solicitors telling people they 'better get out now.'" Many had done so, even before any blacks moved into the area.[84]

Talk of solutions at the workshop varied widely, particularly among the academics and experts. The most interesting and controversial topic of the weekend, however, was the use of housing quotas. Nearly all the panelists addressed the issue, and most endorsed it.[85] What was needed, Lee argued, was the creation of a "power situation whereby just so many Negroes will move into a given area and no more, unless the other people wanted to give their homes away." While acknowledging some "objections" to such an approach, since "the advantages of integration are so great, some sacrifice is worthwhile." The use of quotas "would break down the problem to workable units," Lee concluded, and give white residents reason to be hopeful and active.[86]

The CCHR's main intention had been to bring together experts, policy makers, and activists who were open to the idea of residential integration but unsure of how to bring it about. The gathering allowed the participants to compare notes about what had worked and what had not—and to bring that knowledge back to their neighborhoods. No consensus emerged, aside perhaps from a general sense that local action alone was insufficient and that even the most politically risky ideas—like quotas—should be considered, if they showed promise. The lack of a consensus was indicative of a larger problem: political experience, social science, and legal precedent did not offer a ready-made template for how to advance the cause of residential integration. Neighborhoods that succeeded in making their local housing markets nondiscriminatory remained embedded within a larger metropolitan housing market that was deeply racialized. So few predominantly white communities in the Chicago area were open to black families that the small number that actively practiced nondiscrimination found integration to be increasingly elusive—precisely because of their interracialism. By indicating their openness to integration, they were bound to be swamped by black demands for housing that could not be satisfied elsewhere.

The answer appeared to require an expansion and integration of the metropolitan housing market, as well as a transformation of the rules governing access to that market, but few communities, no matter how well organized, had the political wherewithal to bring that about. Was integration possible without limiting the supply of housing available to a growing black community?

His reputation for gritty pragmatism notwithstanding, Alinsky was an optimist. He believed there was a window of opportunity for black and white Americans to find a new way to live with one another. It would be found on the Southwest Side of Chicago. And quotas might very well be part of the solution.

4
The "Benign Quota," Racial Liberalism, and the OSC

> It is more desirable to make a success of achieving racial democracy than acquiring more shelter for a limited number of colored people at the cost of . . . interracial conflict, strengthening segregation elsewhere in the city . . . and further characterizing Negro occupancy with blight.
> ROBERT WEAVER, *The Negro Ghetto*, 1948

> We, the residents of the Southwest community . . . hereby join together in the Organization for the Southwest Community to promote the well-being of the community and its people, without regard to race, religion or national origin.
> OSC, *Statement of Purpose*, 1959

> We are not bigots. We are not intolerant. We are simply facing facts and we say if integration ever comes, it must come by voluntary methods after a long period of education of both races . . . otherwise, we cannot use our streets after dark.
> HARRY EVERINGHAM, Committee for the Preservation of the Southwest Community, 1960

The Grand Boulevard study, followed by a couple of tense months on the Southwest Side, had hardened Alinsky's conviction that while residential integration was wholly desirable, idealistic calls for brotherhood and the passage of open occupancy laws were naïve and unrealistic means to that end. As long as white homeowners automatically associated black neighbors with the destruction of their communities, residential integration would be resisted. Whites saw only two options: fight or flight. Neither promised anything other than the reinforcement of racial apartheid and the perpetuation of the racialized sense of entitlement and peril that supported it.

Although Alinsky hoped that the POSC might in time convince residents that a third option was indeed viable, he and his organizers nonetheless downplayed this deeper purpose in front of all but the most trusted local allies. Of course, most early participants knew that the success or failure of the association would revolve around its response to the issue of race and place. Opponents of integration hoped to use the POSC as a wall to maintain the community and its present racial composition, while more liberal members sought to integrate the organization first, then the neighborhood. Alinsky anticipated such a battle, believing that partial integration could gain strong support only if it had been negotiated in an organized and democratic forum.

Nicolas Von Hoffman and Msgr. John McMahon also made it clear that no organized force for integration of the Southwest Side would ever emerge without such a forum, and the eventual inclusion of new black residents in it. If a certain degree of initial secrecy and chicanery proved necessary for this to take place, then so be it.

Alinsky chose a surprisingly public forum in which to break the issue out into the open: the Chicago hearings of the US Commission on Civil Rights, in early May 1959. With TV cameras rolling, Alinsky outlined his idea for using local racial quotas to create stable racially integrated neighborhoods. While he had discussed the idea earlier with a number of priests and lay leaders that he trusted, the larger population of the Southwest Side (and the city) were made aware of the POSC's "true" purpose. The organizer's comments, characteristically, were blunt: "No white Chicago community wants Negroes . . . the only places in this city where there is even consideration of an integrated population is where the Negro ghetto has rushed in on the whites who, for various financial reasons, are trying to stick it out." Chicago was the nation's most segregated city, Alinsky insisted, because its white population wanted it that way.

Alinsky stopped short, however, of condemning white resistance as indicative of nothing more than ignorant, immoral racism. Long critical of the attempt by liberal social scientists and race-relations groups to psychologize the white racist, Alinsky instead attempted to understand their underlying interests and perceptions. He cautioned the commission not to dismiss the legitimate fears of community obliteration that had enveloped many white ethnic neighborhoods. While racism and segregation are wrong and destructive, Alinsky insisted, "unless we can develop a program which recognizes the legitimate self-interest of white communities, we have no right to condemn them morally because they refuse to commit hara-kiri." The pattern of containment, decline, transition, and flight appeared to neighborhood whites to be a hard social fact, beyond the ability of individual families or communities to stop. As long as structural forces continued to place whites in the tragic position of seeing interracial living as a direct threat to their interests, paternalistic condemnations of their behavior from on high would do little to break the pattern.

If the housing market were not controlled or altered in some way, Alinsky argued, neighborhoods would continue to rapidly turn from white to black, with the attendant social and economic costs. Any solution had to prevent the swamping of white communities while simultaneously forestalling white flight. On the basis of his experiences on the Southwest Side, Alinsky had come to believe that a "silent majority" of white homeowners was willing to concede a small black presence in exchange for keeping their neighborhood and its institutions stable and predominantly white. Given a chance, he asserted, whites "will not leave. Too many whites have already sold and run, only to sell and run again. They're tired and broke. They are now willing to settle for something less than all-white neighborhoods."

The answer, Alinsky testified, was "a formula of some kind"—a quota—"aiming toward the diffusion of the Negro population throughout the city scene." Alinsky suggested 5 percent to 8 percent as a ballpark figure. This would have to be done on a neighborhood basis, he continued, appealing to the "basic interest" of local institutions and organizations. The passage of open occupancy laws was necessary, Alinsky argued, but a bottom-up approach had a better chance at long-term effectiveness. Private, voluntary efforts to control housing markets had to be developed—and community organizing, Alinsky asserted, was the way to bring it about. Community power groups, Alinsky imagined, could buy homes and buildings for sale, thus allowing some democratic control over the "power of selection and of distribution" of the homes. While such agreements had generally been used in the past to keep blacks out of predominantly white neighborhoods on the Southwest Side, they also provided a potentially benign means for controlling local housing supply. With such market power, an individual, a community group, or a nonprofit corporation could attempt to create and maintain racial balance.[1]

As he had argued in the *General Report*, however, Alinsky insisted that over the long haul, organizing in white neighborhoods would not be enough to break the pattern of violent and rapid turnover. Black community groups were needed as well. The problem, Alinsky continued, was that Chicago did not at present have a black community organization that could "speak for the Negro population . . . they do not have an organized base in terms of their numbers . . . to speak and collectively bargain." Such an organization might be able to turn to a white community organization and say, "'Look, you want one and we want two; you want three and we want four. Now, let's get together and pool our strength and we'll be able to get what we want for all of us.'" Race wouldn't have to enter into it, he concluded; self-interest in a common problem, even across the racial divide, would be enough.

Those who "carp about the morality" of the quota proposal, Alinsky concluded, "offer no alternative." They cry, "'Let there be open occupancy,' and then there is no open occupancy . . . a local open occupancy law would still confront us with . . . securing compliance," and implementation would still demand some kind of quota. Alinsky put forward his proposal as an honest and practical answer to this dilemma. He delicately tried to walk the blurry line between the desirability of stable interracial communities and the rights of individual blacks to participate equally in the housing market.[2]

The "Benign Quota" Debate

Despite the controversy and media attention caused by his provocative presentation and local reputation, Alinsky's proposal was not so unusual. By the late 1950s and early 1960s the growing civil rights movement and the constitutional changes that it had helped to bring about had placed racial integration squarely and urgently on the urban agenda. At the same time, the social and institutional forces that created resegregation and white flight were having profound effects on a generation of Northern city dwellers, provoking a variety of intellectual and political responses. Discussions of and experiments with controlled occupancy—quotas—in both public and private housing were the result. Activists, neighborhood groups, builders, and public housing authorities joined civil rights lawyers and social scientists in a series of discussions of and experiments with the so-called benign racial housing quota.[3]

Advocates of the "benign quota" generally saw it as a temporary expedient made necessary by one undeniable social fact: once blacks attained a certain percentage in a block, project, or development, whites would leave, and resegregation would occur. The fact of a "tipping point" was widely accepted in the urban North, and it underlay most arguments for housing quotas. While scholars and administrators differed over the critical numbers, the idea that whites would not live in a neighborhood that was (or was perceived to be) predominantly black served as the fundamental baseline for policy proposals, court rulings, property appraisals, financing decisions, and the day-to-day actions of real estate agents, homeowners, and prospective home buyers.[4]

Quota proponents lamented the social fact of the tipping point and were generally highly critical of the assumption that blacks automatically depressed property values in predominantly white neighborhoods. A survey of South Side real estate agents in the mid-1960s found that agents overwhelmingly believed that housing prices fell in neighborhoods "threatened" by an influx of black families, as panicked white homeowners unloaded their property. An agent in a changing neighborhood said, "It's the most terrific force and something no one can prevent or change . . . when the Negro begins to get close to a neighborhood, you can no more stop it than you can stop a million tons of snow from rolling down a mountain side." Another agent agreed, concluding that, since *Shelley*, there was "no possible way to prevent these neighborhoods from turning colored, and once they have colored, there is no way to stop them from becoming slums . . . I would predict in 10 or 15 years that the entire South Side will be colored within the city limits. There won't be anything left." Approximately two-thirds of the agents expected segregation to continue, and fully seventy-four of the eighty respondents judged residential integration to be impossible in Chicago and condemned any efforts to bring it about.[5]

These assumptions, which the fair housing activist Charles Abrams called the "racist theory of value," underlay the legal, financial, and marketing infrastructure of the metropolitan housing market, were reinforced by federal policy and structured the behaviors of whites in that market. This theory, Abrams argued, was taught in real estate courses, reproduced in textbooks, circulated in home and real estate magazines, and made the subject of state license exams "in which an applicant who might take a democratic position on the racial issue would be marked wrong." While most real estate agents claimed to engage in restrictive practices because their customers and their professional ethics demanded it, real estate agents in effect were protecting the social and equity capital of white homeowners.[6]

By the 1950s scholars had begun to gather evidence that property values generally did *not* drop when black families moved into an all-white neighborhood, if whites waited it out, instead of flooding the market. Racial transition was caused more by the racially discriminatory dual housing market than the machinations of panic peddlers and blockbusters. Nonetheless, the idea among whites that interracial living automatically led to decline, decay, violence, and the erosion of property values had become the mortar in the walls of residential segregation throughout the nation. Resistance to that idea appeared either extraordinarily brave or self-defeating.[7]

"Even where goodwill, community effort and financing have been maximized," the sociologist Morton Grodzins concluded in 1958, "the psychology of tipping has operated." The only interracial neighborhoods in the nation were those where "limits exist upon the influx of non-whites." Without quotas, he insisted, "there has been a total failure to achieve interracial communities." Where controlled migration has been achieved, Grodzins concluded, "so has interracial living." Saul Alinsky, joined by a small group of activists, scholars, administrators, and entrepreneurs, believed in the possibilities of quotas.[8]

Experiments with and advocacy of benign quotas tended to revolve around either newly constructed suburban private developments or government-owned public housing. White fears of inundation were easier to overcome in larger planned public or "quasi-private" developments, because unified ownership could provide stability by preventing the deterioration of property values and the flooding of the local housing market. While large privately funded interracial suburban projects, such as those developed by Morris Milgram near Philadelphia, did face local resistance, they had the advantage of not threatening to disrupt existing patterns of social, cultural, and institutional interaction. Further, white and black home buyers knew what they were getting into when they purchased one of his homes, and some did so in part for ethical reasons. Racial balance was to be maintained not by the residents, but by an overarching third party—the developer. In practice, until the larger housing market for blacks improved, this would mean the continual rejection of qualified (and often overqualified) black applicants. Given that black families had been almost completely excluded from the Philadelphia suburbs, Milgram's developments did at least help to erode the widespread white suburban fear that integrated neighborhoods were a financial risk while providing a small number of black families with social mobility.[9]

Demonstrated success in interracial living in such projects would have a positive effect throughout the housing market by subverting the racist theory of value. But such unified ownership would be difficult to attain in the private market for urban housing. With the potential exception of large privately developed urban projects (such as Lake Meadows or Prairie Shores in Chicago), which could (though rarely did) control occupancy for the purposes of racial integration, Milgram's use of quotas appeared to have little to teach Alinsky and the POSC. A 1955 study of housing demand in transition neighborhoods like the Southwest Side concluded that such occupation controls would never work in existing neighborhoods.[10]

Although it was unclear whether a group like the POSC had the resources to become a serious player in a local housing market dominated by owner-occupied homes rather than apartments, it most certainly did have the potential economic, political, and social power to pressure local homeowners, bankers, and real estate agents. Quotas, Alinsky hoped, would allow residents of the Southwest Side to envision some kind of social control over what had appeared to be an inevitable outcome. The question, however, was whether the partial sacrifice of racial nondiscrimination was worth the gain of a racially mixed Southwest Side.

The 1954 Supreme Court decision in *Brown* has achieved canonical stature in American law and culture. Most commonly, the ruling has been taken to mean that race has no place in American law—that the law must be, in the words of Justice John Marshall Harlan in his famous 1896 *Plessy* dissent, "color-blind." The state must not use or support any kind of racial classification, except under extraordinary circumstances. In the late 1950s and the early 1960s, this "anticlassification" interpretation predominated among liberals; since the 1970s, it has been the centerpiece of conservative approaches to civil rights. But advocates of the benign quota offered another interpretation, one based on a sophisticated analysis of the structural roots of racial inequality in the metropolitan North. Most intriguingly, they offered an early criticism of color blindness as a means for overcoming racial inequality.[11]

In Jack Balkin's useful formulation, interpretations of *Brown* have revolved around two notions: color blindness and equal citizenship. The color-blindness position at the heart of postwar racial liberalism reflected a fundamental optimism about the American experiment and the ability of the nation to overcome the "aberration" of racism. Racism was the result of irrational individual prejudice, which could be eliminated through education, integration and interracial contact, and formal legal equality. An end to formal legal segregation and discrimination would allow for increased interaction across racial lines, causing racism to eventually wither away. According to this view, the Warren Court had thrown out *Plessy* because it allowed the state to impose racial classifications that stigmatized and harmed individual black citizens. Classifications by race stigmatize blacks and deny them the ability to be considered as individuals.

Those who have supported the equal citizenship rationale in recent decades tend to see Jim Crow segregation as part of a larger system of racial subordination. The law could remedy that subordination or enhance it; racial classifications could be a means to either end. While formal equality under the law was necessary for undermining racial subordination, it was not sufficient. As Balkin puts it, the danger of strict adherence to the color-blind principle is that it "shields from scrutiny practices of subordination that cannot be explained as the result of direct racial classification or hidden racial animus." The *Brown* ruling had thrown out Jim Crow laws in public schooling precisely because they played a critical role in a larger system of racial subordination. The task, then, was to uproot that larger system, which a color-blind reading of *Brown* would not abet.[12]

Quota advocates shared this skepticism of color blindness. Under the equal protection clause of the Fourteenth Amendment, the Supreme Court of the late 1950s ruled on the constitutionality of racial classifications on the basis of their "reasonableness." If a classification was found to be reasonable, then it was constitutional. If quota schemes were conceived and implemented in a "good faith" attempt to follow the law's "true purpose," then courts should find them reasonable and allow them to stand. Because they held that residential segregation in the metropolitan North was part of a larger structure of subordination, quota advocates believed that good-faith efforts to address this should be seen as faithful to *Brown*. Reasonableness had to be determined in context, and experience appeared to show that without some kind of occupational controls, the socially desirable goal of residential integration would not be attained. The housing market would continually re-create the walls of segregation.[13] If the courts condemned "honest efforts to integrate on strictly legalistic grounds," Charles Abrams concluded, they would build up a body of law that was color-blind on the surface but would allow no legal room for "breaking down segregated patterns."[14]

Alinsky, Abrams, and other quota advocates questioned the validity of color blindness as an all-encompassing rule for evaluating policies and practices. Facially neutral jurisprudence was useless if the segregation that continued to subordinate black citizens and impoverish their communities was left untouched. The power and privileges of whiteness are in part dependent upon its transparency—on its status as the normative model, which allows whites to remain blind to the racialized aspects of their identities and to perceive race only when someone else's intrudes on their lives. Color blindness was appealing precisely because of this transparency. While it had an intuitive appeal as an end, as a method for achieving racial equality it could reinforce rather than undermine the hegemony of race, by blunting some of the tools needed to overcome it.[15] Advocates of quotas insisted that the Fourteenth Amendment, and especially *Brown*, required taking race into account in designing a means of implementation—such as the use of benign quotas.[16]

Proponents of the benign quota believed that once interracial living had been established, even on a small scale, it would demonstrate to citizens, developers, and policy makers that it was workable, profitable, and replicable. In response to accusations of tokenism, advocates argued simply, "You have to start somewhere." Quotas, by allaying both white and black fears of the unpredictability of complete racial turnover, would be stabilizing. They were never intended to be permanent and would be phased out when they were no longer needed. As Alinsky put it, the present situation was one of total restriction and segregation, determined by the dual housing market. Flexible and temporary quotas—and, in Alinsky's case, private and voluntary—would break the replication of residential segregation. Simply allowing individuals to freely act in the housing market—or more accurately, assuming that absent quotas, individuals do indeed act freely—would perpetuate segregation, the black ghetto, and its attendant social costs. The color-blind belief that formal legal equality led to a just distribution of results did not hold on the ground and thus should not in the law.

Quotas and Racial Liberalism

Most advocates of some kind of controlled occupancy tried desperately to avoid the term *quota*.[17] Alinsky, not surprisingly, flouted such conventions, and with some relish. Indeed, his lone encounter with Martin Luther King Jr. involved a dispute over the word. Based on a December 1959 statement by King favoring Milgram's use of the term *percentage integration*, Alinsky claimed King as a quota ally on a TV program. After a Lutheran cleric criticized King's support, he sought an apology and retraction from Alinsky, claiming he had been "misinterpreted." Alinsky refused, writing King that progressive developments everywhere employ a quota "as the opening wedge" to stabilize integration. He scolded King for taking cover in the "cool comfortable climate on the mountain-top where one can indulge in self-satisfied, safe, militant denunciation of the evils of segregation." Only when one had "descended into the valleys of implementation," as Alinsky had, did one come face-to-face with the "full violence and anger of every racist Negro-hating group in Chicago." He enclosed copies of his hate mail to prove it. King's own violent encounter with white resistance to integration in Chicago was still in the future.[18]

For many liberal critics of quotas, the abolition of discrimination and segregation would ultimately rest, both legally and politically, on the assertion of individual rights, not group ones. The color-blind model of civil rights, with its privileging of the abstract individual over society and social groups, was deeply rooted in the market economy, American liberalism, and modern citizenship. Under that model, the role of the state is only to ensure the maximum freedom of individuals. Once they are given the freedom to pursue their ends, the result will be a kind of meritocratic justice. Antidiscrimination law at both the state and the federal levels had been based on color blindness, with the overall assumption that equality of opportunity would produce a just distribution of results.[19]

By the late 1950s mainstream civil rights organizations, such as the Southern Christian Leadership Conference and the NAACP, generally articulated their demands in a color-blind discourse, and Martin Luther King Jr. became its best-known and most convincing moral advocate (although his views would later change). The few black civil rights leaders who spoke out in favor of the utility and justice of racial preferences at the national level in the early 1960s (generally in employment, not housing), such as James Farmer of the Congress of Racial Equality (CORE) and Whitney Young of the Urban League, were quickly pressured by their peers to retract their ideas.[20]

The debate over housing quotas reveals some of the theoretical and political fault lines in postwar racial liberalism. Political language since the New Deal has been dominated by a discourse of individual rights, applied to an ever-expanding realm of political, social, and economic life. By the late 1950s, rights consciousness had become fully embedded in the language, expectations, and institutions of liberalism and the postwar state more generally.[21]

In Tom Sugrue's useful formulation, blacks in the postwar era used the language of rights to demand equality, whereas whites used it to demand economic and social security. To many black activists, "equality" implied a just and fair distribution of resources first and foremost, not just the absence of formal legal barriers to opportunity. However, part of the "security" that whites both at the workplace and in their neighborhoods expected the government to protect had been built upon New Deal programs, court rulings, and market institutions that were deeply racialized. Job seniority and the associational rights of white homeowners were seen as crucial bulwarks of the social and economic security necessary for full citizenship for whites. But white demands for the "security" of the unequal distribution of those goods inevitably left racial inequalities intact. Thus, when black activists and eventually the liberal state itself demanded antidiscriminatory hiring and housing, many whites both at work and at home felt that their hard-won security was being threatened by "un-American" social engineering and a demand for racial preferences that ran counter to deeply held self-images of earned status and moral innocence with regard to race. They were asking, in essence, for something blacks hadn't earned, and they had.

Black equality and white security appeared to be a zero-sum situation in large part because of how postwar liberals thought about racism, racial inequality, and discrimination. Integrationists in the 1940s and 1950s tended to see racism as an individual pathology to be addressed through education and moral suasion, and segregation as a moral anomaly that could be attacked in the same way. The civil rights policies built upon these assumptions offered limited tokenism both at home and in the workplace, which at once effected little systematic change and sparked strong white resistance while simultaneously raising expectations among blacks that the rising tide of American prosperity would shortly lift their boats, too.

Most important, the language and administration of postwar civil rights law used an individualized grievance model. As a result, antidiscrimination law was blind to the ways that racial inequalities embedded within the law, the market, and space itself were reproduced even in the absence of clear discriminatory intent. Racial discrimination was seen as something done by someone, to someone, and policy solutions were to be implemented at that level.[22] As Lani Guinier has argued, this minimalist liberal analysis of race, rooted in *Brown*, became dominant, while simultaneously reenergizing white racial consciousness. It allowed courts to "limit constitutional relief to remedying acts of *intentional* discrimination by local entities or individuals." It thus excused inaction—naturalizing de facto segregation, while failing to redress the inequalities in resources, opportunities, and power that stemmed from it. It left the causes and consequences of metropolitan inequality beyond the reach of constitutional redress. They remain there still.[23]

Alinsky saw that the formal legalism of the color-blind approach tended to minimize the extent to which many whites were invested in segregation and racial subordination. It also would invite opposition and backlash from whites, without actually attaining meaningful improvement in the lives of blacks. Unlike real estate agents, developers, and landlords, most homeowners engage in a small number of highly individualistic, chronologically and geographically scattered property transactions in their lives, making them hard to regulate with fair housing mandates. They also made resistance to and resentment of "outside" interference highly likely. As late as 1968, 56 percent of white respondents agreed that whites "have a right to keep Negroes out of their neighborhoods if they want to." As a result, the political price of enacting nondiscrimination laws in many places was token implementation, rendering those laws, according to one observer, "mainly symbolic and ritualistic."[24]

Accordingly, black skepticism about racial liberalism grew. Many of Chicago's black civic leaders doubted whether fair housing laws would make much difference in the daily lives of most blacks. The city had become even more deeply segregated since the war, and few black families had the financial resources to take advantage of a fair housing law, even if an effective one were to be passed. "Open occupancy won't do much to help the Black Belt," said one South Side leader. "I don't think that [it] would desegregate the South Side. In fact, I can't think of anything that *would* desegregate the South Side." Dawson and other black machine politicians also didn't see open occupancy as "good politics," since their power was in part derived from the persistence of segregation.[25]

Particularly with regard to housing and education, local civil rights laws were limited in their effectiveness. Residential segregation was sustained by reinforcing processes, institutions, and markets that stretched across jurisdictions—into the suburbs, in particular. The rhetoric of property rights, home rule, local control of schools and property values, and the free market were all color-blind on the surface, but they were effectively deployed by those resisting change. Further, the inaccurate notion that segregation in the North was de facto and thus not caused or reinforced by the law or the state legitimized this resistance. Most court rulings were limited in the same way.

Alinsky had long despaired of the willingness of his liberal allies to recognize the messiness of grounded pragmatic work, instead favoring the moral high ground, and he found a similar calculus at work in their opposition to the benign quota. Housing markets were already deeply racialized: where buyers chose to live, which neighborhoods real estate agents would show, where financing was available, when sellers elected to place their property on the market and to whom they decided to sell it, the distribution of available buyers for each housing unit, the prices that were anticipated, the prices that were offered, and the way property was appraised and assessed were all heavily influenced by racial assumptions, privileges, and inequalities. Land-use laws, which affected what kind of housing was available and where, were also powerfully shaped by race. Fair housing laws addressed the symptoms of racial subordination, but without addressing the disease. Working-class whites in particular had a substantial investment in segregation, which couldn't be dismissed as solely the result of irrational prejudice. They would see themselves as those most likely to lose out in a color-blind market, while wealthier whites could purchase or zone their way out of the moral tensions imposed by liberal solutions to the "American dilemma."

Laws and educational campaigns promoting racial tolerance and equality would have little effect, Alinsky insisted, unless integration was closely tied to self-interest and necessity. Blacks and whites needed to work together on issues of common interest. "We must leave off having race relations summit meetings where the platitudes echo in the air," Alinsky insisted. "We must go down in the valleys and gutters where the atmosphere is hotter, and where the people and the problems are."[26] While fair housing statutes, race-relations professionals, and groups like the CCHR could be of some help, the social learning necessary for white neighborhoods to associate integration and self-interest emerged most effectively from local experience and leadership, Alinsky held. Whites would discover that blacks were good neighbors only by finding it out for themselves.

To Alinsky, quota advocates had recognized that the real problem was the structure of the metropolitan housing market and decided to make a pragmatic intervention, while racial liberals preferred to ignore that dilemma altogether and keep their beliefs unsullied. Alinsky and other quota advocates wanted a color-conscious sociology, not color-blind legalism.[27] The benign quota, he argued, offered a tangible model for how a mass-based community organization dedicated to interracialism could begin to undermine Chicago's dual housing market. While he agreed that racial discrimination and segregation were structural issues that had to be attacked from above as well as below, Alinsky believed that the close relationship between race and property made local organizing a higher tactical priority than lobbying for open-occupancy laws.[28] He worried that an emphasis on fair housing statutes would provide an organizing focus for homeowner groups, real estate agents, and the politicians beholden to them, especially if the laws were extended—as they needed to be—into the private market.²⁹ Alinsky's two decades of organizing on the white South Side had taught him that government intervention into the ostensibly private housing market on a racial issue would serve only to reinforce the rights-based resistance of whites.³⁰

If integration were going to come, Alinsky insisted, it should occur "as a result of free citizens and free institutions deciding to go ahead with integration at all deliberate speed," not "by government coercion." The cost of such coercion, Alinsky argued, would be "incalculable"; indeed, "use of government coercion for laudable purposes can make slaves of free citizens as rapidly as coercion used for scandalous objectives."³¹ Open occupancy would become politically viable only through local organizing, Alinsky maintained, because it was only through democratic community groups that citizens could understand the functional connections between structural problems and everyday life. "Once people are organized so that they have the power to make changes," Alinsky argued, "then, when confronted with questions of change, they begin to think and to ask questions about how to make the changes." A top-down approach, like that of racial liberals who passed laws but left the racial leadership vacuum in white neighborhoods untouched, guaranteed strong resistance. Wider political reform was unlikely to take place unless grassroots support for it existed, and this would happen only if people began to take action in their own communities. For Alinsky, quotas were a practical way to bite the bullet.³²

A further part of Alinsky's objection to the approach of racial liberals stemmed from the corporatist sociology that informed much of his thinking. With its focus on the state (as rule provider and enforcer) and the individual (as moral actor), racial liberalism contrasted sharply with Alinsky's emphasis on more mediate institutions and social formations. Such entities—which included parishes, neighborhoods, block clubs, wards, community organizations, and local housing markets, as well as racial identities themselves—were of vital importance for Alinsky. Approaches to integration that sought to circumvent these social entities, or that ignored their existence, Alinsky insisted, were bound to fail.³³

For Alinsky the key to bringing about positive social change was to use social experience and the gentle prodding of organizers to induce both individuals and local institutions into ever-broader redefinitions of their interests and identities. Laws and markets were themselves created and shaped through the social behaviors and relationships reinforced by local formations, associations, and identities—not just the relationship between the individual and the state.³⁴ For Alinsky, homeowners and their neighbors, as well as real estate agents, bankers, and businesspeople needed to see how both races suffered in the dual housing market. Only then could an alternative racial geography be envisioned and realized. If the Southwest Side was going to survive as an interracial area, residents would need to imagine a new community identity, defined in part by racial tolerance, considered debate, and a lack of panic. This identity also had to be geographically broader than previous ones.[35]

Alinsky believed that the stranglehold of "keep 'em out" groups over local leadership and common wisdom on race relations had to be broken. Pressure for integration had previously come from outside individuals and institutions like the Catholic Interracial Council and the CCHR, which had no local power or authority. The creation of local integrationist community groups would present residents of "threatened" neighborhoods with another view while strengthening the voices of racially tolerant community leaders and public officials.[36]

Without this kind of local work, Alinsky insisted, changes at higher levels of political authority would have a minimal impact. While never renowned for his theoretical consistency, Alinsky was consistent on one essential point: community organizations were built from the ground up and from the neighborhood outward. For them to root deeply and gradually acquire the power to collectively bargain, they and their members had to acquire an ever-widening sense of social efficacy. For Alinsky, this could be done only by starting with what local groups could control, then moving up and out from there, in terms of both goals and social knowledge. Rallying individuals around an open-occupancy statute, no matter how justified, did not build permanent and mass-based local power. "A people do not break through their previous fatalism of submerged resentment and frustration into open problems which can be faced and dealt with," Alinsky argued, "until they have a mechanism, or a formula for effectively coping with the problems." These mechanisms—like quotas—would have to be local projects that would allow community groups to attack the problems in their neighborhoods, parishes, and apartment buildings.[37]

But Alinsky did not propose to create yet another parochial neighborhood association, all of which were generally too small to amass power in local housing markets. The POSC promised to be local enough to respond to the mundane service requests of its constituent member organizations while still covering enough territory to make a dent in the housing market and, when necessary, the city's political life. Its archdiocesan connections (and funding) also provided the fledgling group with an institutional relationship and citywide perspective. Furthermore, Alinsky envisioned an even broader reach through an alliance between black and white community groups.

Each of Alinsky's organizations was unique and organic, and each would grow and evolve in unpredictable directions. While the POSC (with some steering from IAF staff) might begin to develop the social knowledge and political technology to operate on more than a local level, for Alinsky this was far from preordained and was not to be forced. Thus, while the POSC could make symbolic statements and join alliances with outside groups and interests, it could not leverage power at a higher level until it could firmly and confidently do so locally.[38]

Alinsky was not a political theorist. Much like Franklin Roosevelt, he believed that intervention into social problems had inherent value, even without long-term goals in mind. Moreover, the issues on the Southwest Side were immediate (in the late 1950s in Chicago, 7,800 blocks changed over from white to black residency each year), his proposals were unprecedented, and the POSC's constituents had previously expressed little desire for interracialism of any sort.[39]

While Alinsky cultivated a public persona of single-minded radicalism and conflict for conflict's sake, his approach to community organizing was based heavily on compromise and tactical retreat. He welcomed like-minded individuals and institutions as allies, but Alinsky concentrated much of his energy on bringing his most obvious opponents—such as James Norris and Msgr. Molloy—into the fold. This served two purposes: first, his organizations needed to be representative in order to have legitimacy. If the POSC was to become the effective bargaining agent for the Southwest Side—a community union, or, in a sense, a "shadow government"—then it had to be able to facilitate compromises and aggregate local interests. Second, bringing in potential enemies allowed a community organization to "contain" its opposition constructively. As Alinsky put it, any proposal to end racial segregation was a nonstarter unless it presented the possibility of the "pacification of the white working-class elements in the city," who were the "heart and soul of racial warfare in Chicago." Quotas appeared to offer them a compromise they could accept.[40]

If interracial communities were to be created, Alinsky insisted, it had to be block by block, neighborhood by neighborhood, like the slow drip of water eroding a stone. The change would have to come from the bottom up. Only once residents and community leaders understood the structural innards of the dual housing market, white panic, and racial transition could integration be addressed. Success there would ultimately require the destruction of residential segregation in the metropolitan area as a whole—something Alinsky knew but had not developed the political technology to directly address. His organizing philosophy pushed him to focus relentlessly on what his community groups *could* effectively understand and attack.

To upwardly mobile blacks seeking to buy homes in stable, well-maintained neighborhoods like Chatham and Auburn-Gresham, the dual housing market seemed to threaten the stability of their new communities (and their own budgets and investments) almost as soon as they moved in. To white homeowners in "threatened" areas, the market was an overwhelming, coercive force that appeared to blend with the machinations of the federal government, liberal "do-gooders," and blacks to undermine their social and cultural security, and their propertied citizenship. For Alinsky the common desire that seemed to unite disparate interests was stability—and he wagered that the common institutional space that the POSC provided would help people see that common interest and then to compromise.

Any compromise involves concessions, however, and quotas were no exception. Inevitably, Alinsky's approach promised to make the POSC more conservative than many interracialists (himself included) would have preferred. Most constituents of the POSC's member groups intended to keep the Southwest Side as white as possible. Alinsky's quota proposal was thus presented as a kind of tactical retreat, an "inoculation" against complete racial turnover, and a way for local whites to accept the inevitability of black neighbors without fleeing.

Quotas essentially erased the housing needs of black families from active consideration and focused on how best to pacify whites. The unwillingness of white homeowners to live with a significant number of black neighbors was addressed by limiting *black* housing choices. Worse, the successful implementation of benign quotas in one neighborhood would also make it that much harder for other neighborhoods to integrate, by reinforcing the cultural and economic underpinnings of the dual housing market. The moral compromises and material sacrifices were both balanced much more heavily on the backs of black families than on white ones. In the absence of concerted federal action to open up the suburbs and unwind decades of state support for metropolitan segregation, Alinsky's intense territoriality promised to magnify these dilemmas, not resolve them.

Alinsky was correct to argue that quotas needn't be dismissed simply because they required moral compromises. Selling the viability of interracial living to white homeowners was critical for any significant and lasting residential integration was to take place. But without significant changes in racial segregation throughout the Chicago area, their use in a specific neighborhood would necessarily involve some racial discrimination. Even if a strong community organization were able to fully implement a quota system, the dual housing market would continually undermine it. It was unlikely that the POSC as conceived would be able to act quickly and decisively enough on a broader stage to make sustained integration possible. Still, until the POSC had the willingness, power, and allies to shatter the institutional underpinnings of racial containment, Alinsky was willing to accept the more moderate goal of keeping some part of the Southwest Side white.

"Committee for a Sane Policy Toward Saul Alinsky": Reaction on the Southwest Side

As Alinsky's biographer David Finks described it, the reaction to Alinsky's testimony was almost uniformly negative: "all hell broke loose" in the Chicago media, in national liberal and Protestant circles, and on the Southwest Side. Only in private correspondence and conversations did Alinsky get the sense that some found his stance admirable. Segregationists saw it (accurately) as an attempt, however limited, to permanently integrate neighborhoods, and so condemned it. Black leaders were decidedly mixed in their private responses, although publicly their reactions were quick and negative. A quota "is no solution to the problem," a local NAACP spokesman told the *Christian Science Monitor*. "At best it is a stopgap approach." A. L. Foster, of the black South Side Cosmopolitan Chamber of Commerce, argued that quotas left black housing needs at the mercy of white racism: "The acceptance of Negro families only after the white residents indicate approval smacks too much of paternalism."[41] Liberal white Protestants long suspicious of the racial views of Chicago Catholics in general, and of the archdiocese in particular, were confirmed in their belief that Meyer and Alinsky (and the POSC) were an allied force for segregation in the city.[42]

Through the newspapers, Alinsky tried to clarify some misconceptions about his viewpoint. Critics, he argued, had missed his central point: to achieve a "non-discriminatory open occupancy in housing everywhere." Quotas were a temporarily expedient method of "breaking the present jam" and "getting Negroes and whites to know each other as people." His plan was a "realistic approach" that assured whites that "the entrance of Negro families will not result in total community change," thus encouraging them to remain. If implemented in a "solidly organized" community that was adjacent to the expanding ghetto—one that "sees itself specifically doomed unless it does something"—a quota system would ensure a "non-threatened, non-hostile situation" in which "the Negro family ceases to become a symbol." Once such a community was organized, it could purchase vacant homes and sell them to selected black families of a similar economic background. The quota system would allow blacks to enter "by invitation, not invasion."[43]

Citing "organizational reasons," Alinsky had evaded questions by Civil Rights Commission Chair Fr. Theodore Hesburgh as to whether any of his present community groups might participate in such a project, but his attempt to shield the POSC from scrutiny failed. The press descended on predominantly white neighborhoods, asking what locals thought of Alinsky's quota plan. One reporter asked South Side residents, "If you could have a Negro family of your own choosing in your block and be sure there would not be any more, would you stay in your block?" While some contended that they would stay, most seemed to believe that it was too little, too late: as one respondent put it, "As far as the South Side of Chicago is concerned, it's gone."[44] Neighborhood-improvement associations on the Southwest Side warned that the POSC would "put two Negroes in every block," and IAF organizers were threatened with physical violence. "We were being thrown out of meetings and having doors slammed in our faces," Von Hoffman recalled. "Showing up in some parts of the district meant risking a beating."[45]

Typically, Alinsky took pleasure in the negative reaction, believing it to be in some way cathartic for the city. In a series of whimsical letters to Carl Tjerandsen of the Schwarzhaupt Foundation, Alinsky claimed that there was "method in my madness." The entire city, Alinsky quipped, "is suffering from severe, chronic color constipation, and I was out to administer a sizable mental laxative." He regretted that Tjerandsen hadn't been there to see "the urban bowels move as they have!" Black and white interracialists "have whispered about these things and agreed on this as a pragmatic procedure to try to break through the white curtain" privately, he argued, but it was only then coming to the forefront, as a result of his testimony.[46]

In an interview with the reporter Robert Schultz, Alinsky acknowledged the moral ambiguities of his proposal and conceded that he would be the "first to agree" that his plan was "immoral . . . contrary to the Democratic process." However, he countered, he would "take this means to this end" because he didn't know of any other options. Alinsky also reminded readers that proportions and ratios had already been accepted by the Supreme Court as a realistic approach to desegregation of schools. Furthermore, even open-occupancy laws, when enforced, would still require "the use of a 'ratio,' 'percentage,' or quota device, just as does the desegregation of the schools." While critics claimed that the quota was "restrictive," the situation currently was one of "total restriction." He invited his opponents to offer an alternative.[47]

While much of the criticism vilified Alinsky as a segregationist, ultimately it was local red-baiting attacks from the right that caused Alinsky and the POSC the most difficulty. Professional anticommunist and local resident Harry Everingham attempted to create a united front of homeowners' associations by rhetorically conflating "forced" integration, communism, Alinsky, and the POSC at meetings and in the *Southtown Economist*.[48] The accusation that the POSC intended to "put two Negroes on every block" originated with Everingham and his Committee to Preserve the Southwest Community, and it became the rallying cry for local segregationists. By early summer 1959, according to Fr. Jerome Riordan, just the mention of Alinsky's name "would be like putting a hand grenade in the parking lot and pulling the pin. Everyone would run for shelter." "I had to sneak around hoping that the fear-crazed whites wouldn't recognize me as connected with Alinsky," Von Hoffman remembered, "the guy planning to use the quota idea to bring unprintables into the area in order to flip it racially and make millions."[49]

The IAF's organizers, as well as POSC president O'Toole, found themselves repeatedly summoned before community groups to defend Alinsky and quotas. At a stormy mid-June meeting of the Beverly Area Planning Association, Von Hoffman tried to reassure the assemblage that as far as he knew, quotas were not official IAF policy. Both Von Hoffman and the press were ejected from the meeting, at which point the BAPA voted—over the objections of its president, Merrill Heuss, who served on the POSC's Structure Committee—not to affiliate with the POSC. Anti-Semitism also played a role in the opposition; the Ridge Civic Council voted not to affiliate because the organization had "too many New York people."[50]

The Brainerd Civic Association (BCA), a homeowners' group and member of the BAPA, was an especially sharp critic of Alinsky and the POSC. At a July 20 meeting the group's president, Jane Crawford, read an eighteen-point mimeographed "activity report"—drawn directly from the files of the Chicago Police Department's Red Squad—accusing Alinsky of "left-wing tendencies," and the POSC of being a subversive plot to force integration. Among other things, Crawford claimed that Alinsky was a "sponsor of the league for the advancement of colored people" and "founded the commission against racial disturbance." She also accused Alinsky of driving the meatpacking industry out of Chicago.

Bruce Sagan, publisher of the *Southtown Economist* and a supporter of the POSC, reprinted the report and allowed Alinsky a rebuttal. Predictably, the organizer didn't take the accusations very seriously. He claimed to be "guilty in spades" of most of them and wondered why Crawford didn't also blame him for the flight of the shoe, textile, and copper industries. Sagan took the attack more seriously. He solicited a response from the BYNC's Joseph Meegan, who told the paper that he didn't know of a "tougher anti-Communist" and recommended that readers "ask their local pastors" about Alinsky. Sagan also reprinted the text of Alinsky's quota testimony in full.[51]

By mid-August 1959, Alinsky and POSC leaders concluded that the organization's affiliation with the IAF had become a publicity liability and decided to sever it. While the official relationship was dissolved, the POSC promptly rehired Chambers and Villemas to work as staff organizers, ensuring that Alinsky's influence would still be felt. Von Hoffman was reassigned to Woodlawn, where Alinsky was striving to construct a black community organization, although Chambers and Villemas continued to report to him. And still, the red-baiting of the POSC heated up as the October congress approached.[52]

A little over a week before the congress, St. Kilian's, the Catholic parish that included most of the membership of the BCA, as well as James Norris's East Gresham Community Association, became a heavily contested site. Claiming that Alinsky "has a background that I'm not proud of," and that one of the more active Protestant ministers in the POSC (presumably Rev. Robert Christ) had "Communistic tendencies," Jane Crawford told the parishioners that "we don't feel we need outsiders to come in and tell us what to do." Other members of the BCA and the BAPA agreed, claiming that the existing groups could effectively handle conservation themselves, without the POSC. The effort of the IAF organizers to include the community's more conservative spokesmen paid off at this meeting, however; St. Kilian's priest J. Harold McTigue pushed for the church to affiliate with the POSC, and Norris encouraged his fellow parishioners to "get on with the job of saving our community" by joining. After hearing from both sides, according to the *Southtown Economist*, the seven hundred parishioners were unconvinced by red-baiting and "cries of Quota System," and they voted overwhelmingly to send twenty-four delegates to the POSC's first congress.[53]

Donald O'Toole traveled around the community condemning the attacks, defending the POSC, and continuing to avoid the subject of either quotas or integration. The POSC, the banker told the Englewood Lions Club, "is run by a bunch of guys named Joe . . . [with] blue shirts and callused hands" and by the leaders of area banks and churches who had "noticed a decline in the character of the people who were using their facilities."[54] The problem with Crawford and other critics, O'Toole said, was that they insisted on "reading into this thing more than there is. They don't believe that the motives . . . are as simple as they are, namely to find out what the problems of this community are and decide what to do about them." The purpose of the new group was to create an urban community by "taking advantage of all that is good in city life." But to do that, he concluded, "we must have certain values of suburban living. We must be modern as to buildings and streets, and keep them that way. We must be clean. We must be safe." What Alinsky says, he concluded, "is his business. We are just a bunch of people who are trying to do a decent thing."[55]

At a mid-September rally of 2,500 people inside and outside of the POSC's new office at 849 West Seventy-Ninth Street, O'Toole argued that while "people are leaving our community," the fault lay with residents for not enforcing housing and zoning codes, or taking advantage of institutional and governmental resources. Residents of the Southwest Side "have not been talking to each other about our community during these past years." Rather, "we have confined ourselves to our own parish groups and to our own small neighborhood associations, and we have felt powerless to do anything beyond the limits of these small areas." Msgr. Molloy told the crowd that he was happy to see an organization "designed to keep the neighborhood intact"—a statement that, like O'Toole's, could lend itself to a number of interpretations with regard to racial integration.[56]

An "All-White Cake"? Defining the Southwest

That ambiguity became increasingly difficult to maintain as the congress neared in late October 1959. The focus of conflict quickly turned inward, as members of the various committees tried to determine the geographic boundaries of their "Southwest Community." This was more than just a technical or constitutional question. If the borders were set to exclude predominantly or increasingly black areas—Englewood, in particular—it would increase the chances that the POSC would become an exclusively white organization dedicated to keeping blacks out of the area. For the more conservative and segregationist participants in the POSC, this was precisely why they had joined. If the borders were malleable, however, or extended north and eastward to include areas of present and future black settlement, this virtually assured the long-term acceptance and participation of black families and institutions in both the POSC and the community at large. Chambers, Villemas, and McMahon worked furiously to stabilize a clergy-dominated voting bloc that would push for that outcome.

The subcommittee on boundaries, chaired by James Norris, reported to the larger Structure Committee at a lively meeting in early October. Norris recommended that the borders follow the lines of the nearly hundred groups that had already affiliated with the organization, effectively setting up the POSC as defender of a white Southwest Side. He claimed that there was no intent to discriminate; rather, he simply wanted to avoid a portion of Englewood that was the focus at the time of an urban renewal project, as he did not want the POSC to have to deal with the federal government as a countervailing power in the area.

Given Norris's previous activism as a segregationist, it is difficult to take his claim to nondiscrimination seriously. More likely, he feared the participation of Englewood's growing black population, as well as the scrutiny that a federally funded project in the area might bring. Rev. Christ doubted Norris's intentions and argued that if the POSC gave the impression that it was segregationist, it would "lose the cooperation of all government agencies and be unable to carry out our program of community betterment." The Structure Committee's chair Michael Bukacek, a chemical engineering professor at the Illinois Institute of Technology and head of the liberal Winneconna Lakes Area Improvement Association, agreed, pointing out that he "wouldn't want to stand up at a Senate investigation and tell the nation why this or that organization was excluded." The subcommittee resolution was voted down 14–12, at which point Norris submitted his resignation. Realizing that a walkout by Norris could split the organization, Bukacek declined the resignation and agreed to delay the decision until the next meeting.

Much was at stake here. While Alinsky believed that O'Toole, McMahon, and a number of other POSC leaders had "bought the idea" of using the organization as a tool for controlled integration, he was deeply worried that once the group was built, its broader membership would say, "'Since we are now so strong, why bother with any quota? Why not use this strength to keep Negroes out?' Once the cake is baked there is little that we can do." It was vitally important, Alinsky wrote Carl Tjerandsen, that "the necessary ingredients ... be placed in the cake during its making, or else the chances are that we will get an all-white cake ... rather than have that, I would personally prefer seeing no cake." Bukacek and other POSC leaders thus had to be "kept constantly on the spot so that the raison d'être will not be lost."[57] The following week, the Structure Committee compromised: rather than being defined by specific streets, the "Southwest Community" would include six neighborhoods (Washington Heights, Beverly, Auburn-Gresham-Highland, West Chatham, South Englewood, and Southwest Englewood), the borders of which were vague and could be manipulated on a case-by-case basis.[58]

In the days leading up to the Congress, pressure on the POSC increased from within and without, threatening to split the group. Protestant clergy began to receive heavy moral and political pressure from the liberal Protestant magazine *Christian Century*, from their congregations, and from higher-ups in their denominations. Here again, the tactical decision to avoid open advocacy of integration created problems. In a series of *Christian Century* editorials starting in mid-October, Harold Fey and Walter Kloetzli attacked Alinsky, his quota proposal, and the POSC, as well as the Archdiocese of Chicago.

Kloetzli, who was the head of urban ministry for the Lutheran Church, had met with a number Southwest Side pastors and succeeded in preventing some Lutheran congregations from participating. Fey claimed that the POSC's aim was to build an "iron community curtain" around the white Southwest Side, and prevent blacks from "moving out of racial ghettoes into more desirable neighborhoods." While Protestant and Catholic clergy were at the forefront of the new group, this was largely because they had been "induced to serve as fronts" for a "camouflaged power structure" dedicated to getting around the Supreme Court's banning of restrictive covenants. Protestant ministers in particular, Fey warned, were in danger of becoming tools of a Catholic-dominated segregationist organization.

These segregationist intentions, Fey argued, were clear from the fact that "there are no Negro representatives in the organization" and that the POSC's stated boundaries "coincide neatly with those of the area of white occupancy." The goal of "exclusion of the Negro" was also evidenced by the involvement of Alinsky and the IAF, "the architects of the Back of the Yards Neighborhood Council . . . which continues to be inhabited only by whites."[59] Alinsky, who generally tried to avoid answering his critics in print, privately seethed, dashing off an eighteen-page typewritten response for the IAF board, pieces of which were widely submitted as letters to the editor in the coming months by his staff. On occasion he confronted critics personally. Alinsky had been close friends with Marshall Field III, who had served on the IAF board for years, but the newspaper owned by Field's son, the *Chicago Sun-Times*, ripped the organizer in print for his work on race relations. Spotting Field near the headwaiter's station at the ritzy Tavern Club, Alinsky let him have it: "Marsh, you can take that newspaper of yours and shove it up your ass." Halfway out the door, Alinsky turned with a parting shot: "And make it the Sunday edition." He pushed his fedora back and left.[60]

The mutual hostility between *Christian Century* and Alinsky dated to Fr. Egan's public criticism of the Hyde Park urban renewal project the previous year. It would continue into the mid-1960s, with the IAF's Woodlawn Organization as its eventual target. Some of the magazine's arguments can be dismissed as the result of ignorance and anti-Catholic prejudice. The magazine clearly misunderstood the dispute over boundaries within the POSC and had the motivations of Alinsky and the archdiocese almost precisely wrong—if anything, the "camouflaged power structure" behind the POSC was working for integration, not segregation. Von Hoffman rather bluntly acknowledged these efforts: "Everything concerning race . . . was steered by Saul's stealthy minions," he recalled. "So there was the contradiction: we organized people to determine their own destinies except when we determined them." He remembers Alinsky as unapologetic: "to his way of thinking a majority trying to deprive a minority of basic rights had to be opposed."[61]

The picture of the BYNC drawn by Kloetzli and his allies was largely accurate, but they had no real basis for arguing that the POSC was similar, let alone that Alinsky and the archdiocese were secretly working to bring this about. And the contrast between their blind acceptance of the University of Chicago's good intentions in Hyde Park and their inaccurate accusations of Catholic conspiracy did not speak well for their fairness or knowledge.

Nonetheless, the conflict with *Christian Century* is of some importance, and not only because of its national scope or its immediate impact on the Southwest Side. Kloetzli and Fey stumbled onto some essential dilemmas. They were almost certainly correct that the POSC would seek to limit black in-migration and prevent white flight. Under metropolitan Chicago's racial geography, no urban neighborhood could maintain racial balance without purposefully controlling the housing market and limiting black access to it in some fashion. This was as true for Hyde Park as it was for the Southwest Side. And in both cases, success at doing so threatened to make integration *more* elusive elsewhere in the city, unless open occupancy became a regional reality. Kloetzli and Fey refused to believe that the University of Chicago had done precisely this in Hyde Park.

Alinsky dismissed Kloetzli and Fey as typical liberals, dismissive of messy compromises and far too enamored of the power and sufficiency of legislation and goodwill. The willingness of Kloetzli and Fey to see the best in Hyde Park and the worst on the Southwest Side struck Alinsky as elitist and intolerant. The alternative to quotas wasn't the "open city" from Alinsky's perspective; it was the continuation of ghetto expansion and segregation. Von Hoffman agreed. The question wasn't who was for open or closed cities; rather, "what is at issue is how this is going to be done and when it is going to be done"? The IAF had put forward concrete proposals to break down the "closed city" that were "the best we can think of." If critics didn't like them, "ought they not come forward with the constructive alternative to what we are doing? . . . This is the gravest and most profound domestic issue currently facing America."[62]

Kloetzli, Fey, and other liberal critics missed the importance of Alinsky's experiment on the Southwest Side. If the POSC succeeded, Alinsky believed, it would potentially strike a far more significant blow against the "closed city" than the University of Chicago had. In Hyde Park, the university and its allied groups could speak about integration publicly without sparking white resistance and flight, because of both the economic security of white residents and the economic power of the school to ensure the exclusion of low-income blacks for ostensibly nonracial reasons. As Alinsky would somewhat cynically describe it, Hyde Park whites used their economic assets to buy most of the space needed for them to publicly exercise their moral rectitude; the university purchased the rest. This couldn't be replicated. Most neighborhoods didn't have an institution like the university, and most weren't populated by residents as well-off as those in Hyde Park. The Southwest Side was much more typical of the city as a whole. If sustainable racial integration could be shown to work there, Alinsky reasoned, it could work anywhere. Local critics of the POSC who desired to maintain the Southwest Side as an all-white enclave seem to have understood this.[63]

After POSC volunteers put up signs announcing the congress, they were set upon by a group of twenty "toughs" who tore the banners down and threatened to kill the volunteers if they put them back up. The SPA, BAPA, and other area homeowners' groups lobbied aldermen to have POSC signs removed from nine different intersections, though without success.[64] Everingham and his Committee to Preserve the Southwest Community distributed thousands of copies of an anti-POSC pamphlet on October 23 and at Calumet High School (the site of the Congress) on the morning of October 24.

The pamphlet, which the *Southtown Economist* reprinted, claimed that the Communist Party had been engaged in blockbusting on the South Side for years and was seeking to "create greater tension by forcing Negro residents upon all white neighborhoods." Clergy participating in the POSC, the committee claimed, had been duped into serving as "CATS PAWS for the Communists," rather than "protecting the human rights of private property and self-government." Alinsky and the IAF were fronts for the Chicago communist Herb March, it said, and were financed by "Eastern funds," as was O'Toole's Standard State Bank. Everingham warned homeowners that once the POSC could claim to speak for the majority of property owners on the Southwest Side, it would be able to lean on City Council for "socialist measures" like open occupancy or urban renewal, which were designed to destroy the "private property system." He urged them to "support your local community improvement association" in order to foil the "clever plan."[65] The *Economist* condemned the pamphlet and praised the POSC as "a good try at coping with the problems of our community," and as "American in the full meaning of the word . . . in the spirit of the historical and revered town meeting."[66]

Two nights before the congress, the Structure Committee's boundaries compromise was put to the test when Chambers and Villemas encouraged Auburn Park Methodist Church (which was 90 percent black) to apply for membership. While the *Christian Century*'s criticisms may have had some effect on this action, Alinsky and the IAF organizers made it clear to the POSC's leadership that their continued participation would depend upon the outcome. The vote in the Credentials Committee appeared to be very much in doubt unless integrationists could get some of the more conservative clergy to publicly step forward. Many of those present were anxious—a Methodist minister even arranged to have an open telephone line to his bishop during the meeting. After being reassured that the congregation wasn't a storefront church with a "jackleg preacher" and that it fell within the boundaries, Msgr. Molloy surprised everyone by moving for admittance.[67]

Alinsky's tactic of containing (in both senses) the Southwest Side's more racially conservative forces within the organization had paid off. The key had been the clergy caucus, which Chambers and Villemas had so assiduously encouraged. Molloy's stance was immediately and loudly backed by McMahon, Christ, and other pastors, provoking one observer to remark, "Never have I seen the power of the church so forcefully demonstrated.... Protestants and Catholics were in complete harmony."[68] Fr. Egan described it as a "great victory for Msgr. McMahon," who along with Christ was the driving force for interracialism in the POSC. The clergy caucus would remain the primary (and often exclusive) advocate for integration in the organization in the coming years. As Chambers put it, "Without the involvement of the churches ... you would have had just another anti-Negro group."[69] The IAF staffers were ecstatic; as Von Hoffman wrote, the decision "was completely precedent shattering for that community and any other in Chicago or elsewhere."[70]

"The Day the Chicago Racists Lost": The OSC's First Congress

More than one thousand delegates representing 104 organizations (36 of them churches) gathered in the gymnasium of Calumet High School on a chilly, windy October Saturday in 1959 to hold elections, debate resolutions, and strike the word *provisional* from the name of the community organization.[71] Surrounded by red, white, and blue bunting, the delegates recited the Pledge of Allegiance, then embarked on a ten-hour marathon of parliamentary procedure, constitutional construction, elections, and issue debates. The congress elected Donald O'Toole as president, along with fourteen geographically balanced vice presidents—including James Norris, Rev. Christ, and Msgrs. McMahon and Molloy, as well as two other Protestant ministers, a bank president, a religious school administrator, three laymen, and three homeowners' association presidents.[72]

Despite months of rancor, there was surprisingly little controversy or conflict. Representatives of the Committee to Preserve the Southwest Community distributed leaflets beforehand but otherwise sat quietly in the balcony.

While the delegates from Auburn Park Methodist Church entered a hushed room with an armed guard, only two resolutions stirred significant anger: a resolution proposed by Theodore Voigt of the Southtown Planning Association to exclude the increasingly black area north of West Seventy-fifth street (which was roundly booed) and an attempt by an Auburn Park real estate agent to introduce a loyalty oath (which was voted down).[73] No resolutions or statements dealing with residential integration were proposed; as Christ put it: "We were trying then to build an inclusive organization that would survive. It was not the time to raise the basic issue over which there would dissension and controversy. It would come soon enough."[74]

"Today is historic," O'Toole told the gathering. The people and institutions of the Southwest Side "are gathered here in a solemn and democratic fashion to discuss the future of this community" and to complete the work of the POSC. "In our assault on deterioration and blight," the newly elected president continued, "nothing can be accomplished without unity ... [and] your presence here is evidence that that unity has been achieved." "We can," he concluded, "restore our neighborhoods."[75] The delegates then adopted a statement of purpose for the new Organization for the Southwest Community (OSC): "We feel the cultural, economic, and religious life of the community should be revitalized, and the physical community made a more attractive place in which to live and rear families. We desire to solve these problems in a constructive way, according to the principles of American democracy ... we hereby join together in the Organization for the Southwest Community to promote the well-being of the community and its people, without regard to race, religion or national origin."[76] Thus, while the OSC was pledged to nondiscrimination, and even to the inclusion of blacks, it remained officially silent on the issue of integration. Resolutions, largely focused on community maintenance and ending panic peddling and blockbusting, also avoided the issue. The exception, significantly, was the decision to include Morgan Park, which contained a sizable and long-standing black settlement, within the official boundaries of the organization. Overall, however, the OSC maintained the fiction that its goals were without racial content and focused primarily on keeping the Southwest Side "a more attractive place in which to live"—a functional euphemism that was certainly well understood by most participants.[77]

The Program Committee, chaired by Rev. Christ, successfully proposed ten resolutions that the delegates hoped would allow the OSC to gain some control over the local real estate market, including the establishment of a home-loan fund to attract young families to transitional areas, the creation of a real estate practices committee to fight blockbusting and develop a real estate code of ethics, and a campaign to investigate code violations and encourage housing rehabilitation. IAF staffers hoped that the OSC could use these tools to broadly educate residents about the workings of the dual housing market and take some first steps toward slowing the pace of flight and transition. After the congress let out shortly after midnight, the delegates returned home exhausted but enlivened by the sense that they were about to embark on something unprecedented, exciting, and important.[78]

Integration or Nondiscrimination?

Despite the relative unanimity of the OSC's inaugural Community Congress, internal divisions continued to hamper its depth and effectiveness. While OSC leaders and staff began to make implement many of the resolutions enacted by the Congress, the organization's first year was dominated by an internal struggle to define its official position on integration. It was increasingly difficult for the OSC and its spokesmen to avoid the issue, both locally and in the press. The OSC's ambiguous position sparked widely divergent reactions. Rev. Carl Fuqua, the executive secretary of the Chicago NAACP, praised the group as "a step toward better race relations," while Harold Fey and Walter Kloetzli continued their attacks. Within the community, meanwhile, integrationists and segregationists continued to battle for the soul of the new group.

The writings of Fey and Kloetzli had an immediate impact on the OSC. Two ministers were called to appear before a committee of the Church Federation of Greater Chicago that was airing criticisms of the group and were warned to associate themselves only with community organizations that listed "modification of the city's racially segregative housing pattern" among their main objectives.[79]

One of the OSC's clergy vice presidents was attacked by both his congregation and his religious superior for his participation in the group. The Rev. James Reed was a young liberal assistant pastor from the affluent Beverly Hills Trinity Methodist Church and an active participant in the founding of the OSC as a delegate from the Beverly Hills–Morgan Park Council on Human Relations. In early December 1959, his pastoral relations committee informed Reed that the board of Trinity was opposed to his participation in the OSC because of its unclear position on segregation. They asked him to resign from his office in the OSC or give up his position with the church—which Reed flatly refused to do. Convinced that this demand was motivated by racist opposition to the admittance of black groups to the OSC, Reed told the *Daily News*, "I don't think members can tell me what my responsibilities are in a matter of conscience." Meanwhile, Bishop Charles Brashares, the head of the Illinois Methodist Church, pressured Reed from a different direction:

influenced by the arguments of Fey and Kloetzli, Brashares feared that the OSC was a segregationist group and didn't want any of his clergy associated with it until all the evidence was in. He threatened to transfer Reed to another church if he did not resign from his OSC position. When Reed again refused, Brashares moved him to a church on the North Side.[80]

Reed's case quickly became a rallying point for local ministers, helping to further solidify an integrationist clergy caucus within the OSC. Seventeen Protestant ministers from the area signed a statement supporting Reed and blaming the "forces of prejudice" for his removal. Reed's situation, and the reaction to it, made clear the extraordinary pressure that the organization's vacillation on integration was putting on its leaders.[81] On December 26, O'Toole and other OSC leaders decided to bite the bullet. After a heated Executive Committee meeting, O'Toole issued a statement: "We are against segregation; we, with President Eisenhower, the Supreme Court, and all the nation's moral and religious leaders, favor equality and justice for all people. We have successfully repelled and defeated many vicious attacks by hysterical racists and hate-mongers from within and without our community. Our organization, neither by word, deed nor hint, has ever encouraged any act that is not fully and completely consistent with our laws and the spirit behind them."[82] Four theologians at the University of Chicago, including Dr. Alvin Pitcher of the Church Federation of Greater Chicago, immediately rallied to the OSC's (and Reed's) defense, praising the group as "the first organization of its power and size to state flatly [that] it is opposed to segregation" and encouraging Chicago's Protestant denominational bodies to support it.[83]

O'Toole's endorsement of integration—which really amounted only to a promise that the OSC would abide by the law—was weak, and it said nothing about the possibility of interracial living on the Southwest Side. Indeed, in a spring 1960 article, the OSC president weakened his position further, claiming that while the group had "no racial bias or interest" and stood "squarely for the Constitution of the US," it had "steadfastly refused to accept any characterization as 'segregationist,' 'anti-segregationist,' 'integrationist,' 'pro-integrationist,' or any other title having to do with race relations." The OSC "invite[s] no one into the community, and we bar no one from it. We set no quotas on the members of any race or creed." The task of the OSC, O'Toole concluded, was to "completely control our own community" in order to make it "so desirable that it will attract only the most desirable people, and to establish order which requires each family in the community to live according to the standards of the community."[84]

Despite the OSC's calculated effort to avoid alienating their more racial conservative members, many local segregationists felt betrayed by the

December 26 statement. A number of homeowners' associations voted to resign from the organization, and Harry Everingham continued to attack the OSC and its leaders. An attempt by Msgrs. Molloy and McMahon to persuade the Eighteenth Ward Civic Council to join the OSC prompted a series of critical speeches, radio broadcasts, and editorials. The council, one of the largest organizations in the area, offered the OSC a potential ongoing relationship with Alderman James Murray. Everingham, who had hoped to bring the group into his Committee for the Preservation of the Southwest Community, attacked the OSC in a speech to the council and in a series of editorials published in the *Southtown Economist*. Claiming that the OSC sought to "impose its will over all neighborhood improvement organizations and other civic groups" in the community, Everingham implied that both Molloy and McMahon had been influenced by "radicals and members of communists fronts." McMahon and Molloy were outraged and demanded an apology from the council for providing Everingham with a venue for his attacks.[85]

Everingham continued his public criticisms but retreated from attacks on the two highly regarded pastors, claiming that he had no fight with any church or individual "except Saul Alinsky and his trained men, and those who associate with them to force their will upon us." Claiming to have definitive proof that Alinsky was a "reformed Communist," Everingham asserted that the organizer and his allies were "breeding class hatred as part of their plan to divide and conquer . . . this includes urban renewal and open occupancy laws which are all part of the socialist structure and will lead to the police state." Property owners on the Southwest Side "are not willing to accept integration by force," he continued. "If integration is forced upon them by the OSC, many of the people, perhaps a majority, will sell their homes and move to the suburbs," Everingham argued. "Integrated neighborhoods soon become the most crime-laden in the city, as the records prove." Nonetheless, he concluded: "We are not bigots. We are not intolerant. We are simply facing facts and we say if integration ever comes, it must come by voluntary methods after a long period of education of both races . . . otherwise, we cannot use our streets after dark."[86]

He then attacked the OSC directly, and where it was arguably most vulnerable: its carefully structured ambiguity on residential integration. Why did the organizers give prospective delegates to the first congress the impression that the OSC was being created to keep the community white, he asked readers? Why had O'Toole refused to define the OSC's purposes regarding integration? Why was a loyalty oath defeated at the congress? Why was the OSC harboring individuals such as Max Sonderby, chair of the Welfare and Safety Committee, whose membership in communist front groups "such as the Americans for Democratic Action . . . proves that the OSC is in the hands of radicals, dupes, and subversive influences?" Everingham informed residents that he was working to initiate an investigation of the OSC by the House Un-American Activities Committee.[87]

Everingham's all-out attack quickly backfired, in part out of shock at his attack on Catholic priests. Protestant ministers active in the OSC issued a joint statement supporting McMahon and Molloy, arguing that Everingham's real problem with the Everingham was its "failure to espouse racism and bigotry." McMahon agreed, telling the *Southtown Economist* that he had shown himself "definitely as a racist, hiding under the robes of a crusader against communism . . . he would ask us to preach a religion which would pervert the Sermon on the Mount." Furthermore, by fabricating a communist background for Alinsky, "like all lying demagogues," he had "finally hanged himself."[88] Even Alinsky, who rarely responded publicly to personal attacks got into the act, telling reporters: "I have become inured to the attacks of Communists, Fascists, bigots and professional patriots who squeeze their green out of the red, white and blue. The voices are different, but the stench is the same."[89]

The editors of the *Southtown Economist*, who believed that Everingham had indirectly slurred the cardinal himself, apologized to Meyer, Alinsky, and other local clergy for giving him uncensored access to the paper and declared Everingham's charges "unfounded." By mid-May, Everingham's credibility had essentially evaporated, and much to his chagrin, his attacks had brought the OSC's Protestant and Catholic pastors closer together. The demise of Everingham helped to dampen the credibility and effectiveness of red-baiting by other OSC opponents, but the group's internal divisions remained. Throughout the OSC's first year, the staff and officers struggled to define issues that would start the organization on the road to some kind of community control, without making racial issues a constant and divisive litmus test for its member groups.

"A Real Estate License Is Not a Hunting Permit": The OSC Program

In keeping with Alinsky's approach, Von Hoffman and OSC leaders sought to direct organizational energies toward issues that were immediate, were easily explained, and (where possible) had readily identifiable villains. In its first years, the OSC continued to delicately avoid taking a position on residential integration, opting instead to focus on issues that were related but ostensibly more neutral and immediate: educating residents, stopping blockbusting, and halting racial violence. OSC staffers sought to teach member organizations about the structural roots of neighborhood transition, blockbusting, real estate practices, and the dual housing market. O'Toole and the staff repeatedly stressed issues that would prevent white flight and that might form the basis for an alliance of mutual self-interest between longtime residents and new black ones.

The OSC's stabilization program took both local and citywide approaches. One of the reasons neighborhoods undergoing rapid racial changeover tended to deteriorate quickly was racial discrimination in the housing and credit markets. To combat this, and to aid young families that hoped to change from renting to owning without moving to the suburbs, the OSC convinced three banks (including O'Toole's Standard State) to help fund a Federal Housing Authority–insured Home Loan Program. By the mid-1960s the program had loaned out more than $6 million to nearly six hundred families. Although this fact was not widely publicized for fear of retaliation against the institutions by angry whites, more than 30 percent of these loans went to black families—and that number increased over time.[90]

Writing to Alinsky in 1962, Nicholas Von Hoffman praised the program for "bringing families into the neighborhoods in question who, given the economic opportunity, are eager and able to keep property values up." At the same time, it was "enabling Negro families to purchase housing at interest rates that do not force them to overcrowd and abuse the structures in order to pay for them." Finally, Von Hoffman argued, the program "made it much easier to keep a white population in recently changing neighborhoods . . . slowing the rate of change and diminishing the uglier economic and social consequences of total panic-stricken community changeover." O'Toole agreed with Von Hoffman's assessment; the Home Loan Program had made homeowners aware of their selling options and had caused many residents to take their homes off the market.[91] In 1962 the OSC also set up the Home Modernization Loan Pool, capitalized at just under $1 million, to provide low interest rates and long-term credit for home improvements. The organization also sponsored a series of lectures to encourage the maintenance of standards and instruct residents on how to remodel a home and get financing. By the end of the first year of the program, the OSC was assisting nearly forty remodeling jobs a month.[92]

Through its committees on real estate practices and housing and zoning, the OSC also acted to get zoning and housing codes enforced, to stop real estate speculation and blockbusting, and to assuage white fears of property value losses in integrated blocks. O'Toole, a former real estate agent, was instrumental in helping the OSC to craft an attack on "panic peddlers." While the importance of real estate speculators in the racial turnover of neighborhoods tended to be exaggerated in the popular imagination, they nonetheless provided an identifiable target for local activists and a means by which OSC staffers could educate residents about how racial discrimination enabled speculators to make high profits while harming the interests of both black and white homeowners. Von Hoffman distributed twenty-five thousand copies of a 1959 *Daily News* series on blockbusting, hoping to demonstrate that fear and flight were in large part the creation of self-interested speculators, not the inevitable result of new black neighbors.[93]

Activists on the OSC's two committees informed member organizations like the racially integrated West Chatham Improvement Association that posting For Sale and Sold By signs on homes and apartment buildings was illegal, and that the City Building Department (CBD) was responsible for enforcing those laws but had been lax in doing so. After repeated phone calls to the CBD, the association's members took matters into their own hands in the early spring of 1960. They launched a nighttime raid, tearing down signs and burning them in a vacant lot.[94] The Winneconna Lakes Area Improvement Association, led by chair of the Real Estate Practices Committee Michael Bukacek, took similar action, spearheading an OSC effort to strengthen the authority of the CBD to investigate and punish violators of housing and zoning codes. Member groups began to perform the CBD's investigatory role on the Southwest Side.[95]

The Housing and Zoning Committee processed dozens of code violations each month and engaged in periodic mass removals of Sold By signs in transitional neighborhoods.[96] The OSC also put pressure on property owners who refused to maintain their buildings or who violated housing and zoning codes by illegally subdividing them. While the Southwest Side had few "slum" areas, residents feared that run-down properties—particularly apartment buildings in the northern and northeastern sections of the area—threatened the value of nearby homes and encouraged rapid flight. After complaints about rats and cockroaches to the owners as well as the CBD garnered no results, in August the Gresham Community Council, the East Gresham Community Council, and the Oakdale Community Association organized an OSC picket line, 150 people strong, around a deteriorating apartment building. After a Real Estate Practices Committee report listing eight pages of violations was ignored, in mid-September the OSC chartered a bus and carried the protest to the owner's downtown offices. The Housing and Zoning Committee investigated more than 500 such complaints in 1960 and filed 132 of them with the CBD.[97]

The OSC committees and member associations also aided in the investigation and prosecution of real estate speculators. Two South Side real estate agents were indicted and found guilty for conspiring to cheat and defraud two families in a house deal in a changing neighborhood in 1961, and in November 1962 three members of a local realty company were found guilty of fraud and stripped of their licenses. Citizen research led to the indictment and eventual imprisonment of three members of Boulevard Realty and Mortgage in 1964, on charges of conspiracy and fraud.[98] The indictments had a chastening effect, slowing panic peddling in the northernmost parts of the OSC's territory. Bukacek as well as the editors of the *Southtown Economist* also hoped that it would lay the legal groundwork for an anti-blockbusting city ordinance, which he later persuaded the OSC to endorse. Real estate agents certainly thought the OSC was having an effect: as Bukacek informed the City Club Forum in July 1960, the OSC's campaign to "prove that a real estate license is not a hunting permit" had garnered strong opposition from realty interests accustomed to dealing with block clubs and property owners associations, over whom they had much more influence.[99]

The centerpiece of the OSC's campaign to discipline the real estate industry was its effort to draw up and enforce a code of conduct for housing transactions. Von Hoffman worked with O'Toole and Bukacek in April 1960 to create the Real Estate Code of Ethics, which bound its signatories to avoid scare tactics and the encouragement of panic selling. While the South Side Real Estate Board and the Beverly Suburban Real Estate Board refused to participate, more than thirty firms had endorsed the code by late August 1960—with the OSC threatening to publicize the names of real estate agents who had not. Realtors who resisted were subjected to picketing at their homes and offices. The code targeted speculators spreading rumors through phone solicitations and condemned solicitations on the basis of race, the use of Sold By signs on front lawns, canvassing, and repeated mass mailings.[100]

"On That Somewhat Slippery Rock": The Southwest Side in 1960

As the OSC's second October congress approached, *Chicago Daily News* reporter M. W. Newman evaluated conditions on the Southwest Side. He found residents to be cautiously optimistic, although many were still suspicious of the OSC, and racial transition continued unabated: an average of forty black families moved into the area each month. Newman concluded that although few whites on the Southwest Side welcomed the idea of blacks moving in, most saw it as inevitable. They varied, however, in their opinions on whether white flight was equally unavoidable. Newman informally surveyed residents in the most "threatened" parts of the Southwest Side—in Auburn Park, near Halsted. Many whites on the tree-lined 7500 block of South Union had already fled, he observed, while its new black residents (two families) had "survived their 'baptism of fire'—porch fires, torch tossings." "Most of my neighbors have been nice," a black housewife told the reporter, "but some already are moving." Two white women on the same block confirmed this, telling Newman that while the two black families were good neighbors, they were "concerned over what will follow them" and had decided to move anyway.

A block away, on South Emerald, however, Newman found some OSC activists who planned to stay despite worries about whether their new black neighbors would "behave according to accepted white middle-class standards." Because of the OSC, Newman argued, a number of "men of white skin" had found "virtues they never expected in men of brown skin." A female resident of Ogden Park told him: "Many Negroes improve their property, you know. They're just as good neighbors as anyone else." The wife of Jack Trahey, an OSC activist, informed the reporter: "We are staying. Our reasons are both practical and idealistic. If people will keep calm, we can work this whole matter out." Mrs. Trahey, who proudly displayed the OSC's emblem in her window, insisted that the community organization had taught residents "how to head off panic. We talk things over." She had organized her block for the OSC, and she and her husband were in the midst of remodeling their home. Recently, Trahey had chased off a real estate agent offering to buy the house, telling him, "I believe in integration. Don't you?" One of her neighbors expressed a more calculating opinion, stating: "There is nothing to be gained by running away . . . where can we replace this house at a reasonable cost? We are staying."[101]

However, Newman also found many OSC activists to be almost as ambivalent about the organization as nonmembers—especially when he raised the issue of quotas. Quotas, he found, were talked about constantly in the area. Residents repeatedly referred to the rumors that the OSC advocated a quota of one black family per block, and they differed over whether the community group favored integration or segregation. Msgr. McMahon informed Newman: "Our goal is not to induce Negroes to move in, or to force integration. But if they do move in, it is their right and they should be treated like anyone else." O'Toole echoed this, arguing that the OSC was "trying to maintain a high-standard community and then it doesn't matter who lives in it. We decided not to be 'anti,' not to try to stop the unstoppable." An OSC member who showed Newman around his neighborhood in Ogden Park told him that while they ignored the black family on his block, he was optimistic that if "more white blocks admit just one or two black families," everything would "work out."

The area had no socially integrated blocks, Newman observed, and several of the OSC's member organizations were of the "keep 'em out" school of thought. Many local residents—including members of the OSC—did not agree with the official organizational policy of accepting the right of blacks to move into the area. These sentiments were especially strong in those parts of the Southwest Side that had few black families, including Beverly Hills and Brainerd. Others—perhaps the majority—seemed to walk the same delicate line that the OSC was attempting to. Newman apparently came to the same conclusion as Alinsky's organizers: while the Southwest Side had a small number of integrationists and segregationists, the majority of residents preferred to avoid violence, flight, and the moral implications of racial issues. An Ogden Park housewife rather bluntly summed up a pragmatic approach: "Sure you can burn people out, but suppose you burn the wrong house? It's too risky." The OSC, Newman wrote, "has already eased panic somewhat," and by opening the Great Question for public debate, it had "made it harder for whispers and sneaky rumors to have their way." While the organization "is still divided among itself as to just where it is going . . . it is trying." "On that somewhat slippery rock," he concluded, "the OSC stands."[102]

The rock became even more slippery in mid-October, when the OSC kicked off the first of four televised public hearings in preparation for its annual congress. Anyone with something to say, and a willingness to follow *Robert's Rules of Order*, could take the floor for up to ten minutes. OSC members hotly debated a variety of racial issues before the Real Estate Practices Committee and the Civil Rights Committee, for all of Chicago to see—making it clear that the 1960 congress would be more directly focused on segregation and integration than the previous one. This was not an accident: integrationist clergy like Christ and McMahon joined with Von Hoffman and other staffers in organizing the hearings, inviting a variety of racial liberals from around the city to speak and daring the OSC's more restrictionist members to defend their views before a citywide audience. The list of participants read like a who's-who of Chicago liberals, including representatives from the American Friends Service Committee, the Congress of Racial Equality, the Urban League, and the NAACP, as well as a variety of religious groups.[103]

While the hearings were in part designed to educate the community on the connections between race, housing, and neighborhood stability, they also allowed the integrationist viewpoint to get a full hearing, without placing the OSC staff or its leaders in the politically awkward position of publicly advocating relatively unpopular opinions. A series of speakers from outside the community lauded the new group and pleaded with its members to definitively endorse residential integration and attack the dual housing market. The Rev. Canon William Van Meter, of the Christian Social Relations Committee of the Episcopal Diocese of Chicago, praised the OSC for "show[ing] the way in the changing neighborhoods" and called on the group to "place yourself on record as inviting into your neighborhood any citizens solely on the basis of their being good neighbors." Edward Holmgren, of the Chicago Urban League, urged the OSC to fight for an open-occupancy law, and Fr. John Egan encouraged the organization to focus on "the development of a stable and integrated neighborhood" and to "know the means by which the mechanics and economics of transition to the ghetto can be thwarted," because "nothing else but a stable and integrated society is possible if you are to survive."[104]

Despite growing pressure on the issue of integration, the second congress was surprisingly uneventful. By one estimate, the OSC's membership had grown by more than one-third since the first congress. While a number of property owners' associations from the southern end of the community had withdrawn, more than a dozen member organizations were either all or partially black. The racially moderate agenda of McMahon and Christ largely carried the day, in part because of effective caucusing before the congress and clergy unity. Rev. Christ brought together a caucus of Protestant ministers that worked closely with McMahon and other priests to keep divisive racial issues off the agenda and engineer the election of the OSC's first black executive, from Morgan Park. Perhaps most important, they also successfully urged the creation of the Community Relations Committee to improve race relations and work with government agencies to end restrictive housing practices. While the OSC continued to officially avoid the issue of residential integration, it had begun to take tentative steps toward improving race relations within its own membership.[105]

Shortly after this congress, Alinsky proudly reported to the IAF trustees that, although the organizing process had been "one long extended struggle against fear and entrenched racist opposition," the OSC had come to have more than a dozen all or partially black groups and had elected a black vice president. As a result, Alinsky concluded, the OSC constituted "a major step in developing a voluntary method of laying the ghost of the segregation problem." While the racism of many local whites made Von Hoffman pessimistic about the long-term prospects of preserving the Southwest Side as an interracial community, he agreed that the OSC had "gone further in the field of race relations on a practical level than any other organization that I know of in a major American city." The Chicago Catholic Interracial Council agreed, giving the OSC its annual race-relations award in 1961. The OSC was making significant progress at integrating itself. Whether it could do the same on the Southwest Side—while simultaneously building and expanding its membership—remained to be seen.[106]

5

"And Just All of a Sudden, They Left"

The OSC and the Challenges of Neighborhood Integration, 1961–1969

> We squandered what might have been an opportunity, in 1958, 1965, or 1971, to find a new way for Americans to live with one another. We blew it one family at a time.
> RAY SUAREZ, *The Old Neighborhood*, 1999

> For no problem is a solution more easily stated: white populations should be brought back into the central cities, and Negroes should be allowed to choose freely where they want to live in all areas of central cities and suburbs alike. No solution is more difficult to implement.
> MORTON GRODZINS, "The Metropolitan Area as a Racial Problem," 1958

> Once you have seen a Chicago community crumble under the effects of segregation, you never forget it. The white Chicagoan who keeps his racial prejudice grows more bitter. The white Chicagoan who sees that it was not "the Negro" but segregation that caused the tragedy, gains insight and realization that it is segregation that must go.
> FIFTH WARD ALDERMAN LEON DESPRES, "The Most Segregated City in the North—Chicago," 1962

The postwar white middle class has gained much of its wealth and economic security from home equity that has been amassed in part via housing market segregation and discrimination. Real estate agents, bankers, politicians, courts, neighborhood groups, and the state itself have until fairly recently all worked to guarantee that equity, and to assure white home owners of their right to those guarantees. All-white neighborhoods in both cities and suburbs thus became a kind of "collective property" for the safekeeping of racial privilege. Declarations of home rule and local autonomy, whether articulated by urban neighborhood groups or politically independent suburbs, sought in part to protect the value of that racialized property. When laid upon the broader terrain of fragmented metropolitan political boundaries, this racial mapping has created identities and interests bound to its perpetuation. Housing markets, like all markets, are social and political creations through which power hierarchies are produced and reproduced. The consequences of these racial geopolitics for American politics, race relations, and cities have been profound.

This was part of the landscape on which Saul Alinsky sought to build a community organization dedicated to residential integration in the early 1960s. Alinsky's territorial organizing focus provided him with a keen understanding of just what white homeowners on the Southwest Side of Chicago thought was at stake when black families began to move into their neighborhoods. Above all a pragmatist, Alinsky sought to find a mechanism that would preserve something of what white families valued about their communities while simultaneously helping Chicago's growing and expanding black population.

Alinsky's preference was for his Organization for the Southwest Community (OSC) to use "benign" housing quotas to disperse black families throughout its territory. He believed that whites were ready to concede a small black presence in their neighborhoods in exchange for some degree of stability. By directing the OSC toward the housing market and its institutions, rather than toward the vilification of blacks, this dispersal would provide experiences in interracial living for whites and abet the creation of an alternative racial geography. Was Alinsky right? How could he sell the plausibility of racial retreat and neighborhood stabilization to whites when the "common sense" of segregation told them otherwise? Did a community organization really have the power to control its small part of the regional housing market? And if it had to discriminate against individual black families in order to create an integrated community, was it worth it?

The OSC launched an admirable and unprecedented effort to create an interracial community organization along one of Chicago's most violent and contested racial boundaries in 1959. Although its failure to sustain racial integration was in part a function of specific organizational problems, it was also due to the racialization of urban geographies and identities, and the inability of Alinsky's methods to grapple with problems that were ultimately metropolitan in scope.

Fair Housing, the Median Forum, and the Revolt of the Racial Conservatives, 1961–1962

The conflicts bubbling beneath the surface during the OSC's first year and half quickly crested in March 1961, when the Community Relations Committee informed the OSC Council that it had drafted a letter to the area's political representatives backing an open occupancy bill in the Illinois General Assembly. The irritation of racial conservatives quickly turned to outrage when council members were informed that committee representatives had not come to them seeking a vote of approval, because the letter had already been sent. Incensed, a number of delegates withdrew their organizations from the OSC, arguing that such a law threatened the constitutional rights of white property owners. After a heated debate, two more neighborhood associations walked out, informing reporters, "There is a growing objection to the unethical tactics of the hardcore group of integrationists."[1]

The damage was irreparable, and in the coming weeks the OSC split into warring factions: the Moderate Liberals (MLs) and the more conservative Median Forum (MF). Eighteen months of careful work by staff and activists teaching whites to see acts of nondiscrimination and community maintenance as in their long-term self-interest was shattered, racializing almost every issue that came before a member organization or the OSC in the spring and summer of 1961. As the staffer Edward Chambers described it: "Everything was concentrated around the fact of the changing racial scene. No matter what the issue was—transportation, building codes, zoning, integrated meetings—the votes were always on integration. Three to four hundred people would show up every month . . . the right wing and the liberals would battle it out on the floor in those really hot meetings . . . and the moderate majority would keep carrying the day for justice and equality and dignity. It was a new day for these people." While Chambers was excited at the energy and attention residents had begun to pour into the OSC—making it the public forum that Alinsky had always intended—it was an energy of fission, not fusion.[2]

Although a split was not inevitable, it became difficult to avoid. Auburn-Gresham, Winneconna Lakes, and Washington Heights experienced a series of violent incidents that summer as the pace of racial change accelerated. At the same time, the growing visibility of blacks in the OSC emboldened its integrationist staff and leadership while raising fears that Everingham had been right among white members from Beverly and Brainerd: the OSC had intended to integrate the Southwest Side all along, and would seek to accelerate the migration of blacks into their neighborhoods.

In June, the OSC welcomed the Morgan Park Planning Organization (MPPO) into the group. The MPPO, itself a federation of twenty-five local organizations, would become the strongest and most powerful voice for blacks in the OSC. Its aims included "the promotion of equal opportunities in living accommodations and employment, both locally and generally," as well as the "fostering of integrated institutions and integrated living." The leadership included an Episcopal vicar, the head of a credit union, and the president of a packinghouse union local.[3] Even as the OSC expanded both the size and reach of its stabilization programs, racial conservatives became increasingly convinced that the group no longer represented them. As the third congress approached, the MLs and the Forum began to hold separate meetings. Msgr. McMahon worried privately that the Forum would convince all of the OSC's nonliberal organizations to withdraw.[4]

More than eight hundred people attended the televised pre-Congress hearings in September 1961, as racial liberals from around Chicago put the issue of open-occupancy laws before the OSC and the community. John McDermott, of the Catholic Interracial Council, and Warren Lehman, of the Chicago Urban League, offered forceful arguments for fair housing laws. At a hearing on September 14, McDermott praised the OSC as "the most ambitious and the most serious attempt of any neighborhood in America to cope with the hard problems of the racially changing neighborhood." While he refused to endorse "any system of screening or quotas," McDermott believed the OSC needed to discourage the idea that "one can be neutral about integration" and let events "take their natural course." Integration had to be created, through direct involvement in the housing market. However, he warned, it was not possible to create 'integration in one community.' "It is unfair for just a few communities to face the full brunt of the housing segregation problem," he told the group. "You have a right to demand that all communities do their share in solving this problem." Unless the OSC campaigned "vigorously" for fair housing legislation, the Southwest Side would find it increasingly difficult to be "an island of sanity in a sea of confusion; an island of stable, normal integration in a sea of racial segregation."[5]

Warren Lehman presented perhaps the most convincing argument for an OSC endorsement of open occupancy, echoing Alinsky by connecting fair housing to the interests of whites. Why were white homeowners tempted by the offers of speculators and blockbusters? Lehman asked. As black settlement moved closer, mortgage money began to dry up in white neighborhoods, first for blacks seeking to move in, and then for whites who were suddenly unable to maintain and improve their homes. The lack of financing forced blacks into contract-selling situations, which did threaten property values by eating up money that might have gone to maintenance and by encouraging subdividing. Thus, Lehman concluded, property deterioration, the apparent impossibility of residential integration, and the fight-or-flight mentality were all created by racial discrimination in the real estate financing market.

Nondiscriminatory lending, Lehman argued, would allow both whites and blacks to buy into a neighborhood after it had reached its "tipping point." Such a law, Lehman insisted, "would provide to white people a right that they do not now have. That is the right of selling to whomever they want whenever they want. The right to sell to a prospective white purchaser is now effectively denied to the white man who lives in a community where Negroes also live.

Giving this right to white people will increase the possibility of stabilizing the Southwest community." This persuasively turned the property rights language of open-occupancy opponents on its head: only in a free and open market guaranteed by fair housing laws could whites dispose of their property as they saw fit. Furthermore, Lehman pointed out, to make the Southwest Side an open housing market required a supply of potential *new* white buyers, not just a stable group of long-term residents. But the dual housing market limited the supply of newcomers to one group. Thus, Lehman concluded, an OSC endorsement of the fair housing bill pending in Springfield would not be a suicidal act of liberal idealism; rather, it was an essential step on the road to stability and interracial living. If blacks could buy on the same terms as whites, wherever they chose—and wherever they could afford—Lehman was confident that the ultimate result would be the dispersion of the black population throughout the city. He urged the OSC to take a similar position.[6]

Alinsky strongly supported the passage of civil rights and nondiscrimination laws at all levels of government. But as an organizer, he doubted that legal protections alone could begin to dissolve Chicago's racial geography. He was also skeptical that Mayor Daley would allow any fair housing law to pass that actually had teeth; as a consequence, he feared that a strong push by the OSC for such legislation would divert it from the harder work of changing things on the ground. "He did not trust the courts and legal protections," Von Hoffman remembered. "It had to be backed up by countervailing power." [7]

An approach to residential integration that relied heavily on legal change and municipal enforcement also presented a tactical dilemma: Getting the OSC to officially endorse an open-occupancy law might destroy the group. Advocates of racial exclusion would see it as an open invitation to black families to move to the Southwest Side; they would then either try to capture the OSC, destroy it, or flee it. Interracialists might shift their focus toward the passage and implementation of the law, to the neglect of local organizing and institution building. The ensuing conflict would politicize the issue in such a way as to seriously risk the representative status of the organization. Alinsky was always loath to introduce divisive and explicitly political issues into his organizations. He thought it best to allow the OSC to come to its own conclusions (with help from IAF organizers) on the utility of fair housing legislation.

One hesitates to quibble with Alinsky's reading of the Southwest Side's racial politics. Nonetheless, an important distinction needs to be made between the utility of fair housing laws for an organization trying to maintain residential integration in a transition neighborhood and their importance for breaking down racial segregation in the city as a whole. While Alinsky was certainly interested in destroying the dual housing market everywhere in the Chicago area, his primary focus was on the Southwest Side. To some extent, Alinsky's advocacy of the value of local experiments in residential integration was self-serving, because he didn't know how to effect a larger transformation of racial geography. Alinsky's territorial approach ultimately had limited utility for resolving social problems that were metropolitan in scope.

Fair housing laws in the city and the suburbs could have provided OSC staffers with a conceptual bridge between local and broader issues, as well as focus local residents on building alliances and relationships with outside groups and institutions. If open-occupancy laws were not working, why? Was it the lack of adequate housing for blacks throughout the Chicago area? Was it the discriminatory actions of real estate agents and lending institutions? Was it because of how white homeowners thought about community and property? Was it because these laws needed to apply to the suburbs as well? Was it because federal money subsidized metropolitan segregation, undermining fair housing laws?

These were crucial questions that Alinsky could organize around, building from local experiences to the racial geography of the Chicago area as a whole, with newer and larger targets and alliances along the way. As long as OSC member groups had useful, important, and connected things to do at the local level, there was no reason why advocacy of nondiscrimination laws would siphon energy and attention away from organization building. Without such laws, success on the Southwest Side would make success elsewhere in Chicago only that much more elusive. They promised to cut off the escape routes of white flight, thus increasing the possibilities of racial dispersal and minimizing the moral compromises of local market control. Active advocacy of fair housing was also essential to having a substantial black presence in the OSC.[8]

Perhaps most important, nondiscrimination laws would change the underlying moral and legal presumptions of the housing market, and also the identities and interests shaped by participation in it. Government policies, court rulings, political mobilizations, financial practices, and the professional ethics of real estate agents had all played a role in establishing and reinforcing spatial configurations, identities, and interests based on race by setting rules that made interracial living seem like a profound threat to white homeowners. By altering the rules that had long racialized urban geography, fair housing statutes could begin to dissolve the connections between racial identity and property that had long animated the geopolitics of Chicago.

If the OSC intended to foster an interracial community as the first step in a larger campaign to democratize the city and its housing markets, it needed to challenge the accepted connections of racial identity, space, and power and begin to inscribe new meaning on the region's geography. Law had played a critical role in establishing the ground rules for a segregated Chicago, and law would have to play a part in creating an alternative racial geography.[9]

While open occupancy never came to a vote before the congress in November 1961, virtually every issue debated there centered on racial integration. Although six groups had withdrawn from the OSC, 135 member organizations sent delegates.[10] Black residents were well represented: fourteen black organizations sent fifty-five representatives, and ten integrated groups (at least 25 percent black) sent forty-seven more. Most delegates (especially those from the churches) were unaffiliated, but the two factions (the MLs and the MF) quickly took control of the agenda. Delegates affiliated with the MF donned Uncle Sam hats, nominated floor leaders, lobbied the unaffiliated, and used walkie-talkies to send voting instructions to loyalists. The Gresham police station assigned uniformed officers to the floor, and volunteers manned a first aid station in anticipation of physical violence.[11]

The most heavily contested debate centered on an amendment to the OSC's constitution proposed by racial liberals. The change was designed to abolish vice-presidential term limits, because otherwise McMahon, Molloy and Christ would have to leave their leadership positions, presenting the MF with the possibility of a takeover. According to Rev. Gordon Irvine, assistant minister at Gresham's Seventh Presbyterian Church, both sides were well aware that "the 'hidden issue' in the Constitutional change was race." After hearing a series of criticisms of the amendment by MF supporters, Fr. Andrew Greeley of Christ the King in Beverly wondered aloud whether they weren't "using constitutionality as a guise under which to launch a personal attack on the three clergymen ... because of the brave stand these clergymen have taken on certain controversial questions. I wonder also whether their opposition is something less than honest." The amendment fell just short of acceptance, thus ending the terms of McMahon, Molloy and Christ. The MF caucus then elected seven of the eleven vice presidents, giving them a substantial majority—but the delegates proceeded to elect Molloy as treasurer, McMahon as executive vice president, and Christ as secretary, ensuring liberal control over both the Executive Committee and the staff. The Median Forum had scored a small victory but would not be able to consolidate it.[12]

Rev. Irvine's analysis of the roll-call vote provides some insights into the inner dynamics of the OSC and the influences of religion, clergy leadership, and proximity to the racial frontier. Church delegations voted for the amendment, as did groups that were all or partially black. While delegates from Protestant churches voted overwhelmingly for the amendment (109-0, with twenty-four abstentions), the vote among the larger Catholic contingent was much closer (131-81) and more heavily dependent upon pastoral leadership.

Parishes with priests active in the OSC (St. Sabina, St. Leo, St. Margaret, and Christ the King) voted overwhelmingly for the amendment; those with clergy who were actively hostile to the group (Sacred Heart, St. Justin Martyr, St. Mary of Mt. Carmel) rejected the proposal resoundingly. Only St. Brendan (which split 9-9) and St. Kilian (which voted 16-8 in favor), the parish church for James Norris and many members of the Brainerd Civic Association, appeared to divide over the amendment. Delegates from groups that Irvine defined as "black" voted 55-0 for the measure, while integrated groups approved it 42-3, with two abstentions. Civic groups and neighborhood associations also tended to support the proposal, approving it 79-33, with three abstentions.[13] Opposition to the amendment, not surprisingly, tended to come from delegations that were not led by activist clergy. Leading the way were parent-teacher associations and what Irvine called "service" associations, typified by veterans' groups. Led by Knights of Columbus chapters, Catholic-oriented organizations also voted no.[14]

Perhaps most interestingly, white groups that were less than a mile from the Southwest Side's racial boundaries, and thus faced the imminent threat of racial turnover, were *more* likely to support the OSC's racially liberal leadership and approve the amendment than were those farther away. The reasons were threefold. First, this geographic split was a function of where the OSC's staff had focused its efforts. The upper half of the Southwest Side had been more effectively organized by the group, and the bulk of its most active leadership was based in Auburn Park, Gresham, West Chatham, and Winneconna Lakes—the neighborhoods surrounding St. Leo, St. Sabina, and the Seventh Presbyterian Church. The upper and lower halves of the area had long participated in different neighborhood associations, and the OSC had been unable to alter that pattern. Also, the measure was in part a vote of confidence for well-respected clergy.

Second, with the exception of the Morgan Park delegations, most of the OSC's black and racially integrated member organizations, and most of the Southwest Side's growing black population more generally, were based in the northern end of the community. Interracial participation at the block level through the OSC no doubt had a chastening effect on the racial positions of delegations.

Third, the OSC had succeeded in selling itself to white residents closer to the racial fault line as a force for stability. Beverly, Brainerd, and other neighborhoods to the south, however, remained convinced that the OSC was primarily focused on dispersing black families throughout the Southwest Side—and given the lack of organizational attention paid to the area, they had little evidence to the contrary.

After the third congress, MF groups began to leave the OSC. The final battle came in February 1962, when another Alinsky group—the black-led the Woodlawn Organization (TWO)—protested school segregation and overcrowding by sending so-called truth squads into predominantly white schools on the South Side to discover the number of empty seats, after Superintendent Benjamin Willis refused to release that information. The squads, made up of black parents, were arrested for trespassing, causing a well-publicized furor. Worried that a tepid response from the OSC would serve as a further invitation to black families to move into the area, MF activists urged the group's Education Committee to condemn TWO's protests.

The MF packed the meeting with supporters, and after what one observer called a "vicious, one-sided debate" a resolution passed, condemning the truth squads. In mid-February, the Executive Council held an open session to consider the resolution; more than three hundred OSC activists crowded the auditorium of Seventh Presbyterian Church. Christ and other racial liberals introduced a substitute proposal calling for an investigation of the complaints registered by the Squads, which was apparently defeated by voice vote. When President Fitzpatrick ruled otherwise, MF activists demanded a division of the house, with only delegates voting. The liberal resolution prevailed 53–38, and MF delegates stormed out. Several delegations from the southern end of the community withdrew, and the conservative caucus essentially melted away after the defeat.

"It Might Be Possible That We Can Stay"

In the wake of the conservative departure, the OSC increased its efforts to stem panic, keep white families in the community, and integrate the organization. As the role of black groups increased, the OSC also became much more assertive on broader civil rights issues, including advocacy of a fair housing law in 1963. But as local and city politics became increasingly racialized, the OSC was faced with an ultimately insurmountable maelstrom of white resistance and demographic change.

In 1963 the organization published a homeowners' guide and, perhaps most interestingly, ten thousand copies of a short play titled *How to Use Facts to Change Your Husband's Mind*—which suggested ways for wives to convince their spouses that the Southwest Side had the lonely suburbs beat. The play was targeted at young white families. Jim, a "deducing husband," is informed by Helen, "his discerning wife," that friends had decided to move back to the Southwest Side from the suburbs. Taxes outside the city were high, services were expensive, and they were apparently bothered by their dependency on cars, as well as the (class) homogeneity. When told that Helen was convinced that they should buy a house on the Southwest Side, Jim laments that they can afford only the smaller down payment for a suburban home. "I've got an answer for that too," Helen joyfully reports. "Under the new OSC Home Loan program, Southwest side banks and savings and loan association are making mortgage money available." "Honey," Jim concludes, "you've sold me too." The pamphlet then went on to describe the loan program in greater detail.[15]

While stabilizing the housing market—and in particular, creating the appearance of stability for local whites—was vital for maintaining the Southwest Side as a racially diverse community of middle-class homeowners, it was closely matched in importance by the need to combat crime and racial violence. Transitional neighborhoods had become racial battlegrounds in the early 1960s as white teens assaulted black property, grappled with black youths, and demonstrated in front of homes recently purchased by black families. As the areas of black residence expanded, so did racial violence. In 1962 a black family's garage was burned down, and their windows were smashed. Another black family had its car's tires slashed and their windows broken. After two months of similar incidents, another family gave up and moved out.

The OSC responded by publicizing the names of perpetrators and lobbying for an increased police presence. Through close cooperation between local police and OSC's Law Enforcement and Human Relations Committee, portions of the Southwest Side essentially experienced a kind of community policing. Block captains reported criminal activity both to the OSC and to the police, while the Law Enforcement Committee participated in regular meetings between beat officers and interracial committees of homeowners in transitional areas. In anticipation of what police commanders described as a "long hot summer" in 1964, the OSC requested more plainclothes officers "in neighborhoods where racial clashes are likely." The OSC office had colored maps, pinpointing trouble spots; when one appeared to be critical, the staff would organize block meetings between whites and blacks to open lines of communication and talk about their common interest in stability. The OSC also enlisted the police to crack down on illegal housing conversions.[16]

The OSC's dedicated efforts to stop white racial violence were crucial in sustaining a sense that its member organizations could create an alternative racial geography. By most accounts, incidents of violence against black families moving onto all-white blocks were reduced, particularly in areas heavily organized by the OSC and with the greatest proportion of black involvement in local institutional life. The OSC, Ed Chambers argued, had succeeded in eliminating "90 [percent] of the violence that used to center around changing neighborhoods." According to an official history of the OSC, activists and staff engaged in "hours of 'hand holding' with frightened people, informal meetings on threatened blocks, education through parish bulletins, brochures and flyers, conferences with ministers, priests, and civic leaders," in order to halt the violence and stem the tide of white panic and flight.[17]

These efforts were part of a larger organizational campaign to encourage interracial cooperation, develop black leadership, and increase the organized power of black newcomers.[18] Alinsky's protégés organized racially moderate (and increasingly integrated) neighborhood groups centered on the OSC's most activist churches. With the aid of the Rev. Robert Christ, the West Chatham Improvement Association had become one of the most dedicated and integrated of the OSC's member organizations; the Auburn-Highland Improvement Association and the Winneconna Lakes Area Improvement Association both drew heavily on the resources and parishioners of St. Leo's, while the Gresham Community Council was led largely by activists from St. Sabina's and Seventh Presbyterian.

Blacks increasingly ran for and won organizational offices, and committees were carefully balanced by both race and religion. By 1963, the OSC staffer Barry Menuez reported that the group was "integrated from the top down," in direct contrast to the "old pattern of exclusion, resistance and collapse." The OSC had 140 member groups at its 1965 congress, 40 of which were partially or entirely black. At the same meeting, three black activists—Harold Boysaw from MPPO, John Garner from the Greenview Park Civic Association (near Auburn-Gresham), and Eugene Hyman of the West Chatham Improvement Association—were elected vice presidents.[19]

Interracial block clubs on the edge of transition areas best represented the OSC's successes in race relations. According to the *Chicago Daily News*, when Auburn Park experienced rapid racial turnover during the summer of 1964, OSC activists greeted black families and worked to involve them in community activities "so as to fire their interest in maintaining the neighborhood." The OSC, Menuez informed the paper, had "a working nucleus in every block."[20] Fr. Egan praised the group for bringing the races into close contact, which he found to be "very important in preparation for stabilizing communities and the acceptance of newcomers." Hardly a night went by without "a predominant number of whites discussing, debating or working with some Negroes on community problems." Many area institutions and civic groups now had black members, and "frank and open discussions" had taken the place of "backroom meetings and pessimism."[21]

Interracial organizing within the OSC was surprisingly close to what Alinsky had originally envisioned in the *General Report* in the late 1950s. By 1965, according to Menuez, the block clubs and frequent meetings put together by the Community Relations Committee had succeeded in providing "a forum and clearinghouse for all the complexities of the problems so that Negroes and whites can hammer out differences face to face." White and black community leaders headed all OSC projects and meetings, which were based on "the mutual self-interest of both races." As a result, "grievances were aired," and "lines of communication and cooperation developed." "The OSC," Menuez concluded, "can claim dramatic results over the past five years in reducing the disruptive and demonic elements of racial transition."[22] Ed Murphy of the Real Estate Practices Committee agreed: "There are an increasing number of [white] people in the Southwest Community who realize that peace of mind will come to the people of this community only when they learn to live with Negro neighbors."[23]

Block clubs called on new black residents to welcome them, inform them about the OSC, and invite them to participate. They also brought white and black families together to share concerns, mediate disputes, and dispel divisive rumors. The Community Relations Committee worked to promote better race relations and pressure city bureaucracies to enforce building and zoning codes, as well as the 1963 law prohibiting panic peddling and blockbusting. The liberal clergy caucus played a key role in bringing black and white Southwest Siders together, and in encouraging black delegates to take leadership roles in the OSC. Msgr. McMahon made a point of visiting every black family that moved into his parish, especially those with children who might attend St. Sabina's school. He also pushed the members of his Christian Family Movement chapter to work with Friendship House on a home-visit program between the races. Although some of his white parishioners resented this, others found it to be an exciting opportunity to test the social teachings of their religion through community activism. As John McDermott described it, people were "organizing, meeting their neighbors. Protestant and Catholic churches were talking to each other, communicating . . . there was a euphoria in the neighborhood—that it might be possible that we can stay."[24]

Black Activism and Open Occupancy on the Southwest Side

The OSC's views and actions on civil rights issues were increasingly shaped by growing black assertiveness. The size of the black community within the OSC's boundaries tripled from 1959 to 1965, especially in Auburn-Gresham and Washington Heights, and the group responded by taking stronger pro-civil rights positions and focusing more of its efforts on the immediate needs of the newcomers.

In addition to the Home Loan Program, which provided housing credit insured by the Federal Housing Authority to a growing number of black families, the Education Committee served as a liaison between public schools and the changing neighborhoods. Especially after the black activist Eugene Hynson took over as chair, the Housing and Zoning Committee stepped up monitoring of code violations and, starting in 1963, received complaints about violations of Chicago's fair housing law. In 1965 the OSC set up a mental health clinic and received federal funding to create a Head Start program. After 1966, the organization focused less on racial integration and more on economic development and the improvement of city services in predominantly black neighborhoods, initiating urban renewal projects, lobbying for school construction, protesting overcrowded schools, expanding parks, and encouraging businesses to locate on the Southwest Side.[25]

Predominantly black groups like the Beverly Hills–Morgan Park Council on Human Relations and the MPPO also became increasingly outspoken on employment and fair housing issues, urging white OSC members to attack racial discrimination more aggressively. In March 1962 the MPPO launched Operation Look-In, an attempt to open up some of Chicago's restricted suburbs. Black middle-class families were sent to fourteen developments in nearby suburbs to push for open occupancy. While they received some positive responses, they heard from salesmen in a number of developments that if they sold to blacks, no whites would buy. As one told the group, "All my loans go through the same savings and loan and they don't make loans to Negroes." The OSC's Community Relations Committee established contacts with human relations groups outside the city, demonstrating the organization's increasingly broad analysis of the structures of metropolitan segregation.[26]

In 1964, the MPPO also attacked employment discrimination, launching a classic "don't buy where you can't work" campaign, pulling its funds out of a Morgan Park bank that refused to hire black workers. Local blacks and whites removed more than $100,000 in deposits over a six-week period and launched a successful boycott. The organization continued to monitor the hiring practices of other Morgan Park businesses by periodically sending black "testers" to apply for open positions.[27]

The MPPO and other black organizations persuaded the OSC to push for a citywide open-occupancy law. Activists in the group became increasingly aware of the precariousness of residential integration at the local level, without stronger measures opening up the larger housing market. Declaring that the dual housing market had "hampered the freedom of residence of individuals who meet the economic, moral and cultural standards of many communities in our area," black OSC delegates insisted that only a "metropolitan-wide acceptance of individual families on a basis of their own individual merits" could preserve the Southwest Side as a stable, integrated community.

In February 1963 Alderman Leon Despres proposed two housing statutes: one that prohibited discrimination by real estate agents and another that banned it by property owners. Despres had submitted open-housing ordinances each year since 1955, only to have the Daley machine either send them to defeat or bottle them up in committee. In 1963, however, a number of black aldermen warned the mayor that black middle-class voters—typified by OSC's growing black leadership—had become increasingly critical of the Democratic machine, and that some kind of token housing reform would be necessary to preserve Daley's electoral coalition. The mayor was up for reelection in 1963 and saw an opportunity. He proposed a watered-down version of Despres's ordinance restricting discrimination by real estate agents. According to Arnold Hirsch, by passing a toothless fair housing ordinance Daley could make "a symbolic gesture designed to appeal to civil rights advocates" without posing a threat to the city's white ethnic neighborhoods. According to Despres, who had been shut out of City Council deliberations over the bill, it "was close to being a segregationist's ideal . . . its power to make any change was almost zero." Nonetheless, the racial politics of the 1963 ordinance would play out in much the same way that Alinsky had feared.[28]

Daley asked Alderman James Murray to draft and sponsor the bill. Murray, who represented the Southwest Side's Eighteenth Ward (which included Ashburn and most of Auburn-Gresham), pleaded with Daley not to sacrifice his career on the altar of political expediency. "Mr. Mayor, why me?" Murray wondered. "The people in my ward will destroy me." To Daley, Murray seemed to be the most secure choice among his loyal aldermen: he was a former US congressman, had been on City Council since 1954, and was the son of Thomas Murray, a longtime Chicago unionist, political figure, and racial conservative who at the time was Superintendent Benjamin Willis's biggest defender on the Chicago School Board.[29]

Murray tried to explain the proposed ordinance to his constituents in a series of public meetings, arguing that it would protect white homeowners against blockbusting, and that it would not interfere with the right of property owners to sell or rent to whomever they wished. The *Chicago Sun-Times* agreed, reporting that if the law passed, property owners would still have "full discretion in choosing buyers of their property" and could, if they wished, instruct their real estate brokers not to sell or rent to blacks, without violating the statute. The argument was not well received: Murray was chased out of one meeting and was the target of threatening phone calls and pickets outside his home.[30]

Racial tensions escalated on the Southwest Side and within the OSC. In March 1963, Alinsky ally Msgr. John Egan spoke to the Murray Park Civic Association, which had recently voted to withdraw from the OSC because of its support for the bill and what it saw as a takeover by "the undesirable minority." The priest eloquently and scathingly chastised those assembled in the packed American Legion hall, declaring: "I disagree totally and unequivocally with the principles and objectives of this organization . . . I know there are some among you who accept wholeheartedly and fully the American and Christian concept of the dignity of man, and the right of every man to equality and freedom of opportunity . . . if those who hold these views . . . are in error, then this American Legion hall in which we meet tonight is a monument to hypocrisy and a sad mockery of the lives of these men who are in the American Legion, both living and dead." Like Murray, Egan needed an armed escort to whisk him away from the angry crowd.[31]

Despite the lack of enforcement mechanisms in the proposed statute, the Chicago Real Estate Board (CREB) and dozens of property owners' associations lobbied against it. Both the *Daily News* and the *Tribune* editorialized against the law.[32] Although the machine-backed statute passed by a comfortable margin, the sixteen white aldermen who voted against it represented the largest defection from the machine in Daley's tenure. Alderman Murray's political career came to a rapid end. As Murray put it: "I told all the other Southwest Side aldermen that if we hang together, we won't hang separately. But I couldn't convince them." None of them came to Murray's defense publicly; indeed, the law—and Murray's sponsorship of it—became the pivotal political issue on the Southwest Side for the better part of the decade.

Indicating the limits of the OSC's reach, the Southwest Side became the site of a growing movement opposed to "forced housing" as well as school integration. The fair housing debate coincided with a fall 1963 confrontation between civil rights activists and school superintendent Benjamin Willis over racial segregation. As part of a legal settlement, the Chicago Board of Education allowed a small number of top black students to transfer to predominantly white schools with honors programs. Bogan High, in Ashburn, was one of those schools. Thousands picketed when school opened in September. Willis promptly removed it and fourteen other predominantly white schools from the list. The Board of Education ordered him to reinstate them; he refused. After a court order was issued, he resigned in October 1963—but the Board of Education, under intense pressure from Southwest Side whites, refused to accept it. Willis quickly became a heroic symbol of resistance in Ashburn and across the white Southwest Side. Civil rights groups, organized into the Coordinating Council of Community Organizations (CCCO), responded with a citywide boycott of public schools—nearly a quarter of a million students stayed home or attended "freedom schools" in churches across the South Side.

Yet in the face of such mobilization by blacks, Daley apparently underestimated the hostility of white voters to even symbolic statements in favor of school desegregation and fair housing. While he won the 1963 election, he lost the white vote. Southwest Side whites—previously one of Daley's most loyal voting blocs—used the ballot box to scold the machine's perceived liberalism. Daley would learn his lesson.[33]

On September 1, more than five thousand Southwest Side homeowners, many from Murray's ward, marched to City Hall to protest the bill. The protest was organized by the Property Owners' Coordinating Committee (POCC), a statewide alliance of over 175 neighborhood associations representing over a quarter million homeowners. The POCC was funded by the CREB (they shared office space) and was largely based on the Southwest Side.[34] It contained a number of groups that had formerly belonged to the OSC or were based within its boundaries, including the Auburn Park Improvement Association, the Highland Improvement Association, the North Beverly Improvement Association, and the Southwest Council of Civic Associations (a federation with twelve member groups). The Eighteenth Ward Civic Council rebelled against its own alderman by joining. Included on the POCC's board of directors were representatives of the Brainerd Civic Association and the Beverly Area Planners Association, as well as a number of Southwest Side groups from areas not directly represented by the OSC. Two Southwest Side real estate boards, including the Beverly Suburban Real Estate Board, sent letters and telegrams to Daley and Despres stating their opposition to the fair housing statute.

After the passage of the real estate agent law, the POCC and the CREB led a legal and political charge against fair housing measures and "those forms of legislation which would erode the rights of private property ownership" at both the city and state levels. They were encouraged by a growing national movement of real estate agent groups, lawyers, and property associations that were organizing to repeal similar nondiscrimination laws around the country.[35] In 1964 California overwhelmingly passed Proposition 14, repealing the Rumford Act, a stringent antidiscrimination law enacted the previous year. The referendum gave property owners "absolute discretion" in the sale and rental of their properties. The National Association of Real Estate Boards was heavily involved in the Illinois and California campaigns, as well as others.[36]

In 1964 the POCC and the CREB moved to prevent the passage of fair housing statutes in Illinois and its municipalities with a referendum campaign. Despite substantial support for that campaign on the Southwest Side, the OSC voted to oppose the so-called Referendum on Forced Housing in April, instead encouraging the CREB to support a strong citywide open occupancy law and explain to Chicago's white homeowners "the high cost of maintaining a racial ghetto." Only the opposition of Governor Otto Kerner and a technicality prevented the initiative from appearing on the ballot.[37]

In their arguments against fair housing laws, the POCC and the CREB echoed the language of community, race, and property used in California and elsewhere. "Forced housing" measures, the CREB's president argued, violated property rights, and had "nothing to do with civil rights." Fair housing laws "tell a man he no longer has the right of choice as to whom he may sell, lease or rent his property," so constitute "a serious threat to these basic rights of ours as private property owners." The practice of discrimination had long been recognized as a property right of real estate owners. The home, and the right to choose one's associates, was protected by the Constitution.

"We believe that all people have a right to live wherever they choose if they can afford to do so," the CREB and POCC argued at an inaugural press conference. However, "to attempt to legislate this right through Open Occupancy legislation is to deprive other people of a basic right." According to this ostensibly color-blind perspective, neighborhoods resulted from a series of personal, private choices beyond the legitimate purview of government. Exclusionary practices were essential to the health of white communities, the CREB insisted, and open-occupancy statutes were thus an assault on the rights and security of the average American, as well as the public interest. The board intended to protect the racial capital of white homeowners, much as it had for the previous half century.[38]

The close connection among race, property, and security was echoed in opinion polls and in the voting booth. A 1965 survey of Southwest Side voters found that fully 92 percent opposed a statewide open-occupancy law. The Southwest Side had become a "backlash" district in 1964 and continued to punish Democratic candidates for the better part of the decade, because of their racial liberalism generally and because of the perceived threat to white associational and property rights more specifically. While Murray was not up for election in 1964, representatives to the state legislature were, and fair housing quickly became the dominant issue. The Murray-endorsed machine candidate for state senator lost to a young conservative Republican who ran on an anti–forced housing platform.

In many ways the 1963 city law was a disaster for the OSC, as Alinsky had predicted. It further enflamed racial polarization on the Southwest Side while simultaneously doing little to open up the housing market. Its reach was narrow, and its enforcement mechanisms were weak. Because it didn't cover discriminatory behavior by private market actors, white homeowners' associations used the law to police racial boundaries and protect white neighborhoods, not advance nondiscrimination, integration, and an open housing market. While the CCHR had the power to initiate complaints, its lack of staff and funding, as well as doubts about the effectiveness of doing so, largely restricted it to mediating disputes between white neighborhood groups and real estate operators in transition areas. It became a kind of service agency for individual complainants rather than an enforcement agency.[39]

Rose Helper, who conducted detailed surveys of Chicago real estate agents in the late 1950s and the mid-1960s, concluded that the 1963 law had had little impact, as agents continued to engage in racially restrictive practices. In fact, Mayor Daley had allowed the law to be enacted partly because the CCHR had indicated that other such statutes had not had major impacts of population movements. Other studies of state and local fair housing laws concluded that they did little for non-middle-class blacks while also increasing white political opposition. The National Committee against Discrimination in Housing, for example, found in 1961 that while fair housing laws had been a "potent educational force," the number of black working-class families helped by them was "disappointingly small." Of course, some critics (black and white) opposed addressing integration through legislation altogether, arguing that it distracted everyone from the more important task of expanding both the quantity and quality of black housing.[40]

Yet the OSC continued to support fair housing consistently and publicly. In the spring of 1964, the group launched an anti-blockbusting campaign, in an effort to enforce the weak 1963 law. Plans were made to strengthen block captain contacts in racially changing neighborhoods, to keep the organization informed of possible violations of the law by panic peddlers. In April, the Real Estate Practices Committee set up a file listing the purchase price of all local properties sold in the previous two years, to help both white sellers and black purchasers avoid speculators, "protect themselves from abuses of the land contract for home purchase," and determine fair market prices. "The citizens of this community have demonstrated that we can work out our problems when we removed the unethical operators trying to exploit the situation," chair Max Sonderby told the *Chicago Defender*.

Sonderby wrote to 150 real estate agents for information on sales since the beginning of 1962, asked agents to allow sellers and buyers to meet before closing, and publicized the names of those who were willing to cooperate. The result was a street-by-street index of property prices and recent sales histories, which the committee offered to consult for any buyer. "If we can remove the secrecy in the prices at which property is bought and sold," Sonderby argued, "we can put them [blockbusters] out of business."[41] The list quickly proved useful in Auburn Park in the summer of 1964, when forty homes and apartment buildings were sold in a five-block area at prices that closely reflected a stable market. As one real estate agent informed the *Daily News*, area whites were "waiting for their price" and were largely being replaced by "the right people"—black families with mortgages (not installment contracts) and the financial wherewithal to maintain and improve the properties.[42]

When Governor Otto Kerner proposed an executive order prohibiting discriminatory practices by real estate brokers in July 1966—in the midst of Dr. King's open-housing campaign—the OSC praised the effort: "to the extent that this order is effective, it will provide Negro families with the opportunity to purchase homes throughout the Chicago metropolitan area, thereby taking the pressure off the peripheral areas, giving them an opportunity to stabilize and maintain their integrated status." Even though Kerner's order didn't cover the sale of homes by private individuals, the editors of the *Chicago Tribune* declared it "inconsistent with private property rights." The paper encouraged the Illinois Association of Real Estate Boards to challenge it, which it and the CREB did successfully in 1967.[43]

In the summer of 1966, Rev. King and the Chicago Freedom Movement led open-occupancy marches through Gage Park and Chicago Lawn, just north of OSC territory. While the OSC's West Chatham Community Improvement Association (which by this time was mostly black) joined the campaign, by all accounts the marches were wildly unpopular among Southwest Side white homeowners. The historian James Ralph convincingly argues that virtually the entire area was "in upheaval" in response to the marches, and that most whites did not recognize the legitimacy of the civil rights perspective which inspired the protests. Edward Vondrak, publisher of the racially moderate *Southwest News-Herald*, claimed that the typical white Southwest Side homeowner saw the marches as "a threat to the security of his own community and his own home."[44]

Even the OSC's most well-organized neighborhoods, those surrounding St. Sabina, were strongly affected by the chaos around the marches. The violent responses of whites in Gage Park and Chicago Lawn appeared to confirm the unworkability of racial integration. A survey of Chicago whites in the wake of the marches found that 55 percent believed that race relations had worsened in the previous year and a half, and they were less enthusiastic about integration than they had been a year earlier.[45]

White Southwest Siders turned out in overwhelming numbers in 1966 for Republican Charles Percy (who opposed open-occupancy laws) for US senator, over the incumbent liberal Democrat Paul Douglas. In the 1967 aldermanic races, each incumbent in the five Southwest Side wards was challenged and defeated by a candidate riding the coattails of white backlash. Murray wisely declined to run for reelection in 1967, although Daley did put him up for a circuit court judgeship. He won election to the bench but lost his own ward. The Republican candidate vying to succeed Murray, Robert Mahl, declared: "I am a member of, and will welcome support from, the white backlash." Both houses of the state legislature rejected a proposed Fair Housing Practices Act.

A poll of 692 Southwest Side residents in 1967 showed that 684 of them were against a statewide open-occupancy law. A detailed 1967 survey of five Chicago white neighborhoods—including Ashburn—found that 60 percent of residents believed that they had a right to keep blacks out of their neighborhoods, and that blacks should respect this right. Whites ranked race relations and crime as the two biggest issues facing the city; each can be interpreted as a widespread rejection of residential integration, as well as black activism and protest. That rejection, while more heavily concentrated among homeowners, characterized all socioeconomic groups. As racial transition accelerated on the Southwest Side in the late 1960s, none of the local aldermen encouraged blacks and whites to work together. They chose to exacerbate the politics of "fear, confrontation and divisiveness" instead.[46]

"Just All of a Sudden, They Left"

As late as 1964, John McDermott, of the Catholic Interracial Council, believed that the OSC's efforts had been successful in reducing white fears, slowing down flight from the area, and encouraging "more second thinking" by white homeowners contemplating moves to the suburbs.[47] By attempting to gain some kind of control of the housing market, the OSC had unquestionably dispelled some of the resignation and apathy that had accelerated white flight.

Nonetheless, the upper reaches of the Southwest Side continued to change from white to black, followed in the 1970s by much of the rest of the area. A series of well-publicized racial confrontations along advancing racial boundaries—some of them within the heart of the OSC's territory—were seen as weakening white housing demand.[48] While white residents feared the prospect of black neighbors, it was the perception that the ghetto was moving closer that provoked the greatest panic. Increases in general crime in the area—in particular, the rapid circulation of stories of assaults, muggings, and break-ins—encouraged that perception. Aside from calling for more patrolmen and urging residents to maintain their "eyes on the street," the OSC was powerless to stop such crimes, particularly when perpetrators were outsiders, as was often the case.[49]

As late as 1965, St. Sabina's white parishioners had stayed put, even while those in nearby parishes that had not joined the OSC—such as Little Flower—left. In part this was because so many of McMahon's parishioners were elderly and living on fixed incomes, and thus couldn't afford to risk the financial loss of a panicked sale. Primarily, however, they stayed because McMahon and the OSC gave them some confidence that the neighborhood would remain stable, even as it became more racially diverse. Priest Robert McClory was "amazed at how calm everybody was. In '64 and '65 people were talking . . . saying 'I don't know whether it will work. There's so much violence around . . .' [but] don't worry, Father, we're going to stay if it's at all possible." And then, "just all of a sudden," McClory lamented, "they all left."

In the summer of 1965, Frank Kelly, a seventeen-year-old white member of St. Sabina, got into a shouting match with a black teenager in front of the church's youth center and was shot and killed. His name instantly became a symbol for the fears and doubts of white residents. Fr. Daniel Sullivan recalled that "instantly, instantly, everybody knew that name—Frank Kelly. The horror that spread! The fear that it engendered! Up to that time people had been figuring they were going to buck it out." Already frightened by increases in car theft, purse snatching, and juvenile offenses, as well as by the appearance of panic peddlers the previous year, the OSC's white base quickly collapsed. One thousand families left the parish in 1965, and another thousand fled in 1966—an extraordinary demographic event for a relatively small area.[50] The year 1967 witnessed an increase in both gang violence and organized vigilantism, particularly in Auburn-Gresham, the heart of OSC's white membership.[51]

Despite the OSC's efforts, Auburn-Gresham had the third-fastest rate of racial succession in Chicago from 1960 to 1966, changing from less than 1 percent black to more than 34 percent. By 1970, it was almost completely black. Its "racial replacement rate"—the speed at which dwelling units were vacated by a white family and then occupied by a black one—was the highest in the city by far from April 1965 to April 1966. Fully 14 percent of Auburn-Gresham's housing units were vacated by whites and occupied by blacks during this period. The OSC seems to have had little impact on the speed of racial change, although these numbers do miss variations within the neighborhood, such as between parishes.[52]

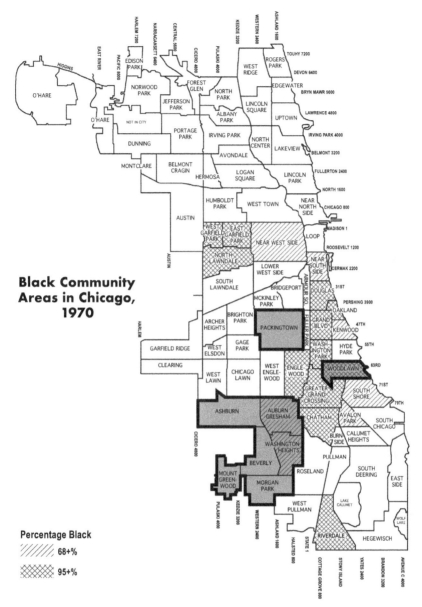

FIGURE 5.1. Racial Transition and Alinsky's three neighborhood organizations in 1970. Adapted by Shana Santow, from Roger Fox and Jerry Szatan, "The Current Economic Status of Chicago's Black Community: A Mid-1970s Overview Report," Chicago Urban League (Winter 1977).

However, by lessening panic and violence, fostering substantial black participation, pushing for property upkeep and the enforcement of housing and zoning codes, disciplining the behaviors of real estate agents, making prices and property values transparent to both buyers and sellers, and using the Home Loan Pool to ensure that black purchasers could afford to own and maintain their new homes, the OSC was able to keep the area economically and physically stable. As a result, many of the more destructive aspects of racial transition on the edge of the expanding ghetto never took hold. By stemming violence and allowing both whites and blacks a shot at fair value in the housing and credit markets, the OSC succeeded in stabilizing the quality and economic status of the community. It never had the power or the support to implement Alinsky's quota proposal, but on a number of blocks it did slow transition and flight long enough to allow interracial cooperation to emerge.

Even though the area around St. Sabina's became virtually all black by 1970, it remained a solid middle-class community and became one of the premier black Catholic parishes in Chicago—and the nation. Half of the new black homeowners in the area were able to get conventional mortgage loans, in addition to those families eligible for the OSC's Home Loan Program. As of 1968, the population of the OSC's territory was approximately 25 percent black, made up largely of middle-class families in quality housing. Washington Heights, for example, was overwhelmingly black and had a median income well above the city average for either race.[53] This was no small accomplishment: it allowed most white families who chose to leave to keep the equity they had built up in their houses, while it assured the black families that moved in that their geographical mobility had a reasonable chance of ensuring their economic and social mobility as well. At the same time, the institutional stability that the OSC helped to create made the Southwest Side that much better a place for them to live.[54]

As Msgr. Egan observed in 1965, in those Catholic parishes that were strongly affiliated with the OSC—St. Leo's and St. Sabina's, in particular—racial turnover was relatively peaceful and took over six years. Neighboring churches that opposed or avoided the organization changed in less than two years. IAF staffers came to believe that the OSC's greatest accomplishment was preventing the area from becoming a slum in the wake of racial change. Racial transition on the Southwest Side may have been inevitable, Nicholas Von Hoffman concluded, but the OSC had "done astonishingly well in making these transitions as peaceful and as slow as possible."[55]

But why was the OSC unsuccessful at creating an integrated neighborhood? Some of the OSC's failures were the unavoidable results of economics, demography, geography, and poor timing; others stemmed from Alinsky's approach and from a lack of resources. The OSC lacked both the time and the capacity to build and maintain a geographically broader membership that was both ideologically and racially diverse. Shaped in part by Alinsky's relentlessly local approach, the group struggled to maintain white demand for housing on the Southwest Side. The OSC tried to remain apolitical in Richard Daley's Chicago, fearing that political participation might further divide the group internally—but doing so prevented its vision of a stable and racially integrated Southwest from getting a broader hearing. Ultimately, however, the OSC's experiment in stable racial integration collapsed because metropolitan segregation remained in place, untouched by community organizing, civil rights activism, and legislation.

OSC's Limited Organizational Reach

OSC staffers faced three enormous tasks in broadening and deepening the organization's reach: sustaining its representativeness by keeping its more racially conservative members, expanding its membership and resource base beyond the core churches and pastors, and integrating the Southwest Side's new black residents—into predominantly white member groups, into leadership positions in the OSC, and into their own community associations. The OSC simultaneously moved to clarify its goals and become capable of grappling with the day-to-day effects of Chicago's Great Question on local residents. While formulating a program and constructing a broadly based organization were both essential tasks, they proved exceedingly difficult to undertake simultaneously.

Small victories would not build the OSC, when all participants could see the larger battle ahead. The effort of OSC staffers to frame local issues as nonracial—as simply matters of community improvement—fooled no one for long. The OSC not only had to formulate a convincing alternative racial geography; it had to do it under severe time constraints. If Alinsky had initiated an organizing campaign in 1949, rather than 1959, he and the OSC might have had the chance to build support for an alternative racial geography that promised to keep the Southwest Side a viable and predominantly white middle-class area. Instead, the OSC had to transform the expectations, interests, and identities of local whites in the midst of racial transition rather than in preparation for it.

The willingness of MF delegates to disaffiliate their organizations from the OSC in early 1962 was indicative of the larger difficulties staffers and activists had in retaining racial conservatives. Some groups left the OSC; many individuals moved to the suburbs, became resigned to racial change, or joined groups affiliated with the restrictionist Property Owners' Coordinating Committee, which began to heavily cut into the OSC's potential base starting in 1963. Given the impending sense of crisis among even the most racially liberal whites, it was virtually impossible for the OSC to stake out a position on Chicago's Great Question that would allow it to serve as a representative public forum. OSC staffers also struggled to expand the group's geographical and political diversity. As a consequence, its power base never grew beyond the core churches in the upper half of the Southwest Side. Servicing St. Leo and St. Sabina (the two largest contributors of money and people) left little time and money "for doing organizational work that will pay off in future contributions," resulting in what Von Hoffman called a "shortage of organizational investment capital."[56]

The racial conservatism of many area priests equaled that of their parishioners, which compounded the difficulties. In a scathing assessment, Von Hoffman told Alinsky in June 1963 that, "with certain notable exceptions, the pastors out on the Southwest Side are practically a caricature, a cartoon, of the sins of omission and commission of the Irish Roman Catholic clergy." Three Catholic churches—Little Flower, St. Brendan, and St. Justin Martyr (Egan's old parish)—were controlled by segregationist priests. In lobbying racially conservative pastors, the OSC's staff director Ed Chambers and Barry Menuez (his successor) had had to engage in "the most humiliating and disgusting kind of belly-creeping." Any attempt to these pastors' parishioners independently was bound to fail, Von Hoffman insisted, both because they were unlikely to challenge clerical authority and because they largely supported their priests anyway.

Given the proclivity of the local clergy to "stand up like the jellyfish they are" in the event of racial crisis, Von Hoffman argued, it was nothing short of "miraculous" that the OSC had gotten as far as it had "against this ocean of anti-Negro sentiment." "Half the time out there," Von Hoffman seethed, "we have had to spend our efforts and ingenuity in trying to pluck these guys out from leading the mob." Until the archdiocese moved to replace or lean on some of the pastors, OSC staffers had "every reason to feel that ultimately the organization is going to go to pieces." Both Egan and Von Hoffman, as well as Donald O'Toole, believed that a stronger moral, financial, and organizational effort by the archdiocese would have allowed the OSC to encompass a greater number of parishes, command broader and deeper community power, direct resources more quickly and effectively to organizing black newcomers, and take greater control over the Southwest Side's housing market.[57]

The principled position of the archdiocese on racial discrimination and segregation was beyond question at the time of the OSC's founding, and the institutional bravery and importance of Cardinal Meyer's willingness to fund the group should not be underestimated. By 1960 the archdiocese had officially become a public foe of racial segregation—the largest and most powerful institution in the city to take such a position. However, these abstract commitments weakened at the local level.[58] Meyer, who became increasingly involved in the theological conferences and controversies of the Second Vatican Council, which opened in the fall of 1962, paid less and less attention to the OSC in particular and Chicago's racial problems in general.[59]

A growing number of Catholics on the Southwest Side resented the increasingly public stance taken by the church on race. During the summer of 1966 the offices of the archdiocesan newspaper, *New World*, were bombarded by letters from Catholics criticizing clergy for their participation in open-housing marches. Former Alinsky ally Msgr. Edward Burke spoke for many when he warned Chicago Catholics early in 1967: "When we fight for the rights of the Negro we cannot overlook the rights of the white person. He has been forced to support, unaided, himself and his family. If he owns property, he purchased it by the sweat of his brow, and is a true Christian when he asks that his possessions not be disturbed." It is unclear whether a greater commitment of Meyer's personal and institutional resources could have altered these divisions, which increasingly afflicted urban parishes throughout the country.[60]

The "threat" of black families moving into parish neighborhoods often precipitated heated arguments over the proper role of clergy and the church in community and public affairs, especially in the few congregations on the Southwest Side with openly liberal priests. In a survey of both Catholic and Protestant white church members on the Southwest Side, John Fish found that support for the OSC hinged in part on beliefs about the proper role of religion and its institutions in public life.[61] Even among those churches that were active in OSC, most parishioners (especially at St. Leo's) didn't support participation in the group and were unaware of who their delegates were and what they did or said at meetings. While churches provided most of the officers, funds, and leadership in the OSC, only fifteen of the sixty-seven area congregations participated to a significant degree. Parishioners at St. Sabina's were generally more active in and aware of OSC activities, but this was largely because of the persistent efforts of McMahon. Most churches on the Southwest Side did not have such leadership. Fish concluded that OSC involvement was "peripheral to the ongoing life of the churches."[62]

By the summer of 1965, Egan estimated that less than half of the Southwest Side's parishes were cooperating with the OSC; at least one parish, St. Thomas More, allowed the ultraconservative John Birch Society to hand out anti-OSC pamphlets after Sunday Mass. Egan himself was physically ousted ("by fellows I'd married or baptized their children," he recalled) from a block club meeting near St. Justin Martyr after discussing residential integration. While Egan and Von Hoffman lamented the inability of the OSC to reach a majority of the Southwest Side's Catholic parishes, the intractable racial conservatism of many residents (and priests) probably played a greater role in limiting the group's organizational reach than did the intermittent support of Meyer and the archdiocese.

Without a substantial and well-organized membership base in the churches of Brainerd, Beverly, and Morgan Park, the OSC had nowhere to disperse the area's growing black population. The viability of quotas—and the ultimate future of racial integration on the Southwest Side—was heavily dependent on the ability of the group to deflect a substantial portion of black housing demand away from white neighborhoods on the racial boundary and toward the area's broader housing market. As long as white homeowners in the southern end of the area refused to open their neighborhoods up to limited black occupancy, and as long as the OSC's staff was unable to convince them of the self-interested wisdom of such an approach, the organization would fail to maintain integration. The OSC needed a handle on the entire housing market of the Southwest Side, if quotas (or less formal migration control) were to be a broadly integrative force.

The lack of "organizational Investment capital" to which Von Hoffman referred also limited the ability of OSC staffers to develop black leaders and groups. While blacks in the upper end of the Southwest Side increasingly joined improvement associations, most of the black-controlled organizations in the area (especially in the early years) were small, new, and relatively impoverished churches. Many of them either could not afford membership dues or had such small congregations that their delegates felt overwhelmed at OSC's monthly and yearly meetings. Staffers turned to the creation of block clubs in increasingly black areas to make up for the weakness of churches. But the staff lacked the time and resources to adequately develop independent black community leaders and groups. While longtime white residents had had the time, resources, and institutions to develop neighborhood social capital and leadership, the formation of such leaders, relationships, and groups among new black residents required active and immediate cultivation. Even the Morgan Park Planning Organization, the main black instrument in the OSC, was created by the staff. Torn by the need to retain white racial conservatives and limited by the lack of resources and support among white delegations for working in the black community, staffers struggled to develop a strong black presence and to redefine the identity of the Southwest Side as an integrated area.[63]

Forward movement within the OSC on race and integration, Von Hoffman wrote Alinsky, was largely a function of the "constant building up of the Negro membership so that it is now well beyond a token representation," which had been accomplished through the "conniving of the staff," both Ed Chambers and Barry Menuez. Blacks had come to make up 25 percent of the membership; they were mostly "middle-class types who have made a reasonably decent adjustment for themselves in life and are happy to live an almost completely but not absolutely segregated existence." This was especially true of those who had moved into the eastern part of Washington Heights, many of whom were among the most economically well-off black families in the city. Von Hoffman found that few black delegates were willing to openly challenge racial conservatives at committee meetings, leaving the battle for residential integration largely in the hands of the OSC's staff director. As long as organized black power within the OSC remained weak and white delegations viewed growing black participation as inherently threatening, Von Hoffman argued, the group would not be able to sustain and expand a membership base dedicated to the advocacy of integration as part of the community's long-term self-interest.[64]

Alinsky himself was well aware that his desire to make the OSC a force for racial integration was not widely shared in the neighborhoods, but he believed that pressure from strongly organized blacks was essential if the Southwest Side was to be integrated. As early as 1961, Alinsky informed the IAF board that while the presence of the OSC had made it reasonably certain that as black families moved in "justice will be done," he despaired of the willingness of the organization's white leadership to move beyond nondiscrimination. "The OSC," he argued, "cannot bring itself to see that more is needed than responding in a humane and equitable way." It lacked the determination to initiate racial integration in large part because it could not "supply its own stimulus." In 1959 and 1960 OSC activists had been "in a state close to panic, and were willing to make many concessions because they seemed unavoidable." However, as the organization had gained in strength and confidence, "the incentive to give ground on the issue" had weakened sharply. Desperation had given way to a more "staid" view once their homes, businesses, and churches no longer seemed "destined for auctioneer's block."

In the long run, Alinsky asserted, black families would have to be dispersed throughout the Southwest Side if the long-term interests of residents of all races were to be served. Blacks were going to continue to move in; the question was whether the ghetto would keep expanding and white neighborhoods and parishes disappearing, or whether the "new population will disperse among the old population," thus allowing "community life" to continue.

The problem, however, was that it was the immediate view of self-interest that had "brought OSC leaders to their present 'neutralist' kind of policy." By not permitting "any organized discrimination and by conceding the Negroes in the area a place in the community councils," the group's leadership hoped to be able to "carry out their entirely laudable principles for neighborhood development and enrichment." Beyond such a point, Alinsky conceded, they saw no reason to go: "they will react responsibly, but they will not act."

The reluctance of OSC leaders to press for racial dispersal would grow as the group gained in strength and accomplishments, Alinsky told the board. "Unless they are soon again forced to recall the ultimate realities of the situation facing them and the rest of Chicago," Alinsky warned, the OSC would become increasingly conservative, making it "immeasurably more difficult for them to go all the way with integration." Above all, the organizer feared that the OSC would follow in the footsteps of the BYNC—the opposite of what he had hoped. After its early victories, the BYNC had been in a position "akin to that of the OSC's now," but it quickly changed from "an innovating force to . . . preserving a status quo." Only a "push from the Negro side" could redirect the OSC, Alinsky wrote. Because blacks "have the greatest, immediate interest in integration, they are the ones who must bring the issue to a head in Chicago," he insisted. Without some kind of black organized strength, Alinsky worried, the OSC would probably follow the segregationist path of the BYNC.[65]

Largely because of the pressures of racial transition and the dual housing market, each day spent attempting to organize newly forming black communities was potentially another day of white flight. This left little time for organizers to bring the races together on an equal basis. In a community as deeply organized as the Southwest Side, and as closely tied to geography and property as an expression of religious identity, social belonging, and financial security, the task of bringing black newcomers into the OSC with whites and expecting them to negotiate as equals was almost hopelessly difficult. With sufficient resources and, most important, time, this would have been a formidable project; without either, the OSC could hope to do little other than help to facilitate the transition of the Southwest Side from a community of white middle-class homeowners to one of black middle-class homeowners.

Stability, Mobility, and White Housing Demand

Alinsky had wagered that "stability" would be the issue around which he could rally white homeowners, priests, business leaders, and new black residents on the Southwest Side. However, as John Fish usefully points out, this word had many potential meanings. If *stability* referred to a low rate of population mobility—whites choosing to stay, and blacks electing not to move in—then the OSC was certainly a failure. Auburn-Gresham would have turned over a substantial portion of its population from 1959 to 1968 regardless of the state of the black housing market. But its proximity to the expanding ghetto, and the persistence of housing discrimination throughout the Chicago area, made this failure virtually unavoidable.[66] But for many people on the Southwest Side, community stability referred not so much to keeping the same residents as to keeping the same type of residents—namely, whites. Throughout most of the previous half century, *stabilizing* had merely been a euphemism for preserving racial homogeneity. In the early years of the OSC, many member groups saw the organization as nothing more than the successor to the Southtown Planning Association: a regional federation of long-standing property owners' associations and block groups dedicated to keeping the Southwest Side white. Delegates from the southern end of the community were especially hopeful that the OSC would play the role of racial gatekeeper and draw a line in the sand a good distance away from them. When it became clear that the OSC wouldn't (and couldn't) keep black families out of the area, racially conservative groups left for federations (like the BAPA and the POCC) that promised to do so. Racial homogeneity probably appealed to all but the most liberal OSC members.

However, if community stability is defined as the maintenance of institutions and services in the midst of population turnover, then the OSC was probably a success. Both the *General Report* and the creation of the OSC were motivated in part by the desire of Cardinals Stritch and Meyer to maintain Catholic institutions in transition neighborhoods and to find a way to keep schools and parishes relevant to the lives of new black residents. Donald O'Toole and the OSC's other activists from the business community hoped to maintain the economic life of local retail stores, banks, factories, and establishments by using the community group to ensure that the purchasing power of the Southwest Side's new residents was comparable to that of those who were leaving.

This definition of community stability is very much connected to the final one that Fish identifies: keeping the Southwest Side as a district of mostly middle-class homeowners, living in quality homes. The OSC was largely successful in bringing this kind of stability about. Alinsky, as we know, believed that the only way to prevent the flight of white families from transition neighborhoods was to reassure them that their communities would remain predominantly white and middle class, both culturally and economically. Efforts at total exclusion of blacks were ineffective and morally wrong, he insisted, and the interests that resistant whites were trying to protect could be better served by allowing a small influx of black families throughout the city.

The OSC's racial moderates (and some of its early exclusionists, like Msgr. Molloy and James Norris) essentially bought this alternative racial geography as a form of racial retreat. Few shared the views of Alinsky, his staff, and the group's racial liberals (Christ, McMahon, Bukacek, and others) that racial integration and dispersion were desirable in and of themselves. Instead, they saw some degree of black residency as inevitable and sought to redefine the Southwest Side as a biracial middle-class community with a stable and significant preponderance of whites. A public stance of nondiscrimination, the acceptance of black members, and an effort to cut down on racial violence resulted from this tactical retreat. This was certainly the majority opinion in the OSC, especially after the MF withdrawal.[67]

Targeting villains (blockbusters and panic peddlers, and to a lesser extent white families considering flight) attracted residents to the group, but it made the exit of whites the locus of organizing while ignoring the other half of sustaining a strong housing market for whites—namely, external demand. Although this focus may have provided a pedagogical means for drawing connections between housing prices, population movements, and racial discrimination in the larger housing market for residents, it was ultimately a faulty analysis of why white neighborhoods on the edge of the ghetto tended to turn over. Speculators certainly could drum up panic, but racial transition was dependent upon a simple economic fact: real estate on the white Southwest Side was worth more to blacks than it was to whites, given black demand, white supply, the quality of housing, the proximity to the expanding black ghetto, and the nature of housing conditions in the metropolitan area overall. And whites were unlikely to move into Southwest Side neighborhoods without some reassurance that the black population was going to remain stable. By presenting transition as a problem mainly of flight and of controls over black in-migration, Alinsky's approach was too inward looking.

While Alinsky's focus was in part a function of his general approach to organizing, it was a common one in the late 1950s and early 1960s. Ingrid Ellen argues that both scholars and practitioners have tended to conflate—mistakenly—the issues of exit and entry. The factors in the decision of a household to leave an area like the Southwest Side may very well have been different from those for families considering a move *into* the area. With their participation in and knowledge of local institutions and social networks—as well as the economic, social, and psychological costs of moving—families already living in transition areas were generally more inclined to stay than financially comparable households were to move into such a neighborhood. Given the persistent population mobility in all urban neighborhoods, the racial stability of the Southwest Side was ultimately more dependent upon the expectations and experiences of those seeking to move in. As Ellen puts it, "entry drives racial change more than exit" in transition neighborhoods.[68]

The few "entry-focused" programs initiated by the OSC were generally inadequate. Affirmative marketing of the neighborhood as a place of interracial tolerance might have attracted some white families, although it probably would have attracted black families in even larger numbers. The OSC did receive some positive publicity—it was the subject of a nationally broadcast television documentary—but it never initiated an organized campaign to sell itself to the white market. The Home Loan Pool was a positive step, although it was undercapitalized and inadequately publicized beyond the core churches and member organizations. A larger consortium of Southwest Side financial institutions perhaps could have initiated a program of pro-integrative mortgages, to provide financial incentives for black families to move onto all-white blocks. However, given the inability of the OSC to strongly organize south of Auburn-Gresham, bankers there could expect strong community counterpressures and were unlikely to go along.[69]

The group did initiate referral services for tenants, but the program was underutilized and geographically limited; the high percentage of housing stock that was owner-occupied also limited its reach. As hard as it was for the OSC to manipulate the nature and direction of housing demand, it was equally difficult to alter the supply, both in quantity and quality. The Southwest Side was made up overwhelmingly of single-family homes and thus did not offer the possibility for oligopolistic control over management or ownership, at least not in such a short span of time. In the renters' market of Hyde Park, the Southeast Chicago Commission (SECC) and the Hyde Park–Kenwood Community Conference had been able to create institutions to centralize control over the ownership and/or management of housing, and then employ racial steering.[70] Similarly, a politically independent suburb like Oak Park successfully used its power to legislate to create and sustain a relatively balanced racial geography beginning in the late 1960s. Without some kind of more formalized authority over its real estate market, the OSC's ability to guarantee racial dispersion and stability was inherently limited.[71]

Ultimately, white homeowners seeking comparable housing standards and amenities in the Chicago area could find neighborhoods farther from the South Side ghetto that were under no imminent threat of racial turnover. This was part of what made integration in one community so difficult. As long as most neighborhoods remained closed to black families, whites could always find somewhere in the metropolitan area where there was no black influx.

In keeping with Alinsky's local approach, most of the actions taken by the group were designed to uphold and improve the area, build social capital, and raise confidence in and expectations for the future of the Southwest Side. This emphasis on what Ellen calls the "structural strength" of the area—its quality-of-life indicators, such as stability, amenities, safety, school quality, and property value appreciation—was certainly important. However, it was bound to make the area attractive to prospective black buyers as well as whites. Housing was in greater demand from blacks than from whites on the Southwest Side because of a restricted black supply, not because certain neighborhoods had experienced some decay in the housing stock. "Decay" was important in its effects on white demand, not in creating an immediate vulnerability to racial transition.

Unless blacks were dispersed into neighborhoods beyond the edge of the ghetto, or unless conditions were heightened sufficiently to price most blacks out of the local market while sustaining white demand within it, as was occurring in Hyde Park, a solely inward-looking approach was bound to fail. Given the age of most residential structures in Auburn-Gresham, its proximity to the ghetto, the limited financial and political resources of both the OSC and its member organizations, and the lack of local authority over zoning, building standards, taxes, and public schools, it was unlikely that the group could re-create the Southwest Side as a community of integrated but white-dominated wealth.[72]

Alinsky's localized analysis was flawed because it failed to account for the fact that all neighborhoods turn over their populations, even when there is no changing racial component. White flight was not necessary for a neighborhood like Auburn-Gresham to turn over in the span of a decade. It mattered for property values, and for the preservation of a stable housing market, perhaps; it almost certainly affected the resilience of social capital in the area. But the economic and demographic facts of race and housing in the Chicago metropolitan area ultimately mattered more than the racial fears of whites.[73]

Given the enormous expansion and exclusionary policies of Chicago's suburbs, the disincentives created by the financial system and federal programs, the beliefs and behaviors of real estate agents, and the strong connections drawn by many white homeowners among race, property, and security of all kinds, sustaining white demand in the area proved to be a daunting task. Without federal action and coalition building that reached beyond the Southwest Side—which Alinsky's approach tended to downplay—the OSC was unlikely to succeed, particularly with the time constraints and the polarizing racial politics.

How could it have been done, if at all? Communities that have had the greatest success in creating stable racial mixing have generally had a number of common characteristics and approaches. Neighborhoods that are distant from concentrated black settlements, have a past history of racial stability, have a high proportion of rental housing, possess a large institutional anchor, are located in metropolitan areas with small and moderately segregated black populations, and have thriving housing markets and strong amenities have generally been able to sustain racial integration. The Southwest Side had none of these things.[74]

An institutional anchor with political power that generated its own housing demand would have made the greatest difference. Presences like universities, hospitals, and military bases have historically been at the core of many racially integrated urban neighborhoods. Hyde Park benefited from the University of Chicago, in terms of both its economic and political power and the constant demand of its largely white, educated middle-class students, faculty, and staff for nearby homes and apartments. The flow of economically stable households seeking to live in the area kept the streets busy and safe, businesses solvent, and the housing market strong.

Despite Alinsky's hopes for the OSC, and for the archdiocese and its parishes, the Southwest Side had nothing comparable.[75] Even if local churches retained some white parishioners, they were unlikely to attract new younger ones. The territorial basis of urban Catholicism was rapidly diminishing, as theological splits, racial conflict, and demographic change led to the suburbanization of Catholic identities and institutions. The OSC itself could not play this role, either. It did not have nearly enough control over the local housing market, or the resources to shore up the structural strength of the entire Southwest Side, or the ability to sufficiently disperse the growing black population. Alinsky's inability to implement quotas was a factor here, as was the fact that so many white neighborhoods in the city and especially in the suburbs continued to exclude black families. To affect the housing market enough would have required federal action to open the suburbs and political organizing by the OSC on a broader geographic plane. Neither occurred.

"An Island of Sanity in a Sea of Confusion?"
Race, Property, and Politics

In what was arguably the most politically involved, active, and organized city in America, the OSC steadfastly avoided traditional politics. In light of the divisions of race, religion, geography, and ideology that already characterized the group, Alinsky and his staff concluded that involving the OSC in electoral politics, and challenging the Daley machine in particular, would be suicide.

This judgment may have been sound, but it clearly limited the OSC's ability to shape the politics of property and racial geography.[76]

While the OSC beckoned white homeowners to envision a racially mixed but predominantly white Southwest, the well-worn treads of Chicago politics reinforced racial segregation. For the OSC to succeed in altering the relationship between race and place on the Southwest Side, it had to venture into the arena where that relationship was forged and reinforced: local politics. The OSC was a regional city organization taking on metropolitan issues that it was unlikely to resolve without a broader political effort.

The importance of politics for issues of race and housing was never more apparent than in the fair housing campaigns of the mid-1960s. While the OSC did (admirably) move toward racial liberalism, exemplified by its endorsement of the 1963 fair housing law, thousands of white homeowners in the area moved very much in the opposite direction. This was done in large part through the political arena, where the only advocates of residential integration tended to be civil rights groups and white liberals with no local base. The absence from political discussions of the OSC and its vision of an alternative racial geography ensured that the possibility of even limited racial integration never entered the debate over Chicago's Great Question. The issue was politicized in terms of fight or flight, and "us" against "them." Alinsky had a pragmatic argument for racial retreat, but it never got a hearing.[77]

Could the OSC have changed this? It may very well have been powerless to overcome the interests and identities developed through the past half century of racial geopolitics on the Southwest Side. Even if the OSC had found a way to enter the larger political arena, it is quite possible that no one would have listened, substantial parts of its membership would have been alienated, and the group would have collapsed.

Nonetheless, integration on the Southwest Side simply was not viable without at least a partial end to racial containment elsewhere in the region. Without that, the only means left to Alinsky and his organizers would have been organizing on a broader geographical scale, to build a constituency for broader solutions to the Great Question than fair housing laws and local goodwill. The OSC needed to make it clear to white homeowners in the Southwest Side that the viability of their neighborhoods was heavily dependent on what occurred elsewhere. To assert or attempt to establish the autonomy of any one part of the region's political economy and social geography was impossible. Ultimately, to achieve geographically broader solutions, the OSC needed to create identities, interests, and coalitions that were equally broad. This could not be done without confronting Chicago's racial geopolitics beyond the Southwest Side, as well as within the OSC's constituents.

Alinsky believed that democratic political organizations had to emerge within small territorial units with natural bonds of unity and identification. This involved using the institutions, leaders, and belief systems of residents to bridge local differences, build horizontal linkages, and create a set of identities and interests that would allow people to understand how their problems were connected to larger issues and institutions. A community organization then would be in a position to mobilize local resources, accumulate power, broaden local participation in institutional decision-making, and win outside acceptance as the area's bargaining agent. This would create a new structural and democratic connection between the community and outside organizations and institutions, and also provide a means for professional organizers to broaden local identities and interests through participation in the give-and-take of pluralist bargaining.

For Alinsky, this approach called for initially vilifying outside groups and institutions to generate a sense of community unity and identity and create the basis for attacking local problems. He certainly took this approach on the Southwest Side. To Alinsky's credit, the OSC never used blacks as its target; most of the group's ire was directed toward real estate agents and blockbusters. In this respect, he tried to weaken the connections drawn by many local whites between neighborhood turnover and their new black neighbors. Simultaneously, however, his quota proposal, and the larger goal of white middle-class predominance, made the protection of white racial capital a high priority—and thus by extension, still posited black in-migration as the primary threat to it. In a racialized social geography this organizing approach promised to reinforce the attitudes and interests that perpetuated resegregation and white flight in the first place, if Alinsky and his staff could not construct a political technology that would broaden the OSC and its goals.[78]

Alinsky's tendency to stress easily winnable issues early on gave the OSC a relentlessly local focus. Influence over city or metropolitan-level actors and processes would have to emerge from a deeply embedded local power base. Alinsky had little confidence in the ability of single-issue groups and "masthead" liberal organizations to seriously affect Chicago's housing market and its politics. Moral suasion had had little influence, and most of the liberal housing organizations found themselves continually rebuffed by both blacks and whites.[79]

Alinsky was probably tactically sound in his insistence that organizing for racial integration had to begin at the local level. But his general aversion to both theory and ideology prevented him from articulating how he saw the relationships between the OSC, its concrete strategies and actions, and the larger structural issues that made integration so elusive. Alinsky's answer ultimately resided in his belief that an alternative racial geography would (and could only) be achieved as a by-product of the OSC's daily struggles and organizational growth.

Alinsky needed to build a community organization prepared to join with groups from throughout the Chicago area to exercise political power, open up housing markets, and challenge the geopolitical identities and interests that upheld racial segregation. In 1961 John McDermott, of the Chicago Catholic Interracial Council, had warned that the Southwest Side would find it increasingly difficult to be "an island of sanity in a sea of confusion; an island of stable, normal integration in a sea of racial segregation." He was correct.[80]

Conclusion

Chicago in the early to mid-1960s was not the most hospitable time or place for efforts to create residential integration. Few neighborhoods even attempted it. The South Side ghetto continued to expand toward Chicago's southern border while whites increasingly decamped to the suburbs, which maintained exclusionary land-use policies. Job and retail growth was increasingly centered in the suburbs as well; the city lost a substantial chunk of its white middle class during the decade. The Daley machine, meanwhile, increasingly tied itself to white homeowners' perceived interests in residential segregation.

If the OSC was to foster stable residential integration, it appeared to have very little time—and a deeply inhospitable political context—in which to do so. Lacking the means, the vision, and the time to assemble a powerful metropolitan coalition, the OSC could obtain only Pyrrhic victories. Good intentions were not enough. While Msgr. McMahon continued to fight the good fight—he came out of retirement to help his by-then-all-black neighborhood organize the Southwest Community Action Coalition in 1971—the OSC essentially evaporated in 1969. The short-lived coalition fought for many of the same goals as its predecessor, but not integration.[81]

By the mid-60s fair housing activists around the country became increasingly convinced that without a frontal attack on metropolitan segregation by the courts and the federal government, local activists struggling for racial justice would be overwhelmed, and equal opportunity would be impossible to achieve. In a 1966 strategy paper for the National Committee against Discrimination in Housing, attorney Richard Margolis noted the growing number of groups like OSC and praised them for their willingness to "stay and stay integrated." But he worried that without immediate action to confront metropolitan segregation, "the people directly at war with galloping segregation" would be overwhelmed by forces beyond their control. They simply could not act at the scale necessary. "They need help," Margolis urged. That help did not materialize in Chicago or elsewhere. It still hasn't. Chicago's suburbs remained almost completely closed to black families. The federal government refused to challenge metropolitan segregation when it had the resources and the clear moral imperative to do so.[82]

"Whiteness," as George Lipsitz puts it, "never has to speak its name, never has to acknowledge its role as an organizing principle in social and cultural relations." One of the crucial ways racial privilege organizes social, political, and economic life is through the construction of a social geography that tends to reinforce it. In the twentieth century, the spatialization of racial hierarchies came to define the way many Americans—black and white—saw cities and their problems, saw themselves, and saw one another. The resulting racial divisions and inequalities continue to limit policy options and life chances for millions of Americans.[83] Given these obstacles, the OSC's efforts are admirable, instructive, and important. Preaching interracialism in Hyde Park was one thing; trying to bring it about by organizing in the "belly of the beast" was quite another. Alinsky's ideas and his efforts have much to teach us about the politics of racial geography in the postwar American city.

The valiant effort of Alinsky and the OSC to run up the down escalator of Chicago's metropolitan racial geography coincided with a renewed push by black Chicagoans to forcefully exert themselves on issues of race and place. This happened within the OSC and in the city as a whole. Sparked by Alinsky's Woodlawn Organization, civil rights groups coalesced into a coherent and effective force for change in the early 1960s. In 1966, Dr. King would join them in an effort to break open Chicago's housing market, focusing on the white neighborhoods just to the north of OSC territory. While the OSC never formally joined this movement, it increasingly found itself taking similar positions. Alinsky had always insisted that integration was impossible without an organized black presence in Chicago. He would put this to the test in Woodlawn.

6

"We Will Not Be Planned For"

The Creation of the Woodlawn Organization

> The very pith and marrow of our work . . . is to create situations in which people can think and act constructively and effectively on the serious moral problems which are theirs. We firmly do believe that when people have the opportunity, they will live up to the highest expectations.
> SAUL ALINSKY TO REV. CHARLES LEBER, April 1959

> There is nobody to speak for the community. A community does not exist in Woodlawn.
> CHICAGO PLANNING DEPARTMENT, March 1962

By the early 1960s, decades of housing and labor market discrimination, as well as political powerlessness, had concentrated black workers in the jobs and industries most vulnerable to economic change and bound them to segregated neighborhoods increasingly devastated by disinvestment, and also poorly served by public schools, city services, and law enforcement. "As a boxed-in minority," Alinsky wrote in the *General Report*, "the paramount objective of the Negroes must be to break through the vexatious physical and social isolation they are held in." Previous attempts had failed, and "the edifice of segregation stands without a tremor." "Whether we are addressing ourselves to the family, the child, housing, juvenile delinquency, residential segregation, job discrimination, low wages or whatever the reader cares to mention in connection with the Negro population," he continued, "we are stymied before we are under sail. No instrument is at hand's reach to work with." A powerful black mass organization, Alinsky believed, was the only way to shake the structure. Without it, black Chicago would "not [be] able to realize its potential force."[1]

Alinsky and his IAF staff created the Woodlawn Organization (TWO) in 1960. TWO's story weaves through many of the larger events, ideas, and mobilizations of the turbulent 1960s—the Freedom Rides, the Chicago Freedom Movement, the War on Poverty, the Black Power movement, and community control. TWO and its members sought to define and institutionalize a philosophy of self-determination by trying to envision an alternative racial geography that lay somewhere between fostering individual social and geographic mobility and "gilding the ghetto." In the process, TWO activists struggled to

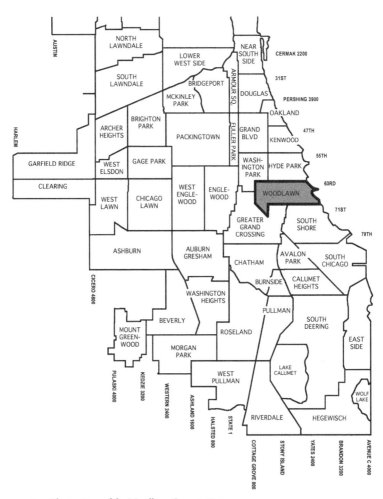

FIGURE 6.1. The territory of the Woodlawn Organization.

articulate a relationship between race and place that enabled them to build power locally while simultaneously attacking the racial inequalities embedded in the housing and labor markets of the Chicago area and in the national welfare state. TWO helped to jump-start Chicago's Black Freedom Movement and played a nationally important role in stretching and defining the limits of

President Johnson's War on Poverty. It was arguably Alinsky's most successful organizing venture.[2]

Woodlawn and the Birth of TWO

By the time Alinsky and his staff arrived in 1960, Woodlawn's ninety thousand residents were overwhelmingly black and increasingly poor. As late as 1950 Woodlawn had been only 17 percent black. Ten years later, after the white housing market there had vanished, blacks made up 89 percent of the population. By 1960, only 8,450 whites were left.[3]

The collapse of industrial employment in the 1950s and 1960s combined with racial discrimination, metropolitan residential segregation, and unequal schooling to devastate black urban neighborhoods. Unskilled and semiskilled black workers and their communities bore the brunt of the loss of urban manufacturing jobs brought on by industrial deconcentration and automation. Job losses were heavily concentrated in black neighborhoods, and new industrial and mercantile facilities were disproportionately located in the suburbs, which used exclusionary zoning to keep blacks out. Between 1955 and 1963 the majority of plant closings in the Chicago area were in the west and south industrial districts, with the south district (which included Woodlawn) losing 7 percent of its plants and 22 percent of its jobs.

From 1963 to 1977, industrial employment in those districts fell another 50 percent. Jobs that were covered by unemployment compensation fell by 4 percent in Chicago's predominantly black neighborhoods in the 1960s, even as the black population expanded by 38 percent. Woodlawn lost about 14 percent of these positions during the decade. In contrast, employment increased by about 5 percent in predominantly white areas, despite a 19 percent decline in the city's white population. The rate of black labor-force participation in Chicago declined from 78 percent to 68 percent from 1959 to 1969, with devastating effects. By 1970, the rate in Woodlawn was 54 percent, among the worst in the city.[4] Conditions were made significantly worse by housing segregation. As jobs fled to or emerged in suburban Chicago, housing discrimination prevented black workers from relocating. The suburbs were 4 percent nonwhite in 1960 and also in 1970, even as 320,000 blacks moved to the city during the decade.

The areas with the most industrial job growth were those farthest from black neighborhoods, and those that lost the most jobs were almost entirely black. "The location of jobs has been radically dispersed," the Chicago Urban League (CUL) found in 1964, "while Negro residential opportunities are still basically confined to the ghettoes." Less than one-fifth of Chicago blacks owned a car, and suburban rail services tended to abandon stations in areas that had flipped from white to black residence. The trains also didn't run late enough to accommodate those working night shifts.

Blacks paid more for their housing and retail purchases than whites, were paid less for comparable work, and faced longer and more expensive commutes than whites. Though not often stated as such, metropolitan open occupancy was clearly an economic issue as much as a civil rights one. Chicago was hardly unique; from 1951 to 1965, manufacturing employment in five metropolitan areas increased by 1.5 million—but it fell by 360,000 jobs inside the cities.[5]

Despite the fair employment laws enacted outside the South since the late 1940s, racial discrimination continued to limit black prospects, particularly in the private sector. The lowering of racial barriers had had no effect on the status of black workers relative to whites, the CUL observed in 1966, particularly for the unskilled. Illinois's Fair Employment Practices Law of 1961 applied only to employers with seventy-five or more workers, leaving most of the city's black labor force unaffected. Even after accounting for differences in age, education, sex, seniority, and length of residence in Chicago, unskilled black workers made twenty-four cents less per hour than whites. Better education seemed to make little dent; black college graduates earned less on average than white high school dropouts. Black workers were shut out of skilled and supervisory positions in the manufacturing sector, as well as the building trades. Increasingly, they were trapped in the lowest-paying service and retail jobs. By the early 1960s, growing numbers of black men were unstably employed or had dropped out altogether as the demand for low-skilled workers dried up. Altogether these forces were creating what the CUL called "an urban peasantry."[6]

Good-paying white-collar jobs were available in the Loop, which was better served by public transit than the suburbs, but job discrimination (particularly in the private sector) and the poor quality of ghetto schools made these positions inaccessible to many blacks as well. While legislation and civil rights activism greatly reduced blatant racial discrimination in the private labor market, as late as 1960 Chicago employment bureaus reported that 98 percent of their white-collar job orders specified no black applicants. New jobs were often filled internally by existing white workers. Racial discrimination was tempered somewhat by civil service rules and credentialing in the public sector and in the independent professions, making the lack of access to quality education all the more important for blacks.[7] In effect, a rung of the ladder of economic opportunity had been removed, limiting the experiences, connections, and skills that would open opportunities for the poorest and least-educated blacks.[8]

Black poverty was also becoming increasingly concentrated geographically as black middle-class families moved out of the traditional South Side ghetto. Woodlawn was becoming more uniformly poor and poorer relative to the city as a whole.[9] Its average family income was only 57 percent of the area mean by the mid-1960s; more than one-fifth of Woodlawn residents received public assistance, and that number was rising. Unemployment in East Woodlawn exceeded 30 percent, while one in six employed residents were paid poverty wages.[10]

By 1970 Chicago had a dozen neighborhoods that were 95 percent or more black; 57 percent of blacks lived in them. Nine of the twelve—including Woodlawn—were below the citywide median income for black families, itself only 70 percent of the white median income. While 21 percent of all black families in Chicago lived in poverty, 29 percent of those living in these virtually all-black neighborhoods did. Unemployment was similarly concentrated geographically; over 25 percent of Chicago's jobless lived in these twelve neighborhoods. As in Grand Boulevard, Alinsky would face the dilemma of trying to build an organization in a community with large numbers of young and poor newcomers, a deteriorating job base, and a fleeing black middle class.[11]

"Dissolving the Walls of Racial Partition": Alinsky's Vision for Woodlawn

Woodlawn was dotted with a number of large churches, small businesses, and neighborhood associations, but rapid change was taking its toll. The speed of racial turnover in Woodlawn—especially in the last three years of the 1950s—left area churches, block clubs, schools, and small businesses in chaos. As of March 1960, 87 percent of Woodlawn residents had moved into their homes in the preceding six years. West Woodlawn did contain a substantial black middle class, but it was precarious. Like similar families in Grand Boulevard, they were worried about the stability of their neighborhoods and the value of their homes and businesses. They were worried about their children as well; schools were increasingly overcrowded and youth unemployment was rising sharply, as was gang activity. Many began to move to more stable neighborhoods to the south, like Chatham. Not surprisingly, black middle-class groups were among the first to reach out to Alinsky. Woodlawn's growing poor population, however, lacked an organized voice.[12]

According to Rev. Arthur Brazier, the young black minister of the Apostolic Church of God, local clergy believed that "within two or three years Woodlawn would become a major slum, unless a vigorous community organization was developed."[13] While the South East Community Conference

(SECC) claimed to represent Woodlawn, it primarily spoke for the University of Chicago, which had real estate interests and ambitions in the area. According to the journalist (and future TWO director) Squire Lance, the SECC had "forfeited any right to speak for the community" by abetting the displacement of thousands of poor black families from Hyde Park. Woodlawn residents deeply distrusted the university and feared that the bulldozers that had rolled over a large part of Hyde Park would soon cross the Midway Plaisance, which separated the two neighborhoods.[14]

Only the Greater Woodlawn Ministerial Alliance appeared to speak for black Woodlawn.[15] In the spring of 1958 it began to discuss the social and physical deterioration of the neighborhood with public officials and community groups. Fr. Martin Farrell, the white pastor of Holy Cross Church, was the catalyst, pressing Alinsky to initiate a project in the area.[16] Woodlawn "must have a neighborhood organizer quickly," he wrote. "It is the most disorganized community in the US." There was little in the way of local leadership, he wrote, but there were "many ordinary people in the community waiting for somebody to lead them to effective democratic organization."[17]

Alinsky sent Nicholas Von Hoffman to assess the area. Von Hoffman largely agreed with Farrell's assessment, particularly in the area east of Cottage Grove Avenue. While West Woodlawn was a working and middle-class district with well-organized block clubs and churches, Von Hoffman told Alinsky, crossing Cottage Grove into East Woodlawn "is like going to another planet." Area residents suffered from increasing crime, overcrowding, a shortage of parks and school space. The police were absent when needed and abusive when present. Housing was old, overcrowded, dense, and in poor condition. About half the units in Woodlawn were in large apartment houses, mostly absentee owned—the greatest concentration of such buildings of any low-income community in Chicago.

East Woodlawn lacked traditional forms of leadership and organization, but Von Hoffman resisted describing the community as disorganized. Rather, East Woodlawn residents were "indifferent to 'community problems' because there is nothing in Woodlawn that would attract loyalty." Leaders and social groupings lacked any kind of vehicle for mass activity and cooperation. Unless a People's Organization is created, Von Hoffman wrote, "Woodlawn will continue to grow as a slum until conditions there will be favorable for total land clearance."[18]

Farrell recruited Charles Leber and Ulysses Blakeley, co-pastors of Woodlawn's venerable First Presbyterian Church. Leber and Blakely—who were white and black, respectively—had been recruited in 1957 by the church's University of Chicago–dominated leadership to lead the rapidly changing congregation.[19] Both men had read Alinsky's *Reveille for Radicals* in seminary. According to them, Woodlawn was "dying for lack of leaders ... it seemed any effort would be futile unless our own people could direct it, choose their own goals and work for them, grow in the process and have a sense again of the rightness of things."[20]

Farrell, Leber, Blakeley, and Brazier met with Alinsky late in 1958. Alinsky told them he would come only if he was invited by a representative group of black residents, and if local churches and institutions could raise enough money up front to keep the organization going for at least two years. Von Hoffman had estimated the cost of running an organization for three years at $143,660. He believed the two qualifications were crucial if he and his organizers, all of whom were white, were to be considered legitimate.[21]

Alinsky argued in a letter to Leber that communities like Woodlawn were "hot with change ... boiling with mobility and daily deterioration into worse and worse slums, communities which have no controlling force with which to cope with any of the problems from without or within." But he was confident that a reorganized civil society might help to create and sustain community identification. As he put it: "The very pith and marrow of our work is the creating of a vehicle that permits the individual a greater say in the circumstances that govern his life ... our job is to create situations in which people can think and act constructively and effectively on the serious moral problems which are theirs. We do firmly believe that when people have the opportunity, they will live up to the highest expectations."[22]

In January 1959, Farrell and the other ministers organized a meeting of Woodlawn clergy. Msgr. Vincent Cooke, of Chicago Catholic Charities, had agreed to underwrite a community organization for $50,000 over three years if the Presbyterians and the Lutherans would do the same. The Presbyterians were more cautious, however, and the Lutheran delegation was strongly opposed to the idea. The OSC critic Walter Kloetzli, the secretary of urban church planning for the National Lutheran Council, demanded that Alinsky himself appear to answer questions. Leber, Farrell, and Blakeley were insistent that an ecumenical alliance was essential for success, so Alinsky agreed to join more than thirty clergy and lay leaders at the Union League Club on February 17.[23]

The meeting was tense. Alinsky was often coy and irreverent when subjected to hostile questioning, but realizing the stakes, he behaved himself. Kloetzli interrogated the organizer about the IAF's methods and history, and his reasons for considering Woodlawn. Woodlawn, Alinsky responded, "has within it representative issues that affect every community in the city of Chicago. What happens in Woodlawn would be significant for urban redevelopment in the rest of the city."[24]

Alinsky outlined four goals for a community organization: first, to make churches more effective in speaking up against and correcting injustice; second, to build sufficient community strength to lobby for public services; third, to provide community representation in conservation and renewal programs; and finally, to develop a "positive climate of hope" for residents.[25] As for his method, Alinsky summarized it thus: "The IAF believes in a revolutionary doctrine: given the opportunity, people in a community can work out their own problems. The issues of a community are those that the people living in the community consider to be important, not those that others may think are important for them."[26]

Despite the harsh questioning, Alinsky left the meeting encouraged. As he put it: "It was the kind of ministers that came to us . . . it meant going into trouble, lots of trouble. If they were willing to, who was I to say I've got other things to do?"[27] While Alinsky didn't discuss the group as a means of breaking down residential segregation, it was clear that his Grand Boulevard vision remained unchanged. An organization in Woodlawn had two goals, he wrote in his 1960 grant proposal to the Schwarzhaupt Foundation: making positive changes in the lives and living standards of residents, and taking "an essential step necessary for the general goal of an orderly progression toward open occupancy in Chicago."[28] Alinsky did not see these as incompatible or potentially contradictory aims. Success in addressing the everyday needs of Woodlawn residents would eventually make the organization powerful enough to address the broader structures that impoverished them economically and politically. It would also help participants to draw connections between their local troubles and larger issues. While he insisted that the citizens of Woodlawn direct the goals and methods of the group, he was confident that they would move toward residential integration.[29]

Residential integration was essential, Alinsky argued. If action were not taken to "begin large-scale residential integration as rapidly as possible," he warned, the city would have to "concede the disappearance of more white communities, the marooning of more churches, and the multiplication of the economic, social and political havoc directly traceable to the Chicago segregation system." Accordingly: "The Negroes have the greatest, immediate interest in integration. They are the ones who must bring the issue to a head in Chicago, as they have already done in the Southern states." The black population must be "dispersed or integrated . . . a black and white solution is doom for cities like Chicago." A black Woodlawn organization was critical to this process, because only "a Negro organization representing immediate Negro self-interest can be the occasion by which the whites see that integration is not only in their own long range self-interest, but also in their self-interest now." Such a group would disabuse whites of the notion that blacks "run down real estate, that they prefer to live by handouts from organized charity and they cannot climb to be more than clients reliant on other people's direction." Whites would thus no longer fear the possibility of black neighbors.[30]

Urban renewal, Alinsky told the IAF board, just moves the ghetto somewhere else and "leaves the tangle of social, political, moral and economic conditions that manufacture a Woodlawn untouched." "The state the people find themselves in, not the houses they live in, lie at the bottom of most of these problems," he argued. We can no longer ignore "low wages, segregation, and the people's general impotence" if the lives of black Chicagoans are to improve. A Woodlawn organization would provide hope, the possibility of individual mobility, and a powerful advocate for black interests and integration.[31] "One way or another the new forces and direction born in the South during the past few years will come tumbling into the northern Negro ghetto," Alinsky told the IAF board. It could either be "a valuable tonic" that would lead to a racially integrated city or "a destructive element taking a reckless and

FIGURE 6.2. The founders of the Woodlawn Organization. *Left to right*: Rev. Arthur Brazier, Fr. Martin Ferrell, Rev. Ulysses Blakely, and Rev. Charles Leber. Box 170, folder 1730, Saul Alinsky Papers, Special Collections, University of Illinois Chicago.

violent course." "We hope," Alinsky wrote, "that the Woodlawn Project will bring forth the first of the two possibilities."[32]

"We Will Not Be Planned For": Building TWO

The IAF began organizing in Woodlawn in 1960, creating a federation of local organizations and civic associations called the Temporary Woodlawn Organization (TWO) early the next year. Much like the BYNC, the temporary organization was "built and maintained by the concurrent pursuit of a wide variety of little issues." Alinsky's organizing approach stressed the importance of giving people something to do, however small; this gave people a sense of efficacy and empowerment, encouraging them (with help) to draw connections between the personal and the political.

Woodlawn was divided into eleven geographical areas, each represented by a TWO vice president. The standing committees—housing, schools, civil rights, social welfare, community maintenance, and consumer practices—encouraged broad community participation and the development of new leadership. Committees also provided concrete benefits to local residents, encouraging membership growth. Typical residents might come to TWO with a complaint or issue, but committees pursued issues only if those residents agreed to actively participate. They would ask the residents to organize a club in their building, church, or neighborhood, which would then join TWO.

Grassroots organizations "must constantly increase the area of participation," Alinsky insisted. "Unless you have the kind of climate and the kind of operation where people begin to develop as people . . . you're not pushing too much of the democratic process." He believed the approach was particularly important in black communities, because "we whites have done such an extraordinary job . . . of brainwashing on the blacks that many blacks do consider themselves second class citizens." "It isn't just getting the services, it's how you get them," Alinsky explained. "It's whether you get them as an independent and an equal . . . instead of this good-hearted, paternalistic, colonial society outside that says 'we're doing this for your own good.'" John Fish describes TWO's approach as "not only to help change the objective conditions in Woodlawn but also to provide the occasions whereby the residents could participate in, even bring about, their own liberation." This effort was particularly critical in East Woodlawn, which lacked the rooted and institutionalized civil society found west of Cottage Grove. There, TWO served as both social movement and ward heeler.[33]

The Housing Committee was typical. When tenants came to it for help with abusive or absentee landlords, they were instructed to call their neighbors together for a meeting that TWO activists would attend. As one reporter described it: "At first the meeting went like most meetings go. One or two people got up and did a lot of loud mouth talking. They said the same old things about how the landlord was evil and was stomping on the people's rights. The people said 'amen' and agreed with the loud talkers but they did not know what to do. The TWO told the people they had to stay cool and not get excited. 'Cold, cool anger which lets you think is what you need,' the TWO representatives said." Tenants would then select someone to research their landlord and relevant city laws. The Housing Committee would organize a negotiating session with the landlord; if the landlord balked or was unreasonable, TWO would formally file complaints with the city. On occasion, it would also organize rent strikes or picket landlords' homes.

As residents formed community groups, TWO grew. It built upon the already-existing civil society when available; when not available, the organization essentially created it. In some cases, TWO sought to subvert and replace existing groups. The Schools Committee, for example, worked with local parent-teacher associations, but if they were found to be "no more than an arm of the principal and not willing to tackle the basic issues concerning education in the ghetto," the committee would organize competing parent education councils.[34]

Unlike Alinsky's other organizations, TWO was led by a large and growing contingent of female activists. Although men usually held the top leadership and staff positions, by 1965 four of TWO's eleven area vice presidents were women. Women were also very active as committee chairs. This was particularly true as TWO became more involved in issues of poverty, welfare, and social services after 1963. Phyllis Hubbard and Ida Davis, for example, led the Housing Committee in its campaign to get absentee landlords to clean up apartment buildings. Ollie Clark was perhaps TWO's most prominent female activist, but she was by no means atypical. Like many upwardly mobile black families in Chicago, the Clarks moved south in the early 1950s, settling in West Woodlawn. Active in block clubs before the IAF arrived, Clark jumped into TWO with both feet, serving as chair or vice chair of virtually every committee at some point. Clark was particularly interested in politics, and in 1966 (at the age of sixty) ran for the state senate as a Republican. While she lost, she was the first black woman in Illinois to receive the endorsement of either political party.[35]

Alinsky's organizers were all white. From the outset, he worried whether this would make it difficult for TWO to sink deep roots in the community. He intended to quickly recruit black staff and pull nonlocal organizers out as soon as feasible. "They knew it would be their own show," he said in 1962.

This effort was largely successful; by 1965, TWO's staff was all black. Robert Squires was one of the first local black residents recruited by Nicholas Von Hoffman. A college graduate, a veteran, and a former Catholic seminarian, Squires had developed strong organizing skills in Catholic settlement houses, which he quickly put to work in Woodlawn during the winter of 1960. Charismatic, funny, streetwise, and diplomatic, Squires struck Von Hoffman as a natural organizer, capable of garnering respect from all classes in the area.

East Woodlawn was Squires's responsibility. He walked the streets daily, speaking to "every bookie, every whore, every policy runner, every cop, every bartender, waitress, storeowner, restaurant owner."[36] He "trained local persons in how to run a meeting, how to overcome opposition, how to instill racial group pride, how to cultivate secondary or new leadership." While more traditional groups, like churches, block clubs, and the clergy association joined quickly, Squires concentrated on the smaller and more informal gatherings that tended to draw Woodlawn's newest and poorest residents: beauty shops, sports teams, janitors' associations, choirs, youth clubs, and pool parlors. He became staff director of TWO in November 1962.[37]

While Alinsky initially served as the public face of TWO, it was led by a series of impressive and increasingly well-known black presidents—beginning with Rev. Arthur Brazier. Described by Von Hoffman as "a man of integrity, intelligence and stem-winding oratorical gifts," Brazier was TWO's most influential leader. He was also its most important public intellectual; his 1969 book *Black Self-Determination* outlined the intellectual evolution of the organization's guiding philosophy. Born in Hyde Park in 1922, Brazier served two years in India and Burma during World War II before returning to Chicago to work as a spot welder and a letter carrier. Ordained in 1951, he was called to Woodlawn's Apostolic Church of God in 1960. With a congregation that was conservative both politically and theologically, Brazier hesitated to get involved in TWO. But Von Hoffman successfully persuaded him that ministry and activism were not incompatible.[38]

By 1962, when a local paper ran a series on TWO alongside a large photo of an intense-looking Brazier—with the caption "POWER"—he had become well known in the city. He struck a public balance between militant rhetoric that expressed well the anger and resentments of black Woodlawn, and more conciliatory tones that implied the willingness of TWO to participate in the ethnic patronage politics of the city in the Daley era. Described as "a big, hungry cat of a man, handsome and well-built, tough and articulate, militant but realistic," Brazier quickly became a leader in Chicago's larger civil rights movement, serving as the first convener of the Coordinating Council of Community Organizations (CCCO), formed in April 1962 to fight racial segregation in public schools. Brazier even contemplated challenging Rep. William Dawson for Congress in 1966.[39]

Lynward Stevenson and Leon Finney also took leadership positions, with the latter succeeding Brazier as president in 1967. Stevenson, pastor of Bethlehem Covenant Presbyterian Church and a onetime classmate of Martin Luther King Jr. at Morehouse, was born in Kentucky and moved to Chicago in 1950. He became active in TWO in 1962, through its Schools Committee. He gained national attention in 1964, when he testified before Congress on federal poverty programs in Chicago, and subsequently chaired TWO's Social Welfare Committee—by 1967, the organization's most important committee.

Born in Mississippi in 1938, Leon Finney grew up in West Woodlawn. As he put it, "I have been on Sixty-Third Street, it seems, all my life." A college graduate and ex-Marine, he ran his family's barbeque business until the Southern Black Freedom Movement inspired him to get involved in his community. Unlike many participants in TWO, Finney carried a strong memory and attachment to the history and institutions of Woodlawn. The black Woodlawn of Finney's youth was populated by professionals and middle-class people, as well as "working folks." There was a "continuity of community" that had changed radically by the early 1960s. This memory inspired the twenty-six-year-old Finney to get involved in TWO in 1964; the next year he joined the paid staff. In 1967 he became president, supervising TWO's increasing involvement in community development. Finney and Alinsky remained close friends until the organizer's death.[40]

The creation of a membership base for the organization was greatly aided early on by the heavy-handed efforts of the University of Chicago to expand its campus. Using federal urban renewal funds, the university wanted to clear a major strip of the neighborhood to establish a buffer zone between itself and the increasingly poor and black population of Woodlawn. As would happen in countless city neighborhoods around the nation in the 1950s and 1960s, the threat of urban renewal would help to foster a strong sense of territorial identity among citizens in the bulldozer's path. In late 1960, the university tried to get immediate city approval to begin clearing land for its South Campus project.

Drawing on the Greater Woodlawn Ministerial Alliance, Von Hoffman quickly assembled forty Woodlawn residents to protest the plan before the City Planning Commission (CPC), and succeeded in getting public hearings scheduled for January 1961. Word of the university plan—and of the fledgling organization's early success—spread in Woodlawn; Von Hoffman had little trouble mobilizing three hundred local citizens to attend. The new group made two demands: any renewal project involving Woodlawn had to be part of an overall plan for the community, and Woodlawn residents had to be involved in all planning and implementation. "We want to build up our area until it is the most outstanding in Chicago, and we want to do it with and for the very people who are living here now," Brazier told reporters. The CPC agreed and ordered the City Planning Department to begin putting together a proposal for the renewal of Woodlawn. "In the past it always seemed as though the University of Chicago ran the city government, but Thursday was a different story," a TWO member observed. "They were listening to us down there . . . not just the university."[41]

Alinsky and his staff had been engaged in an increasingly vitriolic conflict with the University and its liberal supporters for years. TWO's vocal opposition to the South Campus plan merely exacerbated it. As an alumnus and a Hyde Park resident—his son David attended the university's Lab School—the confrontation was often personal for Alinsky. Faculty that he had counted as friends and neighbors avoided him. Occasionally they confronted him directly: Bruno Bettelheim, a world-renowned child psychologist and a concentration camp survivor, bumped into Alinsky and Von Hoffman on the Midway. Bettelheim "raged at Saul, accusing him of organizing the dregs of society—criminals, 'animals,' drug addicts, rapists—and generally letting a scourge loose on decent white people." Alinsky looked at him "with a little crooked smile on his face, puckered his lips, one of his mannerisms, and said in a low-key, quiet voice, 'Bruno, you're full of shit,' and walked on."[42]

It is hard not to be struck by the anti-Catholicism, antiblack racism, and empirical inaccuracy of many of the arguments of these critics. Equally striking is the unquestioning acceptance of the university's good intentions. These were, without exception, liberal men—some of the city's most prominent, in fact. And part of their critique of Alinsky's work was rooted in a more widespread liberal suspicion of his divisive rhetoric and a legitimate worry that organizing in the ghetto would reinforce segregation rather than undermine it. And no one could miss the prominent role of Chicago Catholics in white resistance to black neighbors, in the Back of the Yards and elsewhere. Ultimately, however, the criticisms proved not only wrongheaded but also counterproductive: each salvo fired at Alinsky and his staff increased their legitimacy in the eyes of Woodlawn residents. "One of my problems in Woodlawn was my white skin," he observed. "But . . . a lot of Woodlawn people began saying, 'if those big fat-cat downtown white papers are calling Alinsky a dangerous, no-good son of a bitch, then he must be all right.' "[43]

Starting with an April 1961 letter to the *Chicago Sun-Times* and continuing in a series of articles over the next year, Harold Fey and others contended that Chicago was caught in a battle between two opposing forces: those advocating an "open society" and those seeking a "closed society." Fey put the University of Chicago, the SECC, and Protestant churches in Woodlawn and Hyde Park in the former, and the IAF and the Archdiocese of Chicago in the latter group.

According to Fey, TWO was a tool of forces (the IAF and the archdiocese) determined to circumvent democracy and keep blacks contained in the ghetto. They feared that Woodlawn blacks displaced by the South Campus project would "increase pressures for integration in other areas," like the Back of the Yards. The archdiocese was seeking to save all-white parishes, Fey argued. While the archdiocese couldn't stop the "positive re-development" of Hyde Park and Kenwood by the university and its allies, in Woodlawn it was building the foundation for an IAF-led political movement "whose object is to establish control over American urban society by raising up from its ruins a 'power structure' dictatorship based on slum dwellers." He singled out Woodlawn's Protestant clergy for their participation in TWO: "How can they command respect for Christian moral standards when they advocate and practice the ruthlessness of the class war, magnifying and exacerbating differences?" The goal of TWO, Fey wrote, "is to keep poor people where they are by opposing redevelopment and setting up 'power' organizations to divert their social and political energies against forces making for one pattern of basic civic improvement."[44]

The university, Brazier responded, was hardly a paragon of the "open society," given its decades-long advocacy of racially restrictive covenants and its ongoing efforts to keep blacks from moving into the southeastern corner of Hyde Park. TWO "is overwhelmingly black," Brazier pointed out, "and to say we have a passion to keep ourselves in the slums is utterly ridiculous ... by the very nature of its membership [TWO] is unalterably opposed to racial segregation and discrimination."

Dick Harmon, a seminarian, gathered forty-one signatures from dozens of ministers and theologians on a letter that echoed Brazier. It was published in full in *Christianity and Crisis*, while excerpted versions found their way into Chicago newspapers. They reiterated the sordid racial history of the university, defended the archdiocese, and pointed out that while both the OSC and TWO were on record favoring an open occupancy law, neither the SECC nor the university nor the *Sun-Times* was. The university, "like other institutions, seeks to defend its own property interests, power and control," they pointed out. In the past it had done so with restrictive covenants; more recently it had made use of code enforcement, zoning, and screening. That the black residents of Woodlawn were suspicious of the university was hardly surprising. Indeed, the Archdiocese of Chicago had a better record of opposing racial segregation than either the university or area Protestant organizations.

Sounding a lot like Alinsky, the ministers and theologians insisted that an open society wasn't possible without the exercise of power. "Is the ideal an 'openness' which places no restraint on the powerful?" Ultimately, the only check on the powerful was organizing by the people. "Whatever openness comes to American cities will only come about when presently disorganized Negroes . . . develop structures of power capable of compelling white structures, such as real estate and banking interests, to break down the present pattern of segregation." "That," they concluded, "is what TWO is about." Edgar Chandler, of the Church Federation of Greater Chicago, separately praised TWO's efforts at interfaith cooperation.[45]

While the threat of the bulldozer helped to jump-start the formal creation of TWO, an event a thousand miles away infused it with the energy and moral purpose of a social movement: the Freedom Rides of May 1961. Von Hoffman received a long-distance collect call from a former TWO volunteer who was now working with the Congress of Racial Equality (CORE) on its campaign to integrate interstate bus terminals in the South. The volunteer, like many other Freedom Riders, had been severely beaten. He asked Von Hoffman to organize a benefit for some of the Freedom Riders in Woodlawn. This provided an opportunity to appeal to both middle-class West Woodlawn and the greater neighborhood's growing poor population, which TWO was struggling to reach.

Von Hoffman, who hadn't expected much of a turnout, was stunned by the response. More than eight hundred people jammed St. Cyril's church, while others listened outside on loudspeakers. A passing of the hat garnered $600 for CORE; one of the Riders taught the audience the song "We Shall Overcome." Von Hoffman excitedly called Alinsky to bring the good news. "I think we should toss out everything we are doing organizationally and work on the premise that this is the moment of the whirlwind, that we are no longer organizing but guiding a social movement," he told him. Alinsky hesitated, worried that a morally crusading focus on dramatic action would detract from day-to-day organizing. But as Von Hoffman later reflected, Alinsky had always demonstrated a willingness to "jettison long-held, old ways of organizing" if the circumstances changed." He trusted Von Hoffman's judgment and agreed.[46]

TWO quickly capitalized on the untapped identification of black residents with the southern civil rights movement, by organizing a freedom ride of its own in August: forty-six buses took more than 2,500 black passengers downtown to register to vote, as part of TWO's Voter Cavalcade. It was the largest voter registration event ever at Chicago's City Hall; the chief clerk was forced to add fifty extra workers to the regular Saturday staff of fifteen to accommodate the numbers. This mass registration was done without the assistance of the regular Democratic organization's precinct captains—a clear message to Daley about the potential power of this fledgling black group.[47]

"One of the reasons we are having the cavalcade," Brazier told the press, "is to ignite among minority group members in the north the same spirit that Rev. Martin Luther King and the others have gotten started in the south ... school and residential discrimination is practiced on a wide scale in northern cities, too. Job discrimination is rampant here as well as in the south." Harold York, of the Essex Blackstone Improvement Club, agreed: "We have a bad school situation in our area ... only a united and determined community is going to be able to put an end to that kind of thing once and for all." TWO publicly pledged to make Woodlawn the first 100 percent registered community in the city.[48]

As was evident in the Grand Boulevard study, Alinsky had come to believe that black political power was the key to ending segregation in Chicago. By creating a powerful and politically independent TWO, the cavalcade offered the possibility of real leverage. As a reporter described it: "The local politicians have gone from a position of scoffing and threatening ... to incredulity, to open support of TWO. They are now prominently present at every major meeting, shaking hands and sweating." The cavalcade also familiarized thousands of Woodlawn blacks with TWO and increased both the size and the intensity of community involvement. While the organization still struggled to get support east of Cottage Grove, TWO's growing membership would prove useful in its confrontation with the University of Chicago.[49]

The City Planning Department issued its Woodlawn Plan in March 1962. It was an uncreative mishmash of traditional expert and agency-dominated planning, which called for large-scale demolition and the construction of highrise public housing. The primary goal of the plan was clearly to get the University of Chicago the land it wanted—and to get the city its share of the federal urban renewal money generated by the South Campus project. It had no provisions for citizen input whatsoever. The deputy commissioner of planning summed up the city's sentiments: "There is nobody to speak for the community. A community does not exist in Woodlawn." Woodlawn residents "will be given an opportunity to react."[50]

The plan also completely avoided the fundamental issues of race, segregation, and poverty. "Inasmuch as the municipality is to some extent responsible for the discrimination and the segregation which shapes and gives the environment its leitmotif," Von Hoffman argued, "how is the city's Department of Planning going to do anything about it? In instance after instance the city . . . has used its power to promote and perpetuate segregation and discrimination." The City Planning Department's plan evasively attributed Woodlawn's poverty and deterioration to "certain pressures" being exerted by "general conditions." This is "as diffident a way as could be found to describe the iron wall of segregation that is in large measure responsible for the overcrowding of Woodlawn and other Negro communities," Von Hoffman pointed out. "If they don't have the guts to state the facts, you can imagine how unrealistic and futile whatever they may come up with will be. They want to clean out the Augean stables with a feather duster."[51]

One week after the CPC plan's release, 1,200 delegates from over one hundred organizations gathered in the Grand Ballroom of the Southmoor Hotel for TWO's first Community Congress. Alinsky invited two outside speakers: Martin Luther King's associate Ralph Abernathy and Mayor Richard Daley. The mayor's presence was almost certainly a result of the Voter Cavalcade. Daley promised the convention that urban renewal wouldn't touch Woodlawn "until every individual and group has had a chance to present his recommendations." After rechristening itself the Woodlawn Organization, the delegates adopted self-determination as the organization's goal. TWO would "fight with all its strength to win for the people of Woodlawn the deciding voice in the development of a plan for Woodlawn." "They've been calling us 'welfare chiselers' and 'dependent' and everything else in the book," a delegate told the *Chicago Daily News*. "Now they distrust us for trying things for ourselves." The assembly instructed TWO to use its power to "insure genuine citizen participation in the planning and rehabilitation of our community," by hiring its own planning consultants. Urban iconoclast Jane Jacobs, covering the Woodlawn controversy for *Architectural Forum*, offered her services to TWO.[52]

Social Policy from the Bottom Up: The 1962 Social Policy Planning Memo

In the spring and summer of 1962, TWO began a remarkable and unprecedented exercise in citizen-based urban planning. It hired the architect William Nelson to help citizens understand the city's plan, analyze local problems, articulate community goals, and put together an alternate plan. Von Hoffman, TWO leaders, and Nelson presented study outlines for discussion at dozens of meetings around the community. They created a dictionary of city planning terms to enable residents to understand and criticize the city's proposal, and they assembled slides, maps, and audiotapes documenting Woodlawn's history and present state.[53] Woodlawn was divided up into twenty geographic sections; groups and institutions in each area sent representatives to open meetings in which the city plan was discussed, preliminary local proposals were drafted, and members of a community-wide planning committee were elected. Thousands of residents participated.[54]

In a discussion guide, Nelson and Von Hoffman described and critiqued the city's plan in clear language, summarized the objectives delineated in months of community meetings, and introduced Woodlawn residents to a range of more radical and community-based urban planning ideas. The primary objective for TWO was clear: to create "an environment which is physically attractive, safe, and clean; which is operationally efficient; and which is socially and economically stable and conducive to the development of better individual, family and communal life." Most urban renewal plans failed to understand or appreciate city life, and thus did little to create a "suitable community environment" for an urban neighborhood, Nelson and Von Hoffman argued. "It is the great diversity and mixture of uses which gives the central city its flavor and exciting vitality," they wrote, clearly reflecting the input of Jane Jacobs. Rarely did renewal efforts consider making a predominantly low-income neighborhood more livable for its residents. The city's plan was unacceptable, because it sought to physically eliminate "blighted areas" without resolving the "fundamental problems," Nelson and Von Hoffman wrote. "The people of Woodlawn are human beings whose desires, needs, and ideas should be given chance for expression, whose dignity and rights should be honored, and whose interest should be paramount over any institutional or bureaucratic objective," they argued. Indeed, the City Planning Department's proposal left out the more stable West Woodlawn altogether, ignoring TWO's demand for a comprehensive plan that encompassed the entire Woodlawn community and that tied together physical reconstruction with economic and political empowerment.

At the same time, however, Nelson and Von Hoffman challenged TWO to grapple with the racial dilemmas implied by a grassroots remaking of a segregated community. Segregation and discrimination were fundamental obstacles to making a place like Woodlawn "suitable" in the long run. Would making Woodlawn "an attractive and livable community . . . not result in 'containment' of the Negro community?" Ultimately, Nelson and Von Hoffman concluded, Woodlawn residents "must decide for themselves whether the cause of integration as well as of individual betterment might not be far better served by the dramatic and effective stabilization and rehabilitation of a community through self-determination."[55]

In July 1962, TWO printed the twenty-page Social Policy Planning Memo (SPPM) in the local newspaper, outlining the community's goals. It was an extraordinary document, detailing the range of issues restricting black freedom and offering well-considered solutions. In effect, TWO proposed a radical revamping of urban renewal and the construction of social policy from the bottom up. The memo was sharply critical of the inadequacy and paternalism of the welfare state, the negative assumptions about black communities and capacities embedded in traditional urban development programs, and the inadequacy of Chicago's segregated black schools. The observations and recommendations demonstrated in detail the social learning enabled by TWO's participatory process. Initially focused primarily on stopping the bulldozers, by the end of the summer of 1962 TWO activists had developed a complex understanding of black powerlessness and ways to grapple with it. They had also begun to realize the limits of TWO's reach, given the city's racial politics and the growing poverty of Woodlawn residents.

"Grave questions of policy," TWO argued, "cannot be decided by experts in a democracy." All planning must "increase individual self-reliance and personal freedom" and respect self-determination of the community and the individual. In dealing with social problems, TWO "does not go along with the new fashion of prescribing big doses of social work and social workers to solve the social difficulties tied in with housing . . . the most serious and obvious causes are found in segregation and discrimination. They are not to be resolved by any kind of therapy, but by the people's militant social action."

Citizens must have not just veto power over programs affecting their lives, TWO argued. They must have a role in design and implementation as well. Residents of Woodlawn should be trained to carry out the program and be paid for their work. In addition to providing jobs, this would result in programs staffed by workers with local knowledge. Unless programs were embedded in local civil society and institutions, TWO insisted, they simply wouldn't work. And for this to occur, local citizens had to have the power to act responsibly. "We will not be planned for as though we were children," a TWO spokesman told reporters.

Woodlawn, TWO asserted, was not simply an aggregation of buildings or a group of individuals seeking greener pastures. It was a community, with a representative bargaining agent and a sense of identity. Thus, all planning must seek to preserve Woodlawn for those who live there. This was to be done by preserving and enhancing a healthy diversity of land use and economic status, constructing and protecting public spaces, and focusing on low-rise housing. Rent subsidies were preferable to public housing, because they could be used to break down residential segregation—but if public housing was to be constructed, it should be small scale and dispersed. TWO proposed to set up a nonprofit corporation to develop and rehabilitate housing.[56]

A first stab at defining self-determination, the SPPM challenged not only the Daley machine but also some of the prevailing assumptions about citizenship, power, and representation that underlay the American welfare state. It challenged the managerial model of social change that increasingly defined liberal programs by insisting that ghetto residents suffered from a paucity of power, not just a lack of resources, skills, and opportunities. TWO's vision of black ghetto residents as citizens to be mobilized and empowered, rather than clients to be served, anticipated much of the political ferment that would surround the federal Community Action Program a few years later.

TWO also sought to construct a spatial strategy that balanced the imperatives of building black institutions and local power with attacking the regional racial geography. While acknowledging the power of metropolitan racial segregation, TWO also made an argument about the intrinsic value of black working-class communities and the importance of making them livable. Individual social and geographic mobility was valuable, but so was community viability and stability. In keeping with Alinsky's thinking, TWO decidedly refused to see these imperatives as incompatible.

In early July 1963, seven hundred TWO members staged a sit-in in Daley's office to try to push him and the University of Chicago to the negotiating table. It worked: twenty-five TWO members met with university and city officials on July 16 and reached an agreement. Clearance on university-owned land was to be selected, rather than wholesale, and no clearance was to take place until housing had already been constructed for those displaced. Only vacant buildings would be razed, and no high-rises were to be built. TWO would have veto power over the director of the South Campus–Woodlawn project and have a majority on all committees. The University of Chicago got the land it wanted, but a 13.2-acre area on both sides of Cottage Grove Avenue between Sixty-First and Sixty-Third Streets was offered to TWO, for the construction of mostly middle-income townhouses for the estimated 1,312 families to be displaced by the South Campus project. Financing for Woodlawn Gardens, as TWO named it, would come from the federal government, under section 221(d)3 of the National Housing Act, which allowed nonprofits to obtain federally insured long-term low-interest loans to build middle-class housing.

TWO firmly rejected the Department of Urban Renewal's suggestion of including public housing, fearing that it would result in the geographic "saturation" of low-income projects rather than the construction of scattered units. Middle-income housing, Brazier argued, "is an absolute must . . . there has been nothing for the average man." Fifth Ward alderman Leon Despres agreed, praising the proposed project for "converting a wasted area into good residential land" and "offering hope for a stable, interracial middle income community" on the Hyde Park–Woodlawn border. In partnership with the Kate Maremont Foundation, TWO organized a nonprofit corporation to purchase the Cottage Grove strip and obtain federal funding to build Woodlawn Gardens. The project ultimately housed more than two thousand people in twenty-seven low-rise buildings. Construction contracts were awarded to black businesses, helping to crack Chicago's white-dominated building trades.[57]

Conclusion

Alinsky and Von Hoffman had placed strong emphasis on early victories for TWO, and its initial success in challenging the University of Chicago and the city greatly aided community confidence in its ability. At the same time, however, the SPPM revealed the two interrelated issues that seemed to be of most concern to Woodlawn residents: education and poverty. As the organization sought to build its base beyond the block clubs and churches of West Woodlawn, it would find itself transformed—in ideas, focus, and membership. In the process it would help to reenergize Chicago's Black Freedom Movement.

7

Truth Squads and Death Watches

TWO, Schooling, and Spatial Strategy

> The Woodlawn Organization will not see our youth castrated by junk-heap, dead-end education . . . if they are afraid to send their children to school with ours, then this issue is truly a white man's problem.
> REV. LYNWARD STEVENSON, 1965

> We will go on organizing . . . to speed up integration in our schools. But in the meantime, what is to be our position with reference to ghetto schools that are not going to be integrated in the near future? . . . the old problems still exist.
> TWO STATEMENT, January 1967

By the early 1960s there was a growing recognition among civil rights leaders and the broader liberal left of a looming crisis of structural unemployment in the nation's black ghettos, as young black men increasingly found themselves trapped in communities with declining job prospects. Alarmed by racial disparities in wages and unemployment, discrimination by unions, and high school dropout rates for black teenagers, the NAACP's Roy Wilkins warned Congress in 1963 of a "major economic disaster facing the Negro community."[1] Chicago's opportunity structure was shifting away from the semiskilled and unskilled factory jobs in which black workers were concentrated and toward jobs that required adequate schooling. As devastating as the intersection of segregation, discrimination, and economic change was for neighborhoods like Woodlawn, its impact on young workers was even more debilitating.

The unemployment and labor-force participation rates of young black and white men began to sharply diverge in the late 1950s. The trend was structural rather than cyclical; black youth joblessness continued to climb regardless of the state of the larger economy.[2] From 1950 to 1973, black teenage labor-force participation fell from about 68 percent to 35 percent nationally, while white participation remained stable at 63 percent. By the end of the 1960s, more than 50 percent of black males (and 33 percent of black females) aged sixteen to nineteen were unemployed in Chicago—five times the rate for whites. Nearly 25 percent of black men between the ages of twenty and twenty-four were as well.[3]

Observers have generally viewed Northern black school activism in the decade or so after the *Brown* decision as primarily focused on legal equality and desegregation, separate from demands for economic opportunity. This overlooks the integral place of social and economic rights in civil rights discourse. Black activists had long favored a capacious definition of social and economic rights, and the robust state action necessary to make these rights tangible. The role of the state in creating and reinforcing racial inequalities in schools, housing, and labor markets maintained a boundary between public and private that both protected white privilege and rendered it invisible to some. But TWO and other black groups had little difficulty understanding the ways race, class, and social geography were intertwined. Bringing that understanding to the larger white public—and sparking positive action in response—is a struggle that remains unresolved today.

There was a desperate sense of crisis among parents and activists in the early 1960s—of a ticking time bomb. White politicians and pundits, admiring the tight labor markets and high growth rates that seemed a permanent part of the American economy, opined about the dangers of "rising expectations" among young urban blacks as a possible cause of riots and nationalist militancy. Perceptions at the black grass roots were decidedly different: a generation of young black adults trapped in segregated neighborhoods and schools, without access to the opportunities the state was finally, begrudgingly, acknowledging their right to possess. For groups like TWO, integration was always about leveraging those opportunities. Denied the chance to do this in a time frame that fit the urgency of the situation, black activists across the urban North were forced to consider alternatives.

It was the urgency of this dilemma, more than anything else, that galvanized TWO's activism on education and poverty issues. It is also the critical backdrop for understanding the emergence of black schooling movements across the urban North in the late 1950s and early 1960s. TWO launched a movement for racial desegregation and equality in Chicago's schools that would help to spark a citywide civil rights movement, garnering national attention and ultimately drawing Martin Luther King to the city to launch an attack on residential segregation. By the time of King's arrival, however, TWO had shifted its focus. Frustrated by the intractability of metropolitan segregation and the political ecology that supported it, pushed by the rapid decline of the opportunity structure for Woodlawn's increasingly poor population, and enticed by the resources offered by the War on Poverty, by the mid-1960s TWO had become increasingly focused on community development, poverty, and the reshaping of the welfare state. While the organization never abandoned its commitment to residential and educational desegregation, crisis conditions in Woodlawn demanded an increasingly local focus. Federal urban and economic policy reinforced this spatial strategy, with serious consequences for the fight against metropolitan inequality.

Schooling and the Opportunity Structure in Woodlawn

Racial inequality in Chicago was deeply rooted in the increasing segregation of the public schools. While the segregation of elementary schools was largely in place by 1930, the racial separation of the high schools was mostly a post–World War II phenomenon. By 1964 more than 80 percent of all black students attended schools that were 90 percent or more black. Since 1957, twenty-two new schools had been built. All but one was either all white or all black. Schools that were more than 90 percent black absorbed almost all the increase in black student enrollment between 1950 and 1965.

While this was in part a function of growing residential segregation, it was also the result of decades of deliberate action by public school officials. In 1958, an investigation by the NAACP found that Chicago's public schools were more segregated than could be explained by housing segregation alone. For decades administrators rigidly adhered to a neighborhood school policy and refused to acknowledge or address the plight of black students. The school district even refused to collect or publish data based on race, leaving it to activists to inform the public of the growing crisis. Attendance-area boundaries and feeder patterns were manipulated to maintain segregated schools, both creating and reinforcing white expectations of racially homogeneous schools. The acceleration of segregation and inequality had sparked protest in the black community as early as the 1930s and 1940s, led by the Chicago Urban League (CUL) and the NAACP. While their efforts did force school officials to put aside some of their more overtly racial policies, the overall pattern persisted.

Segregation, in conjunction with ongoing migration from the South, had led to tremendous overcrowding in black schools. While an ambitious construction program in the 1950s (as well as the geographical expansion of the black ghetto) had lessened overcrowding somewhat, it remained almost exclusively a black problem. Nearly half of the black schools ran double-shift schedules, and out of the twenty thousand students on double shift, 80 percent were black. Even so, class sizes were 25 percent larger in predominantly black schools. Nearly half of black elementary schools had more than thirty-five students per classroom, compared to just 12 percent of white elementary schools. Five of the eight mostly black high schools had enrollments 50 percent over the designed capacity. Only four of the twenty-six predominantly white high schools were similarly overcrowded. Indeed, there were nearly twenty-two thousand empty seats in predominantly white schools. In addition, black schools had more uncertified and inexperienced teachers, fewer library books, and a much higher percentage of students living in poverty than mostly white schools. A 1963 study ranked Chicago high schools by the socioeconomic status of surrounding neighborhoods and found that seven of the ten lowest-ranked schools were more than 90 percent black.[4]

Vocational education for black students was segregated and inadequate and did little to address the racial segmentation of the labor market. Most craft-union apprentices were educated at the Washburne Trade School; in 1960, only 26 of its 2,700 students were black. "Almost all of Chicago's major institutions for vocational training and public education operate according to a dualism based on race," CUL researchers argued in 1966. Vocational and public schooling reflected (and reinforced) the discriminatory labor market "by providing inferior educational facilities to Negro pupils" or excluding them altogether.

As a result, the CUL found, "Negro pupils often have difficulty meeting the basic reading and writing requirements of employers." And if they were hired, it was generally for temporary jobs or those with no hope of advancement. Recursively, because black students rarely got jobs that required formal education and advanced training, there was little economic pressure on schools to provide them an adequate education. In effect, the public school system screened black youths out for employers.

Education was a critically important economic tool for blacks, as it had been for much of the century. Even as many racial barriers to white-collar employment began to fall in the 1960s, poverty and inadequate schooling threatened to deprive young blacks of the economic benefits of education. According to the CUL, "the Negro youths' psychological frame of reference about self and future" manifested as "a negative attitude toward school (preparation) and about future job opportunities (incentive). Thus the incentive threshold is low." In addition, schools failed to acknowledge or respect black students' culture, history, and self-worth. Decades of insensitivity experienced by black parents and their children in their encounters with white teachers, principals, and students undermined the foundations of trust and authority essential for learning. Increasing dropout rates in black high schools was one consequence.

In a study from the late 1960s, CUL researchers Harold Baron and Bennett Hymer struggled to describe the nature and totality of racial inequality in the Chicago area. "There is an overriding system of race relations characterized by the social and economic subjugation of the Negro via the whole constellation of institutions," they wrote. While not dictated by law, "the institutions operate almost as though they were ordained by a body of statute." Without immediate action, the CUL concluded, "the children of unskilled Negro workers and the sub-employed are destined to follow in their parents' footsteps . . . employment conditions for unskilled Negro workers will continue to deteriorate so long as no significant changes occur in the school system and the labor market."[5]

It is thus no surprise that the Black Freedom Movement throughout the urban North focused on public education in the late 1950s and early to mid-1960s. While the 1954 *Brown* ruling had certainly provided legal sanction and political inspiration, the movement to improve and desegregate urban schools was also closely tied to a growing awareness of fundamental shifts in the metropolitan opportunity structure. But as the Black Freedom Movement challenged school segregation and inequality, school boards, courts, and the white public responded by defending the concept of the neighborhood school and describing segregated patterns as de facto—the result of housing segregation, itself the product of private market actors, rather than state action (and inaction).

Chicago Schools Superintendent Benjamin Willis, who increasingly became the focus of TWO's and other black organizations' ire, was a strong defender of the neighborhood school idea. Willis refused to collect or acknowledge data on race and school attendance, and he argued that if black educational achievement was inadequate, then neighborhood schooling was the proper remedy. His response to the overcrowding issue was new construction in black neighborhoods, despite vacancies in all-white schools. As Kathryn Neckerman has argued, this pattern of dissembling (which preceded Willis) led to a growing anger and cynicism in the black community about the school system, creating a crisis of legitimacy and trust that affected student classroom performance and parental interactions with teachers and administrators.[6]

Alinsky rightly pointed out that this approach promised, in effect, a return to the "separate but equal" policies invalidated by *Brown*. "Willis will employ any artifice, device or delay to avoid fulfillment of the spirit as well as the letter of the US Supreme Court decision on school desegregation," he argued. Alinsky told a reporter: "No single issue in the US today is more important than integration. Segregation will go when it becomes too damn expensive to keep up. When it becomes expensive, people will spout off that it's immoral, it's unchristian. TWO will make it too damn expensive for city hall, particularly Benjamin Willis, whose arrogance is matched only by his salary."[7]

From an organizer's perspective, Willis was almost too good to be true—a perfect villain and an obvious target. Instead of denying the existence of segregationist school policies, Alinsky remarked, Willis should have shifted blame onto residential segregation. This would have been a "fifteen year job to try to break down the segregated residential pattern of Chicago. We did not have the power to start that kind of conflict." Instead, Willis continued to deny the obvious. His willful ignorance on race mirrored that of the city's political elite as a whole, enabling TWO to easily crystallize the issue and mobilize around it.[8]

In the summer of 1961, the NAACP and the *Chicago Defender* organized Operation Transfer, which encouraged black parents to register their children in less crowded all-white schools on the South Side. Despite widespread overcrowding in predominantly black elementary schools, the Board of Education refused to grant black students transfers. Rev. James Webb and the Chatham–Avalon Park Community Council invited the lawyer Paul Zuber, from the national NAACP office, to help them file a lawsuit in September 1961. Zuber argued that Chicago's neighborhood school policy was unconstitutional. Led by Schools Committee chair Ollie Clark, TWO quickly jumped into the fray, supporting the Webb suit and using hearings and direct-action protests to draw attention to the issues that gave rise to it.[9] In November 1961, more than nine hundred Woodlawn residents crowded into the ballroom of the Southmoor Hotel to participate in TWO-organized hearings. Three public school teachers testified about local conditions; fearful of losing their jobs, they wore hoods and sheets to disguise themselves. Parents told of classes held in basements, attics, and corridors due to overcrowding. Alinsky, who rarely made public appearances in Woodlawn, spoke.

One week later, fifteen Woodlawn parents in black capes began a "death watch" at Board of Education meetings, representing the "mourning of Negro parents for the plight of their children." They sat quietly in the first two rows at each meeting through the winter and spring. When parents in Vernon Park were arrested for holding a sit-in at the overcrowded Burnside School in January 1962, twenty-five ministers of the Greater Woodlawn Pastors' Alliance (GWPA) visited them, and TWO members were arrested in a sympathy sit-in. Burnside had 1,600 pupils housed in a school built for 865; a nearby white school had empty classrooms. TWO also picketed the offices of William Caples, chair of the Board of Education, demanding that the city acknowledge the existence of school segregation and its duty to address it.

In February 1962, after Willis refused to release an inventory of classrooms, a TWO "truth squad" of four mothers took cameras to vacant classrooms in all-white schools to demonstrate that the overcrowding of black schools was caused by purposeful segregation. This was much more than a political stunt; the lack of concrete information about racial imbalance in the schools limited the ability of TWO and other groups to address it. When Mattie Postel, Zephyr Craddock, Josephine Maxwell, and Doris Packnet went to the Kellogg school in Beverly Hills (and found four vacant classrooms), the principal had them arrested on charges of trespassing and disorderly conduct. They were found guilty and given suspended sentences. Schools across the South Side removed "welcome signs," and Woodlawn school officials threatened parents with arrest if they visited their own children's schools.[10]

When white voters rejected a school construction bond in April 1962, Willis built temporary classroom structures made of corrugated steel to house black students. These "Willis Wagons," as TWO dubbed them, demonstrated the unwillingness of either Willis or Daley to grapple with the consequences of racial segregation. By 1964 there were 250 portable classrooms in the city, the overwhelming majority of them in black communities.

Much like his approach to public housing, Daley chose to meet black demands with measures that exacerbated racial segregation, while pacifying white voters. Both Daley and Willis claimed that the public school system needed to remain "above politics," conveniently overlooking the racial politics that had governed decision-making for decades. Willis's defense of the neighborhood school (and Daley's backing of Willis) was widely supported by white Chicagoans and by all the major newspapers. "City officials are well aware that many thousands of white families, justifiably or not, already have fled the city rather than send their children to school with Negroes," the *Chicago Daily News* noted. Of course, strong adherence to the neighborhood school policy was itself a key contributor to racial turnover and white flight. As black families moved into white areas and sent their children to their new neighborhood school, whites were left with few credible objections. Fearing that educational conditions in ghetto neighborhoods would be replicated in their communities, most whites pulled their children.[11]

In May 1962, when word got out that Willis Wagons were to be installed in Woodlawn schools, Rev. Lynward Stevenson and the Schools Committee organized an effective and widely publicized one-day boycott of Woodlawn's Carnegie elementary school. More than 90 percent of Carnegie's 1,350 students participated. More than one thousand Woodlawn parents signed a petition to the state superintendent of instruction demanding public hearings. "Our children are being deliberately and systematically segregated," they argued. Willis Wagons "are an evil instrument to maintain a segregated school system," Rev. William Baird told reporters. "Our only objection is on a simple moral basis that it is wrong to contain Negroes in ghettos," Brazier explained to *Jet* magazine.[12]

While Alinsky's approach emphasized the strategic importance of keeping a local focus, TWO rapidly embedded itself in Chicago's regalvanized civil rights movement. In April 1962 TWO joined with other groups to form a citywide interracial civil rights coalition, the Coordinating Council of Community Organizations (CCCO), with Arthur Brazier as convener. While other CCCO groups had broader profiles, TWO essentially served as the coalition's grassroots base through 1964. The journalist Charles Silberman concluded that "the leadership and organizational strength TWO has provided is the only thing that has kept Chicago's civil rights coalition together." He also praised Brazier as the "principal spokesman on civil rights for Chicago Negroes."[13]

The CCCO jumped into the national spotlight in the summer and fall of 1963. In an effort to get the *Webb* case dismissed, the Chicago Board of Education agreed to two small concessions: a study group, headed by University of Chicago sociologist Philip Hauser, would investigate racial inequalities in the schools and propose solutions, and a transfer plan would be implemented in September to allow a small number of top black students to transfer to predominantly white schools with honors programs.

The transfer program, despite its largely symbolic nature, evoked a violent response from white neighborhoods. Thousands picketed around Bogan High School on the Southwest Side in the fall. Willis promptly removed it and fourteen other predominantly white schools from the list. The Board of Education ordered him to reinstate them; he refused. After black parents won a court order, he resigned in October 1963—but the Board of Education, under intense pressure from Southwest Side whites, refused to accept it and backed up his reduction of the transfer list. Willis quickly became a heroic symbol of resistance across the white bungalow belt. His arguments were given further legitimacy when a US District Court dismissed the *Webb* suit that fall, concluding that plaintiffs hadn't provided enough evidence that school segregation in Chicago was intentional. "De facto segregation resulting from the implementation of a neighborhood school policy, or residential segregation is not enough," the court argued.

In October 1963 the CCCO organized a citywide school boycott to protest racial segregation. It received national attention. Participation was extraordinary: a quarter million students stayed home, roughly half the public school population. TWO played a central role, organizing a conference on direct action at Woodlawn's First Presbyterian Church in July 1963. More than eight hundred delegates from CCCO-member organizations participated in workshops on welfare, housing, school, employment, legislation, and health. While he knew that TWO "could shut up every school in their neighborhood tighter than a drum," Alinsky initially hesitated to involve TWO in the boycott. He acquiesced when the Willis resignation controversy emerged. "The status quo came to the rescue," he observed. The *Chicago Defender* aided the cause by publishing lists of mostly church-sponsored freedom schools that kids could attend instead. Students got involved, too: through the Student Woodlawn Project, organized by a University of Chicago graduate student, youths distributed leaflets in schools and churches.[14]

TWO activists put the Social Policy Planning Memo together in the midst of the 1962 Carnegie school boycott. The context, as well as the process, had a powerful effect on the contents of the document—and ultimately on TWO's strategy. The intransigence of Willis and city officials on desegregation, rapidly escalating youth unemployment, the patent inadequacy of Woodlawn's schools, and the growing activism of poor residents in the organization all combined to give the SPPM a powerful sense of urgency and analytical acuity. TWO activists had come to see poor schooling, the lack of good jobs, and poverty as inseparable. The result was a shift in spatial strategy that would increasingly focus TWO on poverty and local social provision. While never abandoning belief in the desegregation of schools, TWO increasingly privileged local action over structural change.

TWO's critique of Chicago's schools was sharp. Because of school overcrowding, "twenty per cent less money [was] spent per capita" on Woodlawn's black children. More money needed to be spent, to make up for past discrimination. Woodlawn's inadequate schooling was a direct result of a "non-sensical, vicious and demoralizing neighborhood school policy" that was intended to keep "the educational level of Negro children below [that] of white children." Indeed, "segregation has fostered a 'no learn' policy in Woodlawn schools." Low academic standards compounded the problem. A 1967 survey found that 74 percent of students in Woodlawn were "below level" in reading. But children were promoted "regardless of their achievements" while dropouts were "actually encouraged," because discouraged students saw no sense in hanging around school when they were not learning." More than half the students who completed eighth grade did not finish high school; 90 percent of Woodlawn eighth graders either dropped out before their senior year or were "in-school" functional dropouts.

TWO predicted that as a result 35 percent of the students graduating from Woodlawn schools would never hold steady jobs. Discrimination and automation had contributed to Woodlawn's high unemployment, but "children who cannot read or write will never have steady employment." Another consequence would be increased welfare dependency in the adult population. "Every child whom the schools have failed must be supported the rest of his life by the taxpayers of Chicago and the State of Illinois," the memo pointed out. Woodlawn's growing gang problem was another result.

TWO also criticized what was taught in Woodlawn schools. Vocational education was overly stressed while black history was ignored. Yet students shuttled into vocational tracks were facing limited futures—abetted and reinforced by the public school system, as well as discriminatory unions. All trade and vocational schools needed to educate students "how to fight for the jobs . . . [they] are being trained for." Ultimately, however, vocational education needed to be secondary to the liberal arts "unless the idea is to foster de facto segregation of Negroes in the arts, sciences and professions." A liberal education will give students "the tools they need to teach themselves . . . they are the foundation stones of individual self-determination," TWO argued, as well as citizenship. Black history was vital for similar reasons, TWO continued, because "many Negroes have been taught to doubt their own abilities . . . by studying the attainments of other Negroes, past and present, Negro children will gain a healthy pride in their past and hope for their own future."

Solutions had to address segregation and the immediate inadequacies of black schools simultaneously. "Many of Woodlawn's problems cannot be solved in Woodlawn," TWO acknowledged. School integration was the primary example, and it needed to be "the first order of business." Virtually all improvement of daily life in Woodlawn "depends on the integration of our schools." But the memo also suggested a variety of improvements to Woodlawn schools that were independent of citywide integration. Per capita spending needed to be increased and class sizes reduced, particularly in early grades. Lengthening the school day and instituting a compulsory summer session would help to "eliminate the academic double standard." The memo also suggested greater involvement of parents (and TWO) in area schools. "Generations of either mistreatment or patronizing misunderstanding" had led Woodlawn parents to distrust teachers and social workers. Discriminatory hiring within the system merely added to the problem. The solution was to hire parents as teacher aides and form a committee of teachers, administrators, and TWO members for each school. This would also give teachers "a means of learning about the people and what the people want." Finally, improved access to community-run adult education programs, with the promise of jobs for successful graduates, was critical for those who had been already harmed by the Woodlawn schools. By the middle of the decade, frustrated with the lack of meaningful school desegregation, TWO would seek grants and federal funds to implement many of these ideas.[15]

The school campaign had thrust TWO into the forefront of Chicago's Black Freedom Movement. At the same time, the process of the memo provided

Woodlawn activists with a remarkable opportunity to examine black education in a much broader analytical and political frame. Confronted with a rapidly deteriorating opportunity structure, as well as the intractability of Chicago's racial geopolitics, TWO activists began a strategic reassessment. By 1966, when the CCCO and Dr. King launched their campaign to end slums and open housing for blacks throughout the metropolitan area, TWO was focused instead on organizing Woodlawn's poor, improving area schools, and using federal funds to launch locally controlled social services.

The Local Turn: TWO Moves to a New Spatial Strategy

While TWO would continue to parlay the moral legitimacy, spiritual energy, and protest tactics of the civil rights movement into membership, power, resources, and publicity, starting in late 1963 the organization nonetheless began to move toward a new spatial strategy. Driven by Chicago's racial politics and its own organizational needs, as well as a growing awareness of the centrality of poverty to life in Woodlawn, TWO sought to build power locally. Without that, TWO activists decided, black Chicagoans would have little success in altering the conditions under which they lived. They (and Alinsky) came to believe that the CCCO's approach was doomed.

The lack of progress on schools, in particular, provoked a rethinking. A second school boycott, in February 1964, didn't generate the same response as the first one. And even the smallest movement toward school integration by the Board of Education was greeted with vehement resistance in white neighborhoods. The Hauser Report, released in March 1964, confirmed that Chicago schools were thoroughly segregated. Its reform recommendations were mild, but Willis essentially ignored it. The contemporaneous Havighurst Report was more aggressive in advocating purposeful school integration, but its call for a more flexible attendance policy, while empirically (and morally) sound, was a nonstarter politically.[16]

In August 1964 the Board of Education proposed mixing a small number of mostly white and mostly black schools together and redistributing their student populations. When the list of ten pairs of schools was released in November, parents of white students responded with uniform opposition. The Property Owners' Coordinating Committee (POCC), which was engaged in a battle with the OSC on the Southwest Side, threatened a massive white exodus if the board followed through. The board abandoned the plan in January 1965. The CCCO found itself divided, widely criticized, and at a strategic dead-end. While he remained an active participant, Brazier resigned his position as convener in order to tend to affairs more closely in Woodlawn.[17]

Forty-nine Northern public school districts took significant steps toward desegregation between 1962 and 1966. But Chicago was not among them.

Nationally, civil rights groups became increasingly frustrated with the lack of progress on school desegregation, both in the courts and at the local level. The US Supreme Court refused to hear any cases pertaining to school segregation in the urban North, and lower courts issued a series of contradictory decisions. Most revolved around the difficulty of discerning the segregative intent of school officials and whether the fact of racial separation was sufficient to invoke a judicial remedy.

Heightening the frustration, opinion polls reflected a growing white acceptance of school integration in the abstract. But in reality, even good-faith efforts were continually frustrated by the ability of many white parents to withdraw their children from urban public schools and move to the suburbs, an option that simply wasn't available to most black families. Whites viewed their avoidance of integrated schools as the pursuit of social mobility—not the product and producer of white privilege. While the vast majority of blacks continued to support school integration, as did TWO, a growing number of black activists across the urban North became agnostic about the value of desegregation. Some civil rights groups became open to compensatory education programs and experiments with community control of ghetto schools instead.

TWO continued to support school integration, but the crisis facing Woodlawn's young people demanded immediate attention and action. White resistance, legal ambiguities, and political powerlessness thrust TWO activists back upon their own resources.[18] Willis's intransigence on school segregation seemed to mirror the inflexibility of the broader political system. The 1963 mayoral election provided a turning point in Chicago's racial politics. Daley's opponent, Benjamin Adamowski, actively sought white ethnic votes by opposing open housing. He rhetorically linked ghetto expansion and increasing property taxes, both of which were deeply resented by the city's white homeowners. Adamowski won the white vote and nearly toppled Daley. Only the black vote saved him.

For the rest of the decade Daley would use racial issues (like support of Willis) to reorient the geography of his political base toward the Southwest Side bungalow belt, the most racially tense area of the city. In the words of William Grimshaw, "As the racial demands escalated, the machine increasingly took on the retrograde character of a southern white supremacist Democratic party." Rather than accommodate the growing black challenge or put together a racially progressive coalition of blacks and moderate whites—as Edward Kelly had two decades earlier—Daley chose to use political patronage to "wall off the rebellion taking place in the black wards" while further squeezing (and thus further delegitimizing) black machine loyalists.

Leon Despres drafted an insightful (if tongue-in-cheek) memo, describing Daley's post-1963 approach to racial politics: "While controlling the votes of Negro Chicagoans through partisan patronage and the national attraction of the Democratic label, make all necessary concessions to white segregationists by maintaining the pattern of racial housing segregation, school segregation, and social segregation." Ultimately, however, Daley had the wolf by the ears. "Since a pattern of housing and school segregation guarantees a growing ghetto and a declining city," Despres warned, "the segregation policy which wins each election hastens a tragic explosion." A growing number of black voters and activists began to divorce themselves from the machine, use direct action and lawsuits to demand city resources, and seek out alternative means for building power and challenging inequality, generally through local organizing. Middle-class blacks began to seek political independence, while many poor black voters opted out of electoral politics altogether, in favor of other forms of activism. TWO's shift occurred in this context.[19]

A *Chicago Defender* editorial in June 1964 reflected the frustration in the black community with the pace of change and the lack of viable political options. Civil rights legislation, like the 1961 Illinois Fair Employment Practices Law and the 1963 Chicago Fair Housing Ordinance, had deeply racialized city politics while having no appreciable impact on black opportunities. Chicago's Black Freedom Movement seemed to lack energy and focus. Why, the editors asked, is there "no strong day-to-day campaign on the Chicago front in the nation's civil rights battle?" Nahaz Rogers, of the Negro American Labor Council, blamed the machine for blunting the edges of black radicalism and accused some of CCCO's member organizations, like TWO, of refusing to "take strong stands on city-wide problems." While TWO is "possibly the finest community organization in Chicago," Rogers argued, "it does not seem anxious to indulge in militant city-wide projects."

TWO's Lynward Stevenson questioned the automatic association of militancy with citywide direct action. The Chicago movement had not "moved in the right direction," Stevenson told the *Defender*. "We are not aligned with power," he argued. The path to real change started at the grassroots. He encouraged voter registration, selective buying, and "more political activity on the precinct level." Stevenson and TWO had worked hard on Leon Despres's successful reelection in 1963—Daley sought to have him unseated—and would actively support other political allies in the coming years. While there was a place for demonstrations, Stevenson concluded, they were only useful if they were "mass demonstrations. People just look out their windows and laugh at picket lines."[20]

Stevenson's point was very much in keeping with Alinsky's organizing tradition: mobilizing public actions was useful, but only if they were widely supported, were strategically appropriate, and had ongoing grassroots power behind them. While Alinsky appreciated the gains of the CCCO, he was deeply critical of its approach. Movements that relied so heavily on protest and direct action, Alinsky argued, often felt compelled to demonstrate not so much because a particular situation demanded it but because "action, *any action*, was essential to keep the organizations alive." They became captives of their tactics "rather than the masters of power strategy on a broad front," and they struggled to sustain citizen interest between demonstrations. CCCO's 1964 school boycott was an example: the authorities had no reaction, and the "effects of the boycott were over the next day." Alinsky saw this as a "terminal tactic, one that crests, breaks, and disappears like a wave." The CCCO leadership could "console themselves with the 'psychological carry-overs,' 'public displays of support,' and similar prayerful hopes, but as for carrying on the conflict for integration, that was over and done with by the next day." "Nice memory," Alinsky quipped.

Alinsky argued that "The Achilles heel of the civil rights movement" is its inability to develop into a "stable, disciplined, mass-based power organization." "Periodic mass euphoria around a charismatic leader is not an organization," he told *Harper's Magazine* in 1965, obviously referring to Dr. King. "It's just the initial stage of agitation." While this might work in the South, where segregation took the form of overt "public butchery," and the movement could count on the "stupidity of the Southern status quo," in the North racial discrimination—while just as deadly—took the form of a "stiletto" rather than a "broad ax." "You can have 25,000 in a mass demonstration outside City Hall," Alinsky argued, but "Daley is a sophisticated politician, and he is . . . smart enough to know that in a couple of hours they are all going home, and tomorrow everything is going to be just as it was." Daley needed to be convinced that he was faced with a large, powerful, and growing organization that could deliver numbers when the cameras weren't on. "Belatedly many civil rights leaders have been rudely awakened to this situation," Alinsky argued. "It remains to be seen whether they have the skill, sensitivity and above all the infinite patience they will need."[21]

These strategic differences were brought into high relief in June 1966. After months of slow but often effective community organizing on the West Side, Southern Christian Leadership Conference activists began to press King and the CCCO to concentrate on housing discrimination in white neighborhoods. By providing a target (the real estate industry), such a campaign would offer plenty of opportunities for direct action and rapid change. Marches in white neighborhoods would hopefully provoke a surge of national outrage that would force the passage of the fair housing law currently bottled up in Congress. King agreed.

Alinsky and Brazier were among the most vocal critics of the decision, particularly after the riots in the West Side ghetto in July revealed the movement's shallow roots among young black men. Alinsky understood King's focus on national goals, Von Hoffman recalled, but he "believed that an organizer's first responsibility is to the people he has recruited. They joined for better housing or justice or jobs or community self-determination, not to be used in behalf of a grander cause." An open-housing campaign, even if successful, would largely benefit the black middle class. The immediate concerns of poor black Chicagoans, Alinsky argued, would be sidelined. The campaign would also undermine the possibility of interracial coalition by pitting blacks against working-class whites. Alinsky knew well that while whites on the Southwest Side could be easily provoked, the long-term goal of metropolitan desegregation required their pacification, not their antipathy.

"We believe in 100% open occupancy—the right to live where you want," Brazier told the *Chicago Sun-Times*. However, he added, "we also believe in a responsibility to the community where you do live, and this [Woodlawn] is an excellent community . . . it's a dynamic community." While some Woodlawn residents would of course leave—and metropolitan open occupancy would allow them to live wherever they could afford—"we want to preserve this community . . . we want to stay here."[22]

Slow community organizing was more likely to generate long-term change than direct-action mobilizing. "The King operation took on the look of Napoleon before Moscow," Von Hoffman recalled. "A little army stranded inside a vast and hostile terrain." "I think King is finished," Alinsky told the *Washington Post* in July 1966. "He's trapped. He can't get out of [Chicago] in less than ten months to a year and he doesn't know what to do if he stays." The organizer was prescient: in August, King left town and the Chicago Freedom Movement dissipated. Alinsky didn't believe defeat was a learning experience and had little tolerance for losses that could have been avoided. He was dismissive of moral victories. "Not all injustices can be righted," he told Von Hoffman. You have to pick your shots. "The work is too important for sentimentality."[23]

This was not all that divided TWO and CCCO. The CCCO opposed a $195 million Daley-supported municipal bond issue, aimed at leveraging federal funds for street and alley lighting, rapid transit extensions, new sewers, urban renewal, and municipal buildings. The CCCO worried that the money would be used to further buttress racial segregation; for decades city officials had consistently used similar public revenues for racial containment. The lack of black political influence, as well as the racializing of Chicago politics since 1963, made it likely that this pattern would continue.

But TWO, confident in its power to steer resources toward Woodlawn projects, decided to support the bond. "We cannot demand that slums be cleaned up and then deny the city the money to do it," Brazier told the *Chicago Defender*. The editors disagreed. The South Campus experience should have taught TWO activists that Daley would spend the money however he saw fit, they argued in late May 1966. Brazier "gives the impression that he would be satisfied so long as the resources of the bond issues were not used to increase the dimensions of segregation . . . our concern should be with the city's commitments to integration."

Brazier and TWO, however, believed that the CCCO and the *Defender* misunderstood the strategic issue at stake. The city had no "commitments to integration," and the passage or defeat of the bond issue wouldn't create one. This wasn't about symbolism—it was about resources, and the power to leverage them. To create an open and just city, black communities, organizations, and institutions needed power and resources. The bond passed by a 2–1 margin.[24]

TWO remained focused on improving conditions in Woodlawn schools. But desegregation simply didn't appear to be in the offing, at least not in any kind of reasonable time frame or on account of any local pressure. By the fall of 1965 the Johnson administration had also made clear its unwillingness to impose school desegregation. In July 1965 the CCCO had formally complained to the US Office of Education (part of the Department of Health, Education and Welfare), alleging that the Board of Education, in concert with the Chicago Real Estate Board (CREB) and the Chicago Housing Authority, had contrived to maintain the segregation Chicago's public schools. Chicago's actions (and inactions) were in violation of the 1964 Civil Rights Act. The CCCO demanded that Francis Keppel, the commissioner of education, suspend all federal funds to the city's schools. Given the $1.3 billion made available by the Elementary and Secondary School Education Act, in April 1965, this tactic promised real leverage over Daley and Willis. While the desegregation requirements of the 1964 Civil Rights Act were designed to prod Southern schools, Keppel (and Johnson) hadn't anticipated a confrontation in the urban North. CCCO's complaint, however, made a very convincing case. School segregation in Chicago was anything but de facto.

The effort briefly worked. Keppel initiated an investigation of Chicago schools, which largely confirmed the CCCO's complaint. Willis not only stonewalled but proclaimed his intention to use the federal aid mostly for white middle-class schools and the construction of more Willis Wagons. In late September Keppel informed the state of Illinois that he would defer any new federal funds to Chicago schools, declaring the district in "probable noncompliance."

An apoplectic Mayor Daley asked for—and immediately received—a face-to-face meeting with President Johnson in October in New York. Daley was so angry that Johnson was forced to delay a meeting with the pope to hear the mayor out. Upon his return to the White House Johnson gave Keppel— according to one witness—"unstinted hell." Less than a week later, the money was fully restored, and a humiliated Keppel lost his job. School desegregation wasn't coming to Chicago anytime soon. Daley's efforts also led the Department of Health, Education and Welfare to weaken its compliance regulations, with profound long-term effects on school desegregation throughout the urban North. It would be another two years before the department would undertake any other northern investigations and nearly a decade before the US Supreme Court finally took up the issue.

Federal educational funding expanded almost tenfold per year by the end of 1968. Most of the money distributed through Title I of the Elementary and Secondary School Education Act didn't go to poor neighborhoods or low-income students; the portion of it that did go to "educationally deprived" children was dispersed over many different programs, with funding decisions generally made locally. That said, the act's funds did become an ever-increasing percentage of the budgets of urban school systems, including Chicago's. But because the Johnson administration was unwilling to use the money as an opening wedge to attack school segregation in the North, frustrated activists shifted their focus to reforms designed to produce more immediate results for black children: experiments with community control and demands for equal funding. TWO would do the same.[25]

Alinsky and TWO activists argued that this state of affairs required a strategic reassessment. In the early 1960s, according to Brazier, TWO had believed "that if our children could be integrated then the education process would be across the board and equal ... if we could get black kids into schools where the majority of the population was, then education would improve." By the middle of the decade, however, this view had changed. "A complete end to segregation in the schools will come only when Negroes achieve political power," he argued. Only then would they be able to "defeat white racist political bosses" who opposed integration. While TWO continued to support "the right to live, work, go to school and play anywhere we can afford," the group resolved to continue its quest for "tangible equality" through a strategy that represented the "opinions, thoughts, insights and experiences of a large number of black people."[26]

Two frustrating local conflicts in 1965 and 1966 further shaped TWO's evolving views on self-determination, integration, and public education. First, in 1965, the University of Chicago sought federal funds to create an experimental school in Woodlawn, without consulting TWO. Brazier caught wind of the proposal early in 1966 and wrote a scathing letter to federal officials opposing it. "One cause of alienation and low self-esteem" in neighborhoods like Woodlawn, he pointed out acidly, "is being treated like objects, without being respected or consulted by the large bureaucracies that are supposed to be trying to 'help.'" Not only did the US Office of Education reject the proposal—it encouraged the university to find a more collaborative path with both TWO and the Chicago school district.

At virtually the same time, TWO's efforts to foster school integration locally—at Hyde Park High School—ran into difficulties. While located in East Woodlawn, the high school served both neighborhoods. It had a long and illustrious history, but by 1965 it had become overcrowded and dilapidated. After decades of white flight, it was 93 percent black. Under pressure from the HP-KCC, the school district was contemplating building a new high school in southeast Kenwood for Hyde Park students, as well as an elementary school. The HP-KCC feared that the lack of a Hyde Park high school considered viable by white parents would endanger racial balance in the area. The idea, according to Pierre de Vise, was to "dis-annex" predominantly white neighborhoods from predominantly black schools. Advanced placement and honors classes were created in Hyde Park High School as well, to "create predominantly white classes in predominantly Negro schools."[27]

TWO opposed this idea, arguing that it would result in the complete segregation of Hyde Park High and the new school, as well as siphoning off the older school's best teachers. Instead, as part of a larger "Unity Organization," TWO proposed the idea of converting the high school into an educational park with four 1,500-student high schools on a common campus, in order to foster both educational excellence and integration. "Hyde Park must be expanded and improved," Stevenson told the Board of Education in October 1965. "The right of every black child to a decent education demands it."

The Board of Education briefly supported TWO's plan, but then wavered under HP-KCC pressure. TWO threatened in return to bring the issue of racial segregation out into full view by flooding Hyde Park–Kenwood with blacks "in active search of good housing" if the board approved the new school. "The Woodlawn Organization will not see our youth castrated by junk-heap, dead-end education," Stevenson argued in November 1965. "If the HP-KCC wants to withdraw from their share of the struggle, if they are afraid to send their children to school with ours, then this issue is truly a white man's problem," Stevenson told reporters. He assailed the HP-KCC as a "band of confused, frightened whites."[28]

In January 1966, encouraged by Willis, the board approved the construction of a 2,500-student high school for Hyde Park and Kenwood students. The only concession to TWO and other opposed groups was a promise to renovate Hyde Park High School. Stevenson strongly condemned the decision, describing it as "a vote against the black children in Woodlawn." "The segregationists on this Board . . . regard us, who live in Woodlawn, as black animals in the zoo, to be looked at but not respected, and they want nothing but separation from us." TWO only briefly threatened direct action to reverse the decision. If even Hyde Park's white liberals were unwilling to embrace racially integrated schools, what hope was there for citywide change?

By 1966, many TWO activists had become increasingly skeptical of the promises of white racial liberals. "The whites who are against us are not ignorant of the truth. They just do not want to accept the truth," Brazier argued. As a result, "arguing, teaching, educating, pleading, begging and propagandizing will do no good . . . We aren't forgetting about integration, but we aren't waiting for it either . . . we want quality schools now . . . we want good black schools now." Gang violence and youth unemployment in Woodlawn were reaching crisis levels. Improving Woodlawn's all-black schools seemed more immediate, politically feasible, and of greater interest to residents. TWO leadership quickly realized that a focus on community control of Woodlawn schools was likely to be more effective, and better for the organization.[29]

Alinsky concurred. While Woodlawn parents are for desegregated schools, "what they primarily want is to have a better-quality school right now, whether it is around the corner, whether it is segregated or not." Self-determination— and "black power"—"is not the segregationist operation so many people think," he pointed out. "If you are out to get an integrated approach you've got to have the components for it." A powerful black community organization was thus an "elementary step . . . in order to move on towards the integrated patterns." While ultimately black communities lacked the numbers to accomplish their goals alone, independent power was a critical first stage to reaching beyond these limitations. Alinsky did worry, however, about falling into the "trap of separate-but-equal." Many white communities "would be glad to make Negro schools more than equal . . . if only the Negroes would stay in their own communities and stop this constant pressure." The struggle, he concluded, must be "fought on two fronts at once."[30]

TWO never advocated racial separatism, and it remained publicly committed to metropolitan open housing and school integration. TWO continued to call for the use of "imaginative transfer and cluster plans" to break down segregation, and the organization did endorse the school district's Redmond Plan in 1967, which proposed to encourage and sustain integrated schools by manipulating racial balance in transition neighborhoods. The plan capped black enrollment in such areas and bused black students to overwhelmingly white schools, thus putting the primary burdens of desegregation on black families and children.[31] At a well-attended meeting in January 1967, TWO activists grappled with the dilemmas posed by white intransigence and the poor quality of Woodlawn schools. "We will go on organizing and using every form of power to speed up integration in our schools," the group argued. "But in the meantime, what is to be our position with reference to ghetto schools that are not going to be integrated in the near future?" TWO and the CCCO had jump-started a movement for desegregated schools earlier in the decade, but little had changed.

Interracial coalitions in pursuit of the desegregation of public schools remained vital, TWO noted: "Black people, with the aid of their white friends, must come to grips with this problem and solve it." "Separate but equal" was not and never would be viable. The group nonetheless resolved to continue to organize and "develop power" in order to "change our own schools so that our children can have an equal opportunity for good jobs and better homes."[32]

These efforts would lead to the creation of the Woodlawn Experimental School Program (WESP), which ran from 1968 to 1971. Aided by a grant from the Rock River Conference of the Methodist Church, TWO joined with the University of Chicago and the Chicago public school district in July 1967 to propose a federally funded experimental three-school district in East Woodlawn. The project was rooted in TWO's frustration with the district's unwillingness to undertake integration, a growing sense of a youth crisis, and a desire to counter narratives of pathology by showing that black students could achieve at high levels outside of integrated settings.

WESP began in June 1968, with a $1.35 million federal grant that doubled per-pupil spending in participating schools. Like its more famous twin in New York's Ocean Hill–Brownsville neighborhood, the WESP was an experiment in community control. Brazier brought the black educator Barbara Sizemore on board to direct the project. Sizemore, the principal of an all-black high school in Grand Boulevard, saw the main problem as a breakdown in communication and trust between educational stakeholders in neighborhoods like Woodlawn and the exclusion of those most directly affected by public education from school decision-making. Black communities, families, students, and educators had the power to improve things themselves. In her previous position Sizemore had implemented culturally relevant curricula and programming focused on racial pride, student leadership, a cooperative school culture, and community engagement, with great success.[33]

The WESP had a tripartite structure, focused on instruction, research, and the community. School District 14 took the lead on instruction, university professors and graduate students focused on research, while TWO ran the community component. A Woodlawn Community Board governed the program, with seven members each from TWO, the district, and the University of Chicago. Joining elementary, middle, and high schools together in a "stream," the WESP sought to address educational inequality by reducing class sizes and increasing parental and community participation in school affairs. "It is an opportunity for parents to be physically present in the schools, for teachers to have a hand in planning, and for the school to become an integral part of the community," Sizemore said. Each school employed school-community agents to be chosen by TWO, while parents were organized into block-level advisory councils. Parents working as teacher aides could take college classes for credit. TWO and student activists also threatened boycotts to get the school district to appoint more black school principals in Woodlawn and to include more classes on black history.

If rising test scores are any indication, the WESP was a success. This was particularly the case for the elementary and middle schools, where TWO community organizing was most heavily concentrated. The WESP was also a success in offering a variety of volunteer and job opportunities for poor and working-class black women and out-of-school youth. It also fostered the development of community leadership and gave parents a much stronger voice in their children's education. By the summer of 1969, the WCB was increasingly under the control of black Woodlawn residents, many of whom had cut their teeth as activists through their involvement at Wadsworth Elementary. Preliminary findings of university researchers provided hopeful evidence of a workable model. But both the school district and the federal government became increasingly uncomfortable with the experiment. When the initial funding ran out in 1971, it was not renewed. TWO, now led by the more conservative and institutionally focused E. Duke McNeil, chose not to fight the decision.[34]

Conclusion

Driven in part by its experiences with educational work, starting in the mid-1960s TWO's activism became increasingly focused on local improvement and community control of key institutions. As we will see, this shift in spatial strategy was also aided and encouraged by the increasing availability of federal money. President Johnson's War on Poverty did not challenge the patterns of metropolitan segregation and uneven development that were impoverishing neighborhoods like Woodlawn; nor did it seek a fundamental restructuring of the nation's welfare state and labor market policies, to reflect the economic changes that were hammering industrial cities and geographically concentrating poverty. But it did (briefly) offer the possibility of real resources and support for innovative social programming in poor neighborhoods.

TWO and Alinsky could be fairly criticized, perhaps, for a diminishing interest in and activism on behalf of educational and residential integration across the city—its willingness by the middle of the decade to essentially concede one of Alinsky's two "fronts." But this retreat was pragmatic. While some of TWO's inward turn was inspired by Alinsky's approach, and the demands of building and maintaining a large community organization, the repeated unwillingness of public officials at all levels to take affirmative steps toward desegregation had taken its toll.

This shift was also driven by organizational imperatives. Early on, shopkeepers, churches, and block clubs in West Woodlawn were overrepresented in TWO, as Squires and the other organizers struggled to build support among East Woodlawn's poorer population. Some of this was connected to the increasing time and energy spent on direct action and citywide issues and coalitions, much as Alinsky had feared. This situation may have been sustainable in a static community, but Woodlawn was hardly that; as the decade progressed, the population east of Cottage Grove became more typical of the community as a whole. Unemployment, poverty, and violent crime increased, while many working and middle-class residents decamped.[35]

As the Social Policy Planning Memo indicated, TWO's assessment of the obstacles to black freedom in Chicago was evolving, increasingly intricate, and moving toward a more thoroughgoing examination of black poverty and powerlessness. Its strategies were altered accordingly. The kind of social learning promoted by Alinsky's organizing approach enabled TWO activists to draw connections between seemingly disparate issues and to conceptualize programmatic approaches to dealing with them that went beyond direct-action protest. This broadening perspective was also driven by a powerful surge of activism among Woodlawn's poor citizens, which TWO actively sought to harness. Beginning in 1963 they worked to include the poor in the organization at all levels, and to develop campaigns and services to help them. The emergence of poverty as a national issue in 1964 only reinforced this focus.

Under the direction of Edward Chambers, who replaced an exhausted Nicholas Von Hoffman as staff director in 1963, TWO centralized its poverty organizing efforts in the Social Welfare Committee, which was given a salaried secretary, a desk, and a phone. The Rev. Lynward Stevenson was elected chair. This effort would bring in new members, new voices, and new issues, changing TWO into a pathbreaking organization that sought to balance the strategic dilemmas of community empowerment and metropolitan desegregation while simultaneously making social policy from the bottom up.[36]

8

Maximum Feasible Alinsky

TWO and the War on Poverty

> Our youth simply will not accept the old tired slogans, the fatuous, empty talk about workshops, summer camps, recreation, brotherhood and decency. Our youth want jobs... and they demand, and will get, dignity.
> EDITORIAL, *Woodlawn Booster*, August 4, 1966

> If poor people were capable of managing this program, they wouldn't be poor.
> REP. ROMAN PUCINSKI (D-IL), 1965

Residential segregation, racial and gender discrimination in the labor market, and industrial suburbanization all combined to hammer black families and communities in the postwar decades. The visible manifestation of these structural forces—high black housing demand, deterioration of homes and apartment buildings, joblessness, increases in crime, overcrowded parks, schools, and residences—helped to reinforce white prejudices about black families. Few whites understood the structural underpinnings, and Chicago's political, economic, and media leaders generally exacerbated rather than alleviated this state of affairs. Alinsky was coming to understand the uphill nature of this battle through his work with the OSC; Woodlawn would merely show him the other side of the hill.

By 1963 TWO viewed poverty, joblessness, underemployment, and low wages as civil rights issues, inseparable from questions of segregation in housing and education. Strategically, TWO activists now believed that while direct action and citywide change were critical long-term goals, only local organizing would get them there. TWO launched three interrelated campaigns over the decade: employment and job training, organizing Woodlawn's growing poor population, and participation in federal poverty programs. More than perhaps any other grassroots black community organization in the country, TWO sought to attack black poverty from all angles, using internal and external resources. As a result, TWO's experience in the 1960s provides us with a unique perspective on the contours of metropolitan inequality, the limitations of national policy, and the strategic dilemmas faced by local freedom movements.

"The Tide Was Running Out": The Emerging Poverty Crisis in Woodlawn

Efforts to address the devastating intersection of economic change and metropolitan segregation were hampered by the lack of meaningful public discussion of the issue in the early 1960s. The focus among politicians and policymakers was on welfare fraud and black employability, not jobs, adequate incomes, and segregation. Welfare caseloads had been on the rise since the mid-1950s. Black recipients made up a growing percentage of recipients. This accelerated the racializing of public discussion of poverty and social policy, sparking a backlash against welfare that would explode into national politics. Black opportunities were also restricted by a welfare state that was both inadequate and intrusive.

Welfare had become increasingly important for black families. By 1961, 73 percent of welfare recipients in Illinois were black. In May 1963, the Republican-dominated state legislature halted welfare payments in an effort to cap benefits, encourage more intensive casework, and more aggressively prosecute fraud. This caused intense hardship for Woodlawn's poor families. After a two-month delay in relief checks, TWO's Social Welfare Committee organized an emergency meeting to address hunger and prevent a wave of evictions of families receiving Aid to Dependent Children in Woodlawn.[1]

"If the majority of people receiving aid were not Negroes," Brazier argued, "we wouldn't have all of this uproar." Politicians were refusing to consider "the reasons why people are on public assistance," such as "discrimination against Negroes in industry." Brazier joined with other civil rights leaders in connecting both welfare and poverty to job discrimination and low wages. "These opponents of relief do not hire Negroes in their businesses; some do not want them in their unions; do not want to work with them. Yet they tell Negroes to go out and get jobs." As citizens, low-income blacks "are entitled to all the help that is available to the poor," Brazier concluded.[2]

The national conversation about black poverty wasn't much better. Economists and analysts tended to focus on the inadequacies of individual black workers. They generally lacked a structural understanding of black poverty and unemployment, and the extent to which decades of labor market segmentation and discrimination, as well as residential segregation, had rendered black workers and communities especially vulnerable to economic change. After a brief flurry of interest in a more comprehensive national employment regime, labor market policy under Kennedy and Johnson was primarily and increasingly remedial, targeting the motivational and skill deficits of workers on the fringes of an otherwise sound economy. Kennedy's Council of Economic Advisers presumed that macroeconomic policy, in conjunction with antidiscrimination laws and job-training programs for those at the fringes of the labor market, would be sufficient. When civil rights leaders met with Kennedy after the March on Washington, he ignored their demands to create public works jobs, increase and expand the reach of the minimum wage, and attack housing and labor market discrimination. Kennedy talked instead about black family values. With a few patches to the hull, it was assumed, a rising tide would lift all boats.[3]

Unemployment nationally was under 4 percent, leading to an emphasis on black employability rather than blacks' lack of access to living-wage jobs. Poverty was considered a problem of the quality of the labor supply, not the racialized nature of demand, or the lack of available and attainable living-wage jobs for blacks. The inadequacies of the poor were increasingly associated in public discourse with racist tropes of black laziness and white racial innocence, restricting the reach of and political support for more just employment policies. Labor market policy was subsumed under the rubric of social assistance and disconnected from economic policy. Worse, the Chicago Urban League argued, it completely missed the fact that black workers were "locked into definite and inferior sectors of the labor market . . . just as the larger city has confined Negroes to residential ghettos and segregated schools."[4]

Fair employment laws seemed to do little to address the group effects of discrimination, or the structural roots of mass unemployment, particularly for low-skilled blacks. Compensatory programs targeted at blacks, which both Whitney Young and Martin Luther King Jr. called for in 1964, were nonstarters politically. Civil rights leaders also struggled to get unions to challenge white privileges in housing and employment. Frustrated by the failure of liberal legal efforts to break down entrenched patterns of exclusion and segregation, the Black Freedom Movements in Oakland, Philadelphia, and other cities began to demand group preferences and actual jobs instead. This left groups like TWO with a narrow range of options.[5]

As early as 1962, it was clear that the very survival of both TWO and Woodlawn itself would require a better understanding of black poverty, and reaching out to the poor themselves. "The tide was running out in Woodlawn," Von Hoffman reflected. Working-class people with steady jobs—"the one absolute necessity for a long-running community organization, according to the Alinsky playbook"—were a rapidly shrinking percentage of the neighborhood. As a result, businesses and landlords were abandoning the community. "We recognized that no matter how much access to mainstream institutions we might have," Brazier observed, "unless people had jobs, unless people earned money, no matter what doors were opened, they would not have the opportunity to walk through them." In a fascinating survey just days before the March on Washington, the *New York Times* found equal employment opportunity to be the "major concern" of most black activists in Chicago. "Eventually, across the whole nation, the big problem is going to be jobs," Anthony Henry of the American Friends Service Committee argued. "Anything else will be just playing around."[6]

In 1963, TWO began a series of federally funded experiments in job training and employment. For the rest of the decade it insisted that all federal money that came into Woodlawn put their neighbors to work. These initial efforts would draw TWO into Lyndon Johnson's War on Poverty and a broader confrontation with the roots of black poverty.

"Out of the Slough of Ignorance and Poverty": TWO and Employment

In cooperation with University of Chicago faculty, TWO began work on a job-training proposal for Woodlawn's "hard-core unemployed" in May 1963. It focused on workers displaced from skilled jobs, discouraged from finding equivalent work, and generally underqualified for federal job-training services. Traditional programs tended to use entrance tests, often racially biased, that stressed formal education, while ignoring reliability, employment history, and ability to learn on the job. Believing that this screened out black workers, TWO chose to stress precisely those experiential factors. Many of Woodlawn's unemployed were also wary of government agencies, so TWO argued that it could better recruit and counsel participants. The organization received a $76,000 federal grant in July 1964, under the Manpower Development Training Act. On a fifteen-month contract, TWO would work with two hundred of Woodlawn's unemployed.

TWO's program was innovative, focusing on trainees who had tested poorly for federal job-training grants and who had given up looking for work. While training grants were generally aimed at skilled males displaced by automation, TWO included women and the unskilled. Individual trainees were sponsored and mentored by TWO member organizations, and TWO staff workers met with them as well. The emphasis was on group work, to "stimulate supportive interaction, sharing of problems, and ways to cope." Trainees were also encouraged to get involved in community activities. Woodlawn residents staffed the program, while trainees were encouraged to organize clubs—which would then join TWO.

Classes were offered in general industrial work, the metal trades, clerical and sales work, and service work. TWO staff supported participants to get them in the program and keep them there. Trainees with children were given weekly subsidies. After discovering that 25 percent of their trainees suffered from minor but obstructive health problems, TWO and the University of Chicago used federal funds to create a community health-care center. They also sought out funding for a Head Start program for trainees' children. The response was stunning: by August 1966, there were nearly five thousand applications for two hundred slots.

TWO continued to administer job-training grants throughout the decade. Each succeeding grant reflected the social learning of activists and staff, as well as the growing participation of the poor. Under the first grant, TWO's program didn't create jobs for graduates. They sought to address this with a larger grant in 1965 from the Department of Labor's Bureau of Apprenticeship Training, which provided on-the-job training for 350 adults. Graduates were immediately hired, worked for an hourly wage the first day, and took home a paycheck the first week. Nationally, blacks tended to be underrepresented in on-the-job training programs, which were much more likely than more traditional training efforts to connect graduates to good industrial positions. TWO's program placed Woodlawn's unemployed with local merchants, University of Chicago hospitals and clinics, the *Woodlawn Booster*, and downtown hotels and department stores.[7]

TWO also worked to break down discriminatory hiring in Woodlawn stores and service and retail businesses elsewhere in the city. As early as 1962, TWO's Job Discrimination Committee used testers (white and black) to compile a list of businesses they suspected of hiring discrimination, or of hiring blacks only for inferior positions. The state's fair employment law lacked effective enforcement mechanisms; TWO took it upon itself to enforce it. When negotiations and public pressure didn't work, TWO threatened a variety of direct actions, including boycotts and "shop-ins." Marshall Field's, Chicago's most prominent department store, was a target of great economic and symbolic importance—and because it had lots of black customers. "After fifty years of discrimination in hiring," activist Charles Henderson told TWO's newspaper, "it is now time that Marshall Field and other all-white or nearly white firms pay their price. That price is taking on negro employees immediately, regardless of openings presently available, and sharply increasing the amount of on-the-job training for negro employees."

By April 1964, TWO had succeeded in getting 325 jobs for Woodlawn blacks in Marshall Field's stores, as well as dozens of positions (including a black manager) with the grocery chain High-Low Foods. That year, TWO resolved to investigate the building trades and "encourage boycotting of companies that discriminate in their hiring policies or failure to upgrade Negroes." They also worked on integrating the Fire Department and other city agencies.[8]

TWO activists saw job training and the fight for employment as the logical outgrowth of their civil rights activism and a necessary response to poverty. "The fruits of the integration struggle will be of little value if the Negro is too poor to take advantage of them," said Brazier. Through its employment efforts, Lynward Stevenson argued, TWO is "exploding the myth that communities such as Woodlawn are populated by people who do not want to work and are content with doles from the state." The editors of the *Chicago Defender* praised TWO for trying to lift "their brothers out of the slough of ignorance and poverty." By 1966 TWO had trained and placed nearly one thousand Woodlawn men in jobs and broken racial barriers in a number of Chicago's largest retail establishments.[9]

By the middle of the decade TWO had sixty business-related member groups, fifty block clubs, and thirty churches, and it represented nearly forty thousand of Woodlawn's hundred thousand citizens. It had begun to effectively reach the low-income population. It ran a newspaper, was building housing, ran a job-training program, and had secured citizen participation in urban renewal two years before anyone had heard the term *maximum feasible participation*. Thus, when Congress passed the Economic Opportunity Act in August 1964, TWO was organizationally and ideologically ready to push its program of community power and self-determination. TWO committed to "investigate President Johnson's program for the war on poverty with the view toward better educational, business, and job opportunities for the people of Woodlawn."[10]

Maximum Feasible Alinsky? TWO and the War on Poverty

President Johnson launched his War on Poverty at an auspicious moment. As Thomas Jackson points out, there appeared to be some hope that federal policy might finally address the public and private structures of racial inequality: "1963 and 1964 presented the last, best opportunity of the postwar era to institutionalize social democratic policies that could have addressed the growing crisis of joblessness at the heart of the racial and urban crises." Riots in Harlem, Philadelphia, and elsewhere during the summer indicated the scale of the problem. At the same time, the success of George Wallace in Democratic primaries in the North demonstrated a growing white backlash against black demands that would set political limits on Johnson's range of action.

Ultimately, Johnson dismissed calls for job creation and income redistribution, in favor of an attack on poverty along conventional lines of education, social services, and vocational training. Poverty was viewed as a problem of individual development and the social disorganization of poor (and black) communities, not as a function of discrimination and segregation, or of economic restructuring. Johnson assumed the War on Poverty would facilitate individual blacks' mobility into the middle class. The nation, said presidential adviser Daniel Moynihan, had moved "beyond civil rights." This rendered the persistence of structural racial inequality invisible, limiting the reach of the antipoverty campaign.

The most unusual—and confusing—part of Johnson's effort was the call for "maximum feasible participation" of the poor in the management and distribution of services through the Community Action Program (CAP). Some in the new federal Office of Economic Opportunity (OEO), like Sanford Kravitz and Richard Boone, insisted on making the CAP a real tool for empowerment, but in most municipalities efforts were initiated and controlled by local political authorities. Conservatives criticized community action for empowering lawless radicals, fomenting riots, and undermining law and order. Some antipoverty activists viewed CAP as a real opportunity, while others worried that the program was merely an effort to co-opt the civil rights movement and curb more radical demands.

Both Johnson and local politicians were pleased at $300 million that CAP made available, but they did not anticipate—or desire—the frontal challenge to urban power structures the program engendered. While CAP did not cause the political conflicts over race, political power, poverty and resources of the mid-1960s, it did reveal inequalities that were decades in the making and provided Black Freedom Movements with discursive and economic resources. TWO made the most of this.[11]

In his "Open Letter to Sargent Shriver" in October 1964, Lynward Stevenson outlined TWO's plans in the War on Poverty, including a Head Start program, as well as an expanded and comprehensive community-run job-training effort.[12] TWO forwarded the plan to Deton Brooks, the Daley-appointed executive director of the Chicago Committee on Urban Opportunity, the city's OEO-sanctioned Community Action Agency, which was charged with distributing the federal funds. Brooks and the city stonewalled: Daley had no intention of allowing the federal government to fund any politically independent organizations.[13] Brooks publicly questioned TWO's competence, arguing that city experts and agencies could more efficiently and effectively spend federal money. Daley concurred: "It would be like telling the fellow who cleans up to be the city editor of a newspaper."[14]

Around the country, OEO was caught up in similar battles between local politicians and community groups. *Maximum feasible participation* was initially ill defined; when OEO tried to clarify, conflicts escalated. While municipal officials encouraged OEO to downplay the importance of participation, the agency was also under pressure to expand the role of the poor. New York's Adam Clayton Powell, chair of the House Committee on Education and Labor, launched an investigation of the poverty program in eleven cities, and was displeased with the lack of participation. Powell held hearings starting in April 1965 to keep pressure on the OEO. Civil rights groups—TWO prominent among them—also lodged complaints. Activists from within the OEO itself, who saw 'maximum feasible participation' as a way to empower the civil rights movement, also pushed it.

In March 1965 the OEO issued a workbook, cowritten by Richard Boone, to help local agencies include the poor in a meaningful way. Community action, Boone wrote, must help the poor get power and use trained workers to help the poor form "autonomous and self-managed organizations which are competent to exert political influence on behalf of their own self-interest." These organizations could engage in demonstrations. Complaints from local politicians—from Richard Daley, in particular, who sent the OEO a pile of proposals in March that had no provision for participation whatsoever—began to pour into the White House and the OEO.[15]

Rep. Powell sought to target Chicago (and Daley) in particular, and thus gave TWO a prominent role in his hearings. Lynward Stevenson issued scathing criticisms of Daley and Brooks, also garnering national attention. He accused the mayor of subverting the War on Poverty by using it to maintain control of the black poor and feed the patronage system. The charges were certainly accurate: the ninety-nine members of the Chicago Committee on Urban Opportunity's board were all appointed by Daley, and only seven of them resided in poor neighborhoods. The overwhelming majority were machine loyalists, city bureaucrats, business allies, and compliant black aldermen. Brooks appointed the directors of Chicago's twelve neighborhood-service centers, who in turn chose residents for neighborhood advisory councils, but only after clearing them with Democratic Party ward organizations. "The Mayor's power in Chicago's antipoverty drive," wrote the *New York Times*, "is almost absolute."

In Chicago, Stevenson testified, the War on Poverty involved maximum feasible participation of the rich, the precinct captains, and the ward committeemen, not the poor. "Men in Cadillacs meet at champagne luncheons to plan our future while expecting us to stand hat in hand." The city had held up TWO's application for Head Start funds for nearly ten months, Stevenson told the committee. Under Daley, he concluded: "There is no War on Poverty. There is only more of the ancient, galling war against the poor." Rep. Roman Pucinski, a committee member but a Daley loyalist, responded angrily: "If poor people were capable of managing this program, they wouldn't be poor."

In its extensive coverage, the *New York Times* disagreed with the congressman, describing TWO as a "bristling refutation of the argument that the poor are incapable of leadership and self-determination."[16]

Alinsky echoed Stevenson's criticisms in a May 1965 speech. The antipoverty program "is emerging as a huge political pork barrel" and a "form of political patronage," he argued. Daley and other mayors were using federal money to "suffocate militant independent leadership and action organizations which have been arising to arm the poor with their share of power." "There is only one way in which federal funds can be siphoned into the hands of the poor, into the kind of bona fide community action programs," Alinsky concluded. Local authorities must be "bypassed," and the poor must be organized.[17]

Partly in response to the hearings, in May the OEO tried to give the poor further voice by instructing its local Community Action Agencies (CAAs) to identify areas with heavy concentrations of the poor, let residents choose neighborhood advisory councils, and empower those councils both to influence programs in their community and to choose representatives for citywide boards.[18] Powell also persuaded Shriver that organizations separate from official city antipoverty agencies should be able to receive funds directly. As a result, TWO was awarded $77,530 for Head Start and Early Childhood Development programming in June 1965.[19]

Daley was furious. "What in the hell are you people doing?" Daley asked Johnson aide Bill Moyers. "Does the president know he's putting M-O-N-E-Y in the hands of subversives? To poor people who aren't part of the organization?" According to the OEO's Jack Conway, the mayor urged Vice President Hubert Humphrey "to put the blowtorch on us . . . he was mad at us because we had funded TWO."[20]

Embarrassed and angered at TWO's public attacks, Daley met with Stevenson to discuss representation on Woodlawn's local CAA. Daley agreed to allow TWO to submit a list of twenty-one names, of which he would choose at least thirteen for the twenty-five-member committee. Daley surprised TWO by accepting all twenty-one, but then he increased the size of the board to seventy-five, with the remainder nominated by him.[21] Stevenson condemned the mayor as "outright deceitful" and questioned whether Daley was "capable of any sincerity and honesty when dealing with the Negro community." Long plagued by "discrimination, dependency, delinquency and disease," that community was suffering from a new affliction: "Daleyism." "TWO's only recourse," he concluded, "is to take to the streets." Throughout the fall and winter of 1965, TWO tried to use large turnouts at meetings to gain influence on the local board but without success. Daley was determined to shut TWO out of the poverty program. Nationally, the OEO was also buckling under intense political pressure—a process accelerated by the Watts riots. "The mayors for all practical purposes have won their battle," a *New York Times* reporter concluded.[22]

Alinsky was directly involved in the OEO's two most controversial demonstration grants, and each of them played a critical role in the ultimate fate of the antipoverty war: the Community Action Training Center (CATC) in Syracuse, and a TWO job-training program for Woodlawn gang members. In February 1965, the OEO gave its first demonstration grant to the social work professor Warren Haggstrom of Syracuse University to create the CATC. The CATC had three components: research into community organizing and its benefits for the poor, the training of future social workers and ordinary citizens in organizing poor neighborhoods, and the creation of democratic neighborhood councils of the poor. OEO's chief Syracuse investigator, Jack Williams, described the CATC as "the first test of the involvement of the OEO in the Saul Alinsky approach to the problems of the poor." The CATC, it was hoped, would demonstrate just what *maximum feasible participation* meant and what it could accomplish.[23]

Syracuse, however, already had an official War on Poverty agency: the Crusade for Opportunity, dominated by appointees of Republican Mayor William Walsh, and had very little organized input from the poor. OEO officials privately hoped that the CATC's neighborhood councils would eventually take over the Crusade.[24] Haggstrom asked Alinsky to serve as an adviser, and to help teach his student organizers. Alinsky hesitated. He was extremely skeptical about the ability of any community organization to remain independent while receiving federal funds and warned Haggstrom that "the moment they would run into an issue with City Hall, the funds would be turned off." He also worried that the OEO, anxious for rapid results, would rush the organizing forward, endangering the time-consuming process of building an autonomous mass-based organization.

Haggstrom offered to pay Alinsky out of the university's budget, rather than the grant money, and Alinsky reluctantly agreed. While the center was never officially an "Alinsky project," opponents closely identified him with it. Both Haggstrom and his OEO sponsors also believed the project to be "straight Alinskyism," in large part because Alinsky protégé Fred Ross, who had spent the previous decade organizing Mexican American farmworkers in California, trained the social work students.[25]

Under Ross's stern direction, sixteen trainees fanned out into poor districts, organizing "house meetings" in apartment complexes and public housing projects. By late spring 1965 they had assembled neighborhood councils in four of Syracuse's five public housing projects, focused primarily around long-pent-up grievances with the paternalistic Syracuse Housing Authority, the County Welfare Office, and City Hall. The councils also began to register tenants to vote in the upcoming mayoral election.[26]

In his June testimony before the House Republican Task Force on the War on Poverty, Mayor Walsh accused the CATC of improper use of federal funds, claiming that the center was "experimenting with the poor like mice in a laboratory . . . a fight has developed over who owns the poor." The CAP had become a political liability to Johnson, and he quickly responded. "It's not worth it," he angrily told his budget advisers in August. "I think somebody ought to veto these damn fool community action [programs]. Don't you put any money into community action. Just cut it down. You hear that? Just *cut that down*." Johnson told Vice President Humphrey to broker a solution in Syracuse, and the OEO (and the university) began to feel the heat.[27]

Some OEO officials tried desperately to save the CATC. Investigator Jack Williams strongly urged that the OEO not back down. "A precedent of retreat in Syracuse," he argued, "would mean that all community action funds would be administered through a power-structured set up."[28] Many key players in the OEO believed they were "doing Alinsky." A number of officials—Sargent Shriver, Fred Hoehler, Richard Boone, and Lloyd Ohlin—claimed an acquaintance with Alinsky and his ideas. Shriver, as head of Chicago's Catholic Interracial Council in the 1950s, had numerous encounters (some not so friendly) with Alinsky over housing issues and admired his work; Hoehler had written his master's thesis on the Back of the Yards Neighborhood Council; Ohlin had consulted with Alinsky in the early stages of his Mobilization for Youth program on the Lower East Side of New York City, and Boone kept a portrait of the organizer on his office wall.[29]

Many of the key shapers of the CAP openly admitted Alinsky's influence on it, and on the Syracuse demonstration grant in particular. Field reports from Syracuse by OEO inspectors often seemed to be lifted verbatim from Alinsky's writings. According to Frank Mankiewicz, who had been involved in the early planning stages of the War on Poverty: "The purpose of this program [CAP] was to have what you had in Syracuse . . . I don't think you'd want to go running to Congress and rubbing their nose in Saul Alinsky, but the fact of the matter is that philosophically our program was an Alinsky-type program."[30] The goal of the demonstration grant, Jack Williams argued, was "to study, for the first time within an academic discipline, the Alinsky community organizing technique." Clearly, then, a number of OEO officials had Alinsky—or their notion of his ideas, at any rate—very much in mind in the formative months of the CAP.[31]

Early in November 1965, however, Walsh won reelection easily, largely by appealing to a white backlash vote against the CATC and its neighborhood councils. The White House, worried about the 1966 midterm elections, took notice.[32] The grant was renewed at lower levels of the OEO, but deputy director Bernard Boutin, appointed by Johnson to rein in the CAP, recommended that it be rejected. Shriver concurred.[33] The university then terminated its contract with Alinsky, in December 1965. "Shriver and the anti-poverty program he administers have absolutely knuckled under to local politicians," he told the *Chicago Tribune*. "Shriver has made his peace with the welfare industry." Asked by another reporter if he was upset at being fired, Alinsky laughed: "Have you ever been to Syracuse?"[34]

Within a year of the OEO's first expenditure of funds, the War on Poverty was under heavy attack from the left, and at the black grassroots. It was also under attack from Alinsky himself. Always a skeptic of professional social work, he was particularly dismissive of the defanged version of his organizing approach that seemed to be making the rounds at the OEO and in graduate programs.[35] In a widely quoted 1965 article, he famously described the War on Poverty as "a prize piece of political pornography." *Poverty* "means not only lacking money, but also lacking power," Alinsky wrote. "When one lives in a society where poverty and power bars you from equal protection ... and equal participation in the economic and social life of your society, then you are poor." An effective antipoverty program thus needed to "do something about not only economic poverty but also political poverty."

However, Alinsky was deeply skeptical about the willingness of the OEO (and the Johnson administration) to take the political risks necessary to truly organize the poor for power. In all likelihood, maximum feasible participation would offer only the illusion of power, by giving control over limited programs to nonrepresentative individuals rather than trying to organize independent mass-based community organizations empowered to bargain collectively. "The big issue is not whether these councils are one-third poor, but who picks them," Alinsky argued. "Representation requires an organized base." Until the poor "through their own organized power would be able to provide bona fide legitimate representatives of their interests who would sit at the programming table and have a strong voice in both the formulation and the carrying on of the program," he asserted, "I would have serious doubts about any really meaningful program to help and work with the poor."

For the War on Poverty to be effective, Alinsky argued, the OEO would have to bypass city officials and the "social welfare industry," and directly fund "militant independent organization[s] such as TWO." In cities where these groups didn't exist, federal officials could seek out effective indigenous leadership in poor neighborhoods to start the process of "the gathering together of community sources of power" through mass meetings, for the purpose of electing residents to represent the poor—in other words, what the CATC sought to do. The creation of independent, mass-based community organizations, he argued, could do far more for the poor than the expansion of what he called "welfare colonialism." Without an independent power base for the poor, the War on Poverty would just become "an extension of the general welfare program." Government-sponsored community action was unrealistic, he told the *New York Times*, akin to "asking an employer to go ahead and hire a union organizer." The War on Poverty, he concluded, is "the greatest boondoggle and feeding trough that's come along for the welfare industry in years."[36]

TWO leaders were also deeply critical of OEO's apparent retreat. The War on Poverty "hasn't given any real funds to any militant organizations," Stevenson told reporters. "When organized," he insisted, "we don't need a handout. We can demand what's coming to us."[37] At a December 1965 meeting called by Daley, Shriver described the proper role of the poor in the CAP as analogous to that of an architect's client, who "participates" in designing their home while the architect does the actual design. TWO activists toting signs—Double-Dealing Daley Sells the Poor for Power, and The War on Poverty Is a Big Fraud—picketed the hotel where they were meeting. They called for Daley and Shriver to denounce Willis and his policies; for five hundred black families to be moved into Bridgeport, Back of the Yards, Beverly Hills, and other all-white neighborhoods; and for more trade school opportunities for black apprentices.[38]

"Very Much a Movement of the People": The Social Welfare Union

TWO began to consolidate its efforts to organize Woodlawn's poor. In 1965 Rev. Stevenson and the Social Welfare Committee organized the semi-independent Social Welfare Union (SWU), dedicated to collectively representing Woodlawn's growing number of citizens on public assistance. Generally organized at the building level, these were welcomed as member organizations. In 1966, TWO instructed SWU to form a coalition of welfare unions and organizations across Chicago "to direct a city-wide attack against welfare injustices, against the Illinois State Legislature." The SWU advised recipients about their maximum benefits under the law, worked to increase budget allowances, and fought against punitive legislation in Springfield. It developed a reputation within both Woodlawn and the Welfare Department for effectively representing recipients of public assistance, serving as a kind of "ward heeler" for Woodlawn's poor—young mothers in particular. It was TWO's most successful organizing experience among Woodlawn's poor. It significantly expanded the membership base and provided a significant source of new militant and female leadership.[39]

The SWU was part of an emerging national welfare-rights movement in the summer of 1966, which Alinsky's CATC helped to jump-start. That January, the Syracuse activists George Wiley, Bruce Thomas, Rhoda Linton, and others used CATC's federal funds to host the Poor People's War Council on Poverty "to unite grassroots organizations throughout the country to insure total participation by the poor in all aspects of the antipoverty program." The council gathered over six hundred delegates from twenty-one states, including representatives from TWO. That May, TWO activists and dissident student social workers at the University of Chicago held an important conference on the idea of a guaranteed national income. Welfare-rights activists from around the country attended, helping to fuse a series of disparate groups into an emerging national movement. The SWU was formally created weeks later.[40]

Herman Blake, who sat in on SWU meetings while on a fact-finding visit to Woodlawn, found them to be the organizations' best-attended and most energetic gatherings. Worried that he would find TWO to be a top-down group dominated by the middle-class, Blake was reassured by the meetings. Members—virtually all of them female welfare recipients—came dressed in "regular daily clothing," with their children in tow. TWO leaders "welcome the welfare recipients and treat them cordially."

After an opening report by SWU president Annie Jackson, attendees shared experiences and asked questions about welfare regulations, allotments, and grievance procedures. A doctor reported on the newly opened Woodlawn Child Care Center and the availability of free medical services for children. He then marched the entire assembly over to the center for a tour. The next meeting involved a conversation with state representatives about changes in welfare laws. In general, Blake found, TWO fosters a "profound respect... for all points of view regardless of the social and economic status of the person." SWU meetings "gave eloquent witness to the involvement of all levels of the community, and they cooperate with each other very well." TWO's program and its leadership "are both indigenous." It is, he concluded, "very much a movement of the people."[41]

Jackson, a welfare recipient, was typical. Distressed by the paternalism of the Welfare Department, she came to TWO for help. They brought her to an SWU meeting; within a few weeks, she was spending time each day in the TWO office, helping other recipients.[42] Each person who came in was asked to join Jackson in her work and spread the word. Blake found this to be the case in other committees as well; TWO got people "involved in resolving their own problems."⁴³ The Welfare Department responded to SWU demands with increasing speed, Jackson told Blake, because "the organization is so highly feared." The Cook County Director of Public Aid expressed a desire to work closely with the SWU, helping recipients to receive bigger allotments and increased rent allowances.⁴⁴

Of perhaps even greater importance, participation empowered young black mothers beaten down by the paternalism and indifference of the welfare bureaucracy, and the anonymous cruelty of their poverty. Gladys Kyles, a thirty-eight-year-old mother of eleven children and a recipient of public assistance, came to TWO for help getting the heat turned back on in her building. Kyles quickly became a prominent activist in the Social Welfare Committee; in February 1966, she was appointed by the OEO to its National Advisory Council.⁴⁵

In November 1967, Jackson testified before the state legislature's Advisory Committee on Public Aid. Congress had just created a mandatory work requirement (the Work Incentive Program, or WIN) for mothers on public assistance, and capped the percentage of a state's population that could receive welfare. Functionally, this was a caseload freeze. Jackson lamented these punitive measures and the political backlash that had prompted them. "All too often people have been making decisions for poor people, but have not asked us what are our problems," she told the committee. Jackson reminded the elected officials that "welfare recipients do not enjoy being on aid nor do they intend to stay on aid." The SWU and its more than nine hundred members "would gladly take jobs if there was the kind of employment available that would give them dignity and an income that would take them out of poverty . . . we don't want our children to have to grow up and go on public aid." Blake echoed this sentiment: "the general desire," he concluded, "is for independence."⁴⁶

"They Got Nothing to Do, So They Throw the Brick": The TWO Youth Project

TWO's most publicized and important confrontation with Mayor Daley involved an innovative OEO Demonstration Grant to deal with Woodlawn's devastating youth unemployment, and a corresponding wave of gang violence that portended both middle-class flight and a vicious police crackdown. The SWU and local clergy were critical in pushing TWO to grapple with the gang issue. It nearly split the organization along class lines. The conflict ultimately attracted national attention, provoking congressional hearings and contributing to the passage of the Green Amendment in late 1967, effectively ending federal support for maximum feasible participation of the poor in the OEO's programs.

The Blackstone Rangers, the largest gang in the Woodlawn area, had formed in the early 1960s. Initially a small East Woodlawn gang, the Rangers were prompted by increasingly violent turf battles with their rival (West Woodlawn) gang, the Disciples, to begin a massive and brutally violent organizing drive in 1965. The campaign was remarkably successful: Ranger Nation expanded from three thousand members in 1966 to perhaps five thousand members by June 1968 as smaller gangs affiliated with them. But the blocks surrounding Woodlawn Avenue—which divided the Rangers and the Disciples—became a war zone. From June 1966 to May 1967, there were seventy-three gang-related shootings in Woodlawn.

While the violence was the most visible evidence of the Rangers' growing reach, they also demonstrated an astonishing organizing sensibility. When they sought to extend their influence to a neighborhood that already had a gang, they would negotiate its absorption into the Rangers, leaving its leaders considerable autonomy; in unorganized areas, they would move their own leadership in to build an affiliate. One observer compared the expansion to that of the Roman Empire. A more apt analogy might have been TWO—absent the violence, the community group was put together in a similar fashion.[47]

The appeal of the Rangers was evidence not only of a long history of police brutality in black communities but also of a growing political consciousness among poor black youth. Rooted in the common experience of arbitrary white authority on the streets and in the schools and systemic discrimination in the labor market, and catalyzed by empowering school boycotts, working-class black youth culture in Woodlawn took on an increasingly political cast.

When O. W. Wilson was appointed as police chief in 1960, his "stop and frisk" policy dramatically increased confrontations between cops and youth. In 1961, determined to crush gangs, Wilson created the Gang Intelligence Unit (GIU), whose rough tactics merely inflamed the situation. According to Andrew Diamond, "the interface between the police and youths was, in the early 1960s, a radicalizing space." Police brutality, as well as the eroding opportunity structure for young black men, also further politicized—even radicalized—many youth workers as well.[48]

By the mid-1960s, the beginnings of "a radical critique of race and power" had emerged within the everyday spaces of working-class black youth. Those spaces included the Rangers, but also high schools, streets, and recreational areas. The GIU—and many residents—might have seen the gangs as criminals, but the reality was much messier. Gangs often had junior and sometimes "pee-wee" divisions, indicating their broadly representation of the community. Most adults in Woodlawn were well aware of the larger educational and labor market context of gangs because it shaped the opportunities and perceptions of all young people in the area.

The Rangers themselves were divided over how much a politics of black community control should define them—indeed, whether they should be "political" at all. But there was little question that many young men saw them as an avenue to empowerment. That empowerment itself had shifted toward "a mix of Black Power ideas involving racial unity, the struggle for civil rights, community control, and black entrepreneurialism" indicated that what the GIU (and TWO) faced was something much larger than a law-and-order problem. Area high schools experienced an explosion of student black-power politics in the fall of 1967, as the Rangers moved into the spotlight. That the Rangers engaged in violent, criminal, and self-destructive acts is beyond dispute, but its members were thoroughly embedded in the community and the forces that shaped it.[49]

By spring 1966 the walls of buildings in Woodlawn, Kenwood, and Hyde Park were dotted with graphic evidence of their presence: signs reading Black P. Stone, Stone Run It, and Almighty Black P. Stone Nation could be found throughout the area. The Rangers were run by a group of twenty-one leaders, who met frequently to make decisions, plan action, exercise sanctions, and enforce solidarity. The so-called 21 were a charismatic group who increasingly saw themselves as "building something" rather than just monopolizing violence. While the Rangers certainly didn't set themselves up as an alternative to TWO, gang members and their parents largely stood outside its world of block clubs, churches, and social groups. The creation of the SWU locals in 1966 was in part a response to the emergence of the Rangers, who not only threatened social peace in Woodlawn but also the unity of TWO itself if it didn't become more representative of the increasingly young and poor population.

While deeply troubled by the Rangers' violence, some observers were optimistic that the gang's organizational skill could be diverted to more positive ends. "While 'straight' community organizations sweat to produce a dozen members at a meeting," the activist Robert Levin observed, "the Rangers easily draw a thousand. . . . They are *the* organization for the young in a community over one-half of whose population is under 25." The Rangers are "a marvel of organization," said a Woodlawn community worker. "If they were directed properly they could give a lot to the community." "The leaders are the key," observed youth officer Julius Frazier. If they could be convinced to turn their energies toward community support, "the rank and file will follow."[50]

As Rev. Martin Luther King Jr. and the Chicago Freedom Movement shifted to street protests in May 1966, the SCLC held a meeting with over 250 Rangers at the Holy Cross school in Woodlawn, hoping to head off riots. The activists explained nonviolent direct action to the young men. In the wake of the West Side riots that July, Ranger leadership cooperated with TWO, the police, and area ministers to prevent a similar uprising in Woodlawn. A number of Ranger leaders marched with Dr. King into Gage Park in late July; they wore baseball gloves to catch bricks and bottles thrown by angry whites and refused to respond in kind. King publicly praised their restraint. A GIU undercover observer doubted that the Rangers could be fully enlisted in nonviolent direct action. Perhaps unwittingly, he stumbled on a useful explanation: "They were more anxious to get jobs than to be locked up in a sit-down demonstration."[51]

John Fry, a white minister at First Presbyterian and a former Marine, had begun to work with the gang in May 1965. Fry, who liked to call himself the "honky preacher," was outspoken in his belief that the Rangers had "stumbled into the precincts of potential greatness by driving out of the parochial confines of a neighborhood gang. We desire that greatness to be expressed in ways directly beneficial to the youth themselves, and to Woodlawn as a whole." The First Presbyterian Church became a kind of sanctuary for gang members, and Fry and his staff successfully negotiated a number of truces, even convincing the Rangers to let the minister lock up their weapons in the basement. Intrigued by their organizational potential and fearful of the long-term consequences of leaving them and their families outside TWO's influence, Brazier lobbied his organization to support Fry's work. He also opened conversations with the OEO about a job-training program for gang members.[52]

While many activists in TWO respected the aspirations and potential of the gang, as well as their hostility to the police, the organization risked splitting along class and geographical lines. Brazier had a difficult time selling some TWO activists on working with the gang rather than supporting police efforts to destroy it. Middle-class residents of West Woodlawn, who were disproportionately represented in TWO, and lived in Disciples territory, were particularly torn. For decades police activity in Chicago's black neighborhoods had alternated between excessive force and purposeful neglect, even as violent crime and gang violence escalated rapidly.

While black Chicagoans left places like Woodlawn for a variety of reasons, physical safety was near the top of the list. In the late spring of 1967, South Side blacks ranked crime among the biggest issues facing the city, after housing and the cost of living. Public discussion of the rapid escalation of urban crime was generally framed around assumptions of black criminality and white victimhood, as it often still is. The reality, of course, is that black communities often bore the brunt of it. TWO activists were well aware of the larger structural and political forces at work, but crime is generally experienced personally, not politically. Gang violence was particularly troubling, because it tended to affect youth culture in schools, and thus, academic achievement. For those Woodlawn families with the resources to leave, Brazier was proposing a risky gamble.[53]

While Brazier favored efforts to cut down on illegal and violent acts, he was adamant that TWO address the root causes of gang violence. The SWU agreed and worked with Brazier to build support. He spoke at committee meetings throughout the summer of 1966, and the *Woodlawn Booster* was enlisted to praise the Rangers' growing political consciousness. The paper editorialized in early August, "What we have bred in Woodlawn—and across the country, especially in ghetto communities—is a new breed of cat. Our youth simply will not accept the old tired slogans, the fatuous, empty talk about workshops, summer camps, recreation, brotherhood and decency. Our youth want jobs . . . and they demand, and will get, dignity."[54]

TWO was pushed to the breaking point that September, when the school year started. Hyde Park High School became a flash point, as the Rangers sought to drive the Disciples out of it. The resulting violence led many black middle-class parents from West Woodlawn to pull their children out. In conjunction with the Board of Education's January 1966 approval of a new high school for students from Hyde Park, the conflict also completed white flight from the school. A new group, the Concerned Parents of Woodlawn, began to put pressure on both TWO and the police to address the gang issue. Block clubs in more middle-class areas of central and west Woodlawn called on TWO to stop working with Fry. At a contentious meeting of the TWO Schools Committee in late September, a group of forty parents condemned the organization's approach and called for a police crackdown on the Rangers.[55]

While some saw great potential in the Rangers, the police saw in them the seeds of a black Mafia. Local media generally echoed this view. Believing that he had community support, the local police district commander informed the Greater Woodlawn Pastors' Alliance (GWPA) of his intent "to destroy the Ranger organization and arrest the leadership." The police then raided First Presbyterian, taking the weapons Fry had locked up, and arresting over 50 Rangers on a variety of charges. Media coverage inaccurately depicted the church as a weapons depot for gangs, an image the CPD and City Hall did little to correct. The police "believe they have a hunting license to get Rangers," Fry argued.[56]

Brazier urged patience. "TWO is doing more than any other group," he told the Steering Committee. "Others are just talking . . . the solution to this problem doesn't happen overnight. It took a long time coming and it will take a long time to deal with it . . . let us not allow any group to start a campaign to divide TWO. Our strength is in our unity." The GWPA, however, quickly split over the issue. Fry demanded that TWO criticize the police, while Fr. Martin Farrell of Holy Cross Church wanted the organization to censure Fry, condemn gang violence, and support the crackdown. In the November meeting of the TWO Steering Committee, Brazier tried to persuade Farrell not to introduce any resolutions that might jeopardize his ongoing negotiations with the OEO. Farrell refused. After his resolutions were narrowly defeated, he and his allies—mostly block clubs from the area surrounding Holy Cross—walked out. The Steering Committee then voted unanimously to support Brazier's proposal.[57]

While Brazier's inclination had always been to fully involve gang youth in planning and developing its job-training program, much of the impetus for doing so actually came from Jerome Bernstein, deputy director of the Manpower Division of the CAP. Bernstein came to Chicago twice in the spring of 1967 to meet with TWO, Fry, and gang members to design the proposal. In April, Bernstein successfully convinced leaders of both the Rangers and the Disciples to sign a truce, informing them that the OEO would only approve the plan if they did so. The truce held through the April 1968 riots, resulting in a sharp drop in violence, vandalism, and burglaries in Woodlawn.

In its proposal to the OEO, TWO in many ways returned to the intellectual roots of Alinsky's career as an organizer. The group sought to place the gang issue in social and economic context and develop structures for socially productive empowerment. TWO described the Rangers as "an illegitimate structure created to attain legitimate goals" such as "real power and socioeconomic status." Gang members believed they lacked any other vehicle for dealing with the "chaotic conditions with which they are confronted." Traditional youth-serving agencies tended to have a self-selecting clientele, leaving those in the greatest need "physically and psychologically alienated from the agency."

TWO, however, had the experience and community legitimacy to "redirect the energies of the youth gangs of Woodlawn" by building "positive, constructive social programs" that would help young people and the community as a whole. The involvement of gang youth in the crafting of TWO's proposal had "given them a sense of identity with the project as well as hope for the future," and convinced the organization that an OEO-funded project needed to include them in its implementation and governance. TWO's "fundamental philosophy" is that "engagement in real issues restores human dignity." That same approach "will succeed with youth because youth demands . . . a structure within which they can change their own destiny, yet know their elders support them." It is only when they have a stake in the project that it becomes "within their self-interest to make it succeed."[58]

In May and June 1967, while the OEO deliberated, the Rangers and Hyde Park High students staged a nationally publicized musical revue *Opportunity Please Knock*, sponsored by jazz pianist Oscar Brown Jr. More than eight hundred people saw the performance at First Presbyterian. Millions more enjoyed a portion of it on the Smothers Brothers television program. The performance (and the truce) helped to alleviate some of TWO's internal tensions, as did the possibility of federally funded job training for many members' children. For the moment, TWO had succeeded in convincing local activists that the real conflict was between Woodlawn residents (including gang youth) and outside forces (Daley and the police). Delegates to TWO's May 1967 convention enthusiastically endorsed the OEO proposal. The SWU locals were particularly vocal supporters. White House staffer Bill Graham, who visited Woodlawn on President Johnson's behalf in May 1967, informed his boss that Fry's work with the Rangers was "very hopeful."[59]

Daley successfully delayed the proposal for months, but in June 1967 TWO received a direct $957,000 demonstration grant from the OEO, to run through May 1968. The Youth Project began in September. In a July 1967 conversation captured by the National Film Board of Canada, Fry, Alinsky, and Finney discussed the transformative potential of the Rangers. "Here is a group that from the time they first looked at a TV screen they've seen tear gas . . . they've seen police dogs . . . and they've seen a lot of their leaders sort of walk, their civil rights leaders," Alinsky argued. In response, "they've organized into groups like the Blackstone Rangers." It was critical for TWO not to walk. Finney concurred. "The guys are really looking for jobs, you know, . . . and if there's nothing for them to put in their pockets, well, they got nothing to do, so they throw the brick." The solution, they agreed, was to connect them to both TWO and the labor market. Fry added: "We just take all the play from them by actually delivering." Alinsky tended to see adolescent males as "nature's natural fascists," Von Hoffman recalled. The answer was to "keep them busy twenty-four hours a day, never let up . . . never be without a project for them or they will think one up for themselves."[60]

The Youth Project used the existing gang structure and leadership to recruit eight hundred unemployed young men to job-training programs. All were high school dropouts. Students with some work experience and eighth-grade skills in reading and math worked with TWO's on-the-job training program, while those with minimal education and job skills received remedial training first. Trainees were paid $45 a week to take classes and had access to legal and health services. Students received instruction in basic math, reading and adult literacy, "the 'world of work,'" and black history. The instructors for the second track were gang leaders, under professional supervision. Gang members were also hired as community workers, aides, and subprofessionals, at up to $5,200 a year. Xerox was hired to formulate the curriculum, and the Chicago Urban League worked on job development for graduates. By the end of January 1968, thirty-eight gang members were on staff, and more than one hundred had been placed in jobs. Twenty graduates worked at International Harvester; members of the Rangers and the Disciples took buses to suburban jobs together, without incident.

In a September 1967 letter to Joseph Califano, special assistant to President Johnson, Julian Levi of the University of Chicago praised the Youth Project for reducing violent crime and gang tensions in Woodlawn.[61] Unfortunately for TWO, the project had drawn national attention precisely as intense congressional debates over community action, crime, and law and order had begun to shift the parameters of the politically possible in a decidedly conservative direction. President Johnson's efforts to address poverty and racial discrimination in the cities and suburbs of the North were under assault from many directions by early 1967. Polls the previous fall showed that most Americans believed that the Republicans could better handle urban riots and racial violence, and that most whites thought the War on Poverty was doing nothing to stop the unrest—and might even be contributing to it by feeding black frustration and rewarding criminality. Liberals and Democrats were routed in the November 1966 elections.[62]

In October 1964 Johnson had claimed that the best way to address crime and disorder was by attacking poverty. Conservative efforts to question the relationship between the two had gained political credence among white voters since then. "There is indeed a problem of the slums," the conservative *National Review* acknowledged in August 1966. "And there is the problem of rioting and civil disobedience. But the two are not the same problem, and it is a distinctively Liberal fatuity to suppose that they are."

Johnson adviser Harry McPherson nicely summarized the president's dilemma: "We talk about the multitude of good programs going into the cities, and yet there are riots, which suggests that the programs are no good, or the Negroes past saving."[63] Neither explanation held much appeal; at the same time, the various demands coming from black activists and the left for greater community power, an attack on metropolitan residential segregation, and a vast expansion in the size and reach of social programs seemed not viable in the wake of the midterms. While the right exaggerated the (negative) impact of the poverty program, the left attacked it as at best underfunded and overpromised, and at worst, as co-optation and distraction. Johnson and other liberals struggled to find a persuasive balance between the need for both social justice and social order, in rhetoric, policy, and politics.

Frustrated by a lack of reliable ground-level intelligence, in late 1966 Attorney General Nicholas Katzenbach convinced Johnson to send some of his young staffers on secret visits to black neighborhoods around the country. White House aide Sherwin Markman remembers a winter meeting with the boss: "I want to know what's happening in the ghettos," Johnson announced. "If I could go, I'd go myself, but I can't . . . the next best thing is, I'd like some of you fellows, if you would go out there, and live in the ghettos, and then report directly to me." Dozens of young staffers fanned out across the country during the first five months of 1967, trying to get a sense of black views on the War on Poverty and to anticipate the next riot(s). Johnson hoped that this information might help him put together a legislative agenda for 1968 and provide qualitative data—quotes and human interest stories—to buttress that agenda in congressional testimony. Markman and his colleagues were instructed to find a local guide and to stay overnight in the ghetto. For many of them, this was their first extended interracial encounter.[64]

In January 1967, guided by Ken Vallis, a black staffer from the local OEO office, Markman went on a covert mission to the South Side. In a subsequent seven-page memo he made clear that the demand from black activists and organizations for more control over poverty programs was rooted in Mayor Daley's obstructionism, as well as their historical powerlessness. Further riots and the collapse of black support for liberal poverty policy were in the offing if something didn't change. Markman's coworkers heard similar things in other cities.

"For three days and two nights last week I lived and slept in the worst part of the Negro ghetto of Chicago," Markman wrote. "I was fortunate in being able to talk at length, in depth and candidly with a host of people: Negroes who live in the ghetto, Negroes and whites who work with them, idealists, troublemakers, young and old." What he found gave little reason for optimism. Most of his time was spent in Woodlawn. Aside from living in poverty, Markman wrote Johnson, "the people of these ghettos also live with a deep-felt bitterness. It was expressed to me in many forms, but it always came out as a belief that the ghetto Negro lives in a world which is severed from ours." "Hemmed in by the circle of poverty," his informants generally saw government as a kind of foreign enemy—as "part of the white apparatus which created and fosters the perpetuation of the circle." This feeling of "alienation from the governmental structures" had been caused in part by their experiences with the War on Poverty.

Markman's arrival coincided with the beginning stages of Daley's efforts to kill off the Youth Project. He had an extended breakfast with Rev. Brazier and other TWO activists, at which they conveyed their growing frustration with Daley and the War on Poverty. "In almost all instances the response was that the poverty program does not reach the people, and is controlled by the city government," Markman wrote. "The people feel the program is blocked by the local government and thus is not helpful to them. This is why they demand that they have a voice in their own programs and that the money come to them without local government intervention."

The 1966 riots were rooted in legitimate grievances, Markman argued, as were the criticisms of the poverty war coming from black Chicagoans. "Without exception all of the people I spoke with are convinced that the riots of last summer will be repeated, expanded and intensified this year," he told Johnson. Riots "will continue to come," he wrote, and police action was not a sufficient response. "If we do not stop the violence, the backlash will destroy the political base which permits us to go on to the deeper solutions of the problem."

Markman found one "sign of hope," however: The Woodlawn Organization. Describing it as "a completely indigenous group," he praised TWO for its attempts to launch a "total attack on the entire circle of poverty simultaneously." Markman and Brazier had an extensive conversation about the balance between integration and black community building. "They want integration, but he feels that integration must come along with an up-building of their own organization ... [and] their own community," Markman wrote. "He believes that you must attack here and now—education, jobs, labor unions— and then integration will follow." He conveyed most of this exchange to the president: "They believe in ultimate integration," Markman wrote, "but they also believe that they must also (and probably first) create a first-rate community of their own." Although his visit was brief, Markman effectively caught a sense of TWO's strategic dilemma: how to command resources, improvements, and power for Woodlawn while addressing the metropolitan segregation that ultimately limited their access to these things.

While TWO had been an enormous thorn in the side of the Daley machine, the OEO, and the Administration itself, Markman acknowledged, he found its leadership to be "politically sophisticated" rather than purely negative. "The leaders of TWO believe that ultimately they must exercise the greatest possible influence upon the governmental structures" in order to make it more responsive at all levels. "They intend to use TWO as a unified political force. They believe they can thus increasingly force government to listen to them." In other words, Markman told the president, "Rather than merely attacking the power structure they intend to make themselves part of it. In my judgment they are right and they have a very good tool with which to work." Implicit in Markman's praise was his sense that TWO offered a 'responsible' grassroots alternative to groups with more nationalist rhetoric and strategies. Given the alternatives, Markman concluded, groups like TWO "must be encouraged."[65]

In the wake of a growing white backlash against the War on Poverty, fueled by perceptions of it as a "black" program that rewarded radicalism, riots, and lawlessness, Johnson sought to head off the complete destruction of the OEO in April 1967 by increasing the control of local officials over CAAs. After a brief cooling-off period in the wake of that summer's riots in Newark, Detroit, and other cities, the House Committee on Education and Labor took up the issue. Rep. Pucinski, working on Daley's behalf, and with TWO very much in mind, urged the Committee to require that CAAs be run by elected officials, and that all OEO grants be funneled through them. Rep. Edith Green (D-OR) offered an amendment to the Economic Opportunity Act to this effect in October. When Congress enacted the act, Green argued, it "did not intend to legislate a revolution in American politics by establishing another structure of government."[66]

TWO, as well as the CATC, loomed large over the passage of the so-called Green Amendment. The *New York Times* interpreted it as a direct result of events in Chicago and used TWO as its primary case study of the politics of the CAP. "Daley has never been reconciled to the statutory recognition given to the poor," the paper reported. "As rewritten by the committee the bill makes it difficult for the Woodlawn folks to get anti-poverty funds except by courtesy of the Daley organization." While the Green Amendment didn't curtail the political activism of the poor—movements to broaden participation had taken on a life of their own—it did end formal federal support for it.[67]

Daley continued to try to undermine the Youth Project in summer and fall of 1967. He blocked the appointment of a director, encouraged the police to harass students and staff, and publicly implicated the project in criminal activity. The police also harassed any individuals and institutions that sought to work with Rangers. A house owned by the Chicago Theological Seminary, in which Rangers and seminar students lived, was raided ten times between December 1967 and February 1968, each time without probable cause. Twenty-six arrests were made. Seminarians who gave Rangers rides were tailed by the police and threatened with traffic violations.[68]

The OEO contract required that Daley "concur" with TWO in naming a director. In June 1967, an advisory committee of TWO leadership, University of Chicago faculty, and directors of social agencies recommended an ex-probation officer and gang expert from New York for the position. Daley rejected him and encouraged TWO to nominate someone from Chicago. TWO obligingly did so, but the mayor continued to veto its choices. When Daley finally submitted two nominees himself, both candidates refused to be interviewed by TWO. While TWO finally appointed an interim director in November, Anthony Gibbs, the project suffered from Daley's delaying tactics. It struggled to hire professional teachers, and the staff lacked guidance. "It was an effort to punish TWO," a University of Chicago professor told a reporter. While Gibbs helped to right the ship over the winter, the project was unable to overcome Daley's two other efforts to destroy it: police harassment, and a fear-mongering public relations campaign.

Both TWO and the OEO—and the students—struggled to understand the official attitude of law enforcement toward the project. While the Chicago police met daily with TWO staff and participated in regular monitoring meetings with OEO, TWO, and Chicago Committee on Urban Opportunity representatives, the GIU went to great lengths to destroy the Youth Project. Daley reconfigured and reinforced the GIU in March 1967, as a direct response to TWO's activities, giving it a broad mandate to investigate and infiltrate organizations associated with gangs. Fry and the First Presbyterian Church, in particular, was targeted. The GIU also engaged in a concerted campaign to destroy the leadership of the Rangers, mostly through repeated mass arrests of young black men throughout Woodlawn and through the use of agents provocateurs. While nearly all those arrested were either acquitted or never came to trial at all, the harassment discouraged students and employers from participating.

"Our approach is the hard-line police approach," argued Captain Edward Buckney, the head of the GIU. Buckney believed most young gang members were coerced into the Rangers by its older members, so he sought to "cut off the head" of the gang by arresting its senior leadership. "If we could divorce those who religiously believe in it from the community, the others would have a chance to get out," Buckney argued. By giving the Rangers leadership support, funding, and legitimacy, Brazier and Fry were encouraging gang violence, not preventing it, Buckney argued.[69]

Rangers "are hazed, slapped around, insulted, taken in squad cars and dropped in territories of rival gangs, and arrested on the slightest pretext," Robert Levin observed in the spring of 1968. GIU officers regularly entered the four training centers to question participants and disrupt operations. The Rangers leader Jeff Fort was arrested in October 1967 and held for five months without bond or trial, before the charges were finally dropped. Employers, worried about bad publicity, began to back away from the Youth Project.

Hostility from Daley and the GIU threatened not only to destroy the project but also to sow division within TWO if gang warfare was once again unleashed. While the top leadership of the Rangers sought political legitimacy and seemed capable of controlling the membership, the younger second tier lacked the same skills and interests. By destroying the leadership, police actions might create more crime and gang violence in Woodlawn, not less.[70]

On a number of occasions, TWO meetings were interrupted by police raids. Eighteen officers broke up a June 1967 meeting at 1st Presbyterian between Brazier, Finney, Bernstein, and gang representatives. Anthony Gibbs was apprehended in his office in November, for resisting arrest. The charges were quickly dropped. "The oppressive presence of the police is very evident," Herman Blake observed. "The community is saturated with police cars, including an ever-present array of patrolling paddy wagons." "I have lost all faith in the political establishment of this city," a despondent Brazier told the GWPA. "They do not want to stop riots. They will not let people help themselves. They want control, and will stop at nothing to deny independent groups from gaining power." Levin, a VISTA—or Volunteers in Service to America—volunteer assigned to the Community Legal Counsel in Chicago, believed Daley and the GIU's efforts were politically motivated. The Rangers had helped to generate a 70 percent turnout for anti-machine alderman Leon Despres in a recent election, and Daley feared that the Rangers would disrupt the 1968 Democratic National Convention.[71]

In December 1967, the *Chicago Tribune* used information from the GIU and Daley associate Earl Bush to run a series of exposés, many inaccurate, alleging financial improprieties, violence, and drug use at the training centers. The paper also noted that many of the trainees and instructors had criminal records, and some were under indictment, awaiting trial. The articles received national coverage. Congressman Pucinski used them to prompt investigations by the Government Accounting Office (GAO) and the OEO. Pucinski also succeeded in convincing the OEO to fire Jerome Bernstein, depriving the TWO program of its foremost advocate in Washington.

The Investigations Subcommittee of the Senate Committee on Governmental Operations, chaired by the War on Poverty critic John McClellan (D-AR), also sent representatives to Chicago. The investigators occupied the time and energy of Brazier, Gibbs and TWO staff for three months in early 1968, asking questions and poring through documents. A mid-January shooting at one of the training centers added to the pressure and sparked further criticism of the project from Daley, the *Tribune,* and the GIU.[72]

Brazier vented his frustration to the *Chicago Defender*: "Blacks are always accused of doing nothing to straighten out their own neighborhoods. Now, when we are using poverty funds to solve some of these problems, we find that we are still being criticized. . . . but what are we expected to do? Should we throw up our hands and back out?"[73]

The White House staffer Sherwin Markman secretly returned to Woodlawn in February 1968 on President Johnson's behalf and spoke to Brazier at length. While Brazier praised the OEO's courage in "bucking Daley and giving them the experimental program," Markman concluded that his problems with the Mayor and Rep. Pucinski had left the minister "an embittered and disappointed man." Brazier "sees the city hardening in all departments in relation to the Negro community . . . he says he has never seen it this bad before." Police brutality, always a problem in Woodlawn, had greatly increased in previous months. "Militancy is growing," Brazier lamented, and there is "no way in the world it can be stopped." He confidentially expressed a desire to retreat "back to his Church" and cede his leadership role to "more militant people." Markman found this worrisome; in a similar report a year earlier, he had praised TWO as a moderate and integrationist grassroots alternative to black power activism in Chicago.[74]

Despite the harassment, however, the Youth Project persisted. Both the GAO and the OEO cleared the project of any financial malfeasance. The OEO remained publicly supportive. "Inevitably, there will be 'failures' in a project of this nature. But the greatest failure would be to do nothing and let all these teenagers harden into adult criminals," OEO's regional director Alan Beals said. The OEO staffer Denis Orphan concurred: "We knew it was no pie-in-the-sky when we started. But I think we've probably already done some good for 200 people . . . nothing like this has ever been done before by anybody." Woodlawn residents also rallied around TWO. An overflow crowd of four hundred attended a Steering Committee meeting in January to demonstrate their support. Markman, in his letter to Johnson, noted how widespread local support was.[75]

While the investigations by the GAO and the OEO raised legitimate (if intrusive) questions, the same could not be said for McClellan's efforts. Senate investigators hoped to make the case that TWO was using federal funds to foment riots and disorder. Unable to find any evidence, they began to work closely with the GIU. Senate staffers, wrote one reporter, spent months "scrounging around the South Side of Chicago for dirt to discredit the OEO job project." TWO found itself caught in a national battle over 'law and order' and Johnson's War on Poverty. Daley and Pucinski sought to demonstrate that OEO programs that bypassed City Hall were bound to fail, while McClellan hoped to discredit the entire War on Poverty. The GIU fed investigators scandalous and unproven stories about the Rangers, TWO, and the

First Presbyterian Church. It also provided witnesses—generally former gang members seeking revenge or leniency—and McClellan allowed testimony to be given without cross-examination and with immunity from libel suits. Sensationalized stories were fed regularly to the press in the spring of 1968, particularly after the riots surrounding Dr. King's murder in April.[76] The Senate investigation also hindered the efforts of Irving Spergel, the University of Chicago scholar hired by the OEO, to evaluate the project, twice requesting subpoenas of the research records.

And yet sixty-one graduates of the Youth Project had obtained jobs by the end of May 1968. Spergel recommended that the OEO fund the project for two more years. Because of the Rangers positive role in preventing riots, Daley briefly reconsidered his opposition to that renewal and contemplated allowing the appointment of a permanent director. President Johnson followed the controversy closely, waiting on Daley. The GIU apparently talked the mayor out of changing his mind.[77]

The McClellan hearings began in June 1968. The violence of recent months and rising crime rates hovered over them, which opponents of the War on Poverty sought to connect to civil rights groups, "outside agitators," and liberal social policy. Crime rates had increased by double digits each year since 1965 and had climbed 17 percent in the first three months of 1968 alone. A poll in late February found that for the first time a majority of Americans saw "crime and lawlessness" as the most important domestic issue. President Johnson struggled—and failed—to get ahead of the issue.

The Kerner Commission's report on the 1967 riots, released in March 1968, implicitly blamed the limitations of the War on Poverty and explicitly blamed white racism—putting Johnson in a difficult spot. Johnson told one of his advisers that placing the principal blame on white racism "only hurts us when we try to pass laws for the Negro." Frank Meyer confirmed Johnson's worries in the conservative magazine the *National Review*. The commission "placed the blame everywhere but where it belongs, everywhere, that is, except upon the rioters and upon the liberals who . . . prepared the way for the riots by their contempt for social order and their utopian, egalitarian enticements and incitements."[78]

The hearings quickly devolved into a forum for conservative assaults on the White House, the Supreme Court, and liberalism. That summer, conservatives took a firm hold on the nation's political agenda and discourse around crime and social policy. Liberals increasingly stepped away from social policy as the answer to urban crime, falling back on gun control and increased law enforcement. It didn't help that liberalism's most authoritative voice on law and order, Senator Robert F. Kennedy, had been silenced days before the

McClellan hearings opened. This polarizing context didn't bode well for the TWO Youth Project.

McClellan's investigation entailed very little direct examination of the project's accomplishments. Instead, the committee heard from GIU officers and former gang members, who accused Fry and TWO of using taxpayer money to strengthen the Rangers. Illinois Senator Charles Percy encouraged the committee to call project supporters Leon Despres, Julian Levi, and Edwin Berry of the Chicago Urban League to testify, with no success. The hearings "are a fraud," Brazier told the *Defender*. "It is a question of the white power structure trying to wrest control of a grassroots project from the black community."[79]

Both the OEO and the *Chicago Defender* demanded a fair hearing for the project. Bertrand Harding, the acting director of the OEO, pointed out that the GIU had never brought any of its charges to prosecutors or to the OEO. He also questioned McClellan's credibility, given his "apparent eagerness . . . to accept the uncorroborated statements of a Chicago hoodlum, who was never a participant in the program." At least through mid-August 1968, Harding continued to publicly defend the grant. Some means had to be developed to "reclaim these poor, hard-core youth," since traditional efforts by police, churches, schools and job-training programs had all failed. "If we have failed, we have learned valuable lessons that had to be learned." Privately, the Administration believed the primary purpose of the hearings was the destruction and embarrassment of the entire War on Poverty—the community action programs in particular.[80]

In a July 8 editorial, the *Defender* argued that rather than examining baseless accusations, the Senate should investigate whether the program worked, as well as the failure of the police to halt criminal activity in black communities. The TWO project "is now being made the scapegoat for all of the failings of the police department, the schools, and the community at large," it argued. Abner Mikva, an independent Democrat running for Congress to represent Woodlawn and Hyde Park, was equally critical of McClellan: "The US Senate is no cloak to be used by a senatorial nightrider . . . [his] credentials in the area of help for the poor hardly recommend him for the job of evaluating the TWO program."[81]

Brazier finally testified on the tenth day of the hearings. Introduced by Senator Percy as a man of "personal integrity, selflessness and courage," the minister sought to focus on the accomplishments of the project by calmly describing its rationale and its history. "The first year was a little ambitious, and didn't work out quite as well as we thought it should," he acknowledged. "But some of these boys are really trying. We've seen some real behavior changes in a lot of them." Brazier accused Daley of obstructing the program. "The animosity shown to the project by some persons makes it a miracle that this program accomplished what it did," he observed. Brazier lost his temper only once, when he mentioned that the project taught trainees to arrive at their new jobs on time. "Are we going to nurse people all the way through their life?" McClellan asked. "Some people need a tremendous amount of support throughout their life," Brazier responded testily. "We're paying for years of segregation and neglect," he argued; the problems of the ghetto would never be solved without a lot more time and federal money.[82]

Harding ultimately caved to intense political pressure and withdrew his support for renewed funding in August. The reason did not cover Harding in glory: Senator Harry F. Byrd Jr. (D-VA), who sat on the Labor Committee, refused to support Harding's permanent appointment as director if he didn't renounce the project, writing in a public letter that he would not approve "an appointee who shows such a reckless disregard for use of tax funds," without "written assurance that no similar projects will be permitted." Sensing that President Johnson had little stomach for a fight over the project (or his confirmation), Harding gave in. He pointedly refused to concede that the project was a mistake, describing it as one of those "noble experiments" that failed "without imputing guilt or duplicity to the experimenters." He continued to defend it in later hearings, but Harding promised that the OEO would no longer fund projects that "would produce the objectionable results of this particular grant."[83]

While the *Chicago Tribune* celebrated "the end to a sorry experiment" and praised McClellan for performing a "valuable service," Brazier described the end of the project as "tragic." "We brought peace to this community," he told the TWO Steering Committee in September, "and for this we have been maligned across the country." The Project "was directly responsible for reducing violence in Woodlawn. This was the quietest summer we've had in years," Brazier lamented. "But no one is being called . . . to say anything good about the program." Alinsky had predicted that in places where the black poor actually tried to seize power, local and federal officials would act to stop them. TWO's experience with the Youth Project thus came as no surprise to him.

Given its short and frequently interrupted life, it is difficult to evaluate the effectiveness of TWO's project. According to Lois Wille, most Chicago youth workers and "street gang experts" believed the project had been misunderstood and just needed more time. Most of its practices, depicted by its enemies as unorthodox, irresponsible, and inappropriate, were modeled on established and successful gang projects elsewhere in the city. "Either the Senate committee doesn't understand what street-gang work is all about, or it is deliberately trying to make this one project look bad," the director of one

North Side youth agency told Wille. "It could have been any of us up there before that committee." "It is unfair to tag TWO with the criminal activity of the Rangers," argued the YMCA's Bruce Cole. "They were trying to turn kids away from crime by getting them decent jobs . . . these are tough kids, a most volatile source of potential trouble. If we write them off and don't work with them, we're saying 'OK, to heck with you—make as much trouble as you can.'"

When Spergel submitted his final evaluation to the OEO in February 1969, he described the project as "pioneering" and "reasonably successful." He noted a reduction in crime and delinquency in the Third Police District, success in job placement, and the prevention of riots. Only two of the trainees could read at the eighth-grade level when they enrolled, but most advanced two or three grades during the project's short life. "No other youth manpower program ever reached so relatively large a pool of hard-core male delinquent youths," Spergel wrote. He found "no strong programmatic reason for termination or failing to extend the life of the project." Indeed, given that "many powerful groups and organizations acted . . . to encourage the failure of the project," he concluded, "the fact that the project had positive results is remarkable." Whatever its actual and potential impact, the very existence of the program was evidence of TWO's willingness to take innovative risks to radically alter the South Side ghetto's opportunity structure. It was also evidence of the limits of the War on Poverty itself.[84]

Conclusion

As support waned for the War on Poverty—and for more direct attacks on metropolitan racial inequality—liberal and left discussions became bogged down in seemingly irreconcilable dualities, each with its own set of preferred strategies and policies, and often exaggerated by the press: integration versus separatism, universalistic or class-based approaches to organizing and reform versus race-based ones, liberal versus radical, and a focus on federal action and legislation versus an emphasis on local black empowerment. Ultimately, these dualities were far more reflective of how stubbornly embedded racial inequality and white privilege were in the national economy and the metropolitan landscape than of fundamentally different approaches to the American dilemma. As Dr. King learned in Chicago in 1966, black grassroots activism wasn't enough; economic growth wasn't enough; antidiscrimination law wasn't enough; a revamped welfare state wasn't enough. Untying the Gordian knot of race in America required an alchemical mixture of all at once.

Even as the War on Poverty came under increasing attack from all sides, the period between the summer of 1965 and the spring of 1968 gave rise to some remarkably creative rethinking among activists and policy makers about racial and economic inequality in metropolitan areas. TWO played a vital role in this national conversation and would seek to bring many of these ideas together in the Model Cities plan it developed in the last year of the Johnson presidency. Its successes and failures would ultimately reveal much about the limits of federal urban policy, the nation's racial politics, and the future of the American metropolis.

9

Model Cities, TWO, and the Spatial Dilemmas of Metropolitan Segregation

> The Model City Program offers the promise of carrying forward the purging of American cities of the stigma and stain of racism. If this promise is not realized, we will tie around our necks another unbearable albatross.
> FRANK HORNE, National Committee against Discrimination in Housing, April 1967

In both word and deed, civil rights activists and organizations in the North grappled with the dilemmas of metropolitan inequality in the mid-1960s. The period from President Johnson's Howard University speech in May 1965 to the release of the Kerner Commission's report in March 1968—was a defining moment, one of heartbreaking promise and intense intellectual debate and social conflict. Pushed from below, from within, and from the right, liberal policy and politics directly confronted the dilemmas of race and poverty in the metropolitan North. Liberalism faced a reckoning that was decades in the making and, in many ways, of its own making. The encounter ultimately demonstrated the limited analytical reach of American liberalism and the extent to which its racial compromises had limited its political capital. But it also revealed extraordinary visions and possibilities, roads not taken. The paths winding outward from this policy fork are all the more remarkable to us today, when we confront many of the same dilemmas with a radically diminished sense of political and moral efficacy.

For this very brief time, policy makers, activists, and social movements were grappling with metropolitan racial inequality, both on the streets and in the corridors of power. The strategic dilemmas faced by the Black Freedom Movement in the North suddenly erupted into national policy discourse. For a moment, it seemed that President Johnson might use the Model Cities program to directly challenge metropolitan racial segregation, by leveraging civil rights law and the power of the purse to open the suburbs and encourage metropolitan governance. Introduced to Congress in January 1966—the same week that Martin Luther King launched his open-housing campaign in Chicago—Model Cities sought to combine community development and metropolitan desegregation in a frontal attack on the problems of the city.

Simultaneously, the fraying coalition of labor, liberals, and the civil rights movement united in support of the Freedom Budget, released amid the congressional debate over Model Cities. The Freedom Budget argued for an extension of the social and economic rights envisioned by FDR in his 1944 Second Bill of Rights. First proposed by Bayard Rustin at a White House planning conference in November 1965, the Freedom Budget for a time seemed a viable alternative to the far more modest (and politically floundering) War on Poverty. The Kerner Commission report, at the end of this period, proposed fusing together these reform visions, while Martin Luther King, the Woodlawn Organization (TWO), and grassroots activists around the country grappled with connecting local black empowerment and social democratic policy nationally to challenge metropolitan racial inequality.

In combination, the Model Cities program and the Freedom Budget implicitly critiqued the War on Poverty. As proposed, Model Cities recognized the vital connection between black urban poverty and metropolitan segregation while simultaneously valuing black activism and community development. The Freedom Budget was premised on the assumption that racial equality could be attained only through the creation of a robust welfare state and an economic policy aimed toward full employment. These three ideas—color-blind social democracy, activist-driven community development, and metropolitan desegregation—interacted intellectually and programmatically with local pushes from below. From 1966 to 1969, Saul Alinsky's TWO would seek to restructure the American welfare state from the ground up, and to use Model Cities to do it. But by the mid-1970s, all that was left of the three reform visions was an underfunded and mostly privatized version of community development. It left the patterns of metropolitan segregation and inequality in place, setting the stage for yet another racial reckoning a half century later.

Freedom Budget

The Freedom Budget emerged primarily as a critique of social and economic policy under President Johnson. It had its immediate origins in a November 1965 White House planning conference on civil rights. Liberals and civil rights activists, increasingly skeptical of the limitations of Johnson's War on Poverty, were incensed at the August 1965 leak of White House adviser Daniel Patrick Moynihan's report *The Negro Family*. They feared that the study signaled a shift in focus from jobs and income to culture, crime, and the black family. White House staffers saw the conference as an opportunity to reassemble the civil rights coalition, in order to push for further federal action. Bayard

Rustin and A. Philip Randolph took advantage. "The ghetto is the problem," Randolph said in his keynote address, "and it must be destroyed." The only way to prevent riots and defuse the "increasingly explosive socio-racial dynamite in the black ghettos," he concluded, was to deal with unemployment and urban poverty on a color-blind basis. Rustin concurred: "Negro poverty cannot be abolished without the simultaneous abolition of white poverty, and vice versa." They suggested a massive, $100 billion federal attack on poverty and economic insecurity, through full employment and a guaranteed annual income. The press latched on to the idea. President Johnson selected a thirty-member council to plan the 1966 conference, with Randolph as cochair.[1]

The summer of 1966 was a season of defeat, frustration, and division for the civil rights movement, both in Congress and around the country. Fair housing was defeated in Congress and on the streets of Chicago, while Stokely Carmichael's June call for Black Power made manifest the long-simmering strategic, organizational, and generational divisions within the movement. The energies and resources of white leftists, meanwhile, were increasingly focused on the escalating conflict in Vietnam.

The Freedom Budget was released just a week before the November 1966 midterm elections, at New York's Salem Methodist Church. It called for $185 billion in federal spending over ten years to provide full employment, invest in public goods, and eliminate poverty and economic deprivation for all Americans. Describing the budget as a "real *war* on poverty," Randolph tied racism directly to the "workings of our economy." The Freedom Budget was above all else a call for full employment.[2]

The Freedom Budget directly attacked the idea that the poor were in any way qualitatively different from the mainstream. Because most poverty and economic insecurity stemmed from a combination of inadequate employment opportunities and low wages, a full-employment policy was the most direct solution. Tight labor markets, an increased minimum wage, and the elimination of "right-to-work" laws in the South would boost wages, stimulate consumer demand, and eliminate much of the nation's poverty. Economic growth alone would not be sufficient.

The best way to implement a full-employment policy, according to the Freedom Budget, was a massive federal effort to address "unmet social needs— in slum clearance and housing, education and training, health, agriculture, natural resources and regional development, social insurance and welfare programs." Echoing John Kenneth Galbraith's argument that the nation had pursued private wealth at the expense of the public good in recent years, the budget reminded readers that publicly financed social outlays had been stagnant since the beginning of the Korean War. The result was massive pent-up need. "The greatest undeveloped market in the world for our own products is among our 62 million citizens who are still poor or deprived," the authors wrote. By giving them "the opportunity to reshape the sordid physical environment in which they and so many of the rest of us live," a full-employment policy would expand national wealth and generate sufficient tax revenue to pay for the federal expenditures.[3]

The Freedom Budget strongly criticized Johnson's War on Poverty as a piecemeal and underfunded effort that was too focused on the personal characteristics of the poor and unemployed. While "personal deficiencies have a bearing upon the economic condition of many individuals," the report conceded, "it is even more true that deficiencies in nationwide policies and programs, evidencing a default in the national conscience, spawn and perpetuate these personal deficiencies." Improved education, job training, and social services were not enough to lift people out of poverty; at best, they should be "an auxiliary approach to a nationwide full-employment policy."[4]

To enhance purchasing power, put a floor under wages, and protect the vulnerable, the Freedom Budget called for revamping the social safety net. The ultimate goal was a "federally-initiated and supported guaranteed annual income . . . as a matter of right," but as a supplement to a full-employment economic policy, rather than in place of it. A guaranteed annual income not only would help those in need—it would boost the overall economy, by increasing consumer demand. "A steady and growing flow of income to these people . . . will also help to maintain economic growth and a full-employment environment," the authors maintained. When at full employment, the economy had the "productive power to abolish 'freedom from want'" in a decade.[5]

While the impetus for the Freedom Budget came directly from the fractured Black Freedom Movement, the authors hoped that the social democratic rhetoric, class-based analysis, and policy specifics of the proposal might hold the coalition together. This seemed particularly vital after King's retreat from Chicago and the November 1966 "backlash" election, in which whites across the country repudiated liberal advocates of civil rights. Social democrats like Rustin and Randolph believed that racism and racial inequality fed off scarcity and economic insecurity. Because of its focus on economics, they hoped that the Freedom Budget would sustain an interracial coalition while a rising "full employment" tide would lift black boats along with white ones. And benefits from massive expenditures to "wipe out the slum ghettos, and provide a decent home for every American family" would also accrue to blacks.[6]

Both TWO and Alinsky shared the critique of the War on Poverty put forward by the Freedom Budget. Reflecting the growing power of the Social

Welfare Union (SWU) in the organization, in May 1967 TWO called for a federally administered guaranteed annual income. "The welfare system as it now operates serves to perpetuate the conditions that have engulfed the poor . . . and dehumanizes those whom it purports to serve, thus creating a more severe problem for the poor than the poverty in which they are compelled to live," TWO argued. Years of individual and group frustration with Illinois welfare politics led the organization to conclude that only a guaranteed income could ensure individual autonomy from economic want, from dehumanizing eligibility restrictions, and from paternalistic state agencies.[7]

However, TWO's perception of the strategic dilemmas posed by metropolitan inequality extended beyond the social democratic critique embodied by the Freedom Budget. Race mattered, TWO argued, as did black powerlessness. By seeking to elide race both politically and analytically, the budget underestimated its stubborn power in shaping metropolitan inequality, the black condition, and the broader political ecology. Black urban poverty *was* rooted in poor employment opportunities and low wages—but these things, in turn, were rooted in residential and labor market segregation within cities and across metropolitan boundaries. Focused primarily on markets, economic classes, and the state, the budget's authors missed the critical role of place in racializing opportunities and labor markets in the nation's metropolitan areas, and in disempowering black communities. While universalistic social and economic policies would undoubtedly benefit the black poor, black poverty *was* different from white poverty. One did not have to be a black separatist—or a white racist—to see this. The authors of the Freedom Budget simplified a challenge that was, in the end, far more radical.

In their series of "Black Papers" in 1965 and 1966, TWO activists had argued that segregation and black urban poverty were part of a structure of economic, political, and racial privilege and deprivation, not just an aberration in an otherwise fundamentally just society. The ghetto exists because it is profitable, TWO argued, and because black citizens have been rendered powerless by the lure of poverty programs. Employers profit from low wages paid to black workers, unions boost pay for skilled white workers by excluding blacks, the Chicago Real Estate Board makes money off blockbusting and racial steering, and organized crime gains from the "grinding despair and personal disintegration which comes from ghetto life" through gambling and drugs. The cost of the ghetto was passed on to taxpayers, and future generations, through social programs that left segregation in place. Welfare and most War on Poverty programs "are just safety valves, to let off the pressure from within this black cauldron . . . with a pittance thrown out as smokescreen to confuse the public." Rather than share their power and wealth, the powerful "would rather keep black people mis-educated, ill-housed, unemployed, and dependent on an impersonal bureaucracy, and thus broken in spirit."

Universalistic, class-based economic and social policy was important, TWO argued, but black empowerment was also crucial in attacking metropolitan inequality. Federal money, TWO argued, was being used to "buy off our rage against being confined in the ghetto" and to "distract black people from building enough power to break out." As long as poverty programs "'service' people individually, the poor are prevented from organizing collectively, so they do not threaten the position or wealth of those in power." Only independent organizations of the poor, TWO continued, were capable of putting pressure on the walls of the ghetto. "We have spit out the pacifier," a paper concluded. "The safety valve is now out of balance." The root issue is "citizen participation—whether 'maximum feasible participation' of the poor means what it says, or is just a huckster's slogan."[8] "From this moment on," Brazier concluded, "we must understand that we are in a war against extinction . . . either we establish community power, or we shall forever remain at the mercy of poverty, poor housing, inadequate education, and joblessness."[9]

The dilemma for TWO and similar groups was not just how to obtain "community power," whether through federal programs or otherwise. It was also how a spatial strategy rooted in segregated and impoverished space could be used to attack metropolitan segregation and inequality. Asking neighborhoods like Woodlawn to bear the burden of addressing the accumulated consequences of the nation's commitment to the color line was irrational and unjust. But making a virtue of this, even rhetorically, seemed unlikely to generate the leverage necessary for undoing that commitment. While some black freedom groups saw community power as an end in itself, many others—like TWO—had a keen understanding of the dilemmas created by the intertwining of race, class, and social geography. This critique went well beyond the simplistic and paralyzing integration-separatism dichotomy. Since at least the 1930s, Black Freedom Movements have pursued what Nikhil Pal Singh has called "lasting equalitarian transformations" of American life, comfortably combining group-based remedies, grassroots action, calls for social democratic redistribution, and advocacy of integration. TWO was very much a part of this tradition. So was Alinsky.[10]

The Model Cities program seemed to offer federal resources on a scale to fit TWO's emerging vision. While the Freedom Budget conceptualized the dilemmas of metropolitan racial inequality in economic terms, demanding nonracial and universalistic policy solutions, Model Cities was shaped by different, though no less insightful or radical, assumptions. The task force that proposed it understood the obstacle that metropolitan segregation posed to black freedom and recommended that the federal government challenge it directly. Three visions for challenging metropolitan inequality emerged on the left during this period: a social democratic approach to economic and social policy, community development, and metropolitan desegregation. The Freedom Budget embraced the first one. Model Cities, as conceived, combined the other two. TWO would seek to merge all three.[11]

Model Cities

The Model Cities program began with the grandest of ambitions. Walter Reuther, president of the United Auto Workers, came to President Johnson in May 1965 with a vision for attacking the urban crisis in Detroit and other cities. He urged him to set up a committee to design and implement a kind of urban Tennessee Valley Authority "to stop the erosion of life in urban centers among the lower-and-middle income population." The goal was to bring local constituencies together with the federal government to fund massive reconstruction of targeted neighborhoods.[12] After the Watts uprising, a profoundly shaken Johnson empowered Reuther to convene a task force.[13]

The Task Force on Urban Affairs and Housing, chaired by Massachusetts Institute of Technology political economist Robert Wood, met from October to December 1965. In addition to Reuther, the group included Whitney Young of the Urban League, Chicago railroad executive Ben Heineman, Senator (and former Health, Education, and Welfare secretary) Abraham Ribicoff, industrialist Edgar Kaiser, and Kermit Gordon from the Bureau of the Budget, as well as legal scholar Charles Haar.[14]

In its December 1965 report, the task force recommended a sharp break from earlier policies. Criticizing existing efforts as "too small and too diffuse," the group called for a serious federal commitment to both community development and metropolitan coordination. While regionalism was not a new idea, it had generally been emphasized as a way to deal with the administrative and fiscal inefficiencies of rapid suburban growth. The contribution of the task force—driven mostly by Haar—was its effort to tie regionalism to metropolitan inequality, uneven development, and racial segregation, and to propose that the federal government use its financial resources to attack housing segregation by race and class in suburbs as well as cities. Implicit in the report was recognition of the role the federal government had played—and continued to play—in the creation and maintenance of metropolitan segregation.

"Unless the housing of low-income people can be distributed in better fashion throughout the metropolitan areas," the task force argued, "we will continue to develop low-income and racial ghettoes in the central cities." Given the shifting of job opportunities away from the cities, the suburbs had to help alleviate and solve the problems of the urban poor. This could be done through sharing resources, active participation in regional governance, and support of a comprehensive program to meet the housing needs of low- and moderate-income families in the suburbs. The task force urged the Department of Housing and Urban Development (HUD) to enforce suburban compliance with this "metropolitan action program": participation would be "a prerequisite for some federal benefits which accrue largely to the non-poor." The goal was to use HUD and federal money to stimulate new approaches and organizational arrangements at the metropolitan level. In assessing Model Cities proposals, the secretary of HUD needed to give "maximum consideration" to proposals that would "counteract the segregation of housing by race or income."

The task force also sought to remedy the inequities of traditional urban renewal by shifting the focus of federal policy toward community development. The idea was to fund and coordinate local programs to reform the "total environment" of selected poor neighborhoods rather than just focus on physical development. Cities were expected to designate "Model Areas" in which to concentrate and coordinate resources. The poor themselves would participate in planning and governance. Success would be measured not only by improvements in the lives of locals but also by the extent to which revamped neighborhoods were able to attract and keep upwardly mobile blacks and whites. The task force believed that integration by class and race was an essential component of rebuilding these neighborhoods. Those who were dislocated by projects in the Model Areas would be integrated throughout the metropolitan area. Importantly, however, the task force stressed that community development and metropolitan desegregation by race and class had to be pursued with equal gusto if metropolitan inequality was to be unraveled. The task force seemed to offer a policy vision that was comprehensive and metropolitan. As proposed, Model Cities was the first major federal effort to attack metropolitan segregation.[15]

In January 1966, Johnson asked Congress for $2.3 billion to attack neighborhood poverty and to fund metropolitan planning in seventy cities over six years. He made it very clear that he saw Model Cities as part of a larger effort to attack racial segregation. To this end, HUD would appoint a metropolitan coordinator for each city, to help coordinate proposals and programs and to ensure compliance with federal civil rights laws. The goal of the Demonstration Cities and Metropolitan Development Act, Johnson concluded, was to "set in motion the forces of change in great urban areas that will make them the masterpieces of our civilization." Illinois Senator Paul Douglas introduced the bill to the Senate later that month.[16]

Many liberal civil rights groups were excited by the potential of Model Cities. The National Committee against Discrimination in Housing (NCADH), for example, was at the forefront of a growing fair housing movement. A series of research projects on the suburbanization of industrial employment had convinced NCADH activists that metropolitan segregation was the structural linchpin of racial inequality in the North. "Job opportunities are increasingly to be found in areas where Negroes are not permitted to live, while areas where Negroes do live continue to show downhill employment trends," the NCADH found. Fair housing laws would be an "empty opportunity" unless they were accompanied by a massive public effort to create low- and moderate-income housing in the suburbs and on the urban fringe. Recent federal studies on educational inequality also seemed to lend credence to these arguments, for they doubted that equal educational opportunity was possible when poor black students were clustered together.[17]

Only a frontal attack on metropolitan class and race segregation would enable fair housing laws to change conditions on the ground. What was needed, NCADH staffer Frank Horne argued, was a "reorientation of the planning, financing and marketing policies of private and public agencies at all levels from the imposed racism of the ghetto to a consciously created inclusive pattern of integrated occupancy of buildings, projects, streets and neighborhoods." The NCADH demanded that both Health, Education, and Welfare and HUD withhold all grants from suburban areas—including those that funded schools, hospitals, roads, water, and sewer systems—until they created enforceable metropolitan desegregation plans. Model Cities seemed like a perfect vehicle for this effort.[18]

The NCADH also sought to shift the policy priorities of the major civil rights organizations toward metropolitan desegregation, hoping—much like the authors of the Freedom Budget—to reunify the movement in the wake of the white backlash, the emergence of Black Power, and the apparent intellectual and political exhaustion of liberal policy.[19] Most of those organizations saw fair employment, federal enforcement of Southern school desegregation, and voting rights as their major legislative priorities. The NCADH insisted that economic opportunity was fundamentally linked to residential segregation. "Racial restriction in housing now stands like a rock, unmoved by the swirling maelstrom of the current civil rights upsurge," Horne argued. "Separation because of race cuts a wide swath through the entire fabric of American life ... as long as this line of demarcation exists, there will be no fundamental resolution of the so-called problem of race in our country."[20]

The introduction of both a fair housing bill and Model Cities to Congress in early 1966 also seemed to indicate growing recognition of the critical importance of breaking down metropolitan segregation. HUD's secretary Robert Weaver reiterated to Congress in February 1966 that cities needed to "encourage good community relations and counteract the segregation of housing by race or income" to receive Model Cities money. "Improving blighted areas is not enough alone," Weaver argued in an April speech. "We must proceed in tandem with simultaneous moves to open up housing occupancy to all potential customers throughout the whole metropolitan area."[21]

Finally, the NCADH and its allies took heart from the White House Conference on Civil Rights, in early June 1966. The housing portion of the conference's final report was the most extensive and detailed brief for affirmative metropolitan desegregation of the era. Frank Horne and George Schermer, both of the NCADH, wrote most of it. Produced under the aegis of the White House, if not with its concurrence or approval, in the midst of congressional deliberations over Model Cities and fair housing, its radicalism is rather startling.

Federal policy, the report argued, had until very recently been "geared almost exclusively" to the expansion of the white middle-class suburban housing market. New programs aimed at cities and the poor suffered from the "absence of provision for attacking the still inviolate 'white noose' of the suburbs." The report included four housing goals: freedom of choice, an expansion of the supply of low- and moderate-income housing throughout metropolitan areas, a push for racial and class inclusion in the suburbs, and the revitalization and integration of existing ghetto areas.

The report demanded that the federal government use all its "programs and resources ... to promote and implement equal opportunity and desegregation," and that it require "demonstrations of affirmative action to desegregate" from all recipients of federal funds and assistance. "To achieve communities and neighborhoods inclusive of all race and incomes will require a major redistribution of population between city and suburb, [and] a restructuring of the relationship among local governing units in the metropolitan area," the report argued. Current policy, "geared solely to 'ghetto enrichment,'" was insufficient.[22]

Congress debated Model Cities and fair housing during the spring and summer of 1966, and the apocalyptic mood of the time—as well as the impending midterm election—infused the debate. A kind of perfect political storm resulted, sinking the fair housing bill, limiting the reach of Model Cities, foregrounding "law and order," and seemingly closing an already-narrow window for addressing metropolitan segregation. With forty-four cities torn by violent uprisings that year, many Americans came to see Model Cities as "something for the blacks, a way of placating the protestors in the ghettoes," Charles Haar observed. Advocates of the legislation, too, increasingly depicted it as a kind of riot insurance while downplaying its emphasis on regionalism and desegregation.

A coalition of Republicans and Southern Democrats criticized the Model Cities bill, perceiving a federal plot to impose busing for school integration. Representative Paul Fino (R-NY) claimed—not without reason—that Model Cities would enable HUD to put "rent supplement" and "scattered-site public housing" in every suburb, draw up open-housing legislation in every city, and redesign suburban taxes to "pay for slum schools."[23]

In 1966, the provisions establishing an affirmative effort to break down residential segregation were replaced with the requirement that HUD foster "maximum opportunities in the choice of housing." The practicalities of how (or whether) to grapple with housing segregation were essentially left up to the municipal officials who would craft Model Cities' proposals. The fair housing bill met a similar fate: efforts to break a Senate filibuster failed on September 19. "It would have been hard to pass the emancipation proclamation in the atmosphere prevailing this summer," White House staffer Harry McPherson complained to Attorney General Nicholas Katzenbach. Just over half of all Americans believed that the Johnson White House was "pushing integration too fast." At the insistence of Rep. Fino and others, the House passed an amendment to Model Cities clarifying that it could not be used to promote racial balance in schools. This ensured its passage—narrowly—in mid-October 1966, and Johnson promptly signed it on November 3. The Freedom Budget was released the same week.[24]

Dilemmas of Spatial Strategy and the Future of Federal Policy

In many ways the two original components of Model Cities—an emphasis on urban community development and an attack on metropolitan segregation—defined an emerging strategic and intellectual split in the civil rights movement. It was becoming clear that many white voters hesitated to support even nondiscrimination laws, let alone affirmative attacks on metropolitan segregation. Most were unaware of the extent to which patterns of economic and racial segregation had for decades been shaped by government at all levels; as a result, calls for "affirmative action" struck many whites as a demand for "forced" integration of their schools and communities, and an arrogant intervention into the nation's most important "private" market: housing. This rhetoric was reinforced by the National Association of Real Estate Boards as well as many politicians around the country. It had fundamentally undermined Alinsky's work on the Southwest Side.

White opposition to affirmative desegregation was not unanticipated by its advocates. But by 1966, many moderates, liberals, and movement activists were also questioning the emphasis of the NCADH and its allies on metropolitan desegregation. The community development component of Model Cities promised to build on the institutional and neighborhood empowerment organizing in Chicago's Woodlawn and other black ghettos. It appealed to the spatial and uplift rhetoric that so often accompanied that organizing while also offering the possibility of more resources for ghetto communities without provoking white backlash. A remarkably diverse group of activists, academics, and political figures began to coalesce around a ghetto enrichment strategy.

In a series of widely discussed articles in 1966 and 1967, leftist social scientists Frances Fox Piven and Richard Cloward questioned the political and analytical wisdom of a focus on desegregated housing. Liberal advocacy of housing integration had prompted a white backlash that had depleted the political capital necessary for large-scale social, physical, and economic reconstruction of inner-city areas, they argued. A more conservative Congress was even less likely to take appropriate action. In case after case "the issue of racial integration endangered the passage of bills, then emasculated them by the meagerness of appropriations," they argued. "The desperate need for better housing and facilities in the ghetto has been and continues to be sacrificed to the goal of residential integration," they pointed out, citing the history of white resistance to scattered-site public housing. This struggle "has cost the poor, especially the Negro poor, dearly." "If liberals follow their accustomed route and force new contests over desegregation," the Model Cities program will likely "go the way of earlier housing measures, weakened and mangled at each stage of public decision." The coupling of integration with measures to improve existing ghetto conditions "must lead to the defeat of both." The choice, therefore, "is between total defeat and partial victory." Thus, they concluded, "strategies must be found to improve ghetto housing without arousing the ire of powerful segments of the white community."[25]

Further, Piven and Cloward argued, echoing Black Power arguments, "it is also far from clear that integration is always desirable." Segregation and black poverty were the products of a deeper problem: "the lack of adequate Negro power to secure a just share of private and public resources." Housing desegregation wouldn't alter this basic condition—indeed, by fragmenting the black community, it might contribute to it. Blacks, like white ethnics before them, needed a period of separatism in order to build the "organizational vehicles to enable them to compete with whites for control of the major institutions that shape the destiny of the ghetto." There was no reason the black ghetto couldn't serve as a "staging area . . . to build the communal solidarity and power necessary to compel eventual access to the mainstream of urban life."

"The salvation of the mass of ghetto residents is in the social and physical reconstruction of those institutions which shape and mold men and which provide them with meaningful links to the larger society," Cloward told the NCADH as early as May 1966. To accomplish this, "separatism—not integration . . . will be essential." A focus on ghetto "rehabilitation" would be a first step toward "alleviating poverty and toward a more profound integration of Negro life with the mainstream of society than can be achieved by mere spatial redistribution," Cloward argued. It would simultaneously protect the "social bases out of which the political force for more substantial action can be developed."[26]

In 1967 the *New Republic* surveyed the options for "rebuilding the slums." Proposals that sought to harness the power, imagination, and capital of business and nonprofits to solve the urban crisis attracted particularly high praise. Two prominent policy ideas were put forward by Senator Charles Percy (R-IL), who had ousted liberal Democrat Paul Douglas in November 1966, and Senator Robert Kennedy (D-NY). Percy argued that the federal government should stabilize poor urban areas by encouraging widespread home ownership. His legislation would create the quasi-public nonprofit National Home Ownership Foundation, which would offer credit and loan insurance for nonprofits and limited-dividend corporations to build urban housing to sell to low-income residents. Home purchasers, in turn, would be eligible for direct federal subsidies on their mortgages, as well as insurance against foreclosure in case of illness or unemployment. Like Model Cities, such a program could—in theory—push metropolitan desegregation. But Percy's emphasis was on home ownership within the ghetto as an alternative to opening up the suburbs, not as a means to accomplish it.[27]

By the fall of 1966 Senator Kennedy had become a vocal critic of the War on Poverty, and he had used the White House Conference on Civil Rights to gather support for his ideas. He called for public-private partnerships and tax incentives to rebuild ghetto neighborhoods, empower the grass roots, attract outside capital, and create jobs. At his urging, in November 1966 Congress amended the Economic Opportunity Act to include seed money for community development corporations (CDCs), through its Special Impact Program. It led to the creation of the Bedford-Stuyvesant Restoration Corporation, one of the first CDCs.[28]

Because most of these ideas focused on using tax and marketplace incentives to entice capital into ghetto neighborhoods, they created some strange bedfellows: leftists like Piven and Cloward, liberals like Kennedy, moderates like Percy, business elites, and Black Power advocates. Advocates of ghetto enrichment did differ in important ways, of course. Kennedy, Piven, and Cloward favored empowering the black poor to use outside resources to restructure their own communities, while Percy and many business elites were indifferent, or worse, to black empowerment. Although the authors of the Freedom Budget weren't necessarily advocates of a ghetto enrichment strategy, they did believe that flooding inner-city areas with jobs and federal resources was the necessary first step toward racial justice. As strong critics of Black Power, Rustin and Randolph were agnostic at best about the necessity of black empowerment, except as part of a broader multiracial working-class coalition.[29]

Privately, some of Johnson's own advisers agreed that pushing housing desegregation was futile. While various White House task forces continued to advocate for a federal attack on metropolitan segregation, Johnson staffers began to focus on policies and programs that would pump money, capital, and services into the ghettos and that would draw on businesses and market incentives.[30]

This growing emphasis on enrichment-based policies didn't emerge just from policy makers, pundits, and professors. It strongly resonated with black spatial strategies that stressed grassroots control of local institutions, which were increasingly expressed in the rhetoric of Black Power. TWO was part of a broader spectrum of movements that sought to mobilize the black poor to improve their daily living conditions, particularly in the wake of growing frustration with the inability of liberal social policy and jurisprudence to address metropolitan inequality. Many of these groups accepted the geographic concentration of poor blacks as an unalterable given; others saw virtue in it as a catalyst for racial solidarity and cultural flourishing.

In preparing for their 1966 housing task force, Schermer and George Nesbitt grasped the moral and political dimensions of this debate: "Which should have priority: improving conditions where people live now—which may be a matter of making the ghettos more livable and perpetuating segregation—or pressing for programs that will decentralize the ghetto and encourage racially inclusive neighborhoods?" And "are these really mutually exclusive alternatives?" they asked.[31]

The NCADH and its allies insisted that while ghetto enrichment was important, it would never succeed without a concerted effort to undermine metropolitan segregation. Black sociologist Kenneth Clark, introducing an NCADH study, was deeply critical of "attempts to 'prevent riots' by gilding and reinforcing ghettos—trying to make them 'separate but equal.'" "The separatist concept" was being promoted "in the halls of government and among "some white liberals . . . as what the 'Negro' wants and as the answer to his problems," Clark wrote. These efforts had been consistently rejected in surveys of black public opinion and were "bound by the momentum of history to boomerang." The Harvard sociologist John Kain concurred: programs to gild the ghetto, "apart from being objectionable on moral grounds, accept a very large cost in terms of economic inefficiency, while making the solution of many social problems inordinately difficult."[32]

The NCADH concurred with this assessment in its 1967 annual report: if ghettos areas were not "reclaimed as open and integral parts of totally open metropolitan areas," community development would only "fasten down and extend the patterns of racial segregation." Leaving racial and economic segregation untouched would leave poor black cities surrounded by white affluent suburbs that were "increasingly conservative, and indifferent to the problems of the urban core." As a result, the funding necessary to make a ghetto enrichment strategy even remotely viable would be in the hands of suburban-dominated state legislatures and congressional delegations.[33]

The NCADH's two most prominent black activists, Frank Horne and Clarence Funnye, took issue with Piven and Cloward's assumption that emphasis on housing integration by naïve liberals had made the lives of poor urban blacks worse. Funnye found this "flight into sociological fantasy" to be almost precisely incorrect: "government and private enterprise have spent most of the last thirty years actively working to *impede* deghettoization," not confront it. The failure of liberal urban policy wasn't rooted in a stubborn insistence on desegregation but in its refusal to understand it and take it seriously.

"All of our troubles today are the derivatives of segregation," Horne argued, "not of free choice and integration." Piven and Cloward "write as though the racial ghetto has suddenly emerged full-blown from the head of Jupiter, without long historic and economic roots" that lie "outside the ghetto and primarily in the minds and actions of people who are not Negro." The ghetto, Horne pointed out, is "formed and maintained by forces from the outside." It concentrated the negative consequences of poverty geographically while isolating black workers from economic opportunity. Ignoring residential segregation would likely accelerate white flight, eroding the urban tax base and further isolating blacks politically—thus undercutting the racial bargain implicit in the ghetto enrichment strategy. "Any attempt to redevelop the ghetto must be accompanied by a firm commitment to deghettoize," Funnye insisted. "No amount of prettying up, fixing up, paint, plaster and parks can do more than make the ghetto life a little more tolerable."[34]

One might assume that Alinsky would lean toward Piven and Cloward's position. Alinsky's militant language, his calls for the pursuit and exercise of power, his sharp-tongued mockery of moral and spiritual calls for racial brotherhood, and his insistence that racial justice would not be possible unless black communities organized themselves, all led many liberals and moderates to criticize Alinsky and his projects as a force for strengthening the ghetto rather than abolishing it. Others were attracted to Alinsky and his work for precisely the same reasons. The architects of the Community Action Program and many Black Power activists tended to see Alinsky as an ally—as someone who favored a mixture of ghetto enrichment and grassroots militancy. Media coverage of Alinsky in the mid-1960s often depicted him as the person poor black communities called on when they need someone to "bust up the joint," giving credence—depending upon one's inclinations—to either his authenticity as a militant or his status as one of the greatest threats to racial harmony in the urban North. Alinsky, of course, cultivated this chameleon-like aura, although he was much better at making moderates and liberals uncomfortable (and he enjoyed it far more).

But on race, his blunt truthfulness made him a provocateur. He constantly sought to attack the self-images of the age, on both sides of the color line, in a way that no other white public figure did. He insisted that whites accept that racial inequality and segregation were inseparable from the exercise of power—by those who created and maintained it, and by those who sought to challenge and unwind it. And he insisted that blacks not confuse the institution building and grassroots organizing needed to overcome metropolitan segregation with fanciful visions of racial unity and a viable separatism. TWO, notably, followed his lead: at the height of its power, size, and public profile in an era when black urban activism was dominated by the rhetoric of black unity and racial separatism, the group studiously avoided deploying it.

There was much in the idea of Black Power that Alinsky found praiseworthy. The emphasis on black culture and identity "is essential and of prime significance. It must be achieved," he wrote in 1967. But "identity without power is still a second-class identity." Black culture must proceed "hand-in-hand" with organizing. "This nation desperately needs the organized power of our black sector and its representatives in our body politic," Alinsky argued. Black empowerment was important as a means and for its own sake, much as it was for all "have-nots." To him, "ghetto enrichment" would be valuable if it helped blacks to build institutions, social capital, and power. But it could not be an end in itself.

Alinsky was a sharp critic of racial separatism, which he thought was completely unworkable and would give racist whites exactly what they desired.

Alinsky described separatism as a kind of destructive "therapy" that would blind both whites and blacks to the consequences of metropolitan segregation. While fully supporting efforts by TWO to create locally run programs, services, and even businesses, Alinsky always saw these as about empowerment, about process, not as an actual solution to black deprivation. "You set up a black-owned gas station and what have you got? Four jobs. This will accomplish nothing except maybe psychologically," he argued. "Until the blacks have the experience of being exploited by their own people as they were by the whites, this will be a constant thorn."

Alinsky had been grappling with this debate over race and spatial strategy since the late 1950s, though largely through an organizing frame rather than a policy one. His views were shaped by his sociological imagination, which pushed him to examine these questions from the ground up—from the local outward, in other words. When thinking about how to get "from here to there," he didn't expend much intellectual effort envisioning the "there" part. It is safe to say that Alinsky concurred with Funnye and favored deghettoization as the ultimate goal, and for the same reasons. Alinsky also didn't believe deghettoization would be attainable or permanent without grassroots organizing on both sides of the color line and across it.[35]

At a well-attended meeting in January 1967, TWO activists grappled with these same dilemmas. Integration of schools and housing clearly wasn't forthcoming. As a result, they resolved to continue to improve Woodlawn's public schools. But they refused to "get trapped in the pit of the doctrine of 'separate but equal.'" "We will work to integrate schools and housing not only in Chicago, but in those lily-white suburbs that ring our city," TWO concluded. "We will continue to struggle until there is no sanctuary for whites to flee at the first sign of integration." In the absence of a federal emphasis on deghettoization, however, groups like TWO struggled to overcome the dilemmas of spatial strategy that metropolitan segregation imposed.[36]

Model Cities and Metropolitan Segregation

In early 1967, HUD started to put together grant guidelines for Model Cities planning, and applications began to pour in. The NCADH continued to put intense pressure on Secretary Weaver to use Model Cities against metropolitan segregation rather than merely "polish up the ghettos and perpetuate segregation."[37] Instead of "realizing the promise of opening the doors *out of and into* the ghetto for *all* people," Horne lamented, a Model Cities that refused to touch metropolitan segregation would "reap the whirlwind of racial conflict."[38] In the *New York Times*, Wood similarly argued that the federal government had an "enormous—and never to be duplicated—opportunity to act affirmatively to extend housing opportunity. The question before the nation is whether it will do so, or restrict itself to 'polishing up' for the present prisoners and their children the racial ghettos that federal housing policy and the real estate and mortgage banking industries have built."[39]

In February, HUD's secretary Robert Weaver told the president that the NCADH was trying to force him "to come out with a pledge for a positive racial integration in the model cities program." Weaver refused to do so, citing the legislative history of the program, which clearly revealed the intent of Congress. "As long as federal housing laws make no affirmative statements about desegregation, as long as they and their legislative history clearly indicate that certain federal laws prohibit such affirmative action, no administration and no department can successfully establish the affirmative policy the Committee espouses." Weaver also questioned the assumption that community development and racial integration were polar opposites: "The alternative of 'perpetuating the ghetto' vs. dissolving it is without substance," he argued. "We must do both." The NCADH, of course, believed this as well. Their criticism was more profound: community development—and Model Cities—would not work without an affirmative federal attack on metropolitan segregation.[40]

Many municipal officials and conservative activists feared precisely what the NCADH desired: that Model Cities would serve as a kind of stealth fair housing law. Mayors hesitated to apply for funds, fearing that HUD would require local fair housing laws first. In early 1967 the House Appropriations Committee threatened to cut funding for Model Cities if Weaver used it to attack residential segregation. Worried, Weaver called together his staff on March 14.[41]

The next morning, the director of the Model Cities Administration, Walter Farr, gave an exclusive interview to the *Washington Post*. "Desegregated housing is being given a relatively low priority," Farr said. The Model Cities legislation "doesn't permit an 'aggressive' policy of housing desegregation." Therefore, HUD would not insist on the passage of open occupancy laws as a precondition. "We are not pinning it down. We are not telling the mayors what they have to do," Farr stated. "The heart of this program is that they—the local people—have got to do their own planning . . . Our position is that improving the quality of the neighborhoods is more important than dispersal." HUD staffers reiterated Farr's message. Assistant Secretary Taylor publicly hoped that the displaced would be rehoused on an open occupancy basis "primarily through voluntary efforts to open up other neighborhoods to these people from the slums." They were effectively giving local officials a green light to ignore racial and economic segregation when assembling their Model Cities plans.[42]

By the end of the riot-torn summer of 1967, sixty-three cities had received Model Cities planning grants from HUD. Only a handful of them—all directly influenced by the NCADH—included provisions for expanding housing choice beyond the inner city. Model Cities "is largely oriented toward 'ghetto enrichment' coupled with the abandonment of integration," Wood lamented. The money was on its way out the door; whether it would leverage any real change remained to be seen.[43]

Nevertheless, the Woodlawn Organization took the planning process as an opportunity for grassroots utopian dreaming. Over 1968 and 1969, the organization offered a concrete vision of community development and a revamped welfare state. In a sense, it would fuse the social democratic vision of the Freedom Budget with its own take on community empowerment. Although an attack on metropolitan segregation was beyond the power of any community group, TWO arguably took the community-based model of the Great Society as far as it could go—and even that proved too far, both for Mayor Daley and HUD. Afterward, TWO would launch itself into a decades-long career as a national innovator in community development, very much in keeping with the broader trajectory of federal urban policy, which combined government disinvestment with solutions that drew on public-private partnerships and market-based solutions. TWO would build grocery stores, shopping malls, and housing, and garner millions of dollars of foundation and government grants. It would focus on increasing home ownership for the black middle class around Brazier and Finney's East Woodlawn church. Woodlawn, in the meantime, would continue to slide, and metropolitan segregation would shape larger and larger swaths of the American landscape.

Model Cities in Chicago

The Model Cities bill's provisions for citizen participation were deliberately ambiguous. On the surface, the language was strong. HUD required cities to "provide the means for the Model Neighborhood citizens to participate and to be fully involved in policy-making, planning and the execution of all program elements." The question, then, was whether HUD officials would actually withhold millions of dollars from cities that did not sufficiently involve the poor. Given the backlash politics of the period, this was unlikely. And indeed, most cities intended to select participants on Model Areas Planning Councils (MAPCs) by appointment (rather than election), and few included residents of poor communities on their steering committees. Given Daley's ability to project his power nationally, a participatory Model Cities program in Chicago was a long shot.[44]

Never one to pass up federal funds, however, Mayor Daley quickly appointed the machine loyalist Erwin France to run Model Cities in Chicago and submitted a planning grant application in May 1967. Daley proposed four target neighborhoods, including East Woodlawn. It is hardly surprising that he made no effort to consult with local representatives of any of them. Despite worries among HUD staffers about the "lack of involvement of the people most concerned, the poor of the target areas," Chicago received the grant. That success did little to nudge Daley's democratic proclivities.[45]

Brazier and TWO didn't even learn about the planning proposal until Daley mentioned it at a December 1967 meeting. Angered, Brazier strongly encouraged TWO to initiate its own Model Cities planning process. "We are through with plantation politics," he told TWO's Steering Committee. "Those days are over, but just saying so won't make it true. We must close ranks and get the kind of Model Cities program we need."[46]

The timing was fortuitous; the organization was already synthesizing its various programs and ideas into a coherent structure and vision for Woodlawn. In March 1967 the organization had hired a black architecture firm from Cleveland to help develop a plan that would preserve existing structures, encourage home ownership, provide a diversity of housing, and make Woodlawn not just "a Negro community . . . but rather a free American Community in which every race, creed and color will have both the opportunity and the incentive to live in mutual respect and harmony." TWO leaders received positive assurances from HUD officials that a Daley Model Cities plan for East Woodlawn that didn't include the organization would meet with great skepticism in Washington. In early 1968 TWO began to seek out technical help for its own plan.[47]

Despite the opportunity that Model Cities appeared to present, many in TWO were skeptical, in light of the checkered history of public housing, urban renewal, and redlining in Chicago. Black suspicion of Model Cities could be alleviated only if "organized communities play a meaningful and determining role" in designing and running a program "designed for the people of our communities," Brazier concluded.[48]

With four years of running increasingly large programs under its belt since the Social Policy Planning Memo, TWO began to put together a broadly participatory process. Unable to get technical planning assistance from the city or from HUD, TWO instead received a grant from the Community Renewal Society and drew on its ongoing relationship with the University of Chicago's Center for Urban Studies. Since 1964 TWO had partnered with faculty to create an experimental school district, a mental health center, a child health clinic, a legal aid facility, and a social service center in Woodlawn. Each facility had a TWO Citizens Advisory Board that met frequently with professional staff and used citizens as staffers ("subprofessionals") and community agents. While many Woodlawn residents were skeptical of the university, a core of faculty activists had earned the trust of TWO activists. They decided to use TWO's existing committee structure to put together a Model Cities plan, aided by a faculty task force affiliated with each committee. The committees already had leadership and experience with problem analysis and planning development, so the plan could be assembled quickly.[49]

Daley began to assemble MAPCs in the four target areas in the spring of 1968. He appointed half the members outright, with ward organizations controlling most of the rest. More than 10 percent of MAPC members held Model Cities jobs, in direct violation of HUD regulations, and many more held municipal patronage jobs. Of the twenty-three members on the East Woodlawn MAPC, ten—including the chair—didn't even live in the neighborhood. Brazier criticized this as typical of the city's "paternalistic plantation methods."[50]

TWO's strategy ran along two tracks. First, it would put together its own Model Cities plan with broad community participation, enabling the organization to claim that its plan—unlike Daley's—met HUD regulations. Second, TWO would refuse to participate in the MAPC for East Woodlawn, unless it was given majority control. This would prevent Daley from being able to claim community support. If Daley wanted to get his plan accepted by HUD, he would have to incorporate TWO ideas and representatives. In other words, he would have to negotiate. TWO activists declared they would submit their Model Cities plan directly to HUD, though they knew the regulations clearly indicated that all proposals had to come from the city. But as long as HUD took its requirements for citizen participation seriously, TWO could leverage its people and its ideas into Daley's process.

Daley, not surprisingly, directly challenged TWO's efforts. Through a combination of threats, patronage, and flattery, in June 1968 he convinced seven TWO activists to serve on the East Woodlawn MAPC. TWO promptly expelled them from leadership positions. Simultaneously, Daley sought to publicly discredit TWO's ability to assemble and administer a Model Cities plan, by encouraging GIU harassment and federal investigation of the Youth Project. This latter tack had the added benefit of tying up the time and energy of TWO's leadership for months. The McClellan hearings opened in June 1968, just as Daley appointed the East Woodlawn MAPC and TWO launched its planning process. About 250 members of TWO's Planning Council gathered at St. Cyril's on June 22 to outline local problems and assemble the political machinery for running its Model Cities planning process.[51]

By mid-August, the process had solidified. The task forces would bring summaries of previous discussions and ideas to meetings, which committee members would revise until they were "satisfied that the task force really understood them."[52] Proposals were often "criticized mercilessly," and more often than not, according to faculty participant William Swenson, "the suggestions of the Task Force members were completely revamped by the community members." Proposals were then forwarded to the Planning Council, which worked with its own task force to prevent duplication, keep the planning focused, and keep communication constant and moving both ways. Faculty knew how to speak bureaucratic lingo and fix community-driven goals and programs to HUD requirements, but the community "continued to provide the substantive ingredients."[53]

John Fish estimated that at least five hundred Woodlawn residents were directly involved in the process. The plan was presented to the Planning Council in November, and then to a series of community hearings, with thousands in attendance. Subsequent revisions were made and approved before three hundred TWO members in December. To demonstrate to HUD the contrast between its participatory process and the city's, TWO excluded faculty from the final deliberations.[54]

Social Policy from the Bottom Up: TWO's Model Cities Plan

TWO's Model Cities plan, released in December 1968, offered a profound critique of the welfare state and essentially proposed to rebuild it from the bottom up. Most Model Cities plans proposed little more than an extension of agency services and governance structures. TWO, in contrast, envisioned a kind of local participatory social democracy, with Woodlawn residents collectively running a comprehensive network of child and adult educational programs, health centers, and nonprofit housing developments. This structure would be underpinned by a guaranteed annual income for Woodlawn residents, funded by the federal government and administered by a TWO-affiliated entity.

Poor communities, TWO argued, are not simply an aggregation of individual cases, each with its own logic and self-contained causes. Community and individual problems are interrelated and cannot be split up "in terms of conventional categories of educational, medical, social welfare, or legal approaches" just to facilitate administration. Poverty is experienced both individually and collectively, and its causes are structural. Conventional approaches to urban poverty involved the expenditure of enormous amounts of money and political capital, did little to alleviate human suffering, and left poor communities atomized, stigmatized, and passive. They did nothing to develop and use existing community structures to involve poor citizens in identifying, understanding, and addressing common problems. Agency professionals determined program goals, rather than the community and its needs.[55]

TWO's plan proposed to make Woodlawn residents "sources of wealth, not just consumers of it," by radically changing the focus and governance of the welfare state. The goal was to end "the massive disbursements of aid through hierarchies of bureaucratic agencies," which were merely ameliorative, and move toward public investment and the self-transformation of the community. Citizen participation and public investment were critical "to rid the community of the shame of dependency, and help it to become self-supporting."[56]

TWO proposed making public assistance simpler, less intrusive, and more generous. Politically and racially motivated demands for either punitive or rehabilitative welfare programs—such as the 1967 Work Incentive Program—had detracted from their primary function: income maintenance. They had also resulted in paternalistic and intrusive eligibility practices that stigmatized the poor and harmed the truly needy. Thus, TWO called for welfare to be separated from social services and for grants to be adequate and virtually unconditional. In effect, TWO proposed to implement a guaranteed annual income plan. Eligibility for financial assistance would be determined solely by an individual declaration of need. Grants would be large enough to meet all ordinary needs, so recipients would not have to undergo the demeaning process of constantly requesting budget changes and special allowances from agencies—a major complaint of SWU activists.

In Illinois, a family of four with no income was eligible for an annual public assistance grant of $2,544, not including special allowances. Household budgets were closely supervised. Under TWO's plan, that family would receive $4,078, with budget responsibilities left entirely to them. Because poverty in Woodlawn was as much a function of low wages as lack of employment, families with one or more employed members would also be eligible for public assistance, up to $5,250 a year. The primary objective was to "ensure every neighborhood resident a minimum income sufficient to meet reasonable family needs." Punitive welfare programs assumed that poor people wouldn't work unless forced to do so. Rehabilitative programs were premised on the idea that people lived in poverty because of some individual deficiency, which could be cheaply remedied without addressing broader questions of powerlessness, low wages, economic restructuring, and metropolitan segregation and discrimination. The guaranteed annual income TWO proposed was based on a structural understanding of poverty and a respect for the dignity of poor people as citizens.[57]

Variations on a guaranteed annual income had caught the fancy of policy makers, activists, and intellectuals across the political spectrum in the late 1960s, reflecting an emerging consensus that the welfare system was flawed. In January 1967, President Johnson indicated a willingness to study income maintenance proposals. In response, cities inserted income guarantee experiments into their Model Cities planning grant proposals. Fifteen of the sixty-three municipalities that won the first round of grants in June 1967—including Newark, Boston, and Oakland—intended to study or experiment with negative income taxes, family allowances, and "fatherless child insurance." Most of them were on a much smaller scale than TWO's, however, and all had their origins in collaborations between city officials and academics—not in community deliberations.[58]

TWO also proposed to aim social services at the entire population of Woodlawn, not just the poor. Services just offered to the poor, TWO argued, were generally underfunded, badly run, and poorly regarded. Under its plan, poor citizens could make use of a wide range of local services, but their access to income maintenance would be an entirely separate matter. Whenever feasible, vouchers or cash should be provided, turning recipients into "consumers." TWO proposed moving away from the notion of a two-tiered welfare state by creating comprehensive "social utilities" designed to "enhance the normal growth and development" of all Woodlawn residents. This included health-care services, which would be provided regardless of ability to pay, by a nonprofit public community corporation that would pool money from private insurance and public programs.[59]

TWO also proposed a radical governance strategy, befitting its emphasis on self-determination. Referred to somewhat ambiguously as decentralized centralization, the plan called for a geographically dispersed welfare state dedicated to organizing and outreach, governed by a local entity called the Core. The Core would be a nonprofit public corporation that would effectively serve as a kind of neighborhood government, with free membership for all Woodlawn residents. Essentially, the Core would be TWO's service arm. Existing TWO efforts in education, job training, and housing would be placed under this new institution, and new ones would be created.

The hundred-person Community Governing Board would set policy and choose officers. Forty members of the board would be elected annually by the membership. Community organizations and institutions would appoint the remainder, for three-year terms. The Core would represent the community before private institutions and all levels of government and would be legally eligible to receive public and private funds, to contract for services, and to own and operate facilities. For example, the Core would use public assistance funds to administer a guaranteed annual income for Woodlawn residents; it would also combine public resources and private insurance to provide health care for all as well.[60]

In addition to further work in public education, the Core would create the nonprofit Housing and Economic Development Corporation (HEDC) that would encourage resident ownership, the scattering of public housing, the construction of low-rise apartment buildings, and a diversity of income, family-types and zoning across Woodlawn. The TWO-KMF Development Corporation would be governed by the HEDC, which would in turn spin off other local CDCs. TWO believed that the HEDC could stimulate local business, build industrial parks, offer relevant vocational training, and foster job development. TWO's job-training programs would be merged into the Career Vocational Institute, also governed by the HEDC. "Any investment [in Woodlawn] . . . which does not encourage the growth of a self-supporting community is surely wasted," TWO concluded, "and only granting meaningful community control will stimulate such growth."[61]

Using its recent work with Woodlawn public schools as a model for thinking about how to foster community control of social programs, TWO proposed to carry out its Model Cities plan through neighborhood-based agencies with citizen boards. [62] These agencies, or "pads," would each serve a two- or three-block area and would be staffed by local residents, making them, in effect, vehicles for local employment and job training. They would function as outreach centers providing residents with easy access to all manner of service. Public and private social agencies were encouraged to create administrative units focused on Woodlawn and to locate services in the pads. Unlike traditional social agencies, the focus would be on early diagnosis, prevention, and treatment. Community agents and staff at each pad were to be hired by an open committee of representatives from neighborhood organizations and would serve as advocates for residents before public and private agencies. Agents and staff would reach out to residents through churches, schools, social groups, political organizations, businesses, and door-to-door canvassing. Unlike social service professionals, these agents would "likely share the individuals' experiences and culture, and thus would be easier to approach and talk to." They would compile a complete dossier for a family visit, and then help the family coordinate decisions about its own future.

Like the SWU and some of TWO's other committees, the pads would serve residents while organizing them. Community agents would bring groups and individuals together to work on common problems. This would treat Woodlawn citizens as both ends and means, "rather than the passive object of expanded professional service and study." The citizen, TWO argued, is "strengthened by knowing that he is central to the process of re-creating his community, and that professional services and particular operating measures offered him are pliable or replaceable." Such a structure would allow programs to adhere closely to local needs in a nonintrusive way while also embedding them into local civil society. When joined with a guaranteed annual income, TWO concluded, such a structure would truly address Woodlawn's problems while respecting the dignity of citizens, families, and neighborhoods.

TWO's Model Cities plan called for slightly more than $19 million for its first year and $146 million over five years. Brazier demanded that Daley hold off on submitting his plan to the City Council until "widespread public hearings can be held," and he threatened to go to HUD if the mayor continued to ignore Woodlawn residents.[63] The problem for TWO, however, was that by January 1969, HUD was in new hands—Richard Nixon's. In the waning days of the Johnson administration, HUD had clarified its citizen participation regulations. Most of it was aimed directly, if subtly, at the Chicago stalemate. While criticizing cities for substituting "the appearance of participation" for the real thing, HUD also encouraged "militants" to negotiate rather than hold out for control. The implication was that if TWO agreed to participate in the East Woodlawn MAPC, HUD would make sure Daley adhered to its regulations and kept his promises. In January 1969, TWO allies, Alderman Leon Despres and the newly elected state representative Abner Mikva, brokered a compromise. The East Woodlawn MAPC would be enlarged to thirty-two members. TWO would appoint nine of them; when added to the seven individual TWO members already there, the organization would have 50 percent. In exchange, Erwin France promised that TWO's plan would get a fair hearing.[64]

Brazier and Stevenson presented the compromise to a rowdy Steering Committee meeting. It was a tough sell. They were confident that TWO could unify its sixteen members, grab one or two others, and get its Model Cities plan through the MAPC. HUD had already made it clear that TWO's plan aligned closely with both the spirit and the letter of the Model Cities law. The pressure would then be on Daley (and on HUD). If the mayor rejected or ignored the decision of one of his own MAPCs, and HUD enforced its own regulations, Daley could lose out on tens of millions of dollars of federal funding. Activists on the Steering Committee, however, had just spent the previous six months deeply involved, emotionally and intellectually, in a collective reenvisioning of their community. They were intensely committed to what they had created. Many saw the compromise as a capitulation. Brazier urged them to be pragmatic. If any portion of TWO's vision were to become a reality, it would have to come through the official process. On January 27, the Steering Committee concurred.[65]

Model Cities plans for the four target areas were to be presented to the City Council on March 13. This didn't leave much time for TWO to organize and present its case. Daley, not surprisingly, made it harder. At the first meeting of the reconstituted East Woodlawn MAPC, the Daley forces stunned TWO representatives by presenting a thirty-four-page plan for immediate approval. Staffers from an array of public and private agencies strongly urged passage. Not only had it not been circulated beforehand; the exact same plan had been presented to all four MAPCs at the same time. Clearly written by city officials, it was a listing of 137 different projects under nine categories, to be parceled out to over forty public and private agencies, with no mention of the specific problems, ideas, or institutions of the individual neighborhoods. Federal money would be mostly funneled through existing city bureaucracies, including the Chicago Transit Authority, the Board of Health, the Department of Streets and Sanitation, and the Board of Education. Contracts and jobs would be given to political loyalists. It narrowly passed, enabling Daley to claim that his Model Cities process met HUD requirements. TWO representatives walked out.[66]

After weeks of public pressure, the CDA agreed to call a special meeting of the MAPC to consider TWO's plan—on March 10, just three days before the City Council meeting. Aldermen already had copies of Daley's plan, which had by then metastasized into a 2,300-page document "of almost unlimited patronage, limited handouts and massive removal," according to Leon Despres. TWO hired a court reporter to document the MAPC meeting, hoping to gather information that might give it some leverage with HUD. Even if the East Woodlawn MAPC succeeded in passing part or all of the TWO plan, it was very unlikely that it would get to City Council in time for full consideration. TWO concluded that its only play left was HUD. While MAPC approval might not have any impact on what Daley presented to HUD, it would provide TWO with a more convincing argument for the inadequacy of the participation component of the official plan.

In its presentation TWO strongly criticized the lack of community involvement in Daley's Model Cities proposal, taking it apart point by point. In health care, for example, while both plans included the construction of health centers and a five-hundred-bed hospital, TWO's plan proposed community ownership of the facilities and the creation of the locally run "pad" centers. With regard to law enforcement, TWO pressed for citizen advisory boards as well as an independent neighborhood law firm to provide a broader range of services than legal aid. In housing, the city proposal called for private and public institutions to help blacks secure financing for ownership. TWO strongly preferred the creation of neighborhood development corporations "to be set up, owned and operated by the community," to make capital available for home ownership and small businesses. Daley's plan offered jobs and control to machine loyalists and city agencies; TWO's focused on local control and the employment and training of Woodlawn residents. The contrast couldn't have been clearer.

TWO also urged the MAPC to include some of their employment and economic development proposals. The city plan excluded TWO's guaranteed annual income proposal and rarely proposed using local residents to run or deliver new services. The city proposal did not include community-owned and community-run insurance and transportation companies, for example; TWO's did. The city also refused to back TWO's effort to fold the WESP into Model Cities. "In most cases," TWO representatives argued, "the MAPC has not made strong plans for community stabilization in Woodlawn." The MAPC voted to accept TWO's proposal "for study" by its subcommittees, which would meet the day before the City Council hearing. The subcommittees adopted most of TWO's plan, but the full MAPC—almost certainly under Daley's orders—stalled. When it finally approved most of it in April, it was too late: Daley's plan was on the fast track to City Council approval.

With the City Council vote looming, Nixon's newly appointed HUD secretary, George Romney, visited Chicago. Romney reiterated the new administration's intent to give local elected officials full control over Model Cities programs. TWO participated in a heated meeting with Romney and joined other groups in strongly criticizing the lack of community voice in the city's plan. Brazier told the secretary that the MAPCs were packed with unrepresentative individuals on the city payroll. Romney was emphatic that residents would not under any circumstances have the "ultimate control" in planning or implementing the program. "Let me make this very clear," he told the gathering. "There is no logical way to substitute neighborhood residents for elected officials, and we're not going to do it." The City Council considered Daley's plan on April 25. The mayor refused to recognize Despres, who tried to argue on TWO's behalf, until after the television cameras had left the room. City Council approved Daley's plan, 41–7.[67]

TWO was unable to convince HUD to reject the Chicago proposal. In May 1969 HUD banned exclusive initiation of projects by citizen groups, making explicit what had been ambiguous—federal support of resident participation was finished. Nixon's "new federalism" handed control to public officials, not citizen groups. "Model Cities is just a marriage between urban renewal and the Poverty Program," a TWO spokesman lamented. After briefly attempting to affect MAPC elections in April 1970, TWO activists decided that fighting for greater control over federal programs wasn't worth the effort. "The City of Chicago will resist with all its resources any efforts toward community control," Brazier concluded. TWO, like similar groups, shifted its focus to community economic development through private-public partnerships. Most of the Model Cities funds distributed in Chicago from 1969 to 1972 were used to grease the wheels of the Democratic machine. Nearly half went to "administrative expenditures," generally of dubious value. Most of the rest was disbursed through sweetheart contracts to machine loyalists. Woodlawn saw little benefit.[68]

Conclusion

Despite TWO's best efforts, Woodlawn rapidly declined as a viable mixed-income community in the 1960s and 1970s. In 1960, just over eighty thousand people lived there. A decade later, the population had fallen by 36 percent, to fifty-two thousand. The core of the neighborhood lost 41 percent of its population in the 1960s, more than any other Chicago community. By 1990 it had tumbled another 50 percent; more than half of area residents were on some sort of public assistance.

Accompanying this was an enormous reduction in the economic, social, and political resources that had made Woodlawn a livable place—and that had made a grassroots organization like TWO possible. The decline of employed adults made neighborhood institutions like churches, block clubs, stores, banks, and medical offices difficult to sustain while simultaneously weakening formal and informal social controls. Redlining crippled the housing market; when the Southeast National Bank closed its Woodlawn branch in 1971, the neighborhood was left without a single financial institution. Crime and gang violence escalated, further accelerating Woodlawn's depopulation. By 1990 most of its commercial and industrial establishments were gone. "The once lively streets . . . have the appearance of an empty, bombed-out war zone. The commercial strip has been reduced to a long tunnel of charred stores, vacant lots littered with broken glass and garbage, and dilapidated buildings."[69]

Most observers in the 1970s blamed Woodlawn's collapse on its most visible manifestations—gang violence and arson. There were more than 1,600 fires in 1970 alone, destroying two hundred buildings. There is little doubt that these things played an important role in the collapse of the housing market, the flight of Woodlawn's remaining middle class, and the deterioration of the social capital and associational life necessary for safety, business viability, and collective action. But the deeper roots of Woodlawn's suffering were already in place when TWO was organized and increasingly visible in the early 1960s. Deindustrialization and metropolitan segregation were geographically concentrating the black poor in neighborhoods like Woodlawn—unhindered by public action and reinforced by an increasingly conservative national politics.

The opportunity structure for Chicago's unskilled black workers collapsed in the late 1960s and early 1970s, just as Woodlawn's population was becoming younger and poorer. The unemployment rate for black men between the ages of sixteen and nineteen exceeded 50 percent in the early 1970s; nearly one-third of young black women were in the same position. The reasons for high youth unemployment were not difficult to discern. The decline in manufacturing jobs in the city and the higher requirements for the living-wage jobs that remained led to a rapid decline in entry-level jobs for unskilled workers. Educational disparities made it harder for young black workers to qualify for living-wage positions and kept higher education well out of reach for too many. The geographic concentration of unskilled, young, and inexperienced blacks created increased competition for the limited number of low-paying positions that remained, keeping unemployment high and wages low. By the mid-1970s, Woodlawn's labor-force participation rate was barely 50 percent, and its overall unemployment rate was just under 19 percent.[70]

In the wake of the Model Cities conflict, TWO formed one of the first community development corporations. The Woodlawn Community Development Corporation (WCDC), launched in 1972, tried to attract moderate and middle-income families to the area through housing rehabilitation and construction, technical and financial assistance to jump-start local enterprise, and large-scale commercial real estate development. It had little success until the 1990s, when the market for middle-class housing began to revive near the university. Gentrification sparked fears of displacement among many low-income residents, while TWO found itself in the ironic position of supporting a revived South Campus plan to build condos and single-family homes for the black middle class. The population finally stabilized, and the percentage of Woodlawn residents living in poverty fell from 50 percent in 1990 to 39 percent a decade later. Unfortunately, as in so many similar neighborhoods, the foreclosure epidemic in the '00s hit Woodlawn hard—particularly its new black homeowners. Woodlawn continues to be profoundly shaped by the structures of metropolitan inequality, which the WCDC is powerless to stop.[71]

The fault, of course, doesn't lie with TWO. Thousands of other CDCs have emerged in poor urban neighborhoods in the past five decades, aided by federal subsidies and private foundations. They face the same limitations. Poor people don't fight wars of position on grounds of their own choosing. The push by TWO and other Black Freedom Movement groups for community development was a reaction to the limitations imposed both by the politics of racial geography and by a nation unwilling to challenge metropolitan segregation. TWO took whatever slack in the political system that was available and tried to use it to build opportunities for individual mobility, patronage, and group political power.

After the summer riots of 1967, the community development component of Model Cities moved to the forefront of Johnson's urban policy. Congress weakened the power (and budget) of the Model Cities metropolitan coordinators, while various public officials put forward detailed proposals for investing in ghetto neighborhoods. Both foreshadowed the future direction of urban policy much more than the NCADH or the task force that created Model Cities did. In 1968 the Office of Economic Opportunity began to make grants to CDCs. The Ford Foundation began to fund model CDCs around the country, including TWO's. Other private grant-making entities followed suit.[72]

The dilemma, however, was that, like the War on Poverty, the emerging community development focus tended to reinforce the idea that the struggle for racial justice had to be not only local and community-based but also centered on public-private partnerships and market-based policies. Intellectually and strategically, it severed desegregation from community development, in favor of the latter. By the end of the decade foundations and grassroots activists were firmly focused on local work and a reduced public sector, further weakening support for attacks on metropolitan segregation and inequality that crossed boundaries of race, class, and territory. This approach offered the possibility of pleasing multiple constituencies: white suburbanites, who feared desegregation of their schools and neighborhoods; Black Power advocates; white liberals; self-help conservatives; and politicians of both parties, who sought riot prevention that wouldn't alienate key voting blocs. Rather than serving as a tool to begin to unwind metropolitan segregation, Model Cities ultimately solidified the "gild the ghetto" approach to urban policy. President Nixon and the federal courts would later lock it into place, where it remains. Outside of law enforcement and the criminal justice system—which would receive absolutely massive and ever-growing government funding and support, with devastating results in Woodlawn and elsewhere—the decades to come would result in the narrowing legitimacy of the public sector.[73]

This should not, of course, minimize TWO's accomplishments or its importance. Despite limited resources, Woodlawn activists got jobs and developed skills and political experience for themselves, and they gained better housing, health care, legal representation, early childhood education, and income support for poor people. They also made public institutions more accountable. TWO activists had to master the intricacies of property law, mortgage financing, landlord-tenant relations, building codes, zoning, and federal programs, among other things. They had to do research, keep track of hearings, and mobilize turnout at protests and meetings.

As Carl Tjerandsen, president of a foundation that provided funding for TWO, remarked, "Almost no individual would ever be likely to acquire the range and depth of knowledge indicated above ... in short, it was the group, the organization which made it possible to assemble the information and through discussion achieve an understanding of it. The group was essential to the motivation to undertake the task because it was the power of TWO to make a difference, to solve a problem, that encouraged its members to begin so arduous a task." TWO, in the words of Alinsky organizer Edward Chambers, "became the teacher of how one functions in society."[74]

Because the Great Society provided neither employment nor widespread collective representation of the poor, and because it did nothing to break down discrimination in metropolitan housing and labor markets, it brought the strategic dilemmas of the black struggle into high relief. Could ghetto residents organize themselves to control their own communities, while simultaneously working with other social forces capable of reorganizing the metropolitan landscape?

For reasons of class as well as race, black activists had long favored a capacious definition of social and economic rights and the robust state action necessary to make those rights tangible. By the early 1960s, it had become clear that liberal efforts to extend those rights to blacks had failed to achieve the structural changes in the welfare state and in labor and housing markets that were needed. Despite major civil rights victories later in the decade, the state at all levels continued to exacerbate racial segregation, institutionalize white privilege, and accelerate uneven development in metropolitan areas. Much of the public discussion of black activism in the mid- to late 60s revolved around the supposed integration-separatism dichotomy, missing the more profound critique of the American opportunity structure embedded in the effort of groups like TWO to connect social democratic policy with metropolitan desegregation and grassroots community development.

TWO stands as an example of both the potential and the limits of independent black community organizing as an antipoverty strategy. While it amassed considerable power locally, the causes of black poverty in Woodlawn lay in larger structures, and the unwillingness of the nation to confront the ongoing consequences of metropolitan segregation. TWO was never able to assemble the power and authority to reach the point at which local action generates larger social reform—that kind of alchemical mixture of local power and social movement capable of fundamentally reorienting social priorities.

Conclusion

Mending Walls and Building Bridges

> Men hate each other because they fear each other. They fear each other because they don't know each other. They don't know each other because they can't communicate with each other. They can't communicate with each other because they are separated from each other.
> REV. MARTIN LUTHER KING JR., 1957

> Spatial segregation ... is opportunity segregation.
> LEGAL SCHOLAR JOHN A. POWELL, 2008

In a fascinating and prescient 1958 book, the University of Chicago political scientist Morton Grodzins discussed the problems of race and housing in the postwar American metropolis. Like Saul Alinsky, he had spent years analyzing the causes and consequences of racial segregation and white flight in Chicago. Grodzins had coined the term *tipping point* and joined his Hyde Park neighbor in calling for the use of benign quotas to foster neighborhood integration. But he had become increasingly worried about the growing "city-suburban bifurcation of races." Metropolitan segregation promised devastating economic, political, and moral consequences for cities.

"The total picture for the future, if present trends are unaltered," Grodzins declared, "is that segregation will continue and probably increase rather than decline." If race and class were to become "increasingly coterminous" with the boundaries of cities and their surrounding suburbs, cities would be faced with a "wide range of deleterious consequences" that would place at risk "the preservation and further development of many facets of urban American life, for whites and Negroes alike." For Grodzins this was the justification for "taking all positive steps possible to end the present patterns of segregation."[1]

A decade later, despite unprecedented economic growth, a federal War on Poverty, and the flowering of an extraordinary interracial movement aimed squarely at the American dilemma, metropolitan segregation remained very much in place. In the years since, it has expanded even farther, stubbornly resisting all efforts to undermine it, including those of Saul Alinsky, the OSC, and TWO. In the absence of a concerted federal effort to unwind metropolitan segregation, Alinsky-style local activism was unable to leverage sufficient power and resources to do the job. Embedded within a metropolitan social geography it couldn't reshape, the OSC was confronted with a Hobson's choice: use all possible means to pursue racial exclusion, or focus on making racial transition slower and a bit more civil. The story of TWO and Woodlawn, essentially a case study of the "ghetto enrichment" approach, demonstrated that separate simply could not be meaningfully equal.

Voices in favor of an attack on metropolitan segregation did not disappear, of course. Indeed, one of the most remarkable things about the late 1960s is the stubborn and often passionate persistence of desegregation advocates within the executive branch, despite political retrenchment after the 1966 midterm elections. President Johnson was somewhat vexed that each urban task force he appointed seemed to call for metropolitan desegregation, even as he was casting about for alternative and more politically viable approaches to the urban crisis.[2]

Charles Haar in particular continued to press the issue. In October 1967 Haar sent Johnson a detailed confidential memo sketching out four possible futures of American cities and race relations: the "Armed Fortress," the "Pacified Ghetto," the "Mini-Ghetto," and the "Vanishing Ghetto." Haar—the principal author of Model Cities—was HUD's assistant secretary for metropolitan development, as well as the chair of Johnson's Task Force on Suburban Problems, and he was the administration's most forceful advocate of attacking metropolitan segregation. The secret memo, written over many late nights, aimed to get the policy apparatus to "sit back a little bit and think about the whole picture," Haar recalled.

In the first scenario, "Armed Fortress," white America "turns its back" and "digs into suburban enclaves," leaving the black ghetto increasingly isolated and subject to police power. Riots become even more commonplace, and "humanitarians . . . retreat before the rising demands of the middle class that streets be made safe." Spending on both Model Cities and the War on Poverty is "drastically reduced," leading to further resentment and ghetto violence. White flight accelerates, as does the movement of jobs and institutions to the suburbs. Remaining in the city are poor blacks, middle-class blacks with "scant hope of escaping to suburbia," and only the poorest of whites. These population shifts lead to the election of a growing number of black mayors, who are ultimately powerless to deliver jobs and opportunities. The Republican Party, meanwhile, moves rightward in order to appeal to white families "with a newly vested interest in maintaining the suburban status quo."

Haar's second future, the "Pacified Ghetto," entails a grand bargain between the white suburbs and increasingly black cities. Whites fund federal urban programs in exchange for "preserving their freedom to make their communities exclusionary." Blacks unify around an enrichment agenda, under which "conditions of life in the ghetto are slowly improved." Central cities and suburbs engage in a "process of collective bargaining," in which the "relatively luxurious programs for physical development of the suburbs—open space, sewer and water, transportation—are traded off for more social welfare programs for central cities." With a "pacified Negro community reaping the benefits of massive federal aid through the Model Cities program," metropolitan areas are divided into "separate but equal slices." While this scenario might seem sustainable, Haar cautioned, it would do nothing to fix the isolation of blacks in the city from economic opportunity, and geographically concentrated poverty would undermine the quality of urban schools.

In the third scenario, the "Mini-Ghetto," Haar imagined the passage of a strong fair housing bill in 1968, which included single-family homes. The suburbs finally open up—but in a kind of checkerboard pattern. Many blacks leave the city and arrange themselves in suburban areas largely along class lines, reflecting the persistence of exclusionary zoning and other restrictive land-use policies. Poorer black families concentrate in older inner-ring suburbs, where they encounter many familiar struggles: concentrated poverty, inadequate social services and schools, and white flight. Indeed, circumstances are in some ways worse, since these communities lack the tax and job bases of the city. Parts of the city are gentrified. Overall, "there is less of a cleavage between central city and suburb," as disparities are "evened out." Metropolitan segregation persists, although largely because of class-based exclusions.

Haar called the final scenario the "Vanishing Ghetto." Here, fair housing law is coupled with the elimination of suburban exclusionary restrictions, federal policies aimed explicitly at racial and economic desegregation, and the creation of a guaranteed annual income for all. A "deliberate effort" is made by the federal government to "open up all local governmental units throughout metropolitan areas fairly evenly to newcomers." States outlaw exclusionary zoning, allowing blacks to freely make mobility decisions based on job opportunities, public school quality, and proximity to public transit. Because of dispersal, suburban whites "lose fear of inundation," and integrated communities result. While blacks lose the political control that geographical concentration might provide, "they do benefit from the housing, public facilities and civic services enjoyed by their white neighbors." Essentially, the "Vanishing Ghetto" restated Haar's original vision of Model Cities. While it was "unrealistic as a short run goal," he conceded, "as an ideal, it needs stating."

Haar was hardly neutral about these four policy options. "At the moment," he concluded, "we are wavering somewhere between Scenarios I [the Armed Fortress] and II [the Pacified Ghetto]." But Haar wrote the memo "to generate consensus on the fourth scenario." As long as the federal government could "avoid the appearance of compulsion," it might be possible to use strong fair housing laws, financial incentives, and legal challenges to bring the nation somewhat closer to the "Mini-Ghetto." Nonetheless, Haar concluded, the more likely outcome was either the "Armed Fortress" or the "Pacified Ghetto." Even the "Pacified Ghetto" would require "a major change in residential movement and in public policies." While the memo did shape discussions within HUD, and among some White House staffers, Johnson's margin comments were dismissive: "Interesting, but too pessimistic."[3]

No reorientation of federal urban policy was forthcoming, at least not in the direction that Haar hoped. Despite a promising start, urban policy under Nixon narrowed. George Romney, a prominent civil rights voice within the Republican Party, was appointed as secretary of Housing and Urban Development (HUD). As an eyewitness to Detroit's explosive 1967 black riot and the grievances that provoked it, Romney understood how the federal government had promoted segregation in the past and the more positive role it could play in the future. At his confirmation hearing, Romney denounced the Federal Housing Administration, saying it has "built a high-income white noose basically around these inner cities, and the poor and disadvantaged, both black and white, are pretty much left in the inner city."

Romney had every reason to think that he had the resources, capacity, and political and constitutional support to unwind metropolitan segregation. The 1968 Housing and Urban Development Act called for the construction of twenty-six million housing units, including six million for low- and moderate-income families that would be federally subsidized. And the law had given the federal government the resources and capacity to decide where they would be built; the 1968 fair housing law, as Romney saw it, demanded that he use it to "loosen the white noose." While he deferred to Nixon's New Federalism on Model Cities grants, Romney quietly developed a series of programs and proposals that put HUD (and Nixon) on a collision course with metropolitan segregation—and those who preferred to leave it untouched. That group included the increasingly suburban base of the Republican Party.

Operation Breakthrough was designed to build low- and moderate-income housing in the suburbs. While it wasn't aimed at racial integration, Romney intended to use HUD funding to either entice or coerce suburbs into revoking exclusionary zoning laws. Open Communities, however, was directly aimed at the racial integration of the suburbs. Hidden even from the White House, by the summer of 1969 Romney and his staff had taken a full inventory of all federal programs that could be used to open the suburbs, and had even drawn up a list of possible target areas (including suburban Cook County, outside Chicago).

They were deeply critical of their predecessors. The Kennedy and Johnson administrations, despite all their rhetoric, "lacked the political fortitude to deal with urban problems on a metropolitan-wide basis," noted HUD undersecretary Richard Van Dusen in the fall of 1969. Instead, "they poured large amounts of money into the ghettos." "The white suburban noose around the black in the city core is morally wrong, economically inefficient, socially destructive, and politically explosive," one staffer wrote to Romney in August 1969. Using the promise of federal funds, HUD began to put both programs into practice during the first half of 1970. Romney went to Congress in May 1970 to get legislative authority to use coercion as well.[4]

Angered at Romney's secrecy, and under increasingly intense pressure from suburban officials, Nixon took control of housing policy in October 1970. In the spring of 1971, he impounded federal funds allocated by Congress for low-income housing construction, effectively alleviating pressure on his suburban constituency. Federal funding for infrastructure and education continued to flow into suburbs, even as most of them maintained exclusionary practices. Nixon made his position explicit between December 1970 and June 1971, declaring that the federal government did not have the legal authority to "force" racial and economic integration of the suburbs. While he would enforce nondiscrimination law, he insisted that racial segregation in the suburbs was a by-product of economic considerations, not discrimination. Privately, he even considered introducing a constitutional amendment banning federal efforts to force educational and residential integration. Romney was pushed out after the November 1972 election. "Nixon's policy," according to Charles Lamb, who served on the US Commission on Civil Rights in the mid-1970s, "was consciously designed to protect the status quo, to shield suburbs from economic, and thus racial, integration. Its political intent was to preserve the Republican political base for years to come."[5]

While federal retrenchment on metropolitan segregation began under Johnson, it was locked into place under his successor. Through political rhetoric, policy priorities, and judicial appointments, Nixon essentially derailed whatever civil rights momentum remained from the Johnson administration. Title VIII of the Civil Rights Act of 1968—the Fair Housing Law—could be interpreted narrowly, as a prohibition against discrimination. Or it could be seen as requiring HUD to affirmatively promote racial and economic integration. In essence, this was the dilemma Alinsky had grappled with in the *General Report* and in the OSC: would antidiscrimination laws be enough to foster integration and undermine racial inequality, or was more purposeful action required? Between 1967 and 1969 the US Supreme Court issued a series of rulings that suggested a more capacious interpretation of civil rights law with regard to housing—an interpretation that Romney shared. Nixon, however, adhered to the narrower view. Between 1969 and 1972 he appointed four justices to the Supreme Court who concurred with his interpretation.[6]

Advocates of a frontal challenge to metropolitan inequality suffered a mortal blow in the Court's *San Antonio v. Rodriguez* (1973) and *Milliken v. Bradley* (1974) decisions, which essentially placed racial segregation and its consequences beyond the reach of constitutional remedy. One might also include the *Warth v. Seldin* (1975) and *Village of Arlington Heights v. Metropolitan Housing Development Corporation* (1977) decisions, which severely limited the situations in which federal courts might hear legal challenges to exclusionary zoning.

In *Rodriguez*, the Court rejected the argument that inequitable school financing—whether within a district or across jurisdictional boundaries—violated the equal protection clause of the Fourteenth Amendment. *Milliken* was of even greater consequence—the most important Supreme Court decision on civil rights since *Brown*. The justices overturned a lower court that had ordered a comprehensive metropolitan area–wide desegregation plan for Detroit and the fifty-three suburban school districts around it. Given the role of government at all levels in creating a racially segregated housing market in the Detroit area, Judge Stephen Roth had argued, "school district lines are simply matters of political convenience and many not be used to deny constitutional rights."

Roth's ruling finally opened up the question of metropolitan segregation for constitutional consideration. In a 5–4 decision, however, the Supreme Court struck down Roth's ruling, contending that suburban districts should not be held responsible for Detroit's segregated schools and praising local control as a social good. "It may seem the easier course to allow our great metropolitan areas to be divided up into two cities—one white, the other black," Justice Thurgood Marshall dissented. "But it is a course, I predict, our people will ultimately regret." By 1977 constitutional and political barriers had been thrown up around metropolitan segregation that remain in place today. Ever since, federal courts have consistently construed civil rights and fair housing law narrowly, viewing metropolitan social geography as the product of individual choices within a nondiscriminatory market—a kind of black box, beyond the legitimate capacity of government action to control. Or, given the role of white opportunity hoarding in perpetuating inequalities, perhaps the "box" belongs to Pandora, too politically explosive to open.[7]

Federal urban policy since 1967 has focused primarily (and weakly) on improving the quality of ghetto neighborhoods (and their residents) by devolving resources and power to municipal authorities, using tax credits and subsidies, and encouraging public-private partnerships and community development corporations, not on the forces that create and sustain metropolitan inequality. As part of his New Federalism, Nixon sought to give states and localities "wide administrative leeway" in proposing and implementing federal programs. This effort was embodied by the February 1974 Housing and Community Development Act (HCDA), which merged federal housing programs—including Model Cities—into one Community Development Block Grant, with weakened federal oversight. It also created Section 8 low-income housing vouchers.

While the HCDA required the spatial deconcentration of housing opportunities for the poor—because the Fair Housing Act arguably did the same—this has had a minimal effect on the direction of federal policy, because of the inability (and often, unwillingness) of HUD to compel compliance. When HUD secretaries under Democratic presidents Carter and Clinton tried to punish recalcitrant suburbs, congressional and local opposition stopped them. HUD has ignored the requirement altogether under Nixon's Republican successors. Regulatory enforcement of fair housing and lending laws has similarly fluctuated. Regardless of the occupant of the White House, however, the trajectory of federal urban and social policy has persisted. The HOPE VI program and the Low-Income Housing Tax Credit dominate federal urban housing policy today, and despite some recent progress, both have generally reinforced racial and economic segregation. Efforts to expand homeownership in poor urban neighborhoods have also not touched metropolitan segregation and its consequences. In the process, they have left poor and minority communities vulnerable to the ups and downs of the housing market and the depredations of underregulated financial institutions while walling them off from most of the purported benefits of homeownership.[8]

Since the early 1980s in particular, mass incarceration has also become a kind of de facto urban policy; the criminal justice system at all levels has targeted poor black communities like Woodlawn, sweeping up an extraordinary number of young men, with devastating consequences. The withdrawal of public resources and attention from metropolitan inequality has been mirrored (and exacerbated) by private disinvestment. That disinvestment, in turn, has been encouraged by deregulation and the refusal to acknowledge that governments and institutions can (and do) shape markets—they don't just respond to them. Particularly since 1980, federal and local governments have emphasized privatization, decentralization, economic competitiveness, and creating a favorable "business climate." Policy makers in both parties have deployed the rhetoric of decentralization and localism—for education, as well as urban policy more generally.[9]

This approach enjoys support from free-market advocates on the right as well as many activists on the left. Politically, it has granted both political parties a kind of cheap policy grace, presenting the appearance of doing something about poverty and urban problems, but without the political and economic costs of confronting metropolitan segregation, economic insecurity, and an inadequate welfare state. This persistent localism has had profound and intensifying consequences.[10]

Alinsky and the Stubborn Persistence of Metropolitan Segregation

American metropolitan areas, especially in the decades after World War II, have been characterized by a deeply racialized social geography and the ensuing racial geopolitics. Saul Alinsky's experiences on the South Side of Chicago demonstrate the centrality of this politics in limiting the number and stability of integrated neighborhoods, and the effectiveness of locally based organizing in creating and sustaining them. They also shed light on the consequences of metropolitan segregation for black ghetto neighborhoods, and the limitations of an "enrichment" strategy. Alinsky's career overlapped with two national windows of opportunity to make our social geography more just: the late 1940s and the mid- to late 1960s. Both opportunities were missed. We may have the good fortune to have another one; in recent years, racial segregation and its consequences have moved to the forefront of national political discourse for the first time in almost fifty years, thanks to an explosion of black activism, scholarly advocacy, court action, and new regulatory policy. As a consequence, this history may have much to teach us.

Racial segregation *matters*, not just in the past but in the present. The good news is that more and more Americans now live in nonhomogeneous places. The bad news is that segregation by race and especially class still powerfully shapes opportunities and life chances, particularly in older postindustrial metropolitan areas. The number of Americans living in high-poverty neighborhoods has nearly doubled since the start of the twenty-first century. Poor black and Latino families in particular are increasingly likely to live in such areas. This trend began before the Great Recession and has continued unabated. Its roots are in the broader structures of metropolitan inequality, not in the ebbs and flows of the economy.[11]

Pathbreaking scholarship by Patrick Sharkey, Robert Sampson, Raj Chetty, and others starkly demonstrates that our failure to address these inequities has isolated millions of black families from opportunities, with cascading social and economic impacts across generations. For children especially, prolonged exposure to concentrated neighborhood disadvantage has deeply negative consequences for cognitive development, physical and mental health, educational achievement, future earnings, and overall well-being. Racial segregation leaves too many Americans cut off from good schools, healthy environments, job opportunities, safe streets, the protection of the law, and full membership in the polity. Most whites have far more access to neighborhoods with stronger labor markets, better-performing schools, and cleaner air and water, and they have generally been able to hoard opportunities—individually and collectively—to protect that access.[12]

Metropolitan segregation today is not the result of individual choice in a nondiscriminatory "free" market. It is not a rapidly ebbing vestige of our tortured racial history. Patterns of social geography, whether shaped by race or class, are not just constructed—they are sustained. These patterns are determined by social and political choices, with enormous consequences. "A country that condemns segregation as a malady of its past," writes Angela Glover Blackwell, "must own up to the legacy of exclusion, disinvestment, and disadvantage this practice has left in its wake—and do something to change it."[13]

The primary way race continues to shape opportunity in the United States is through social geography. The economic changes that undermined Woodlawn and other ghettos in the 1960s—principally deindustrialization and the hollowing out of the metropolitan opportunity structure—metastasized subsequently. As a result, black inner-city residents were isolated both socially and physically from expanding suburban labor markets and economic and educational opportunities. They also suffered the consequences of disinvestment, financial deregulation, and the expansion of the carceral state, as well as the nation's overall abdication of public responsibility for equal opportunity. The shifting of economic risks onto workers and communities has made many more Americans, regardless of race, economically insecure. But because job access, social capital, educational opportunity, the ability to acquire and grow wealth, and even health and physical safety are so closely tied to where one lives (or can live), metropolitan segregation has afflicted the afflicted and comforted the comfortable to a much greater extent than is generally acknowledged.

As Melvin Oliver and Thomas Shapiro have demonstrated, it is at the intersection of wealth and social geography where we see that white advantage and black disadvantage are both cumulative and related. It is there we find home ownership, school attendance patterns, and access to the labor market—all of which either provide transformative assets across generations, or deny them. It is there we can see the weight of our racial history and how it continues to elevate some while impeding others. In other words, race shapes life chances and access to primary social goods through place above all else—not through individual acts of discrimination and insult. As Oliver and Shapiro note, "The accumulation of wealth for some whites is intimately tied to the poverty of wealth for most blacks . . . practically every circumstance of bias and discrimination against blacks has produced a circumstance and opportunity of positive gain for whites."

For most Americans, home ownership is their primary form of wealth. Even though homeownership rates for blacks are lower than whites' (45 percent compared to 74 percent in 2021), and homes appreciate far more slowly in minority and integrated neighborhoods, black wealth is twice as likely as white wealth to be tied up in home equity. But because of unequal access to mortgage and housing markets, as well as the "racial valuing of neighborhoods on the basis of segregated markets," racial wealth disparities remain enormous. Black families were locked out of the massive buildup of home equity over the past seven decades, which provided millions of white families with opportunity-leveraging assets across generations—a head start, essentially. Residential segregation has suppressed black home equity while boosting the wealth accumulation of white homeowners, in effect reproducing white advantage (and black disadvantage) with each generation.[14]

Metropolitan racial segregation geographically concentrated the most exploitive causes of the housing market boom of the early 2000s, as well as the consequences of its collapse. Subprime loans and foreclosures were spatially concentrated in low- to moderate-income communities, in neighborhoods of color in particular. Minority households were more than three times as likely as whites to end up with risky loans. Since the start of the Great Recession in late 2007, racial segregation has combined with financial deregulation and discriminatory financial markets to disproportionately strip middle-class black families and neighborhoods of billions of dollars of assets. While the wealth of American families overall fell about 29 percent during the Great Recession, the decline for blacks was far greater, at 48 percent. The ratio between the median wealth of whites and that of blacks is higher now than it was in 2007. Borrowers of color collectively lost between $164 billion and $213 billion in housing wealth as a result of subprime loans alone. Metropolitan segregation thus remains at the very heart of racial inequality.[15]

American metropolitan areas remain racially segregated for a variety of reasons, but the strong connections among race, place, and property continue to undermine efforts to attack urban problems. Where white metropolitan residents live, whom they live near, the educational decisions they make for their children, whom they consider desirable neighbors, what they value about their properties and their neighborhoods, and the direct economic benefits of home ownership are all deeply tied to race. The racial geopolitics that resulted, especially after the Second Great Migration of blacks beginning in the early 1940s, continues to affect how urban and suburban residents (both white and black) map the social terrain, envision social change, and make housing decisions. The creation of white identity and the racial geopolitics that have both shaped and reflected it are central to understanding the politics and social geography of metropolitan areas, the persistence of racial and economic segregation, and the limits to place-based efforts to address the resulting problems.

The story of Saul Alinsky makes the deep roots of this racial politics very clear. It also makes clear how difficult it is to effectively confront them through local action and neighborhood-based urban policy. This raises some important cautions for those seeking progressive change today. The use of local place-based strategies alone to attack poverty, segregation, inequality, and uneven development—whether undertaken by government or by private entities—can exacerbate the very lifeways that have caused these problems in the first place if it is not accompanied by metropolitan-level analysis and organizing.

The Limits of Place-Based Policy and Activism

Writers and policy makers on both the right and the left differ about how to address the consequences of metropolitan segregation, but they have generally agreed that the solutions lie in a privatized, market-based, decentralized, and "color-blind" version of Haar's "Pacified Ghetto": fixing, repairing, or enabling inner-city communities (or their residents). That is, the focus isn't on geographic concentration by race and class—it is on managing its consequences, without disrupting (or even acknowledging) the fundamental cause. For the right, welfare reform, deregulation, faith-based initiatives, and the right market incentives will fix communities, individuals, and schools. Frustrated by devolution and retrenchment at the federal level and the persistence of jurisdictional fragmentation in metropolitan areas, and disillusioned by the structural limitations of the welfare state, the left has increasingly looked to local grassroots organizing to sustain social justice and further democratic change. Community development, the construction of social capital, home ownership, and more funds for city schools, it is hoped, will uplift the urban minority poor. "The standard progressive approach of the moment," Ta-Nehisi Coates wrote in 2015, "is to mix color-conscious moral invective with color-blind public policy." When trying to deal with the "effects of white supremacy," he concludes, the liberal approach "is simple—talk about class and hope no one notices."[16]

Despite the growing ideological divisions of our age, there has been a surprising political convergence on issues related to urban policy, criminal justice, education, social services, and housing. From the spread of charter schools, to the expansion of home ownership through financial deregulation, to the drastic shift in the welfare state toward social services and tax credits (and away from entitlements), it is apparent that left and right agree on much more than is commonly assumed. Virtually all these points of agreement either ignore or exacerbate racial and economic segregation. The Obama administration's embrace of urban charter schools, school choice, and the use of market models for the assessment of students, teachers, and schools was emblematic of this convergence—it co-opted the language of community, equal opportunity, and civil rights, while restricting access and reinforcing inequality. Race to the Top grants went to charter school expansion, not to interdistrict experiments with integration. Despite a lack of evidence of the efficacy of this approach and growing empirical support for the educational value of school integration by class as well as race, educational inequalities are rarely discussed in terms of segregation, housing policy, land-use laws, and the intersection of inequality and social geography.[17]

In an age of greatly diminished expectations—the "twilight of common dreams," as Todd Gitlin once put it—positive public action to unwind metropolitan segregation has come to be seen as unrealistic, unnecessary, or paternalistic. Substantive racial equality, in short, remains elusive. Boundary-crossing coalitions remain similarly elusive. Policy and activism that does not seek to address and unwind metropolitan segregation will do little to trouble the inequalities of wealth and life chances that white opportunity hoarding has sewn into the fabric of American life. The idea that urban neighborhoods can and should regenerate themselves naturalizes racial segregation. Making the role of government in shaping opportunity and social geography even more invisible has made it that much harder for Americans to see these things as ones that can and should be changed. It allows white suburbanites to believe that their wealth is unrelated to the deprivation in nearby cities and inner-ring suburbs.

Organizing for Metropolitan Justice

While Alinsky was never able to connect the OSC and TWO (let alone the BYNC) to broader coalitions capable of attacking metropolitan segregation, he was aware of its ultimate necessity. In the IAF's 1960 annual report, for example, Alinsky advised that projects should be organized "not only for . . . [their] effects within the community," but as an integral part of a coordinated attack on residential segregation. "We believe that this holistic springboard offers the only hope for possible success." By the end of the 1960s, his conviction about such coalitions had hardened. "The only way you can have integration is for the whole city to open up, almost simultaneously," he told *Harper's Magazine* in 1970. "Otherwise, when just one community opens up, whether by black initiative or blockbusting, the pressure is so great that the community just turns over." "We have to adjust our vision," he told a college audience in January 1969. "We have already moved into a regional way of life," he argued, with Chicago as just one neighborhood in a metropolitan area of over "thirteen hundred authorities and jurisdictions." As he gruffly put it in 1969, "a political idiot knows that most major issues are national, and in some cases international in scope. They cannot be coped with on the local community level."[18]

Alinsky didn't see this as a retreat from the grassroots organizing that had made him famous. The problem of scale, of course, has long vexed democratic theorists and social justice activists. Local decision-making, Alinsky had always asserted, offers opportunities for meaningful civic engagement, as citizens can act through familiar institutions to draw connections between the issues they experience and the broader political and economic ecology. But he also recognized that local institutions, identities, and conditions were embedded in broader structures of inequality, which too often fragmented efforts to understand and overcome them.

Alinsky was deeply influenced by the principle of subsidiarity, an idea drawn from Catholic social thought. Subsidiarity requires that as many decisions as possible should be left to the local level, where citizens are more likely to be directly engaged. More conservative thinkers have used subsidiarity as an intellectual basis for criticizing strong state action. But the emphasis on the local in Catholic social thought was a means to a more important end. According to the theologian Edward Verstraeten, subsidiarity is based on an ethical imperative for communal, institutional, or governmental action to create the social conditions for the full development of the individual. That meant that while local action was preferred, if broader action was needed to pursue that ethical imperative, then so be it. While Alinsky was no theologian, his approach to organizing was similar.[19]

In the wake of the 1968 election, Alinsky became increasingly worried that the vast white suburban middle class would retreat behind an ideological and political privatism that not only would undermine opportunities for multiracial and multiclass coalitions—it would undermine democracy itself. Organizing, therefore, needed to "center upon America's white middle class. That is where the power is . . . large parts of the middle class . . . must be activated," Alinsky argued. "They're alienated, depersonalized, without any feeling of participation in the political process, and they feel rejected and hopeless . . . now it's up to us to go in and rub raw the sores of discontent, galvanize them for radical social change. We'll give them a way to participate in the democratic process . . . We'll not only give them a cause, we'll make life goddamn exciting for them again." New Left and Black Power dreams of a transformational alliance of minorities, students, and the white poor were delusional, according to Alinsky. Even if such a coalition were assembled, he argued, it would still have to "find supporters among the [three-quarters] of our people who are middle class."

"The 'silent majority' now are hurt, bitter, suspicious, feeling rejected and at bay," Alinsky argued. Living in "illusions of partial escape," they were increasingly likely to "drop out into a private world, the non-existent past," rather than engage public issues as active citizens. Their participation and faith in broader public institutions—and their optimism about American citizenship as a common enterprise—was in danger of eroding. The result would be a paranoid politics shaped by the "law of survival in the narrowest sense." "This is the so-called Silent Majority . . . , and it's here that the die will be cast and this country's future decided for the next 50 years."[20]

While middle-class instincts were fundamentally conservative, Alinsky acknowledged, "the realities of their daily lives drill it home that the status quo has exploited and betrayed them . . . there's a second revolution seething beneath the surface of middle class America—the revolution of a bewildered, frightened and as-yet-inarticulate group of desperate people groping for alternatives—for hope." Once the suburban middle class had been mobilized—Alinsky thought economic insecurity, corporate power, and perhaps environmental issues would provide the initial spark—"it will be natural for it to seek out allies among the other disenfranchised." Metropolitan desegregation by race and class could be presented in terms of enlightened mutual self-interest, but on a geographical and political scale capable of bringing about transformational change. If the left didn't take advantage of this opportunity, more reactionary forces and tendencies certainly would. "If we don't win them," Alinsky argued in his 1971 *Rules for Radicals*, "Wallace or Spiro T. Nixon will."[21]

Alinsky and the IAF created the Citizens Action Program in the late 1960s, both as a laboratory school for training community organizers and as an experiment in metropolitan coalition building. The group, originally named the Campaign against Pollution, started in November 1969 in response to a weather inversion that caused a cloud of polluted air to hang over the Chicago area for almost a week. From the beginning, the Citizens Action Program focused on issues and interests that affected local communities but that originated in broader structures and processes.

In many ways, the Citizens Action Program's approach to organizing wasn't much different from previous Alinsky groups: it retained the organization-of-organizations format and used confrontational tactics to embarrass prominent political and economic institutions into action. Importantly, however, the program sought to work on a broader geographical plane, using issues that were regional in scope.[22] "The most important issues which affect a neighborhood—property taxes, pollution, mortgage loans, etc.—are determined outside the neighborhood by major economic forces," Citizens Action Program organizer Paul Booth said in 1973. "A citywide, militant organization was the only way people could begin to deal with these problems."[23]

Most importantly, the Citizens Action Program brought together people of different races, classes, and neighborhoods to address redlining and neighborhood deterioration. It began a campaign to expose the decisions of private investors and panic peddlers, Federal Housing Authority abuses and bank lending policies, and the influence of all these groups on city government. The Citizens Action Program campaigned to get pledges from people to withdraw their money from financial institutions that practiced redlining and deposit it in banks that agreed to invest in city neighborhoods. More than $120 million in "greenlining" pledges were collected by April 1975. The group successfully pressured the governor of Illinois to investigate redlining and other federal abuses; his report, along with community lobbying, led to the passage of a law—which became a national model—prohibiting redlining and requiring disclosure of mortgage loan information. After negotiations with and demonstrations against the Federal Home Loan Bank of Chicago, the bank confirmed the existence of redlining. This led to a city ordinance prohibiting redlining by any institution that accepted city deposits.

The Citizens Action Program succeeded in shifting the focus of white neighborhood anger away from blacks and toward the institutions largely responsible for divisive racial geopolitics. Individuals and groups that spun off from the program helped to lead the movement which resulted in the Home Mortgage Disclosure Act (1975) and the Community Reinvestment Act (1977), which have helped to reverse at least some of damage done to inner cities by the politics of racial geography.[24]

The post-Alinsky IAF has attempted to build similar coalitions. Its most ambitious effort has again been in Chicago: United Power for Action and

Justice (UPAJ). The result of a decade-long crusade by Alinsky's friend and ally Msgr. John Egan, efforts to organize a regional federation of community, labor, and religious groups that crossed the boundaries of class, race, ethnicity, and jurisdiction culminated in a massive founding convention—with ten thousand people in attendance—at the University of Illinois Chicago in October 1997. In the years since, the UPAJ has fought for affordable housing in the suburbs and throughout the city, among many other issues.[25]

Efforts by the Gamaliel Foundation (an IAF-like network of community organizations) to engage in "community-based regionalism" also offer great promise and get even closer to a frontal attack on metropolitan segregation. Gamaliel issued a Statement on Regional Organizing in 2001. Because "most important decisions are being made at a regional, national and global level," Gamaliel called on its affiliates to recognize "that the power and significance of a neighborhood group has diminished." In response, the foundation resolved to assist in the creation of "large metropolitan organizations that bridge divisions of race, class and political boundaries." If groups like this can assemble solid working coalitions across jurisdictional boundaries, it would present an unprecedented opportunity to construct a strong political constituency dedicated to an alternative metropolitan geography.

Across the country, a growing number of local activist groups—often rooted in community development corporations—are focusing on regional equity issues. Analytically, according to Manuel Pastor, Chris Benner, and Martha Matsuoka, these organizations see that the "most challenging urban problems are created by our patterns of metropolitan development." Practically, they pursue metropolitan strategies focused on housing and economic development, acknowledging the limitations of both "traditional community development" and federal policy. Politically, they see potential for progressive organizing and sustainable coalition building at the regional level. By focusing on economic competitiveness and sustainability, as well as more traditional issues of racial and economic justice, they are able to build relationships with business and environmental interests as well.[26]

There is a growing recognition that the fair housing and community development movements have too often worked at cross-purposes. Despite their common origin in the effort to address what Elizabeth Julian calls the "twin evils of Jim Crow: separate and unequal," in recent decades they have moved in parallel (and sometimes conflicting) policy universes. In large part this reflects the legislative environment: state laws fragment metropolitan political jurisdictions, federal policies reinforce this fragmentation, and court rulings hold segregation to be outside the realm of constitutional concern. As a consequence, fair housing policy and advocacy have overemphasized individual acts of discrimination, while leaving systemic structures of racial exclusion unchallenged. They have also failed to make common cause with community-based social justice efforts to deal with the consequences of metropolitan segregation for neighborhoods, community institutions, and families.

The community development movement, despite far more resources and political support than the fair housing movement, has been unable to make separate equal. Community development corporations do have a long list of important accomplishments, to be sure. In the absence of meaningful metropolitan-level policy from the federal government, they have admirably tried to fill the breach. The benefits have been both tangible (improved schools, the construction of affordable housing, increased investment capital) and intangible (social capital and empowerment). Their use of the Community Reinvestment Act to challenge the lending practices of large financial institutions has brought trillions of dollars of capital into urban neighborhoods. Community development corporations have also done essential work at the local and state levels on home foreclosures and community reinvestment in the wake of the Great Recession. Yet they have had limited effect on the larger structures of metropolitan segregation and inequality, in part because they take those structures as given. As a consequence, David Rusk argues, the community development movement finds itself "running up a down escalator." Too often, their efforts disproportionately benefit landowners, businesses, and the upwardly mobile, while leaving the ultimate causes of impoverishment, disinvestment, and inequality unchallenged. To tweak Ira Katznelson's famous formulation, these "metropolitan trenches" systematically segregate resources from needs and activism from analysis and organizing at the scale needed to further social justice in meaningful ways.[27]

Since the mid-1960s, solutions to the urban dilemma have too often been viewed in terms of the people-versus-place dichotomy: that policy and activism should focus either on community development (place) or on facilitating individual mobility. Place-based policies have predominated in recent decades, though largely through a privatized, market-based, and inadequately resourced model. The results have been disappointing. With the exception of public housing vouchers and a few small-scale experiments, federal urban policy has rarely pursued people-based efforts. Federal policy is place based, yet ignores how metropolitan segregation concentrates poverty and opportunity. It is person-based, yet is privatized, fragmented, inadequately funded, often punitive, and limited.[28]

Metropolitan approaches have gained increasing traction in some states and localities in the past two decades with some notable successes.

Montgomery County, Maryland, has used land-use and zoning laws to provide and disperse low- and moderate-income housing and to pursue the economic integration of its public schools. Research seems to indicate that integrative housing policy is critical for school desegregation to really stick—and that economic integration of schools and communities has a powerful impact on student achievement.

In the Minneapolis area, meanwhile, state legislator Myron Orfield and the Met Council have had success assembling political coalitions between the city and its surrounding inner-ring suburbs to foster a broader sharing of low- and moderate-income housing (and revenues) throughout the metropolitan area. At the state level, Oregon and (to a lesser extent) Washington have both encouraged regional land-use planning, for the purpose of reining in suburban sprawl. The New Jersey Supreme Court, in its 1975 and 1983 *Mt. Laurel* decisions, ordered each municipality in the state to meet its "fair share of the regional need for low- and moderate-income housing." Bruce Katz, David Rusk, William Julius Wilson, and others have argued that only regional efforts like these have any hope of diminishing structural problems.[29]

Metropolitan efforts at the federal level have been more limited. The Moving to Opportunity and Gautreaux experiments focused on dispersing small numbers of poor and often minority families from ghettos to suburbs and outlying urban areas. The results have provided growing evidence for the benefits of unwinding metropolitan segregation. Neither, however, focuses on increasing the supply of low- to moderate-income housing in the suburbs, and thus leaves land-use laws and powers untouched. They are also very small in scale. In 2016 HUD issued a promising regulation designed to increase the purchasing power of housing vouchers in high-opportunity zip codes in twenty-three metropolitan areas—the so-called Small Market Area Rents program. But it never really got off the ground before Obama's second term ended, and it didn't include any commitments to expand the supply of low- to moderate-income housing in high-opportunity neighborhoods.[30]

All these efforts are praiseworthy because they make explicit the connection between opportunity and social geography. They require participants (and opponents) to draw connections between issues that the politics of racial geography have allowed us to keep separate for so long: the relationship between suburban riches and urban poverty, private wealth and public squalor, white privilege and black deprivation, sprawl and city disinvestment, and white middle-class anxiety and the "Robin Hood in reverse" economic and tax policies of the past three decades.

The US Supreme Court's important decision in the July 2015 *Inclusive Communities* fair housing case brought some of the tensions between "community development" and desegregation to the forefront. In Texas, the Inclusive Communities Project (ICP) had sued the state Department of Housing, accusing it of funneling the vast majority of federal low-income housing tax credits into high minority and low-income neighborhoods in Dallas. The ICP argued that because Texas was reinforcing racial segregation ("gilding the ghetto," as they said in Alinsky's day), it was violating the federal Fair Housing Act. Even if there was no direct evidence of racial motivation, ICP argued, there was more than ample information to demonstrate the disparate and disproportionate impact on minorities. The state countered that it was revitalizing poor neighborhoods in Dallas, through the construction of affordable housing in the places where those on low-incomes lived, and that this was a legitimate policy goal without racial motivation.

Justice Anthony Kennedy's majority opinion definitively affirmed that the 1968 Fair Housing Act's primary goal was to move the nation "toward a more integrated society." The ruling also upheld the use of 'disparate impact' as a policy tool for pursuing that goal.[31] Just one week later, President Obama's HUD announced new rules to guide jurisdictions receiving federal housing funds on how to "affirmatively further" the desegregation goals of the 1968 law. These rules hold that each state and locality that receives federal housing and community development funds must take affirmative steps to measure and address racial segregation, and remove barriers to housing choice in areas of opportunity in housing, jobs, education, and transportation. To help localities see, understand, and surmount these barriers, HUD created an innovative database that identified racially and ethnically concentrated areas of poverty. Municipalities would be held accountable for addressing these patterns (and for not exacerbating them). The data were to be shared with community groups and activists, enabling those most affected by metropolitan inequality to hold public officials accountable for the equity impact of their actions (and inactions). Easily understandable evidence could now be produced that pointed the way toward solutions or provided the smoking gun for political and legal action. These developments, alongside the emerging Black Lives Matter movement, pried open a window of opportunity—wider than at any time in nearly a half century—to begin to unwind metropolitan segregation. Walter Mondale, one of the principal authors of the Fair Housing Act, expressed hope in 2015 that the "unfinished business" of the law might finally be addressed.[32]

Unfortunately, the following occupant of the White House didn't share these commitments. Indeed, Donald Trump (and his father before him) had a long and stained history of racial discrimination in his real estate dealings and of racist provocations. Claiming that Obama's commitments to fair housing and opportunity constituted "mandated social engineering," Trump's HUD secretary Ben Carson suspended them. In his 2020 reelection campaign, Trump even tried to use the Obama policies as a racist cudgel to drive white suburban voters away from Democratic nominee Joe Biden. A Biden administration, Trump argued, would "eliminate single-family zoning, bringing who knows into your suburbs, so your communities will be unsafe and your housing values will go down." It is a good sign that this Nixonian script wasn't well received by most suburban voters, who now generally reside in communities that are more racially diverse than they were fifty years ago. Then again, Nixon's earlier successes in fighting off challenges to the comprehensive restructuring of metropolitan opportunity had created a safe space where generations of subsequent white suburban opportunity hoarding could operate—unchecked by the Constitution and unchallenged by federal policy. The actions Obama and Biden had committed to were far more incremental than what was on the table in the late 1960s and early 1970s. Trump's race-baiting didn't play because the threat didn't resonate.[33]

The Biden administration, to its credit, has committed itself strongly to racial equity. On his first day in office the president issued an executive order on it, noting that both the COVID-19 pandemic and the Black Lives Matter movement had exposed inequalities and "highlighted the unbearable human costs of systemic racism." The order called for an "equity assessment" across the entire federal government and the disaggregation of all federal data sets by race, among other variables. It also committed to allocating resources "to address the historic failure to invest sufficiently, justly and equally in underserved communities, as well as individuals from those communities." Another order directed HUD to reverse Trump administration actions that "undermined fair housing principles." Biden also laid out plans to address racial inequalities in wealth, boost black homeownership, and increase rental housing in high-opportunity neighborhoods.[34]

In June 2021, HUD reinstated the Obama-era "affirmatively further" rule. Importantly, however, it doesn't require jurisdictions to use federal data tools to analyze local barriers to integration and then submit plans to dismantle them. HUD will struggle to enforce the requirement that communities take meaningful action against metropolitan segregation, if they aren't required to analyze housing patterns, concentrated poverty, and disparities in access to jobs, quality schools, and public transportation. 'This doesn't reverse the damage of the Trump administration," lamented UCLA law professor Jonathan Zasloff. "What gets measured gets dealt with." On the other hand, the Biden administration had also committed itself to investing billions of dollars in low- and moderate-income housing. In a sense, HUD secretary Marcia

Fudge is in a somewhat similar position to George Romney in 1969: a legal and moral imperative to desegregate, and tools and resources to put that obligation into action across the metropolitan landscape. Whether the Biden administration can balance its pledge to pump resources into underserved communities with a commitment to addressing unequal opportunities at the metropolitan level remains to be seen.[35]

Ultimately, of course, the tension between these two things is a false one, a zero-sum situation set up by the structures of metropolitan segregation. Community development can only succeed if it is embedded in a larger context of regional equity. The legal scholar john a. powell and the Kirwan Institute, as well as Angela Blackwell and PolicyLink, have offered an intellectual and policy framework that seems ideally suited for bridging these dilemmas. The goal is to forge a movement aimed at equitable and sustainable development, regional equity, and the creation of "inclusive communities of opportunity." This framework seeks to balance the need for urban revitalization with an effort to disconnect social geography from unequal access to the opportunity structure. "Regional equity," Blackwell argues, is based on a "deep understanding of how metropolitan development patterns structure the life chances and social and economic opportunities of residents, and the ways in which uneven spatial development reinforces old racial and class divides, while creating new ones." The goal is to ensure that everyone, regardless of where they live, can access the essential ingredients of economic and social success, using a variety of policy and organizing tools at all levels to bring this about—inclusionary zoning, community benefit agreements, transit-oriented development, land-use regulations, and of course federal programs and dollars.

"Housing location is the primary mechanism for accessing opportunity in our society," powell argues. It shapes the quality of schools, the quality of public services, access to employment and to transportation, as well as public safety. "Spatial segregation," therefore, is "opportunity segregation." Policy and activism must be focused on the "creation and preservation of affordable housing" across metropolitan regions and must be "deliberately and intelligently connected on a regional scale to high performing schools, sustained employment, adequate and affordable transportation, and institutions that facilitate civic and political engagement." The emphasis must be on providing housing choice in communities of opportunity rather than on economic or racial integration as such. This perspective acknowledges that because so much poverty is likely to remain spatially bounded in the near future, enrichment strategies remain vital, particularly for the provision of public goods, and the maintenance of social networks and institutions. But ultimately, metropolitan segregation remains the structural linchpin of racial inequality in America.[36]

Metropolitan segregation distracts citizens and community groups from the atrophy of the nation's opportunity structure in the past five decades. Much as Alinsky feared, it has contributed to the rising influence of conservative narratives that posit inequality as the natural and inevitable result of markets, individual choice, and merit. The result is an underdeveloped sociological imagination and an impoverished vision of the commonweal. The atrophy of the commons, so often lamented, can be attributed to many things. In the United States, at least, racial and economic segregation have greatly exacerbated the weakness of the public sphere, by atomizing and privatizing experiences and interests that have their origins in broader structures and deeper historical patterns properly amenable to common governance. The resulting garrison impulse is unsustainable; in the era of Donald Trump, it has put the very future of our democracy at risk. As demographic change creates an America that is younger and more diverse, metropolitan segregation is like kindling for the wildfire of white nationalist demagoguery. "The existence of segregated residential patterns helps politicians draw safe districts for white voters," argues fair housing activist and former HUD official Elizabeth Julian. Breaking down some of these barriers, she concludes, could "defuse some of the explosive dynamics that gave rise to Trump." Metropolitan regions with the highest rates of inequality and segregation (by class as well as race) tend to have the lowest rates of social mobility and the most stagnant economies. We also know that our current system doesn't generate enough affordable housing, even for middle-class families, and that segregation as well as restrictive land-use laws are part of the reason. The current circumstance may work well for a "favored quarter," perhaps. But it otherwise diminishes us all.[37]

It is a classic progressive dilemma to wonder and theorize about the proper level of focus, when there seems so much to do, and all problems seem connected. Alinsky's story doesn't tell us that local activism is useless as a tool for confronting metropolitan segregation and its consequences. What it may tell us is that organizing must ultimately be directed toward changes in the law and in the distribution of political power, and toward the creation of geographically broad coalitions across race, class and jurisdiction. I don't want to create a straw man out of present-day community organizations. Many of them—including the IAF—don't operate like Alinsky groups did. In many places they have prevented a kind of freefall while enabling the disadvantaged to marshal resources and hope. But for most the basic focus remains local, in the sense that the issue of racial and economic segregation is put aside, in favor of marshaling resources and political power to benefit a specific place.

Ultimately, however, government and civil society must focus on solutions to the problems of cities that are informed by the insight that place and the distribution of primary social goods have been and still are related, and that seek to break that connection. Devising policies that take that seriously means assembling coalitions that do so as well. A neighborhood or community segregated by race or class is not just a place where poor and black (or rich and white) people live. It is a social structure that embeds injustice into our daily lives and that foments identities and politics that fragment efforts to overcome it.

Social justice, as well as the future of our democracy, demand that we break the politics and ways of thinking that have grown up around metropolitan segregation. Without a conscious effort to unwind our unjust social geography, efforts by government and civil society will replicate the fragmentation that frustrated Alinsky and that divides us today. But that effort can be made. We have to believe, as Robert Frost wrote, that there is something "that doesn't love a wall, that wants it down."

Acknowledgments

When a book takes as long to come out as this has, one accumulates a lot of red in the ledger. I was in my midtwenties, single, and in graduate school at Penn when this began as a doctoral thesis. I completed it a few weeks shy of my fifty-fifth birthday, as a tenured college professor, happily married with two amazing teenage children. I have lived a truly blessed life, filled with all the joys, bruises, and sorrows that make our endless numbered days meaningful. And here and there, when circumstances allowed it, I've also chipped away at "the Alinsky book." The past three decades have been filled with good, soul-filling work: teaching, activism, and civic engagement on educational equity, racial justice, humanities education for veterans, the economically excluded, and more. Needless to say, when Michael Katz, Walter Licht, and Tom Sugrue (and before that, Bruce Laurie) first tried to show me how to do this work, the long odyssey that followed wasn't part of the plan. Of course, today I understand something—many things—that I didn't back then: the odyssey is the thing, not the plan.

To paraphrase Gertrude Stein, silent gratitude is of no use to anyone. When one is younger, gratitude isn't that easy to access. It is very tempting to think that where one is and where one is going depends primarily on whatever talents, energies, and ambitions you can bring to bear. Ties to others can help or hinder, and in the youthful charge forward, one rarely stops to think or reflect on such things. However, time and circumstance have long since taught me that these ties hold me up and hold me together, and that few things are more important or fulfilling than letting people know it.

In some ways, this book is better for the long gestation period. For one thing, I have a more functional and defensible mixture of knowledge, humility, and wisdom than I did then. As often happens with age, I am more aware of contingency, contradiction, and the tragic sensibility—of limited human beings, trying to make choices under conditions that are generally not of their own choosing.

More concretely, this book has greatly benefited from decades of remarkable scholarship on the history of racial inequality in the metropolitan areas of the North, and its intersection with law, housing markets, public policy, and identity. The work of Tom Sugrue and Arnold Hirsch towered over this book from the outset, as will be immediately apparent to any reader. Tom literally towered over it, as teacher, adviser, and intellectual mentor. But my meandering path also allowed me to learn from the scholarship of Wendell Pritchett, Tom Jackson, Matthew Countryman, Martha Biondi, Robert Self, David Freund, Amanda Seligman, Beryl Satter, Sheryll Cashin, Richard Rothstein, John McGreevey, Gary Gerstle, and countless others. Several of them have shaped this book (and its author) directly. Wendell, David, and Tom have been generous role models, colleagues, and friends for decades. Amanda and Matthew spent countless hours combing through earlier iterations of this book, providing priceless feedback not only on ideas, sources, and arguments but also on structure and syntax. I met Richard somewhat late in the game, but as a model of engaged scholarship he convinced me that what I was working on could and should speak to the present. Thanks, all of you.

The good people at the University of Chicago Press have patiently stuck with me over the years, for which I am incredibly grateful. Doug Mitchell believed in this project from the earliest stages, kept the dim flame flickering as it expanded in size, and served as an engaging correspondent and intellectual interlocutor throughout. Tim Mennel, who stepped in when Doug retired, has been a lifesaver. One of my many flaws (exemplified by what you are reading now) is a lack of brevity. Quite simply, this book has always been too damn long. I'm terrific at editing other people's work and lousy at editing my own. Tim's empathetic scalpel—and belief in the book—is the main reason you have it in front of you today. Thanks.

Most of the research for this book was completed some years ago, at a wide variety of libraries and archives: University of Illinois Chicago Special Collections, University of Chicago Special Collections, the Chicago Historical Society (now the Chicago History Museum), the Archives of the Archdiocese of Chicago, the National Archives II, and the Lyndon B. Johnson and Richard Nixon Presidential Libraries, among others. My profound thanks not only to the archivists and librarians who assisted me but also to their colleagues, who fulfilled my extensive photocopying requests and made my research experience an exciting adventure. A special shout-out to the Richard Nixon impersonator I met while standing at the urinal bank at the presidential library in

ACKNOWLEDGMENTS

Yorba Linda for asking me—in character, and with great conviction—about my research. Part of me would have preferred for this odd encounter to have taken place at the Lyndon Johnson library instead. Then again, if you've heard the LBJ urinal story, perhaps it's for the best.

While I never had the pleasure of meeting Saul Alinsky—I'm old, but not that old—I did have the opportunity to converse with several people in his personal and professional circle. Nicholas Von Hoffman was supportive at the very earliest stages, before I really had a sense of what I was trying to say. Msgr. Jack Egan regaled my soon-to-be-wife, Shana, and I with some terrific Alinsky stories over several hours, helping me to better understand what they were really trying to do on the Southwest Side. I struck up a friendship with Alinsky's son David, who shares his father's impish wit, and always seemed to be delighted that I was trying to use his dad's work to tell a bigger story. While teaching at Fordham and Gonzaga, I periodically met older Jesuits, all of whom seemed to have an "Alinsky story" of one sort or another. While this book is really an intellectual biography, my hope is that it presents an Alinsky that these good people might recognize. And that the man himself might recognize too. My apologies, Saul, for lacking the courage to put the middle finger picture on the cover.

My colleagues in the History Department at the University of Massachusetts–Dartmouth have been supportive of me and my family since I arrived there in 2004. I've been department chair for most of the years since, and their kindness, generosity, and passionate commitment to making our community a supportive place for faculty and students alike has made me feel very much at home. Shana and I have grappled with some challenging health circumstances over the years, which could easily have derailed things for me professionally. That they have not is because Gerard, Bob, Anne, Len, Betty, Gail, Steve, Linsun, Bridget, Cristina, Matt, Tim, Len, Brian, Paula, Richard, Ilana, Crystal, Sue, Carol, and so many others have had my back. I am proud to be among you. I'd also like to thank the deans of the College of Arts and Sciences—Bill Hogan, Jen Riley, and Pauline Entin—who have all supported my work personally and professionally. I'm particularly grateful for the Publication Subvention Grant I received in 2022.

A decade or so ago, I had the great good fortune to coauthor a book with my father, Len Santow. The best part of the experience, by far, was the writing of it—trying to find common ground between our very different views and disciplines, and to engage each other as equals with valuable things to say. From my earliest memories until the present, my dad and my mom, Sharon, have always made me feel like what I do and say (and write) matters—even if they would do or say something entirely different. They raised my sister

Debbie and I to be independent thinkers, and above all to believe that education matters. I've tried to do the same for my kids, and I am eternally grateful for their guidance and generosity right up to the present.

Maya and Micah, you began this journey with me warmly packed into baby carriers during department meetings, singing songs and sharing hopes and dreams as I drove you to daycare and preschool, and eating snacks out of the vending machine in my building. You've really only been dimly aware of this book, I think. And that's a good thing, though you have become increasingly aware of the racial injustices at the heart of it and called to speak out in your own way. While your lives have mostly been made gentle by circumstance, you've also been made painfully aware from a very young age how important it is to hold tight to those you love. Today, as young adults, you are brilliant, creative, funny, generous, and loving. You take nothing for granted, a kind of wisdom I'm still struggling to acquire. There is nothing I'd rather do than spend time with your mom and the two of you. What a gift. Thank you.

If the readers of this book find the maps to be useful, you can thank my wife, Shana, for that. I can do one thing reasonably well, and you are holding it. As anyone who has ever been around Shana can tell you, she can do pretty much anything and do it well: architecture, photography, graphic design, gardening, metalwork, painting, fundraising, baking, web design. Shana, we met almost exactly twenty-five years ago, when you dropped your phone number in my book bag at a steak restaurant in Philadelphia. It unnerves me still to think of what my life would have been like if you hadn't the chutzpah to put it there, and if I hadn't had the dumb luck to come across it. On our first date we picked at our food while your passion for everything—travel, architecture, creativity, life—washed over me. I cried on the drive back home after dropping you off, knowing that whatever my life had been before that night, it was about to become so much richer and deeper than I ever thought possible.

The decades since have been filled with adventure, and babies, and dogs, and dear friends, and laughter, and a relationship of love and companionship that has made me indescribably happy. It has also been filled with cross-country moves, challenges, oncologists, and pain and suffering that you do not deserve—but that you've handled with grace and dignity. Even in the midst of your own travails, you run to help others with theirs. You are, and have always been, the best person I know. It is said that the body keeps score, a kind of map the topography of which manifests the physical and emotional scars of a human life well lived. Your "map" reflects that journey. Mine does too. All I can say is that there isn't any place in this world or the next I want to visit, if it isn't with you. We travel well together, I think. Thank you.

Notes

Introduction

1. For discussions of social geography, see David Harvey, *Consciousness and the Urban Experience*, Johns Hopkins University Press, Baltimore (1985), 24; Ira Katznelson, *Marxism and the City*, Oxford University Press (1993), 143.

2. Patrick Sharkey, *Stuck in Place: Urban Neighborhoods and the End of Progress toward Racial Equality*, University of Chicago Press (2013); Robert J. Sampson, *Great American City: Chicago and the Enduring Neighborhood Effect*, University of Chicago Press (2012).

3. David Delaney, *Race, Place and the Law: 1836–1948*, University of Texas Press, Austin (1998), 6–7, 9, 13, 96, 103–4.

4. For a few examples, see especially Nikole Hannah-Jones's award-winning 2014–2015 investigation for ProPublica, "Segregation Now: Investigating America's Racial Divide," http://www.propublica.org/series/segregation-now. See also Richard Rothstein's best-selling book *The Color of Law: A Forgotten History of Our Government Segregated America*, W. W. Norton, New York (2017). See also Richard Rothstein, "How Government Policies Cemented the Racism That Reigns in Baltimore," *American Prospect*, Apr. 29, 2015; Emily Badger, "The Long, Painful and Repetitive History of How Baltimore Became Baltimore," *Wonkblog* (blog), Apr. 29, 2015, http://www.washingtonpost.com/blogs/wonkblog/wp/2015/04/29/the-long-painful-and-repetitive-history-of-how-baltimore-became-baltimore/; "Historian [Richard Rothstein] Says Don't 'Sanitize' How Our Government Created Ghettos," *Fresh Air*, May 14, 2015, http://www.npr.org/2015/05/14/406699264/historian-says-dont-sanitize-how-our-government-created-the-ghettos; German Lopez, "Riots Are Destructive, Dangerous, and Scary—But Can Lead to Serious Social Reforms," Vox.com, Apr. 30, 2015. The *Atlantic Monthly*'s online CityLab series also published dozens of articles in 2015 presenting historical and sociological scholarship on segregation, poverty, and racial inequality to a popular audience.

5. Claudia Rankine, "The Condition of Black Life Is One of Mourning," *New York Times Magazine*, June 22, 2015.

6. Nicholas Von Hoffman, *Radical: A Portrait of Saul Alinsky*, Nation Books, New York (2011), 5; "Bringing It All Back Home: Interview with Saul Alinsky," *Rolling Stone*, Mar. 4, 1971.

7. Rabbi William Berkowitz, ed., *Conversation With . . .* , Bloch Publishing, New York (1975), 60; Von Hoffman (2011), 11, 127.

8. Von Hoffman (2011), 142–43, 210; Bernard Doering, ed., *The Philosopher and the Provocateur: The Correspondence of Jacques Maritain and Saul Alinsky*, University of Notre Dame Press, South Bend, IN (1994), 5.

9. Saul Alinsky, *Rules for Radicals: A Practical Primer for Realistic Radicals*, Random House, New York (1971), 4–5.

10. Von Hoffman (2011), 30, 33, 36; Saul Alinsky, *Reveille for Radicals*, Vintage Books, New York (1971 ed.), 47.

11. Marion K. Sanders, *The Professional Radical: Conversations with Saul Alinsky*, Harper and Row, New York (1970), 31 and 37. *The Professional Radical* is an anthology of interviews that Sanders did with Alinsky for *Harper's* magazine; the quotes are from their 1965 interview.

12. Saul Alinsky, *Reveille for Radicals*, University of Chicago Press, Chicago (1946), 19–22; "Saul Alinsky on Goldbrick Radicals," *Boston*, Dec. 8, 1970; Von Hoffman (2011), 127; Eric Norden, "Interview with Saul Alinsky," *Playboy*, Mar. 1972, 76; Sanders (1970), 50.

13. On postwar political theory, see Robert Westbrook, *John Dewey and American Democracy*, Cornell University Press, Ithaca, NY (1993); Russell Hanson, *The Democratic Imagination in America: Conversations with Our Past*, Princeton University Press, Princeton, NJ (1985); Edward Purcell Jr., *The Crisis of Democratic Theory: Scientific Naturalism and the Problem of Value*, University Press of Kentucky, Lexington (1973); Robert Bellah, Richard Madsen, William M. Sullivan, Ann Swidler, and Steven M. Tipton, *"Habits of the Heart": Individualism and Commitment in American Life*, University of California Press, Berkeley (1985). Alinsky's embedded notion of citizenship contrasts sharply with the liberal rights-based notion dominant in the postwar United States and resembles that of communitarian theorists of the past two decades.

14. Alinsky (1946), 37, 40, 192. See also Alinsky's 1962 "Citizen Participation and Community Organization in Planning and Urban Renewal," 17; David Finks, *The Radical Vision of Saul Alinsky*, Paulist Press, New York (1984), 33.

15. Maritain, who was a regular correspondent with Alinsky, wrote extensively about the critical role of mediating structures in democratic communities in his books *Integral Humanism: Temporal and Spiritual Problems of a New Christendom*, University of Notre Dame Press, South Bend, IN (1968), and *Man and the State*, Hollis and Carter, London (1954). On subsidiarity, see Edward J. Verstraeten, "Solidarity and Subsidiarity," in *Principles of Catholic Social Teaching*, ed. David Boileau, Marquette University, Milwaukee, WI (1998), 119, 135. The Alinsky-Maritain correspondence can be found in Doering (1994). Maritain discusses Alinsky's organizations and subsidiarity on p. xxvii.

16. Alexis de Tocqueville, *Democracy in America*, ed. Henry Steele Commager, Oxford University Press, London (1947), 513.

17. Fred Crosson, "Catholic Social Teaching and American Society," in *Principles in Catholic Social Teaching*, in *Principles of Catholic Social Teaching*, ed. David Boileau, Marquette University, Milwaukee, WI (1998), 170–71.

18. Alinsky to Maritain, Letter I, n.d. [probably 1943 or 1944], in Doering (1994), 11.

19. Norden, "Interview with Saul Alinsky" (1972), 76–78; "Bringing It All Back Home: Interview with Saul Alinsky," *Rolling Stone*, Mar. 4, 1971.

20. Alinsky (1971), 12–13, 125.

21. Alinsky (1971), xxv–xxvi, 23.

22. Maritain to Robert Hutchins, May 27, 1951; Maritain to Alinsky, Nov. 5, 1962; and Maritain to Alinsky, Sept. 14, 1964—all in Doering (1994), 47–48, 105–6. See also Tom Gaudette, "Good Stories and Hard Wisdom," in *After Alinsky*, ed. Peg Knoepfle, Sangamon State University Press, Springfield, IL (1975), 113; Berkowitz (1975), 262.

23. National Film Board of Canada, *Encounter with Saul Alinsky* (documentary film), pt. 2, 1967.

24. In 1947 his first wife, Helene, died while trying to save their daughter and another child from drowning. A few years later Alinsky fell in love with another woman, Babette Stiefel, who was stricken with polio and died. See Von Hoffman (2011), 153; Sanford Horwitt, *Let Them Call Me Rebel*, Vintage Books, New York (1992), 237–38.

Chapter One

1. Chicago Community Inventory, *Population Growth in the Chicago SMA* (1958), 12; Chicago Community Inventory, *Local Community Fact Book: Chicago, 1960*, University of Chicago Press (1963), 8–9. See also Arnold Hirsch, *Making the Second Ghetto: Race and Housing in Chicago, 1940-1960*, Cambridge University Press (1983); Otis Duncan and Beverly Duncan, *Negro Population of Chicago: A Study of Racial Succession*, University of Chicago Press (1957); David Wallace, "Residential Concentration of Negroes in Chicago" (PhD diss., Harvard University, 1953).

2. On credit discrimination against black families in Chicago, see Chicago Commission on Human Relations, *Mortgage Availability for Non-Whites in the Chicago Area: A Report* (Apr. 1963). See also Chicago Commission on Human Relations, *Selling and Buying Real Estate in a Racially Changing Neighborhood* (June 1962) and *The Growing Negro Middle Class in Chicago* (Sept. 1962).

3. Rick Halpern, *Down on the Killing Floor: Black and White Workers in Chicago's Packinghouses, 1904-1954*, University of Illinois Press, Champaign (1997), 21; Robert Slayton, *The Back of the Yards: The Making of a Local Democracy*, University of Chicago Press (1986), 12–13, 21–26; James Barrett, *Work and Community in the Jungle: Chicago's Packinghouse Workers, 1894-1922*, University of Illinois Press, Champaign (1990), 37–41; Thomas Jablonsky, *Pride in the Jungle: Community and Everyday Life in Back of the Yards Chicago*, Johns Hopkins University Press, Baltimore (1993); Agnes Meyer, "An Orderly Revolution," *Washington Post*, Jan. 4–9, 1945. For data and observations on the residents of the area in the early twentieth century, see Charles Bushnell, "Some Social Aspects of the Chicago Stock Yards," *Journal of Sociology* 7, nos. 3–6 (1901–1902), 145–70; John Kennedy, *Wages and Family Budgets in the Chicago Stock Yards District*, University of Chicago Press, Chicago (1914); Edith Abbott and Sophonisba Breckinridge, "Housing Condition in Chicago, Ill.: Back of the Yards," *American Journal of Sociology* 16 (Jan. 1911); Edith Abbott and Sophonisba Breckinridge, *The Tenements of Chicago, 1908-1935*, University of Chicago Press, Chicago (1936); Alice Miller, "Rents and Housing Conditions in the Stock Yards District of Chicago, 1923" (MA thesis, University of Chicago, 1923).

4. On work in the packinghouses, see Barrett (1990), 21–30, 146; John Commons, ed., "Labor Conditions in the Slaughtering and Meat Packing Industry," *Trade Unionism and Labor Problems*, Ginn and Company, Boston (1905), 243–45; Slayton (1986); Halpern (1997); Roger Horowitz, *Negro and White, United and Fight! A Social History of Industrial Unionism in Meatpacking, 1930-1990*, University of Illinois Press, Champaign (1997).

5. See John McGreevy, *Parish Boundaries: The Catholic Encounter with Race in the 20th Century Urban North*, University of Chicago Press (1997), 10–11; Slayton (1986), 144; Barrett (1990), 78; Stock Yards Community Clearing House, "1918 Community Study." March is quoted in Slayton (1986), 148.

6. Slayton (1986), 13, 50, 118, 148; Gurney Breckenfeld, "Chicago: Back of the Yards," in *The Human Side of Urban Renewal*, ed. Martin Millspaugh and Gurney Breckenfeld, Washburn Press, Baltimore (1960), 184.

7. Slayton (1986), 31; Louise Montgomery, *The American Girl in the Stockyard District*, University of Chicago Press, Chicago (1913), 4; Thomas Dyja, *The Third Coast: When Chicago Built the American Dream*, Penguin Books, New York (2013), 85. See also Hirsch (1983), 188–96; Margaret Garb, *City of Dreams: A History of Home Ownership and Housing Reform, 1871–1919*, University of Chicago Press, Chicago (2005). On home ownership in Packingtown, see Slayton (1986), 31–37, 126; Dominic Pacyga, "Crisis and Community: The Back of the Yards, 1921," *Chicago History* 6, no. 3 (Fall 1997); Jablonsky (1993), 103–4. On Catholics and homeownership more generally, see Olivier Zunz, *The Changing Face of Inequality: Urbanization, Industrial Development, and Immigrants in Detroit, 1880–1920*, University of Chicago Press, Chicago (1982); Tom Sugrue, *Origins of the Urban Crisis: Race and Inequality in Postwar Detroit*, Princeton University Press, Princeton, NJ (1996); Stephen Thernstrom, *Poverty and Progress: Social Mobility in a Nineteenth Century City*, Harvard University Press, Cambridge, MA (1964); McGreevy (1997).

8. James Grossman, *Land of Hope: Chicago, Black Southerners and the Great Migration*, University of Chicago Press, Chicago (1991), 127.

9. William Tuttle, *Race Riot: Chicago in the Red Summer of 1919*, Atheneum Books, New York (1970), 119; Halpern (1997), 39.

10. On the 1919 riot, see Tuttle (1970). See also Alma Herbst, *The Negro in the Slaughtering and Meat Packing Industry in Chicago*, Houghton Mifflin, Boston (1932); Halpern (1997), 47; Barrett (1990), 47–49. On the Back of the Yards during the 1919 riot, see Chicago Commission on Race Relations, *The Negro in Chicago* (1922), 115; Barrett (1990), 222–23; Halpern (1997), 66–69; Tuttle (1970); Breckenfeld (1960); Lizabeth Cohen, *Making a New Deal: Industrial Workers in Chicago, 1919–1939*, Cambridge University Press (1990); Grossman (1991), 210.

11. Margaret Garb, "Drawing the 'Color Line': Race and Real Estate in Early Twentieth-Century Chicago," *Journal of Urban History* (July 2006), 774, 779. See also Margaret Garb, *City of Dreams: A History of Home Ownership and Housing Reform, 1871–1919*, University of Chicago Press, Chicago (2005).

12. On real estate practices and racial segregation, see Charles Abrams, *Forbidden Neighbors: A Study of Prejudice in Housing*, Harper and Brothers, New York (1955); Luigi Laurenti, *Property Values and Race: Studies in Seven Cities*, University of California Press, Berkeley (1960); Robert Weaver, *The Negro Ghetto*, Harcourt Brace and Co., New York (1948); Zorita Mikva, "The Neighborhood Improvement Association: A Counter-Force to the Expansion of Chicago's Negro Population" (MA thesis, University of Chicago, 1951); Egbert Schietinger, "Racial Succession and Changing Property Values in Residential Chicago" (PhD diss., University of Chicago, 1953); Brian J. L. Berry, *The Open Housing Question: Race and Housing in Chicago, 1966–1976*, Ballinger, Cambridge, MA (1979); Horace Cayton and St. Clair Drake, *Black Metropolis: A Study of Negro Life in a Northern City*, Harcourt Brace and Co., New York (1945); Rose Helper, *Racial Policies and Practices of Real Estate Brokers*, University of Minnesota Press, Minneapolis (1969); David Freund, *Colored Property: State Policy and Racial Politics in Suburban America*, University of Chicago Press, Chicago (2007); Jeffrey Hornstein, *A Nation of Realtors: A Cultural History of the 20th Century American Middle Class*, Duke University Press, Durham, NC (2005). The *Hyde Park Herald* quote comes from Arnold Hirsch, "E Pluribus Duo? Thoughts on 'Whiteness' and Chicago's 'New' Immigration as a Transient Third Tier," *Journal of American Ethnic History* (Summer 2004), 19.

13. Garb (2006), 781–82; Gregory Alexander, *Commodity and Propriety: Competing Visions of Property in American Legal Thought, 1776–1970*, University of Chicago Press, Chicago (1997), 145–51; Freund (2007).

14. Hirsch (2004), 24.

15. The Chicago Area Project was established by sociologist Clifford Shaw, of the Institute for Juvenile Research; he insisted that effective community efforts to fight juvenile delinquency had to be run by local residents, with the help of a trained delinquency worker (like Alinsky). Shaw believed that youth crime was rooted in structural problems affecting the community as a whole, and he instructed his fieldworkers to seek out local groups and leadership (rather than outside social work agencies) to organize solutions. The project was tremendously influential in postwar criminology. See Clifford Shaw and Ernest Burgess, *The Jackroller: A Delinquent Boy's Own Story*, University of Chicago Press, Chicago (1930); Finks (1984), 13–14; Donald Reitzes and Dietrich Reitzes, *The Alinsky Legacy: Alive and Kicking*, JAI Press, Greenwich, CT (1987); Robert Halpern, *Rebuilding the Inner City: A History of Neighborhood Initiatives to Address Poverty in the United States*, Columbia University Press, New York (1995).

16. Sheil would later introduce Alinsky to Marshall Field III, who would help finance the Industrial Areas Foundation in its early years. On Meegan and Alinsky, see Finks (1984), 16–17. On young priests in Packingtown, see Slayton (1986), 201; Nicholas Von Hoffman, *Radical: A Portrait of Saul Alinsky*, Basic Books, New York (2010), 106.

17. Saul Alinsky, *Reveille for Radicals*, University of Chicago Press, Chicago (1946), 20, 22; Reitzes and Reitzes (1987), 28–29; Pacyga (1981), 7; Rick Halpern interview with Vicky Starr, Aug. 4, 1986, United Packinghouse Workers of America Oral History Project (UPWAOHP), State Historical Society of Wisconsin, Madison; Halpern interviews with Herbert March, July 15, 1985, and Oct. 21, 1986, UPWAOHP; Halpern (1997), 156.

18. Alinsky (1946), 77. For other writings that lay out Alinsky's organizing strategies, see Saul Alinsky, "Community Analysis and Organization," *American Journal of Sociology* (May 1941); "A Note on Community Conservation and Community Organization" (paper presented before the National Council of Catholic Charities, Sept. 29, 1953), Alinsky Papers, Special Collections, University of Illinois Chicago (hereafter Alinsky Papers); "From Citizen Apathy to Participation" (paper presented at Sixth Annual Conference of the Association of Community Councils of Chicago, Oct. 19, 1957), Alinsky Papers; "X-Raying Community Organizations" (paper presented to the Mississippi Valley Tuberculosis Conference, Oct. 13, 1961), Alinsky Papers; "Citizen Participation and Community Organization in Planning and Urban Renewal" (paper presented to Chicago Chapter of the National Association of Housing and Redevelopment Officials, Jan. 1962), Alinsky Papers; Saul Alinsky, *Rules for Radicals: A Practical Primer for Realistic Radicals*, Vintage Books, New York (1971); Reitzes and Reitzes (1987), 28–62; Joan Lancourt, *Confront or Concede: The Alinsky Citizen Action Organizations*, Lexington Books, Toronto (1979); Robert Bailey Jr., *Radicals in Urban Politics: The Alinsky Approach*, University of Chicago Press (1974); Robert Fisher, *Let the People Decide: Neighborhood Organizing in America*, Twayne Publishers, Boston (1984).

19. Alinsky (1946), 85, 88.

20. Back of the Yards Neighborhood Council, "The Call to a Community Conference" (1939), Alinsky Papers; interview with Vicky Starr, Aug. 4, 1986; interviews with Herbert March, July 15, 1985, and Oct. 21, 1986, UPWAOHP. On the relationship between local parishes and unions, see Slayton (1986), 200–203, 210–11; Sanford Horwitt, *Let Them Call Me Rebel*, Alfred A. Knopf, New York (1989), 69–71; Bernard Kahn, "The Catholic Church and Its Relationship to the Back of the Yards Neighborhood Council: A Study in Community Political Behavior" (MA thesis, University of Chicago, 1949).

21. See Slayton (1986), 202–5 and 227.

22. In 1909, fewer than one in five whites working in the stockyards had been born in the United States; by 1928, that ratio had increased to better than one in four. Barrett (1990), 42, 271–73; Cohen (1990), 7, 207, 249; James Barrett, "Americanization from the Bottom Up: Immigration and the Re-making of the Working Class in the United States, 1880–1930," *Journal of American History* (Dec. 1992).

23. On race and the meatpacking workforce in Chicago, see Roger Horowitz, *"Black and White, Unite and Fight": A Social History of Industrial Unionism in Meatpacking, 1930–1990*, University of Illinois Press, Champaign-Urbana (1987); Barrett (1990), 49; Halpern (1997), 131–33, 146–47.

24. Hirsch (2004), 9–10, 14–15.

25. Halpern (1997), 97; Cohen (1990), 339.

26. Arnold Hirsch, "The Cook County Democratic Organization and the Dilemma of Race, 1931–1987," in *Snowbelt Cities: Metropolitan Politics in the Northeast and Midwest since World War II*, ed. Richard Bernard, Indiana University Press, Bloomington (1990), 63–90. On Kelly, race, and public housing, see Roger Biles, *Big City Boss in Depression and War*, Northern Illinois University Press, DeKalb (1984), 135–37; Robert Spinney, *City of the Big Shoulders*, Northern Illinois University Press, DeKalb (1999), 204.

27. Halpern (1997), 158; "Race, Ethnicity, Neighborhood and Class: The Yeasty Chicago Brew," *Social Policy* (Spring 2002), 63–64. See also interview with Richard Saunders, Sept. 13, 1985, UPWAOHP. The PWOC's assistant national director, Hank Johnson, was black. He was also a good friend of Alinsky's; they traveled across the country together during the war and met with union locals.

28. Hoehler (1947), 23; "Race, Ethnicity, Neighborhood and Class" (2002), 65.

29. On the council's early racial progressivism, see Alinsky to Herbert March, Oct. 3, 1946, file 167, Alinsky Papers; Alinsky to James Wilson, Jan. 7, 1964, Msgr. John Egan Papers (hereafter Egan Papers), Special Collections, University of Notre Dame, Notre Dame, IN; Meyer (1945); John Martin, "These Three Certain Wise Men," *McCall's* (n.d.), Alinsky Papers; Alinsky, "Outline of Community Planning Program for the Section on State and Community Planning for Health" (presentation to the National Health Assembly, Washington, DC, n.d.), Alinsky Papers; "Invocation Address by the Most Rev. Bernard Sheil before the Annual Community Congress of the BYNC on January 27th 1943," Sheil Papers, Chicago Historical Society (CHS), Chicago; "The Call to a Community Congress of the BYNC," Jan. 27, 1943, Back of the Yards Public Library; Alinsky to James Wilson, Jan. 7, 1964, Egan Papers; Stephen Becker, *Marshall Field III*, Simon and Schuster, New York (1964), 358; Halpern (1997); Hoehler (1947); Horwitt (1989). The Office of Civilian Defense wrote to Meegan in 1942 praising the council's leadership and interest in "the welfare of Negro citizens" and asking for its continued help in lessening racial prejudice as part of the war effort. Loring Moore to Meegan, Racial Relations Adviser, Sixth Civilian Defense Region, Office of Civilian Defense, Nov. 6, 1942, Alinsky Papers.

30. Gary Gerstle, *American Crucible: Race and Nation in the Twentieth-Century*, Princeton University Press, Princeton, NJ (2002). "The Call to a Community Congress of the BYNC," Jan. 27, 1943, and "Invocation Address by the Most Rev. Bernard Sheil before the Annual Community Congress of the BYNC," Jan. 27, 1943, Back of the Yards Neighborhood Council Papers, Chicago Public Library, Chicago.

31. *Chicago Community Fact Book* (1960), 8–9. See also Chicago Community Inventory (1958), 12; Berry (1979), 402; Brian Berry and Irving Cutler, *Chicago: Transformations of an Urban System*, Ballinger Press, Cambridge, MA (1976), 55; Gregory Squires, Larry Bennett, Kathleen

McCourt, and Philip Nyden, *Chicago: Race, Class, and the Response to Urban Decline*, Temple University Press, Philadelphia (1987); Hirsch (1983), 27–29.

32. See Abrams (1955), 110; McGreevy (1996). See also John Ottensmann and Michael Gleeson, "The Movement of Whites and Blacks into Racially Mixed Neighborhoods: Chicago 1960–1980," *Social Science Quarterly* (Sept. 1992); Leonard Rieser, "An Analysis of the Reporting of Racial Incidents in Chicago, 1945–50" (MA thesis, University of Chicago, 1951), 15. More generally, see Hirsch (1983), chap. 2.

33. Abrams (1955), 116; Nicholas Lemann, *Promised Land: The Great Black Migration and How It Changed America*, Vintage Books, New York (1992), 71–73; Berry (1979), 403–5. There was a net decline of 41,500 white homeowners in Chicago in the 1960s. See Berry and Cutler (1976), 30.

34. See "Housing and Race in Chicago: A Preliminary Analysis of 1960 Census Data" (prepared by Chicago Urban League, July 1963), 9–10. By 1970, vacancy rates in the area that defined the 1960 Black Belt exceeded 6 percent, and blacks no longer suffered from a housing shortage—although access to the suburbs remained restricted. Berry and Cutler (1976), 55; Berry (1979), 405; Allan Spear, *Black Chicago: The Making of a Negro Ghetto, 1890–1920*, University of Chicago Press, Chicago (1967), 148–49; Cayton and Drake (1945), 12, 204; "Statement of Robert C. L. George, Executive Director, Greater Chicago Council against Discrimination," Investigation of Housing (1955), 249–51, Hearings before the Committee on Banking and Currency, House of Representatives, 84th Cong., 1st sess., Nov. 21–23, 1955, pt. 3, Chicago.

35. See Advance Mortgage Corporation, "Midwest Minority Housing Markets," Dec. 1, 1962, 30; Chicago Commission on Human Relations, "The Growing Negro Middle Class in Chicago," Sept. 1, 1962, 3.

36. Led by a Catholic priest named Francis Lawlor, whites in West Englewood would eventually attempt, unsuccessfully, to draw a hard-and-fast racial boundary at Ashland Avenue in the late 1960s. On Lawlor, see Berry (1979), esp. chap. 7; Dominic Pacyga and Ellen Skerrett, *Chicago: City of Neighborhoods*, Loyola Press, Chicago (1986), 496–98.

37. On the 1949 events in Englewood, see "Blame Indifference of Chicago Cops For Mob Attacks on Negroes, Jews," *Chicago Defender*, Nov. 26, 1949; Hirsch (1983), 55–56.

38. Dominic Pacyga, "Chicago's Ethnic Neighborhoods: The Myth of Stability and the Reality of Change," *Ethnic Chicago: A Multicultural Portrait*, ed. Melvin Holli and Peter Jones, Eerdmans, Grand Rapids, MI (1995), 614–15.

39. It also created a sense of precariousness for the black middle class, who struggled to maintain stability in their new neighborhoods and feared that the ghetto would follow them as white people and white capital fled. A decline in city services, law enforcement, and accessibility to credit was presumed (and generally did) follow. Hirsch (2004), 21; Will Cooley, *Moving Up, Moving Out: The Rise of the Black Middle Class in Chicago*, Northern Illinois University Press, DeKalb, IL (2018); Mary Pattillo and Annette Lareau, *Black Picket Fences: Privilege and Peril among the Black Middle Class*, University of Chicago Press, Chicago (2013).

40. On restrictive covenants, see Richard Brooks and Carol Rose, *Saving the Neighborhood: Racially Restrictive Covenants, Law and Social Norms*, Harvard University Press, Cambridge, MA (2013); Jeffrey Gonda, *Unjust Deeds: The Restrictive Covenant Cases and the Making of the Civil Rights Movement*, University of North Carolina Press, Chapel Hill (2015); Robert Fogelson, *Bourgeois Nightmares: Suburbia, 1870–1930*, Yale University Press, New Haven, CT (2005); Wendy Plotkin, "Deeds of Mistrust: Racial Restrictive Covenants in Chicago, 1900–1953" (PhD diss., University of Illinois Chicago, 1999); David Delaney, *Race, Place and the Law, 1836–1948*,

University of Texas Press, Austin (1998); Mark Tushnet, *Making Civil Rights Law: Thurgood Marshall and the Supreme Court, 1936-1961*, Oxford University Press, New York (1994); Clement Vose, *Caucasians Only: The Supreme Court, the NAACP, and the Restrictive Covenant Cases*, University of California Press, Berkeley (1959); Louis Washington, "A Study of Restrictive Covenants in Chicago" (MA thesis, University of Chicago, 1948); Herman Long and Charles Johnson, *People v. Property: Race Restrictive Covenants in Housing*, Fisk University Press, Nashville, TN (1947); Bernard Sheil and Loren Miller, *Racial Restrictive Covenants*, Chicago Council against Racial and Religious Discrimination, Chicago (1946); Robert Weaver, *Hemmed In: The ABC's of Restrictive Covenants*, American Council on Race Relations, Chicago (1945).

41. On New Deal housing policies, see Price Fishback, *Well Worth Saving: How the New Deal Safeguarded Homeownership*, University of Chicago Press, Chicago (2013); Freund (2010); John Bauman, Roger Biles, and Kristin Szylvian, eds., *From Tenements to the Taylor Homes: In Search of an Urban Housing Policy in Twentieth-Century America*, Penn State University Press, University Park, PA (2000); Arnold Hirsch and Raymond Mohl, *Urban Policy in Twentieth-Century America*, Rutgers University Press, New Brunswick, NJ (1993); Gail Radford, *Modern Housing for America: Policy Struggles in the New Deal Era*, University of Chicago Press, Chicago (1996); Kenneth Jackson, *Crabgrass Frontiers*, Oxford University Press, New York (1985); Ronald Tobey, Charles Wetherell, and Jay Brigham, "Moving Out and Settling In: Residential Mobility, Home Owning, and the Public Enframing of Citizenship, 1921-1950," *American Historical Review* (Dec. 1990).

42. Arnold Hirsch, "Searching for a 'Sound Negro Policy': A Racial Agenda for the Housing Acts of 1949 and 1954," *Housing Policy Debate* (2000), 419, 429-31. The idea of a "two-tiered" housing policy comes from Radford (1996).

43. Hirsch (1990); H. E. F. Donohue, *Conversations with Nelson Algren*, Hill and Wang, New York (1963), 330.

44. Hirsch (1983); Hirsch (1990); Spinney (1999), 204; Roger Biles, *Richard J. Daley: Politics, Race, and the Governing of Chicago*, Northern Illinois University Press, DeKalb, IL (1995), 17.

45. On Alinsky and the PHA, also see "Charges Mayor with Failure on Housing Issue," *Chicago Tribune*, Apr. 20, 1950. The PHA included many religious groups, as well as the packinghouse union. On Hunt's tenure as superintendent, see Kathryn Neckerman, *Schools Betrayed: Roots of Failure in Inner-City Education*, University of Chicago Press, Chicago (2007), 88-89, 92-103.

46. Hirsch (2000), 395, 398-99, 404-5, 408; Janet Abu-Lughod, *Race, Space and Riots in Chicago, New York and Los Angeles*, Oxford University Press, New York (2007), 67-70; Reginald Isaacs, "The 'Neighborhood Unit' Is an Instrument for Segregation," *Journal of Housing* (Aug. 1948).

47. Hirsch (1983); Hirsch (1990); Spinney (1999), 204; Biles (1995), 17; Neckerman, (2007), 94, 97; "Jones Blasts Segregation in Chicago Public Schools," *Chicago Defender*, Sept. 27, 1958.

48. Nelson Algren, *Who Lost An American?*, Macmillan, New York (1963), 141-42.

49. By 1947, half of the sixty thousand packinghouse workers in Chicago were black; black membership in the union was 50 percent and rising. See Fred K. Hoehler, "Community Action by the United Packinghouse Workers of America-CIO in the Back of the Yards Neighborhood of Chicago" (MA thesis, University of Chicago, 1947), 12-13; interview with Herbert March, July 15, 1985, UPWAOHP; Mike Miller interview with Jane and Herb March (n.d.), in author's possession.

50. Alinsky quoted in "Major Race Riot in Chicago Seen: Saul D. Alinsky Says His City Is on Verge of Serious Clash of Negroes and Whites," *New York Times*, Dec. 11, 1946. See also Alinsky to Herbert March, Oct. 3, 1946, file 167, Alinsky Papers; Hoehler (1947), 15, 33.

51. See Hoehler (1947), 13; Meyer (1945); Elizabeth Butters interview with Leon Beverly, Dec. 16, 1970, 11, Labor Oral History Project, box 1, Roosevelt University Library, Chicago; Halpern (1997).

52. Breckenfeld (1960); McGreevy (1996); Eileen McMahon, *What Parish Are You From? A Chicago Irish Community and Race Relations*, University Press of Kentucky, Lexington (1995); Gamm (1999); John Ottensmann and Michael Gleeson, "The Movement of Whites and Blacks into Racially Mixed Neighborhoods: Chicago 1960–1980," *Social Science Quarterly* (Sept. 1992).

53. Gary Gerstle, *Working-Class Americanism: The Politics of Labor in a Textile City 1914–1960*, Cambridge University Press, New York (1989); Barrett (1992); Sugrue (1996); Cohen (1990).

54. Barrett (1987), 102n12; "Back of the Yards Shows City How to Whip Blight," *Chicago Sun-Times*, Jan. 10, 1954. See also Jane Jacobs, *Death and Life of Great American Cities*, Random House, New York (1961), 298, for her short but informative discussion of the council.

55. Amanda Seligman, *Block by Block: Neighborhoods and Public Policy on Chicago's West Side*, University of Chicago Press, Chicago (2005), 87; Dyja (2013), 7.

56. Article by M. W. Newman, *Chicago Daily News*, Apr. 24, 1959; Breckenfeld (1960).

57. On the July 1953 meeting, see BYNC, "The Future of the Back of the Yards" (July 1953), CHS; "Yards Group Spurs Blight War," *Chicago Sun-Times*, Jan. 11, 1954; BYNC, "The History of the Fifteenth Year"; "Neighborhood Comes Back by Itself—in Five Years," *Cleveland (OH) Press*, Oct. 8, 1958. On savings and loans in the area, see *Chicago Sun-Times*, Jan. 11, 1954; Msgr. Thomas Meehan, "Conservation in Back of the Yards: A Report on the Past, Present, and Future" (1963), box 24, BYNC Correspondence folder, Egan Papers; John Kuenster, "The Neighborhood That Came Back" (Mar. 1956), unidentified clipping, Egan Papers.

58. On the conservation program, see BYNC, "Conservation by 'We the People Back of the Yards'" (1953), CHS; Breckenfeld (1960); "Back of the Yards Shows City How to Whip Blight," *Chicago Sun-Times*, Jan. 10, 1954; BYNC, *The History of the 15th Year of the BYNC* (Nov. 1954), Back of the Yards Public Library, Chicago. See also "Back of the Yards Area Winning War against Blight," *Chicago Sun-Times*, Feb. 6, 1955; BYNC, *Twenty-First Annual Report* (1960), 3–4, "Neighborhood Comes Back by Itself," *Cleveland Press*, Oct. 8, 1958, "Back of the Yards Miracle," *Cleveland (OH) Press*, Oct. 10, 1958, Alinsky Papers; Nicholas Von Hoffman to Charles Liddell, Executive Director of the Federation of South End Settlements in Boston, Jan. 21, 1959, Alinsky Papers; Msgr. Thomas Meehan, "Conservation in Back of the Yards: A Report on the Past, Present and Future," box 24, BYNC Correspondence folder, Egan Papers. On the key role of clergy, see BYNC, *1959 Annual Report*; "Fierce Pride Spurs Yards Blight Fight," *Chicago Sun-Times*, Jan. 13, 1954; *Chicago Daily News*, Apr. 24, 1959.

59. Erwin Knoll and Jules Witcover, "'Guerilla Attacks' Won One War for 'Poor'—Alinsky's Back of the Yards in Chicago Is Now Dignified, Next Target," *Syracuse (NY) Herald-Journal*, June 7, 1965; M. W. Newman, *Chicago Daily News*, Apr. 24, 1959; Breckenfeld (1960); Slayton (1986), 222.

60. The CCHR statements are from the *Chicago Daily News*, Aug. 9, 1963, 36. See also Knoll and Witcover (1965); Slayton (1986); Breckenfeld (1960); "Confessions of a Blockbuster," *Saturday Evening Post* (1962).

61. *Chicago Daily News*, Aug. 9, 1963, 36; Breckenfeld (1960), 182.

62. University of Chicago trustees, in the words of Hutchins's successor Leonard Kimpton, contributed money to "buy, control and rebuild our neighborhood" beginning in the mid-1940s. See "Statement to Alumni," Feb. 1955, Lawrence Kimpton Papers (hereafter Kimpton Papers), Special Collections, University of Chicago Library, University of Chicago, Chicago. On racially

restrictive covenants, conservation, and urban renewal in Hyde Park more generally, see Peter Rossi and Robert Dentler, *The Politics of Urban Renewal: The Chicago Findings*, Free Press, New York (1961), 54, 84–86; Hirsch (1983), 145–50; Stewart Winger, "Unwelcome Neighbors," *Chicago History* (Spring-Summer 1992), 63–64; Julia Abrahamson, *A Neighborhood Finds Itself*, Harper and Brothers, New York (1959); Mikva (1951); Abrams (1955), Plotkin (1999). One of the best-known Supreme Court covenant cases—*Hansberry v. Lee* (1940)—involved a University of Chicago–funded defense of covenants drawn up to keep black families out of the Washington Park subdivision of Woodlawn.

63. Hirsch (1983), 153, 159–63. In preparing an outline for a board of trustees meeting on the subject, Chancellor Kimpton wrote, "Tear it down and begin over again. Negroes." Lawrence Kimpton, "Outline for Board of Trustees Meeting," Jan. 14, 1954, Kimpton Papers. See also Biles (1995), 51; "Clouter with Conscience," *Time*, Mar. 15, 1963. Donald Murphy managed a revolving fund of $500,000 for the university to buy Woodlawn property, renovate it, and resell it in the immediate postwar years; in the 1950s, school trustees allocated $4 million for the fund. See Winger (1992), 69; "Citizens Hit Crime Rate in Hyde Park," *Chicago Daily Tribune*, Mar. 23, 1952. Alinsky was invited to attend the community meeting that led to the creation of the SECC. On the SECC's objectives, see Rossi and Dentler (1961), 79–84.

64. On the founding of the HP-KCC, see Hirsch (1983), 137–40; Rossi and Dentler (1961), 103–6; Abrahamson (1959). The phrase "inevitability of interracialism" is used by Rossi and Dentler (1961), 104.

65. Abrahamson (1959), 290, 299, 301.

66. See Abrahamson (1959), 295–301; Hirsch (1983), 140, 142, 152. In its September 1956 press release, the HP-KCC argued that "the establishment of one successful interracial neighborhood will do more in the long run to solve the housing problem of Chicago's minority groups than any other single factor."

67. Winger (1992), 56–73; Biles (1995), 13; Hirsch (1983), 135–37, 152–53; Adam Cohen and Elizabeth Taylor, *American Pharoah*, Little Brown, Boston (2000), 209–10.

68. "Chicago's Black Belt Expands, but Never Cracks," *Chicago Defender*, May 20, 1963. The Hyde Park urban renewal project accomplished its goals. From 1960 to 1970, the population of the area declined by more than a quarter. Average income in the area jumped by 70 percent while the black population dropped 40 percent. Most of those who were displaced were poor and black. They likely relocated to public housing elsewhere in the city, to the ghetto, or to white working-class communities at its edge. See Cohen and Taylor (2000), 212.

69. For Hirsch's discussion of how the university (through the SECC and HP-KCC) was able to portray its conservation and renewal plans as a function of racial idealism, see Hirsch (1983), 137, 146, 148–49, 185; Winger (1992) makes a similar statement, 72; On the relationship between the SECC and the HP-KCC, see Hirsch (1983), 137–38; Rossi and Dentler (1961), 144–46; Abrahamson (1959).

70. Alinsky's ally and close friend Fr. John Egan joined him in public criticism of the Hyde Park project. Daniel Cantwell, Ed Marciniak, Sargent Shriver, and other activists in the Catholic Interracial Council (CIC) were critical of Egan because his opposition easily lent itself to the impression that the archdiocese supported segregation. For worries by Catholic interracialists about the appearance of the church's opposition to the project, see Cantwell to Shriver, June 12, 1958; Ben Heineman to Shriver, June 6, 1958—all in the Daniel Cantwell Papers (hereafter Cantwell Papers), CHS. See also an editorial by Marciniak in the summer 1958 issue of *Work* in which he criticizes Catholic opposition to the plan. Catholic faculty at the university also

protested to the archdiocese about its position—see McGreevy (1996), 131. For Egan's views, see statement by the Cardinal's Conservation Committee on the Hyde Park–Kenwood Urban Renewal Plan issued by the Very Rev. Msgr. John J. Egan, Executive Director, June 11, 1958, box 20, folder 20-24, Cantwell Papers. For examples of Egan's opposition to the Hyde Park–Kenwood project, see "Trojan Horse in Our Cities," *Ave Maria*, May 10, 1958; "Both Sides of Hyde Park–Kenwood Redevelopment," *New World*, May 2, 1958; "More Housing . . . Less Segregation," *New World*, May 16, 1958; and his speech before the Annual Convention of the Association of Community Councils of Chicago, May 21, 1958, Alinsky Papers. See also Hirsch (1983), 172.

71. Breckenfeld (1960); Alinsky quote is from "Annual Report to the Board of Trustees of the IAF," Dec. 12, 1963, 10.

72. Alinsky claimed in 1962 that he had tried to work within some of the council's member organizations to build a rival group within Packingtown. Although there is no evidence of this, he did reportedly approach Meegan about integrating the area and was sternly rejected. See Georgie Ann Geyer, "Friend or Foe?" *Chicago Life*, July 21, 1962; Von Hoffman (2010), 51–52.

73. "Agenda: IAF Meeting of 12/14/61," box 11a, Dr. George Shuster "misc. IAF" folder, George Shuster Papers, Special Collections, University of Notre Dame, Notre Dame, IN.

74. Radio interview of Alinsky by Len O'Connor, Fall 1965, audiotape 12, Len O'Connor Papers, CHS; "Alinsky Takes Churches Where the Action Is," *National Catholic Reporter*, Nov. 3, 1965; Von Hoffman (2010), 53; Norden (1972), 76.

75. National Film Board of Canada, "Deciding to Organize," July 1968, transcript, 4.

Chapter Two

1. Saul Alinsky, "A Note on Community Conservation and Community Organization" (presentation to the National Conference of Catholic Charities [NCCC], St. Louis, July 29, 1953), Alinsky Papers, Special Collections, University of Illinois Chicago (hereafter Alinsky Papers).

2. Saul Alinsky, "If I Were a Negro," *Negro Digest* (Apr. 1946).

3. Margery Frisbie, *An Alley in Chicago: The Ministry of a City Priest*, Sheed and Ward, Kansas City, MO (1991), chap. 9; Nicholas Von Hoffman, *Radical: A Portrait of Saul Alinsky*, Nation Books, New York, 2010, 130–31.

4. Frisbie (1991), chap. 8.

5. Alinsky, *IAF 1957 Annual Report*, 12, Msgr. O'Grady Papers (hereafter O'Grady Papers), Special Collections, Catholic University of America. See also *General Report*, pt. I, chap. 3, 54–55, Alinsky Papers; *Report to the Archbishop of the Conservation Committee of the Archdiocese*, Nov. 1958, box 43781.02, p. 14, ACC folder, Meyer Papers (hereafter Meyer Papers), Archives of the Archdiocese of Chicago.

6. Alinsky, *IAF 1957 Annual Report*, 25, O'Grady Papers.

7. *General Report*, pt. I, 1; *General Report*, pt. I, chap. IV: Summary of Recommendations, 68; Alinsky to Stritch, memo, Nov. 14, 1957, Alinsky Papers.

8. *General Report*, pt. I: What the Study Has Discovered, 6–7; chap. II, sec. C, 36–38.

9. Alinsky to Stritch, memo, Nov. 14, 1957, 7, Alinsky Papers.

10. *General Report*, pt. IV, chaps. 7–8, 49–50, 54; *General Report*, pt. IV: 1958 Chicago—A Place to Live, 23.

11. *General Report*, pt. I, chap. II, sec. C, 18.

12. Alan Anderson and George Pickering, *Confronting the Color Line: The Broken Promise of the Civil Rights Movement in Chicago*, University of Georgia Press, Athens (1986), chap. 2.

13. Anderson and Pickering (1986), 63–66. The extent to which the CCHR's shift in emphasis was driven by events in neighborhoods along the edge of the expanding ghetto is evident in its annual reports: *The People of Chicago: Five Year Report, 1947–51, of the Chicago Commission on Human Relations* (1952); Arnold Hirsch, *The Making of the Second Ghetto*, Cambridge University Press, Cambridge (1983), 177–79, 214–15, 245–46.

14. See Hirsch (1983), 215; John McGreevy, *Parish Boundaries: The Catholic Encounter with Race in the Urban North*, University of Chicago Press, Chicago (1996), 85.

15. Kathryn Neckerman, *Schools Betrayed: Roots of Failure in Inner-City Education*, University of Chicago Press, Chicago (2007), 98–103.

16. Unidentified clipping, Oct. 20, 1965, manuscript collection, Ely Aaron Papers, University of Illinois Chicago; *General Report*, pt. I, chap. IV: Interracial Organizations, 53; Hirsch (1983), 246.

17. *General Report*, pt. I, chap. IV: Interracial Organizations, 60. See also Walter Jackson, *Gunnar Myrdal and America's Conscience*, University of North Carolina, Chapel Hill (1990); David Southern, *Gunnar Myrdal and Black-White Relations: The Use and Abuse of an American Dilemma, 1944–1969*, Louisiana State University Press, Baton Rouge (1987).

18. Hirsch (1983), 214–17. On civil rights groups in Chicago during the 1950s, see Arvarh Strickland, *History of the Chicago Urban League*, University of Illinois Press, Champaign (1966); William Grimshaw, *Bitter Fruit: Black Politics and the Chicago Machine 1931–1991*, University of Chicago Press, Chicago (1992); Christopher Reed, *The Chicago NAACP and the Rise of Black Professional Leadership*, Indiana University Press, Bloomington (1997); Jeffrey Helgeson, *Crucibles of Black Empowerment*, University of Chicago Press, Chicago (2014).

19. For historical accounts of this scholarship, see Jackson (1990); Hirsch (1983); Southern (1987). E. Franklin Frazier was perhaps the foremost scholar of damage. For examples, see Daryl M. Scott, *Contempt and Pity: Social Policy and the Image of the Damaged Black Psyche, 1880–1996*, University of North Carolina Press, Chapel Hill (1997).

20. *General Report*, pt. I, chap. III: Prejudice and Integration, 48–49; *General Report*, sec. F, chap. IV, 74.

21. Frisbie (1991), chap. 8.

22. *General Report*, pt. I, chap. II, sec. C, 13–15; *General Report*, pt. III: The Grand Boulevard Report, sec. B: Types of Surveys, xii.

23. Alinsky to Stritch, memo, Nov. 14, 1957, 5–6, Alinsky Papers.

24. *General Report*, chap. I: General Conditions in Chicago, sec. B—Expansion of Negro Residential Areas, 2–3; chap. III: Prejudice and Integration, 50.

25. *General Report*, pt. I, chap. I, 7.

26. Alinsky to Stritch, memo, Nov. 14, 1957, 7, Alinsky Papers.

27. *General Report*, pt. III, chap. IV: Housing, 10.

28. Chicago Community Inventory, *Local Community Fact Book: Chicago, 1960*, University of Chicago Press, Chicago (1963); Chicago Fact Book Consortium, *Community Fact Book*, Chicago Review Press, Chicago, (1980).

29. See Grimshaw (1992), 96–97, on population dispersal, class differentiation, and black politics in Chicago in the 1950s. On poverty in Grand Boulevard, see Pierre de Vise, *Chicago's Widening Color Gap* (Interuniversity Social Research Committee Report No. 2) (Dec. 1967), 58–66, 82.

30. Dominic Pacyga and Ellen Skerrett, *Chicago: City of Neighborhoods*, Loyola University Press, Chicago, 1986, 352; *General Report*, pt. III, chap. III: Present Population, 6.

31. Pacyga and Skerrett (1986), 353–54; Roger Biles, *Richard J. Daley: Politics, Race, and the Governing of Chicago*, Northern Illinois Press, DeKalb (1995), 89–90; Thomas Dyja, *The Third Coast: When Chicago Built the American Dream*, Penguin Books, New York (2013), 365.

32. *General Report*, pt. III: The Grand Boulevard Report, chap. VIII: Politics, 56

33. *General Report*, pt. III: The Grand Boulevard Report, sec. C: Summary of Conclusions, xvi; Biles (1995), 91–93; Ben Joravsky and Eduardo Camacho, *Race and Politics in Chicago*, Community Renewal Society, Chicago (1987), 19.

34. Joravsky and Camacho (1987), 18; Grimshaw (1992), 66; Dempsey Travis, *An Autobiography of Black Politics*, Urban Research Institute, Chicago (1986), 155.

35. On Dickerson, see Robert Blakely and Marcus Shepard, *Earl B. Dickerson: A Voice for Freedom and Equality*, Northwestern University Press, Evanston, IL (2007); "Earl Dickerson Denies Guild Is Communist," *Chicago Defender*, June 26, 1954; "Sunday Is Earl B. Dickerson's Day," *Chicago Defender*, Dec. 5, 1970; "NAACP to Cite Dickerson," *Chicago Defender*, Oct. 20, 1975. See also "Dickerson Names to Illinois Fair Employment Group," *Chicago Defender*, Sept. 21, 1961; "Rejection of Dickerson 1st Such Move in a Decade," *Chicago Defender*, Nov. 2, 1961; "GOP Blocks Earl Dickerson," *Chicago Defender*, Nov. 1, 1961.

36. Arnold Hirsch, "The Cook County Democratic Organization and the Dilemma of Race, 1931–1987," in *Snowbelt Cities*, ed. Richard Bernard, Indiana University Press, Bloomington (1990), 63, 85; Barbara Ferman, "Chicago: Power, Race, and Reform," in *Big City Politics in Transition*, ed. H. V. Savitch and John Clayton Thomas, Sage Publications, New York (1991), 51.

37. *General Report*, pt. I: What the Study Has Discovered, 39; chap. V: Why the Weakness of the Negro Position—The Crux of the Problem, 66.

38. Milton Rakove, *Don't Make No Waves, Don't Back No Losers: An Insider's Analysis of the Daley Machine*, Indiana University Press, Bloomington (1975), 256–81.

39. Hirsch (1990); Joravsky and Camacho (1987), 23–24.

40. *IAF General Report*, sec. F: Politics, 31, Alinsky Papers. On Dawson, see Grimshaw (1992), Charles Branham, "Black Chicago: Accommodationist Politics before the Great Migration," in *The Ethnic Frontier: Essays in the History of Group Survival in Chicago and the Midwest*, ed. Melvin Holli and Peter d'A. Jones, Eerdmans, Grand Rapids, MI (1977), 211–62; Leon Despres, *Challenging the Daley Machine*, Northwestern University Press, Evanston, IL (2004), 86.

41. "Chicago Seeks Violence Cure: City Cross Section Ask Mayor to Act," *Chicago Defender*, July 19, 1947. The group consisted of representatives from most of Chicago's Kelly-era racially liberal community: the NAACP, the Chicago Council against Racial and Religious Discrimination, the CIO Council, the Chicago City Club, the Catholic Youth Organization, the Anti-Defamation League, the American Civil Liberties Union, and the Independent Voters of Illinois.

42. Strickland (1966), 172–75; Hirsch (1983), 61–62, 246–47.

43. On Williams, the Urban League, and the Committee to End Mob Violence, see Strickland (1966), 172–74; Hirsch (1983), 246–47; James Q. Wilson, *Negro Politics: The Search for Leadership*, Free Press, New York (1960), 63–64, 111, 140–43, 160–61; Reed (1997), 167; "Demand Mayor's Ouster," *Chicago Defender*, Dec. 3, 1949; "Report Williams under Fire," *Chicago Defender*, July 16, 1955; "Sidney Williams Fired by Chicago Urban League," *Chicago Defender*, July 23, 1955.

44. Reed (1997), 163, 166; Neckerman (2007), 96–97.

45. Adam Cohen and Elizabeth Taylor, *American Pharoah*, Little, Brown, Boston (2000), 204–7; James Ralph, *Northern Protest: Martin Luther King Jr., Chicago and the Civil Rights Movement*, Harvard University Press, Cambridge, MA (1993), 240; Reed (1997), 162–63, 166, 189; Travis (1997), 260–61, 270; Wilson (1965), 63–64, 162, 283, 288; *Chicago Defender*, Dec. 14, 1957;

No Shake Up in NAACP—Jones," *Chicago Defender*, Dec. 28, 1957. On Abner, see "Willoughby Abner Dies," *Chicago Defender*, Dec. 4, 1972. On the NAACP's efforts to expose and address the extent of intentional segregation in Chicago's public schools, see "NAACP Wants Chicago Schools Desegregated," *Chicago Defender*, Dec. 15, 1956, and "NAACP Reports on School Bias," *Chicago Defender*, Feb. 23, 1957.

46. *General Report*, pt. I, chap. IV: Interracial Organizations, 54–56, 68; *General Report*, pt. III: The Grand Boulevard Report, sec. B: Types of Surveys, xiii; General *Report*, pt. I, chap. II, sec. C, 39.

47. *General Report*, sec. F: Politics, 34; *General Report*, pt. III: Grand Boulevard Report Synopsis, ii–iii. See also Chicago Fact Book Consortium, *Local Community Fact Book, Chicago Metropolitan Area: Based on the 1970 and 1980 Censuses*.

48. *General Report*, pt. I, chap. I, sec. C: Class Structure and Social Conditions in Chicago, 11–13; *General Report*, pt. III: The Grand Boulevard Report, chap. V: Protestant Churches, 61.

49. *General Report*, sec. F, chap. VI: Courses of Action, 78.

50. *General Report*, pt. I, chap. I, sec. D: Religion, 17–18; chap. V: Protestant Churches, 20–21.

51. Alinsky to Stritch, memo, app. I, Nov. 14, 1957, Alinsky Papers.

52. *General Report*, app. I; Wilson (1960), 125–26; Swift and Company ended hog-dressing production in 1952 and ceased all pork operations in Apr. 1957. Wilson and Company had closed its plants two years earlier. See Chicago Fact Book Consortium (1980); Rick Halpern, *Down on the Killing Floor: Black and White Workers in Chicago's Packinghouses, 1904-1954*, University of Illinois Press, Champaign (1997).

53. *General Report*, pt. I, chap. III, 63–65; "Race, Ethnicity, Neighborhood and Class: The Yeasty Chicago Brew," *Social Policy* (Spring 2002), 67–68.

54. Chap. VII: Unions, 47–48, 59; *General Report*, pt. III: The Grand Boulevard Report, sec. C: Summary of Conclusions, xviii.

55. *General Report*, sec. F, chap. VI: Courses of Action, 76.

56. *General Report*, pt. III: The Grand Boulevard Report, sec. C: Summary of Conclusions, xx–xxii.

57. *General Report*, chap. VI, sec. C: Can White Sponsors Do the Job, 79.

58. *General Report*, pt. I: What the Study Has Discovered, 7; *General Report*, sec. F, chap. VI: Courses of Action, 71, 73.

59. *General Report*, pt. I, chap. V: Protestant Churches, 20–21.

60. *General Report*, pt. I, chap. VI, sec. D: Two Types of Proposals, 83; *General Report*, pt. III: The Grand Boulevard Report, sec. C, xxii; chap. IV: Housing, 15–16.

61. *General Report*, app. I; Alinsky to Stritch, memo, Nov. 14, 1957, 7, Alinsky Papers.

62. *General Report*, chap. III: Prejudice and Integration, 49, 51–52.

63. *General Report*, pt. I, chap. III, 62.

64. Alinsky to Stritch, memo, Nov. 14, 1957, 7–8, Alinsky Papers.

65. Alinsky to Stritch, memo, Nov. 14, 1957, 8, Alinsky Papers.

66. Alinsky to Stritch, memo, Nov. 14, 1957, 4, Alinsky Papers.

67. Alinsky to Stritch, memo, Nov. 14, 1957, 8–9, Alinsky Papers.

68. Alinsky to Stritch, memo, Nov. 14, 1957, 5, Alinsky Papers.

69. See Wilson (1960), 151; Peter Rossi and Robert Dentler, *The Politics of Urban Renewal: The Chicago Findings*, Free Press, Glencoe, IL (1961), chap. 6.

70. Wilson (1960), 202–3; St. Clair Drake, "Profiles: Chicago," *Journal of Educational Sociology* 17 (Jan. 1944), 261–71; Rossi and Dentler (1961), 65.

71. Wilson (1960), 185–86, 195; Preston Smith II, "The Quest for Racial Democracy: Black Civic Ideology and Housing Interests in Postwar Chicago," *Journal of Urban History* (Jan. 2000), 136. See also Preston Smith II, *Racial Democracy and the Black Metropolis: Housing Policy in Postwar Chicago*, University of Minnesota Press, Minneapolis, 2012. The phrase "spatial strategy" comes from David Delaney, *Race, Place and the Law, 1836–1948*, University of Texas Press, Austin (1998), 103–4.

72. *General Report*, pt. I, chap. VI, 86–89.

73. Wilson (1960), 193–97; Delaney (1998).

74. Msgr. John Egan, videotaped interview by Mark Santow, Aug. 1997, Chicago, in the author's possession. See also Sanford Horwitt, *Let Them Call Me Rebel*, Alfred A. Knopf, New York (1989), 318–19.

75. O'Grady to Meyer, Oct. 3, 1958, folder CBC General Correspondence, ACC folder, Meyer Papers.

76. *General Report*, pt. I, chap. III, 63–65; Steven Avella interview with Egan, Oct. 19, 1981, 1, and "The Definition and Purpose of the ACC and the Functions of its Executive Office," memo to Meyer, Mar. 10, 1959, CBC General Correspondence, ACC folder, Meyer Papers. See also Frisbie (1991), chap. 11, and "Memo in Preparation for the Meeting with Archbishop Meyer," ca. Feb. 1959, box 8, Msgr. John Egan Papers, Special Collections, University of Notre Dame, Notre Dame, IN. On Meyer and race, see Avella, *This Confident Church: Catholic Leadership and Life in Chicago, 1940–1965*, University of Notre Dame Press, South Bend, IN (1992), 299.

77. *General Report*, pt. I, chap. IV: Summary of Recommendations, 68.

Chapter Three

1. M. W. Newman, "South Side Neighborhood Works for Racial Peace," *Chicago Daily News*, Sept. 1, 1960.

2. For works that examine the transition and disappearance of white ethnic city neighborhoods, and their effects on identity and politics, see Beryl Satter, *Family Properties: Race, Real Estate, and the Exploitation of Black Urban America*, Metropolitan Books, New York (2009); Ray Suarez, *The Old Neighborhood*, Free Press, New York (1999); Gerald Gamm, *Urban Exodus: Why the Jews Left Boston and the Catholics Stayed*, Harvard University Press, Cambridge, MA (1999); Louis Rosen, *South Side: The Racial Transformation of an American Neighborhood*, Ivan R. Dee, Chicago (1998); Tom Sugrue, *Origins of the Urban Crisis*, Princeton University Press, Princeton, NJ (1996); Alan Ehrenhalt, *Lost City: Discovering the Forgotten Virtues of Community in the Chicago of the 1950s*, Basic Books, New York (1995); Alexander Von Hoffman, *Local Attachments: The Making of an American Neighborhood 1850–1920*, Johns Hopkins Press, Baltimore (1994); Hillel Levine and Lawrence Harmon, *The Death of an American Jewish Community: A Tragedy of Good Intentions*, Free Press, New York (1992); J. Anthony Lukas, *Common Ground: A Turbulent Decade in the Lives of Three American Families*, Alfred A. Knopf, New York (1985); Jonathan Reider, *Canarsie: The Jews and Italians of Brooklyn against Liberalism*, Harvard University Press, Cambridge, MA (1985); Eleanor Wolf, Charles LeBeaux, Shirley Terreberry, and Harriet Saperstein, *Change and Renewal in an Urban Community: Five Case Studies of Detroit*, Praeger, New York (1969); Vincent Giese, *Revolution in the City*, Fides Publishers, Notre Dame, IN (1961).

3. Dominic Pacyga and Ellen Skerrett, *Chicago: City of Neighborhoods*, Loyola University Press, Chicago (1986), chaps. 14–15; John Fish, *The Edge of the Ghetto: A Study of Church Involvement in Community Organization*, Seabury Press, New York (1966), 3; Newman (1960). In 1960,

58 percent of housing units on the Southwest Side were owner-occupied, although this varied with individual communities. See Chicago Community Inventory, *Local Community Fact Book: Chicago, 1960*, University of Chicago Press, Chicago (1963).

4. Eileen McMahon, *What Parish Are You From? A Chicago Irish Community and Race Relations*, University Press of Kentucky, Lexington (1995), 159; Pacyga and Skerrett (1986), 496–98; John Egan, "OSC—An Evaluation, October 1965" (prepared by Office of Urban Affairs of the Catholic Bishop of Chicago, Nov. 2, 1965); "OSC Proposals for Planning and Renewal," Mar. 1962, box 38, OSC file, Msgr. John Egan Papers (hereafter Egan Papers), Special Collections, University of Notre Dame, Notre Dame, IN.

5. Newman (1960); Egan (1965).

6. On transition in rental areas, see Arnold Hirsch, *Making the Second Ghetto: Race and Housing in Chicago, 1940–1960*, Cambridge University Press, New York (1983), 31; Giese (1961), 11–13; Will Cooley, *Moving Up, Moving Out: The Rise of the Black Middle Class in Chicago*, Northern Illinois University Press, DeKalb (2018); "The Management of Neighborhood Change" (abridged proceedings of citywide workshop held Apr. 10–12, 1959, in Lake Geneva, WI), Chicago Commission on Human Relations, 8.

7. Giese (1961), 22.

8. Cooley (2018); Richard Taub, D. Garth Taylor, and Jan D. D. Dunham, *Paths of Neighborhood Change: Race and Crime in Urban America*, University of Chicago Press, Chicago (1984), 15–16; Giese (1961), 25, 47; Chicago Community Inventory, *Chicago Community Fact Book* (1950), 183; Chicago Community Inventory (1960), 103.

9. M. W. Newman and Harry Swegle, "The Panic Peddlers," 9 pts., *Chicago Daily News*, Oct. 13–Oct. 22, 1959. The OSC ran off thousands of copies of this series to educate local groups about the structural causes of transition and flight.

10. Wendy Plotkin, "Deeds of Mistrust: Race, Housing, and Restrictive Covenants in Chicago 1900–1953" (PhD diss., University of Illinois Chicago, 1999), 64.

11. Newman and Swegle (Oct. 13 and Oct. 16, 1959).

12. Newman and Swegle (Oct. 14 and Oct. 19, 1959). In 1962, the *Saturday Evening Post* published the article "Confessions of a Block Buster" in which a Chicago real estate speculator argued that the policies of the Chicago Real Estate Board ensured the continual tipping and resegregation of changing neighborhoods, and that the city had over one hundred blockbusters like himself. He asked his critics to stop blaming him until they could answer the questions, "What alternative can you provide for my function? Would you try to influence your bank or savings-and-loan association to begin lending to Negroes? Would you help remove the pressure on 'busted' areas by welcoming a Negro family into your block?" Beryl Satter, in her 2009 book *Family Properties*, offers a fascinating and detailed description of block busters on the West Side.

13. Gaudette was later an organizer for an Alinsky-sponsored group in Austin, a white middle-class community on the city's western fringe. See Robert Bailey, *Radicals in Urban Politics: The Alinsky Approach*, University of Chicago Press, Chicago (1974); Jean Lancourt, *Confront or Concede: The Alinsky Citizen-Action Organizations*, Lexington Books, Lexington, MA (1979).

14. On Gaudette's group, see Newman and Swegle (Oct. 15 and Oct. 22, 1959); Nellie Dora, "Community Problems in Chatham," from *The Management of Neighborhood Change* (Conference Publication, Chicago Commission on Human Relations, Apr. 10–12, 1959), 9. In the early 1960s, the Chatham–Avalon Park Community Council became one of the founding members of the CCCO, the coalition that sparked the Chicago Freedom Movement.

15. On WACA, see *Chicago Daily News*, Oct. 22, 1959; Giese (1961), chap. 4.

16. Giese looked upon the early months of Alinsky's Provisional Organization for the Southwest Community with some interest, declaring: "If the effort fails, we will have lost the urban battle and we will have lost face around the world in our manner of handling race relations. The whole world is watching." Giese (1961), 78; "The 'Big Change' in Chatham-Avalon: Middle Class South Side Area Battles for Orderly Integration," *Chicago Daily News*, May 8, 1959; "The Chicago Wall," *Chicago Defender*, Oct. 4, 1962; Murray Friedman, "The White Liberal's Retreat," *Atlantic Monthly*, Jan. 1963, 43; Patrick Reardon, "Solid Citizens: Through Hard Work and Vigilance, Chatham Has Remained Strong, Will New Residents Be as Committed?" *Chicago Tribune*, June 7, 1998; Cooley (2008), 104, 268–69. For a recent account of the Chatham–Avalon Park Community Council's efforts to keep Chatham middle class, see Aaron Schutz, "'If That's Snobbery, Then I'm a Snob': The Successful Fight to Create a Black, Middle-Class Enclave in Chatham, 1955–1960," *Journal of the Illinois State Historical Society* 133, nos. 3–4 (Fall–Winter 2020).

17. Rosen (1998), 144, 121–22. In addition to L. K. Northwood and Ernest A. T. Barth, *Urban Desegregation: Negro Pioneers and Their White Neighbors*, University of Washington Press, Seattle (1965), Tom Sugrue has a useful discussion of black pioneers in Detroit during the same time period, in *Origins of the Urban Crisis*, Princeton University Press, Princeton, NJ (1996), 188–90, 216. See also Cooley (2018).

18. Don Gold, "In God She Trusts," *Ladies Home Journal*, Nov. 1963; Thomas Dyja, *The Third Coast: When Chicago Built the American Dream*, Penguin Books, New York (2013), 373–75.

19. Marvin Caplan, "The Last White Family on the Block," *Atlantic Monthly*, July 1960, 56; Carl Rowan, "Why Negroes Move to White Neighborhoods," *Ebony*, Aug. 1958.

20. Dora (1959), 9.

21. Newman and Swegle (Oct. 21, 1959).

22. Newman and Swegle (Oct. 21, 1959).

23. Mark Satter, "Land Contract Sales in Chicago: Security Turned Exploitation," *Chicago Bar Record*, Mar. 1958; Chicago Commission on Human Relations, *Selling and Buying Real Estate in a Racially Changing Neighborhood* (June 1962); *Chicago Defender*, July 2, 1962; *Chicago Sun-Times*, July 21, 1962; *Chicago's American*, July 20, 1962; Satter (2009), 59, 75.

24. Sugrue (1996), 216–17; Karl Taeuber and Alma Taeuber, "The Negro as an Immigrant Group: Trends in Economic and Racial Segregation in Chicago," *Journal of American Sociology* (Jan. 1964); J. Saunders Redding, *No Day of Triumph*, Harper and Brothers, New York (1942), 17; Anthony Downs, "Alternative Futures for the American Ghetto," *Daedalus* (Fall 1968), 1333.

25. James Langland, ed., *The Chicago Daily News Almanac and Year-book for 1927*, Chicago Daily News, Chicago (1926), 822–41; Egan (1965), 2; Alinsky, *IAF Annual Report* (1960), 10, Alinksy Papers; Andrew Diamond, *Mean Streets: Chicago Youths and the Everyday Struggle for Empowerment in the Multiracial City, 1908–1969*, University of California Press, Berkeley (2009), 179–83, 222; David Remnick, *The Bridge: The Life and Rise of Barack Obama*, Alfred A. Knopf, New York (2010), 129.

26. The exception here is East Morgan Park, which had contained a large black settlement since the 1920s, and the eastern section of Washington Heights, which became a black middle-class homeowner's area in the 1950s.

27. On Groebe and BAPA in the late 1940s, see Zorita Mikva, "The Neighborhood Improvement Association: A Counter-Force to the Expansion of Chicago's Negro Population" (MA thesis, University of Chicago, 1951), 72–75, 85. Nearly 82 percent of the housing units in Beverly were owner-occupied in 1960, with a median value of almost $25,000—much higher than in Auburn-Gresham, just to the north. Morgan Park, Washington Heights, and especially Beverly had a

higher percentage of professionals in the workforce than the city average. *Chicago Community Fact Book* (1960), 159, 165, 231. On Beverly Hills-Morgan Park, see Pacyga and Skerrett (1986), chap. 15. On the black community in Morgan Park, see Cooley (2008), 131.

28. Mikva (1951), 72–98; Plotkin (1999), 82–83.

29. On covenants on the Southwest Side, see Plotkin (1999), chap. 4; Herman Long and Charles Johnson, *People vs. Property: Race Restrictive Covenants in Housing*, Fisk University Press, Nashville, TN (1947), 50–51; Mikva (1951), 24–26, 52, 63, 72–74; Gerald Sullivan, *The Story of Englewood, 1835–1923*, Foster and McDonnell, Chicago (1924); Martin Meyerson and Edward Banfield, *Politics, Planning and the Public Interest: The Case of Public Housing in Chicago*, Free Press, Glencoe, IL (1955), 107, 113, 116.

30. Mikva, in his study of improvement associations, claims that SPA was "greatly influenced by real estate interests." Most of its officers as of 1951 had heavy investments in expensive commercial property in the area. On Rathje and McDonnell, see Meyerson and Banfield (1955), 107–8.

31. See Chicago Community Inventory (1950), 279. See also Dominic Pacyga, "Chicago's Ethnic Neighborhoods: The Myth of Stability and the Reality of Change," in *Ethnic Chicago: A Multicultural Portrait*, Eerdmans, Grand Rapids, MI (1995).

32. The Illinois Redevelopment Act of 1941 set the bureaucratic groundwork that was later used by the South East Chicago Commission (SECC) and the University of Chicago in efforts to redevelop Hyde Park and Kenwood. See Hirsch (1983), 36; Julie Abrahamson, *A Neighborhood Finds Itself*, Harper Brothers, New York (1959), 196–97; Rossi and Dentler (1961).

33. Hirsch (1983), 37; Mikva (1951). See also Louis Washington, "A Study of Restrictive Covenants in Chicago (MA thesis, University of Chicago, 1948), 14; Chicago Council against Racial and Religious Discrimination, *Chicago's Neighborhood Improvement Associations* (1943). See also Meyerson and Banfield (1955), 107–8.

34. See Mikva (1951), 81–83. Local community papers were often crucial to the growth of neighborhood organizations. See League of Women Voters of Chicago, "Neighborhood Organizations," Oct. 1961, box 38, OSC file, Egan Papers.

35. The term *economic cold war* is Alinsky's. See Alinsky, *IAF Annual Report* (1961), Alinksy Papers.

36. Mikva (1951), 85; Sanford Horwitt, *Let Them Call Me Rebel: Saul Alinsky, His Life and Legacy*, Alfred A. Knopf, New York (1989), 342–43.

37. See *Urban League Newsletter*, Nov.–Dec. 1957, Alinsky Papers, Special Collections, University of Illinois Chicago (hereafter Alinsky Papers).

38. Alinsky, *IAF Annual Report* (1961), Alinksy Papers.

39. See Leonard Rieser, "An Analysis of the Reporting of Racial Incidents in Chicago, 1945–50" (MA thesis, University of Chicago, 1951), 15; Hirsch (1983), 55. On the 1949 violence, see Hirsch (1983); *Report of the Chicago Commission on Human Relations*, Dec. 10, 1949, 16.

40. On crime in the area, see "What Happens When White Neighbors Refuse to Panic?" *Chicago Daily News* Sept. 3, 1960; McMahon (1995), 161–65; *Southtown Economist* issues from Aug. 30, 1961, Apr. 22, 1962, May 20, 1962, Aug. 22, 1962, and Aug. 18, 1963; Horwitt (1989), 325; Chicago Community Inventory (1960), 151; Fish (1966), xvi–xvii.

41. Fish (1966), 5–7.

42. See John McGreevy, *Parish Boundaries: The Catholic Encounter with Race in the 20th Century Urban North*, University of Chicago Press, Chicago (1996); Steven Avella, *This Confident Church: Catholic Leadership and Life in Chicago, 1940–1965*, University of Notre Dame Press, South Bend, IN (1992). The importance of Catholic identity on the Southwest Side was indicated

by the fact that the *Southtown Economist* listed properties by parish—a method local real estate agents took note of. See also McMahon (1995), 78–81, 91, 96, 113–15.

43. On the state of race relations in Auburn-Gresham and Greater Grand Crossing in the late 1940s, see Shirley Star, "Interracial Tension in Two Areas of Chicago: An Exploratory Approach to the Measurement of Interracial Tension" (PhD diss., University of Chicago, 1950).

44. McMahon (1995), 131, 133, 136–38. See also McGreevy (1996), Avella (1992), Fish (1966), 3; Chicago Community Inventory (1960); Horwitt (1989), 323; Margery Frisbie, *An Alley in Chicago: The Ministry of a City Priest*, Sheed and Ward, Kansas City, MO (1991), chap. 12. McMahon came from the St. Charles Borromeo parish, which had changed from white to black—although he succeeded in keeping the parish school integrated for two decades before transition.

45. See McMahon (1995), 159; Fish (1966), 3; Horwitt (1989), 323–25.

46. By 1959, the credit union had 732 members and an operating budget of $1.4 million; it later served as a model for the OSC's Home Loan Fund. See McMahon (1995), 77.

47. See John McMahon, "Conservation at St. Sabina's," *Catholic Charities Review*, Jan. 1954, 11–13.

48. John McMahon, "Talk," *Seraph*, May 1957, 3.

49. See Frisbie (1991), chap. 12.

50. Fish (1966), 9.

51. Interview with Egan, Nov. 14, 1976, in David Finks, *The Radical Vision of Saul Alinsky*, Paulist Press, New York (1984), 123.

52. Finks (1984), 124. See Egan to Meyer, Jan. 5, 1959, CBC General Correspondence, ACC folder, Meyer Papers (hereafter Meyer Papers), Archives of the Archdiocese of Chicago.

53. See Alinsky, "The Urban Immigrant" (presented at Notre Dame conference Roman Catholicism and the American Way of Life, Feb. 13, 1959), file 292, Alinsky Papers, for his version of the January meeting and the days that followed. Minutes of Pastors Meeting in Christ the King Parish, Jan. 6, 1959, Alinsky Papers. See also Harold Cross, "Cardinal Endorses Organization of Southwest Community," *Southtown Economist* Jan. 17, 1960, 1.

54. Charles and Bonnie Remsberg, "In the Vanishing Slums of Chicago," *Catholic Digest*, July 1963. The words are Egan's. On Egan's relationship with the IAF, see Egan, "The Archdiocese Responds," *Church in Metropolis*, Summer 1965.

55. Frisbie (1991), chap. 12; Horwitt (1989), 331.

56. Martinez quoted in McMahon (1995), 139.

57. Nicholas Von Hoffman, *Radical: A Portrait of Saul Alinsky*, Nation Books, New York (2010), 55–57; Fish (1966), 10.

58. Finks interview with Chambers, Sept. 15, 1977, in Finks (1984), 128; Chambers and Von Hoffman to Egan, Aug. 7, 1961, file 334, Alinsky Papers.

59. See Von Hoffman to Alinsky, memo, June 21, 1963, Alinsky Papers.

60. See Robert Christ, "The Local Church in a Community Organization" (n.d.), box 38, p. 13, Egan Papers, for comments by a local Protestant minister on the relationship between the POSC and area improvement groups.

61. See Horwitt (1989), 342.

62. See Von Hoffman to Alinsky, memo, June 21, 1963, Alinsky Papers. See also Avella (1992), 239, who concurs with Von Hoffman that the pastors of the Southwest Side were "among the toughest of the old Irish barons and would not come together easily in so controversial a project." On Egan and anticommunism, see Donald O'Toole to Egan, Oct. 3, 1960, OSC correspondence file, box 39, Egan Papers; Daily Reports by Egan, Oct. 24, 1960, box 66, Egan Papers.

63. See *Southtown Economist*, Sept. 6, 1959; *Auburn Park Times: Souvenir Edition Commemorating 75th Anniversary of St. Leo Parish*, Oct. 31, 1957, file 343, Alinsky Papers; and Frisbie (1991), chap. 6, for descriptions of Molloy and his parish. See also Horwitt (1989), 328–31.

64. See "Charge Catholic Priest Bars Negroes at St. Leo," *New Crusader*, Oct. 1, 1960; "Parish Notes," *St. Leo Weekly*, Aug. 26–31 file, box 24, Catholic Interracial Council Papers, Special Collection, Catholic University of America Library; Von Hoffman (2010), 59–62.

65. *St. Leo Weekly*, Aug. 5, 1959.

66. Interview with St. Leo's parishioners Grace Benzig and Terence O'Rourke, in McMahon (1995), 145.

67. Von Hoffman (2010), 62.

68. See McMahon (1995), 149.

69. See Horwitt (1989), 331.

70. McMahon (1995), 146.

71. See Christ (1962), 3–5, Horwitt (1989), 333. John Fish, in his firsthand account of the OSC, claims that Christ later became the most influential and active person in the organization. Fish (1966), 8.

72. Alinsky to IAF Board, memo, Nov. 30, 1960, "Articles Appearing in the Christian Century Magazine Oct. 1959–March 1960," Alinsky Papers.

73. Christ (1962), 10–11.

74. On religious balance and participation in OSC, see McMahon (1995), 146–7; Fish (1966), 14–15; Christ (1962).

75. *Chicago Daily News*, May 25, 1959; Newman (1960).

76. Studies of communities—both urban and suburban—that have attempted to create "intentional integration" in the past few decades have generally agreed that the economic security of whites plays a key role in determining their willingness to participate. See Harvey Molotch, *Managed Integration: Dilemmas of Doing Good in the City*, University of California Press, Berkeley (1972); Juliet Saltman, *A Fragile Movement: The Struggle for Neighborhood Stabilization*, Greenwood Press, New York (1990); Don DeMarco and George Galster, "Prointegrative Policy: Theory and Practice," *Journal of Urban Affairs* 15 (1993); W. Dennis Keating, *The Suburban Racial Dilemma: Housing and Neighborhoods*, Temple University Press, Philadelphia (1994); Ingrid Ellen, *Sharing America's Neighborhoods: The Prospects for Stable Racial Integration*, Harvard University Press, Cambridge, MA (2001).

77. A lawyer sympathetic to residents of the Southwest Side trying to keep their neighborhoods and public facilities all white told the *Bulletin* in 1961 that their community could "become another Englewood, Chatham, Woodlawn, or hypocritical Hyde Park. Or it can become a hated but happy community." The economic and political advantages of Hyde Park, in this rendering, allowed its institutions and residents to essentially buy their way out of the racial dilemmas of containment and flight, and from this position of power then criticize poorer white neighborhoods for falling short of their more virtuous and tolerant behavior. See *The Bulletin*, Aug. 3, 1961, Alinsky Papers. See also Hirsch (1983), 66.

78. *General Report*, chap. VI, sec. D: Two Types of Proposals, 85.

79. Alinsky, "Citizen Participation and Community Organization in Planning and Urban Renewal" (speech before Chicago chapter of the National Association of Housing and Redevelopment Officials, Jan. 29, 1962), published by IAF, Alinsky Papers.

80. *General Report*, pt. IV: 1958 Chicago—A Place to Live, chap. XV: Conservation, 128–35.

81. Alinsky (1962); "X-Raying Community Organizations" (speech to the Special Interest Sessions of the Mississippi Valley Tuberculosis Conference, Oct. 13, 1961), Alinsky Papers; Abrahamson (1959), 331; Hirsch (1983), 140–41.

82. Abrahamson (1959), 330–31; Alinsky, *IAF General Report*, pt. I, chap. VI.

83. Chicago Commission on Human Relations, *The Management of Neighborhood Change* (abridged proceedings of citywide workshop, Apr. 10–12, 1959, Lake Geneva, WI), Chicago Commission on Human Relations Papers, Special Collections, University of Illinois Chicago.

84. Testimony by John Lee, "Community Problems in Winneconna Lakes," Chicago Commission on Human Relations (1959), 12–13.

85. University of Chicago sociologist Peter Rossi, who was intimately familiar with the efforts of the Hyde Park–Kenwood Community Conference (HP-KCC) to maintain racial integration in its neighborhood, advocated the use of a quota system "on grounds involving economics (ability to pay)." Only through an approach that restricted the proportion of blacks in an area could interracial neighborhoods be maintained, Rossi insisted. While acknowledging the paradox that "discrimination can be used to break down discrimination," the sociologist concluded that only quotas would allow whites and blacks to share the same institutions, and thus hasten the ability of blacks to "move rapidly into cultural parity with the whites." Rossi (1959), 20.

86. Chicago Commission on Human Relations (1959), 14.

Chapter Four

1. For integrationist examples, see Edward Rutledge and William Valentine, "Market Area Agreements—An Old Device Put to New Use," *Journal of Intergroup Relations* (Summer 1961). The private interracial housing developer Morris Milgram used a similar tool in Deerfield, Illinois, and in the Philadelphia suburb Concord Park, where his corporation retained the right of first purchase on homes offered for sale to maintain racial balance. While neither the University of Chicago nor the HP-KCC was party to an option agreement (or admitted the use of quotas), both took comparable steps to attain a monopoly position in their part of the urban housing market—through real estate purchases and a tenant referral service, respectively.

2. Testimony of Saul Alinsky before the US Commission on Civil Rights, Chicago, May 5, 1959, 769–81. For newspaper coverage, see "Urges Negro Quota in White Areas Here," *Chicago Daily News*, May 5, 1959, "How Negro Home Quotas Would Work: Sociologist Alinsky Outlines Method of Combating Ghettoes," *Chicago Daily News*; "What Chicagoans Say about Plan," *Chicago Daily News*, May 7, 1959; "Calls Quotas Segregation Solution Here: Alinsky Tells Plan at Civil Rights Quiz," *Chicago Daily Tribune*, May 6, 1959; "'Planned Dispersion' of Negroes," *Chicago Sun-Times*, May 8, 1959; "Quota Plan," *Chicago American*, May 6, 1959; "The Housing Inquiry," *Chicago Defender*, May 13, 1959.

3. The National Lawyers Guild discussed it at annual meetings, and the Commission on Race and Housing, initiated by the Fund for the Republic, issued reports that discussed it in some detail. The National Committee against Discrimination in Housing dedicated a third of its 1958 annual conference to the benign quota.

4. Countless writers discussed the notion of a tipping point. For a sample, see Robert Weaver, "Integration in Public and Private Housing," *Annals of the American Academy of Political and Social Science* (Mar. 1956); Morton Grodzins, *The Metropolitan Area as a Racial Problem*, University of Pittsburgh Press, Pittsburgh, PA (1958), 6 (offering 25 percent as "the limits of a

neighborhood's tolerance for interracial living"); Eunice and George Grier, *Privately Developed Interracial Housing: An Analysis of Experience*, University of California Press, Berkeley (1960), 65 (arguing that 25 percent to 33 percent black was a "practical composition"); and Chester Rapkin and William Grigsby, *The Demand for Housing in Racially Mixed Areas*, University of California Press, Berkeley (1960) (whose study of West Philadelphia convinced them that quotas of some kind were necessary to generate white demand in transition areas). John McDermott, chair of Philadelphia's Commission on Human Relations when Milgram built Concord Park, and later chair of the Chicago Commission on Human Relations, told the National Committee against Discrimination in Housing in 1956 that when blacks reach 30 percent to 40 percent "in a given block, the situation becomes shaky and stability is threatened." See McDermott, "Eight Observations about Neighborhood Stabilization," Philadelphia Commission on Human Relations, Oct. 12, 1956. See also McDermott, "Helping the Panic Neighborhood: A Philadelphia Approach," *Interracial Review* 28 (1955). The battles over race and place that characterized the postwar Northern city are incomprehensible without this ideological and structural backdrop. Charles Abrams, *Forbidden Neighbors: A Study of Prejudice in Housing*, Harper and Brothers, New York (1955), is perhaps the best account of the origins of these assumptions.

5. In 1966 James Downs, chair of the Real Estate Research Corporation and former head of Chicago's City Planning Commission, believed that the city's white homeowners still assumed that a few black neighbors led to complete racial transition. See "Chicago: A Big City Meets Its Problems," *US News and World Report*, Mar. 28, 1966; Rose Helper, *Racial Policies and Practices of Real Estate Brokers*, University of Minnesota Press, Minneapolis (1969), 103, 107–8. See also "The Negro Housing Market from a Real Estate Broker's Point of View: An Illinois Survey," in *Open Occupancy vs. Forced Housing under the Fourteenth Amendment: A Symposium on Anti-Discrimination Legislation, Freedom of Choice, and Property Rights in Housing*, ed. Alfred Avins, Bookmailer, New York (1963), which confirms the same findings through a survey of real estate agents in Chicago, its suburbs, and downstate.

6. Abrams (1955), 158. David Delaney, *Race, Place and the Law, 1836–1948*, University of Texas Press, Austin (1998), 159, argues that judicial findings of fact in racially restrictive covenant cases "took racial segregation as a given, something that goes without saying." On the gatekeeping function of real estate agents and the extent to which the very definition of professional ethics for agents included the preservation of white property and associational rights, see Helper (1969), 117.

7. On scholarly debates over the effects of race on property values and prices, see Homer Hoyt, *One Hundred Years of Land Values in Chicago*, University of Chicago Press, Chicago (1933); Robert Weaver, *The Negro Ghetto*, Harcourt Brace, New York (1948), 293; Abrams (1955), chap. 13; Abrams, "The New 'Gresham's Law of Neighborhoods'—Fact or Fiction," *Appraisal Journal* (July 1951); Belden Morgan, "Values in Transition Areas," *Review of the Society of Residential Appraisers* (Mar. 1952); Luigi Laurenti, "Effects of Nonwhite Purchases on Market Prices of Residences," *Appraisal Journal* (July 1952); *Property Values and Race* (1960), 47; Egbert Schietinger, "Racial Succession and Changing Property Values in Residential Chicago" (PhD diss., Department of Sociology, University of Chicago, 1953); Schietinger, "Racial Succession and Changing Property Values in Residential Chicago," in *Contributions to Urban Sociology*, ed. Ernest Burgess and Donald Bogue, University of Chicago Press, Chicago (1964); Rapkin and Grigsby (1960); Otis Duncan and Philip Hauser, *Housing a Metropolis: Chicago*, Free Press, Glencoe, IL (1960), 203–4; Karl Taeuber and Alma Taeuber, *Negroes in Cities: Residential Segregation and Neighborhood Change*, Aldine, Chicago (1965), 25; Martin Bailey, "Notes on the Economics of Residential Zoning and Urban Renewal," *Land Economics* 42 (1966); David Karlen, "Racial Integration and

Property Values in Chicago," Department of Sociology, University of Chicago (Apr. 1968); Richard Muth, *Cities and Housing: The Spatial Pattern of Urban Residential Land Use*, University of Chicago Press, Chicago (1969); Helper (1969), 95; Harvey Molotch, *Managed Integration: Dilemmas of Doing Good in the City*, University of California Press, Berkeley (1972); Brian Berry, *The Open Housing Question: Race and Housing in Chicago 1966–1976*, Ballinger Publishing, Cambridge, MA (1979), chap. 16.

8. Grodzins (1958), 7.

9. On Milgram, see Tom Sugrue, *Sweet Land of Liberty*, Random House, New York (2009), 231; "An Example of Open Housing" (remarks by Irving Leos of Modern Community Developers to the National Board of the YMCA in March 1959), *YMCA Magazine*, May 1959. See also Oscar Cohen, "The Benign Quota in Housing: The Case For—and Against," *Anti-Defamation League Bulletin*, Jan. 1959. Other than chapter 7 of Sugrue's 2009 book, there is little scholarship on Milgram or his developments. See Milgram, "Commercial Development of Integrated Housing" (Summer 1960), and *The Good Neighborhood*, Norton Books, New York (1977); Kenneth Jackson, *Crabgrass Frontiers*, Oxford University Press, New York (1985).

10. Rapkin and Grigsby (1955), 71. See also R. J. Anderson, "An Analysis of the Possible Impact of Anti-Discrimination on the Home Building Industry," in Avins (1963).

11. Judicial opinions and law review articles from the late 1950s and early 1960s make it clear that benign quotas, aside from being politically unpalatable, were on shaky constitutional ground as well—in part because of their implicit recognition of group over individual rights, as well as their expansive interpretation of *Brown*. While the Supreme Court had not handed down a ruling on housing quotas, state and federal circuit courts had, rejecting the method as in violation of the Fourteenth Amendment and contrary to the precedents set in the *Buchanan*, *Shelley*, and *Brown* cases. Indeed, as of this writing, the Supreme Court had still not ruled definitively on the constitutionality of integrative quotas. On quota case law post-1968, see L. M. Vodar, "The Use of Racial Housing Quotas to Achieve Integrated Communities: The Oak Park Approach," *Loyola University of Chicago Law Journal* 6 (1975); "Oak Park: Reverse Steering and Racial Quotas," in Berry (1979); Comment, "Tipping the Scales of Justice: A Race-Conscious Remedy for Neighborhood Transition," *Yale Law Review* 90 (1980); Comment, "Benign Steering and Benign Quotas: The Validity of Race-Conscious Government Policies to Promote Residential Integration," *Harvard Law Review* 93 (1980); B. S. Gelber, "Race-Conscious Approaches to Ending Segregation in Housing: Some Pitfalls on the Road to Integration," *Rutgers Law Review* 37 (1985); R. A. Smolla, "In Pursuit of Racial Utopias: Fair Housing, Quotas, and Goals in the 1980s," *Southern California Law Review* 58 (1985); D. Bishop, "Fair Housing and the Constitutionality of Governmental Measures Affecting Community Ethnicity," *University of Chicago Law Review* 55 (1988); M. A. Kushner, "The Legality of Race-Conscious Access Quotas under the Fair Housing Act of 1968," *Cardozo Law Review* 9 (1988); George Galster, "Neighborhood Racial Change, Segregationist Sentiments, and Affirmative Marketing Policies," *Journal of Urban Economics* 27 (1990); W. Dennis Keating, *The Suburban Racial Dilemma: Housing and Neighborhoods*, Temple University Press, Philadelphia (1994).

12. Jack Balkin, *What Brown v. Board of Education Should Have Said*, New York University Press, New York (2001), 13. For examples of the anti-subordination and equal citizenship interpretation, see Charles Black Jr., "The Lawfulness of the Segregation Decisions," *Yale Law Journal* 69 (1960); Owen Fiss, "Groups and the Equal Protection Clause," *Philosophy and Public Affairs* 5, no. 107 (1976); John Charles Boger, "Willful Colorblindness: The New Racial Piety and the Resegregation of Public Schools," *North Carolina Law Review* 78 (Sept. 2000).

13. By the early 1960s, defenders of the benign quota had begun to put together a legal defense of race consciousness and group rights, which would later play a key role in the construction of affirmative action case law. See Robert A. Horn, *Groups and the Constitution*, Stanford University Press, Palo Alto, CA (1956); Thomas A. Cowan, "Group Interests," *Virginia Law Review* 44 (1958). See also Alfred Blumrosen, *Modern Law: The Law Transmission System and Equal Employment Opportunity*, University of Wisconsin Press, Madison (1993); Paul Moreno, *From Direct Action to Affirmative Action: Fair Employment Law and Policy in American 1933–1972*, Louisiana State University Press, Baton Rouge (1999), 141–43. Advocates of quotas in public housing also asserted that the Supreme Court's ruling in *Brown v. Board of Education* (1954), due to the role of federal programs, policies, and agencies in the growth and maintenance of racial segregation, encompassed an "affirmative duty" to further integration—not simply to stop segregation. Because quotas worked and were based on ratios that could be "scientifically" determined, they were reasonable and thus constitutionally permitted. See Victor Navasky, "The Benevolent Housing Quota," *Howard Law Journal* 6 (1960); Charles Abrams, "The Quota System," foreword to *Equality*, ed. Robert L. Carter and Charles Abrams, Pantheon Books, New York (1965).

14. Abrams (1965).

15. Attorney Peter Marcuse made a similar argument in *Journal of Intergroup Relations*, contending that "taking the facts of race into direct account may sometimes be appropriate to achieve actual equality" and may in fact be an implementation of the equal protection clause, rather than a violation of it. See Marcuse, "Benign Quotas Reexamined," *Journal of Intergroup Relations* (Spring 1962), 111–13. Similar arguments, of course, have been and are used to defend affirmative action in employment and school admissions—perhaps most famously by Supreme Court Justice Harry Blackmun, who argued in the important *Bakke* case: "To get beyond racism, we must first take account of race. There is no other way." *University of California Regents v. Bakke*, 438 U.S. 265, 407 (1978) (Blackmun, J., writing separately). See also Orlando Patterson, *The Ordeal of Integration*, Civitas, Washington, DC (1997), chap. 5; John Skrentny, *The Ironies of Affirmative Action*, University of Chicago Press, Chicago (1996); Ian Haney Lopez, *White by Law: The Legal Construction of Race*, New York University Press, New York (1996), chap. 6; and Neil Gotanda, "A Critique of 'Our Constitution Is Color-Blind,'" *Stanford Law Review* 44 (1991).

16. For Abrams, the *Brown* decision itself left the door open for race-conscious policies, because it "not only shattered the unsavory separate but equal doctrine but also exposed the more savory doctrine of 'color blindness' to reexamination." Since segregation (of schools, in this case) was determined to have detrimental effects on black children, whether de jure or de facto, the state had a responsibility to use positive means to break it up, which could not be done by being colorblind. Bickel (1962), 71. Address of Charles Abrams before the Teachers' Guild on the Occasion of the Presentation of the John Dewey Award to Thurgood Marshall, Mar. 2, 1957, NAACP Papers, III-J-6, Library of Congress, Washington, DC; Dan Dodson, "Can Intergroup Quotas Be Benign?" *Journal of Intergroup Relations* (Autumn 1960), 14. See also Moreno (1999), 137.

17. As George Grier and Eunice Grier put it in their study of integrated private housing developments, "Of all the emotion-provoking aspects of interracial housing, few are capable of producing more heat than 'quotas.'" The Griers found that both black and white interracialists willing to accept policies of managed integration balked at the word *quota*—"professional workers in intergroup relations" in particular. One commentator claimed that advocates of controlled integration "exhibit a carefully thought-out sort of schizophrenia: it's okay to use a quota—in fact, it's necessary—but you should never talk about it." See Grier and Grier (1960); Moreno (1999), 140n7.

18. King told the reporter that "percentage integration" was "all right as . . . an attempt to set an example in a community to prove that integration can work." He claimed that Milgram's Modern Community Developers was "working in line with our democratic creed." See *Chicago Daily News*, Dec. 16, 1959; King to John Wagner of the National Lutheran Council, Dec. 15, 1960; Wagner to Alinsky Dec. 29, 1960; Alinsky to Wagner and King, Jan. 3, 1961—all in box 20, IAF correspondence, Egan Papers. See also Thomas Jackson, *From Civil Rights to Human Rights: Martin Luther King Jr. and the Struggle for Economic Justice*, University of Pennsylvania Press, Philadelphia (2006), 126.

19. Black activists had challenged this notion of color blindness as early as the 1940s, particularly with regard to job discrimination. As Martha Biondi, Robert Self, and others have convincingly demonstrated, the Black Freedom Movement in the urban North was focused primarily on desegregation and full equality in housing, employment and schooling. The legal apparatus of New Deal liberalism appeared to be a promising means to that end, but black activism wasn't necessarily wedded to its color-blind methodology. The inability of postwar racial liberals to see the black urban condition in its structural complexity—in terms of both employment and housing—was poorly timed and tragic. As Biondi describes it, when Cold War liberalism displaced its more socially democratic Popular Front predecessor in the early 1950s, it simultaneously submerged the economic plight of blacks and delegitimized the kinds of mass mobilization likely to give voice to it. Martha Biondi, *To Stand and Fight: The Struggle for Civil Rights in Postwar New York City*, Harvard University Press, Cambridge, MA (2003), 265, 269–70; Anthony Chen, "The Hitlerian Rule of Quotas": Racial Conservatism and the Politics of Fair Employment Legislation in New York State, 1941–1945," *Journal of American History* (Mar. 2006).

20. Farmer and especially Young made a number of public statements in the months before the hearings on the 1964 Civil Rights Act advocating race conscious means to achieve equality. Farmer advocated proportional racial hiring as early as the winter of 1962–1963 but backtracked during the hearings; Young, whose 1963 call for an "American Marshall Plan" for blacks included "discrimination in favor of Negro youth," and a condemnation of the tokenism that color blindness produced, also retreated under pressure. While Bayard Rustin and A. Phillip Randolph privately supported many of Young's ideas—they would collaborate on the Freedom Budget three years later—they worried that any discussion of group rights or quotas would endanger the civil rights bill. Skrentny (1996), 3, 9, 22, 27, 32–34; Charles and Dona Hamilton, *The Dual Agenda: Race and Social Welfare Policies of Civil Rights Organizations*, Columbia University Press, New York (1997), 129–30, 132.

21. As the historian Tom Sugrue and others have shown, a redefinition of the relationship between the state, entitlement and citizenship was at the heart of the "second" New Deal, demonstrated most clearly in President Roosevelt's 1944 Second Bill of Rights, in which the president guaranteed a series of positive social rights to such things as "a useful and remunerative job," "adequate protection from the economic fears of old age, sickness, accident and unemployment," and "a decent home. See Tom Sugrue, "The Tangled Roots of Affirmative Action," *American Behavioral Scientist* (Apr. 1998); Franklin Roosevelt, "Message to Congress on the State of the Union," in *The Public Papers and Addresses of Franklin D. Roosevelt*, ed. Samuel L. Rosenman, Harper and Brothers, New York, (1950), 13:32–44. On FDR's 1944 address, see Cass Sunstein, *The Second Bill of Rights*, Basic Books, New York (2006).

22. See Sugrue (1998); Skrentny (1996); Moreno (1999). See also Joseph Robison, "Legislation against Bias—Possibilities and Limitations," *Journal of Intergroup Relations* (Winter 1959–1960), 40–41, who criticized the reliance of enforcement of fair housing laws on the initiative of

individual complainants and drew parallels between antibias laws and the 1935 National Labor Relations Act.

23. Lani Guinier, "From Racial Liberalism to Racial Literacy: *Brown v. Board of Education* and the Interest-Divergence Dilemma," *Journal of American History* (June 2004), 96. See also Michael Klarman, "How *Brown* Changed Race Relations: The Backlash Thesis," *Journal of American History* (June 1994).

24. Lynn Eley and Thomas Casstevens, *The Politics of Fair Housing Legislation: State and Local Case Studies*, Chandler Publishing, San Francisco (1968), 15, 381.

25. James Q. Wilson, *Negro Politics: The Search for Leadership*, Free Press, New York (1960), 198.

26. Alinsky, *IAF Annual Report* (1960), 6-8, Alinksy Papers.

27. These contrasting terms are from Moreno (1999), 137. Attorney Peter Marcuse makes a similar argument in "Benign Quotas Reexamined," *Journal of Intergroup Relations* (Spring 1962), 111-13.

28. See Peter Marcuse, "Benign Quotas Reexamined," *Journal of Intergroup Relations* (Spring 1962), 108-9, for a brief discussion of fair housing laws from the pro-quota point of view. See also Robison (Winter 1959-1960).

29. Shifting the burden of racial justice into the realm of legal discourse had been an effective spatial strategy for the NAACP and other advocacy groups throughout the twentieth century, but it did provide the opposition with the opportunity to deploy a rights-based discourse in response, particularly in the case of the private housing market. As the Chicago law professor Alfred Avins rather caustically put it at a 1963 symposium on "forced" housing, "the short of the matter is that anti-discrimination legislation in practice is a grave infringement on property rights," and as an act of social engineering "is as flagrant a violation of basic human rights and dignity as can be found in the worst totalitarian system ever devised." A number of lawyers, scholars, and real estate experts criticized nondiscrimination laws as in violation of the basic private property rights protected by the Fourteenth Amendment. For a fascinating series of articles on this subject, see Avins (1963).

30. Alinsky worried that such an aroused racial geopolitics might also undermine political support for public housing. As president of the Public Housing Association (PHA) during the explosive battle over Chicago's Carey Ordinance in the late 1940s, he was well aware of the galvanizing potential of nondiscrimination laws, especially when they gave the appearance of an alliance between blacks, the federal government, and white liberals. On the PHA, see Martin Meyerson and Edward Banfield, *Politics, Planning and the Public Interest: The Case of Public Housing in Chicago*, Free Press, New York (1955), 139. For a contemporary example of tactical doubts about integration, see Frances Fox Piven and Richard Cloward, "Desegregated Housing: Who Pays for the Reformers' Ideal?" *New Republic*, Dec. 17, 1966; "The Case against Desegregation," *Social Work* (Jan. 1967).

31. Alinsky, *IAF Annual Report* (1960), 9, Alinksy Papers.

32. Saul Alinsky, *Rules for Radicals: A Practical Primer for Realistic Radicals* (1971), 105-6. See also Alinsky, *Reveille for Radicals*, University of Chicago Press, Chicago (1946), 167; Alinsky, "From Citizen Apathy to Participation" (1957) (presented at the sixth annual Fall Conference of the Association of Community Councils of Chicago), 9.

33. Alinsky (1946), 40, 192.

34. See Alinsky (1946). On the role of social experience and learning in broadening interests and identities, see Alinsky, "The Morality of Power," (1961), 22-23, 27.

35. For an interesting discussion of how the Chicago suburb of Oak Park succeeded in redefining its community identity in the face of racial change—underwent a "normative reconstruction"—see Carole Goodwin, *The Oak Park Strategy: Community Control of Racial Change*, University of Chicago Press, Chicago, 1979, 127.

36. Abrams (1955), 338–39.

37. Alinsky, "Citizen Participation and Community Organization in Planning and Urban Renewal" (speech to Chicago chapter of the National Association of Housing and Redevelopment Officials, Jan. 29, 1962), published by IAF, 13.

38. See Saul Alinsky, "The Morality of Power" (address before the University of Notre Dame Symposium, June 28, 1961, 22–23, 27) for a sample of his thoughts on these subjects.

39. Karl Taeuber and Alma Taeuber, "The Negro as an Immigrant Group: Trends in Economic and Racial Segregation in Chicago," *Journal of American Sociology* (Jan. 1964).

40. Ben Joravsky, "Alinsky's Legacy," in *After Alinsky: Community Organizing in Illinois*, ed. Peg Knoepfle, Sangamon State University Press, Springfield, IL (1975), 7. See also *General Report*, pt. I, chap. VI, 86–89, Alinsky Papers, Special Collections, University of Illinois Chicago (hereafter Alinsky Papers).

41. "Letter to the Editor," *Chicago Sun-Times*, May 15, 1959; "Chicago Scrutinizes Racial Housing Quota," *Christian Science Monitor*, Mar. 8, 1960. Wilson argues that while the public reaction of black political, civic, and religious leaders was negative, private opinion on quotas was mixed. See Wilson (1960), 194–95.

42. These arguments are best exemplified in editorials published in the liberal Protestant *Christian Century* in 1959 and 1960, condemning Alinsky, the OSC, and the Chicago archdiocese for attempting to build "iron community curtains" on the South Side of Chicago. See "No Iron Community Curtain," Oct. 21, 1959; "Machiavelli in Modern Dress," Nov. 11, 1959; "New Power Structure Grows in Chicago," Nov. 18, 1959; as well as a number of letters to the editor. *Christian Century* continued this line of reasoning in 1961 and 1962, defending the University of Chicago in its battles with Alinsky's black Woodlawn Organization. Meyer's testimony in particular—written by Nicholas Von Hoffman, delivered by Fr. Egan, and widely publicized as an endorsement of the idea of quotas—sparked controversy. Liberal Catholics, such as Daniel Cantwell of Chicago's Catholic Interracial Council, tried to defuse Meyer's testimony by insisting that the cardinal "was not discussing or advocating particular strategies or techniques." On the other hand, many Chicago Catholics wrote to Meyer, the CIC, and other entities to voice their sense of betrayal at the church's integrationist position. Memo, n.d., box 8, folder 2, Daniel Cantwell Papers, Chicago Historical Society, Chicago.

43. Robert Schultz, "How Negro Home Quotas Would Work: Sociologist Alinsky Outlines Method of Combating Ghettoes," *Chicago Daily News*, May 7, 1959; Alinsky to editor of *Chicago Daily News*, May 26, 1959, published on May 29, 1959.

44. "What Chicagoans Say about Plan," *Chicago Daily News*, May 7, 1959.

45. *Catholic World*, Aug. 1960. See also David Finks, *The Radical Vision of Saul Alinsky*, Paulist Press, New York (1984), 126; Nicholas Von Hoffman, *Radical: A Portrait of Saul Alinsky*, Nation Books, New York (2010), 65. Alinsky found himself being pulled into highly publicized debates with such local luminaries as labor activist Sidney Lens, Edwin Berry of the Urban League, and Rev. Carl Fuqua of the Chicago NAACP. Churches and associations around the city held meetings and discussions on the "quota issue"; one Hyde Park congregation hosted a gathering of the Committee for a Sane Policy toward Saul Alinsky. See *Chicago Defender*, May 26, 1959; *Chicago Daily News*, June 11, 1959; *Hyde Park Herald*, Aug. 26, 1959. Berry and Fuqua tentatively

supported the idea, while Lens (who was white) condemned it as wrong, unworkable, and legally questionable. See "Open or Closed Cities—A Reply to Replies," *Christian Century*, June 7, 1961.

46. Alinsky to Tjerandsen, May 22, 1959, Emil Schwarzhaupt Foundation Papers, Special Collections, University of Chicago, Chicago (hereafter ESF Papers). See also Alinsky to Tjerandsen, June 1, 1959, ESF Papers; Alinsky to Adolph Hirsch, May 28, 1959, box 26, folder 6, ESF Papers, in which Alinsky claimed to have "recently stepped hard on a great many morally swollen and pompous toes in this town."

47. Schultz (1959); Alinsky to editor of *Chicago Daily News*, May 26, 1959, published on May 29, 1959.

48. Everingham and his organization We, the People were aided by the Chicago Police Department's Red Squad, which harassed IAF organizers and fed him information on Alinsky obtained from the Federal Bureau of Investigation. Information published by Everingham in pamphlets and press statements was in large part taken verbatim from informational index cards in the possession of the Red Squad, leading the author to the conclusion that anticommunist groups on the South Side were in frequent contact with the Chicago Police Department.

49. Von Hoffman (2010), 65.

50. "Super Civic Group Meets Resistance," *Chicago Tribune*, June 21, 1959; *Southtown Economist*, Aug. 19, 1959.

51. *Southtown Economist*, Aug. 16, 1959.

52. Eileen McMahon, *Which Parish Are You From? A Chicago Irish Community and Race Relations*, University Press of Kentucky, Lexington (1995), 144; John Fish, *The Edge of the Ghetto: A Study of Church Involvement in Community Organization*, Seabury Press, New York (1966), 16; *Southtown Economist*, Aug. 23 and Aug. 26, 1959.

53. *Southtown Economist*, Oct. 18, 1959.

54. *Southtown Economist*, Oct. 18, 1959.

55. *Chicago Daily News*, Oct. 15, 1959.

56. On the rally, see *Chicago's American*, Sept. 15, 1959; *Southtown Economist*, Sept. 16, 1959.

57. Alinsky to Tjerandsen, May 22, 1959, ESF Papers.

58. *Southtown Economist*, Oct. 4, 1959; Fish (1966), 11; *Chicago Daily News*, Oct. 15, 1959.

59. "No Iron Community Curtain!" editorial, *Christian Century*, Oct. 21, 1959.

60. Alinsky to IAF Board, "Memorandum on *Christian Century* Articles 10/59–3/60," June 1960, Alinsky Papers; Von Hoffman (2010), 143–44.

61. Von Hoffman (2010), 56–57.

62. Nicholas Von Hoffman to Richard Harmon, "Memorandum," May 9, 1961, Alinsky Papers.

63. The *Christian Century* attack heightened already significant fears by local Protestants of Catholic domination of the POSC. Before the IAF entered the community, institutional cooperation between Catholics and Protestants on the Southwest Side had been virtually nonexistent. The controversy over the archdiocese's opposition to the Hyde Park–Kenwood urban renewal plan, the participation of many local priests and lay Catholics in neighborhood racial violence, and the persistence of anti-Catholicism had generally rendered many of Chicago's liberal Protestants automatically skeptical of the church's racial politics. Kloetzli in particular warned Southwest Side ministers that Alinsky's "organization of organization" focus would allow Catholics to pack the POSC's membership rolls by enlisting the dozens of sodalities and groups affiliated with each parish—regardless of the extent to which these groups overlapped. To deal with these suspicions, Chambers and Villemas scrambled to ensure that the participatory structures of the

new group were strictly balanced, by effectively allowing each parish only one delegation. The problem with this approach, however, was that the organizers were unable to tap into the rich institutional webbing and social capital that the cultural infrastructure of urban Catholicism nurtured. This emphasis on religious balance, according to Von Hoffman, quickly led to "serious problems as far as depth and closeness of organizing goes" and served as "an abiding handicap in the building of the organization and the continuing of it." With only two (and later three) staff organizers, the POSC faced an uphill climb in its efforts to sink deep roots in the community. Von Hoffman to Alinsky, memo, June 21, 1963, 3, Alinsky Papers

64. *Southtown Economist*, Oct. 18, 1959.

65. *Southtown Economist*, Oct. 25, 1959; Fish (1966), 16.

66. *Southtown Economist*, Oct. 22 and Oct. 25, 1959.

67. See McMahon (1995), 140; Sanford Horwitt, *Let Them Call Me Rebel: Saul Alinsky, His Life and Legacy*, Alfred A. Knopf, New York (1989), 354–55; Fish (1966), 11; Chambers interview with Finks, Sept. 15, 1977, in Finks (1984), 128.

68. Unidentified observer quoted by Fish (1966), 11.

69. Robert Christ, "The Local Church in a Community Organization" (1962), 11; Egan quoted in Margery Frisbie, *An Alley in Chicago: The Ministry of a City Priest*, Sheed and Ward, Kansas City, MO (1991), chap. 12. Chambers quoted in Fish (1966), 13.

70. Von Hoffman to Richard Venecho of St. Mary of the Lake Seminary, May 2, 1961, folder 423, Alinsky Papers.

71. Interestingly, primary accounts of the congress differ on the weather; Msgr. Egan, who even in 1998 remembered it as "dramatic, magnificent," and one of the most inspiring days of his life, recalls October 24 as a beautiful day. See Frisbie (1991), chap. 12; Santow interview with Egan, in author's possession.

72. *Chicago Daily News*, Oct. 26, 1959; "New Power Structure Grows in Chicago," *Christian Century*, Nov. 18, 1959.

73. *Southtown Economist*, Oct. 25 and 28, 1959; Frisbie (1991), chap. 12; Stanley Koven, "The Day the Chicago Racists Lost," *Catholic World* (n.d.), Egan Papers.

74. Christ, quoted in Fish (1966), 12, 17–18.

75. *Southtown Economist*, Oct. 25, 1959.

76. Donald O'Toole, "Halting the Flight to Suburbia," *Commerce* (Apr. 1960).

77. Interestingly, the South Shore Commission, created around the same time as the OSC a few miles to the east, experienced an almost identical dilemma over the extent to which the inevitability of a growing black population demanded an integrationist response. The commission also vacillated on the issue and retained a language of the "good community" that allowed activists (black and white) to converse about group goals while avoiding racial issues—a practice that was occasionally useful but led to a wide variety of criticisms of the commission from both integrationists and exclusionists. See Harvey Molotch, *Managed Integration: The Dilemmas of Doing Good in the City*, University of California Press, Berkeley (1972), 72–74.

78. See *Southtown Economist*, Oct. 25 and 28, 1959; Fish (1966), 11–12.

79. Christ (1962), 7, box 38, Egan Papers. Rev. Douglas Still, executive secretary of the Social Welfare Department of the Church Federation, supported the OSC. During a 1962 speech to the Midwest Area World Mission Institute, Still congratulated the organization for making racial integration one of its main objectives and castigated Harold Fey and other critics for "ignorance of the facts [rather] than objective assessment of them." He also endorsed the use of quotas at approximately 20 percent to 25 percent, because beyond that ratio "white people move out because

they feel they cannot maintain and protect the cultural institutions of the community"—the schools, especially. See "Church Federation Aide Backs Quota Integration in Housing," *Chicago Sun-Times*, Aug. 11, 1962.

80. *Chicago Daily News*, Dec. 23 and 24, 1959, and Jan. 14, 1960; *Southtown Economist*, Jan. 6, 1960; Fish (1966), 19.

81. On Reed, see "Fate of Rev. Reed to Be Told Sunday," *Southtown Economist*, Jan. 6, 1960; *Chicago Daily News*, Dec. 23 and 24, 1959, and Jan. 14, 1960; Fish (1966), 19. According to Rev. Christ, redbaiting of local Protestant clergy also helped to unite ministers active in the OSC. See Christ (1962), 7.

82. Fish (1966), 19.

83. *Chicago Sun-Times*, Dec. 31, 1959. Reed remained at his church on the North Side, and thus had to resign his OSC post, since he no longer lived in the area. Interestingly, the battle to fill Reed's OSC vacancy was a close one: at a meeting in late April of the Executive Council, Walter Douglas (who was white) of the Marlboro Improvement Association narrowly defeated the Rev. Harold Burris of Auburn Park Methodist, the OSC's first black member organization. See *Southtown Economist*, Apr. 24, 1960.

84. O'Toole (1960), box 38, OSC file, Egan Papers.

85. *Southtown Economist*, Apr. 17 and 20, 1960; Fish (1966), 19; *Chicago Daily News*, Apr. 19, 1960; *Southtown Economist* Apr. 20 and 24, 1960.

86. *Southtown Economist*, Apr. 24, 1960.

87. *Southtown Economist*, May 8, 1960.

88. *Southtown Economist*, Apr. 27, 1960.

89. *Southtown Economist*, May 8, 1960.

90. First and foremost, the loan program was intended to help local parishes keep young families, by satisfying their desires for homeownership locally. See Office of Urban Affairs of Archdiocese of Chicago, "Program and Accomplishments of OSC," Apr. 1961, box 38, OSC file, Egan Papers.

91. Von Hoffman to Alinsky, June 5, 1962, file 307, Alinsky Papers. On the Home Loan Program, see "Panic Sales of Homes at End Here," *Southtown Economist*, Jan. 27, 1960, 1; Donald O'Toole, "Remarks on the OSC," Feb. 4, 1960, Egan Papers; *Southtown Economist*, Oct. 31, 1962; "OSC Home Loans Marks Fourth Year," Dec. 25, 1963, 1; "Hail OSC Home Loan Program," Jan. 19, 1964; "Program and Accomplishments of OSC," Apr. 1961, box 38, OSC file, Egan Papers; "OSC Progress Report 1962," 2, box 38, OSC file, Egan Papers; Barry Menuez, "Notes for Address to Clergy," Apr. 1, 1963, 4, box 38, OSC file, Egan Papers; "Committee Report of OSC 1962," folder 307, Alinsky Papers.

92. Barry Menuez, *Church in Metropolis* (Summer 1965), 31; Egan (1965), 9; Von Hoffman to Alinsky, memo, June 5, 1962, file 307, Alinsky Papers; Charles and Bonnie Remsberg, "In the Vanishing Slums of Chicago," *Catholic Digest* (July 1963); "Program and Accomplishments of OSC" (1961); "OSC Progress Report" (1962); "Committee Report of OSC" (1962), file 307, Alinsky Papers; Menuez (1963); "OSC Reports Rise in Remodeling," *Southtown Economist*, Aug. 15, 1962, 1.

93. *Southtown Economist*, Apr. 24, 1960; M. W. Newman, "OSC's War on Blockbusters and Panic Peddlers," *Chicago Daily News*, Sept. 2, 1960; Michael Bukacek, WLAIA, address to the City Club Forum, July 18, 1960, box 38, OSC file, Egan Papers. In another attempt to head off some of the tactics used by blockbusters on the Southwest Side, the OSC Welfare and Safety committee used its growing relationship with the Chicago Police Department to have officers

removed from outside the homes of new black residents, because blockbusters had been "using the presence of armed policemen as a weapon to stir fear and distrust in running down the value of a neighborhood." *Southtown Economist*, Apr. 24, 1960.

94. Newman (1960); *Southtown Economist*, Oct. 26, 1960. The WCIA's liberal position on race (as well as its growing black membership) became evident in the mid-1960s, when the group became a member of the Coordinating Council of Community Organizations (CCCO), the local federation which helped to spearhead the Chicago fair housing campaigns of the Rev. Martin Luther King Jr. and his Southern Christian Leadership Conference. See James Ralph, *Northern Protest: Martin Luther King Jr. and the Civil Rights Movement*, Harvard University Press, Cambridge, MA (1993), 95.

95. Bukacek to the City Club Forum (1960), and "Testimony of Egan," box 38, OSC file, Egan Papers. The Chicago Building Department was notorious for being understaffed, corrupt, and inefficient—see Mike Royko, *Boss: Richard J. Daley of Chicago*, E. P. Dutton, New York (1971), 101.

96. By 1962 the OSC was processing an average of thirty-five complaints a month, many of which dealt with illegal conversions. "OSC Progress Report 1962"; Menuez (1963); *Southtown Economist*, Oct. 28, 1964; Fish (1966), 32. On the efforts to remove Sold By signs, see "Committee Report of OSC 1962," file 307, Alinsky Papers.

97. *Southtown Economist*, Oct. 26, 1960; Newman (1960). The Gresham Community Council was organized by members of Christ's Seventh Presbyterian church, which the building was near. Finks (1984), 129.

98. On November 10, 1962, three members of the Spector Real Estate Company were found guilty of fraud and embezzlement, had their licenses revoked, and were sentenced to prison. The OSC also succeeded in getting a member of the Dobbins Real Estate Company convicted and fined for door-to-door blockbusting harassment. See "Two Get Fraud Sentences," *Southtown Economist*, Aug. 7, 1960, 1; "OSC Progress Report 1962," box 38, OSC file, Egan Papers; "Blockbuster Fined," *Southtown Economist*, July 29, 1962, 1; "Plan to Spur Prosecution of 'Block Busters,'" *Chicago Sun-Times*, July 27, 1962.

99. Newman (1960); *Southtown Economist*, Oct. 26, 1960; Fish (1966), 21; Bukacek to City Club Forum (1960).

100. Michael Bukacek, chair of the Real Estate Committee, received phone death threats in 1960, during the initial organizing push for the Code. On the Code of Ethics, see "Blockbusting Is Prime Target of OSC Committee," *Southtown Economist*, Mar. 20, 1960, 1; "OSC Will Continue 'War' on Blockbuster Tactics," *Southtown Economist*, July 13, 1960, 1; "Southwest Side Gets Tough in War on Panic Peddlers," *Chicago Daily News*, Sept. 2, 1960; "OSC Moves to Combat Speculators," *Southtown Economist*, Apr. 19, 1964; "OSC Indexes Prices to Stabilize Home Sales," *Human Relations News of Chicago* (May 1964); Patrick Stanton, "OSC Progress Detailed for 5 Years," *Southtown Economist*, Oct. 28, 1964. See also Fish (1966), 32.

101. Jack Trahey later (in 1963) served as the chair of the OSC's Real Estate Practices Committee—one of the most important positions in the organization. See *Southtown Economist*, Jan. 13, 1963.

102. M. W. Newman, *Chicago Daily News*, Sept. 1–3, 1960.

103. *Southtown Economist*, Oct. 26, 1960; "Urban Problems OSC Meet Topic," *Chicago Defender*, Oct. 12, 1960; Fish (1966), 22. WTTW broadcast the hearings on television, which took place on four consecutive Wednesday evenings.

104. *Southtown Economist*, Oct. 26, 1960; "Testimony of Egan," box 38, OSC file, Egan Papers.

105. *Southtown Economist*, Oct. 26, 1960; "Daily Press to Air Neighborhood Faults on Video," *Chicago Defender*, Nov. 2, 1960; *Midwest Magazine*, Dec. 4, 1960; Alinsky, *IAF Annual Report* (1960), 10, Alinksy Papers; Fish (1966), 21.

106. Von Hoffman to Richard Vanecho, of St. Mary of the Lake Seminary, May 2, 1961, file 423, Alinsky Papers; "Agenda: Industrial Areas Foundation Meeting of Dec. 14th, 1961," 7, George Shuster Papers, box 11a, "miscellaneous IAF" folder, Special Collections, University of Notre Dame, Notre Dame, IN.

Chapter Five

1. "Quit Southwest Side Group in Open Occupancy Row," Mar. 3, 1961, 1, "OSC Rows over Issue," *Southtown Economist*, Mar. 19, 1961, 1; League of Women Voters of Chicago, "Neighborhood Organizations," Oct. 1961, 9, box 38, OSC file, Msgr. John Egan Papers (hereafter Egan Papers), Special Collections, University of Notre Dame, Notre Dame, IN; John Fish, *The Edge of the Ghetto: A Study of Church Involvement in Community Organization*, Seabury Press, New York (1966), 23; Memorandum for File, Aug. 25, 1962, Egan Papers; Eileen McMahon, *Which Parish Are You From? A Chicago Irish Community and Race Relations*, University Press of Kentucky, Lexington (1995), 154. The legislation, which would have given all citizens the legal right to buy, sell, or rent housing in any neighborhood or area of their choice, was later voted down by the Illinois General Assembly. See Rose Helper, *Racial Policies and Practices of Real Estate Brokers*, University of Minnesota Press, Minneapolis (1969), 278.

2. M. David Finks interview with Chambers, Sept. 15, 1977, quoted in Finks, *The Radical Vision of Saul Alinsky*, Paulist Press, New York (1984).

3. On the MPPO, see "Admit New Morgan Park Group at June OSC Meet," *Chicago Defender*, June 26, 1961. The union activist, Jesse Vaughn, was treasurer of MPPO.

4. Chambers and Von Hoffman to Egan, "Police Activity in Connection with Race Violence on the Southwest Side," box 35, Egan Papers; *Southtown Economist*, Aug. 30, 1961; Memorandum for File, Aug. 25, 1962, Egan Papers.

5. Statement by John McDermott, Executive Director, Catholic Interracial Council, to Public Hearing #3, OSC, Sept. 14, 1961, Alinsky Papers, Special Collections, University of Illinois Chicago (hereafter Alinsky Papers); "Catholic Council Urges Fair Housing Legislation," *Chicago Defender*, Sept. 19, 1961.

6. Statement of Chicago Urban League at Public Hearing of OSC, Sept. 18, 1961, box 38, OSC file, Egan Papers.

7. Nicholas Von Hoffman, *Radical: A Portrait of Saul Alinsky*, Nation Books, New York (2010), 151.

8. The sociologist Morton Grodzins, in his seminal 1958 essay "The Metropolitan Area as a Racial Problem," advocated a combination of "consciously contrived" experiments with controlled integration at the local level—quotas—and rigorous fair housing laws throughout the metropolitan area. Unless the suburbs were opened, the local benefits of quotas would do nothing but cause problems elsewhere in the city. See also Grodzins, *The Metropolitan Area as a Racial Problem*, University of Pittsburgh Press, Pittsburgh, PA (1958), 16–18. Anthony Downs later made a similar argument, which included advocacy of quotas. See Downs's Sept. 1, 1970, Senate testimony, *Senate Select Committee on Equal Educational Opportunity, Part 5: De Fact Segregation and Housing Discrimination*, 2966.

9. For a discussion of race, geography and power, see David Delaney, *Race, Place and the Law: 1836–1948*, University of Texas Press, Austin (1998), 6–8, 13–14; Richard Ford, "The Boundaries of Race: Political Geography in Legal Analysis," *Harvard Law Review* 107 (1994); Richard Ford, "Urban Space and the Color Line: The Consequences of Demarcation and Disorientation in the Postmodern Metropolis," *Harvard Blackletter* 117 (1992). On the law, space, and social relations more generally, see Nicholas Blomley, *Law, Space, and Geographies of Power*, Guilford, London (1994); Allan Pred, *Making Histories and Constructing Human Geographies: The Local Transformation of Practice, Power Relations, and Consciousness*, Westview Press, Boulder, CO (1990); Jennifer Wolch and Michael Dear, eds., *The Power of Geography: How Territory Shapes Social Life*, Unwin and Hyman, Boston (1989).

10. Among many other groups, member delegations included the Southtown Little and Pony Leagues, the Whistler PTA, the Southtown Hebrew Congregation, and the Toboggan Club—providing a sense of the diverse social and cultural roles played by OSC organizations. See *OSC Proposals for Planning and Renewal*, Mar. 1962, box 38, Egan Papers.

11. "Congress 'Duel' Looms," *Southtown Economist*, Nov. 1, 1961, 1; "OSC Election Upset," *Southtown Economist*, Nov. 8, 1961, 1, 6; Fish (1966), 23; Rev. Gordon Irvine, "Analysis of the Roll Call Vote on a Constitutional Change at the Third Annual Congress of the OSC" (May 1963), file 308, Alinsky Papers.

12. Fish (1966), 25; Irvine (May 1963), 1–4, 7; *Southtown Economist*, Nov. 8, 1961, 6.

13. The largest delegations from a black group were the Greenview Park Community Council and the Holy Name of Mary (a Catholic group), with eight members each. The other black groups included three churches (Auburn Park Methodist Church, the first integrated member organization in the OSC, Morgan Park Assembly Church, and Beth Eden Baptist), one parent-teacher association (the Bates PTA), and three neighborhood groups (Morgan Park Civic League, Winneconna Lakes Area Improvement Association, and the MPPO). The two largest integrated groups (25 percent of either race) were the Wentworth PTA and the West Chatham Improvement Association. Irvine (1963), 8.

14. Parent-teacher associations voted overwhelmingly against the amendment, 172–36, while service groups and agencies rejected the measure by a vote of 77–28, with nine abstentions. The biggest Knights of Columbus chapter, the Perez Council Knights, was also a large no bloc. Irvine (1963), 8.

15. The play, *How to Use Facts to Change Your Husband's Mind*, was written by Patrick Stanton of the Publicity and Home Buyers Committee, Alinsky Papers; *Southtown Economist*, Oct. 24, 1962.

16. "The Community That Lifted Itself by Its Own Bootstraps," *Midwest Magazine*, Dec. 4, 1960; Newman, *Chicago Daily News*, Sept. 3, 1960; *Southtown Economist*, Aug. 30, 1961, 1; Fr. John Egan, "The OSC—An Evaluation" (1965), 8, Egan Papers; "Program and Accomplishments of OSC," Apr. 1961, box 38 OSC file, Egan Papers; "OSC Progress Report" (1962), box 38, OSC file, Egan Papers; "Report of the Law Enforcement and Safety Committee," 1962, file 307, Alinsky Papers; "Negroes Branch Out—Mostly in Peace," *Chicago Daily News*, July 21, 1962; Barry Menuez, "Notes for Address to Clergy," Apr. 1, 1963, box 38, OSC file, Egan Papers; Nicholas Von Hoffman to Saul Alinsky, memo, June 21, 1963, Alinsky Papers; "S. West Unit, Cops Map Fight on Area Crime," *Chicago Defender*, Apr. 4, 1964; "Cops Pledge to Halt Summer Race Violence," *Chicago Defender*, May 20, 1964; Chambers and Von Hoffman, "Police Activity in Connection with Race Violence on the Southwest Side," memo to Fr. John Egan, box 35, Egan Papers.

17. "Negroes Branch Out—Mostly in Peace" (1962); "OSC Progress Detailed for 5 Years," *Southtown Economist*, Oct. 28, 1964. In November 1960 Alinsky confidently informed the IAF board that the Southwest Side "is a very changed area today as compared to over against two years ago. Most of the organized forms of resistance to Negroes have been smashed, and in its place have been planted constructive and sound programs calculated to help members of both races." Alinsky, *IAF Annual Report* (1960), 10, Alinsky Papers.

18. Egan, "Program and Accomplishments of OSC" (Apr. 1961); Menuez (1963), 5; "OSC" (Oct. 1968).

19. Menuez (1963), 5; Egan (1965), 1; *Southtown Economist*, Nov. 4, 1965; *Chicago Tribune*, Nov. 5, 1965.

20. "Auburn Park Residents Refuse to Panic Over Racial Change," *Chicago Daily News*, July 10, 1965.

21. Egan (Apr. 1961), 2–3, and "OSC Progress Report" (1962), 2, box 38, OSC file, Egan Papers.

22. Community Relations Committee report (1962), file 307, Alinsky Papers; Menuez (Summer 1965), 31.

23. "S.W. Community Unit Launches Intensive Plan for Progress," *Chicago Defender*, May 3, 1965.

24. McMahon (1995), 151, 160–62; Margery Frisbie, *An Alley in Chicago: The Ministry of a City Priest*, Sheed and Ward, Kansas City, MO (1991), chap. 12.

25. Interreligious Council on Urban Affairs, "Community Organization Notebook," Oct. 1968, box 10021.10, Human Relations and Ecumenism folder, Archives of the Archdiocese of Chicago (hereafter AAC); Sanford Horwitt, *Let Them Call Me Rebel: Saul Alinsky, His Life and Legacy*, Alfred A. Knopf, New York (1989), 437.

26. Undated MPPO press release, box 35, Egan Papers; "'Look In' Campaign Brings Mixed Results," *Chicago Defender*, July 16, 1963.

27. "Boycott Morgan Park Bank," *Chicago Defender*, June 17, 1964; "Morgan Park Bank Boycott Gets Results," *Chicago Defender*, June 30, 1964.

28. Arnold Hirsch, "The Cook County Democratic Organization and the Dilemma of Race, 1931–1987," in *Snowbelt Cities: Metropolitan Politics in the Northeast and Midwest since World War II*, ed. Richard Bernard, Indiana University Press, Bloomington (1990), 80; Roger Biles, *Richard J. Daley: Politics, Race, and the Governing of Chicago*, Northern Illinois University Press, DeKalb (1995), 92–93; Leon Despres, *Challenging the Daley Machine*, Northwestern University Press, Evanston, IL (2005), 92–95.

29. On the Willis controversy, see chapter 7.

30. On Murray, see Ben Joravsky and Eduardo Camacho, *Race and Politics in Chicago*, Community Renewal Society, Chicago (1987), 33; James Ralph, *Northern Protest: Martin Luther King Jr. and the Civil Rights Movement*, Harvard University Press, Cambridge, MA (1993), 116, 279n68; *Southwest News-Herald*, Jan. 5, 1967, 1, 10–11.

31. "OSC Slates Race Talk," *Chicago Defender*, July 24, 1963; "Priest Rebukes Biased Southwest Group for Fostering Segregation," *Chicago Defender*, Mar. 14, 1963.

32. At public hearings on the bills in August, the president of the CREB insisted that the proposed statute, by restricting the right of choice in property sale or occupancy, served as a "restriction on human rights." The bill, passed on September 1, 1963, forbid real estate agents from discriminating on the basis of race, color, religion, national origin, or ancestry and made panic peddling illegal. Importantly, however, it did not restrain property owners from discrimination. On the law, see "The Realtor: Real Estate Dealer, Plus," *Chicago Daily News*, May 17,

1963; *Chicago Tribune*, July 5, 1963; Mike Royko, *Boss: Richard J. Daley of Chicago*, E. P. Dutton, New York (1971), 142; Thomas Landye and James Vanecko, "The Politics of Open Housing in Illinois," in *The Politics of Fair Housing Legislation: State and Local Case Studies*, ed. Lynn Eley and Thomas Casstevens, Chandler Publishing, San Francisco (1968), 86–91; Biles (1995), 95; Helper (1969), 278–79.

33. "Open Occupancy Is Wrong," *Southwest News-Herald*, May 2, 1963, 2, and Aug. 1, 1963, 2; Ralph (1993), 115, 128. See *Southtown Economist*, Sept. 22, 1963, on the OSC's decision to support both Murray and the new law.

34. See "An Introduction to POCC," *Chicagoland's Real Estate Advertiser*, Feb. 7, 1964, 10; "Realtors Hire Lawyers to Fight City Housing Law," *Chicago Daily News*, Sept. 19, 1963; "Kerner Defends Open Occupancy," *Chicago Sun-Times*, June 14, 1964; "Housing Referendum Dead— NAREB Will Not Go to Court," *Chicagoland's Real Estate Advertiser*, Sept. 1, 1964; Ralph (1993), 154; Rose Helper, *Racial Policies and Practices of Real Estate Brokers*, University of Minnesota Press, Minneapolis (1969), 278–80.

35. By 1966, more than fifty states and cities had adopted fair housing measures—though, importantly, none had been approved by public referendum. Indeed, places as varied as Berkeley, Akron, Tacoma, and the State of California had defeated such statutes. See Eley and Casstevens (1968); on California, see Raymond Wolfinger and Fred Greenstein, "The Repeal of Fair Housing in California: An Analysis of Referendum Voting," *American Political Science Review* (Sept. 1968).

36. Detroit passed a similar law, by a comparable margin. John Denton's book *American Apartheid* provides the most definitive account of the National Association of Real Estate Boards' legal and political strategy with regard to fair housing legislation. On the 1964 California referendum—which passed by a vote of nearly 2–1 and prevented open-occupancy laws from being passed in the future, in additional to voiding the 1963 Rumford Act—see Thomas Casstevens, *Politics, Housing and Race Relations: California's Rumford Act and Proposition 14*, University of California Press, Berkeley (1967); Raymond Wolfinger and Fred Greenstein, "The Repeal of Fair Housing in California: An Analysis of Referendum Voting," *American Political Science Review* (Sept. 1968); Eley and Casstevens (1968); "Anti-Rights Plan Winning on Coast," *New York Times*, Nov. 4, 1964, 34; "Coast Rights Chiefs Map Plan to Void Fair Housing Setback," *New York Times*, Nov. 5, 1964, 18; "Proposition 14's Chances of Survival in the Courts," *New York Times*, Nov. 6, 1964; Helper (1969), 281–82; John H. Denton, *Race and Property*, University of California Press, Berkeley (1964); Stephen Meyer, *As Long as They Don't Move Next Door: Segregation and Racial Conflict in American Neighborhoods*, Rowman and Littlefield, Lanham, MD (2000). For a comparison of the Detroit and California referenda, see Harlan Hahn, "Northern Referenda on Fair Housing: The Response of White Voters," *Western Political Quarterly* (Sept. 1968), 483–95. In 1966 the California Supreme Court ruled that the law was unconstitutional, and the US Supreme Court concurred the following year. Detroit's Home Owners Ordinance was later invalidated as well. The 1963 Berkeley referendum, like the statewide one, actually overturned a fair housing ordinance passed previously by the City Council. On Berkeley, see *New York Times*, Apr. 4, 1963, 25.

37. "Organization Chart: Property Owners' Coordinating Committee," Oct. 28, 1964, box 47, Egan Papers; Helper (1969), 283; "An Introduction to the POCC," *Chicagoland's Real Estate Advertiser*, Feb. 7, 1964, 10; *Southtown Economist*, Apr. 8, 1964; *Chicago Defender*, Apr. 11–17, 1964; "Housing Referendum Dead" (1964). On the POCC and the CREB, see Ralph (1993), 154; Eley and Casstevens (1968).

38. For some examples of this language of race and property from the early 1960s—which was ubiquitous and offers fascinating insights into how white privilege was deeply imbricated into metropolitan geography—see Denton (1964); Alfred Avins, ed., *Open Occupancy vs. Forced Housing under the Fourteenth Amendment: A Symposium on Anti-Discrimination Legislation, Freedom of Choice, and Property Rights in Housing*, Bookmailer, New York (1963). The arguments of the POCC and the CREB reflected those of the National Association of Real Estate Boards (NAREB), as laid out in its nationally distributed pamphlet *Property Owners' Bill of Rights* (June 1963). The NAREB made the same arguments in its successful opposition to President Johnson's fair housing in 1966—see box 164, National Committee against Discrimination in Housing Papers (hereafter NCADH Papers), Amistad Research Center, Special Collections, Tulane University Library, New Orleans. See also Helper (1969), 278, 283–84; Ralph (1993), 187; Ellen Frankel Paul and Howard Dickman, eds., *Liberty, Property, and the Foundations of the American Constitution*, State University of New York Press, Albany (1989). For a contemporary critique of NAREB's arguments on property law, see Joseph Robison, "Ghettos, Property Rights and Myths," *Frontier* (June 1964).

39. Chicago Commission on Human Relations, *Report of Complaints Received* (Apr. 1967); Eley and Casstevens (1968), 93; Joravsky and Camacho (1987); Despres (2005), 94–95; Amanda Seligman, *Block by Block: Neighborhoods and Public Policy on Chicago's West Side*, University of Chicago Press, Chicago (2005), 176–78.

40. James Q. Wilson, *Negro Politics: The Search for Leadership*, Free Press, New York (1960), 150; William Collins, "The Housing Market Impact of State-Level Anti-Discrimination Laws, 1960–1970," *Journal of Urban Economics* 55, 534–64; Thomas Landye and James Vanecko, "The Politics of Open Housing in Chicago and Illinois," in Eley and Casstevens (1968), 86–90. On the Chicago statute, its enforcement, and the political battles before and after, see Joravsky and Camacho (1987), 33; Ralph (1993), 102, 209, 279n68; Eley and Casstevens (1968); Helper (1969); NCADH, *Trends in Housing* (May–June 1961). As of 1963, the typical complainant to antidiscrimination agencies was black and relatively well educated. See National Committee against Discrimination in Housing, *Trends in Housing* (Sept.–Oct. 1963), 3. For a discussion of enforcement problems by an opponent of fair housing laws and the argument that "the average Negro needs a house, not a lawsuit," see Alfred Avins, "Anti-Discrimination Legislation in Housing: A Denial of Freedom of Choice," and John Herbert Tovey, "Discrimination, Anti-Discrimination Legislation, and Freedom of Choice in Housing: A Dialogue," in Avins (1963).

41. "Open War against Blockbusters," *Chicago Defender*, Mar. 7, 1964.

42. "OSC Indexes Prices to Stabilize Home Sales," *Human Relations News of Chicago* (May 1964); "Southwest Group in Blockbusting Drive," *Chicago Defender*, May 4, 1964; Patrick Stanton, "OSC Progress Detailed for 5 Years," *Southtown Economist*, Oct. 28, 1964. See also Fish (1966), 32; "OSC Moves to Combat Speculators," *Southtown Economist*, Apr. 19, 1964; "Auburn Park Residents Refuse to Panic over Racial Change," *Chicago Daily News*, July 10, 1965; Menuez (Summer 1965), 30.

43. See Eley and Casstevens (1968). Resolution, Beverly Hills–Morgan Park Council on Human Relations (n.d.), file 307, Alinsky Papers; MPPO resolution to OSC Congress Regarding Race Relations (n.d.), file 307, Alinsky Papers; Fish (1966), 27. On the 1966 order, see "The Back Door to Open Housing," *Chicago Tribune*, July 15, 1966; "Kerner Receives Praise on Open Occupancy Stand," *Chicago Defender*, July 18, 1966.

44. *Southwest News-Herald*, Aug. 4, 1966, 1, 10. Ralph defines the Southwest Side as Chicago Lawn, Gage Park, Ashburn, Auburn-Gresham, Archer Heights, Clearing, Garfield Ridge, West

Elsdon, Brighton Park, and West Lawn, as well as the diminishing white neighborhoods in the western half of West Englewood. Aside from Auburn-Gresham and parts of Englewood, much of this territory was outside the boundaries of the OSC, although most of these neighborhoods were demographically, economically and culturally similar—made up of largely lower middle-class Catholic homeowners, many of whom had left neighborhoods closer to downtown as the ghetto expanded. Most of these neighborhoods also shared common political boundaries—the Eighteenth Ward encompassed most of the area. On the marches, see Ralph (1993); Alan Anderson and George Pickering, *Confronting the Color Line: The Broken Promise of the Chicago Rights Movement in Chicago*, University of Georgia Press, Athens (1986); David Garrow, ed., *Chicago 1966: Open Housing Marches, Summit Negotiations, and Operation Breadbasket*, Carlson Publishing, Brooklyn, NY (1989); Gene Marine, "'I've Got Nothing against the Colored, Understand,'" *Ramparts* (Nov. 1966); Lee Rainwater, "Making the Good Life: Working-Class Family and Life-Styles," in *Blue-Collar Workers: A Symposium on Middle America*, ed. Sar Levitan, McGraw-Hill, New York (1971), 204–29.

45. Donald Bogue and Richard McKinlay, "Militancy for and against Civil Rights and Integration in Chicago: Summer 1967" (Interuniversity Social Research Committee, Report #1), Community and Family Study Center, Chicago (1967), 49–50; Maurice Moore, *A Study of Integrated Living in Chicago*, University of Chicago Press, Chicago (1968); McMahon (1995), 170; Ralph (1993), 221; Joravsky and Camacho (1987), 42.

46. Illinois didn't enact a fair housing law until two years after the 1968 passage of a federal law. A new Illinois constitution, ratified in 1970, built into the state's laws new protections against racial discrimination in housing and employment. Ben Joravsky, *Chicago* (Aug. 1986), 99; Joravsky and Camacho (1987), 33, 37, 42; *Human Relations News of Chicago* (Sept. 1963); "Murray Defends Law," *Southtown Economist*, Sept. 15 and 22, 1963. On Eighteenth Ward politics, see David Freeman, *Chicago Politics Ward by Ward*, Indiana University Press, Bloomington (1988), 124–26; *Southwest News-Herald*, Mar. 16, 1967, 1; Ralph (1993), 279n69. On political backlash, see Ralph (1993), 116, 222; Donald Bogue and Richard McKinlay, *Militancy for and against Civil Rights and Integration in Chicago: Summer 1967* (Research Report, Interuniversity Social Research Committee—Chicago Metropolitan Area, Report No. 1), University of Chicago Press (Aug. 1967), 4, 13, 16, 47–50; Seligman (2005), 180.

47. "OSC Progress Detailed for 5 Years," *Southtown Economist*, Oct. 28, 1964.

48. An October 1963 bombing of a black-owned home in the 8900 block of South Parnell was part of a six-month wave of racial attacks in the area. A brawl following a high school basketball game in January 1964 prompted a special meeting of the OSC's Law Enforcement Committee to "suppress the rumors that run rampant through the community after an incident of this type" and to demand that the police keep the group—and thus the public—informed about the details of such crises. Nonetheless, racial change and the violence that occasionally accompanied it continued. "Blast Won't Halt Move, Says Negro," *Daily News*, Oct. 24, 1963; "OSC Acts to Avert Bias Acts," *Southtown Economist*, Jan. 29, 1964; "OSC Acts in School Game Fight," *Southtown Economist*, Jan. 26, 1964.

49. For examples of reporting on crime, see "OSC Says Crime Down," Aug. 30, 1961, 1; "Crime Up in Gresham," May 20, 1962, 1; "Crime Up in Gresham," Apr. 22, 1962, 1; "Gresham Crime Is Up," Aug. 22, 1962, 1; "Demand More Police," June 12, 1963, 1; "Gresham Crime Up," *Southtown Economist*, Aug. 18, 1963, 1.

50. McMahon (1995), 165–68.

51. "Teen Gang Activities Boil in Southwest Area," *Chicago Defender*, Feb. 23, 1967.

52. For data on racial transition on the Southwest Side in the 1960s, see McMahon (1995); *Chicago Community Fact Book: 1970 and 1980*; Chicago Urban League, "Where Blacks Live: Race and Residence in Chicago in the 1970s" (Spring 1978); *Chicago Sun-Times*, Jan. 13, 1967, 4; Ralph (1993), 278n65; Chicago Community Inventory, *Local Community Fact Book: Chicago, 1960*, University of Chicago Press, Chicago (1963); Hospital Planning Council for Metropolitan Chicago, *Chicago Regional Hospital Study* (Dec. 1966); Roger Fox and Deborah Haines, *Black Homeowners in Transition Areas*, Chicago Urban League, Chicago (1981); Harvey Molotch, *Managed Integration: Dilemmas of Doing Good in the City*, University of California Press, Berkeley (1972), 136–37, 144; McMahon (1995), 178–80. It should be noted also that Washington Heights and West Englewood—communities generally considered to be within the OSC's boundaries—also underwent very rapid racial transition from 1960 to 1966, although neither area changed as quickly as did Auburn-Gresham (which had a smaller black population than either in 1960).

53. In 1970 Auburn-Gresham and Washington Heights had median family incomes that were above the city average, although these neighborhoods' black residents tended to be poorer than their white neighbors. Roger Fox and Jerry Szatan, "The Current Economic Status of Chicago's Black Community: A Mid-1970s Overview Report," Chicago Urban League Research and Planning Department, Chicago (1977), 12–17; Inter-Religious Council on Urban Affairs (Oct. 1968); *Chicago Community Fact Book* (1970). The IRCUA was run by Msgr. John Egan.

54. Fish's useful discussion of the limitations and accomplishments of the OSC, with which I generally agree, are found in Fish (1966), 132–34.

55. Egan (1965); Menuez (1963), 4; Von Hoffman to Alinsky, June 21, 1963, Alinsky Papers.

56. *Southtown Economist*, Oct. 31, 1962. In 1962, St. Sabina's contributed $15,000 to OSC—by far the largest contribution. Christ the King gave $2,500, and Molloy's St. Leo's gave $1,275. Box 56, Office of Urban Affairs Correspondence folder, Egan Papers.

57. Von Hoffman to Alinsky, memo, June 21, 1963, Alinsky Papers; McMahon (1995), 178. On O'Toole's perspective, see Horwitt (1989), 433–34.

58. In 1960 Meyer convened a clergy conference, "The Catholic Church and the Negro in the Archdiocese of Chicago," at which the cardinal gave a well-publicized speech advocating integration, condemning parish priests for a lack of moral leadership, and endorsing the policies of the OSC. Meyer chided local priests who participated in "anti-Negro sentiment" and the "anti-Negro activities of any group in his community," declaring that "in this urgent matter of understanding between the races . . . it is the responsibility of the priest to form public opinion rather than to follow it." In conclusion, Meyer commended the OSC as a model for parish-level interracialism. Meyer, "The Mantle of Leadership," in *The Catholic Church and the Negro in the Archdiocese of Chicago*, Archdiocese of Chicago, Chicago (1960); "Discrimination and the Christian Conscience (1958)," in *Pastoral Letters of the American Hierarchy*, ed. Hugh Nolan, Our Sunday Visitor, Huntington, IN (1971). See also John McGreevy, *Parish Boundaries: The Catholic Encounter with Race in the 20th Century Urban North*, University of Chicago Press, Chicago (1996), 180. Meyer also issued a directive to Chicago priests early in 1961 to eliminate racial discrimination in Catholic institutions—particularly schools. See "Notes from COPE AFL-CIO," Feb. 15, 1961, box 43781.03, Cantwell—Recent Correspondence folder, Meyer Papers (hereafter Meyer Papers), Archives of the Archdiocese of Chicago.

59. Chambers to Egan, Oct. 18, 1962, and Meyer to All Local Pastors, Mar. 3, 1961, in box 43786.02, CBC General Correspondence, Southwest Community Organization folder, Meyer Papers. Msgr. Egan worked hard to keep Meyer's interest in the OSC. Priests that were active in the group "have not received the wholehearted support of the clergy in the OSC area," Egan

informed him, "and this failure to cooperate . . . only tends to weaken the organization's accomplishment of its excellent purpose and goals." Egan to Meyer, Apr. 12, 1964, Meyer Papers.

60. See Burke, "Let's Do Some Thinking for a Change," box 11, folder 4, Daniel Cantwell Papers, and "letters in support of Burke," Cantwell Papers, box 11, Chicago Historical Society (CHS); *Chicago Sun-Times*, Jan. 22, 1967, 3; *National Catholic Reporter*, Feb. 1, 1967, 3; McGreevy (1996), 189–92; Ralph (1993), 127–28, 147, 208; Charles Dahm, *Power and Authority in the Catholic Church: Cardinal Cody in Chicago*, University of Notre Dame Press, South Bend, IN (1981); William Osborne, *The Segregated Covenant: Race Relations and American Catholics*, Herder and Herder, New York (1967).

61. Fish found that the three most significant differences between supporters and critics of OSC in 1965 (the year of the survey) were attitudes toward racially changing neighborhoods, the Freedom Movement (whether it moving "too fast"), and the proper social role of religion. Fewer than 10 percent of those who identified themselves as anti-OSC wanted to live in integrated neighborhoods, compared to 34 percent of those who were pro-OSC—not a very high percentage in either case. A majority of both groups believed that the civil rights movement was moving too fast—most likely comparable to national trends, by 1965. See Fish (1966), 110–19. As McGreevy shows, the reforms of Vatican II also exacerbated these divisions. See McGreevy (1996), 182, 207.

62. Fish found that participation in OSC was generally seen as something that "social action types" did; their actions were tolerated more than endorsed. Fish (1966), 13–14, 139–44.

63. League of Women Voters (1961), 9; McMahon (1995), 149. On the strategic shift to creating block clubs in black neighborhoods as a way of introducing them into the OSC without causing a series of pitched racial battles within older community groups, see Menuez (Summer 1965), 31; Interreligious Council on Urban Affairs (Oct. 1968). OSC staffers also created a Women's Auxiliary in the late 1960s, in part to broaden black participation.

64. Von Hoffman to Alinsky, memo, June 21, 1963, Alinsky Papers.

65. Alinsky, *IAF Annual Report* (1961), Alinsky Papers.

66. In Auburn-Gresham, for example, 42 percent of local residents older than age 5 lived in a different dwelling in 1960 than in 1955. While some may have moved within the neighborhood, this is nonetheless a significant population turnover—and before large-scale black in-migration. Statistically, most Chicago communities replaced 5 percent to 10 percent of their populations each year—leading to almost complete turnover in one or two decades. Chicago Community Inventory (1960). To indicate just how mobile the nation's urban population was in the 1950s and 1960s, Auburn-Gresham's percentage of new residents was substantially lower than the average Chicago community, which had just under 60 percent of its residents living in different dwellings in 1960 than in 1955. See also Molotch (1972), 171–72; Anthony Downs, "Alternative Futures for the American Ghetto," *Daedalus* (Fall 1968), 1339–40.

67. Menuez (Summer 1965), 29.

68. Ingrid Ellen, "Sharing America's Neighborhoods: The Changing Prospects for Stable Racial Integration" (PhD diss., Harvard University, 1996), 102, 118; Ingrid Ellen, *Sharing America's Neighborhoods: The Prospects for Stable, Racial Integration*, Harvard University Press, Cambridge, MA (2000). Anthony Downs made a similar argument—see Downs (1968), esp. n. 22.

69. Shaker Heights, Ohio, is the best-known community to have initiated pro-integrative financial programs, albeit two decades after the creation of the OSC. The Home Loan Pool was integrative, but its efforts were necessarily concentrated in too small an area to ultimately be effective. See Brian Cromwell, "Prointegrative Subsidies and Their Effect on Housing Markets:

Do Race-Based Loans Work?" (Working Paper 9018, Federal Reserve Bank of Cleveland, OH, 1990); Don DeMarco and George Galster, "Prointegrative Policy: Theory and Practice," *Journal of Urban Affairs* 15 (1993); Ellen (1996), 326.

70. In the mid-1960s, the South Shore Commission, which represented a community with a much larger percentage of multiunit housing than the Southwest Side, utilized a tenant referral service and an alliance with the area's larger real estate management company to maintain a 50–50 racial balance in real estate transactions. The commission, unlike the OSC, self-consciously tried to "manage" integration in this way, aided by the amount of rental housing in the area. See *South Shore Scene* (Dec. 1966); Molotch (1972), 117–18.

71. On Oak Park, see L. M. Vodar, "The Use of Racial Housing Quotas to Achieve Integrated Communities: The Oak Park Approach," *Loyola University of Chicago Law Journal* (1975); Carole Goodwin, *The Oak Park Strategy: Community Control of Racial Change*, University of Chicago Press, Chicago (1979); Brian J. L. Berry, "Oak Park: Reverse Steering and Racial Quotas," in *The Open Housing Question: Race and Housing in Chicago, 1966–1976*, Ballinger Publishing, Cambridge, MA (1979); Alysia Tate, "A Tale of Two Towns: Evanston, Oak Park Struggle to Keep Racial Balance," *Chicago Reporter*, June 1998. On "intentional integration" more generally, see Norman Bradburn, Seymour Sudman, and Galen Gockel, *Side by Side: Integrated Neighborhoods in America*, Quadrangle Books, Chicago (1971); Juliet Saltman, *Open Housing as a Social Movement: Challenge, Conflict and Change*, Lexington Books, Lexington, MA (1971); *A Fragile Movement: The Struggle for Neighborhood Stabilization*, Greenwood Press, New York (1990); Downs (1973); Gary Orfield, *Toward a Strategy for Urban Integration: Lessons in School and Housing Policy from Twelve Cities*, Ford Foundation, New York (1981); George Galster, "Neighborhood Racial Change, Segregationist Sentiments, and Affirmative Marketing Policies," *Journal of Urban Economics* (1990); Don DeMarco and George Galster, "Prointegrative Policy: Theory and Practice," *Journal of Urban Affairs* (1993); W. Dennis Keating, *The Suburban Racial Dilemma: Housing and Neighborhoods*, Temple University Press, Philadelphia (1994); Philip Nyden, Michael Maly, and John Lukehart, "The Emergence of Stable Racially and Ethnically Diverse Urban Communities: A Case Study of Nine US Cities," *Housing Policy Debate* (1997).

72. On structural strength, see Ellen (1996), 97. See also Richard Taub, D. Garth Taylor, and Jan D. D. Dunham, *Paths of Neighborhood Change: Race and Crime in Urban America*, University of Chicago Press, Chicago (1984). Only 15 percent of Auburn-Gresham's housing units had been built since 1940, and the median value of the community's owner-occupied units was $17,900 in 1960—higher than many homes in the suburbs but less than the city median and not expensive enough to serve as a means of racial containment. Only Beverly Hills–Morgan Park, with housing units that were 82 percent owner-occupied and had a median value of $25,000, had the capability of pricing all but the wealthiest black families out of the area—an effort that both communities, led by the Beverly Area Planning Association (BAPA), attempted in the late 1960s. See *Chicago Community Fact Book* (1960), 156–57; Dominic Pacyga and Ellen Skerrett, *Chicago: City of Neighborhoods*, Loyola University Press, Chicago (1986); Berry (1979); Taub et al. (1984).

73. Molotch (1972), 171, 173.

74. Ellen (1996), 98–101, 310–12. Most studies have assumed that areas with a high percentage of homeowners are more likely, not less likely, to be racially stable; Alinsky certainly believed this. Ellen argues, however, that because homeowners care more about the future structural strength of their surrounding neighborhood, they will be more fearful than renters of a growing black population—largely because of expected effects on property values and the higher transaction costs involved in moving if the racial balance changes. Homeowners will thus leave

changing neighborhoods at lower levels of black presence if they think that presence will continue to grow. Arguably, the religious identity of the homeowners conditions this somewhat, although given the advanced age of most homeowners on the Southwest Side, she is probably correct. For an opposite view on home ownership and neighborhood change, see W. A. Schwab and E. March, "The Tipping Point Model: Prediction of Change in the Racial Composition of Cleveland, Ohio Neighborhoods, 1940–1970," *Environment and Planning* 12 (1980).

75. See McGreevy (1996), 261–63, on these changes in urban Catholicism; the term *absentee market* refers to the "pool of potential buyers and renters of housing units" who didn't live in the area but who served as the "broad general market for housing of that type in the metropolitan area." See Downs (1973), 70. On the importance of institutions as anchors, see Ellen (1996), 101.

76. David Llorens, "The Long 'Negro' Spokesman in Chicago's City Council," *Negro Digest* (Dec. 1966); Barbara Ferman, "Chicago: Power, Race, and Reform," *Big City Politics in Transition*, ed. H. V. Savitch and John Clayton Thomas, Sage Publications, New York (1991).

77. Joseph Kling and Prudence Posner, "Class and Community in an Era of Urban Transformation," in *Dilemmas of Activism: Class, Community and the Politics of Local Mobilization*, ed. Joseph Kling and Prudence Sarah Posner, Temple University Press, Philadelphia (1990), 36; Robert Fisher, *Let the People Decide: Neighborhood Organizing in America*, Twayne Publishers, Boston (1984), 58.

78. See Kling and Posner (1990), 33; Fisher (1984); Donald and Dietrich Reitzes, *The Alinsky Legacy: Alive and Kicking*, JAI Press, Greenwich, CT (1987), 37.

79. Arnold Hirsch makes a similar argument, observing that citywide organizations like the CCHR, the CHA, and the CIC all frequently found themselves arrayed against locally based groups and unable to secure a solid foothold in the neighborhoods for more liberal views on race and housing. See Arnold Hirsch, *Making the Second Ghetto: Race and Housing in Chicago, 1940–1960*, Cambridge University Press, New York (1983), 210–12; "Memo, Re: Problems Confronting CIC in Its Dealings with Clergy" (n.d.), CIC papers, Chicago Historical Society, Chicago.

80. Statement by John McDermott, Executive Director, Catholic Interracial Council, to Public Hearing #3, OSC, Sept. 14, 1961, Alinsky Papers.

81. Robert McClory, "Defunct OSC Rises Again," *Chicago Defender*, Aug. 18, 1973.

82. Richard Margolis, "Toward a Strategy for NCDH," May 1966, box 39, folder 33, Frank Horne Papers, Amistad Research Center, Tulane University, New Orleans.

83. George Lipsitz, "The Possessive Investment in Whiteness: Racialized Social Democracy and the 'White' Problem in American Studies," *American Quarterly* (Sept. 1995), 369.

Chapter Six

1. *General Report*, pt. I, chap. V: Why the Weakness of the Negro Position—The Crux of the Problem, 66, Alinsky Papers, Special Collections, University of Illinois Chicago (hereafter Alinsky Papers).

2. On Woodlawn and the TWO, see Nicholas Lemann, *The Promised Land: The Great Black Migration and How It Changed America*, Alfred A. Knopf, New York (1991); Sanford Horwitt, *Let Them Call Me Rebel: Saul Alinsky, His Life and Legacy*, Alfred A. Knopf, New York (1989); John Hall Fish, *Black Power/White Control*, Princeton University Press, Princeton, NJ (1973); Arthur Brazier, *Black Self-Determination: The Story of the Woodlawn Organization*, Eerdmans, Grand Rapids, MI (1969). On the civil rights movement in Chicago, see Roger Biles, *Richard J. Daley: Politics, Race, and the Governing of Chicago*, Northern Illinois University Press, DeKalb (1995);

James Ralph, *Northern Protest: Martin Luther King Jr., Chicago, and the Civil Rights Movement*, Harvard University Press, Cambridge, MA (1993); Arnold Hirsch, "The Cook County Democratic Organization and the Dilemma of Race, 1931–1987," *Snowbelt Cities: Metropolitan Politics in the Northeast and Midwest since World War II*, ed. Richard Bernard, Indiana University Press, Bloomington (1990); David Garrow, ed., *Chicago 1966: Open Housing Marches, Summit Negotiations, and Operation Breadbasket*, Carlson Publishing, Brooklyn, NY (1989); Alan Anderson and George Pickering, *Confronting the Color Line: The Broken Promise of the Civil Rights Movement in Chicago* (Athens: University of Georgia Press, 1986).

3. By 1966, Woodlawn was over 98 percent black. Philip Hauser and Evelyn Kitagawa, *Local Community Fact Book, 1950*, Chicago Community Inventory, University of Chicago, Chicago (1953); "Population and Housing Data for the Woodlawn Community," May 1960, assembled by Nicholas Von Hoffman, from preliminary census reports, Alinsky Papers; Von Hoffman to Farrell, memo, Mar. 17, 1958, Alinsky Papers; Evelyn Kitagawa and Karl Taeuber, *Local Community Fact Book: Chicago Metropolitan Area, 1960*, Chicago Community Inventory, University of Chicago, Chicago (1963); Pierre de Vise, "Chicago's Widening Color Gap" (Interuniversity Social Research Committee Report No. 2) (Dec. 1967), 146; Carl Tjerandsen, *Education for Citizenship: A Foundation's Experience*, Emil Schwarzhaupt Foundation, Santa Cruz, CA (1980), 236; Winston Moore, Charles Livermore, and George Galland Jr., "Woodlawn: The Zone of Destruction," in *City Scenes: Problems and Prospects*, ed. J. John Palen, Little Brown, Boston (1977), 228.

4. In a 1968 study of five metropolitan areas, the National Committee against Discrimination in Housing (NCADH) found that more than 62 percent of valuation permits for new industrial buildings and 52 percent of those for mercantile establishments from 1960 to 1965 were for construction in the suburbs. See NCADH, "The Impact of Housing Patterns on Job Opportunities," 1968, box 121, folder 3, NCADH Papers, Amistad Research Center, Tulane University, New Orleans. See also Joel Rast, *Remaking Chicago: The Political Origins of Urban Industrial Change*, Northern Illinois University Press, DeKalb (1999), 14, 24–27; Northeastern Illinois Planning Commission, "Industrial Development," Oct. 1965; Illinois State Employment Service, "Employed Workers Covered by the Illinois Unemployment Compensation Act, 1955–64," June 1965; Thomas Sugrue, *Origins of the Urban Crisis*, Princeton University Press, Princeton, NJ (1996), 143–47; Chicago Urban League, "The Negro Labor Market in Chicago, 1966"; Thomas Jackson, *From Civil Rights to Human Rights: Martin Luther King Jr. and the Struggle for Economic Justice*, University of Pennsylvania Press, Philadelphia (2007), 135; Roger Fox and Jerry Szatan, "The Current Economic Status of Chicago's Black Community," Chicago Urban League, Chicago (1977), 89–99; Roger Fox and Jerry Szatan, "The Current Economic Status of Chicago's Black Community: A Mid-1970s Overview Report," Chicago Urban League Research and Planning Department (1977), 29, 53, 74, 91, 95.

5. Fox and Szatan, "Current Economic Status" (1977), 21–23; De Vise (Dec. 1967), 75–78; Chicago Urban League, "The Unskilled Negro Worker in the Chicago Labor Market" (1964), 7–8; Chicago Urban League, "Negro Labor Market," 7; John Kain, "The Big Cities Problem," *Challenge* (Oct. 1966); John Kain, "The Distribution and Movement of Jobs and Industry," *Metropolitan Enigma*, US Chamber of Commerce, Washington, DC (1967); Chicago Department of City Planning, "Industrial Movements and Expansions 1947–1957" (1961); NCADH, "The Impact of Housing Patterns on Job Opportunities" (1968), 21–24; John McDonald, *Employment Location and Industrial Land Use in Metropolitan Chicago*, Stipes, Champaign, IL (1984), 11–12; Anthony Downs, "The Future of American Ghettos" (paper delivered at American Academy of Arts and

Sciences Conference on Urbanism, Oct. 1967); Anthony Downs, "Alternative Futures for the American Ghetto," *Daedalus*, Fall 1968.

6. De Vise (1967), 77–80; US Bureau of the Census, "Survey of Economic Opportunity" (Spring 1966); David Taylor, "The Unskilled Negro Worker in the Chicago Labor Market," Chicago Urban League (1967); Leon Moses et al., "Plant Relocation Study," Transportation Center, Northwestern University, 1963; Chicago Urban League, "Negro Labor Market," 4–5; "Chicago: Racial Tensions Increasing," *New York Times*, Aug. 26, 1963; Fox and Szatan, "Current Economic Status" (1977), 41–44.

7. Kathryn Neckerman, *Schools Betrayed: Roots of Failure in Inner-City Education*, University of Chicago Press, Chicago (2007), 38, 44–46.

8. Sugrue (1996), 143–47; Chicago Urban League, "Negro Labor Market"; Jackson (2007), 135.

9. The average income gap between Woodlawn and Chicago widened in the 1950s. At the same time, the relative gap between Woodlawn residents declined. In 1950, those with the lowest incomes made 66 percent of those with the highest incomes; in 1960, they made 82 percent. Herman Blake, "Report on TWO, 1967," Schwarzhaupt Foundation, 89, Emil Schwarzhaupt Foundation Papers, Special Collections, University of Chicago, Chicago (hereafter ESF Papers); Ruth Moore, "Woodlawn: Urban Forces in Conflict," *Chicago Sun-Times*, Apr. 9, 1961.

10. De Vise (1967), 58–60, 66; Tjerandsen (1980), 236; *Chicago Defender*, May 12, 1960; Chicago Department of City Planning, "Statistics," Dec. 27, 1961, Ruth Moore Papers, box 8, Chicago Historical Society (CHS), Chicago.

11. In 1966 and 1970, 20 percent of Chicago's black workers earned poverty-level wages; another 10–12 percent were unemployed or out of the workforce completely. Fox and Szatan, "Current Economic Status" (1977), 11–15, 52, 58; Mayor's Council of Manpower and Economic Advisors, "Unemployment-Labor Force Policy" (Apr. 1976).

12. Herman Blake, "Report on TWO, 1967," 88, ESF Papers; Brazier (1969), 25; Brian Berry, "Commercial Structure," Northeastern Illinois Planning Commission (May)1965; Von Hoffman (1960); Kitagawa and Taeuber (1960); James Briggs Murray interview with Rev. Arthur Brazier, June 7, 1991, 8–9; Arnold Hirsch, *Making the Second Ghetto: Race and Housing in Chicago, 1940–1960*, Cambridge University Press, New York (1983).

13. Brazier (1969), 24; Floyd Mulkey, "Historical Sketches of Organizations in Woodlawn," Oct. 8, 1962, TWO file, CHS; Hampton Price, "Christmas Letter from an Inner-City Pastor to His Friends," Feb. 16, 1961, box 29, folder 14, ESF Papers; Julian Levi, "The Neighborhood Program of the University of Chicago," Office of Public Information of the University of Chicago (Aug. 1961), 7.

14. Squire Lance, "Woodlawn: Have Its Organizations Failed?" *The Bulletin*, Aug. 17, 1961. Lance eventually served as the first executive director of TWO; later, he worked on the IAF staff and as an official with the National Urban League. In 1975 he ran, unsuccessfully, to replace Leon Despres on City Council. "Lance Joins Walker Drive," *Chicago Defender*, July 13, 1972, 8; Leon Despres, *Challenging the Daley Machine*, Northwestern University Press, Evanston, IL (2005), 122.

15. Lance (1961); Tom Jenkins to D. E. Machelmann and W. K. Brussat, memo, July 29, 1954, Despres Papers, box 182, folder 1, CHS; Von Hoffman to Farrell, memo, Mar. 17 1958, Alinsky Papers.

16. Farrell had heard Alinsky speak at meetings of Cardinal Samuel Stritch's Conservation Council back in 1952, when Stritch had called together over 150 pastors from Catholic parishes

across the city and advised them to resist efforts by some of their parishioners to keep certain groups out of their neighborhoods. Alinsky had outlined a plan for a citywide network of neighborhood organizations, and Farrell was impressed. See Cardinal Stritch, "Speech to Chicago Pastors," Nov. 26, 1952, Msgr. John O'Grady Papers, Special Collections, Catholic University of America Library; and Alinsky, "Speech at National Conference of Catholic Charities Annual Meeting," Sept. 29, 1953, Alinsky Papers.

17. Martin Farrell to Alinsky, Feb. 22, 1958, Alinsky Papers.

18. Von Hoffman to Farrell, memo, Mar. 17, 1958, Alinsky Papers; Nicholas Von Hoffman, "Reorganization in the Casbah," *Social Progress* (Apr.)1962, 39–40; Horwitt (1989), 397. The Welfare Council of Metropolitan Chicago determined that only 51 percent of housing units in Woodlawn were "sound" in 1960, as opposed to 77 percent for the city as a whole. Data from Research Department, Welfare Council of Metropolitan Chicago, Nov. 3, 1967, Welfare Council Papers, CHS.

19. See Leber and Blakeley, "The Great Debate in Chicago," *Presbyterian Life*, June 15, 1961; David Finks, *The Radical Vision of Saul Alinsky*, Paulist Press, New York (1984), 137; historical sketches of Woodlawn organizations, by Floyd Mulkey, submitted to CHS, Oct. 8, 1962, TWO File, CHS.

20. Quote is from Blakeley, cited in Ernestine Cofield, "Ministers vs. Evils of Urban Renewal," *Chicago Defender Magazine*, Nov. 19, 1962.

21. David Finks interview of Martin Farrell, Feb. 22, 1977, cited in Finks (1984).

22. Alinsky to Charles Leber, Apr. 1959, Alinsky Papers.

23. See Brazier (1969), 16; Archbishop Meyer to Martin Farrell, Sept. 25, 1959, folder 43, Alinsky Papers.

24. Georgie Geyer, "Woodlawn: A Community in Revolt," *Chicago Scene*, June 7, 1962.

25. Alinsky, "Sixteen Questions," Mar. 1959, Alinsky Papers. See also Tjerandsen (1980), 239.

26. Geyer (1962).

27. Ernestine Cofield, "Found: A General to Lead a Slum Army," *Chicago Defender Magazine*, Nov. 20, 1962.

28. Blake (1967), 97. Alinsky received a three-year grant of just under $70,000 in November 1960.

29. Cofield, "Found" (1962).

30. Alinsky, *IAF Annual Report* (1960), 7–8, 16, Alinksy Papers.

31. Alinsky, *IAF Annual Report* (1960), 17, Alinksy Papers.

32. *General Report*, pt. I, chap. IV: *Summary of Recommendations* (1957), 68, Alinsky Papers; Alinsky, *IAF Annual Report* (1960), 12, Alinsky Papers.

33. National Film Board of Canada, "Building an Organization," July 1968, transcript, 9–10; John Fish, *The Edge of the Ghetto: A Study of Church Involvement in Community Organization*, Seabury Press, New York (1966), 96–97.

34. Phil Morris, "How Group Subdued Chiseling Landlord," *Chicago Courier*, July 21, 1962; "The People Speak," *Chicago Defender*, Feb. 25, 1963, 12; "TWO Now 'Dealing in Dozens' to Get Slumlords to Fix Up Flats," *Chicago Defender*, Dec. 28, 1963, 4; Brazier (1969), 35; Blake (1967), 121–24. For a fascinating example of how TWO pressured local landlords, consult the 1968 National Film Board of Canada documentary *A Continuing Responsibility*.

35. "Report of the Nominating Committee, Fourth Annual TWO Convention," May 14, 1965, The Woodlawn Organization file, CHS; "The People Speak", 12; "TWO Now 'Dealing in Dozens,'" 4; "It's an Uphill Battle for Mrs. Ollie Clark," *Chicago Defender*, Oct. 20, 1966, 2; "Ollie

Clark Wins Praise," *Chicago Defender*, Nov. 5, 1966, 10; "Neighborhood Groups in Fest for Black Judicial Candidate," *Chicago Defender*, Oct. 31, 1970, 39. On the issue of gender and Alinsky's organizing approach, see Randy Stoecker and Susan Stall, "Community Organizing or Organizing Community: Gender and the Crafts of Empowerment," *Gender and Society* 12, no. 6 (1998).

36. Cofield, "Found" (1962); "TWO Evaluation," June 24, 1964, Church Federation of Greater Chicago records, box 52, file 1, CHS; Horwitt (1989), 397–98.

37. Robert Squires continued to be politically active after his years with TWO; he later served as administrative assistant to Fifth Ward alderman (and TWO ally) Leon Despres and as head of the Employment Department of the Chicago Commission on Human Relations. "Commission on Human Relations: Works to Assure Justice, Equal Opportunity for All," *Chicago Defender* June 26, 1965, C28; Cofield, "Found" (1962); Finks (1984), 147; Nicholas Von Hoffman, "Finding and Making Leaders," Alinsky Papers.

38. Nicholas Von Hoffman, *Radical: A Portrait of Saul Alinsky*, Nation Books, New York (2010), 58; Horwitt (1989), 418.

39. On Brazier, see William Braden, "Rev. Brazier in Profile: For Rights Leader, Power is the Prize," *Chicago Sun-Times*, Apr. 19, 1964; James B. Murray interview with Arthur Brazier, June 7, 1991, at the Schaumburg Center in New York City; Horwitt (1989), 418–19; Finks (1984), 156; Anderson and Pickering (1987), 120 and 129; "Brazier May Buck Dawson," *Chicago Defender*, Oct. 26, 1965, 1.

40. On Lynward Stevenson, see "Profile of a Leader: Reverend Lynward Stevenson, 'Mr. Poverty,'" *Woodlawn Observer*, Jan. 19, 1967. On Finney, see James B. Murray interview with Leon Finney, June 8, 1991, Schaumburg Center; "Woodlawn Winning Acclaim under TWO's Leon Finney," *Chicago Defender*, Dec. 15, 1973, 3.

41. TWO press release from late January 1961, "South Campus Dropped: Community Program Started"; Squire Lance, "Woodlawn: TWO Is Born, Starts War with University," *The Bulletin*, Aug. 24, 1961.

42. Von Hoffman (2010), 144–45.

43. Marion Sanders, *The Professional Radical: Interviews with Saul Alinsky*, Harper and Row, New York (1970), 45.

44. Harold Fey, "The Open Society," *Chicago Sun-Times*, Apr. 16, 1961; "Open or Closed Cities?" *Christian Century*, May 10, 1961; Walter Kloetzli, "Letter to the Editor," *Christian Century*, May 31, 1961.

45. Kloetzli (1961).

46. Horwitt (1989), 399–402; Von Hoffman (2010), 183.

47. Finks (1984), 134–35; "1000 Set for Loop Registration," *The Bulletin*, June 17, 1961; Report from Kenneth Gillis to Leon Despres, Aug. 26, 1961, Despres Papers, box 182, file 1, CHS; Ernestine Cofield, "Political Power Shown by Mass Bus Ride to City Hall," *Chicago Defender Magazine*, Dec. 2, 1962; Von Hoffman (2010), 136.

48. TWO, "2000 Chicago-Style Freedom Riders Ready" (press release), n.d., Alinsky Papers; TWO, "TWO Readies Massive Chicago Freedom Ride: 1500 to City Hall to Register to Vote" (press release), n.d., Alinsky Papers.

49. While Grand Boulevard was in machine territory, Woodlawn was not. It occupied portions of Wards 5, 6, and 20, none of which Dawson controlled. The Fifth Ward alderman Leon Despres was a political independent and TWO ally who had known Alinsky for thirty years. The independent black alderman Charles Chew, who frequently referred to his black machine-supported colleagues as "the Silent Six," described Despres (who was white) as the City Council's

"only Negro." The Sixth Ward representative became a reliable supporter in the wake of the registration drive. Arnold Hirsch, "The Cook County Democratic Organization and the Dilemma of Race, 1931–1987," in *Snowbelt Cities: Metropolitan Politics in the Northeast and Midwest since World War II*, ed. Richard Bernard, Indiana University Press, Bloomington (1990), 80; Roger Biles, *Richard J. Daley: Politics, Race, and the Governing of Chicago*, Northern Illinois University Press, DeKalb (1995), 92–93. On black politics in Chicago, see Harold Gosnell, *Negro Politicians: The Rise of Negro Politics in Chicago*, University of Chicago Press, Chicago (1935); James Q. Wilson, *Negro Politics: The Search for Leadership*, Free Press, New York (1960); William Grimshaw, *Bitter Fruit: Black Politics and the Chicago Machine, 1931–1991*, University of Chicago Press, Chicago (1992); Geyer (1962).

50. Department of City Planning, "Proposal for a Program to Meet the Long-Term Needs of Woodlawn," Mar. 1962; Ruth Moore, "Woodlawn Plan: 'Total' Renewal," *Chicago Sun-Times*, Mar. 16, 1962; Jane Jacobs, "Chicago's Woodlawn—Renewal by Whom?" *Architectural Forum*, May 1962; Nicholas Von Hoffman to William Nelson, Apr. 10, 1962, Alinsky Papers.

51. Von Hoffman to Nelson, Apr. 10, 1962, Alinsky Papers.

52. Geyer (1962); Horwitt (1989), 418–20; *Woodlawn Booster*, Mar. 21, 1962; Charles Silberman, *Crisis in Black and White*, Random House, New York (1964), 345; Alinsky, *IAF Annual Report* (1960), 16, Alinsky Papers.

53. "Study Outline: Preliminary Phase of 'Woodlawn Plan' Discussion," Alinsky Papers.

54. Von Hoffman to Nelson, Apr. 10, 1962, Alinsky Papers.

55. "Woodlawn Plan Discussion Guide" (prepared for TWO by Nelson and Associates), June 8, 1962, Alinsky Papers.

56. "Social Policy Planning Memo," *Woodlawn Booster*, July 25, 1962; Geyer (1962); "Social Welfare Report . . . A New Faith," *Woodlawn Booster*, Oct. 31, 1962, box 8, "Woodlawn 1961–62" folder, Ruth Moore Papers, CHS. See also Ernestine Cofield, "A Blueprint to Secure Community's Future," *Chicago Defender Magazine*, Dec. 3, 1962.

57. Repeated government delays in Chicago and Washington continually pushed back final approval and construction for years, however, taking up a great deal of TWO's time and energy. Finally, in July 1967 the TWO-KMF Development Association was officially designated as the developer-builder of the project, and the land was transferred from the city to TWO in November 1968. Construction began the next month. The project was an enormous and unprecedented accomplishment. Unfortunately, Woodlawn Gardens did not fulfill its original purpose in providing housing for those displaced. A substantial portion of Woodlawn's middle class had departed the area in the intervening years, while inflation and parking requirements forced TWO to decrease the number of units and increase rents. An effort by TWO to participate in a federal rent subsidy program to enable low-income residents to live in Woodlawn Gardens failed. "Agreement Reached between Mayor Daley and TWO on 7/16/63," Alinsky Papers; "Rev. Brazier Opposes 'Negro Removal' Plan," *Chicago Defender*, July 17, 1963, 1; Blake Report, 106; "TWO Tells Details of Cottage Grove Project," *Chicago Defender*, Mar. 24, 1964, 3; KMF and TWO, "A Comprehensive Plan for the Development of Cottage Grove Avenue (60th through 63rd)" (joint press release), Mar. 24, 1964, Church Federation of Greater Chicago, box 52, file 1, CHS; "TWO-Maremont Foundation's Great Contribution to Chicago," *Chicago Defender*, Mar. 28, 1964, 1; "Survey Eyes Housing Needs in Woodlawn," *Chicago Tribune*, Apr. 12, 1964, 2; *TWO Newsletter*, Apr. 17, 1964; William Braden, "Rev. Brazier in Profile," *Chicago Sun-Times* Apr. 19, 1964; "Groups Seek to Buy Land for Housing," *Chicago Tribune*, Sept. 6, 1964, 1; "City May Launch Project," *Chicago Tribune*, Nov. 28, 1964, 1; "South Side Land Sale Approved," *Chicago*

Tribune, June 30, 1967, B8; "Break Ground for Woodlawn Homes Project," *Chicago Tribune*, Dec. 4, 1968, 4; Fish (1973), 71–77.

Chapter Seven

1. Statement of Roy Wilkins, Civil Rights: Hearings before Subcommittee Number 5 of the House Committee on the Judiciary, 88th Cong., 1st sess., 1963.

2. The black-white income gap closed substantially in the 1940s, a result of tight labor markets, civil rights activism, unionization, and government action. It opened again in the 1950s and early 1960s, as the economy stagnated, manufacturing deconcentrated, and interracial coalitions atrophied. Only the relatively large number of wage earners in black families (wives and mothers, predominantly) enabled their family incomes to keep pace with whites in the Chicago area in the supposedly prosperous 1960s.

3. Roger Fox and Jerry Szatan, "The Current Economic Status of Chicago's Black Community: A Mid-1970s Overview Report," Chicago Urban League Research and Planning Department (1977), 28–29, 50–52, 58–60, 104–7, 124–25; Pierre de Vise, "Chicago's Widening Color Gap" (Interuniversity Social Research Committee Report No. 2) (Dec. 1967), 77–80; US Bureau of the Census, "Survey of Economic Opportunity," Spring 1966; David Taylor, "The Unskilled Negro Worker in the Chicago Labor Market," Chicago Urban League (1967); Bayard Rustin, "A Negro Leader Defines a Way Out of the Exploding Ghetto," *New York Times*, Aug. 13, 1967; "The Social and Economic Status of the Black Population in the US," *Current Population Reports*, series P-23, no. 54, July 1975, table 9, 25; Mayor's Council of Manpower and Economic Advisors, "Unemployment-Labor Force Policy," Apr. 1976; Thomas Maloney, 'Wage Compression and Wage Inequality between Black and White Males in the United States, 1940–1960," *Journal of Economic History* 54 (1994), 358–81.

4. "Chicago's Growing Racial Crisis," *Chicago Defender*, Mar. 4, 1963, 9; "Chicago's Black Belt Expands, but Never Cracks," *Chicago Defender*, May 20, 1963, 9; Robert Havighurst, "The Public Schools of Chicago: A Survey for the Board of Education of the City of Chicago," Chicago Board of Education (1964); Philip Hauser et al., "Report to the Board of Education of the City of Chicago by the Advisory Panel on Integration of the Public Schools," Mar. 31, 1964; "Freedom Day I Shook the Machine" (flyer), box 78, folder 2, Leon Despres Papers, CHS; William Vrame, "A History of School Desegregation in Chicago since 1954" (PhD diss., University of Wisconsin, 1971); John Rury, "Race, Space, and the Politics of Chicago's Public Schools: Benjamin Willis and the Tragedy of Urban Education," *History of Education Quarterly* (Summer 1999); De Vise (1967), 83, 101; Kathryn Neckerman, *Schools Betrayed: Roots of Failure in Inner-City Education*, University of Chicago Press (2007), 84–87, 95; Michael Homel, *Down from Equality: Black Chicagoans and the Public Schools, 1920–1941*, University of Illinois Press, Champaign-Urbana (1982); Elizabeth Todd-Breland, *A Political Education: Black Politics and Education Reform in Chicago Since the 1960s*, University of North Carolina Press (2018), 27.

5. David Green, "Vocational Education and Race in the Chicago Public Schools: Three Historical Case Studies and Implications for Current Reform," *Urban Review* 24, no. 1 (1992); Neckerman (2007), 58, 125; John Coons, "Civil Rights USA: Public School Sites in the North and West, 1962 Chicago," US Commission on Civil Rights (1962); Chicago Urban League, "The Unskilled Negro Worker in the Chicago Labor Market" (1964), 8; Chicago Urban League, "The Negro Labor Market in Chicago, 1966," 9–14; Chicago Urban League, "Proposed Project in Guidance for Negroes in Chicago," box 29, folder 7, Daniel Cantwell Papers, Chicago Historical Society

(CHS); Harold Baron and Bennett Hymer, "The Negro Worker in the Chicago Labor Market," in *The Negro and the American Labor Movement*, ed. Julius Jacobsen, Anchor Books, Garden City, NY (1968), 258–77; Edwin Berry, "Jobs, Poverty and Race," *Negro Digest*, Sept. 1964; *Chicago Sun-Times*, "Survey Finds Discrimination in White-Collar Jobs," Jan. 21, 1968; John Morgan and Richard Van Dyke, "White-Collar Blacks: A Breakthrough?" American Management Association (1970), 15–16.

6. In 1967 the Board of Education member Warren Bacon told reporters that Willis and the board had gerrymandered school districts for years to maintain segregation. *Chicago Daily News*, Feb. 20, 1967; US Office of Education, "Analysis of Certain Aspects of Chicago Public Schools under Title II of the Civil Rights Act of 1964," Jan. 1967; "Aide Tells Why He Quit: 'Poor and Can't Learn' School Attitude Decried," *Chicago Sun-Times*, Aug. 6, 1967; Neckerman (2007), 97.

7. "Two Who Seek to Clean Up Chicago," *Chicago Defender*, Jan. 13, 1964, 25; "Found: A General to Lead a Slum Army," *Chicago Defender*, Nov. 20, 1962; David Llorens, "The Lone 'Negro' Spokesman in Chicago City's Council," *Negro Digest*, Dec. 1966.

8. "Chicago's Black Belt Expands", 9; Rury (1999), 131; Saul Alinsky, *Rules for Radicals: A Practical Primer for Realistic Radicals*, Vintage Books, New York (1971), 133.

9. *New Crusader*, "NAACP Misses Boat; Parents Take Over School Bias Suit," Sept. 17, 1961; Dionne Danns, *Something Better for Our Children: Black Organization in the Chicago Public Schools, 1963–1971*, Routledge, New York (2003), 26–27; Andrew Diamond, *Mean Streets: Chicago Youths and the Everyday Struggle for Empowerment in the Multiracial City, 1908–1969*, University of California Press (2009), 246; Tom Sugrue, *Sweet Land of Liberty*, Random House, New York (2008), 452–54.

10. "TWO Throws Full Support Behind Efforts to End Segregation in Chicago Schools," *Chicago Defender*, Sept. 25, 1961, 5; "1500 Overflow School Board," *Chicago Defender*, Oct. 17, 1961, 1; "TWO Maps Plan to Integrate Schools Here," *Chicago Defender*, Jan. 24, 1962, 2; "Parents Picket 'Slum' School," *Chicago Defender*, Jan. 30, 1962, 1; Ernestine Cofield, "The Battle of Woodlawn: 'Death Watch' against School Segregation," *Chicago Defender*, Nov. 27, 1962, 9; "200 Picket Chicago School Board for Integration," *Jet Magazine*, Nov. 2, 1961, 46; Todd-Breland (2018), 33; Crystal Sanders, *A Chance for Change: Head Start and Mississippi's Black Freedom Struggle*, University of North Carolina Press, Chapel Hill (2016).

11. Amanda Seligman has a fine discussion of the dilemmas of the neighborhood school idea in chapter 5 of her *Block by Block: Neighborhoods and Public Policy on Chicago's West Side*, University of Chicago Press, Chicago (2005). "City's Racial Problems in Willis' Lap," *Chicago Daily News*, July 6, 1962.

12. Adam Fairclough, *To Redeem the Soul of America: The SCLC and Martin Luther King Jr.* (Athens: University of Georgia Press, Athens, 1987); Horwitt (1989), 406, 430–31; Lois Wille, "Mayor Daley Meets the Movement," *The Nation*, Sept. 30, 1965; James Ralph, *Northern Protest: Martin Luther King Jr., Chicago, and the Civil Rights Movement*, Harvard University Press, Cambridge, MA (1993), 20–23; Alan Anderson and George Pickering, *Confronting the Color Line: The Broken Promise of the Civil Rights Movement in Chicago*, University of Georgia Press, Athens (1986)), 90 and 99; "Truth Squad Found Guilty," *Chicago Defender*, May 16, 1962, 1; Cofield (1962), 9; M. David Finks, *The Radical Vision of Saul Alinsky*, Paulist Press, New York (1984), 150–51; Carl Tjerandsen, *Education for Citizenship: A Foundation's Experience*, Emil Schwarzhaupt Foundation, Santa Cruz, CA (1980), 247–48; John Hall Fish, *Black Power/White Control*, Princeton University Press, Princeton, NJ (1973), 12–65; Elinor Richey, "The Slum That Saved Itself," *Progressive*, Oct. 1963, 26–29; Ralph (1993), 17; "TWO Policy and Resolutions Report, May

1963," Alinsky Papers, Special Collections, University of Illinois Chicago (hereafter Alinsky Papers); "Chicago School 'Strike' Protests Mobile Classes," *Jet Magazine*, May 31, 1962, 19; "50 Picket Chicago's Mobile Classrooms," *Jet Magazine*, June 7, 1962, 52.

13. Charles Silberman, *Crisis in Black and White*, Random House, New York (1964), 346; On the creation of the CCCO, see "The Struggle for Equality," *Chicago Defender*, July 31, 1962, 11; Anderson and Pickering (1986), 295–97; Ralph (1993), 17–18; Danns (2003), 37–41.

14. Silberman (1964), 346; "Politics Charges Fly on 'Warehouse School': Classroom Empty, Church School Full as Parents Boycott," *Chicago Defender*, Feb. 2, 1963; "Rights Advocates Plan Session on 'Direct Action,'" *Chicago Defender*, July 17, 1963, 6; "Hit Willis Wagons in Englewood Community," *Chicago Defender*, July 29, 1963; "Willis Wagon Foe Is Vocal in Bias Fight," *Chicago Defender*, Sept. 4, 1963; "Integration: Willis Wills Out," *Time*, Oct. 11, 1963; "School-by-School Story of Boycott," *Chicago Defender*, Oct. 23, 1963; "Integration: De Facto Superintendent," *Time*, Nov. 1, 1963; Diamond (2009), 246–47; Marion Sanders, *The Professional Radical: Interviews with Saul Alinsky*, Harper and Row, New York (1970), 43–44; Danns (2003); Todd-Breland (2018), 22–27.

15. "Social Policy Planning Memo," *Woodlawn Booster*, July 25, 1962; Cofield (1962), 9; "TWO Policy and Resolutions Report," May 1963, Records of the Church Federation of Greater Chicago, box 52, folder 1, CHS; "Woodlawn Experimental Schools District Counseling Program to Prevent Dropouts," Jan. 1969, 2. TWO later received funding from the government and Methodist Church sources to organize Woodlawn parents.

16. Alinsky testified before Hauser's fact-finding committee in January 1964. Transcript of James B. Murray interview with Arthur Brazier, June 7, 1991, Schaumburg Center, New York; Philip Hauser et al., "Report to the Board of Education of the City of Chicago by the Advisory Panel on Integration of the Public Schools," Mar. 31, 1964; Robert J. Havighurst, *The Public Schools of Chicago: A Survey for the Board of Education for the City of Chicago*, Board of Education of the City of Chicago, Chicago (1964).

17. Seligman (2005), 135–37.

18. Christopher Chandler, "Increased Segregation Reported in City's Public Schools," *Chicago Sun-Times*, Sept. 27, 1966, 18; Lois Wille, "Chicago Schools Get an 'F,'" *Chicago Daily News*, Oct. 8, 1966, 3; Fish (1973), 176; Mary Herrick, *The Chicago Schools: A Social and Political History* (1981), 324–25; Gregory Squires, Larry Bennett, Kathleen McCourt, and Philip Nyden, *Chicago: Race, Class, and the Response to Urban Decline*, Temple University Press, Philadelphia (1987), 131; Danns (2003), 44–46.

19. William Grimshaw, *Bitter Fruit: Black Politics and the Chicago Machine, 1931–1991*, University of Chicago Press, Chicago (1992), 103, 115–19, 124–25; Len O'Connor, *Clout: Mayor Daley and His City*, Avon Books, New York (1975), 178–79; Larry Bennett, "Postwar Redevelopment in Chicago: The Declining Politics of Party and the Rise of Neighborhood Politics," in *Unequal Partnerships: The Political Economy of Urban Redevelopment in Postwar America*, ed. Gregory Squires, Rutgers University Press, New Brunswick, NJ (1989), 170; Adam Cohen and Elizabeth Taylor, *American Pharoah*, Little Brown, Boston (2000), 302; Sugrue (2008), 464.

20. "Chicago Rights Fight Seen in Sad Shape," *Chicago Defender*, June 6, 1964, 1.

21. Rabbi William Berkowitz, *Conversations With . . .* , Block Publishing, New York (1975), 269; Sanders (1970), 50–52; Alinsky (1971), 153; Alinsky, "Action to Equality of Opportunity," IAF, 1963, Welfare Council of Metropolitan Chicago Papers, box 350, file 6, CHS; Ralph (1993), 27.

22. Von Hoffman (2010), 33; William Braden, "Rev. Brazier in Profile," *Chicago Sun-Times*, Apr. 19, 1964; David L. Lewis, *King: A Biography*, University of Illinois Press, Champaign-Urbana (1978), 320.

23. According to James Ralph, the SCLC's Bernard LaFayette tried to reach out to TWO and other Chicago community organizations after the strategic shift but with no success: "local groups never became the real backbone of the open-housing initiative." Ralph (1993), 93, 102–4, 119, 205; Despres (2005), 96–98; Fish (1973), 110; Von Hoffman (2010), 33, 36, 76. For a sense of the debate among black activists in Chicago about integration in 1966, see "White Backlash," *Chicago Defender*, Oct. 15, 1966.

24. "TWO Backs Municipal Bond Issue," *Chicago Defender*, May 25, 1966, 3; "TWO and the Bonds," *Chicago Defender*, May 29, 1966, 1; "Chicago Vote Indicates Daley Retains His Power," *New York Times*, June 16, 1966; Ralph (1993), 95

25. Douglass C. Cater files, folder "Civil Rights Bill: Complaints under Title VI," LBJ Library; "Chicago Is Facing School Aid Fight," *New York Times*, June 30, 1965; "Rights Group Asks US to Cut off Aid to Chicago Schools," *New York Times*, July 6, 1965; "Chicago Officials Warn on Schools," *New York Times*, July 7, 1965; "Chicago Story—City Hall and Civil Rights," *New York Times*, Oct. 17, 1965; Ralph (1993), 182; James Patterson, Brown v. Board of Education: *A Civil Rights Milestone and Its Troubled Legacy*, Oxford University Press, New York, 138–40; Cohen and Taylor (2000), 351–53; Biles (1995), 115; Allen Matusow, *The Unraveling of America: A History of Liberalism in the 1960s*, Harper, New York (1986), 200–203; Anderson and Pickering (1986), 178–81; Sugrue (2009), 469–70; Todd-Breland (2018), 60.

26. Brazier (1969), 139, 141, 142–43. See also Phil Norris, "Freedom Coming Too Slowly for Members," *Chicago Courier*, July 14, 1962.

27. De Vise (1967), 109.

28. On the controversy over the proposed experimental school in Woodlawn, see Fish (1993), 179–80, and Todd-Breland (2018), 69–70. "Proposal for Expansion of Hyde Park High School into Secondary Educational Park: An Outline," Aug. 10, 1965, box 86, folder 2, Beadle Records, Special Collections, University of Chicago, Chicago; "TWO Raps Ben's Hyde Park Plan," *Chicago Defender*, Sept. 11, 1965; "Southsiders Picket a School Project," *Chicago Defender*, Sept. 22, 1965; De Vise (1967), 107–8; "TWO Threatens HP-Kenwood 'Block-Busting': Stevenson Irritated by White Battle for Segregated Classes," *Chicago Defender*, Nov. 24, 1965, 1; "Policy and Resolutions," n.d., Woodlawn Organization Collection, CHS; "Four Groups to Eye 'Education Park," *Chicago Defender*, Feb. 1, 1966.

29. "TWO, Unity Unit Rap Board Plan on School," *Chicago Defender*, Jan. 27, 1966, 4.

30. "Freedom Coming Too Slowly for Members," *Chicago Courier*, July 14, 1962; *TWO News*, Oct. 27, 1965, 1; *TWO News*, Dec. 1, 1965, 3; Fish (1973), 90–93, 176; "TWO Urges Negroes to Back Busing Plan," *Chicago Defender*, Jan. 24, 1968, 8; "Busing Conflict Dims as Blacks Seek Better Neighborhood Schools," *Chicago Tribune*, Dec. 14, 1969, 16; Brazier (1969), 24; National Film Board of Canada, "Through Conflict to Negotiation," July 1968, transcript, p. 9; Sanders (1970), 49.

31. On the Redmond Plan, see Seligman (2005), chap. 5.

32. "TWO Vote Drive Continues; Takes Position on Schools, Housing," *Woodlawn Observer*, Jan. 19, 1967.

33. See Barbara Sizemore, *Walking in Circles: The Black Struggle for School Reform*, Third World Press, New York (2008); Todd-Breland (2018), 50–67.

34. On the Woodlawn Experimental School Program, see TWO, "1967 Policy and Resolutions," box 181, folder 4, Leon Despres Collection, CHS; "Experimental School Plan is Disclosed," *Chicago Tribune*, Dec. 11, 1967, 2; "OK Woodlawn Pilot School," *Chicago Tribune*, Jan. 7, 1968, 1; "Parents Help 'Take Apart' Their Schools," *Chicago Tribune*, July 21, 1968, 14; "Principal Seeks School Transfer in Row With TWO," *Chicago Defender*, Sept. 10, 1968, 1; "TWO Issues Threat

to School Board: A Black Principal—Or Else," *Chicago Defender*, Oct. 16, 1968, 1; "Experimental School Board to Turn Community Wishes into Realities in Woodlawn," *Chicago Tribune*, June 1, 1969; "Residents Ready to Work in Woodlawn Schools," *Chicago Tribune*, June 15, 1969, 3; "Woodlawn Schools Give Parents Planning Role," *Chicago Tribune*, June 8, 1969, 3; "Pupils Show Gains in Woodlawn Tests," *Chicago Tribune*, Feb. 25, 1970, 10; Fish (1973), chap. 4; De Vise (Dec. 1967), 104–5; Morris Janowitz and David Street, "Urban School Systems: Strategies for Change," Center for Social Organization Studies, University of Chicago (1966); John Lyons, *Teachers and Reform: Chicago Public Education 1929–1970*, University of Illinois Press, Champaign-Urbana (2008), 174; Todd-Breland (2018).

35. *Chicago Maroon*, May 22, 1964, 1. See also Harold Fey, "The Industrial Areas Foundation: An Interpretation" (1965), box 48, folder 3, Church Federation of Greater Chicago Papers, CHS.

36. Von Hoffman left to work for the *Chicago Daily News* and moved on to a very successful career as a journalist. Von Hoffman (2010), 46; Nicholas Lemann, *The Promised Land: The Great Black Migration and How It Changed America*, Vintage Books, New York (1991), 101–2; Joan Lancourt, *Confront or Concede: The Alinsky Citizen-Action Organizations*, Lexington Books, Lexington, MA (1979), 116; Tjerandsen (1980), 253.

Chapter Eight

1. Frances Fox Piven and Richard Cloward, *Regulating the Poor: The Functions of Public Welfare*, Vintage Books, New York (1971), table 4; "Chaos in Chicago: Democracy Northern Style," *Liberator*, May 1963; "TWO Rips Maremont, State Okay Delayed," *Chicago Defender*, Feb. 7, 1963, 4; Tom Sugrue, *Sweet Land of Liberty: The Forgotten Struggle for Civil Rights in the North*, Random House, New York (2008), 383–84. For another example of state-level political backlash against expanding welfare rolls in the nation's cities, see Annelise Orleck, *Storming Caesar's Palace: How Black Mothers Fought Their Own War on Poverty*, Beacon Press, Boston (2005).

2. *Woodlawn Booster* May 1, 1963; Robert Hess and June Tapp, "An Evaluation of a Community-Based Manpower Training Program," University of Chicago, 1965, 4; "TWO Rips Maremont, State Okay Delayed," *Chicago Defender*, Feb. 7, 1963, 4; "Maremont Stand on Relief Wins S. Side Backing," *Chicago Defender*, Apr. 29, 1963, 4; "GOP Challenged on Relief Issue by TWO Parley," *Chicago Defender*, May 6, 1963, 4; *TWO Newsletter*, Apr. 17, 1964.

3. President Kennedy used the phrase "a rising tide lifts all boats" in an October 3, 1963, speech in Heber Springs, Arkansas, commemorating the opening of the Greers Ferry Dam. Kennedy used the phrase often to defend his fiscal policies against accusations of pork-barrel politics but also from those who sought more liberal and redistributive programs.

4. Margaret Weir, *Politics and Jobs: The Boundaries of Employment Policy in the United States*, Princeton University Press, Princeton, NJ (1992), 62, 69; Harold Baron and Bennett Hymer, "The Negro Worker in the Chicago Labor Market," in *The Negro and the American Labor Movement*, ed. Julius Jacobsen, Anchor Books, Garden City, NY (1968), 258–77; Chicago Urban League, "The Negro Labor Market in Chicago, 1966."

5. Thomas Jackson, *From Civil Rights to Human Rights: Martin Luther King Jr. and the Struggle for Economic Justice*, University of Pennsylvania Press, Philadelphia (2007), 12, 133, 136–37; Sugrue (2008), 156; Kent Germany, *New Orleans after the Promises: Poverty, Citizenship and the Search for the Great Society*, University of Georgia Press, Athens (2007), 151–52; Chicago Urban League, "The Negro Labor Market in Chicago, 1966," 12. On the growing emphasis on jobs in black urban movements, see Robert Self, *American Babylon: Race and the Struggle for Postwar*

Oakland, Princeton University Press, Princeton, NJ (2003); Matthew Countryman, *Up South: Civil Rights and Black Power in Philadelphia*, University of Pennsylvania Press, Philadelphia (2007); Martha Biondi, *To Stand and Fight: The Struggle for Civil Rights in Postwar New York City*, Harvard University Press, Cambridge, MA (2003).

6. Nicholas Lemann, *The Promised Land: The Great Black Migration and How It Changed America*, Vintage Books, New York (1991), 101–2; "The Woodlawn Organization," Pratt Institute Center for Community and Environmental Development, Schaumburg Center, New York Public Library; "Chicago: Racial Tensions Increasing," *New York Times*, Aug. 26, 1963.

7. Robert McKersie and William Swenson, "Neighborhood Economic Development," *Delivery Systems for Model Cities: New Concepts in Serving the Urban Community*, University of Chicago Center for Urban Studies, Chicago (1969), 53; *TWO Newsletter*, Apr. 17, 1964; TWO, "Proposal for a Community Action Program for the Greater Woodlawn Area," n.d., TWO file, Chicago Historical Society (CHS); *Chicago Maroon*, June 11, 1967; Connie Seals, "Human Relations Beat," *Chicago Defender*, Jan. 30, 1965, 4; Herman Blake, "Report on TWO, 1967," Schwarzhaupt Foundation, 89, 110, Emil Schwarzhaupt Foundation Papers, Special Collections, University of Chicago, Chicago (hereafter ESF Papers). For data on black participation in federal job-training programs, see National Committee against Housing Discrimination, "The Impact of Housing Patterns on Job Opportunities" (1968). The job-training program for youth in gangs is discussed later in this chapter.

8. Ernestine Cofield, "Square Deal Campaign Cracks Down on Cheating Merchants," *Chicago Defender*, Nov. 29, 1962; *Woodlawn Booster*, July 31, 1963; *TWO Newsletter*, Apr. 17, 1964; *Chicago Daily News*, Nov. 7, 1963.

9. A consequence of TWO's ever-larger job-training programs was that much of the leadership's time and energy was spent on proposing and administering them. In one year TWO's budget grew from $30,000 to $1,000,000, and its staff increased from six to thirty. Stevenson later argued that TWO's lack of participation in King's 1966 open-housing campaign was in part a function of this. "TWO Program," *Chicago Defender*, Dec. 31, 1964, 11; Steven Lovelady, "Private Poverty War Stresses Self-Help," *Wall Street Journal*, Feb. 18, 1966, 6; TWO, "Retraining the Hard-Core Unemployed through a Grass-Roots Community Organization," Sept. 1, 1965; *Chicago Maroon*, June 11, 1967; Fish (1973), 78–79.

10. Charles Silberman, *Crisis in Black and White*, Random House, New York (1964); *TWO Newsletter*, Apr. 17, 1964.

11. Germany (2007), 99–100; Jackson (2007), 170, 192–94.

12. "Open Letter to Sargent Shriver," *TWO Newsletter*, Oct. 21, 1964.

13. Lois Wille, "TWO Wants to Know: Will We Share in Poverty Funds?" *Chicago Daily News*, Apr. 7, 1965.

14. Wille, *Chicago Daily News*, Apr. 7, 1965; Adam Cohen and Elizabeth Taylor, *American Pharoah*, Little, Brown, Boston (2000), 318–19.

15. Office of Economic Opportunity, "Community Action Guide" (1965), 17–18; Brian Henry Smith, "The Role of the Poor in the Poverty Program: The Origin and Development of MFP" (MA thesis, Columbia University, New York, 1966), 78–83; Michael Gillette, *Launching the War on Poverty: An Oral History*, Oxford University Press, New York (1996), 196; Noel Cazenave, *Impossible Democracy: The Unlikely Success of the War on Poverty's Community Action Programs*, State University of New York Press, Albany, NY (2007), 143–44.

16. "Representative Powell Has Allies in Poverty War," *Chicago Defender*, Apr. 4, 1965; Rowland Evans and Robert Novak, "Inside Report: Powell and Poverty," *Chicago Tribune*, Apr. 15,

1965; "Dawson, Powell Duel in War on Poverty," *Chicago Sun-Times*, Apr. 18, 1965, 12; Wille, *Chicago Daily News*. Apr. 5-9, 1965; Congressional Testimony of Lynward Stevenson before the House Committee on Labor and Education, Examination of the War on Poverty, printed in *TWO Newsletter*, Apr. 14, 1965; "Poverty War Is Sham Tool of Local Democrats: TWO," *Chicago Defender*, Apr. 14, 1965, 1; "Poverty Witness Impugns Another," *New York Times*, Apr. 14, 1965; "Defends Anti-Poverty Program in Hearing," *Chicago Defender*, Apr. 15, 1965; "Chicago Program Disputed," *New York Times*, Apr. 18, 1965; "Daley Is Opposed on Poverty Drive," *New York Times*, July 23, 1965; Cohen and Taylor (2000), 318–19.

17. Saul Alinsky, "The War on Poverty—Political Pornography," *Journal of Social Issues* (Spring 1965). The article was based on a talk given to the Institute for Policy Studies on May 26, 1965.

18. OEO, "Community Action Memo #3," OEO Inspection Division, RG 381, National Archives II, College Park, MD (National Archives II).

19. "TWO Gets Poverty $," *Chicago Defender*, June 22, 1965, 3.

20. Lemann (2001), 167; Gillette (1996), 208; Cazenave (2007), 152.

21. "'Poverty' Deal Irritates TWO," *Chicago Defender*, July 21, 1965, 1.

22. "TWO Sets March, Demands 'War' Probe," *Chicago Defender*, July 22, 1965, 3; "Despres, TWO Questioning Poverty Petitions," *Chicago Defender*, Jan. 13, 1966, 1; "'Long Hot Summer' Here and in Dixie," *Chicago Defender*, July 22, 1965, 3; Jackson (2007), 234; Joseph Loftus, "Mayors Win Fight on Poverty Funds," *New York Times*, Aug. 15, 1965.

23. Address by Sanford Kravitz, May 21, 1965, and Williams memo, Apr. 27, 1965, box 54, Syracuse file, OEO Inspection Division, RG 381, National Archives II. The grant was for $314,000.

24. See Robert Pickett, "The Genesis and Development of the CATC of Syracuse University, 1964–1966," Jan. 1967, rough draft, University College papers, Special Collections, Syracuse University, Syracuse, NY; boxes 54–55, Syracuse file, OEO Inspection Division, RG 381, National Archives II.

25. Saul Alinsky, "You Can't See the Stars through the Stripes" (proceedings of National Workshop on the Urban Poor: Manpower and Consumer Potentials, US Chamber of Commerce, Washington, DC), Mar. 1968.

26. *Syracuse Post-Standard*, Mar. 19, 1965; Clampitt to Haddad, memo, Apr. 17, 1965, box 55, Syracuse file, OEO Inspection Division, RG 381, National Archives II; interview with Robert Pickett, War on Poverty Oral History Project, 25–26, Columbia University Oral History Library. On Housing Authority, see *New York Times*, June 24, 1965.

27. Charles Walker to Lyndon Johnson, Apr. 12, 1965, and Williams to Ed May, memo, Oct. 19, 1965, box 55, Syracuse file; Williams report, Apr. 27, 1965, box 54, OEO; President Lyndon Johnson with Charles Schultze, Elmer Staats, and Joseph Califano, Aug. 18, 1965, Citation #8555, office conversation preceding conversation with Dwight Eisenhower, tape WH6401.01, Recordings, Lyndon B. Johnson Presidential Library (LBJPL), Austin, TX; Germany (2007), 100. The *Syracuse Herald-American*, on August 1, estimated that the neighborhood councils had registered four thousand tenants (80 percent of them Democrats) by early August. See also *Rochester Democrat and Chronicle*, June 21, 1965; *Rochester Times-Union*, June 11, 1965; *Syracuse Herald Journal*, June 26, 1965.

28. Williams report to Shriver on Syracuse, Apr. 27, 1965, box 54, Syracuse file, OEO Inspection Division, RG 381, National Archives II; Jenkins to Haddad and Clampitt, confidential memo, Aug. 29, 1965; Jenkins to Haddad, Clampitt, and Williams, confidential memo, Aug. 24, 1965, box 55, Syracuse file, OEO Inspection Division, RG 381, National Archives II.

29. Interview with Sargent Shriver, excerpted in Gillette (1996), 36; Hoehler's thesis, "Community Action by the United Packinghouse Workers of America: The C.I.O. in the Back of the Yards Neighborhood of Chicago," was completed at the University of Chicago in 1947; Alinsky to Carl Tjerandsen, of the Emil Schwarzhaupt Foundation, Feb. 16, 1961, box 29, folder 14, ESF Papers, University of Chicago Special Collections. Ohlin and Alinsky also had the same thesis adviser at University of Chicago—Ernest Burgess; Lemann (1991), 152.

30. Interview with Frank Mankiewicz, by Gillette (1996), 202.

31. Williams memo, Apr. 27, 1965, box 54, Syracuse file, OEO Inspection Division, RG 381, National Archives II.

32. On election, see *Daily Orange*, Oct. 26, 1965, and Aug. 29, 1965; Williams report on Syracuse, Apr. 27, 1965; Williams to Ed May, Oct. 19, 1965, box 55, Syracuse file; *Syracuse Herald-Journal*, Oct. 27, 1965, and Nov. 30, 1965; *Rochester Times-Union*, Nov. 3, 1965; *Syracuse Post-Standard*, Nov. 25, 1965.

33. *Syracuse Herald-Journal*, Sept. 24, 1965, Nov. 25, 1965, and Dec. 1, 1965; Barbara Carter, "Sargent Shriver and the Role of the Poor," *The Reporter*, May 5, 1966; *Syracuse Post-Standard*, Dec. 2, 1965; Williams to Ed May, Dec. 1, 1965, box 55, Syracuse file.

34. Gillette (1996), 202, 205, 207–8; "'Poverty War Mislabeled': Saul Alinsky," *Chicago Tribune*, Dec. 23, 1965; "Syracuse University Drops Activist Radical," *New York Times*, Dec. 22, 1965; Lawrence Davis, "Syracuse: What Happens When the Poor Take Over," *The Reporter*, Mar. 21, 1968, 19–21.

35. At one point in the mid-1960s he managed to convince the president of a university to let him take an examination being administered to doctoral candidates in community organization. "Three of the questions were on the philosophy of and motivations of Saul Alinsky," he wrote in *Rules for Radicals*. "I answered two of them incorrectly." Saul Alinsky, *Rules for Radicals: A Practical Primer for Realistic Radicals*, Vintage Books, New York (1971), 169.

36. Alinsky (Spring 1965); "Daley Is Opposed on Poverty Drive"; "Behind the Mask," *American Child* (Nov. 1965); "The Poor and the Powerful," in *Poverty and Mental Health*, ed. Milton Greenblatt, American Psychiatric Association (Jan. 1967); "Syracuse University Drops Activist Radical"; "Poverty War Mislabeled"; "The Tough Line on Poverty . . . The Ways of a Professional Agitator," *The Observer*, Feb. 15, 1966.

37. Rev. Lynward Stevenson and A. L. Smith to Clifford Alexander, Associate Special Counsel to the President, Oct. 8, 1965, Gen FG1 8/7/65–12/1/65, White Central Files FG, LBJPL; "Poverty Funds Bypass Militants: TWO Head," *Chicago Defender*, Dec. 20, 1965, 12.

38. "TWO Protests: Mayor, Shriver Defend Conduct of Poverty War," *Chicago Defender*, Dec. 7, 1965, 1; *New York Times*, Dec. 7, 1965, 27; Cazenave (2007), 153.

39. "Hyde Park Voices, November 1967," box 181, file 4, Leon Despres Papers, CHS; "TWO Evaluation," June 24, 1964, Church Federation of Greater Chicago records, box 52 file 1, CHS; *Woodlawn Booster*, May 1, 1963; *TWO Newsletter*, Apr. 17, 1964; "Policy and Resolutions," n.d., Woodlawn Organization Collection, CHS; Arthur Brazier, *Black Self-Determination: The Story of the Woodlawn Organization*, Eerdmans, Grand Rapids, MI (1969), 35; William Swenson, "The Continuing Colloquium on University of Chicago Demonstration Projects in Woodlawn," Center for Urban Studies, University of Chicago (Nov. 1968); Herman Blake, "Report on TWO, 1967," 89, 114, ESF Papers.

40. A dissident social workers' union in Chicago supported TWO's efforts and issued a "Manifesto for a More Humane Welfare System" in 1966, denouncing the paternalism of the system and calling for more generous benefits. Eleanor Rosebrugh, "Syracuse Group Serves as

Host, Poverty 'War Council' Born," *Syracuse Post-Standard*, Jan. 17, 1966, 1; Cazenave (2007), 156–58; Felicia Kornbluh, *The Battle for Welfare Rights: Politics and Poverty in Modern America*, University of Pennsylvania Press, Philadelphia (2007), 35–38; George Martin and Elinor Paulson, "The Ad Hoc Committee for a Guaranteed Income," *Guaranteed Annual Income Newsletter* (June 1966); Jacqueline Pope, *Biting the Hand That Feeds Them: Organizing Women on Welfare at the Grassroots Level*, Praeger, New York (1989); Nick Kotz and Mary Lynn Kotz, *A Passion for Equality: George A. Wiley and the Movement*, W. W. Norton and Co., New York (1979); "A Manifesto for a More Humane Welfare System," *Social Action* (Nov. 1966).

41. Blake (1967), 114, 139–40.
42. Blake (1967), 116–17.
43. Blake (1967), 123.
44. Blake (1967), 117.
45. Blake (1967), 117; "Mom of 11 on Poverty Group," *Jet Magazine*, Feb. 10, 1966, 6.
46. *Hyde Park Voices*, Nov. 1967, box 181, file 4, Leon Despres Papers, CHS; "TWO Urges Lawmakers, Assist Ghetto Dwellers," *Chicago Defender*, Nov. 21, 1967, 8; Blake (1967), 114; Kornbluh (2007), 97–100; Jackson (2007), 345. On WIN, see Gilbert Steiner, *The State of Welfare*, Brookings Institution, Washington, DC (1971), 43–50; Alan Zundel, *Declarations of Dependency: The Civic Republican Tradition in US Poverty Policy*, State University Press of New York, Albany (2000), 81–91.

47. Robert Levin, "Gang-Busting in Chicago," *New Republic*, June 1968; "A Proposal for the Training of Four-Hundred Out-of-School Youths of the Woodlawn Community," submitted to the OEO by the Reverend Arthur M. Brazier, President, the Woodlawn Organization, box 4, "Chicago" folder, Sherwin Markman Papers, LBJPL.

48. Andrew Diamond, *Mean Streets: Chicago Youths and the Everyday Struggle for Empowerment in the Multiracial City, 1908–1969*, University of California Press, Berkeley (2009), 254–55.

49. Diamond (2009), 257, 262, 265, 291.

50. James McPherson, "Chicago's Blackstone Rangers," *Atlantic Monthly*, May 1969; Fish (1973), 119; "The Gangs: A Thorn in the Ghetto's Side," *Chicago Defender*, Dec. 17, 1966; "Sees Gang Leader Need: Success of TWO Plan to Depend on Their Help," *Chicago Tribune*, Dec. 4, 1966.

51. Diamond (2009), 268.

52. John Fry, "A Statement Regarding the Relationship of the 1, Presbyterian Church and the Blackstone Rangers," Oct. 1966; Lois Wille, "Inside Ranger Gangs," *Chicago Daily News*, Aug. 3, 1966, 1; "'You'd Better Watch Out,' Rev. Fry Warns McClellan," *Chicago Defender*, July 1, 1968. See also John R. Fry, *Fire and Blackstone*, Lippincott Press, Philadelphia (1969); John R. Fry, *Locked Out Americans: A Memoir*, Harper and Row, New York (1973); Morton Kondracke and June Carey, "Youth Gangs Grow, Fear More Strife," *Chicago Sun-Times*, June 5, 1966, 4; *Woodlawn Booster*, June 1, 1966, 1; John Hall Fish, *Black Power/White Control*, Princeton University Press, Princeton, NJ (1973), 119.

53. Will Cooley, in his 2008 dissertation, convincingly argues that black middle-class reactions to and perceptions of crime had a powerful impact on mobility decisions. See Will Cooley, "Moving Up, Moving Out: Race and Social Mobility in Chicago 1914–1972" (PhD diss., University of Illinois, 2008), 274, 322; The Interuniversity Social Research Committee—Chicago Metropolitan Area, "Militancy for and against Civil Rights and Integration in Chicago: Summer 1967" (Report No. 1, Aug. 1, University of Chicago Press, Chicago (1967), 21–24.

54. Fish (1973), 127; *Woodlawn Booster*, Aug. 4, 1966.

55. Noble DeSalvi, "Angry Demand for Police Crackdown," *Daily Calumet*, Sept. 28, 1966.

56. *Woodlawn Booster*, Oct. 18, 1966; Fish (1973), 128–30; John Fry, "History of Ranger Activity, Summer 1966," Oct. 1966, box 94, file 8, 7–9, Leon Despres Papers, CHS.

57. Fish (1973), 132–34; TWO, "Total Manpower Demonstration Program for 700 Unemployed Young Adults," Application to OEO, Nov. 1966, 1.

58. "A Proposal for the Training"; TWO (Nov. 1966).

59. "TWO Denies Gang Charge," *Chicago Defender*, June 22, 1968; Fish (1973), 136–39; McPherson (1969); Bill Graham's report on his visit can be found in box 352, "Ghetto Visits" folder, Office Files of White House Aides, James Gaither, LBJPL. The White House fellow Sherwin Markman, who made a similar visit in January 1967, also left with a positive impression, particularly of the role of the Rangers in suppressing riots on the South Side during the prior summer. See Markman, "Chicago Trip 1968" folder, Markman Personal Papers, LBJPL.

60. National Film Board of Canada, "A Continuing Responsibility," July 1968; Nicholas Von Hoffman, *Radical: A Portrait of Saul Alinsky*, Nation Books, New York (2010), 26–27.

61. "Woodlawn Poverty War Grips Gangs," *Chicago Tribune*, June 18, 1967; "Teen Violence, Frustration Plaguing TWO," *Chicago Defender*, Jan. 10, 1968; "TWO Struggling for Respectability," *Chicago Defender*, Jan. 15, 1968; "Brazier Gives Defense, Answers 'Watts' Query," *Chicago Defender*, June 22, 1968; "Memorandum: The Woodlawn Organization's $927,000 Manpower Demonstration Grant Which Involves Two Chicago Gangs," Bill Ferrell to [unspecified], Jan. 6, 1968, Ex WE 9 1/3/68–1/22/68, White House Central Files WE, box 31, LBJPL; Bertrand Harding, Acting Director of the OEO, "Memorandum for the President: The Woodlawn Organization," June 25, 1968, Ex WE 9 5/1/68–7/9/68, White House Central Files WE, box 32, LBJPL; Julian Levi to Joseph Califano, with attachment, Sept. 7, 1967, Gen LA2 8/26/67–10/15/67, White House Central Files LA, LBJPL.

62. Hazel Erskine, "The Polls: Demonstrations and Riots," *Public Opinion Quarterly* 31 (Winter 1967–1968), 673–74; Michael Flamm, *Law and Order: Street Crime, Civil Unrest and the Crisis of Liberalism in the 1960s*, Columbia University Press, New York (2005), 82.

63. "Bulletin," *National Review*, Aug. 2, 1966; Nimetz to Califano, Aug. 9, 1967, box 58, White House Office Files of Joseph Califano, LBJPL; Flamm (2005), 94–98.

64. Sherwin Markman interview, 24–25, LBJPL; David Carter, *The Music Has Gone Out of the Movement: Civil Rights and the Johnson Administration, 1965–1968*, University of North Carolina Press, Chapel Hill (2009), 175–76.

65. "Ghetto Visits" folder, Office Files of the White House Aides, James Gaither, box 352; Sherwin Markman to the President, Jan. 17, 1967, Personal Papers of Sherwin Markman, box 4, LBJPL; May 9, 1967, WHCF, Ex WE9, box 29, LBJPL; Markman, "Notes," n.d., "Chicago Trip 1968" folder, Markman Papers, box 4; Sherwin Markman, "American Ghettoes: Our Challenge and Response," Apr. 5, 1967, WHCF, Ex WE9, Mar. 12, 1968–Apr. 30, 1968, box 31, LBJPL; Diamond (2009), 247–48.

66. Cazenave (2007), 167–69; Congressional Record, Proceedings and Debates of the 90th Congress, First Session, vol. 113, pt. 23, Nov. 1–9, 1967, 31416.

67. "Poverty: Everybody's Whipping Boy," *New York Times*, Oct. 22, 1967; Cazenave (2007), 169–72.

68. Levin (1968).

69. According to Andrew Diamond, the GIU files—released to the public in 1981—confirm what most TWO activists suspected at the time of the Youth Project: the unit systematically engaged in infiltration and sabotage to destroy the program. Harding, "Memorandum for the President"; McPherson (1969), 83–84; Diamond (2009), 277.

70. McPherson (1969), 77; Fish (1973), 153; "Sees Gang Leader Need: Success of TWO Plan to Depend on Their Help," *Chicago Tribune*, Dec. 4, 1966; "Blackstone Rangers, Street Gang Investigated by Senate Panel, Demanding Share of Power in Chicago," *New York Times*, Aug. 3, 1968. The OEO noted the impact of police harassment and bad publicity on the CUL's ability to find employment for the trainees. See Harding, "Memorandum for the President."

71. Blake (1967), 133; Fish (1973), 150–53; "South Side Story," *New Republic*, July 6, 1968, 13–14; Levin (1968).

72. "Poverty Warriors in Chicago," *Chicago Tribune*, Dec. 23, 1967; "TWO Class: Naps, Dice and Comic Books," *Chicago Tribune*, Dec. 23, 1967; "Rev. Brazier Responds to OEO Threat," *Chicago Defender*, Jan. 30, 1967; Fish (1973), 157–58.

73. "Teen Violence, Frustration."

74. "Chicago Trip 1968" folder, Sherwin Markman Papers, box 4, LBJPL.

75. The GAO investigation also found GIU and press reports that the Youth Project had kept jailed staffers on the payroll to be inaccurate. Due to a clerical oversight, only one such individual had been kept on and for less than twenty-four hours. Harding, "Memorandum to the President," Mar. 27, 1968, Ex WE 9 1/3/68–1/22/68, White House Central Files WE, box 31, LBJPL; "Statement by Alan Beals Concerning the Woodlawn Association," OEO Public Affairs Office, Dec. 22, 1967, Ex WE 9 1/3/68–1/22/68, White House Central Files WE, box 31, LBJPL; Fish (1973), 159; "TWO Struggling for Respectability," *Chicago Defender*, Jan. 15, 1968; "Rev. Brazier Responds to OEO Threat."

76. Levin (1968); "South Side Story," *New Republic*, July 6, 1968.

77. Morton Kondracke, "Evaluator Urges Two More Years to TWO Project," *Chicago Sun-Times*, July 19, 1968; Robert Novak, "How Ranger Probe Started," *Chicago Sun-Times*, July 12, 1968; Rowland Evans and Robert Novak, "Chicago Police behind Probe into Blackstone Rangers Affair," *Washington Post*, July 12, 1968, A21; Fish (1973), 159–61; I. A. Spergel, C. Turner, J. Pleas, and P. Brown, "Youth Manpower: What Happened in Woodlawn" (unpublished ms.), University of Chicago, School of Social Service (1969), 345; Memo from Bertrand Harding to President Johnson, June 25, 1968, Bertrand Harding Personal Papers, box 49, LBJPL.

78. Flamm (2005), 125, 140; George Gallup, *The Gallup Poll: Public Opinion, 1935–1971*, Random House, New York (1971), 2107–08; Harry McPherson, *A Political Education: A Washington Memoir*, University of Texas Press, Austin (1972), 376; Frank Meyer, "Liberalism Run Riot," *National Review*, Mar. 26, 1968, 283.

79. Fish (1973), 161; "Brazier Gives Defense"; "TWO Denies Gang Charge."

80. Ramsey Clark to Harry McPherson, "Demand by Senate Permanent Subcommittee on Investigations for OEO internal documents," Aug. 28, 1968, folder FG 11-15 Office of Economic Opportunity, document 8d, confidential file, box 21, LBJPL; Harding, "Memorandum for the President."

81. "Poverty Unit Denies Knowledge of a Weapons Cache in Chicago," *New York Times*, June 24, 1968; "End of TWO Project Could Bring Crime Rise," *Chicago Defender*, July 8, 1968; "Democratic Candidate Raps McClellan Probe," *Chicago Defender*, July 18, 1968.

82. "TWO Leader Defends Use of US Funds," *Chicago Tribune*, July 10, 1968.

83. Senator Harry F. Byrd Jr. to Bertrand Harding, Aug. 19, 1968, and Harding to Byrd, Aug. 21, 1968, box 49, "Woodlawn Organization Hearings" folder, Harding Personal Papers, LBJPL; "Poverty Chief to Bar Gang Project Funds," *Chicago Tribune*, Sept. 4, 1968; "The Lame, Halt and Poor," *New Republic*, Sept. 14, 1968; "How Permanent Is This Burial," *Chicago Tribune*, Sept. 6, 1968. On Harding's October testimony defending the rationale for the Youth Project, see "TWO

Project Worth Cost, OEO Chief Tells Senators," *Chicago Sun-Times*, Oct. 11, 1968; "OEO Director Backs Giving Aid to Gangs," *Chicago Tribune*, Oct. 11, 1968, "Antipoverty Chief Backs Aid to Gangs," *New York Times*, Dec. 12, 1968.

84. "The End to a Sorry Experiment," *Chicago Tribune*, Aug. 2, 1968, 10; Fish (1973), 173; "TWO Work Defended by Brazier," *Chicago Sun-Times*, Sept. 6, 1968; Lois Wille, "TWO Gang Project: Did It Fail?" *Chicago Daily News*, undated clipping (probably late June 1968). See also Irving Spergel, *Reducing Youth Gang Violence: The Little Village Gang Project in Chicago*, Alta Mira Press, Lanham, MD (2006), 12–14; Diamond (2009), 278.

Chapter Nine

1. The economist Leon Keyserling, the sociologist Herbert Gans, and the socialist Michael Harrington spent the spring and summer of 1966 helping put the proposal together. Kevin Yuill, "The 1966 White House Conference on Civil Rights," *Historical Journal* 41, no. 1 (Mar. 1998); John D'Emilio, *Lost Prophet: The Life and Times of Bayard Rustin*, University of Chicago Press, Chicago (2004), 418–19, 422, 437; Thomas Jackson, *From Civil Rights to Human Rights: Martin Luther King Jr. and the Struggle for Economic Justice*, University of Pennsylvania Press, Philadelphia (2007), 257–58; "Slum Plea Made at Rights Parley," *New York Times*, Nov. 18, 1965; White House Conference, "To Fulfill These Rights: Council's Report and Recommendations to the Conference," June 1–2, 1966; "Dr. King Studies Plan to Repudiate 'Black Power,' " *New York Times*, Oct. 10, 1966; Hazel Erskine, "The Polls: Demonstrations and Riots," *Public Opinion Quarterly* 31 (Winter 1967–1968), 673–74; David Carter, *The Music Has Gone Out of the Movement: Civil Rights and the Johnson Administration, 1965–1968*, University of North Carolina Press, Chapel Hill (2009), 99; Michael Flamm, *Law and Order: Street Crime, Civil Unrest and the Crisis of Liberalism in the 1960s*, Columbia University Press, New York (2005), 82.

2. "10-Year Plan Aims at Poverty's End," *New York Times*, Oct. 27, 1966; " 'Budget' to End Poverty Stirs Capital Skepticism and Sympathy," *New York Times*, Oct. 28, 1966; D'Emilio (2003), 431–32, Edmund Wehrle, "Guns, Butter, Leon Keyserling, the AFL-CIO, and the Fate of Full-Employment Economics," *Historian*, 66 (2004); Leon Keyserling, "Guaranteed Annual Incomes," *New Republic*, Mar. 18, 1967, 20–23.

3. A. Philip Randolph Institute, *A "Freedom Budget" for All Americans: Budgeting Our Resources, 1966-1975, to Achieve "Freedom from Want,"* 4, 23–27, 63, 65; Bayard Rustin, "A Negro Leader Defines a Way Out of the Exploding Ghetto," *New York Times*, Aug. 13, 1967; Daryl Michael Scott, "The Politics of Pathology: The Ideological Origins of the Moynihan Controversy," *Journal of Policy History* 8, no. 1 (1996); National Committee against Discrimination in Housing, *The Impact of Housing Patterns on Job Opportunities* (1968).

4. A. Philip Randolph Institute, *Freedom Budget*, 1, 11, 39, 41. Dr. King, an early supporter of the Freedom Budget, concurred. The poverty war would fail "if it substitutes a 'welfare' approach for much-needed economic reforms aimed at the creation of more jobs," he argued. Only full employment, a guaranteed annual income, and political empowerment could free blacks "from the smothering prison of poverty." National Advisory Commission on Civil Disorders, Transcripts and Agenda of Hearings, July 29–Nov. 9, 1967, box 5, 2811, Record Group (RG) 220, National Archives II.

5. A. Philip Randolph Institute, *Freedom Budget*, 13, 27, 41, 59. Dr. King announced his support for a guaranteed minimum income in his October 1967 testimony before the Kerner Commission. The idea of a guaranteed annual income was surprisingly mainstream in the

mid-1960s. The 1966 Report of the National Commission on Technology, Automation, and Economic Progress—which was appointed by Johnson—called for it. Office of Economic Opportunity director Sargent Shriver endorsed it as well, although he agreed with the authors of the *Freedom Budget* that full employment had to come first. Even the US Chamber of Commerce held a symposium on it, shortly after the Freedom Budget was released. Perhaps most famously, free market economist Milton Freedman proposed using a "negative income tax" for the same purpose. Its policy descendent, the Earned Income Tax Credit, is the nation's largest antipoverty measure today. See "T.R.B. from Washington," *New Republic*, Dec. 17, 1966, 4.

6. A. Philip Randolph Institute, *Freedom Budget*, 12, 19–20, 44–50.

7. George Lardner Jr., "Alinsky Finds Distrust for OEO," *Washington Post*, Apr. 20, 1966, A4; Saul Alinsky, "The Poor and the Powerful," *Poverty and Mental Health*, ed. Milton Greenblatt et al. (Psychiatric Research Report No. 21), American Psychiatric Association (Jan. 1967), 28; William Swenson, "The Continuing Colloquium on University of Chicago Demonstration Projects in Woodlawn," Center for Urban Studies, University of Chicago (Nov. 1968).

8. "A TWO Black Paper: Concerning 1415–21 East 61st Street, and the Forces That Made It a Slum," Nov. 19, 1965; "TWO Black Paper Number Two: Poverty, Power and Race in Chicago," *TWO Newsletter*, Dec. 9, 1965.

9. James B. Murray interview with Arthur Brazier, June 7, 1991, 16, Schaumburg Center; William Swenson, "The Continuing Colloquium on University of Chicago Demonstration Projects in Woodlawn" (1968), Center for Urban Studies; Arthur Brazier, *Black Self-Determination: the Story of the Woodlawn Organization*, Eerdman's, Grand Rapids, MI (1969), 142.

10. Nikhil Pal Singh, *Black Is a Country: Race and the Unfinished Struggle For Democracy*, Harvard University Press, Cambridge, MA (2004), 53.

11. Interestingly, Rep. John Conyers (D-MI) proposed the Full Opportunity Act in October 1967, which would sweep all three visions into one—it called for a federal attack on metropolitan segregation, a guaranteed annual income, and a Freedom Budget–style investment in job creation. It didn't pass. See box 165, folder 24, National Committee against Discrimination in Housing Papers, Amistad Research Center, Tulane University (hereafter NCADH Papers).

12. Alexander von Hoffman, "Let Us Continue: Housing Policy in the Great Society, Part One," Joint Center for Housing Studies, Harvard University, Cambridge, MA, Apr. 2009, and "Into the Wild Blue Yonder: The Urban Crisis, Rocket Science, and the Pursuit of Transformation Housing Policy in the Great Society, Part Two," Joint Center for Housing Studies, Harvard University, Cambridge, MA, Mar. 2011, 6–7; Walter P. Reuther to President Lyndon B. Johnson, memo, May 13, 1965, box 5, folder "Urban Renewal–Slum Clearance, 11/23/63–12/31/65," Gen HS 2 7/1/67, Lyndon B. Johnson Presidential Library (LBJPL), Austin, TX. The Report of the Task Force on Metropolitan and Urban Problems (listed as the Outside 1964 Task Force on Metropolitan and Urban Affairs) can be found at the LBJPL. The task force, chaired by Massachusetts Institute of Technology political economist Robert C. Wood, submitted its report to the president in November 1964.

13. Wendell Pritchett, "White Urban Crisis? Regionalism, Race, and Urban Policy 1960–1974," *Journal of Urban History* (Jan. 2008), 271–73; Nelson Lichtenstein, *The Most Dangerous Man in Detroit: Walter Reuther and the Fate of American Labor*, Basic Books, New York (1995), 402; Wendell Pritchett, *Robert Clifton Weaver and the American City: The Life and Times of an Urban Reformer*, University of Chicago Press, Chicago (2008), 284; Lawrence Levinson, "Through a Glass Lightly: Reminiscences of the Model Cities Act and LBJ's Dance with Legislation," in *Lyndon Baines Johnson Remembered*, Eakin Press, Austin, TX (2003), 101–10; Robert

Dallek, *Flawed Giant: Lyndon Johnson and His Times, 1961–1973*, Oxford University Press, New York (1998), 317; Joseph Califano, *Inside: A Public and Private Life*, Public Affairs, New York (2004), 130.

14. Jack Conway generally attended meetings on Reuther's behalf. Bruce Stave, "A Conversation with Charles M. Haar: Urban History and the Great Society," *Journal of Urban History* 25 (1998); Charles Haar, *Between the Ideal and the Reality: A Study in the Origin, Fate, and Legacy of the Model Cities Program*, Little, Brown, Boston (1975); Alexander von Hoffman, 'Let Us Continue" (2011), 26–31; Bernard J. Frieden and Marshall Kaplan, *The Politics of Neglect: Urban Aid from Model Cities to Revenue Sharing*, Massachusetts Institute of Technology Press, Cambridge, MA (1975); Edward Banfield, "Making a New Federal Program: Model Cities, 1964–1968," in *Policy and Politics in America: Six Case Studies*, ed. Allan Sindler, Little, Brown, Boston (1973), 125–58; John Sasso and Priscilla Foley, *A Little Noticed Revolution: An Oral History of the Model Cities Program and Its Transition to the Community Development Block Grant Program*, Berkeley Public Policy Press, Berkeley, CA (2005).

15. Report of Subcommittee on Topic 1, Interagency 1965 Task Force on Urban Affairs and Housing (Weaver, Chairman), 5, 7–9, 12, LBJPL; Pritchett (2008), 274; Haar (1975); "Proposed Programs for the Department of Housing and Urban Development," War on Poverty Papers, reel 15, LBJPL; Pierre de Vise, "Chicago's Widening Color Gap" (Interuniversity Social Research Committee Report No. 2, Dec. 1967), 128–29.

16. Johnson's speech was quoted in NCADH, "Model Cities and Housing Desegregation," 1967, 5, box 163, folder 40, NCADH Papers. See also Charles Haar Oral History, 50, LBJPL; Robert Clifton Weaver Oral History, 38, LBJPL; Haar (1975), 57, 64; Robert Halpern, *Rebuilding the Inner-City: A History of Neighborhood Initiatives to Address Poverty in the United States*, Columbia University Press, New York (1995), 118; Pritchett (2008), 285–86; Pritchett (Jan. 2008), 274–76; "Sweeping Shifts Are Mapped for Cities by Presidential Panel," *New York Times*, Nov. 15, 1965; "Move On to Save Bill to End Slums," *New York Times*, May 24, 1966; "Cities Bill Passes Main Test," *New York Times*, Oct. 16, 1966.

17. Jack Wood Testimony before the Subcommittee on Housing of the U.S. Senate Committee on Banking and Currency, Aug. 22, 1967, box 165, folder 6, NCADH Papers; Jack Wood testimony to National Commission on Urban Problems, Sept. 6, 1967, box 172, folder 2, NCADH Papers; NCADH, "The Impact of Housing Patterns on Job Opportunities," 1968, box 121, folder 3, NCADH Papers; Anthony Downs, "Alternative Futures for the American Ghetto," *Daedalus* (Fall 1968), 1364; James Coleman et al., *Equality of Educational Opportunity*, US Department of Health, Education and Welfare, Government Printing Office, Washington, DC, 1966; US Civil Rights Commission, *Racial Isolation in the Public Schools*, US Government Printing Office, Washington, DC, 1967.

18. NCADH, "A Housing Program for All Americans," Oct. 1964, box 19, folder 8; NCADH, "Ten Year Plan," Oct. 1964, box 39, folder 29, Frank Horne Papers, NCADH; Jack E. Wood Jr., "America's Racial Ghettos," *The Crisis*, Dec. 1965; Report, Notre Dame Conference on Federal Civil Rights, Feb. 1966, box 42, folder 1, Frank Horne Papers, NCADH; NCADH, "Model Cities and Housing Desegregation," 1966, 26, box 163, folder 40, NCADH Papers; NCADH, "NCDH Position Regarding Proposed Federal Anti-Discrimination Housing Legislation," Apr. 28, 1966, National Association of Home Builders Archive (NAHBA), Washington, DC; NCADH, "The Impact of Housing Patterns on Job Opportunities," 1968, box 121, folder 3, NCADH Papers; Report of the Notre Dame Conference on Federal Civil Rights, published in *Notre Dame Lawyer* 41, no. 6 (1966), box 42, folder 1, Horne Papers, NCADH. On the public law–private law distinction,

see Leonard Rubinowitz and Ismail Alsheik, "A Missing Piece: Fair Housing and the 1964 Civil Rights Act," *Howard Law Journal* 48 (2005).

19. NCADH leaders participated directly in the administration's internal debates about fair housing legislation and executive orders, meeting with Vice President Humphrey in May 1965, with Justice Department lawyers and the US Civil Rights Commission in the fall of 1965, and with White House staffer Harry McPherson in January 1966. Those members of the executive branch who were most interested in an aggressive federal attack on metropolitan segregation used NCADH materials in memos and task force reports; the Bill of Particulars was submitted in Apr. 1966, at McPherson's request. A petition from the NCADH's regional conference in Los Angeles arrived at the White House in November 1966, just after the election. The petition can be found in the Office Files of Harry McPherson, box 67, LBJPL. On the 1966 Task Force on Civil Rights, see "Memorandum: Priority Proposals of the Civil Rights Task Force," Dec. 5, 1966, James Gaither Office Files, box 372, LBJPL.

20. NCADH, "A Housing Program for All Americans," Oct. 1964, box 19, folder 8, and Frank Horne, "Achieving Integration in Housing: A Few Concepts and Procedures" (presentation to the Fair Housing Conference held by the NCADH, June 29, 1965), box 33, folder 23, Frank Horne Papers, NCADH; Richard Margolis, "Toward a Strategy for NCDH," May 1966, box 39, folder 33, Frank Horne Papers, NCADH; L. S. Rubinowitz, "A Missing Piece: Fair Housing and the 1964 Civil Rights Act," *Howard Law Journal* 48, no. 3 (2005).

21. In their April 1966 Senate testimony in favor of the Model Cities bill, Jack Wood of the NCADH and Paul Davidoff of Americans for Democratic Action praised the potential of the legislation for remaking the social geography of the nation. The new program should "specifically call for the dispersal of racial and income ghettos" and "deliberately promote residential integration of income and race, "Davidoff argued. Local officials should be required to show that their proposals would not lead to greater segregation in the affected neighborhoods and in the city. House of Representatives Subcommittee on Housing, *Demonstration Cities, Housing and Urban Development and Urban Mass Transit*, 89th Cong., 2nd sess., Feb. 28, 1966, Government Printing Office, Washington, DC, 33–34, 46; Robert Weaver, Speech to Roosevelt Day Dinner of the Americans for Democratic Action, Cleveland, OH, Apr. 16, 1966, box 171, folder 4, NCADH Papers. Davidoff and Wood testified before the Subcommittee on Housing of the Senate Banking and Currency Committee on Apr. 25, 1966. Paul Davidoff, "Testimony," box 163, folder 44, NCADH Papers.

22. Housing Committee, "Report and Recommendations to the Conference," White House Conference "To Fulfill These Rights," May 14, 1966, NAHBA. More generally, see "White House Conference to Fulfill These Rights" folders, Federal Records, LBJPL. Frank Horne, "Model Cities–Promise and Threat" (speech to plenary session, NCADH Regional Conference in New York City, Apr. 13–14, 1967), box 33, folder 31, Horne Papers, NCADH; "Urban Rebuilding Priority Is Urged," *Washington Post*, May 12, 1966; NCADH, "Model Cities Local Action Guidelines" (1966), box 121, folder 2, NCADH Papers; NCADH, "Model Cities and Metropolitan Desegregation: A Program for Grassroots Action," Apr. 1967, box 121, folder 3, NCADH Papers.

23. For Fino's arguments, see 89th Cong., 2nd sess., *Congressional Record* 112 (Oct. 13, 1966), 26,612–26,614, 26,624–26,625. Haar (1975), 76–81, 83; Pritchett (2008), 298; Edward Schmitt, *President of the Other America*, University of Massachusetts Press, Amherst (2010), 138–42; Jackson (2007), 271–77.

24. For a colorful overview of the "long, hot summer" of 1966, see Rick Perlstein, *Nixonland: The Rise of a President and the Fracturing of America*, Simon and Schuster, New York (2009),

especially 120-27. Harry McPherson to Nicholas Katzenbach, Sept. 20, 1966, Select Civil Rights Files of Harry McPherson, CRDJA (*Civil Rights during the Johnson Administration, 1963-1969*, ed. Steven Lawson), pt. I, reel 11, 0643-52; "Signing of Model Cities Bill Ends Long Struggle to Keep It Alive," *New York Times*, Nov. 4, 1966; "Demonstration Cities Bill Passed by House, 178-41," *New York Times*, Oct. 15, 1966; "Johnson 'Demonstration Cities' Plan Gets Lift as Senate Passes $900 Million Version," *Wall Street Journal*, Aug. 22, 1966; NCADH, "Model Cities and Housing Desegregation," 1966, 6, box 163, folder 40, NCADH Papers; Von Hoffman (2011), 32; Haar (1975), 88; Pritchett (2008), 298-99; Levinson (2003), 101-10; Dallek (1999), 317-20; *Gallup Opinion Index* (Nov. 1966); James Sundquist, *Politics and Policy: The Eisenhower, Kennedy and Johnson Years*, Brookings Institution, Washington, DC (1968), 281.

25. Frances Fox Piven and Richard Cloward, "Desegregated Housing: Who Pays for the Reformers Ideal," *New Republic*, Dec. 17, 1966; Piven and Cloward, "The Case against Urban Desegregation," *Social Work* 12 (1967).

26. Stokely Carmichael and Charles Hamilton's book *Black Power* was published in 1967. Richard Cloward, "Community Action for Housing Desegregation: Strategies and Problems" (paper written for NCADH), May 1966; Piven and Cloward, "Desegregated Housing" and "Case against Urban Desegregation."

27. On Percy's proposal, see S. 1592, A Bill to Charter a National Homeownership Foundation, 90th Cong., 1st sess., reprinted in *Housing Legislation of 1967*, 1414-46, 1517-42; Alex Campbell, "'Chuck' Percy: Republicanism's New Frontier," *New Republic*, Nov. 18, 1967, 15-17; Warren Butler, "An Approach to Low and Moderate Income Home Ownership," *Rutgers Law Review* (Fall 1967); Christa Lew Carnegie, "Homeownership for the Poor: Running the Washington Gauntlet," *Journal of the American Planning Association* (May 1970).

28. In addition to boosting the policy profile of CDCs, which became an increasingly important part of federal urban policy in subsequent years, Kennedy also laid the conceptual groundwork for what later became enterprise zones. On Kennedy's ideas, see Statement of Hon. Robert F. Kennedy, Subcommittee on Executive Reorganization, *Federal Role in Urban Affairs*, 1966, 25-47; "Urban Rebuilding Priority Is Urged," *Washington Post*, May 12, 1966; "Kennedy Offers Plan on Ghettos," *New York Times*, May 19, 1966; "Federal Aid to Cities Hit as Shopworn," *Washington Post*, Aug. 16, 1966; "To Save a Slum," *Newsweek*, Nov. 20, 1967; "Tax Incentives to Encourage Housing in Urban Poverty Areas," Hearings before the Committee on Finance, US Senate, 90th Cong., 1st sess., Sept. 14-16, 1967; Jack Newfield, "A Few Rays of Hope," *Life Magazine*, Mar. 8, 1968, 83-94; Alexander von Hoffman, "Calling Upon the Genius: Housing Policy in the Great Society, Part Three," Joint Center for Housing Studies, Harvard University, Cambridge, MA (Mar. 2010); Alice O'Connor, "Swimming against the Tide: A Brief History of Federal Policy in Poor Communities," in *Urban Problems and Community Development*, by Ronald Ferguson and William Dickens, Brookings Institution, Washington, DC (1999), 105-8; Frank Mankiewicz, "The Origins of Enterprise Zones," *Washington Post*, Oct. 30, 1992.

29. James Ridgeway, "Rebuilding the Slums," *New Republic*, Jan. 7, 1967; Robert Semple, "The Slum Planners," *New Republic*, July 1967. The Semple article describes the Percy and RFK plans in some detail. Both were aimed at low- and moderate-income urban families rather than the very poor; Kennedy's plan focused mostly on rental housing, whereas Percy's stressed home ownership. Percy's proposal to create the National Homeownership Foundation, which he introduced to the Senate in April 1967, was eventually enacted into law by the 1968 Housing and Urban Development Act. HUD had already initiated an experiment to use loan guarantees to entice builders to construct low-income housing, including the TWO-KMF development corporation. On the HUD

experiment—Section 221(d)(3)—that helped to spark the CDC movement that Senator Kennedy desired, see "Press Release," Apr. 28, 1967, box 171, folder 4, NCADH Papers.

30. Transcript, Ramsey Clark oral history interview, Apr. 16, 1969, 1, LBJPL; Lamb, 35–36; *Public Papers of the Presidents: Lyndon Johnson* (1967), bk. I, 189–90; "'Fair Housing' Again in Rights Bill," *US News and World Report*, Feb. 27, 1967, 69. On the politics of law and order during this period, see Michael Flamm, *Law and Order: Street Crime, Civil Unrest and the Crisis of Liberalism in the 1960s*, Columbia University Press, New York (2005). At almost the same time that the Johnson administration moved away from an attack on metropolitan segregation, it retreated on crime policy, too—shifting from an emphasis on fighting poverty to gun control and more police.

31. George Schermer, George Nesbitt, and Robert Greene, "Agenda Paper VI: Housing and the Neighborhood," Nov. 1965, Federal Records, White House Conference to Fulfill These Rights, box 12, LBJPL.

32. For an economic critique of ghetto enrichment policies during this period, see Louis Winnick, "Place Prosperity vs. People Prosperity: Welfare Considerations in the Geographic Redistribution of Economic Activity," *Essays in Urban Land Economics in Honor of the Sixty-Fifth Birthday of Leo Grebler*, UCLA Real Estate Research Program, Los Angeles (1966). Winnick, an economist with the Ford Foundation, worried that such policies would tie people to places they might be better off leaving. John Kain, Testimony to the Kerner Commission, Nov. 2, 1967, Transcript of Hearings, 3256, box 6, Kerner Commission Records, LBJPL; see also John Kain and Joseph Persky, "Alternatives to the Gilded Ghetto" (paper prepared for the Economic Development Administration Research Conference), US Department of Commerce, Fall 1967.

33. Housing Committee, "Report and Recommendations to the Conference," May 14, 1966, 120, White House Conference "To Fulfill These Rights," National Association of Home Builders Archive (NAHBA), Washington DC; NCADH, *Annual Report* (1967), 9, box 73, folder 8, NCADH Papers; Wood testimony to National Commission on Urban Problems, Sept. 6, 1967, box 172, folder 2, NCADH Papers. The commission, chaired by former Illinois senator Paul Douglas, had its origins in President Johnson's 1965 Message on Cities. Public hearings were held in eighteen cities between May and October 1967, just as Model Cities planning funds were being distributed.

34. Funnye's strong support for what he called "deghettoization" was shaped by his professional background as an architect with a doctorate in urban planning, as well as his activism—he was the chair of the New York City chapter of the Congress of Racial Equality (CORE) from 1964 to 1965 and later served as field director for NCADH. Clarence Funnye, "Toward Deghettoization: A Proposal for Decisions in Housing and Planning in New York City," memo to Mayor-elect John Lindsay, Idea Plan Associates, Mar. 1966, box 42, folder 2, Frank Horne Papers, NCADH; Clarence Funnye, "The Imperative of Deghettoization," *Social Work*, Apr. 1967; Frank Horne to Jason Nathan, Oct. 11, 1967, box 13, folder 14, Horne Papers, NCADH; Clarence Funnye, "Black Power and Deghettoization: A Retreat to Reality" (1969), NCADH Papers, box 121, folder 6, NCADH; Clarence Funnye, "Judgment at St. Louis," report on hearings of the U.S. Civil Rights Commission on Planning, Jobs and Housing in the Suburbs, Jan. 1970, box 172, folder 18, NCADH Papers.

35. Tom Sugrue, *Sweet Land of Liberty: The Forgotten Struggle for Civil Rights in the North*, Random House, New York (2008), 399–402; Marion K. Sanders, *The Professional Radical: Conversations with Saul Alinsky*, Harper and Row, New York (1970), 84; Lois Wille, "Inland Forum: That Man Alinsky Loves a Good Hassle," *Inland Architect* (Feb. 1969), 27; Saul Alinsky, "You

Can't See the Stars Through the Stripes," *Proceedings of the National Workshop on The Urban Poor: Manpower and Consumer Potentials* (Mar. 1968); Saul Alinsky, "Afterword," *Reveille for Radicals*, Random House, New York (1968), 213.

36. "TWO Vote Drive Continues; Takes Position on Schools, Housing," *Woodlawn Observer*, Jan. 19, 1967.

37. Dr. King put a more positive spin on the community development component of Model Cities, arguing in March 1967 that it held out the promise of ghetto rehabilitation in partial compensation for the nation's failure to integrate the suburbs. In part this was a reaction to continued stonewalling by Mayor Daley and the Chicago Real Estate Board on implementing their end of the 1966 summit agreement. But King also continued to believe that metropolitan desegregation was essential. "I see no more dangerous development in our society than the constant growth and building and development of predominantly negro central cities ringed by white suburbs," he told the Kerner Commission in October 1967. NCADH Press Release, Jan. 15, 1967, box 165, folder 6, NCADH Papers; "U.S. Implementing Model Cities Bill," *New York Times*, Jan. 12, 1967; "'Fair Housing' Again in Rights Bill," 69; NCADH, *How the Federal Government Builds Ghettoes*, Feb. 1967; "Rights Group Says Government Helps to Build Ghettoes," *New York Times*, Feb. 9, 1967; "Federal Government Gets Shelled for 'Building Ghettos,'" *Chicago Defender*, Feb. 25, 1967, 5; Summary Report, Task Force on Cities 1966, James Gaither Papers, box 383, "Misc. Materials Re: Cities 1966" folder, LBJPL; Jackson (2007), 295, 299, 301; King testimony, National Advisory Commission on Civil Disorders, Transcripts and Agenda of Hearings, July 29–Nov. 19, 1967, 2792, RG 282, box 5, LBJPL.

38. Frank Horne, "Model Cities: Threat and Promise" (speech to NCDH Executive Committee, Apr. 13, 1967), box 303, HUD; Rutledge and Wood, letter to the editor, *New York Times*, June 1, 1967.

39. For example, HUD guidelines required all proposals to include an analysis of the problems of model areas. This analysis had to be based on "awareness of how these conditions came about," and should be "put in a metropolitan context." This would inevitably lead to a discussion of residential segregation, Wood argued. Similarly, HUD guidelines required that the analysis be "coupled with evidence of a commitment and capacity to develop a program that will make a substantial impact on those problems." Thus, if a Model Cities proposal included weak measures to attack segregation, activists could challenge it locally and nationally. Section F of the HUD guidelines required proposals to demonstrate "marked progress" in reducing "social and economic disadvantages, ill health, and underemployment." How could any Model Cities program do this, without pushing for more low- and moderate-income housing in suburbs and outlying urban areas, where the jobs increasingly were? Section J of the HUD guidelines required Model Cities programs to contribute to a "well balanced city with maximum opportunities in the choice of housing accommodations for all citizens for all income levels." No Model Cities plan could accomplish this without focusing on integration beyond the narrow boundaries of its model area. NCADH, "Urban Crisis and the Ghetto System: A Program for Grassroots Action" (Nov. 1966), NCADH Papers; NCADH, "Model Cities Local Action Guidelines" (1966), box 121, folder 2, NCADH Papers; NCADH, "Model Cities and Housing Desegregation," 1967, box 163, folder 40, NCADH Papers; Rutledge and Wood, letter to the editor; *Trends in Housing* (May 1967).

40. Robert C. Weaver to the President, Feb. 9, 1967, Ex HU 2-2 Housing 12/10/66–4/30/67 folder, White House Central Files Subject File HU, box 48, LBJPL; HUD Press Release, Feb. 8, 1967, box 171, folder 4, NCADH Papers.

41. NCADH, "Model Cities and Housing Desegregation," 1967, 6–7, box 163, folder 40, NCADH Papers.

42. "What Holds Off Model Funds," *Milwaukee Sentinel*, Mar. 24, 1967; "Model Cities Told to Eliminate Bias in Slum Rebuilding," *New York Times*, Mar. 18, 1967; "Model Cities Program Prohibits Discrimination," *St. Petersburg (FL) Times*, Mar. 26, 1967; Pritchett (2008), 313.

43. The St. Louis Model Cities plan proposed creating a private Metropolitan Housing Corporation to find and/or build low-and-moderate income housing in the suburbs. On the St. Louis experience, see Colin Gordon, *Mapping Decline: St. Louis and the Fate of the American City*, University of Pennsylvania Press, Philadelphia (2008); Edward Rutledge and Jack Wood to Robert Weaver, telegram, May 5, 1967, and Weaver to Rutledge and Wood, May 11, 1967, box 71, folder 9, NCADH Papers; NCADH Annual Report, 1967, box 73, folder 8, NCADH Papers.

44. US Department of Housing and Urban Development, Model Cities Administration. *Program Guide: Model Neighborhoods in Demonstration Cities*, HUD PG-47, Government Printing Office, Washington, DC (Dec. 1967), 3, 20; Jackson (2007), 258; Kent Germany, *New Orleans after the Promises: Poverty, Citizenship and the Search for the Great Society*, University of Georgia Press, Athens (2007), 197–98; Haar (1975), 82–88, 173–78; Nicholas Lemann, *The Promised Land: The Great Black Migration and How It Changed America*, Vintage Books, New York (1991), 199; Community Legal Council, "Citizen Participation in Chicago's Model Cities Program: A Critical Analysis," May 15, 1968.

45. "Chicago Advanced Review," May 18, 1967, "Chicago Trips 1968" folder, Sherwin Markman Personal Papers, box 4, LBJPL; John McClain, "Initial Visit with Chicago," Chicago Trips 1968 folder, Markman Personal Papers, box 4, LBJPL.

46. John Hall Fish, *Black Power/White Control*, Princeton University Press, Princeton, NJ (1973), 242.

47. TWO, "1967 Policy and Resolutions," Leon Despres Papers, box 181, folder 4, Chicago Historical Society (CHS); Fish (1973), 244.

48. Arthur Brazier, "Introduction," *Delivery Systems for Model Cities: New Concepts in Serving the Urban Community*, University of Chicago Center for Urban Studies, Chicago (1969), 11–13.

49. TWO received a $65,000 grant from the Community Renewal Society. For a detailed description of the TWO–University of Chicago partnership, see Julian Levi to Joseph Califano, Sept. 9, 1967, Gen LA2 8/26/67–10/15/67, White Central Files LA, LBJPL, 2–3; Fish (1973), 257.

50. Community Legal Council, "Citizen Participation in Chicago's Model Cities Program: A Critical Analysis," May 15, 1968; "Model Cities Personnel Draws Group's Wrath," *Chicago Defender*, July 14, 1968, 2; Lemann (1991), 198–99; Adam Cohen and Elizabeth Taylor, *American Pharoah*, Little, Brown, Boston (2000), 490–92.

51. Fish (1973), 245–46, 250.

52. William Swenson, "The Continuing Colloquium on University of Chicago Demonstration Projects in Woodlawn: Aspects of a Major University's Commitment to an Inner-City Ghetto," Center for Urban Studies, University of Chicago (Nov. 15, 1968), 248.

53. Swenson (1968), 120.

54. Swenson (1968), 119; "TWO in Model City Proposal: TWO Urges New Model Cities Program," *Chicago Defender*, Nov. 13, 1968, 1; "Woodlawn Project Is Proposed Providing Jobs, Care, Renewal," *Chicago Tribune*, Nov. 13, 1968; "Woodlawn vs. Chicago City Hall," *Washington Post*, Nov. 29, 1968, A12; Fish (1973), 250.

55. Jack Meltzer and William Swenson, "New Principles and Mechanisms in the Model Cities Plan of TWO," in *Delivery Systems for Model Cities* (1969), 15; Harold Richman, "Financial Assistance and Social Services: Major Issues and Guiding Principles," *Delivery Systems for Model*

Cities (1969), 45; Woodlawn Organization, *Woodlawn's Model Cities Plan*, Whitehall Company, Chicago (1970), 26.

56. Meltzer and Swenson (1969), 16.

57. Richman (1969), 45–47; Eddie Williams, "The Model Cities Plan of the Woodlawn Organization–An Abstract," *Delivery Systems for Model Cities* (1969), 87.

58. In a February 1967 press conference, Washington proposed to make a guaranteed minimum annual income the "keystone" of the Model Cities program. George W. Grier, director of the DC Office of Program Coordination, suggested that every family in the district be given "an income it at least can live on," perhaps as much as $4,000 a year. Nothing resembling this idea appeared in the city's final planning grant application, however. Already worried that the new "backlash Congress" would gut Model Cities funding over housing desegregation, HUD officials strongly urged Grier to drop the proposal, and he did. Given this, it was unclear how HUD would react to TWO's far-reaching ideas. William Chapman, "Income Guarantee Eyed for Poor," *Washington Post*, Dec. 17, 1967, A1.

59. Richman (1969), 46–47; Meltzer and Swenson (1969), 21.

60. Meltzer and Swenson (1969), 17–20.

61. Robert McKersie, "Neighborhood Economic Development," *Delivery Systems for Model Cities* (1969), 51–53; Williams (1969), 91, 98.

62. See chapter 7. On the Woodlawn Experimental School Program, see also TWO, "1967 Policy and Resolutions," Leon Despres Papers, box 181, folder 4, CHS; "Experimental School Plan Is Disclosed," *Chicago Tribune*, Dec. 11, 1967, 2; "OK Woodlawn Pilot School," *Chicago Tribune*, Jan. 7, 1968, 1; "Parents Help 'Take Apart' Their Schools," *Chicago Tribune*, July 21, 1968, 14; "Principal Seeks School Transfer in Row with TWO," *Chicago Defender*, Sept. 10, 1968, 1; "TWO Issues Threat to School Board: A Black Principal—Or Else," *Chicago Defender*, Oct. 16, 1968, 1; "Experimental School Board to Turn Community Wishes into Realities in Woodlawn," *Chicago Tribune*, June 1, 1969; "Residents Ready to Work in Woodlawn Schools," *Chicago Tribune*, June 15, 1969, 3; "Woodlawn Schools Give Parents Planning Role," *Chicago Tribune*, June 8, 1969, 3; "Pupils Show Gains in Woodlawn Tests," *Chicago Tribune*, Feb. 25, 1970, 10; Fish (1973), chap. 4; De Vise (Dec. 1967), 104–5; Morris Janowitz and David Street, "Urban School Systems: Strategies for Change," Center for Social Organization Studies, University of Chicago (1966); John Lyons, *Teachers and Reform: Chicago Public Education 1929–1970*, University of Illinois Press, Champaign-Urbana (2008), 174.

63. Indicative of the exclusion of community residents and the vast gulf between how the Daley administration and TWO saw the future of Woodlawn, HUD and the city approved the construction of a 246-unit high-rise apartment building at 64th Street and Stony Island Avenue. TWO had favored lower-density development for years and was particularly outraged that construction was going forward in the midst of its grassroots effort to develop a comprehensive community plan. The developer described TWO's exclusion directly: "I did not communicate with Woodlawn representatives," he told reporters, "because I didn't have to." See "21-Story Building Going Up Despite Woodlawn's Protest," *Chicago Defender*, Apr. 14, 1968, 1; "Woodlawn Project Is Proposed Providing Jobs"; "Ex-Model Cities Chief Tells Why He Quit," *Chicago Sun-Times*, Dec. 13, 1968, 50; *Woodlawn Observer*, Dec. 18, 1968, 1; "TWO Asks Delay of Model Cities Plan," *Chicago Defender*, Dec. 19, 1968, A10.

64. US Department of Housing and Urban Development, Model Cities Administration, "Citizenship Participation in Model Cities" (Technical Assistance Bulletin No. 3), Government Printing Office, Washington, DC (Dec. 1968), 14–15; Fish (1973), 260–61.

65. Fish (1973), 261–63.
66. Fish (1973), 264–65.
67. Romney was familiar with TWO. While considering a run for the White House, Romney had visited Woodlawn in September 1967. Brazier took him on a tour of the neighborhood, and Romney praised TWO's work. "TWO's Rev. Brazier Is Host to Romney," *Chicago Defender*, Sept. 2, 1967; "Woodlawn Model City Panel Views TWO Version of Plan," *Chicago Defender*, Mar. 16, 1969, 3; "Model Cities Aid Ok'd by Council," *Chicago Sun-Times*, Apr. 26, 1969, 1; Fish (1973), 267–69.
68. Fish (1973), 268–73; "Coalition Demands Model Cities Voice," *Chicago Defender*, Apr. 24, 1969, 1; "Push Private Model Cities Plan," *Chicago Defender*, May 8, 1969, 1; "Woodlawn Sets Campaign," *Chicago Defender*, Apr. 2, 1970, 4; Dudley Post, "Requiem for Model Cities," *New Republic*, Apr. 14, 1973, 13–15; Von Hoffman (Mar. 2011), 34–35; Lemann (2001), 251; Cohen and Taylor (2000), 490–92; "Model Cities Plan Attacked Thru Suit," *Chicago Tribune*, Aug. 6, 1969.
69. Winston Moore, Charles Livermore, and George Galland Jr., "Woodlawn: The Zone of Destruction," *City Scenes: Problems and Prospects*, ed. J. John Palen, Little, Brown, Boston (1981); William J. Wilson, *When Work Disappears: The World of the New Urban Poor*, Random House, New York (1996), 5–6, 44.
70. Nicholas Von Hoffman, "When the Change Comes by Fire," *Washington Post*, Dec. 8, 1971; Roger Fox and Jerry Szatan, "The Current Economic Status of Chicago's Black Community: A Mid-1970s Overview Report," Chicago Urban League Research and Planning Department (Winter 1977), 51, 53, 56, 106–7; Mayor's Council of Manpower and Economic Advisors, "Unemployment-Labor Force Policy" (Apr. 1976), 58–60.
71. Celeste Garrett, "Woodlawn Has a Bold Vision: Renewal Already Making Its Mark," *Chicago Tribune*, Dec. 22, 2002.
72. For a fascinating discussion of the origins of the Ford Foundation's involvement in CDCs, see Karen Ferguson, "Organizing the Ghetto: The Ford Foundation, CORE, and White Power in the Black Power Era, 1967–1969," *Journal of Urban History* (Nov. 2007); Pritchett (Jan. 2008), 276–77. On RFK's CDC ideas, see Address by Senator Robert F. Kennedy, Conference on the Revitalization of Harlem, Jan. 21, 1966, New York, RFK Senate Papers, Speeches and Press Releases, box 2, JFK Library, Boston; Address by Senator Robert F. Kennedy, NAACP Legal Defense Fund Banquet, May 18, 1966, RFK Senate Papers, Speeches and Press Releases, box 2, JFK Library; Schmitt (2010), 125.
73. Sugrue (2008), 402.
74. Carl Tjerandsen, *Education for Citizenship: A Foundation's Experience*, Emil Schwarzhaupt Foundation, Santa Cruz, CA (1980), 257 and 665.

Conclusion

1. Morton Grodzins, *The Metropolitan Area as a Racial Problem*, University of Pittsburgh Press, Pittsburgh (1958).
2. Attorney General Nicholas Katzenbach convened a Justice Department Task Force on Civil Rights in September 1966, just after the defeat of fair housing and the narrowing of Model Cities. It recommended the use of federal funds to induce suburbs to change zoning laws to "facilitate the construction of non-ghetto open housing within economic reach of low-and-moderate income nonwhites." The president's Task Force on Civil Rights, convened at the same time, essentially took the housing recommendations of the White House Conference on Civil

Rights, and sent them to the president. "It is probably no exaggeration to say that low-income urban families will never find adequate housing, no matter how much federal assistance is offered, unless some way can be found to break down the locally imposed barriers that prevent such families from moving out" of the ghetto, the group told Johnson. The Task Force on Education recommended that the federal government push a "reasonable mixture" of public school students by race and class across metropolitan boundaries, and encourage the equalization of school funding at the state level. A year later, two task forces chaired by Charles Haar—one on new towns, another on suburban problems—reiterated the necessity of a federal attack on metropolitan segregation. Most famously, the Kerner Commission came out directly in favor of it in March 1968, pointedly arguing that an urban policy that focused exclusively on rebuilding inner-city neighborhoods would doom the nation to a permanent racial division. See "Memorandum: Priority Proposals of the Civil Rights Task Force," Dec. 5, 1966, Department of Justice, Offices Files of the White House Aides, James Gaither, box 372, LBJPL; Paul N. Ylvisaker to the President, July 7, 1967, box 4, Task Force Reports, 1966 Task Force on Cities folder, LBJPL; Joseph Califano to Robert Weaver, Aug. 25, 1967, box 78, "Task Force on Housing and Urban Development, 1968" folder, Office Files of the White House Aides, Joseph Califano, LBJPL.

3. Charles M. Haar, "Thinking the Unthinkable About Our Cities: A Scenario in Four Parts," Oct. 18, 1967, Office Files of Joseph Califano, box 77, LBJPL; "Memorandum for the President," Aug. 18, 1967, Office Files of Harry McPherson, box 20, LBJPL. For more on the memo, and the context in which it was written, see Roger Biles, "Thinking the Unthinkable about Our Cities: Thirty Years Later," *Journal of Urban History* (Nov. 1998); Bruce Stave, "A Conversation with Charles M. Haar: Urban History and the Great Society," *Journal of Urban History* (Nov. 1998).

4. To get a sense of Romney's ideas, see his speech before the Town Hall of California, Apr. 17, 1970, RG 207, General Records of the Dept. of HUD, Office of the Under Secretary, Staff Correspondence, 1969–1972, box 35, National Archives II. On Operation Breakthrough and Open Communities, see Charles Lamb, *Housing Segregation in Suburban America Since 1960: Presidential and Judicial Politics*, Cambridge University Press, New York (2005), 60–84; Chapin, undated memo, attached to Memo from Van Dusen to Romney, Aug. 15, 1969, Romney Papers, box 10, Bentley Historical Library, Ann Arbor, MI. See more generally RG 207, General Records of HUD, Office of the Under Secretary, Subject Files of Richard C. Van Dusen, 1969–1972, box 10, National Archives II.

5. Lamb (2005), 84, 97, 144, 160–63.

6. Lamb (2005), 9, 47, 247.

7. *Milliken v. Bradley*, 418 U.S. 717 (1974), at 741–42, 815; Paul Dimond, *Beyond Busing: Inside the Challenge to Urban Segregation*, University of Michigan Press, Ann Arbor (2005), 26–118; Tom Sugrue, *Sweet Land of Liberty*, Random House, New York (2008), 482–87.

8. Patricia Harris, HUD secretary under Carter, developed new regulations in October 1977 that would enable her agency to punish suburbs that refused to alter their zoning laws to allow more low- and moderate-income housing. Congress, under suburban political pressure, refused to approve them. From that point forward, Community Development Block Grants primarily channeled federal funds into inner-city public housing and rent subsidy programs (Section 8) without providing suburban alternatives. Lamb (2005), 163–79; Pritchett (Jan. 2008), 281; "Ford Signs Bill to Aid Housing: $11.9 Billion Authorized for 3 Years Gives Localities Greater Control in Plans," *New York Times*, Aug. 23, 1974. For critiques of the segregative impact of HOPE VI and the Low-Income Housing Tax Credit, see john a. powell, "Reflections on the Past, Looking to the Future: The Fair Housing Act at 40," *Indiana Law Review* 41 (2008), 607, 619, Elizabeth Julian,

"Fair Housing and Community Development: Time to Come Together," *Indiana Law Review* 41 (2008), 567–69; Florence Wagman Roisman, "The Power of the Supreme Court's Decision in the Fair Housing Act Case, TDHCA v. ICP," *Poverty and Race* 24, no. 4 (July–Aug. 2015); Kirk McClure, Anne Williamson, and Hye-Sung Han, "The LIHTC Program, Racially/Ethnically Concentrated Areas of Poverty, and High Opportunity Neighborhoods," *Texas A&M Journal of Property Law* 6 (Dec. 2020), 89. For a summary of research, and efforts during Obama's second term to mitigate the segregative impact of LIHTC, see Poverty and Race Research Action Council, "The Low Income Housing Tax Credit," https://www.prrac.org/fair-housing/the-low-income-housing-tax-credit/.

9. For a similar argument, see Kevin Fox Gotham, "Blind Faith in the Free Market: Urban Poverty, Residential Segregation, and Federal Housing Retrenchment, 1970–1995," *Sociological Inquiry* (Feb. 1968).

10. For a detailed—and less critical—account of this shift in federal urban policy, see David Erickson, "Community Capitalism: How Housing Advocates, the Private Sector, and Government Forged New Low-Income Housing Policy, 1968–1996," *Journal of Policy History* 18, no. 2 (2006). See also Thomas J. Sugrue, "All Politics Is Local: The Persistence of Localism in Twentieth-Century America," in *The Democratic Experiment: New Directions in American Political History*, ed. Meg Jacobs et al., Princeton University Press, Princeton, NJ (2004), 302–26, at 304.

11. On the increase in the number of black and Latino Americans living in neighborhoods of concentrated poverty, see Elizabeth Kneebone, Carey Nadeau, and Alan Berube, "The Reemergence of Concentrated Poverty: Metropolitan Trends in the 2000s," Brookings Institution Metropolitan Policy Program (Nov. 2011); Alana Semuels, "The Resurrection of America's Slums," *CityLab* (blog), Aug. 10, 2015; Paul Jargowsky, "The Architecture of Segregation: Civil Unrest, the Concentration of Poverty, and Public Policy," Century Foundation (Aug. 2015); August Benzow and Kenan Fikri, "The Expanded Geography of High Poverty Neighborhoods," Economic Innovation Group (May 2020).

12. Raj Chetty, Nathaniel Hendren, and Lawrence F. Katz, "The Effects of Exposure to Better Neighborhoods on Children: New Evidence from the Moving to Opportunity Experiment," Harvard University and the National Bureau of Economic Research (May 2015); Raj Chetty and Nathaniel Hendren, "The Impacts of Neighborhoods on Intergenerational Mobility: Childhood Exposure Effects and County-Level Estimates," Harvard University and the National Bureau of Economic Research (2015); Douglas Massey, "The Social Science of Affordable Housing," *Housing Policy Debate* (June 2015), 634–38. For research and commentary on racial and economic segregation in the early twenty-first century, see Myron Orfield and Thomas Luce, "America's Racially Diverse Suburbs: Opportunities and Challenges," Institute on Metropolitan Opportunity (July 2012); Sean Riordan and Kendra Bischoff, "Growth in the Residential Segregation of Families by Income, 1970–2009," US2010 (Nov. 2011), http://www.s4.brown.edu/us2010/Data/Report/report111111.pdf. Gary Orfield and Chungmei Lee, "Historic Reversals, Accelerating Resegregation and the Need for New Strategies," UCLA Civil Rights Project/Proyecto Derechos Civiles (Aug. 2007), http://civilrightsproject.ucla.edu/research/k-12-education/integration-and-diversity/historic-reversals-accelerating-resegregation-and-the-need-for-newintegration-strategies-1. On opportunity hoarding, see Sheryll Cashin, *White Space, Black Hood: Opportunity Hoarding and Segregation in the Age of Inequality*, Beacon Press, Boston (2021); and Richard Reeves, *Dream Hoarders: How the American Upper Middle Class Is Leaving Everyone Else in the Dust, Why That is a Problem, and What to Do about It*, Brookings Institution, Washington, DC (2018).

13. Angela Glover Blackwell, "How Obama's New Housing Rules Help Fight Modern-Day Segregation," *The Nation*, July 15, 2015.

14. Melvin Oliver and Thomas Shapiro, *Black Wealth/White Wealth: A New Perspective on Racial Inequality*, Routledge Press, New York (2005); Thomas Shapiro, *The Hidden Cost of Being African American: How Wealth Perpetuates Inequality*, Oxford University Press, New York (2004). See also Dalton Conley, *Being Black, Living in the Red: Race, Wealth and Social Policy in America*, University of California Press, Berkeley (1999); Heather Beth Johnson, *The American Dream and the Power of Wealth: Choosing Schools and Inheriting Inequality in the Land of Opportunity*, Routledge, New York (2015); Dorothy Brown, *The Whiteness of Wealth*, Crown Publishing, New York (2021).

15. See Rakesh Kochhar and Anthony Cilluffo, "How Wealth Inequality Has Changed in the US since the Great Recession, by Race, Ethnicity and Income," Pew Research Center (Nov. 2017); Thomas Shapiro et al., "The Roots of the Widening Racial Wealth Gap: Explaining the Black-White Economic Divide" (research and policy brief), Institute on Assets and Social Policy (Feb. 2013); Ylan Mui, "For Black Americans, Financial Damage from Subprime Implosion Is Likely to Last," *Washington Post*, July 12, 2012; Isabel Wilkerson, "Race to the Bottom: How the Recession Hurled African-Americans Backward in Time," *New Republic*, Mar. 18, 2012; Rakesh Kochhar et al., "Wealth Gaps Rise to Record Highs Between Whites, Blacks, Hispanics," Pew Research Center (July 2011); Darrick Hamilton, "Race, Wealth and Intergenerational Poverty," *American Prospect*, Aug. 14, 2009; IASP, "The Racial Gap Increases Fourfold" (research and policy brief, May 2010); Melvin Oliver, "Sub-Prime as a Black Catastrophe," *American Prospect*, Sept. 2008.

16. Ta-Nehisi Coates, "Color-Blind Policy, Color-Conscious Morality," *Atlantic Monthly*, May 13, 2015.

17. For critiques of charter schools, see Diane Ravitch, "The Myth of Charter Schools," *New York Review of Books*, Nov. 11, 2010. See especially *The Death and Life of the Great American School System*, Basic Books, New York (2010); Erica Frankenberg et al., "Choice without Equity: Charter School Segregation and the Need for Civil Rights Standards," Civil Rights Project (Jan. 2010). On Obama's urban policies, see Ariella Cohen, "The Oracle of Urban Policy," *Next American City* (Spring 2010); Manuel Pastor, "Putting Poverty in Its Place," *American Prospect* (Sept. 2009). On the educational value of racial integration of public schools, see Rucker Johnson, *Children of the Dream: Why School Integration Works*, Basic Books, New York (2019).

18. Saul Alinsky, "Industrial Areas Foundation Annual Report," 1960, Alinsky Papers, Special Collections, University of Illinois Chicago (hereafter Alinsky Papers); Marion Sanders, *The Professional Radical: Interviews with Saul Alinsky*, Harper and Row, New York (1970), 86; Saul Alinsky, speech to the College Colloquium on the Plight of the Cities, Michigan State University (Jan. 1969).

19. Sanders (1970), 69; Edward J. Verstraeten, "Solidarity and Subsidiarity," in *Principles of Catholic Social Teaching*, ed. David Boileau, Marquette University Press, Milwaukee (1998), 119, 135.

20. "Playboy Interview Saul Alinsky: A Candid Conversation with the Feisty Radical Organizer, *Playboy*, Mar. 1972, 60; Saul Alinsky, *Rules for Radicals: A Practical Primer for Realistic Radicals*, Vintage Books, New York (1971), 189–90.

21. Alinsky (1971), 184, 187, 189; Alinsky interview, *Playboy* (1972), 61, 177.

22. Derek Shearer, "CAP: New Breeze in the Windy City," *Ramparts* (Oct. 1973); Joan Lancourt, *Confront or Concede: The Alinsky Citizen-Action Organizations*, Lexington Books, Lexington, MA (1979), 26–28; Rose and Rothstein, "The CAP Story: Working Class Reformers," *Chicago Reader* (Oct. 1974).

23. Shearer (1973), 14.

24. On the Citizens Action Program, see David Emmons, "Community Organizing and Urban Policy: Saul Alinsky and Chicago's Citizens Action Program" (PhD diss., University of Chicago, 1986); Henry Scheff, "Issues and Communities: The CAP Model of Organizing," *Focus/Midwest* 11, no. 69 (n.d.); Ron Dorfman, "Greenlining Chicago: The Citizens Action Program," *Working Papers* 3 (Summer 1975); Lancourt (1979); Gregory Squires, Larry Bennett, Kathleen McCourt, and Philip Nyden, *Chicago: Race, Class, and the Response to Urban Decline*, Temple University Press, Philadelphia (1987), 141–42; Shearer (Oct. 1973). On the broader national movement to address red-lining and its consequences, see Rebecca Marchiel, *After Redlining: The Urban Reinvestment Movement in the Era of Financial Deregulation*, University of Chicago Press, Chicago (2020).

25. On the early years of UPAJ, see Robert McClory, "Reviving the Energy for Action and Justice," *National Catholic Reporter*, Jan. 15, 1999; Thomas Lenz, "Building a Force for the Common Good," *Shelterforce* (Sept.–Oct. 1998); David Moberg, "New City-Suburban Coalition Tackles Shared Social Problems," *North Shore Magazine*, Jan. 1998; Steve Kloehn, "Activists Powered by Faith, Not Plans," *Chicago Tribune*, Oct. 20, 1997; "Grassroots Organizing Coming to Suburbia," *Chicago Tribune*, July 15, 1996. For an optimistic view of today's IAF and the possibility for multiracial coalitions, see William Julius Wilson, *The Bridge over the Racial Divide: Rising Inequality and Coalition Politics*, University of California Press, Berkeley (1999), esp. chap. 3. The UPAJ's website has links to news stories about their more recent campaigns. For an example, see Michelle Gallardo, "Hundreds of Chicago residents meet with Mayor Lori Lightfoot to air concerns about violence, housing inequality," ABC7Chicago.com, Sept. 23, 2019.

26. On Gamaliel's work, which has focused on transportation policy and employment, see Victor Rubin, *Regional Equity*, Routledge Press, New York (2016); Todd Swanstrom, "Regionalism, Equality and Democracy," *Urban Affairs Review* 42, no. 2 (Nov. 2006); R. Kleidman, "Community Organizing and Regionalism," *City and Community* 3 (2004). On community-based regionalism more generally, see Manuel Pastor Jr., Chris Benner, and Martha Matsuoka, *This Could Be the Start of Something Big: How Social Movements for Regional Equity are Reshaping Metropolitan America*, Cornell University Press, Ithaca, NY (2009), quotes at 2–3.

27. Peter Dreier, "The Supreme Denial of Integration," *Shelterforce* (Oct. 2007); David Rusk, *Inside Game/Outside Game: Winning Strategies for Saving Urban America*, Brookings Institution, Washington, DC (2001). On CDCs, see Peter Dreier, John Mollenkopf, and Todd Swanstrom, *Place Matters: Metropolitics for the Twenty-First Century*, University Press of Kansas, Lawrence (2014); Rusk (2001); Pablo Eisenberg, "Time to Remove the Rose-Colored Glasses," *Shelterforce* (Mar.–Apr. 2000); Randy Stoecker, "The CDC Model of Urban Development: A Critique and Alternative." *Journal of Urban Affairs* 19 (1997), 1–22; Nicholas Lemann, "The Myth of Community Development," *New York Times Magazine*, Jan. 9, 1994; Herbert Rubin, *Renewing Hope within Neighborhoods of Despair: The Community-Based Development Model*, State University Press of New York, Albany (2000); Neil Peirce and Carol Steinbach, *Corrective Capitalism: The Rise of America's Community Development Corporations*, Ford Foundation, New York (1987); Rachel Bratt and William Rohe, "Challenges and Dilemmas Facing Community Development Corporations in the United States," *Community Development Journal*, advance online publication (2005), 63–78; William Simon, *The Community Economic Development Movement: Law, Business, and the New Social Policy*, Duke University Press, Durham, NC (2001).

28. Elizabeth Julian, "Fair Housing and Community Development: Time to Come Together," *Indiana Law Review* 41 (2008). To get a sense of the people-versus-place debate, see Randall

Crane and Michael Manville, "People or Place? Revisiting the Who versus the Where of Urban Development," *Land Lines* (July 2008); Edward Goetz, *The One-Way Street of Integration: Fair Housing and the Pursuit of Racial Justice in American Cities*, Cornell University Press, Ithaca, NY (2018); and the fascinating exchange between David Imbroscio, Edward Goetz, Rolf Pendall, and Katherine Einstein in *Urban Affairs Review* in 2019. See also Edward Goetz, "Poverty-Pimping CDCs: The Search for Dispersal's Next Bogeyman," and the response to Goetz's article by Myron Orfield, Will Stancil, Thomas Luce, and Eric Myott, all in *Housing Policy Debate* 25, no. 3 (2015).

29. On efforts in Montgomery County, see Heather Schwartz, "Housing Policy Is School Policy: Economically Integrative Housing Promotes School Achievement in Montgomery County, Maryland," Century Foundation (2010); Karen Destoral Brown, "Expanding Affordable Housing through Exclusionary Zoning: Lessons from the Washington Metropolitan Area," Brookings Institution (2001), 5, http://www.brookings.edu/es/urban/publications/inclusionary.pdf; Florence W. Roisman, "Opening the Suburbs to Racial Integration," *Western New England Law Review* 23 (2001), 78–9. On the Mt. Laurel decision, see Douglas Massey et al., *Climbing Mount Laurel: The Struggle for Affordable Housing and Social Mobility in an American Suburb*, Princeton University Press, Princeton, NJ (2020); Alan Mallach, "The Betrayal of Mount Laurel," *Shelterforce* (Mar.–Apr. 2004); David Kirp, John P. Dwyer, and Larry A. Rosenthal, *Our Town: Race, Housing, and the Soul of Suburbia*, Rutgers University Press, New Brunswick, NJ (1995); Charles Haar, *Suburbs under Siege: Race, Space and Audacious Judges*, Princeton University Press, Princeton, NJ (1996). On the new regionalism, see Rusk (2001); Dreier et al. (2000); Myron Orfield, *Metropolitics: A Regional Agenda for Community and Stability*, Lincoln Institute of Land Policy, Boston (1998); *American Metropolitics: The New Suburban Reality*, Brookings Institution, Washington, DC (2002); Dreier et al. (2014); Bruce Katz, ed., *Reflections on Regionalism*, Brookings Institution, Washington, DC (1999).

30. On the Small Market Area Rents program, see Rachel Cohen, "The Fight for the Suburbs," *New Republic*, Jan. 17, 2018. On Moving to Opportunity and Gautreaux, see Chetty, Hendren, and Katz (May 2015); Chetty and Hendren (2015); Xavier DeSousa Briggs, *Moving to Opportunity: The Story of an American Experiment to Fight Ghetto Poverty*, Oxford University Press, New York (2010); Xavier DeSousa Briggs, *The Geography of Opportunity: Race and Housing Choice in Metropolitan America*, Brookings Institution, Washington, DC (2005); John Goering, *Choosing a Better Life? Evaluating the Moving to Opportunity Experiment*, Urban Institute Press, Washington, DC (2003); Edward Goetz, *Clearing the Way: Deconcentrating the Poor in America*, Urban Institute Press, Washington, DC (2003); James Rosenbaum and Leonard Rubinowitz, *Crossing the Class and Color Lines: From Public Housing to White Suburbia*, University of Chicago Press, Chicago (2000); Owen Fiss, *A Way Out: American Ghettoes and the Legacy of Racism*, Princeton University Press, Princeton, NJ (2004).

31. For more on the Supreme Court's decision in *Inclusive Communities Project v. TDHCA*, and the renewed debate about place-based versus mobility-based policy, see "Discussion 15: Moving Up or Moving Out," Dream Revisited, Furman Center, July 2015, http://furmancenter.org/research/iri/home?utm_source=Furman+Center+Mailing+List&utm_campaign=66380b8037-Housing_Starts_Aug_29&utm_medium=email&utm_term=0_ea37468da6-66380b8037-173374481; Angela Glover Blackwell, "How Obama's New Housing Rules Help Fight Modern-Day Segregation," *The Nation*, July 15, 2015; Richard Rothstein, "The Supreme Court's Challenge to Housing Segregation," *American Prospect*, July 5, 2015; Florence Wagman Roisman, "The Power of the Supreme Court's Decision in the Fair Housing Case, TDHCA v. ICP," *Poverty and Race* 24, no. 4 (July–Aug. 2015); Sarah Treuhaft, "Seizing the Moment to Affirmatively Further

Fair Housing," *Rooflines*, June 3, 2015; Thomas B. Edsall, "Where Should the Poor Live?" *Opinionator* (blog), Aug. 5, 2015; John Eligon, "A Year after Ferguson, Housing Segregation Defies Tools to Erase It," *New York Times*, Aug. 8, 2015; Peter Dreier, "Philanthropy's Misguided Ideas for Fixing Ghetto Poverty: The Limits of Free Markets and Place-Based Initiatives," *Non-Profit Quarterly* (Mar. 2015).

    32. For more on the HUD rules, released in July 2015, and their potential impact, see Glover Blackwell (2015); Rothstein (2015); Wagman Roisman (July–Aug. 2015); Treuhaft (2015); Alana Samuels, "Can Better Data Help Solve America's Housing Problems?" *Atlantic Monthly*, July 8, 2015; Emily Badger, "Obama Administration to Unveil Major New Rules Targeting Segregation across the US," *Wonkblog*, July 8, 2015, http://www.washingtonpost.com/news/wonkblog/wp/2015/07/08/obama-administration-to-unveil-major-new-rules-targeting-segregation-across-u-s/; Ruth Gourevitch and Solomon Greene, "Federal Fair Housing Data Highlight the Need for Action to Reverse the Nation's Legacy of Segregation," Urban Institute, June 28, 2018.

    33. Alana Samuels, "Trump Administration Puts on Hold on Obama-Era Desegregation Effort," *Atlantic Monthly*, Aug. 2017; Editorial, "America's Federally Financed Ghettoes," *New York Times*, Apr. 7, 2018; Kristen Capps, "With Justice Kennedy's Retirement, Fair Housing is in Peril," *Bloomsberg.com*, June 28, 2018; Toluse Olorunnipa and Colby Itkowitz, "Trump Tires to Win Over 'Suburban Housewives' with Repeal of Anti-Segregation Housing Rule," *Washington Post*, July 23, 2020; Emily Badger and Nate Cohn, "Why Trump's Blunt Appeals to Suburban Voters May Not Work," *New York Times*, July 30, 2020.

    34. The White House, "Executive Order on Advancing Racial Equity and Support for Underserved Communities Through the Federal Government," Jan. 20, 2021, https:/www.whitehouse.gov/briefing-room/presidential-actions/2021/01/20/executive-order-advancing-racial-equity-and-support-for-underserved-communities-through-the-federal-government/.

    35. Tracy Jan, "HUD to Reinstate Obama-Era Fair Housing Rule Gutted under Trump—Minus the 'Burdensome' Reporting Requirement," *Washington Post*, June 9, 2021.

    36. See john a. powell, "Reflections on the Past, Looking to the Future: The Fair Housing Act at 40," *Indiana Law Review* 41 (2008); john a. powell, "The Housing Crisis: How Did We Get Here? Where Do We Go?" *Shelterforce* (Fall–Winter 2009). For more on powell's ideas, go to http://kirwaninstitute.org/research/opportunity-communitieshousing/index.php. For more on Angela Glover Blackwell, see "Regional Equity and the Quest for Full Inclusion" (2008), http://www.policylink.org/site/apps/nlnet/content2.aspx?c=lkIXLbMNJrE&b=5136581&ct=6997399.

    37. The phrases "favored quarter" and "garrison impulse" come from Sheryl Cashin, *The Failures of Integration: How Race and Class Are Undermining the American Dream*, Public Affairs, New York (2004), 169–70, 179. Elizabeth Julian is quoted in Rachel Cohen, "The Fight for the Suburbs," *New Republic*, Jan. 17, 2018.

Index

Page numbers in italics refer to figures.

Abernathy, Ralph, 201
Abner, Willoughby, 63, 65
Abrahamson, Julia, 46
Abrams, Charles, 31, 113, 116, 346n16
activism, 4; black, 5, 217–18, 260, 347n19; citizen, 5; community, 157; grassroots, 4, 218–19, 260; limits of place-based policy and, 305–6. *See also* Alinsky, Saul; community organizing
Adamowski, Benjamin, 217
African Americans: atmosphere of white hostility encountered by, 90; exclusion of low-income, 132–33; family incomes of, 369n2; flight of middle-class, 60; Great Migration of, 21; history of, 215; limited economic advancement since the civil rights era of, 3–4; upwardly mobile, 123; wealthier, 59; working-class communities of, 204. *See also* black leaders; black middle class; black migration; race; Southern blacks
Aid to Dependent Children (ADC), 107
Algren, Nelson, 37–38
Alinsky, Saul, 1, 4–16, *8*, 24, 90, 95, 116–17, 123–32, 145, 150, 173–74, 179–84, 190–99, 325n24, 349n45; Alinsky-Maritain correspondence, 324n15; community organizing of, 53–59, 111, 123, 134, 147, 176, 181–82, 191, 219; critique of liberal racial orthodoxy of, 54–59; critique of organizational methods of HP-KCC of, 106; fieldwork on juvenile delinquency, 23; *The General Report* (1957), 51–59, 77, 105, 111, 157, 175, 184; "left-wing tendencies" of, 127; reputation of, 36; *Reveille for Radicals*, 6, 190; *Rules for Radicals*, 6–7, 9, 13; union organizing of, 23–26. *See also* activism; community organizing

American Bankers Association, 91
American Dream, 82
American Friends Service Committee, 144
American Legion, 160
Americans for Democratic Action, 139
anti-fascism, 9–10
anti-Semitism, 127
Architectural Forum, 201
Arizona, 5
Auburn-Gresham proposal, 75
Auburn-Highland Community Council, 107
Auburn-Highland Improvement Association, 100, 156
Auburn Park Improvement Association, 161
Auburn Park Methodist Church, 133, 135

Back of the Yards Neighborhood Council (BYNC), 9, 19, 25–26, 31–33, 37–54, 74–76, 127, 131–32, 174, 193; Community Congress of the, 25, 29; creation of the, 23–26, 70; interracial unity of the, 36, 40, 71; negative image of the, 68; and race, 27–30; Race Relations Committee of the, 29, 39; segregationist path of the, 174; territory of the, *18*
Baird, Rev. William, 212
Balkin, Jack, 115
Baltimore, 3, 5
banks, 42–44, 101; lending practices of, 83, 88, 95; local, 105, 155. *See also* mortgages
Baron, Harold, 209
Barrett, James, 26
Barron, Hal, 44
"benign quota" debate, 112–16, 124, 147, 346n13. *See also* housing; quotas

INDEX

Berkowitz, Rabbi William, 7, 15
Berry, Edwin, 51
Bettelheim, Bruno, 197
Beverly Area Planning Association (BAPA), 90–92, 127, 133, 161, 175
Beverly Hills–Morgan Park Council on Human Relations, 136, 158
Beverly Hills Trinity Methodist Church, 136
Beverly Suburban Real Estate Board, 142, 161
Bindman, Aaron, 33
black community organizations, 59, 64–66, 71–72, 76; black churches and, 64–65; union locals and, 66. *See also* churches; community organizing
Black Freedom Movement, 4, 40, 185, 196, 205, 210, 215, 218, 347n19
black leaders, 61, 72, 75; liberal, 73. *See also* African Americans
black middle class, 32, 38, 47, 59, 64–73, 83–88, 103, 158, 173, 377n53; flight of the, 60, 71, 188; political independence of the, 218; precarious condition of the, 188, 329n39; solid community of the, 168; spirit of political insurgency among the, 67. *See also* African Americans; middle class
black migration, 27, 53, 64. *See also* African Americans
Black Panther Party, 64
black political action, 2–4, 28, 61–62, 200. *See also* politics
Black Power Movement, 184
Blakeley, Ulysses, 189–90, *192*
blockbusting, 34, 83–84, 93, 95, 97, 135, 139–41, 149, 159, 164. *See also* housing; real estate speculation
block clubs, 142, 172, 189, 195; meetings of, 172
Booth, Heather, 6
Boulevard Realty and Mortgage, 142
Boysaw, Harold, 156
Brainerd Civic Association (BCA), 91, 127–28, 153, 161
Brashares, Bishop Charles, 136–37
Brazier, Rev. Arthur, 188–90, *192*, 196–200, 204–5, 212–13, 216, 220–25; *Black Self-Determination*, 195
Breckenfeld, Gurney, 40, 44–45
Brown v. Board of Education (1954), 57, 114–18, 207, 210, 345n11, 346n13; "separate but equal" policies invalidated by, 210, 346n16
Buffalo, 5–6
building standards, 178
Bukacek, Michael, 130, 141–42, 176
Burke, Msgr. Edward, 53, 171
Burns, Ben, 52

California, 5, 161–62
Caples, William, 211

Carey, Archibald, 37, 73, 90
Carey Ordinance, 37, 90, 348n30. *See also* Chicago
Carmichael, Stokely, 1
Catholic Church, 12, 43, 105, 153, 350n63; Archdiocese of the, 11, 52–54, 77–78, 104–6, 125, 130–32, 170–72, 179, 198–99; black parishes of the, 168; civil society of the, 41; clergy of the, 10, 23, 29, 52–53, 170–71; cultural and institutional life of the, 103; depopulation of established parishes of the, 53; ethnic differences in the, 20; hierarchy of the, 23; on home ownership, 20–21, 35, 44; parishes of the, 52, 82, 94, 96, 168, 172, 175, 179, 198; priests of the, 99, 139, 341n62; religiously sanctioned territorial sensibility of the, 40–41, 44, 54, 77, 179; schools of the, 175; and white racism, 197. *See also* Catholic schools; Christianity; churches; Office of Urban Affairs (OUA)
Catholic Interracial Council (CIC), 55–57, 122, 145, 149, 165, 182, 332n70, 349n42
Catholic schools, 84, 94. *See also* Catholic Church; education
Catholic Youth Organization, 23
Chambers, Edward, 96, 98, 100, 128–29, 133–34, 148, 155, 170, 173, 228
Chandler, Edward, 199
Chatham-Avalon Park Community Council, 85–86, 211
Chatham Improvement Association, 85
Chavez, Cesar, 6
Chicago: Areas of Black Residence in Chicago, *81*; Ashburn, *80*, 159–61, 165, *167*; Auburn-Gresham, *18*, 74–75, 78, *80*, 83, 91–94, 103, 123, 130, 148, 157–59, 166, *167*, 175–78, 341n43, 360n53, 361n66; Auburn Park, 83, 99, 135, 142, 153, 156, 164; Back of the Yards, 4, 17, *18*, 19–51, 69–70, 74, 92–96, 197–98; Beverly Hills, *80*, 82–83, 90–98, 130, 144, 148, 153, *167*, 172, 212; Black Belt, 29, 31–32, 36–37, 41, 45–46, 59, 64, 67, 72, 82–83, 88–94, 107, 119, 329n34; Black Community Areas (1970) in, *167*; Brainerd, 144, 148, 153, 172; Bridgeport, 39; Calumet Heights, 86; Chatham, *18*, 59, 74, 83–87, 93, 102, 107, 123, 188; Chicago Lawn, *18*, 37, 164; City Building Department (CBD), 141; City Council, 28, 37, 47, 62, 133, 159; City Hall, 200; civil rights in, 37–38, 55, 62; East Chatham, 85; East Gresham, 83; East Washington Heights, 102; Englewood, 33, 37, 49, 59, 74, 82–83, 91–93, 99, 129–30; ethnic nationalism in, 20; Far South Side, 39; Gage Park, *18*, 33, 164; Grand Crossing, 83, 93, 102, 341n43; Great Question of, 170; Gresham, 152–53; Halsted, 142; Highland, 91, 98; Hyde Park, *18*, 30, 45–52, 59, 74, 78, 102–7, 131–33, 177–83, 189, 195–98, 205, 223–24, 331n62, 332n68, 342n77; Jewish West Side, 7; Kenwood, *18*,

INDEX

59, 198, 223–24; Lawndale, 107; Lincoln Park, 107; Marquette Park, 33; Morgan Park, *80*, 90, 92, 135, 145, 153, *167*, 172, 339n26; Mount Greenwood, *80*, 83, *167*; North Englewood, 102; North Kenwood, 102; Ogden Park, 143–44; race relations in, 19, 38, 53, 68–69, 216; South Deering, *18*, 37; South Englewood, 83, 88, 98, 130; South Side, 5–6, 17–22, 27–36, 40–42, 47–49, 54, 61, 68–74, 82, 87, 113, 119–21, 126, 211–12, 349n42; Southwest Englewood, 130; Southwest Side, 4, 33, 74, *81*, 82–111, 114, 122–34, 137–82, 213, 216–17, 220, 340n42, 342n77, 356n17, 358n44; Urban Renewal Department, 204; Vernon Park, 211; Washington Heights, *80*, 83, 90, 130, 148, 158, *167*, 168, 173, 339n26, 360n52; Washington Park, 46, 59–60; West Chatham, 83, 130, 153; West Englewood, 33, 92, 329n36, 360n52; West Side, 94, 219–20; white-dominated building trades of, 205; Winneconna Lakes, 107, 148, 153. *See also* Carey Ordinance; Chicago Board of Education; Chicago Housing Authority (CHA); Chicago Police Department; City Planning Commission (CPC); City Planning Department; Grand Boulevard; Illinois; meatpacking plants; Organization for the Southwest Community (OSC); Packingtown; Robert Taylor Homes; South Campus project; urban renewal; Woodlawn

Chicago Area Project, 23, 327n15
Chicago Board of Education, 38, 159–61, 211, 213, 216, 221–23. *See also* education
Chicago Catholic Charities, 53, 95, 190
Chicago City Bank and Trust, 92
Chicago Commission on Human Relations (CCHR), 31, 44–45, 55–57, 87–88, 107, 120, 122, 163, 334n13, 344n4
Chicago Daily News, 43, 45, 79, 84–85, 101, 136, 141, 156, 160, 164, 201, 212
Chicago Defender, 17, 28, 163, 211, 214, 218, 221
Chicago Fair Housing Ordinance (1963), 218
Chicago Freedom Movement, 164, 184, 220
Chicago Housing Authority (CHA), 28, 37–38, 56, 61–62, 90, 221. *See also* housing
Chicago Police Department, 127, 350n48, 352n93
Chicago Presbytery, 101
Chicago Real Estate Board (CREB), 90–91, 160–64, 221. *See also* housing
Chicago Sun-Times, 131, 159, 197–98, 220
Chicago Title and Trust, 91
Chicago Tribune, 160, 164
Chicago Urban League (CUL), 44, 51, 55, 63, 93, 186–87, 208–10
Christ, Rev. Robert, 100–101, 128, 130, 134–35, 144–45, 152–56, 176
Christian Century, 98, 104, 130–33, 349n42, 350n63
Christian Family Movement, 157

Christianity, 13; of the white middle class, 38. *See also* Catholic Church; churches; religion
Christianity and Crisis, 198
Christian Science Monitor, 125
Christian Social Relations Committee of the Episcopal Diocese of Chicago, 144
churches, 64–66; Baptist, 65, 67; impoverished, 172; network of social organizations of the black, 65; Protestant, 64–65, 94, 134, 137, 350n63; Protestant and Catholic, 157, 171; Protestant and Catholic clergy, 96, 131, 133–34, 139, 145, 198. *See also* black community organizations; Catholic Church; Christianity; church-labor alliance; social ministry
Church Federation of Greater Chicago, 136–37, 199
church-labor alliance, 66. *See also* churches
Cincotta, Gail, 6
citizenship: Alinsky's embedded notion of, 324n13; endless responsibilities of, 14; equal, 115; European immigrants and, 23; modern, 117. *See also* democracy
City Club Forum, 142
City Planning Commission (CPC), 91, 196, 201. *See also* Chicago
City Planning Department, 197, 200–2. *See also* Chicago
civic nationalism, 37; wartime, 40
civil rights: activists for, 36–37, 63, 160, 187; coalition for, 37–38, 55, 213; color-blind model of, 117; discourse of, 207; issues of, 154, 162, 187; organizations for, 117, 161, 180, 217, 334n18. *See also* civil rights movement
Civil Rights Act (1964), 221, 347n20
Civil Rights Commission, 125
civil rights laws, 118–19, 150, 218. *See also* law
civil rights movement, 2–6, 28, 55–57, 112, 195, 207, 213, 216–19; advocates in the, 159; issues of the, 157; leaders of the, 206, 219; southern, 199. *See also* civil rights
civil service rules, 187
Clark, Ollie, 211
class, 3–4, 217
Clinton, Hillary, 6
Cold War, 10; red-baiting of the, 38
color blindness, 117, 119–20. *See also* race
Committee for Home Front Unity (Los Angeles), 55
Committee to End Mob Violence (CEMV), 52, 55, 63
Committee to Preserve the Southwest Community, 109, 127, 133–34, 138
Communist Party, 24
communists, 27, 133, 138–39
Community Action Program, 204
community development corporations, 6

community federation, 5. *See also* community organizing
Community Fund, 63
community organizing, 4–6, 9, 13–14, 23–26, 67, 74–75, 82, 143, 188–90, 219–20, 306–17; black, 54, 67, 111; democratic, 25, 181; funding of, 190; interracial, 147, 157; major experimental approach in, 53–59; racially progressive and integrated, 6, 51–52, 96–97, 120; slow, 220. *See also* activism; Alinsky, Saul; black community organizations; community federation; interracial cooperation; People's Organizations; politics
Community Reinvestment Act (1977), 309
Congress of Industrial Organizations (CIO), 26, 39–40
Congress of Racial Equality (CORE), 117, 144, 199
Connecticut, 7
conservation, 38, 41, 43, 45, 47–48, 51, 77; failure of, 54; program of parish, 95; and stabilization, 94
conservatives, 10, 12, 96, 98–100; racial, 147–54, 169–70, 172–75
controlled occupancy, 116. *See also* housing
Cook County Democratic Party, 60
Cooke, Msgr. Vincent, 53, 95, 190
Coordinating Council of Community Organizations (CCCO), 161, 195–96, 213, 216–22, 225, 353n94
corruption, 36
Cosmopolitan National Bank, 85
Crawford, Jane, 127–28
crime, 23, 84, 89, 93, 155, 165–66. *See also* juvenile delinquency; violence
cultural pluralism, 26

Daley, Mayor Richard, 38, 47, 61–65, 99, 150, 159–65, 169, 179, 200–204, 212, 217–22
Daley machine, 159, 182, 195, 204; black loyalists of the, 218. *See also* politics
Dan Ryan Expressway, 65
Davis, Ida, 194
Dawson, Congressman William, 37, 60–67, 73, 119, 196
Dawson machine, 64–65, 74
Delaney, David, 4
democracy, 6, 9–15, 49–50, 55, 135, 198; BYNC as a model of local, 44; in political organizations, 181, 201–5; social action as practice of, 11, 203. *See also* citizenship; politics
Democratic National Committee (DNC), 60
Democratic Party, 36–38, 98; southern white supremacist, 217
desegregation, 1–2, 220–21; black activists on the value of, 217; legal equality and, 207; as a practical impossibility, 69; residential, 207; school, 126, 161, 207, 210, 214–17, 221–25; of the South Side of Chicago, 119. *See also* racial integration

Despres, Leon, 62, 159, 161, 205, 218; "The Most Segregated City in the North–Chicago," 146
Detroit, 55
de Vise, Pierre, 223
Diamond, Andrew, 90
Dickerson, Earl, 61
discrimination. *See* racial discrimination
Douglas, Paul, 165
dual housing market, 17, 27, 31–34, 48, 52, 62, 71, 88–89, 101, 113, 116, 120–24, 136, 140; destruction of the, 150–51; pleas to attack the, 68, 144; pressures of the, 174. *See also* housing
Dyja, Thomas, 21, 42

Eastern European meatpackers, 5
East Gresham Community Association, 92, 98, 128, 141
Economist, 133
education, 14, 28, 56, 119, 205–16; adult education program, 66, 215; Black Freedom Movement as focused on public, 210; church-sponsored freedom schools in, 214; lack of access for blacks to quality, 187, 200, 206–9, 212–15; liberal, 215; lived experience of race in, 56; Northern black school activism, 207, 210; predominantly black elementary, 211; program of intercultural, 56; racism to be eliminated through, 115; vocational, 209, 215. *See also* Catholic schools; Chicago Board of Education; Model Cities; public schools; school segregation
Egan, Fr. John, 15–16, 52–53, 57, 60, 66, 76–78, 95–100, 106, 131, 134, 145, 156, 160, 168, 170–72, 310, 332n60, 351n71, 360n59
Eighteenth Ward Civic Council, 138
Eisenhower, President Dwight, 137
Elementary and Secondary School Education Act (1965), 221–22
Ellen, Ingrid, 176–77, 362n74
Emil Schwarzhaupt Foundation, 66
emotion, 15, 104, 287; emotional scars, 322
employment discrimination. *See* labor market discrimination
Englewood Civic Association, 90–91
Englewood Lions Club, 128
environmental pollution, 6, 20
equality, 2, 9; desire of blacks for, 59, 118; formal legal, 115; racial, 29, 39; treating each other with, 69. *See also* justice
Essex Blackstone Improvement Club, 200
Everingham, Harry, 109, 126–27, 133, 138–39, 148, 350n48

factionalism, 57, 63
fair employment laws, 187. *See also* law
Fair Employment Practices Law (1961), 187, 218
Fair Housing Act, 5

INDEX

fair housing campaigns, 180, 182, 353n94. *See also* housing
fair housing laws, 119–20, 151, 161–62, 165, 180, 347n22, 354n8, 357n36, 358n40, 359n46. *See also* housing; law
Farmer, James, 117, 347n20
Farrell, Fr. Martin, 78, 189–90, *192*
fascism, 28
Federal Home Loan Bank of Chicago, 309
Federal Housing Act (1949), 38, 43
Federal Housing Act (1954), 38, 43
Federal Housing Administration, 35, 43, 89, 140, 158
federal housing agencies, 42. *See also* housing
federal housing policy, 2, 35. *See also* housing
Ferguson, 3, 5
Fey, Harold, 130–32, 136–37, 197–98
Field, Marshall, III, 131
Finks, Fr. David, 97, 125
Finney, Leon, 196
Fish, John, 97, 171, 174–75, 193, 342n71, 361n61
Floyd, George, 5
Foster, A. L., 125
Fourteenth Amendment, 115–16
Freedman, Milton, 381n5
freedom, 50; black, 203, 227; personal, 203. *See also* free speech; self-determination
Freedom Budget, 263–68, 380n4, 381n5, 381n11
Freedom Rides, 184, 199–200
free speech, 26. *See also* freedom
Fuqua, Rev. Carl, 136

Garb, Margaret, 22
Garner, John, 156
Gaudette, Tom, 15, 53, 85–86
geography, 3; racial, 309, 358n38; regional, 151; urban, 35
Georgia, 60
Gerstle, Gary, 29
ghetto: black, 2–6, 22, 33, 74–75, 86, 95, 110, 162, 178, 186–87, 204–6, 212; deterioration of life in the, 2, 95, 186–87, 190; empowerment of residents in the, 55, 204; expansion of the, 53–54, 60, 73–76, 83, 88–89, 97–102, 132, 168, 173–75, 182, 208, 217–18, 334n13; integrated neighborhoods on the edge of the, 54, 76, 84; overcrowding in the, 54, 87; rehabilitation of the, 386n37; second, 65; South Side, 22, 30–33, 84, 101; white neighborhoods on the edge of the, 34–35, 37, 41, 54, 176. *See also* housing
GI Bill, 77
Giese, Vincent, *Revolution in the City*, 83–84, 86–87
Grand Boulevard, *18*, 32–33, 54–76, 95, 109, 188, 191, 200, 367n49; development of a mixed-income neighborhood in, 59; gradual impoverishment of, 60; overcrowding in, 59; Protestant churches of, 64–65; public schools of, 225; as a "slum" area, 65; union locals of, 66. *See also* Chicago
Grand Boulevard–Packingtown proposal, 74–75
Great Depression, 19, 26–27, 30, 33, 42, 46, 59, 82
Greater Woodlawn Ministerial Alliance, 189, 196
Greater Woodlawn Pastors' Alliance (GWPA), 211
Great Migration, 21–22, 30
Greeley, Fr. Andrew, 98, 152
Greenview Park Civic Association, 156, 355n13
Gresham Community Council, 141, 156
Grimshaw, William, 217
Grodzins, Morton, 113; "The Metropolitan Area as a Racial Problem," 145, 354n8
Groebe, William, 90
Grossman, James, 21
Guinier, Lani, 118

Halpern, Rick, 28
Hansberry, Lorraine, *A Raisin in the Sun*, 87
Hansberry v. Lee (1940), 61, 332n62
Harlan, Justice John Marshall, 114
Harmon, Dick, 198
Harper's Magazine, 219
Hauser, Philip, 213
Hauser Report, 216
Havighurst Report, 216
Hayes, Charles, 40
Head Start program, 158
Helper, Rose, 163
Hesburgh, Fr. Theodore, 125
Heuss, Merrill, 127
Highland Improvement Association, 161
Hirsch, Arnold, 23, 27, 34, 36, 56, 61, 159, 332n69, 363n79
Hoehler, Fred, 39
Hoffman, Abbie, 10
Holmgren, Edward, 145
Holy Name Society, 95
home improvements, 140. *See also* housing
Home Loan Program, 140, 158, 168, 177
Home Mortgage Disclosure Act (1975), 309
Home Owners' Loan Corporation, 35
Horne, Frank, 38, 262
Horwitt, Sanford, 98
House Un-American Activities Committee, 139
housing: black homeowners, 90, 114, 140–41; black shortage of, 68, 75–76, 85, 172, 329n34; Catholic homeowners, 103–4, 358n44; democratic control over the local market for, 82; deterioration of, 95, 149; fair, 149–54, 161; federal, 17; home ownership, 20–22, 32–33, 41, 82, 362n74; illegal housing conversions, 42, 155; inner-city affordable, 6, 67–68; interracial, 346n17; metropolitan open, 225; middle-class,

housing (cont.)
  204–5; older low-income, 65; private, 38, 48, 65, 73, 75–76, 101, 113–14, 162, 346n17, 348n29; problems of, 66–67; race and, 56, 67–68, 82, 94–95, 119–20, 178, 180, 185; real estate values, 44; rental, 83, 140, 203, 362n70, 384n29; shortage of, 30, 32, 48, 68, 75; structural forces of, 68; white homeowners, 22, 34–36, 82–89, 109, 112–14, 124, 141, 147–51, 159–64, 172, 177–80, 186, 217, 329n33. *See also* "benign quota" debate; blockbusting; Chicago Housing Authority (CHA); Chicago Real Estate Board (CREB); controlled occupancy; dual housing market; fair housing campaigns; fair housing laws; federal housing agencies; federal housing policy; ghetto; home improvements; housing discrimination; housing segregation; Model Cities; mortgages; open occupancy; public housing; quotas; racial integration; racial transition; real estate agents; real estate speculation; redlining; suburbs; white flight
housing discrimination, 17, 22, 28, 32–37, 40, 140, 162, 175, 200, 220; fight for laws against, 40, 117–19; segregation and, 67–68, 146, 184, 186. *See also* housing; housing segregation; racial discrimination
housing segregation, 5, 17, 32–38, 46, 54–59, 67–68, 75, 119, 140, 146, 149, 200, 208–13, 218; breaking down, 203, 262–94; city-wide, 59, 186; federally subsidized, 151; stubbornness of, 295, 302–5. *See also* housing; housing discrimination; racial transition; segregation/segregationists; white flight
How to Use Facts to Change Your Husband's Mind (OSC), 154
Hubbard, Phyllis, 194
Hunt, Harold, 37, 56
Hunt, Lester, 53, 57, 60, 66
Hutchins, Robert, 15, 46
Hyde Park Herald, 22
Hyde Park–Kenwood Community Conference (HP-KCC), 46–47, 72, 102–4, 106, 177, 223–24, 332n66, 343n85
Hyman, Eugene, 156
Hymer, Bennett, 209
Hynson, Eugene, 158

idealism, 15
identity: Catholic, 103, 340n42; collective, 26; community, 83, 203; European immigrant, 22–23; home ownership and, 41; local ethnic and class, 25–26, 41–42; racial, 21–22, 26–27, 36, 79, 121, 151; religious, 41, 174; social, 35; territorial, 41, 51, 76, 79
ideology, 9, 12, 50; aversion to theory and, 181; black civic, 73

Illinois, 161. *See also* Chicago
Illinois Association of Real Estate Boards, 164
Illinois General Assembly, 147
Illinois Institute of Technology, 130
Illinois Redevelopment Act (1941), 92, 340n32
immigrants: European, 21–23, 26–28; home ownership of, 20–23; in meatpacking plants, 328n22; in Packingtown, 19, 26; Southern and Eastern European, 27–28
Industrial Areas Foundation (IAF), 5–6, 53, 58–67, 77, 90, 95–101, 123–36, 145, 173, 190–93, 198, 327n16, 350n48
industrial employment, 26, 90, 186–87. *See also* labor
inequality: in housing, 207; in labor markets, 207; racial, 4–5, 11, 38, 115, 118, 183, 185, 207–16, 229; in schools, 186–87, 207, 210, 213; segregation and, 208–10; structural, 57, 79. *See also* racial discrimination; racial hierarchy; racial segregation; racism
integration. *See* racial integration
interracial cooperation, 27, 30, 34; as coalition building, 36, 225; in desegregation of public schools, 225. *See also* community organizing
interracial marriage, 84
Irvine, Rev. Gordon, 152–53

Jackson, Mahalia, 86–87
Jacobs, Jane, 201–2
Jefferson, Thomas, 1
Jet magazine, 212
Jim Crow, 1, 115
John Birch Society, 171
Johnson, President Lyndon, 1–2, 186, 221–22, 227
Jones, Theodore, 63
Judaism, 12–13. *See also* religion
justice, 173; criminal, 5; meritocratic, 117; organizing for, 306–17; racial, 4, 56, 71, 117, 348n29. *See also* equality; social justice
juvenile delinquency, 23–24, 70, 184, 327n15. *See also* crime

Kansas City, 5
Kate Maremont Foundation, 205
Kelly, Frank, 166
Kelly, Mayor Edward, 28, 36, 90, 217
Kennedy, President John F., 373n3
Kennedy, Robert F., 1, 384n28
Kennelly, Mayor Martin, 37–38, 61–63
Keppel, Francis, 221–22
Kerner, Governor Otto, 162, 164
Kimpton, Chancellor Lawrence A., 47
King, Martin Luther, Jr., 1, 33, 117, 196, 200–201, 207, 219–20, 295, 347n18, 380n5, 386n37; open housing campaign of, 164, 216, 220
Klein, Benjamin "Benny the Broker," 85

INDEX

Kloetzli, Walter, 130–32, 136–37, 190, 350n63
Knights of Columbus chapters, 153

labor: labor market, 23, 36, 186–87, 209; organized, 26, 28, 64–65; strikes, 21; unskilled black, 187, 206, 210. *See also* industrial employment; labor market discrimination; meatpacking plants; white-collar employment
labor market discrimination, 28, 56, 158, 184, 187, 200; education and, 209; fight for laws against, 29, 40; racial and gender, 229. *See also* labor; racial discrimination; unemployment
Lance, Squire, 189, 365n14
Land Clearance Commission, 90
law: and culture, 114; fair housing, 149–54, 158, 162–63; federal housing, 37–38; land-use, 120; nondiscrimination, 40, 117–19, 150–51, 161, 348n29; open occupancy, 46, 126, 145–51, 162–65, 198, 357n36. *See also* civil rights laws; fair employment laws; fair housing laws
Leber, Rev. Charles, 184, 189–90, *192*
Lee, John, 107
Lehman, Warren, 149–50
Lewis, John L., 6
liberals, 10–11, 144, 197, 206; black, 28; "masthead" liberal organizations, 181; New Deal, 347n19; postwar, 118; white, 28, 58, 73–74, 86, 125, 170, 180, 224. *See also* racial liberalism
Lipsitz, George, 183
living-wage movement, 6
Lutheran Church, 131

magazines, 5. *See also* media
Mahl, Robert, 165
March, Herbert, 20, 39, 133
Marcuse, Peter, 346n15
Margolis, Richard, 182–83
Maritain, Jacques, 7, 12–13, 15, 17, 53, 324n15
market economy, 117
Martinez, Peter, 97
Marxism, 10
mass culture, 25
Mayor's Committee on Race Relations, 28
McClory, Robert, 166
McDermott, John, 149, 157, 165, 182
McDonnell, William, 91
McGreevy, John, 20
McMahon, Eileen, 94
McMahon, Msgr. John, 78, 94–101, 110, 129–30, 134, 138–39, 143–52, 157, 165, 171, 176, 182, 341n44; *Seraph* (parish newsletter), 95
McTigue, J. Harold, 128
meatpacking plants, 6, 19, 21, 23–24, 127; black workers in the, 27, 30, 39, 49, 330n49; decline of the, 44, 66; immigrants in the, 328n22; Mexican workers in the, 30; skilled workers in the, 33;

403

white workers in the, 27, 39. *See also* Chicago; labor
media, 5, 11; coverage of racial transition by the, 84. *See also* magazines; newspapers; online publications; television
Meegan, Joseph, 23, *24*, 25, 29–30, 43–45, 48, 74–77, 127, 328n29
Menuez, Barry, 156–57, 170, 173
Merriam, Robert, 46
Methodist Church, 136; Rock River Conference, 225
Mexican Americans, 5–6
Meyer, Cardinal Albert, 77–78, 96, 99, 105, 125, 139, 171–72, 175, 349n42, 360n58
middle class, 77, 189, 196; apartment communities of the, 83; biracial, 176; homeowners of the, 155; interracial community of the, 105–6, 205; white, 82–83, 92, 95, 143, 146, 169, 174, 181; white Catholic, 82, 94. *See also* black middle class
Mikva, Abner, 258, 287
Milgram, Morris, 113–14, 117, 343n1
Minneapolis, 3
Mississippi, 196
Model Cities, 262–94, 386n37, 386n39, 388n58. *See also* education; housing
Molloy, Msgr. Patrick, 99–100, 123, 129, 134, 138–39, 152, 176; *St. Leo Weekly*, 99–100
Montgomery, Louise, 21
morality, 13–15
moral skepticism, 15
Morehouse College, 196
Morgan Park Improvement Association, 90–91
Morgan Park Planning Organization (MPPO), 148, 156, 158, 172
mortgages, 33–34, 88, 95; black families with, 164; federally insured, 35; money supply for, 149; program of pro-integrative, 177; in the suburbs, 43. *See also* banks; housing
municipal interracial commissions, 55
Murphy, Ed, 157
Murphy, George, 85
Murray, James, 138, 159–62, 165
Murray, Thomas, 159
Murray Park Civic Association, 160

National Advisory Commission on Civil Disorders (Kerner Commission), 1–2, 4
National Association for the Advancement of Colored People (NAACP), 40, 55, 63–67, 73, 117, 125, 136, 144, 206–8, 211, 336n45, 348n29; Legal Defense and Educational Fund, 61
National Association of Housing and Redevelopment Officials, 105
National Association of Real Estate Boards, 161
National Committee against Discrimination in Housing, 163, 182, 262, 343n3

National Conference of Christians and Jews, 39
National Housing Act, 204
nationalism, 29
National Lutheran Council, 190
national welfare state, 185
Neckerman, Kathryn, 210
Negro American Labor Council, 218
Negro Digest, 52
Nehemiah Housing projects, 6
Nelson, William, 201–2
New Deal, 6, 12, 26, 28–29, 41, 79, 117–18; labor movement of the, 10, 41
New Left, 7, 9–10
Newman, M. W., 79, 142–44
newspapers, 5, 212; city, 79; foreign-language, 20; local community, 340n34. *See also* media
New World, 171
New York, 28; Ocean Hill–Brownsville neighborhood, 225
Nichols, Mike, 72
nondiscrimination, 130; in lending, 150–51; public stance of, 176
Norquist, Grover, 12
Norris, James, 92, 98–100, 123, 128–30, 134, 153, 176
North Beverly Improvement Association, 161
Northern cities, 17, 21, 41, 112, 200, 344n4

Oakdale Community Association, 141
Obama, Barack, 6
Office of Urban Affairs (OUA), 78. *See also* Catholic Church
O'Grady, Msgr. John, 77, 95
online publications, 5. *See also* media
open occupancy, 46, 71–77, 106, 111, 119–22, 133, 152, 158, 187, 220; laws of, 46, 126, 145–51, 162–65, 198, 357n36; nondiscriminatory, 125. *See also* housing
Operation Look-In, 157–58
Operation Transfer, 211
opportunity structure, 208–16
Organization for the Southwest Community (OSC), 33, 52, 80, 82, 99, 135–83, 198, 216, 342n71, 351n77, 355n10, 361n61; activists of the, 143, 173, 175; Civil Rights Committee, 144; Community Relations Committee, 145, 147, 157–58; creation of the, 175; critics of the, 190; Education Committee, 154, 158; Executive Committee, 152, 154; first congress of the, 134–36, 145; Home Loan Program, 155; Home Modernization Loan Pool, 140; Housing and Zoning Committee, 141, 158; Law Enforcement and Human Relations Committee, 155, 359n48; leaders of the, 174; Median Forum of the, 148–49, 152, 154; Moderate Liberals of the, 148, 152; Program Committee of the, 135; racial moderates of the, 176; Real Estate Practices Committee, 141, 144, 157, 163; second congress of the, 145; stabilization programs of the, 140–54; *Statement of Purpose* (1959), 109; third congress of the, 154; Welfare and Safety Committee of the, 138. *See also* Chicago
Orthodox Judaism, 10, 12. *See also* Judaism
O'Toole, Donald, 95, 101, 127–30, 133–43, 170, 175

Pacem in Terris Peace and Freedom Award, 15
Packinghouse Workers Organizing Committee (PWOC), 19–20, 23–30, 328n27
Packingtown, 17–50, 64, 167; decrepit housing of, 42; local union meetings in, 39; older priests of, 23; organizing in, 23–26, 58, 70, 333n72; racial division in, 19–22, 27, 30, 39; as trouble spot, 69. *See also* Chicago
Paine, Thomas, 10
People's Organizations, 11, 25–26, 51, 189. *See also* community organizing
percentage integration, 117
Percy, Charles, 165
Philadelphia, 28, 114
Pitcher, Dr. Alvin, 137
Playboy magazine, 7, 49
Plessy v. Ferguson, 114–15
Poitier, Sidney, 87
police, 155; brutality of the, 5
political insurgency, 67
political theory, 11
politics: action in, 56; black power in, 2–4, 28, 61–62, 200; community organizations and, 67–68; democratic, 6, 13; local, 180; racial, 4, 19, 36–37, 61, 150, 159, 203, 212, 216–18, 221, 350n63; urban and suburban, 79. *See also* community organizing; Daley machine; democracy
Pope John XXIII, 15
Popular Front, 12; coalition of the, 40; interracial alliance in the style of the, 52; labor movement of the, 9
Port Huron Statement, 6
poverty, 1–4, 26, 36, 60, 64–65, 71, 78, 89, 186–88, 194, 200–209, 214–27; federal poverty programs, 196, 229–61; percentage of students living in, 209. *See also* racism; unemployment
Powell, John A., 295
prejudice, 9, 52, 120, 328n29; anti-Catholic, 131; and ignorance, 56; irrational individual, 115; white, 52, 56–57. *See also* racism
property owners' associations, 89–90, 102, 142, 145, 160, 175
Property Owners' Coordinating Committee (POCC), 161–62, 170, 175, 216
property rights, 35, 150, 162. *See also* rights
property taxes, 217
Provisional Organization for the Southwest Community (POSC), 101–10, 114, 122–35, 350n63;

Credentials Committee, 134; Structure Committee of the, 129–30, 133; volunteers of, 133
public housing, 37–38, 43, 73, 212, 332n68, 390n8; administration of, 55; high-rises of, 65, 200; government-owned, 114; integration of, 62, 73; and private housing, 48, 76; projects of, 60, 73, 200, 204; racial change in, 84; rent subsidies as preferable to, 203; as restricted to the ghetto, 61; as small scale and dispersed, 203–4. *See also* housing
Public Housing Association (PHA), 37, 52, 62, 330n45, 348n30
public opinion, 35
public schools, 2, 28, 178; all-black, 223–25; citywide boycott of, 161, 213, 216, 219; dropout rates for black teenagers in, 206, 209, 214; federal funding for, 222–23, 225; improvement of, 221; inferiority in, 64, 187–88, 206–9, 214–15, 223–25; integration of, 90, 206, 210; Jim Crow laws thrown out of, 115; liberal efforts to fight racism in the Chicago, 56, 207; new construction of, 208, 210; and the opportunity structure in Woodlawn, 208–16; overcrowding in the, 154, 158, 188, 208–12, 214, 223; and politics, 212; racial change in the, 84, 217; teachers in the, 211, 215; transfer plan in the, 213; vocational tracks in the, 215; white middle-class, 222; "Willis Wagons" in the, 212, 222. *See also* education; school segregation
Pucinski, Rep. Roman, 229

quotas, 143, 172, 181, 346n13, 346n17, 349n45, 354n8; and racial liberalism, 116–25; system of screening or, 149. *See also* "benign quota" debate; housing

race, 3–4, 26, 35, 50, 68–69, 120, 200, 207; BYNC and, 27–30; changing politics of, 30–36; hegemony of, 116; and housing, 56, 67–68, 82, 94–95, 119–20, 178, 180, 185; liberal thinking about, 55, 118; political ecology of, 54; and property, 120; and racial boundaries, 75; real estate solicitations on the basis of, 142; and segregation, 60, 71, 75, 97. *See also* African Americans; color blindness; race relations; racism; whiteness
race relations, 6, 19, 31, 51–57, 68–70, 105, 120, 131, 145–46, 341n43; and crime, 165; overriding system of, 209; successes in, 156; worsening of, 164. *See also* race; racism
racial containment, 89–93, 180, 362n72. *See also* racial geography
racial discrimination, 1, 47, 56–57, 63–65, 73, 88–90, 118–20, 170, 186–87, 201–3; eradication of, 40; racial conflict and, 44; in the real estate financing market, 149. *See also* housing discrimination; inequality; labor market discrimination; racial segregation; racism
racial geography, 35–36, 74–75, 77, 79–108, 122, 151, 155; alternative, 147, 151–52, 169, 176, 180–84; politics of, 40, 82, 180, 183; transformation of, 30. *See also* racial containment; racial geopolitics; social geography
racial geopolitics, 146, 180, 182, 348n30. *See also* racial geography
racial hierarchy, 3–4; spatialization of, 4, 183. *See also* inequality
racial integration, 29, 58–60, 68, 97, 121, 131, 135, 152, 179–80, 207; controlled, 130, 346n17; failure of, 147; intentional, 342n76; organized force for, 110, 183; partial, 109; permanent, 125; of predominantly white communities, 108–10; as "pressing necessity," 70; as residential integration, 69–77, 82, 102–16, 124, 135–39, 144–45, 149–51, 163–65, 172–74, 180–82, 191; as school integration, 90, 206, 210, 213, 215–17, 223–25; and self-interest and necessity, 120; sustainable, 124, 133, 147, 169; unworkability of, 164. *See also* desegregation; housing
racial liberalism, 28, 36–39, 47–49, 56, 63, 96, 102–3, 120–21, 144, 149–54, 176, 180; black skepticism about, 119; limits of, 106; postwar, 73, 115–17; quotas and, 116–25; social science and, 57–58. *See also* liberals
racially restrictive covenants, 22, 35, 44, 55, 59, 61, 90–91, 102, 131, 344n6
racial segregation, 1–5, 21–38, 45–47, 54, 60–62, 71, 82, 119–24, 143–50, 160, 170, 182, 191, 201–5, 221, 346n13; Catholic archdiocese as public foe of, 171, 199; consequences of, 79, 212; denial of the existence of, 37; dilemmas of, 262–94; protests against, 213; regionwide, 76; social, 218. *See also* housing segregation; inequality; racial discrimination; school segregation; segregation/segregationists
racial theory of value, 22, 35, 113–14
racial transition, 52–54, 74–75, 82–89, 93–95, 99, 123, 153–56, 165, 169, 176, 344n4, 360n52; neighborhoods of, 141, 147, 166, 167, 175, 225, 341n44, 360n52; pressures of, 174; structural roots of, 140; and white flight, 212, 329n39. *See also* housing; housing segregation; white flight
racism, 50, 69, 110, 115, 197; appearance of, 47; and bigotry, 139; images in politics and culture of, 36; in Packingtown, 19–22, 27, 30, 39; white, 57, 64, 125, 145, 210. *See also* inequality; poverty; prejudice; race; race relations; racial discrimination
Raisin in the Sun, A (Hansberry), 87
Rakove, Milton, 62
Ralph, James, 164, 372n23
Rankine, Claudia, 5

Rathje, Frank, 91
real estate agents, 22, 34, 42–44, 57, 77, 83–93, 101, 112–14, 119–21, 135, 140–42, 146, 163–64, 178; discriminatory actions of, 151, 356n32; professional ethics of, 151; real estate industry, 220. See also housing; real estate speculation
real estate code of ethics, 142
real estate speculation, 83–85, 88–89, 95, 140–42, 149, 163, 176, 338n12. See also blockbusting; housing; real estate agents
Reardon, Sean, 3
red-baiting, 23, 30, 37, 57, 63, 98, 126, 128, 133, 139
redlining, 6, 83, 89, 309. See also housing
Redmond Plan, 225
Reed, Rev. James, 136–37, 352n83
Referendum on Forced Housing, 162
religion: of Alinsky, 12–13; as democratic faith, 50; discrimination on the basis of, 356n32; proper social role of, 361n61. See also Christianity; Judaism
Ridge Civil Council, 127
rights: language of, 117–18, 150, 162; social, 347n21. See also property rights
Riordan, Fr. Jerome, 127
riots, 1, 93, 378n59; and national militancy, 207; race, 69; in the West Side ghetto, 220. See also violence
Robert Taylor Homes, 60, 62. See also Chicago
Rochester, 6
Rogers, Nahaz, 218
Rolling Stone magazine, 7, 13
Roosevelt, President Franklin, 123, 347n21
Rosen, Louis, 86
Rowan, Carl, 87
Rubin, Jerry, 10

Sagan, Bruce, 127
Sampson, Robert, 3
school segregation, 9, 37, 203, 213, 218, 221–22, 346n16; denying the existence of, 210–11; intransigence on, 217; and overcrowding, 154, 208–9. See also education; public schools; racial segregation; segregation/segregationists
Schultz, Robert, 126
Schwarzhaupt Foundation, 126, 191
Sears, 92
Second Great Migration, 17, 32
Second Vatican Council, 171
segregation/segregationists, 4, 37, 49–52, 74–75, 97, 110, 116, 125–37, 143, 183, 200–208, 224–25; black political power as the key to ending, 200; in Chicago's political system, 54–56, 119; "common sense" of, 147; formal legal, 115. See also housing segregation; racial segregation; school segregation
selective buying, 218

self-determination, 203–4. See also freedom
self-interest, 13–15, 69–70, 148, 174; in a common problem, 111; individual, 15; institutional, 15; white, 59
Seventh Presbyterian Church, 152–54, 156
sexuality, 84
Sharkey, Patrick, 3
Shaw, Clifford, 23, 327n15
Sheil, Bishop Bernard, 23, 29–30, 327n16
Shelley v. Kraemer (1948), 32, 35, 37, 46, 91–92, 102, 112
Silberman, Charles, 213
Sinclair, Upton, The Jungle, 19, 44
Sizemore, Barbara, 225
Slayton, Robert, 20, 44
social analysis, 55
social geography, 3–4, 35–36, 183, 207, 383n21; of Chicago, 17–21, 30, 36–37, 40, 75; racialized, 181, 358n38. See also racial geography
social justice: humanism and, 13, 49; struggle for, 4, 7, 13, 53. See also justice; social ministry
social ministry, 6, 199. See also churches; social justice
Social Policy Planning Memo (SPPM), 201, 205, 214–16, 227
social scientists, 58, 110
social services, 216
Social Welfare Union (SWU), 241–43
social workers, 203, 215; union of, 376n40
Sonderby, Max, 138–39, 163–64
South Campus project, 196–98, 200, 204. See also Chicago; Woodlawn
Southeast Chicago Commission (SECC), 46–47, 177, 188–89, 198, 340n32
Southern blacks, 17, 21, 64. See also African Americans
Southern Christian Leadership Conference, 117, 219–20
South Side Cosmopolitan Chamber of Commerce, 125
South Side Real Estate Board, 142
Southtown Economist, 91–92, 126–28, 133, 138–39, 142, 340n42
Southtown Land and Building Corporation, 92
Southtown Planning Association (SPA), 90, 92, 133, 135, 175, 340n30
Southtown Realty and Development Corporation, 92
Southwest Community Action Coalition, 182
Southwest Council of Civic Associations, 161
Southwest Neighborhood Council, 91
Southwest News-Herald, 164
Squires, Robert, 195, 227, 367n37
stability, 174–79
Standard State Bank, 101, 133, 140
St. Clair Drake, John, 72

Stevenson, Rev. Lynward, 196, 206, 212, 218–19, 223–24, 228
Still, Rev. Douglas, 351n79
St. Paul, 5, 10
Stritch, Cardinal Samuel, 53, 77, 175, 365n16
Student Woodlawn Project, 214
Suarez, Ray, *The Old Neighborhood*, 146
subsidiarity, 12, 307, 324n15
suburbs: black access to the, 329n34; exclusion in the, 89, 186–87; fair housing in the, 151, 389n2, 390n8; home ownership in the, 140; interracial projects in the, 113; lonely, 154; moving to the, 169, 182, 217; politically independent, 146, 177; restricted, 158; white, 35, 84, 183. *See also* housing
Sugrue, Tom, 89, 118, 347n21
Sullivan, Fr. Daniel, 166
Supreme Court. *See* US Supreme Court

Taub, Richard, 84
taxation, 35, 178
television, 5, 177. *See also* media
Texas, 6
Tjerandsen, Carl, 126, 130
Tocqueville, Alexis de, 11–12
Trahey, Jack, 143
transportation, 35; public, 187; suburban rail services, 186–87
Tuttle, William, 21

unemployment, 1, 19, 67, 232–34; black, 186–88, 206; high, 71, 214; racial disparities in wages and, 206; youth, 24, 188, 206, 214, 224. *See also* labor market discrimination; poverty
union activists, 23–26, 39; black, 40. *See also* unions
Union League Club, 190
union organizing, 9, 19–20, 23–26, 28. *See also* unions
unions: discriminatory, 206, 215; leaders of, 65; limits to interracial cooperation of the, 71; meetings of, 26, 39, 65; mobilizing the memberships of, 65–66. *See also* union activists; union organizing
union-sponsored voting drives, 66
Union Stockyards, 19–21, 23
United Packinghouse Workers Association (UPWA), 40, 66, 70
United Power for Action and Justice (UPAJ), 309–10
United States, 4, 222
University of Chicago, 45–47, 72, 102–6, 132, 137, 179, 189, 196–200, 204–5, 223–25, 331n62, 340n32
University of Chicago Law School, 61
University of Chicago Settlement House, 27
Urban League, 47, 67, 116, 144–45, 149

urban manufacturing. *See* industrial employment
urban neighborhood groups, 146, 148, 153
urban planning, 201–5
urban populism, 10
urban renewal, 37–38, 43–44, 47, 129–33, 158, 192, 196; federal money for, 200; for Hyde Park, 332n68; for Woodlawn, 200–205. *See also* Chicago
US Commission on Civil Rights, 110
US District Court, 213
US Housing Authority, 38
US Office of Education, 221, 223
US Supreme Court, 35, 44, 59, 115, 126, 131, 137, 210, 217, 222, 345n11, 394n31. *See also* Warren Court

Van Meter, Rev. Canon William, 144
Veterans Administration, 35
Villemas, Joe, 96, 98, 128–29, 133–34
violence: covenant of, 44; gang, 224; local, 21, 52; and organized resistance to the expansion of the ghetto, 75–76, 220; physical, 45, 126; racial, 31, 42, 52–58, 63, 90, 93–97, 102, 139, 155, 350n63, 359n48; racial transition and, 56, 84, 97, 100, 148; threats of, 93, 133; violent containment of the "Black Belt," 59; white, 35, 39, 53, 56–57, 87, 89–90, 117, 155, 213. *See also* crime; riots
Vischer, Robert, 12
vision: of a corporatist arrangement of organized racial groups, 68; of human goodness, 15; of oneself as American, 26
Voigt, Theodore, 135
Vondrak, Edward, 164
Von Hoffman, Nicholas, 7, 9, 16, 49, 53, 79, 90–100, 106, 110, 126–34, 139–45, 150, 168–73, 189–90, 195–202, 205, 220, 228
voter registration, 218

War on Poverty, 1, 6, 184, 186, 207; Woodlawn Organization (TWO) and the, 229–61
Warren Court, 115. *See also* US Supreme Court
Washburne Trade School, 209
Washington, DC, 4
Washington, Harold, 64
Washington Post, 220
Weaver, Robert, 73; *The Negro Ghetto*, 109
Webb, Rev. James, 211
Webb v. Board of Education of the City of Chicago (1963), 213
Welfare Council of Chicago, 96
welfare state, 35, 194, 203–4; reshaping of the, 207; welfare dependency in the, 214
Wellstone, Paul, 6
West Avalon Community Association, 86
West Chatham Community Improvement Association, 141, 156, 164
White Citizens Council in the South, 97

white-collar employment, 187. *See also* labor
white flight, 4, 17, 31–34, 58, 73, 79, 93–97, 101–4, 112, 165, 174–78, 182, 329n39; decades of, 223; and integration, 76; prevention of, 140–43, 151; racial transition and, 212; structures of, 123. *See also* housing; housing segregation; racial transition
white neighborhood associations, 22
whiteness: and Catholicism, 40–41, 82; of "new" immigrants, 23; power and privileges of, 116; and racial pogroms, 27–28; spatial expressions of, 4, 210; value of, 89. *See also* race
Wilkins, Roy, 206
Williams, Sidney, 63
Willis, Benjamin, 37–38, 154, 159–61, 210–17, 221–24, 370n6
Wilson, James, 72–73
Winneconna Lakes Area Improvement Association (WLAIA), 107, 130, 141, 156
women, 194
Wood, Elizabeth, 37, 61
Woodlawn, 4, 74, 78, 101–2, *167*, *185*, 186–217, 220–25, 229–94, 365n9, 367n49; black, 195–96, 224; East, 189, 193–95, 223–27; experimental school in, 223; urban renewal for, 200–205, 262–94; West, 188–89, 196, 199, 202, 205, 221, 227; Woodlawn Gardens, 204–5, 368n57. *See also* Chicago; South Campus project; Woodlawn Organization (TWO)
Woodlawn Booster, 229
Woodlawn Experimental School Program (WESP), 225–26
Woodlawn Organization (TWO), 52, 64, 131, 154, 183–205, *185*, 193–228, 349n42, 374n9; activists of, 224; birth of the, 186–88, 200; Community Congress of the, 201; founders of the, *192*; Housing Committee of the, 193–94; Model Cities plan of, 283–90; Schools Committee of the, 194, 196, 212; Social Welfare Committee, 196; TWO-KMF Development Association, 368n57; Voter Cavalcade, 200–201; Youth Project, 243–60. *See also* Woodlawn
Woodlawn Plan, 200
working-class whites, 17, 34, 41, 62, 75, 220; investment in segregation of, 120; pacification of, 123–24; policing of racial boundaries by, 90
World War I, 20–22, 27, 30, 59–60, 102
World War II, 4, 11, 17–19, 23, 28–29, 35, 39, 42–43, 55–56, 82, 195, 208

York, Harold, 200
Young, Whitney, 117, 347n20
youth, 84

Zuber, Paul, 211